International Law and Empire

HISTORY AND THEORY OF INTERNATIONAL LAW

General Editors

NEHAL BHUTA

Professor of Public International Law, European University Institute

ANTHONY PAGDEN

Distinguished Professor, University of California Los Angeles

BENJAMIN STRAUMANN

Alberico Gentili Senior Fellow, New York University School of Law

In the past few decades the understanding of the relationship between nations has undergone a radical transformation. The role of the traditional nation state is diminishing, along with many of the traditional vocabularies which were once used to describe what has been called, ever since Jeremy Bentham coined the phrase in 1780, 'international law'. The older boundaries between states are growing ever more fluid, new conceptions and new languages have emerged which are slowly coming to replace the image of a world of sovereign independent nation states which has dominated the study of international relations since the early nineteenth century. This redefinition of the international arena demands a new understanding of classical and contemporary questions in international and legal theory. It is the editors' conviction that the best way to achieve this is by bridging the traditional divide between international legal theory, intellectual history, and legal and political history. The aim of the series, therefore, is to provide a forum for historical studies, from classical antiquity to the twenty-first century, that are theoretically informed and for philosophical work that is historically conscious, in the hope that a new vision of the rapidly evolving international world, its past and its possible future, may emerge.

International Law and Empire

Historical Explorations

Edited by
MARTTI KOSKENNIEMI
WALTER RECH
MANUEL JIMÉNEZ FONSECA

OXFORD
UNIVERSITY PRESS

OXFORD

UNIVERSITY PRESS

Great Clarendon Street, Oxford, OX2 6DP,
United Kingdom

Oxford University Press is a department of the University of Oxford.
It furthers the University's objective of excellence in research, scholarship,
and education by publishing worldwide. Oxford is a registered trade mark of
Oxford University Press in the UK and in certain other countries

Published in the United States of America by Oxford University Press
198 Madison Avenue, New York, NY 10016, United States of America

British Library Cataloguing in Publication Data
Data available

Library of Congress Control Number: 2016958345

ISBN 978-0-19-879557-5

Series Editors' Preface

Ever since the Romans created the 'law of nations' as a law open to both Roman and non-Roman citizens, what Jeremy Bentham in the eighteenth century baptized 'International Law' has been inextricably bound up with the pursuit of Empire. It was, however, the European overseas expansion which began with the Conquest of America, and ceased only after 1945, that determined how the relationship between a possible world legal order and the use of military force beyond the boundaries of the state might be understood. As Carl Schmitt noted in 1951 'for four hundred years from the sixteenth to the twentieth centuries the structure of European international law (*Völkerrecht*)' had been 'determined by a fundamental course of events; conquest of a new world'. It was this he claimed, which had given rise to what he called 'the traditional Eurocentric order of international law'. Throughout much of the early period the law of nations was seen as an instrument for creating order in an increasingly globalized world, and for restraining the more egregious accesses of the European colonial powers. When in the nineteenth century it acquired both the status of an independent branch of law, and an immense international prestige, it became also the prime vehicle for securing the progress of the civilization which the West believed that it would inevitably bring to the rest. Since the collapse of European overseas empires, however, international law has been systematically denounced as less an instrument for a benign world order than as an often thinly-veiled legal justification for world domination by the European empires, subsequently joined by the United States; and its practitioners have been cast increasingly as, in Immanuel Kant's famous phrase, the 'sorry comforters of mankind' who prophesy peace while devising ingenious arguments for propagating war.

Both positions were—and often continue to be—unduly simplistic. True, the conception of an inter-state law is without doubt of Western origin and was, indeed, frequently used as a means for furthering the expansionist aims of the European imperial powers. It is also the case that Kant's 'sorry comforters' were, in great part, concerned with establishing the terms of the justice of wars to be waged against predominately non-European powers. But it is also true as Martti Koskenniemi argues here that 'like empire—law is also understood to express values and principles that give a "constitutional" dimension to the society it governs, making a "legal community" out of the mass of individuals bound by it'. That was certainly how most of the earlier practitioners of the 'law of nations' saw their task and broadly speaking that is how most modern international lawyers see theirs.

This book is an attempt make sense of the highly complex, shifting, and allusive relationship between law and empire by examining key aspects of its history across the globe from AD to the present. It takes a broad and nuanced view of what constitutes 'international law' and, more problematical still, what constitutes an 'empire'. For all too often the easy dismissal of international law as the mere instrument of empire depends upon a willfully ill-defined, all-embracing, notion of both. This book, while never dropping into the simple association of 'empire' with all and any kind of hegemony or military and economic power, nevertheless takes the term 'empire' to express, as its Latin original did, a wide spectrum of both theories and practices of power across states and peoples. Similarly 'international law' is understood by the authors to include not merely the formal structure of legal discourses, but also institutions, colonial, administrative and diplomatic practices, and their like. No study of international law and empire, however conceived, can escape being largely Eurocentric, if only because both 'international law' and 'empire' as they have been understood over the past five hundred years are European concepts. They are by no means, however, exclusively European phenomena. The book, therefore, also examines non-European imperial locations: South America, China, the Malay Archipelago, Maghreb Africa, and the Ottoman Empire, bringing to it a global reach few previous studies have attempted.

Having been pronounced moribund in the 1960s, international law has since the beginning of this century returned in force. The Westphalian nation-state may still be the prime centre of sovereign power. But international agencies of one kind or another, the United Nations, the International Court of Justice, the International Criminal Court, the International Labor Organization, the International Maritime Organization, the World Trade Organization and so on—together with the ubiquitous concept of 'human rights'—are steadily diminishing its power. In this world international law has become, in the words of James Crawford and Martti Koskenniemi, 'a ubiquitous presence in global policy-making as well as in academic and journalistic commentary.' If indeed Hans Kelsen's Kantian vision of a world order—of an 'empire'—ruled over not by hegemonic powers but by an autonomous, self-referential legal system seems somewhat less of a utopian fantasy than it once did, then we badly need to know more about the histories of the entanglements of international law and empire. The chapters in this book, in their often very different ways, will go a long way towards achieving that end.

The Editors, August 2016

Preface

In the present global scenario, characterized by the increasing impact of international and transnational legal processes on societies, economies, and natural environments across the world, a growing body of literature is drawing attention to the relationship between international law and 'empire'.[1] Whereas in the nineteenth century—and again in the interwar period and the 1990s—international law was recurrently hailed as a vehicle of civilization and progress, its dark sides are now systematically scrutinized,[2] and recent historiography has provided rich critical analyses of the involvement of the modern law of nations in imperial projects.[3] This book aims at drawing out the complexity and ambivalence of that imperial involvement and of international law's role in structuring world governance. The volume thus illustrates how empire and international law have historically been conceptualized in interaction with one another, and how international legal rules, discourses, and institutions have operated in a variety of imperial settings. By carrying out this investigation all chapters expand on recent critiques of Western imperialism while constantly acknowledging the nuances and ambiguities of the international legal language and, in some cases, the possibility of counter-hegemonic claims being articulated through the vocabulary of international law.

To bring to the surface diverse imperial phenomena and the diversity of historical instances of international and 'imperial' juridification, this book adopts wide-ranging notions of both international law and empire. International law here refers to discourses as well as institutions, diplomatic practices, and modalities of colonial administration, legitimated by doctrines ranging from the universalist law of nature and nations of early modern times to the 'exceptional' colonial law of the late nineteenth century. Similarly, empire is broadly conceived as a form of political and economic power potentially encompassing influence and legal authority

---

[1] Jörg Fisch, *Die europäische Expansion und das Völkerrecht* (Steiner 1984); Anthony Pagden, *The Fall of Natural Man: The American Indian and the Origins of Comparative Ethnology* (Cambridge University Press 1987); Emmanuelle Jouannet and Hélène Ruiz Fabri (eds), *Impérialisme et droit international en Europe et aux Etats-Unis* (Société de législation comparée 2007); Anne Peters and Bardo Fassbender (eds), *The Oxford Handbook of the History of International Law* (Oxford University Press 2012); Luigi Nuzzo, *Origini di una scienza: diritto internazionale e colonialismo nel XIX secolo* (Klostermann 2012); Andrew Fitzmaurice, *Sovereignty, Property and Empire, 1500–2000* (Cambridge University Press 2014); Arnulf Becker Lorca, *Mestizo International Law: A Global Intellectual History 1842–1933* (Cambridge University Press 2014); Anthony Pagden, *The Burdens of Empire: 1539 to the Present* (Cambridge University Press 2015).

[2] David Kennedy, *The Dark Sides of Virtue: Reassessing International Humanitarianism* (Princeton University Press 2004).

[3] See, for instance, Martti Koskenniemi, *The Gentle Civilizer of Nations: The Rise and Fall of International Law 1870–1960* (Cambridge University Press 2001); Antony Anghie, *Imperialism, Sovereignty, and the Making of International Law* (Cambridge University Press 2005); China Miéville, *Between Equal Rights: A Marxist Theory of International Law* (Haymarket Books 2006).

as well as military control over foreign populations, subject to different degrees of negotiation. This power can manifest itself through state-sponsored colonization, occupation by settlers, and/or strategies of diplomatic and economic pressure, frequently justified by legitimizing narratives. Obviously adopting broad concepts of empire and international law does not mean that one should not make an effort to clarify them, which is the historian's permanent hermeneutic task, but rather that one should be cautious about defining these concepts in a fixed way given the problematic normative implications of the latter undertaking.

The chapters of the book refer to various imperial locations such as North and South America, China, the Malay Archipelago, the Maghreb and the Ottoman regions, Africa, as well as central Europe. To be sure, because most chapters focus on European imperialism, they may remain liable to the charge of Eurocentrism. However, this does not mean that non-Europeans' agency is absent from the book. In fact, several contributors specifically emphasize the way in which non-European actors negotiated the terms of imperial rules and thereby participated in shaping the concrete features of empire in particular contexts.

In order to avoid essentialist representations of Europe and 'the other', the sections of this volume are not divided along cultural lines or world regions. Rather, the book is structured around a set of thematic areas relevant for a critical historical investigation of law and empire. In its four parts, the book addresses the epistemological (Part I), ideological/discursive (Part II), practical/institutional (Part III), and normative issues (Part IV) raised by the interplay between international law and empire. These parts are preceded by an introductory essay by Martti Koskenniemi providing a rich historical and theoretical canvas for the following chapters and situating the volume in the ongoing debate on international law's role in the shaping of empire.

Part I of the volume, 'Epistemologies of Empire and International Law', problematizes the very conceptual framework in which Western legal and political commentators have couched imperial phenomena. This section achieves this goal in three ways. Firstly, in the chapter 'Provincializing Grotius: International Law and Empire in a Seventeenth-Century Malay Mirror', Arthur Weststeijn attempts to destabilize the Eurocentric paradigm of traditional legal historiography by examining non-Western legal sources and vocabularies as well as non-Western readings of Western legal authorities. This theoretical move 'provincializes' the West and inverts the established centre/periphery interpretative dynamics which have defined the dominant account of international legal history. Secondly, Stefan Kroll calls for differentiated and context-related conceptualizations of imperialism, in particular including the notion of hegemony. His piece 'Indirect Hegemonies in International Legal Relations: The Debate of Religious Tolerance in Early Republican China' deals with the debate on religious freedom and Confucianism that took place in early twentieth-century China. He proposes a notion of 'indirect hegemony' as a way of highlighting the impact of European normative vocabularies on local legal languages and structures while not obscuring the persistent capacity of local actors to create hybridized versions of those languages for their own political projects. Finally, Walter Rech's chapter 'International Law, Empire, and the Relative Indeterminacy of Narrative' highlights the fact that imperial and international legal projects have constantly been promoted by specific historical narratives, yet with varying effects. Rech uses the expression 'relative indeterminacy' to stress that although a plurality of narratives have been deployed to justify empire throughout ancient and modern history, only some of them, for instance progressivism and providentialism, proved particularly suitable for the purpose of imperial legitimization.

Part II, devoted to the 'Legal Discourses of Empire', investigates the way in which the language of the law of nations was used, both within and outside Europe, to advance imperial and colonial ends. In his chapter 'The Concepts of Universal Monarchy and Balance of Power in the First Half of the Seventeenth Century—A Case Study', Peter Schröder focuses on the imperial vocabularies put forward by Tommaso Campanella and the Duke of Sully. Schröder shows that, despite the apparent normative contradiction between Campanella's doctrine of universal monarchy and Sully's theory of the balance of power, both vocabularies were advanced to support the equally hegemonic projects of Spain and France. The imperial projects of early modern Spain are also at the core of Randall Lesaffer's 'Between Faith and Empire: The Justification of the Spanish Intervention in the French Wars of Religion in the 1590s', which draws attention to declarations of war as tools for modern power politics. Lesaffer argues that while the legal arguments asserted in early modern declarations of war were rooted in the traditional just war doctrine, the declarations themselves can be best understood as rhetorical devices for convincing domestic and foreign audiences of the legitimacy of one's imperial project. Manuel Jiménez Fonseca's chapter '*Jus gentium* and the Transformation of Latin American Nature: One More Reading of Vitoria?' also looks at Spanish imperialism, but moves the focus from Europe to Spain's American possessions. Intervening in the debate on the historical importance of Francisco de Vitoria's work, he argues that one aspect of Vitoria's articulation of Spanish economic rights in America that has been under-examined is the way in which they legitimized the Spanish appropriation of Latin American ecosystems. From a similar critical perspective, José-Manuel Barreto's '*Cerberus*: Rethinking Grotius and the Westphalian System' reformulates the conceptual framework within which European imperialism has been classically understood. Drawing on Grotius' work and intellectual political and economic history, he claims that although international law has traditionally been defined as a law largely made by and for states, in fact there are two additional forms of international legal subjectivity: empire and the company. In Barreto's depiction, the state, the empire, and the company embody the three main facets of European imperialism. Julie Saada continues this critical engagement by contributing to the historiographical debate on the normative ambivalence of Western liberal thinking in her piece 'Revolution, Empire, and Utopia: Tocqueville and the Intellectual Background of International Law'. She draws out the ambivalence of liberalism by presenting simultaneously analogous and conflicting theories such as Tocqueville's liberal conservatism and Quinet's anti-clerical republicanism in the context of the French colonial involvement in Algeria.

'Managing Empire: Imperial Administration and Diplomacy' is the title of Part III, which addresses the institutional and organizational dimensions of empire,

including diplomatic practices as means to secure imperial power and/or autonomy from imperial centres. All chapters in this section underline the exploitative
nature of colonial relations and pay special attention to the complex ways in which
imperial administrations and diplomacies have historically operated. Christian
Windler's 'Towards the Empire of a "Civilizing Mission": The French Revolution
and Its Impact on Relations with the Ottoman Regencies in the Maghreb' thema-
tizes the contrast between early modern and late modern European diplomatic
relations with non-Europeans. By analysing the shifting dynamics in treaty-making
and customary relations between France and North African regencies at the turn
of the nineteenth century, he shows that the move from international legal pluralism to a more muscular imperialism took place precisely at the time when Western
nations proclaimed a universalistic and egalitarian creed in the aftermath of the
American and French revolutions. Describing a similar historical trajectory at the
level of both diplomacy and imperial administration, PG McHugh examines the
changing modalities of British imperialism in North American settler colonies in 'A
Comporting Sovereign, Tribes, and the Ordering of Imperial Authority in Colonial
Upper Canada of the 1830s'. He argues that whereas before the nineteenth century
the First Nations of Upper Canada enjoyed a certain degree of political and legal
autonomy from a distant Crown, by the first decades of the nineteenth century
they directly fell under British jurisdiction, thus turning from acknowledged participants in the law of nations into passive subjects of a paternalistic empire. The
issue of imperial administration is also treated in Luigi Nuzzo's chapter 'Territory,
Sovereignty, and the Construction of the Colonial Space'. This piece describes the
way in which European jurists in the second half of the nineteenth century conceptualized the exceptional nature of non-European territories with reference to
notions such as suzerainty and *terra nullius* to legitimize the exercise of particular
forms of Western legal authority over them. This engagement also resulted in the
creation of a special 'colonial law' applied, for instance, on African soil.

Part IV, 'A Legal Critique of Empire?', closes the book by emphasizing the possibility of critique in international law. While the previous parts underline the
exploitative aspects of international law as traced throughout modern history,
this section suggests that international legal language has sometimes been used
to oppose empire. Importantly, however, most chapters in Part IV are less assertive regarding the tangible and long-term transformative effects of this critique.
This is the line of reasoning followed by Umut Özsu in 'An Anti-Imperialist
Universalism? *Jus Cogens* and the Politics of International Law', which traces
the development of *jus cogens* in the Cold War period to stress that apparently
universal legal vocabularies often emerge out of competition between contrasting and even clashing political agendas. Still, Özsu notes that radical political
agendas get necessarily diluted by being articulated through an ambivalent and
legalistic diplomatic language; hence his scepticism about the structural transformative power of international legal critique. Focusing on the same historical
period, Hatsue Shinohara's chapter 'Drift towards an Empire? The Trajectory
of American Reformers in the Cold War' describes how competing visions of
international law and order played out in the shaping of the modern disciplines

of international law and international relations in the United States. In particular, she contrasts Quincy Wright's pluralistic conception of international law and critical warnings against the drifts of American imperialism with Charles Fenwick's enthusiastic endorsement of the United States' foreign policies of the Cold War era. In his chapter '*Imperium sine fine*: Carneades, the Splendid Vice of Glory, and the Justice of Empire', Benjamin Straumann also takes up the topic of the clash between competing visions of the world, in particular between universal justice and state interests, at the roots of both ancient and modern normative discourses. He retraces the Carneadean debate on the rightfulness of empire to show that arguments for justice and peace, on the one hand, and glory and the reason of state, on the other, should carefully be drawn out and not conflated as has been common in recent historical scholarship. Like Özsu and Shinohara, Straumann accounts for the possibility of articulating a critical vision of international affairs through the language of the law of nations, though all authors tend to agree that the effective outcome of this critique should not be overestimated. Bringing the book to closure, Andrew Fitzmaurice's chapter 'Scepticism of the Civilizing Mission in International Law' reconstructs a critical Western tradition of the law of nations from Montaigne through to Pufendorf, Kant, and nineteenth-century international lawyers, which unveiled the inconsistency of Western claims to cultural superiority vis-à-vis non-Europeans. Still, Fitzmaurice points out that some of these sceptical authors nevertheless justified European imperial policies for the sake of national interest, and their doctrines never fully escaped established Eurocentric frames of thought. This preoccupation with the Eurocentric character of Western legal discourse ideally links Fitzmaurice's chapter back to Weststeijn's opening piece.

As all previous sections, Part IV shows that international legal language as exemplified by notions such as 'progress', 'humanity', and 'civilization' remains highly contested, and that it is precisely the ambivalence of this language that allows it to serve imperial and anti-imperial purposes alike. While those concepts, historically and to date, tend to be viewed in opposite camps as either humanitarian or oppressive, their semantic ambivalence and indeterminacy allows them to be deployed for different political agendas in different contexts. All contributions to this book thus call for a sustained engagement with the contextual and situated relationship between international law and empire.

Contents

List of Contributors

José-Manuel Barreto, PhD (London), teaches History and Theory of International Law at the Universidad de los Andes, Bogotá. He works on the decolonization of human rights and international law, and explores their history and theory in the context of modern imperialism. His research also addresses questions about the relations between art, the 'turn to emotions' and the human rights culture, and about how to defend human rights telling stories. He edited *Human Rights from a Third World Perspective: Critique, History and International Law* (Cambridge Scholars Publishing 2013), and has been a Postdoctoral Researcher at the Humboldt University of Berlin and the Kate Hamburger Kolleg-University of Bonn.

Andrew Fitzmaurice is Professor of History at the University of Sydney. He is the author of *Sovereignty, Property and Empire, 1500–2000* (Cambridge University Press 2014) and *Humanism and America* (Cambridge University Press 2003). He is currently completing a micro-history of nineteenth-century international law.

Manuel Jiménez Fonseca is a PhD candidate at the Erik Castrén Institute of International Law and Human Rights (University of Helsinki) where he has been part of the research project 'Intellectual History of International Law: Empire and Religion'. Prior to joining the Institute he has worked for various NGOs and social movements in Spain, Honduras, and Mozambique. His research interests lie primarily in international legal historiography as well as the areas of human rights, development, and social justice.

Martti Koskenniemi is Academy Professor of International Law at the University of Helsinki and Director of the Erik Castrén Institute of International Law and Human Rights. He was a member of the Finnish diplomatic service in 1978–94 and of the International Law Commission (UN) in 2002–06. His main publications include *From Apology to Utopia: The Structure of International Legal Argument* (Cambridge University Press 1989/2005) and *The Gentle Civilizer of Nations: The Rise and Fall of International Law 1870–1960* (Cambridge University Press 2001).

Stefan Kroll is a postdoctoral researcher at the Cluster of Excellence 'Normative Orders' as well as the chair of International Organizations at Goethe University Frankfurt. Kroll holds a doctoral degree in social sciences and was awarded the Otto-Hahn Medal of the Max-Planck-Society 2011. His research is focused on international norms and adjudication, world society, and the history of international law.

Randall Lesaffer (Bruges, 1968) studied law and history at the universities of Ghent and Leuven. From the latter university he obtained his PhD in law in 1998. Since 1999, he has been Professor of Legal History at Tilburg University, where he also served as dean of the law school from 2008 to 2012. He is also Professor of International and European Legal History at the University of Leuven. His work focuses on the early-modern law of nations in Europe.

PG McHugh is Professor of Law and Legal History at the University of Cambridge. He is the author of *Aboriginal Societies and the Common Law* (2005) and *Aboriginal Title* (2011), both for Oxford University Press.

Luigi Nuzzo is Professor of Legal History at the University of Salento and fellow of the Alexander von Humboldt Foundation. He has been a Research Fellow at the Max Planck Institute for European Legal History, the University of California at Berkeley, New York University, and the European University Institute. His research focuses on the history of international law.

Umut Özsu is an assistant professor of law and legal studies at Carleton University. He is the author of *Formalizing Displacement: International Law and Population Transfers* (Oxford University Press 2015), and is currently working on a book about the legal dimensions of the post-1945 wave of decolonization.

Walter Rech is a postdoctoral researcher at the Erik Castrén Institute, University of Helsinki. His main research interests are in international political theory and the history of international law. His publications include *Enemies of Mankind: Vattel's Theory of Collective Security* (Brill 2013) and 'Rightless Enemies: Schmitt and Lauterpacht on Political Piracy' (2012) 32 Oxford Journal of Legal Studies.

Julie Saada is Professor at Sciences Po Law School (Paris) and the author of *Hobbes et le sujet de droit: Contractualisme et consentement* (Editions du CNRS 2010), *Guerre juste, guerre injuste: Théories, histoire et critiques* (with C. Nadeau, Presses Universitaires de France 2009), *Penser la guerre: Conflits contemporains, théorie politique et débats normatifs* (Presses de l'université de Lyon 2015), and *Juger les crimes de masse: Approches critiques* (with R. Nollez-Goldbach, Pédone 2014).

Peter Schröder is Senior Lecturer in Early Modern History at University College London. His main research interest focuses on the history of political thought and he has published widely in this field. His latest monograph *Trust in Early Modern International Political Thought, 1598–1713* is forthcoming with Cambridge University Press. He has been visiting professor at universities in Paris, Rome, and Seoul, and held numerous visiting research fellowships.

Hatsue Shinohara is Professor of International Relations at the Graduate School of Asia-Pacific Studies, Waseda University. Her recent publications include *US International Lawyers in the Interwar Years: A Forgotten Crusade* (Cambridge University Press 2012). She received her PhD in History from the University of Chicago.

Benjamin Straumann is Alberico Gentili Senior Fellow at New York University School of Law. He is the author of *Roman Law in the State of Nature: The Classical Foundations of Hugo Grotius' Natural Law* (Cambridge University Press 2015), and, most recently, of *Crisis and Constitutionalism: Roman Political Thought from the Fall of the Republic to the Age of Revolution* (Oxford University Press 2016).

Arthur Weststeijn is Director of Historical Studies at the Royal Netherlands Institute in Rome. He is the author of *Commercial Republicanism in the Dutch Golden Age* (Brill 2012) and specializes in early-modern intellectual history, with a specific focus on the Dutch colonial empire in a global context.

Christian Windler is Professor of Early Modern History at the University of Bern. He is the author of *Lokale Eliten, seigneurialer Adel und Reformabsolutismus in Spanien (1760–1808), Das Beispiel Niederandalusien* (Steiner Verlag 1992; Spanish translation: Universidad de Sevilla 1997), and *La diplomatie comme expérience de l'Autre: Consuls français au Maghreb (1700–1840)* (Librairie Droz 2002). He recently co-edited *Protegierte und Protektoren: Asymmetrische politische Beziehungen zwischen Partnerschaft und Dominanz (16. bis frühes 20. Jahrhundert)* (with T Haug and N Weber, Böhlau Verlag 2016).

Introduction: International Law and Empire—Aspects and Approaches

Martti Koskenniemi

I

In present jurisprudential orthodoxy 'Law's Empire' has come to signify the incessant search for coherence and unity in law: the effort to construct 'principles' collecting the disparate positive law materials under values on which the legal system is supposed to stand. These 'principles' do not exist on their own, but are the work of jurists' collective imagining designed to explain the law as more than just a random collection of rules, as a meaningful human activity designed to attain objectives valuable for the whole (legal) community.[1] Ronald Dworkin's well-known theory contains just one of the many ways in which lawyers across history have tried to move from the banal facts of legal positivity—the making and applying of rules by authoritative institutions—to something larger that would unify those rules, and with them the totality of legal subjects, under some ethos or teleology. Dworkin's intuition that this situation might be described as 'empire' taps on at least two important features we associate with law. One is the connection to power. Law—like empire—is about channelling, justifying, and opposing power, separating force from authority and creating relations of subordination that help maintain order in society. But—like empire—law is also understood to express values and principles that give a 'constitutional' dimension to the society it governs, making a 'legal community' out of the mass of individuals bound by it. Law's 'imperial' dynamic tends to make it an all-encompassing aspect of citizen's lives. So understood, 'law's empire' comes close to the 'rule of law', the view that human relations ought to be determined by predetermined legal rules administered by accountable officials in transparent legal processes.

In liberal and international jurisprudence, law's empire is an altogether necessary, positive quality that gives expression to the essential unity of the law and the community created by it. This dimension of the matter can scarcely be better

---

[1] Ronald Dworkin, *Law's Empire* (Harvard University Press 1986).

International Law and Empire: Historical Explorations. First Edition. Martti Koskenniemi, Walter Rech, and Manuel Jiménez Fonseca. © Martti Koskenniemi, Walter Rech, and Manuel Jiménez Fonseca 2016. Published 2016 by Oxford University Press.

highlighted than by drawing attention to the assessment by the twentieth century's most brilliant jurist, Hans Kelsen, of the work of Dante Alighieri's *De monarchia* from 1314. Writing in bitter exile from his admired Florence, the Ghibelline Dante inserted in this work a celebration of the (Holy Roman) empire as a guarantor of 'universal peace ... the best of those things that are ordained for human happiness'.[2] Kelsen, who chose Dante's political thought as the subject of his doctoral dissertation, ended his study by expressing his admiration to the 'scientific precision' and the 'deep insight in the nature of the thing that separated it with advantage from turn of the 13th century publications in State theory'. Kelsen highlighted Dante's relentless pursuit of the 'principle of unity' expressed in the position of the secular empire at the top of the political hierarchy of the world. Dante rejected nationalism and wished to separate the spiritual power from the secular one, though as Kelsen noted, the period's religious atmosphere did not allow the poet to bring *sacerdotium* unambiguously under imperial power. Kelsen admired the legally defined nature of Dante's world monarchy, understood as an office designed to act for the good of the subjects ('*minister omnium*'). It was bound by law: '*die Macht des Herrschers von den Rechtsschanken begrentzt sei.*'[3] The emperor may not work against the law because his very office is constituted by the law and for its realization: 'all jurisdiction is prior to the judge who exercises it ... the emperor, precisely as emperor, cannot change it, because he derives from it the fact that he is what he is.' Dante had completely accepted—so Kelsen—the Germanic idea of the internal relationship between statehood (in this case imperial statehood) and the law, each constituting and conditioning the other. 'With this kind of understanding of the relation of state and law the supposition of the complete determination of highest state power by law becomes obvious.'[4]

It is no surprise that Kelsen was sympathetic to Dante's view of empire as a creature of law and the imperial office as its executor. After all, a very similar view lay at the heart of Kelsen's own *Reine Rechtslehre*. Having sat at the feet of another jurist from the Austro-Hungarian Empire, Georg Jellinek, Kelsen came to reject the suggestion by the older professor of a dualism between state and law, the separation of a sociological and a juridical perspective on statehood. Kelsen thought that there was no such thing as an independent 'sociological conception of the state'. The state was a *legal* notion through and through so that even those who wished to study the operation of state institutions sociologically first needed to learn to know the norms that allowed reading some action as that by an 'institution of a state'. There was no independent empirical access to the world of statehood. That world could only be described 'sociologically' once the mass of empirical facts had first been organized through the application of the (legal) concept of statehood on it.[5]

The neo-Kantian Kelsen was doubtless drawn to Dante owing to the latter's logical and hierarchical notion of empire as an expression of the unity of humankind.

---

[2] Dante, *Monarchy* (P Shaw ed, Cambridge University Press 1996) I iv (8).
[3] Hans Kelsen, *Die Staatslehre des Dante Alighieri* (F Deuticke 1905) 89.   [4] Ibid 91.
[5] Hans Kelsen, *Der soziologische und der juristische Staatsbegriff* (2nd edn, Mohr 1928).

Kelsen himself always stressed the unity of law as a principle of legal knowledge, operating through the hierarchical system of the '*Stufenbau*', a series of normative derivations from higher to lower levels that guaranteed the validity of individual norms and the legal competence of actors in the legal system. The system was united at the top by the famous '*Grundnorm*' that guaranteed the system's unity analogously to the way the imperial seat stood over provincial magistrates.[6] Like Kelsen, Dante, too, operated his *reductio ad unum* as a peacekeeping device. In a world with many authorities with unclear relations of subordination (the situation of Northern Italy in the fourteenth century par excellence), there will be constant conflict and general insecurity. There must somewhere be the highest authority. As Dante formulates the conclusion drawn by generations of international jurists (but not only by them): '… mankind is most a unity when it is drawn together to form a single entity, and this can only come about when it is ruled as one whole by one ruler, as is self-evident'.[7]

The idea of unity as humankind's natural *telos* became quite an important part of the natural law tradition in early modernity where it peaked in eighteenth-century Scottish conjectural history, proceeding in 'stages' towards ever higher forms, finally uniting in the establishment of 'commercial society' everywhere. Among twentieth-century international lawyers, this teleology was given expression in the speculation about modernity and interdependence gradually leading to integration and to a worldwide 'international legal community'.[8] The view of this as a *legal* community was forcefully suggested in the 1990s by the rise of new international institutions—the World Trade Organization (WTO, 1995), the International Criminal Court (ICC, 1998), and the intense activity under human rights and environmental regimes. Always critics of sovereign statehood, international lawyers interpreted globalization at the end of the twentieth century as a moment in which humankind would be uniting under institutions with increasingly intrusive legal competences.

But such a view of 'law's empire' has always had its detractors. Many German interwar jurists argued that the first public international institutions such as the League of Nations were actually a hegemonic imposition by Western states on the vanquished belligerents. These jurists highlighted the coercive aspects of international law, the way it operated as an instrument of a de facto sovereign, situated *outside* the law and determining its content in view of its interests.[9] The most widely read English-language general history of the field today, Wilhelm Grewe's *The Epochs of International Law*[10] embodies such an (anti-Kelsenian) view of the law as an instrument of power radiating its influence over its neighbours. From this

---

[6] Hans Kelsen, *Introduction to Problems of Legal Theory* (Bonnie Litschewshi Paulson and Stanley L Paulson trs, Clarendon 1992) 55–75.

[7] Dante, *Monarchy* (n 2) I viii (13).

[8] For a celebration of the theme of moving towards a legal community, see the essays in Ulrich Fastenrath et al (eds), *From Bilateralism to Community Interest: Essays in Honour of Judge Bruno Simma* (Oxford University Press 2011).

[9] See eg the essays collected in Carl Schmitt, *Positionen und Begriffe im Kampf mit Weimar—Genf—Versailles 1923–1939* (Duncker and Humblot 1988).

[10] Michael Byers tr, De Gruyter 2000.

perspective, the history of international law is a history of imperial centres succeeding each other in their effort to dominate over the rest. This view resonates with postcolonial studies that likewise examine the history of international law in the context of imperial expansion. Antony Anghie's influential *Sovereignty, Imperialism and the Making of International Law*[11] has been followed up by a rich scholarship focusing on the many ways in which international law has facilitated European world domination. These studies have read the international history from the Spanish colonization of the 'Indies' in the sixteenth century to the civilizing mission of the nineteenth century as well as contemporary projects of development and human rights as successive efforts for expanding Western hegemony. Earlier histories used to admire jurists such as Alberico Gentili, Hugo Grotius, Emer de Vattel, and John Westlake as cosmopolitan humanitarians. A new generation has focused on the many ways their writings helped to justify the imperial activities of their clients. This is the darker legacy of law's empire where the desire for political autonomy and self-determination has been suppressed by everybody's unconditional subordination to imperial power.

The project 'History of International Law: Empire and Religion' from which the ensuing essays emerge aimed to study international law's 'imperial ambivalence', the way in which the history of international law may be assessed from the two contrasting viewpoints discussed above. Kelsen and Dworkin offer an attractive perspective of law as an instrument for the unity of humankind—Grewe and Anghie open a view on international law as an instrument of expansion and hegemony. However one sees international law's origin, whether one traces it to Roman law, Spanish sixteenth-century theologians, the German academic tradition of *jus naturae et gentium*, French enlightenment universalism, or sees it begin with the 'gentle civilizers' at the end of the nineteenth century, it is impossible to miss the utopian urge in the relevant texts and events. International lawyers celebrate that urge but have also been enchanted by it and in the process become blind to its hegemonic dimensions. The operation of international legal principles is a fundamentally contested datum so that what is viewed by one as humanitarian mission appears for another as an exercise of naked power. Law is one of the vocabularies—perhaps the leading vocabulary—through which we seek to persuade audiences about the justness of our views and the injustice of those put forward by our adversaries. The adversary process continues from the courtroom and the academy into popular debates about the pros and cons of particular actions: humanitarianism or empire? Below I shall briefly outline some contexts where international law and empire have come together in ways that illuminate the ambivalences of their cooperation. These notes are intended to highlight some current conversations about international law's history in which the 'imperial ambivalence' has played some role. They are also meant to indicate some possible ways of future research in this field.

---

[11] (Cambridge University Press 2003).

II

The first vocabulary through which European jurists addressed the issue of empire was Roman (civil) law. Under Roman law the emperor was '*Dominus mundi*' [D 14.2.9] and Dante and many of his contemporaries believed that Rome had ruled the world justly. Romans were the noblest people, always acting for the good of the community: 'The Roman people were ordained by nature to rule.'[12] Whether the Romans themselves believed this, it did not originally lead them to apply Roman law across the world. Instead, they devised the *jus gentium* to cover the relations between citizens and non-citizens. By the time of Justinian's code (AD 530), however, *jus gentium* had received a number of different formulations, some of which collapsed it into instinctual natural law or a Stoic law of 'reason', others defining it as a kind of positive law in force among all nations. This ambiguity would extend to later understandings of the meaning of the 'law of nations' as well, giving it flexibility and normative power that would consecrate the policies of European rulers while assuming the unity of humankind under the principles of Christian ethics.[13]

By the time of Charlemagne, Frankish rulers had begun to address their regime in imperial terms, reaffirming its legitimacy by seeking confirmation from the pope in Rome. The mélange of Christian universalism and Roman imperial ideology contributed, as is well known, to the struggle between the church and the emperor in which both sides were nevertheless in agreement that Christendom's lawful power extended throughout the world. The first clear articulation of world government under Christian institutions arose from the Gregorian church reforms in the eleventh century. This was expressed in Gratian's *Decretum* (*c.*1140), a collection of religious texts and papal decrees, equipped by a series of interpretative glosses designed to ensure the coherence of the whole. Even as the Church subscribed to the theory of the 'two swords' that separated the spiritual from temporal power, ambitious popes argued that the emperor possessed his sword and authority only 'at the request or sufferance of the ecclesiastical realm'.[14] In a famous apology a leading Augustinian scholar of the turn of the fourteenth century argued that the pope was not merely a successor of Peter but a 'vicar of Christ', possessing rights of jurisdiction and property over the entire world.[15]

The civil lawyers of the fourteenth century, for their part, argued that denying that the emperor was the 'Lord of the World' was perhaps heretical.[16] Nevertheless, they knew that the Justinian code could not be applied as such to the developments

---

[12] Dante, *Monarchy* (n 2) II vi (46).

[13] The best exposé of the many contrasting understandings of *jus gentium* is Peter Haggenmacher, *Grotius et la guerre juste* (Presses Universitaires de France 1983) 311–57.

[14] On the papal empire, see James Muldoon, *Empire and Order: The Concept of Empire, 800–1800* (Palgrave Macmillan 1999) 64–86.

[15] RW Dyson, *Giles of Rome's On Ecclesiastical Power: A Medieval Theory of World Government* (Columbia University Press 2004) II x–xii (162–211).

[16] Cecil N Woolf, *Bartolus of Sassoferrato: His Position in the History of Medieval Political Thought* (Cambridge University Press 1913) 24–25.

in Europe. Already early in the thirteenth century Pope Innocent III had accepted
that the French king recognized no secular superior in his realm—a declaration on
which French jurists rapidly developed a whole theory of the king as the 'emperor
in his realm'.[17] The meaning of that expression was anything but clear, however,
especially with regard to feudal nobles not immediately agreeable to viewing their
subordination to the king in terms of the authoritarianism of Roman public law.
In France and in northern Italy, jurists began to make a distinction between the
ideal world of the Justinian code and the de facto exclusive territorial powers of the
French king and North Italian *signori*. When Henry of Luxembourg was elected
the King of Romans in 1308, France's Philip the Fair sent him a letter expressing
astonishment that Henry would assume that the title provided him with some sort
of lordship over France.[18]

The continuation of the Roman Empire—and with it, the idea of someone being
'Lord of the World'—was deeply embedded in Christian eschatology. Especially
German jurists pointed to the prophesy in the Book of Daniel of the 'four empires'
according to which the Roman Empire would extend until the end of the world
and Christ's second coming. Because historical time still persisted, it had to be the
case that Rome was still present in some relevant sense—and the imperialist faction of German jurists had no doubt that after a series of 'imperial translations' it
lay in the hands of the 'Holy Roman Empire of the German Nation'. The idea of
a world empire was deeply embedded in medieval and early modern Christianity.
Dante expressed the many reasons—theological, philosophical, and practical-
political—that demanded a 'reduction to one'. With many leaders, conflict would
be unavoidable. This idea also inspired seventeenth-century German imperialists.
And yet, many contemporaries would view the insistence by the court in Vienna
that it was the imperial capital, with authority over all German lands, as nothing
short of Habsburg hubris itself responsible for constant conflict among the German
estates. It took a first real imperial historian, Hermann Conring from Helmstedt,
to argue that the Roman Empire never ruled the whole world, either in fact or in
law. Today, he argued, the imperial title gave nothing but 'control over the city of
Rome, the pope, the exarchate of Ravenna, and certain towns outside the borders
of the Lombard kingdom'.[19] From the fact that imperial Rome had been finished
with the conquest by the German tribes it followed that Roman law was not automatically binding in Germany and even less as some kind of a universal law.[20] The
German king (whether or not he carried the title of 'Roman Emperor') did not
rule over anything but Germany as a separate though a large and powerful State.
There was no longer any such universal empire, 'even a small independent state as,

---

[17] See eg Jacques Krynen, *L'empire du Roi: Idées et croyances politiques en France XIIIe-XVe siècle* (Gallimard 1993) 384–414.

[18] See eg Andreas Osiander, *Before the State: Systemic Political Change in the West from the Greeks to the French Revolution* (Oxford University Press 2007) 285–96.

[19] Hermann Conring, *New Discourse on the Roman-German Emperor* (C Fasolt ed and tr, Arizona Center for Medieval and Renaissance Studies 2005), XXVIII (37).

[20] Ibid XLIV–V (63–64).

for example, the republic of Ragusa, enjoys exactly the same rights of sovereignty [*maiestas*] as a larger one'.[21]

III

That the vocabulary of empire was reduced into a German eccentricity in seventeenth-century Europe did not mean that it would not have lived in Europe's relations with the extra-European world. It is doubtful if Charles V of Burgundy ever thought of himself as a *Dominus Mundi* as he was elected as head of the Holy Roman Empire in 1519. But there was no lack of courtiers who shared the view of Charles' influential Chancellor, the Italian lawyer Mercurio Gattinara, an admirer of Dante's *De monarchia*, who used the rhetoric of the *Reconquista* to argue for a 'new Rome' extending from Europe to the newly acquired overseas territories.[22] But the Spanish empire in the 'Indies' had great significance for the history of international law. The famous memorandum of 1513, composed by the legal advisor to King Ferdinand, Juan Manuel Palacios Rubios, expressed the view that Spanish rule in its American territories was based on the Pope's lordship over all the world but also that Indians were human beings and enjoyed *dominium* over their goods and communities.[23] The reality of the conquest was of course very different. Royal legislation such as the laws of Burgos and subsequent efforts to regulate the behaviour of the conquerors and the *encomenderos* remained largely ineffectual. The interest of international lawyers has been directed instead to the campaign by the Dominican theologians to use the vocabulary of natural law and the law of nations (*jus gentium*) taken from the writings of Thomas Aquinas to determine the respective rights of the native population and the Spanish conquerors. Although the famous *Relectio* of 1539 by Francisco de Vitoria on the Indians was not that distant from the memorandum of 1513, nineteenth- and early twentieth-century Catholic jurists have hailed its humanitarian sentiments as the 'origin' of present international law.[24]

But whatever Vitoria's motives for applying natural law and the *jus gentium* to the native populations in America, recent research has stressed the way none of this was to indicate any equality between the 'Indians' and the Spanish. Even subsequent members of the Salamanca school were sometimes embarrassed about the suggestion that the Spanish would be entitled to send military forces across native territory on the basis of a supposed *jus communications* and that, although forcible

[21] Ibid LVI (81).

[22] On Gattinara's imperial designs (that concentrated in Europe rather than in the Americas), see especially John M Headley, 'The Habsburg World Empire and the Revival of Ghibellinism' in David Armitage (ed) *Theories of Empire 1450–1800* (Ashgate 1998). See further, John M Headley, *The Emperor and his Chancellor: A Study of Imperial Chancellery under Gattinara* (Cambridge University Press 1983). For the imperial arguments of the Navarrese jurist and royal counsellor Miguel de Ulzurrum in a 1525 treatise *Catholicum opus imperiale regeminis mundi*, see David A Lupher, *Romans in the New World. Classical Models in Sixteenth Century Spanish America* (University of Michigan Press 2003) 46–49.

[23] Juan Lopez de Palacios Rubios, *De las Islas del Mar Océano* (Fondo de cultura económica 1954).

[24] See eg Ernst Nys, *Les origines du droit international* (Castaignes 1894).

conversion was prohibited, Indians still had a duty to listen to preaching.[25] The argument is now well established that natural law bound the American populations in a normative frame of which the Europeans were the authoritative interpreters. Somewhat like 'Christianity' (to which it was closely tied), natural law had little appreciation for the worldview of Native Americans, their customs, or laws. Whether or not it was applied out of humanitarian concern, its effect was to subordinate the native peoples to European government.[26]

As French colonization of North America got under way in the seventeenth century, very little attention was paid to any legal argumentation. The *Compagnie de Nouvelle France* was set up after the Dutch and English models as a joint stock company. Vice-royalty was allocated to an ally of Richelieu's but the chancellor remained in personal charge of the company's operations.[27] No attention was paid to indigenous title as the company allocated lands to partners with the assumption that metropolitan laws would automatically extend thereto.[28] Land-rights were sometimes justified by 'discovery' but no well-articulated theory, even less one of *terra nullius* (a much later concoction), was utilized.[29] In 1663 the company gave up its rights to the Crown that developed a program to increase settlements, for instance, by turning unused *seigneuries* into crown lands and re-allocating parts to new settlers. Abuses were tackled by regulation in 1711 that remained in force until the end of the French presence in Canada. The French ruled their mainland and Caribbean colonies sometimes through private companies, sometimes directly under the king. Absolutist France had very little concern with justifying its imperial activity by law, even less by an 'international' law purportedly standing over the king. No doubt the most interesting piece of French imperial legislation was the *Code noir* of 1685 that regulated French slavery in the colonies and stayed in force way beyond the revolutionary period. The study of that law as well as the later *code d'indigénat,* a series of administrative and legislative provisions that was applied in Algeria from the conquest (1830) onwards but then expanded in the 1870s to 1890s to French colonies in Senegal and further in Indochina would be especially interesting as they included racially and culturally inspired measures of coercion designed to prevent popular dissatisfaction from turning into rebellion that may

---

[25] See Frank B Costello, *The Political Philosophy of Luis de Molina* (1535–1600) (Roma Institute Historium 1974) 128–32.

[26] See especially Anghie, *Sovereignty, Imperialism and International Law* (n 11).

[27] Helen Dewar, 'Souveraineté dans les colonies, souveraineté en metropole: le role de la Nouvelle-France dans la consolidation de l'autorité maritime in France, 1620–1628' (2011) 64 Revue d'histoire de l'Amérique française 63, 86–91.

[28] Edward Cavanagh, 'Possession and Dispossession in Corporate New France, 1600–1663: Debunking a "Juridical History" and Revisiting Terra Nullius' (2014) 32 Law & History Review 97, 98, 109, 113–25.

[29] Benton and Straumann make the useful point that the Roman law concept of *res nullius* was compatible with seemingly different justifications such as discovery, occupation, and conquest and that some of this plurality followed from the way it could be—and was—invoked to defend both private law claims of property and public law claims of jurisdiction: Lauren Benton and Benjamin Straumann, 'Acquiring Empire by Law: From Roman Doctrine to Early Modern European Practice' (2010) 28 Law & History Review 1.

have inspired some of the recent laws providing exceptional powers in dealing with foreigners.[30]

Nor did the British make much use of natural law or the *jus gentium* in the expansion either in North America or the East Indies. As is well known, expansion in both directions took place predominantly with the instrumentality of the private company—though the charters of the companies, enacted under the royal prerogative, were sometimes articulated as coming under *jus gentium*. It is by now largely assumed that Blackstone's famous adage of international law as part of the law of England could not really be defended by common law practice.[31] The law of nations was taught in civil law courses at Oxford and applicable within the High Court of Admiralty and a few other prerogative courts. But it was not part of the common law. The fact that it was so closely associated with Roman law made it possible to integrate it in academic treatises celebrating policies of empire—this is how the Protestant refugee and civil law professor Alberico Gentili used it.[32] But mostly British expansion took place by private actors such as the Virginia or East India Company waging war or concluding treaties with local rulers. The resulting arrangements often resembled feudal landholding, and the question whether the East India company ruled over Bengal as a sovereign or a private company after 1757 remained open until the Charter Act of 1813 finally included the statement that 'undoubted sovereignty' over all company territories belonged to the Crown.[33] This summarized almost half a century of efforts to deal with the problems of territorial government in India without undermining the expansion of the company's Asian trade.

It was only in the nineteenth century, at the time of formal colonization, that international law began to exert a distinct role in the European occupation and government of 'uncivilized territory' and in the formation of European extraterritoriality and consular jurisdiction regimes in China, Japan, the Middle East, and those parts of Africa deemed civilized enough for some sort of formal arrangement.[34] The laws applicable to occupation of colonial territory and set up in the network of colonial treaties in the nineteenth century are nowadays the subject of increasing research.[35] So is the question of the legal treatment of native communities especially in the British

---

[30] See further, Olivier Le Cour Grandmaison, *Coloniser—Exterminer: Sur la guerre et l'État colonial* (Fayard 2005).

[31] William S Holdsworth, 'The Relation of English Law to International Law' (1941–42) 26 Minnesota Law Review 141. See further, William S Holdsworth, *A History of English Law* (Methuen 1937) Vol 10, 370–72.

[32] See Alberico Gentili, *De jure belli libri tres. Vol II The Translation* (Clarendon 1933) Ch xiv, 61–66.

[33] See CH Philips, *The East India Company 1784–1834* (Manchester University Press 1961) 181–91.

[34] See Turan Kayaoglu, *Legal Imperialism: Sovereignty and Extraterritoriality in Japan, the Ottoman Empire, and China* (Cambridge University Press 2010).

[35] See eg Mamadou Hebié, *Les accords conclus entre les puissances coloniales et les entités politiques locales comme moyens d'acquisition de la souveraineté territoriale* (Presses Universitaires de France 2015); Mieke van der Linden, *The Acquisition of Africa 1870–1914: The Nature of Nineteenth-Century International Law* (Wolf 2014); Saliha Belmessous (ed), *Empire by Treaty: Negotiating European Expansion, 1600–1900* (Oxford University Press 2015).

colonial world.[36] The research often suggests that a change in European attitudes took place sometime in the early nineteenth century. Until that time, principles of natural law had been applied—however one-sidedly—to European relations with non-Europeans. With the consolidation of the sovereignty principle, however, non-European territories became free for unlimited plunder and occupation. Not qualifying as 'sovereign', they could be subordinated under any conditions the European power thought useful. For two reasons I remain sceptical of that thesis. First is the jurisprudential one that it seems impossible to separate 'natural law' clearly from positive law and sovereign power. Behind every sovereignty there is some kind of an ideology that justifies it but is visible only once the (positive) legal routines are disturbed—and every natural law needs positivity to make itself applicable in the world. The two are completely intertwined aspects of any configuration of power and ideas about power.[37] Second is a related, historical consideration. The jurists of the late nineteenth century continued to be inspired by naturalist arguments and the (naturalist) theory of universal history proceeding by stages to increasing 'civilization'. They were often, in fact usually, critics of sovereignty and nationalism and if they did support formal occupation of colonial territory by their states, they did this out of total disillusionment to the way private companies and adventurers had been behaving. The work of civilization could only be undertaken through applying formal governmental powers over native territory.[38] To absolve natural law from responsibility in the European colonization of the late nineteenth and early twentieth centuries is to remain blind to the way liberal humanitarianism, feeding on natural law, contains an imperialist impulse.

IV

The studies of international law and empire have largely concentrated on the expansion of European formal empire across the globe. This is as true of the political realist histories such as those by Wilhelm Grewe as of postcolonial histories by Anghie and many of his followers. The focus of the study is on states and sovereignty. But much of Europe's expansion took place through private operators, colonial or trading companies, and by way of private contract and the exercise of the right of private property. When historians of international law discuss Vitoria's writings on the lawfulness of the Spanish conquest of the Indies, they have in mind his famous

---

[36] Out of a wealth of literature, see Robert A Williams, *The American Indian in Western Legal Thought: The Discourses of Conquest* (Oxford University Press 1990); Christopher Tomlins, *Freedom Bound: Law, Labour and Civic Identity in Colonizing English America* (Cambridge University Press 2010); Paul McHugh, *Aboriginal Societies and the Common Law: A History of Sovereignty, Status, and Self-Determination* (Oxford University Press 2005); Lisa Ford, *Settler Sovereignty: Jurisdiction and Indigenous People in America and Australia* (Harvard University Press 2011).

[37] This argument is at the core of my *From Apology to Utopia: The Structure of International Legal Argument* (Reissue with a new epilogue, Cambridge University Press 2005).

[38] See my *The Gentle Civilizer of Nations: The Rise and Fall of International Law 1870–1960* (Cambridge University Press 2001) 98–177.

relectiones on just war and the powers of sovereign dominion. Much less attention is given, however, to the massive discussion on the principles having to do with the expansion of commerce in Europe and beyond that was triggered by the import of silver from the American colonies. The most significant contribution of the 'Salamanca school' was, arguably, the discussion of principles of property and contract that would fit the new commercially oriented world while still seeking to balance the requirements of this new morality (and law) with Christian ethics.[39] New studies of Hugo Grotius, by contrast, regularly do mention his role as the legal counsel for a private company—the Dutch East India Company (VOC)—perhaps also noting the defence of the Company's plundering of Portuguese navigation as both just public and just private war. This suggests that it did not really matter whether to take a private or public law approach. It is all a matter of perspective.[40] If one relates this to the way the United Provinces were ruled by an oligarchy of leading families from each of the provinces (the same families sat in the company's famous Heeren XVII) the question may further be asked about the appropriate frame in which Dutch expansion in general should be understood: an imperial or a commercial venture? If the better response is that it was both one and the other, then it can only be regretted that by far most attention has been directed to the period from the perspective of public international law.

In British imperial history it has been much more common to focus on the decisive role of private actors and the emergence of the 'empire of free trade' at the beginning of the nineteenth century that enabled the century to become one of British overseas predominance. Underlying this are the important changes that took place in the eighteenth-century understandings of commercial law as influentially articulated in a series of cases decided by the Chief Justice of the King's Bench, Lord Mansfield, widely known as 'the father of English commercial law'.[41] To take just one example, in the case of *Miller v. Race* (1758), it was held that defences usually available under the common law would not apply to bills of exchange or bank notes. 'The reason of all these cases is', Mansfield wrote, 'because the usage of trade makes the law' and applies 'even against express Acts of Parliament'.[42] Britain was of course exceptionally dependent on the new instruments applicable in international commerce and as Mansfield realistically noted, 'not a tenth part of the trade in this kingdom could be carried on without them'; because general consent gave these notes the value of money—they were called 'paper money'—they must be treated as such.[43] Mansfield even accepted that judicial notice was to be taken of

---

[39] I have argued this in 'International Law and Empire: The Real Spanish Contribution' (2011) 61 University of Toronto Law Journal 1. See further Wim Decock, *Theologians and Contract Law: The Moral Transformation of the Ius Commune (ca. 1500–1650)* (Nijhoff 2013).

[40] See generally Jonathan Israel, *Dutch Primacy in World Trade 1585–1740* (Clarendon 1989) 16–17, 69–73.

[41] See eg S Todd Lowry, 'Lord Mansfield and the Law Merchant: Law and Economics in the Eighteenth Century' (1973) 7 Journal of Economic Issues 605.

[42] *Miller v. Race* in *Notes of cases argued, and adjudged, in the Court of King's Bench, and of some determined in the other high courts [1753–1759]* (Clarke 1825).

[43] Ibid, 1152, 1154.

mercantile custom. No specific proof was needed but the Court was presumed to know such custom because it was 'law'. For that purpose, he invited into the King's Bench juries consisting of merchants that would have the required knowledge of the commercial practices.

The relations of public law and private law—or sovereignty and property as I have elsewhere put this—are much closer than standard histories of the role of law in imperial expansion suggest. The case of Britain is perhaps an extreme example to the extent that around 1600, as the English began their search for trade routes and settlement, this would take place by chartering private merchants and companies to carry out practically all of this activity. For example, Queen Elizabeth issued a charter in 1581 to twelve of the richest London merchants for a seven-year trade monopoly in the whole of Middle East.[44] Organized initially on a joint stock basis the Levant Company was authorized to make laws and ordinances for the government of English activities in the enormous area allocated to it on the standard condition that they would 'not be contrary or repugnant to the laws, estates or customs of our realm'.[45] In exchange the company was expected to pay the Crown an annual fee of 500 pounds and its ships were regularly commissioned for privateering activities, ensuring 'enormous quantities of sugar without having to pay for it'.[46] The Company's director William Harborne was appointed ambassador but his salary was paid by the company. Harborne was also authorized to appoint consuls across the Ottoman realm and to take action to secure the implementation of the privileges by often-recalcitrant Turkish officials. But the Levant Company was only one among a large number of English trading ventures whose monopoly bound tightly together the interests of the Crown and the merchant elite. The state acted vigorously to prevent 'interloping' and sometimes—as for instance with the Russian Czar in 1623—agreed with foreign rulers for joint implementation of the monopoly. This reflected the growing sense that trade was a matter of policy and that England's wealth and power were completely tied up with that of its leading merchants. How to understand the close dependence of state power with the activities of private merchants became the task of a new genre of writing that moved freely between expositions of new commercial practices, discussion of the legal regulation of those practices, and recommendations for mercantile policy.[47]

---

[44] 'The Letters Patents, or Privileges Granted by her Majestie to Sir Edward Osborne ...' in Richard Hakluyt, *The Principal Navigations, Voyages, Traffiques and Discoveries of the English Nation* (James MacLehose and Sons 1904) Vol V, No 53. See further Alfred C Wood, *A History of the Levant Company* (Routledge 1964) 11; John P Davis, *Corporations: A Study of the Origin and Development of Great Business Combinations and their Relation to the Authority of the State* (Franken 1971) 88–92. Kenneth R Andrews argues, however, that the English interest at this stage was exclusively commercial: *Trade, Plunder and Settlement: Maritime Enterprise and the Genesis of the British Empire* (Cambridge University Press 1984) 90–91.

[45] 'The Letters Patents ...' in Hakluyt (n 44).

[46] Robert Brenner, *Merchants and Revolution: Commercial Change, Political Conflict, and London's Overseas Traders 1550–1653* (Verso 2003) 19.

[47] The standard work is Gerard Malynes, *Consuetodo vel Lex Mercatoria, or the Antient Law-Merchant* (London 1629).

As American colonies were beginning their rebellion in the eighteenth century, writers such as David Hume and Adam Smith suggested that granting them independence while maintaining intense commercial contacts would be best for everyone. This position was shared by the former governor of Massachusetts, Thomas Pownall, commenting on transatlantic relations from a natural law perspective. In the fifth edition of his *Administration of the Colonies* (1774) Pownall suggested giving up the old, wholly 'artificial' colonial system. The metropolis and the colonies were to be pulled together 'by a general, common and mutual principle of attraction'. This would be the 'general commercial interest which is most extensive, necessary and permanent, [and] settles and commands the market'. Universal free trade would, he surmised, create a 'grand marine dominion, consisting of our possessions in the Atlantic, and in America, united in a one [sic] center; where the seat of government is'.[48] In a later work Pownall suggested that the 'old system of Europe' was to be replaced by a new one based on 'nature', namely the realization that:

men and nations should be free, reciprocally to interchange, and respectively as their wants mark the course, [their] surpluses, that this Communion of Nations with each other ... ought to be thus enjoyed and exercised to the benefit and interest of each, and to the common good of all.[49]

V

Critics of formal empire in the nineteenth century highlighted the benefits of free trade for everyone—above all to commercial nations that would be able to bring the most competitive products on the international market. With their vast pool of colonial resources, advanced technologies and efficient production chains, Britain was looking to become the 'workshop of the world' where its industries and merchants would come to dominate the world of trade. For free traders such as 'Cobden, and, indeed the men of Manchester generally, the fight for free trade was a fight for all that was good, true and just'.[50] In the 1830s and 1840s, Britain unilaterally opened its markets for international trade and in the 1860s sought to make the system multilateral. In this way, Arrighi writes, Britain created 'worldwide networks of dependence on, and allegiance to, the expansion of the wealth and power of the United Kingdom'.[51] Even as protectionism was all but over, a wholly international system of commercial exchange had seen the light of day in which Britain was the principal beneficiary. Anne Orford has recently discussed the role of law in the creation of the 'free trade state' by reference to the emergence of

[48] Thomas Pownall, *The Administration of the British Colonies* (5th edn, Walter 1774) vol I, 10, 5–10.
[49] Thomas Pownall, *A Memorial most Humbly Addressed to the Sovereigns of Europe on the Present State of Affairs between the Old and the New World* (2nd edn, London 1780) 115.
[50] Bernard Semmel, *The Rise of Free Trade Imperialism: Classical Political Economy, the Empire of Free Trade and Imperialism 1750–1850* (Cambridge University Press 1970) 162.
[51] Giovanni Arrighi, *The Long Twentieth Century: Money, Power and the Origins of Our Times* (Verso 2010) 56.

new systems of production and distribution of food at this time, noting that the end of mercantilism was not the end of empire—at least 'if empire is understood to involve structured systems of exploitation'.[52] The narrative of how the economic system was assumed to operate as a self-regulating machine, separated from the social world of nation states and domestic politics has of course been well told by Karl Polanyi: 'Instead of economy being embedded in social relations, social relations are [now] embedded in the economic system.'[53] But even as the economic ideology of the nineteenth century suggested that trade would operate as a 'self-regulating system', the occasional gunboat was nevertheless needed to make sure it would operate without disruption. As the greatest foreign investor in Latin America after 1820, Britain would reluctantly but regularly use or threaten to use force in reaction to uncompensated seizure of British funds, for example.[54]

The formal expansion of European sovereignty through annexation or settlement far from exhausts the history of 'international law and empire'. To have a grasp on the way material and spiritual resources have been distributed in the twentieth century requires examining the background rules of private law, contract, and property that lay out the conditions under which relations of de facto dependence are created under ostensible 'free trade' arrangements between private companies, merchants, and investors of large trading nations and the rest of the world. Two directions have begun to dominate the treatment of 'international law and empire' in the contemporary world. First are the new histories dealing with the postcolonial states' efforts in the United Nations and elsewhere in intergovernmental institutions to receive voice as sovereign equals with the old colonial powers. Scholars are keen to understand what happened to the early embrace by international institutions of the 'New International Economic Order', including such connected projects as technology transfer to the Third World and the distribution of proceeds from the extraction of seabed mineral resources at the Law of the Sea Conference (1974–82). Where did 'permanent sovereignty to natural resources', UNESCO's 'new international information order', or the commodity agreements once imagined as the centre of international development, disappear?[55] No doubt, such new work is fed by present-day concerns. As the United Nations celebrated its 70th anniversary, its objective to create a more just and peaceful world seems no closer than it was in 1945. Global inequality is rising—according to studies carried out by Oxfam and Credit Suisse last year, one per cent of the world population owns more than the

---

[52] Anne Orford, 'Food Security, Free Trade, and the Battle for the State' (2015) 11(2) Journal of International law and International Relations 1, 42.

[53] Karl Polanyi, *The Great Transformation: The Political and Economic Origins of Our Time* (Beacon 2001) 60.

[54] It has been assessed that alongside innumerable threats of force, there were at least forty cases of military intervention by Britain in Latin America during 1820–1914. Charles Lipson, *Standing Guard: Protecting Foreign Capital in the Nineteenth and Twentieth Centuries* (University of California Press 1985) 54.

[55] Sundhya Pahuja, *Decolonising International Law: Development, Economic Growth and the Politics of Universality* (Cambridge University Press 2013); Luis Eslava, Michael Fahkri, and Vasuki Nesiah (eds), *Bandung, Global History and International Law: Critical Pasts and Pending Futures* (Cambridge University Press 2016).

other 99 per cent combined and that 69 per cent of that wealth lies in Europe and North America with a share of the world population of only 18 per cent.[56] In other words, if 'empire' is today pursued within and through intergovernmental cooperation—through development cooperation, intervention in 'failed states', post-conflict reconstruction, international criminal trials and so on, then it is clear that international law still stands quite at the heart of it. No conclusion has been reached in the debate on the relations between human rights and empire, either, but, as in all universalist thinking, hegemonic ambition looms large.

The second cross between international law and empire lies in the way the 'governance' of the international world has been increasingly moving beyond formal diplomatic institutions and public international law into 'hybrid' institutions where experts meet with private and public 'stakeholders' to decide on policy by reference to flexible standards, benchmarking, and efficiency optimization. It is trite to speak of the rise of a transnational law that operates largely through contract and property relations and consolidates the alienation of an international economic system from territorial political contestation. The rise of new types of 'regulatory law', codes of best practice, and other informal types of regimes of opportunity and constraint determine a large sphere of the actions by international institutions, companies, investors, and global elites, national and international. I have elsewhere argued that students desiring to find out the ways in which law enables, structures, channels, and opposes international power ought to turn their attention from 'sovereignty' to 'property' and examine the ways of operation of what could be called 'the empire of private law'.[57] Perhaps the most striking example of this in the present is the massive outpouring of interest in the international law of investments; especially significant is investor-state arbitration (ISDS) included in the more than 3000 bilateral investment treaties and in the proposals for Trans-Pacific and Transatlantic trade and investment treaties (TPP and TTIP). The proposal to lift disputes between a foreign investor and a host state from the jurisdiction of the latter, to be adjudicated in international arbitration panels consisting of investment experts applying global minimum standards is of the greatest interest for the history of international law and empire. It proposes to generalize a nineteenth-century colonial practice that began in Latin America, was generalized in the 'Hull formula' in the 1930s of a demand for 'full compensation', and was formalized in the aftermath of a series of nationalization cases emerging from the newly independent states in the 1960s.[58]

The point of ISDS, as of much new law in the fields of the economy, human rights, anti-terrorism, and the environment, is to remove matters of great importance from the context of domestic law and policy, into the hands of networks of

---

[56] Oxfam, 'Having it All and Wanting More, Report on Inequality' (2015) <http://policy-practice.oxfam.org.uk/publications/wealth-having-it-all-and-wanting-more-338125?cid=rdt_havingitall> accessed 16 November 2015; Credit Suisse, 'Global Wealth Report 2015' 6 <https://publications.credit-suisse.com/tasks/render/file/?fileID=F2425415-DCA7-80B8-EAD989AF9341D47E> accessed 16 November 2015.

[57] Martti Koskenniemi, 'Expanding Histories of International Law' (2016) 56 American Journal of Legal History 104.

[58] Ibid.

international experts at global institutions. At the outset of the new millennium Hardt and Negri published a much-debated work on *Empire* that examined the rise of a global system of rule without a centre by reference to Hans Kelsen's views about an autonomous, self-referential legal system regulating behaviour across the world. The authors suggested that a 'constitutionalization of a supranational power' had been under way for much of the twentieth century through the UN and other formal bodies but had now entered a 'paradigm shift' in which an 'imperial sovereignty' was emerging from the multifarious activities carried out under wholly global economic and technological institutions. Kelsen, they claimed, had understood this (and perhaps Dante as well) even as his views remained purely formalistic.[59] The years after the publication of that work have powerfully nuanced its conclusions. But Dante's '*reductio ad unum*' still captures the legal imagination. The global is still seen as somehow grander, truer, and better than the (merely) local and the objective of ambitious men and women criss-crossing the world at their conferences is still to weave a single web of law that would finally encompass a universal system of peace and welfare. It is hard to think of a more significant motive for research in the history of international law and empire than the ambivalence of such an enterprise.

Bibliography

'The Letters Patents, or Privileges Granted by her Majestie to Sir Edward Osborne …' in Hakluyt, Richard, *The Principal Navigations, Voyages, Traffiques and Discoveries of the English Nation* (James MacLehose and Sons 1904)

Alighieri, Dante, *Monarchy* (P Shaw ed, Cambridge University Press 1996)

Andrews, Kenneth R, *Trade, Plunder and Settlement: Maritime Enterprise and the Genesis of the British Empire* (Cambridge University Press 1984)

Anghie, Antony, *Sovereignty, Imperialism and the Making of International Law* (Cambridge University Press 2003)

Arrighi, Giovanni, *The Long Twentieth Century: Money, Power and the Origins of Our Times* (Verso 2010)

Belmessous, Saliha (ed), *Empire by Treaty: Negotiating European Expansion, 1600–1900* (Oxford University Press 2015)

Benton, Lauren and Straumann, Benjamin, 'Acquiring Empire by Law: From Roman Doctrine to Early Modern European Practice' (2010) 28 Law & History Review 1

Brenner, Robert, *Merchants and Revolution: Commercial Change, Political Conflict, and London's Overseas Traders 1550–1653* (Verso 2003)

Cavanagh, Edward, 'Possession and Dispossession in Corporate New France, 1600–1663: Debunking a "Juridical History" and Revisiting terra Nullius' (2014) 32 Law & History Review 97

Conring, Hermann, *New Discourse on the Roman-German Emperor* (C Fasolt ed and tr, Arizona Center for Medieval and Renaissance Studies 2005)

---

[59] Michael Hardt and Antonio Negri, *Empire* (Harvard University Press 2000) 7–8.

Costello, Frank B, *The Political Philosophy of Luis de Molina* (1535–1600) (Roma Institute Historium 1974)

Credit Suisse, 'Global Wealth Report 2015' 6 <https://publications.credit-suisse.com/tasks/render/file/?fileID=F2425415-DCA7-80B8-EAD989AF9341D47E> accessed 16 November 2015

Davis John P, *Corporations: A Study of the Origin and Development of Great Business Combinations and their Relation to the Authority of the State* (Franken 1971)

Decock, Wim, *Theologians and Contract Law: The Moral Transformation of the Ius Commune (ca. 1500–1650)* (Nijhoff 2013)

Dewar, Helen, 'Souveraineté dans les colonies, souveraineté en metropole: le role de la Nouvelle-France dans la consolidation de l'autorité maritime in France, 1620–1628' (2011) 64 Revue d'histoire de l'Amérique française 63

Dworkin, Ronald, *Law's Empire* (Harvard University Press 1986)

Dyson, RW, *Giles of Rome's On Ecclesiastical Power: A Medieval Theory of World Government* (Columbia University Press 2004)

Eslava, Luis, Fahkri, Michael, and Nesiah, Vasuki (eds), *Bandung, Global History and International Law: Critical Pasts and Pending Futures* (Cambridge University Press 2016)

Fastenrath, Ulrich, et al (eds), *From Bilateralism to Community Interest: Essays in Honour of Judge Bruno Simma* (Oxford University Press 2011)

Ford, Lisa, *Settler Sovereignty: Jurisdiction and Indigenous People in America and Australia* (Harvard University Press 2011)

Frégault, Guy and Trudel, Marcel, *Histoire du Canada par les texts*, tome 1 (Montréal 1963)

Gentili, Alberico, *De jure belli libri tres: Vol II The Translation* (Clarendon 1933)

Grandmaison, Olivier Le Cour, *Coloniser—Exterminer: Sur la guerre et l'État colonial* (Fayard 2005)

Grewe, Wilhelm G, *The Epochs of International Law* (Michael Byers tr, De Gruyter 2000)

Haggenmacher, Peter, *Grotius et la guerre juste* (Presses Universitaires de France 1983)

Hardt, Michael and Negri, Antonio, *Empire* (Harvard University Press 2000)

Headley, John M, *The Emperor and his Chancellor: A Study of Imperial Chancellery under Gattinara* (Cambridge University Press 1983)

Headley, John M, 'The Habsburg World Empire and the Revival of Ghibellinism' in David Armitage (ed) *Theories of Empire 1450–1800* (Ashgate 1998)

Hebié, Mamadou, *Les accords conclus entre les puissances coloniales et les entités politiques locales comme moyens d'acquisition de la souveraineté territoriale* (Presses Universitaires de France 2015)

Holdsworth, William S, *A History of English Law* (Methuen 1937) Vol 10

Holdsworth, William S, 'The Relation of English Law to International Law' (1941–42) 26 Minnesota Law Review 141

Israel, Jonathan, *Dutch Primacy in World Trade 1585–1740* (Clarendon 1989)

Kayaoglu, Turan, *Legal Imperialism: Sovereignty and Extraterritoriality in Japan, the Ottoman Empire, and China* (Cambridge University Press 2010)

Kelsen, Hans, *Die Staatslehre des Dante Alighieri* (F Deuticke 1905)

Kelsen, Hans, *Der soziologische und der juristische Staatsbegriff* (2nd edn, Mohr 1928)

Kelsen, Hans, *Introduction to Problems of Legal Theory* (Bonnie Litschewshi Paulson and Stanley L Paulson trs, Clarendon 1992).

Koskenniemi, Martti, *The Gentle Civilizer of Nations: The Rise and Fall of International Law 1870–1960* (Cambridge University Press 2001)

Koskenniemi, Martti, *From Apology to Utopia: The Structure of International Legal Argument* (Reissue with a new epilogue, Cambridge University Press 2005)

Koskenniemi, Martti, 'International Law and Empire: The Real Spanish Contribution' (2011) 61 University of Toronto Law Journal 1

Koskenniemi, Martti, 'Expanding Histories of International Law' (2016) 56 American Journal of Legal History 104

Krynen, Jacques, *L'empire du Roi: Idées et croyances politiques en France XIIIe-XVe siècle* (Gallimard 1993)

Linden, Mieke van der, *The Acquisition of Africa 1870–1914: The Nature of Nineteenth-Century International Law* (Wolf 2014)

Lipson, Charles, *Standing Guard: Protecting Foreign Capital in the Nineteenth and Twentieth Centuries* (University of California Press 1985)

Lowry, S Todd, 'Lord Mansfield and the Law Merchant: Law and Economics in the Eighteenth Century' (1973) 7 Journal of Economic Issues 605

Lupher, David A, *Romans in the New World: Classical Models in Sixteenth Century Spanish America* (University of Michigan Press 2003)

Malynes, Gerard, *Consuetodo vel Lex Mercatoria, or the Antient Law-Merchant* (London 1629)

McHugh, Paul, *Aboriginal Societies and the Common Law: A History of Sovereignty, Status, and Self-Determination* (Oxford University Press 2005)

Miller v. Race in *Notes of cases argued, and adjudged, in the Court of King's Bench, and of some determined in the other high courts [1753–1759]* (Clarke 1825)

Muldoon, James, *Empire and Order: The Concept of Empire, 800–1800* (Palgrave Macmillan 1999)

Nys, Ernst, *Les origines du droit international* (Castaignes 1894)

Orford, Anne, 'Food Security, Free Trade, and the Battle for the State' (2015) 11(2) Journal of International Law and International Relations 1

Osiander, Andreas, *Before the State: Systemic Political Change in the West from the Greeks to the French Revolution* (Oxford University Press 2007)

Oxfam, 'Having it All and Wanting More, Report on Inequality' (2015) <http://policy-practice.oxfam.org.uk/publications/wealth-having-it-all-and-wanting-more-338125?cid=rdt_havingitall> accessed 16 November 2015

Pahuja, Sundhya, *Decolonising International Law: Development, Economic Growth and the Politics of Universality* (Cambridge University Press 2013)

Philips, CH, *The East India Company 1784–1834* (Manchester University Press 1961)

Polanyi, Karl, *The Great Transformation: The Political and Economic Origins of Our Time* (Beacon 2001)

Pownall, Thomas, *The Administration of the British Colonies* (5th edn, Walter 1774) Vol I

Pownall, Thomas, *A Memorial most Humbly Addressed to the Sovereigns of Europe on the Present State of Affairs between the Old and the New World* (2nd edn, London 1780)

Rubios, Juan Lopez de Palacios, *De las Islas del Mar Océano* (Fondo de cultura económica 1954)

Schmitt, Carl, *Positionen und Begriffe im Kampf mit Weimar—Genf—Versailles 1923–1939* (Duncker and Humblot 1988)

Semmel, Bernard, *The Rise of Free Trade Imperialism: Classical Political Economy, the Empire of Free Trade and Imperialism 1750–1850* (Cambridge University Press 1970)

Tomlins, Christopher, *Freedom Bound: Law, Labour and Civic Identity in Colonizing English America* (Cambridge University Press 2010)

Williams, Robert A, *The American Indian in Western Legal Thought: The Discourses of Conquest* (Oxford University Press 1990)

Wood, Alfred C, *A History of the Levant Company* (Routledge 1964)

Woolf, Cecil N, *Bartolus of Sassoferrato: His Position in the History of Medieval Political Thought* (Cambridge University Press 1913)

PART I

EPISTEMOLOGIES OF EMPIRE
AND INTERNATIONAL LAW

1

Provincializing Grotius: International Law and Empire in a Seventeenth-Century Malay Mirror

*Arthur Weststeijn**

Hugo Grotius, long considered a founding father of modern international law, has undergone a remarkable revision in recent scholarship. Over the past decade, a series of publications, especially by Peter Borschberg, Martine van Ittersum, and Eric Wilson, have significantly altered the long-dominant interpretation of Grotius as architect and disinterested champion of a universally applicable notion of the law of nations. In these recent publications, Grotius is presented in a different and much less favourable light: as a clever but highly compromised author who consciously developed a structure of legal reasoning to offer the nascent Dutch Republic the intellectual armoury for attaining colonial supremacy overseas.[1] With this new interpretation, the scholarly emphasis has shifted from *De iure belli ac pacis*, traditionally considered to be Grotius' masterwork, to his earlier treatise *De iure praedae*, written on the explicit request of the board of the Dutch East India Company (VOC) between 1604 and 1606. This work, though never published in its day and only rediscovered in its entirety in the nineteenth century (a short excerpt of it was published in 1609 as *Mare liberum*), now counts as the foundational backbone of Grotius' political stance and of the onset of Dutch colonialism in South East Asia. From a founding father of international law, Grotius has turned into a founding

* This chapter originates from a discussion with Romain Bertrand and Stefania Gialdroni at the École française de Rome in 2013, organized by Guillaume Calafat and François Dumasy. I would like to thank all of them, especially Guillaume, for their inspiration, and the editors of this volume for their useful remarks on an earlier version.

[1] Martine van Ittersum, *Profit and Principle: Hugo Grotius, Natural Rights Theories and the Rise of Dutch Power in the East Indies (1595–1615)* (Brill 2006); Eric Wilson, *The Savage Republic: De Indis of Hugo Grotius, Republicanism, and Dutch Hegemony in the Early Modern World System (c.1600–1619)* (Martinus Nijhoff 2008); Peter Borschberg, *Hugo Grotius, the Portuguese and Free Trade in the East Indies* (NUS Press 2011). See also Hans W Blom (ed), *Property, Piracy and Punishment: Hugo Grotius on War and Booty in* De iure praedae: *Concepts and Contexts* (Brill 2009). Fundamental for the new interpretation has been Edward Keene, *Beyond the Anarchical Society: Grotius, Colonialism and Order in World Politics* (Cambridge University Press 2002).

father of a Dutch empire by law. Surely, there are few other examples of such a swift and radical shift in the status of a universally cherished mastodon of early modern legal thought.

There is, however, a problem with this new interpretation of Grotius—for all its indubitable merits. Or perhaps it is better to say there is a certain irony to it, which seems to have escaped some of its proponents. The irony is that in the interpretation of Grotius as a colonial ideologue, the point of reference and of departure in the analysis generally remains located in Western Europe, to be more precise in Holland. Implicit (and sometimes explicit) to the earlier dominant view on Grotius as a godfather of the Westphalian system was that the West counted as the birthplace and thereby centre of international law, degrading other areas of the globe to the peripheries of its history. The new interpretation of Grotius, perhaps rightly, emphasizes the 'imperial' characteristics of this Eurocentric focus. Clearly, the professed aim is now to take a much more critical stance, unmasking and thereby delegitimizing the colonial or imperial agenda that underlay Grotius' writings. Yet in doing so, the new interpretation continues enacting a dramatic play of global interaction where the European attitude dominates the stage: the protagonist Grotius plays the part of ingenious plotter, Dutch colonial agents happily perform his schemes in South East Asia—and the indigenous peoples are not much more than onlookers behind the scenes who passively undergo the spectacle. Europe, in other words, remains the norm, and the intellectual history of Dutch colonialism continues going mainly in one direction, from centre to periphery. The irony, of course, is that this interpretation merely seems to confirm Grotius' alleged own project of imposing Western norms of international law on non-Western societies. By presenting Grotius' writings as a mouthpiece of Dutch imperialism, the new interpretation risks maintaining the imperial structure of centre and periphery that Grotius himself helped to create.[2]

The question, then, is whether it might be possible to turn the equation. Is there a way to look at the Dutch empire by law in South East Asia from a different perspective, collapsing the dominant hierarchy of centre and periphery? Or to put it differently: is it possible to 'provincialize' Grotius?[3] An earlier hint in this direction has already been given in the pivotal work of Charles H Alexandrowicz, one of the most significant proponents of the traditional interpretation of Grotius. In *An Introduction to the History of the Law of Nations in the East Indies* from 1967, Alexandrowicz argued that Asian-European relations in the early modern period rested on an inclusive notion of the law of nations; Grotius, as one of the founders of this law of nations, used his knowledge of Asian legal sources to argue the case of the VOC. According to Alexandrowicz, it is 'possible to assume that Grotius in formulating his doctrine of the freedom of the sea found himself encouraged by what

---

[2] It should be added that in my own publications on seventeenth-century Dutch colonialism, I have blatantly taken a Eurocentric focus, discussing only Dutch sources. This essay can therefore be seen as an immodest attempt to problematize the limits of my own research.

[3] I am of course, indebted to Dipesh Chakrabarty, *Provincializing Europe: Postcolonial Thought and Historical Difference* (Princeton University Press 2000) for this term.

he learned from the study of Asian maritime custom'.[4] Grotius, in other words, embodied the universal background to international law that Alexandrowicz advocated. This interpretation has been adopted in comparable studies, such as the work by Ram Prakash Anand.[5] Nonetheless, it seems to have been largely the result of wishful thinking. As Peter Borschberg has shown recently, Grotius knew virtually nothing of Asian customs, legal codes, or even mere geography. Borschberg's verdict is categorical: 'The "Alexandrowicz thesis" extolling Grotius' supposed familiarity with Asian commercial and maritime practices cannot be sustained by any stretch of the imagination.'[6]

The attempt at provincializing Grotius by starting with Grotius himself has thus failed. The obvious alternative is to forget about Grotius for a while, and to focus all attention to Asian sources only. That, however, is easier said than done, for the simple reason that very few substantial sources of the period are left. In *L'histoire à parts égales*, a wonderful analysis of the European-Asian encounter around 1600, Romain Bertrand explains how little mention is made in contemporary indigenous accounts of the arrival and increasing presence of the Dutch in South East Asia. One explanation, Bertrand argues, is that the Dutch were simply not very significant from the South East Asian point of view—they were mere 'flies in the milk', in the felicitous phrasing of the twentieth-century Dutch writer Willem Walraven quoted by Bertrand.[7] Another explanation is perhaps equally prosaic: many indigenous sources of the period are no longer available, being never printed and sometimes even destroyed during the advance of colonial rule.

However, there is an exception, which receives its due share in Bertrand's work: the treatise *Taj al-Salatin* ['The Crown of All Kings'], composed by the author Bukhari al-Jauhari in 1603 in the Sultanate of Aceh in north Sumatra, a strong regional power and centre of Islamic scholarship that had diplomatic ties with the Dutch and had sent an embassy to the Dutch Republic one year before. The treatise, written in Malay in Arabic script, discusses the responsibilities and duties of rulers and subjects; it can be characterized as an example of the 'mirror for princes' genre, probably partly derived from earlier Persian sources. Little is known about the author, but his name betrays that he probably originated from the Kingdom of Johor in the south of the Malay Peninsula. In 1603, the year *Taj al-Salatin* was composed, an alliance between Johor and the Dutch captain Jacob van Heemskerck resulted in the seizure of the Portuguese vessel *Santa Catarina* in the Johor River

---

[4] Charles H Alexandrowicz, *An Introduction to the History of the Law of Nations in the East Indies* (Clarendon Press 1967) 65. For recent criticism of Alexandrowicz' general thesis, see Robert Travers, 'A British Empire by Treaty in Eighteenth Century India' in Saliha Belmessous (ed), *Empire by Treaty: Negotiating European Expansion, 1600–1900* (Oxford University Press 2014).

[5] Ram Prakash Anand, *Origin and Development of the Law of the Sea: History of International Law Revisited* (Martinus Nijhoff 1983) 80.

[6] Borschberg, *Hugo Grotius* (n 1) 145. See also Cornelis G Roelofsen, 'The Sources of *Mare Liberum*: The Contested Origins of the Doctrine of the Freedom of the Sea' in WP Heere (ed), *International Law and its Sources* (Kluwer 1988).

[7] Romain Bertrand, *L'histoire à parts égales: Récits d'une rencontre Orient-Occident (XVIe–XVIIe siècle)* (Seuil 2011) 449.

estuary. The seizure gave rise to much controversy, and to uphold its legitimacy, Hugo Grotius was asked to write a legal defence. Thus originated *De iure praedae*.[8]

Taj al-Salatin, then, proves to be promising material for a comparison with Grotius since it is an exact contemporary to *De iure praedae* written in a connected political and diplomatic context—yet on the other side of the globe. Opening up a small but highly exceptional window onto the panorama of the royal courts in the Malay-speaking world, the treatise discusses issues such as sovereignty, justice, the social contract and the right of rebellion that are also central in Grotius' writings and in European political thought in general around 1600.[9] At the same time, its survival proves that *Taj al-Salatin* was widely circulated throughout South East Asia, whilst Grotius' treatise, apart from *Mare liberum*, remained unpublished and was read only by a few. Accordingly, a contextualized reading of *Taj al-Salatin* makes it possible to approach Grotius, and thereby the Dutch empire by law in South East Asia, from a 'peripheral' perspective. Such an exercise could be characterized as a clear-cut example of comparative (and loosely connected) global intellectual history, in line with the recent categorization of approaches in this burgeoning field by Samuel Moyn and Andrew Sartori.[10] Yet the aim of this chapter is to go further by posing a hypothetical question from the (admittedly rather dodgy) realm of if-history: if South East Asian readers had read Grotius, how would they have read it? *Taj al-Salatin* allows for such an exercise in if-history: an exercise in provincializing Grotius that is also an exercise in establishing the possibilities of commensurability between East and West. *Taj al-Salatin*, a treatise conceived as a mirror of princes, thus serves as a Malay mirror that reflects the oddities of international law and empire in its Grotian guise.

'Pearls for the Ears of the Mind': Structure and Contents of *Taj al-Salatin*

Taj al-Salatin is a performative treatise with a title as a speech-act: as Bukhari explains in the introduction, the book's title, 'Crown of all Kings', entails the effect of the book, for whoever reads it attentively will know how to be a true king, his crown being thus legitimized by the book. In twenty-four chapters, Bukhari unfolds the appropriate guidance on moral conduct and political statecraft, explicitly

---

[8] On the seizure of the *Santa Catarina* and the making of *De iure praedae*, see the detailed analysis in van Ittersum, *Profit and Principle* (n 1), and Peter Borschberg, 'The Seizure of the *Santa Catarina* Revisited: The Portuguese Empire in Asia, VOC Politics and the Origins of the Dutch-Johor Alliance (c.1602–1616)' (2002) 33 Journal of Southeast Asian Studies 31.

[9] Bertrand, *L'histoire à parts égales* (n 7) 348–74.

[10] Samuel Moyn and Andrew Sartori (eds), *Global Intellectual History* (Columbia University Press 2013), especially Moyn and Sartori, 'Approaches to Global Intellectual History'. Cf as well Takashi Shogimen and Cary J Nederman (eds), *Western Political Thought in Dialogue with Asia* (Lexington 2009). For a typical example of comparative history of international law focusing on Grotius and Islam, see Christoph Stumpf, 'Völkerrecht unter Kreuz und Halbmond: Muhammad al-Shaybani und Hugo Grotius als Exponenten religiöser Völkerrechtstraditionen', (2003) 41 Archiv des Völkerrechts 83.

addressing an audience of (future) kings and their advisors, officials, and subjects. The text is interspersed with passages from the Qur'an and the Hadith literature, Persian poetry, and historical references to pagan and Muslim rulers, as well as other texts from the Persian mirrors of princes genre, the so-called *andarz*, for example to the late fifteenth-century ethical treatise *Aklaq-e mohseni*.[11] Various manuscripts of the work survive; the first edition was published, with parallel Dutch translation, in 1827 by the Dutch colonial official and linguist (and veteran of the battle of Waterloo) Philippus Pieter Roorda van Eysinga.[12]

The treatise begins with an extensive exhortation to self-knowledge and the knowledge of God. Starting from the hadith 'he who knows himself knows his Lord', Bukhari, most likely a Sunni Muslim, developed the foundational premises of his worldview combining anatomical theories with mystical Sufi teaching.[13] The central message is that true self-knowledge recognizes the physical condition of mankind and the ensuing equality of all and man's subservience to Allah. A detailed survey of the human body and its conception in the womb, with references to Hippocrates, Galen and Aristotle, leads to the admonition 'to think about yourself and know yourself and to contemplate the greatness of the Lord of Hosts, who has created all out of a drop of water and whose entire existence is a secret'.[14] This divine origin of mankind necessitates that one should not neglect one's body, but also realize one's humbleness; modesty is essential since all human excellence is a mere reflection of Allah.

At the same time, man is also inherently weak, being a slave to his passions, which are the result of the four elements that constitute the human body. In line with the classical theory of humorism, Bukhari emphasized the precarious balance of bodily fluids that determine human appetite and health. The resulting passions

[11] M Ismail Marcinkowski, 'Taj al-Salatin' *Encyclopaedia Iranica* (2009) <http://www.iranicaonline. org/articles/taj-al-salatin> accessed 10 December 2014. On the linguistic aspects of *Taj al-Salatin*, see Philippus Samuel van Ronkel, 'De Kroon der Koningen' (1899) 41 Tijdschrift voor Indische taal-, land- en volkenkunde van het Koninklijk Bataviaasch Genootschap van Kunsten en Wetenschapen 55. Van Ronkel claimed the text to be entirely copied from a (lost) Persian original. This view is questioned in Taufik Abdullah, 'The Formation of a Political Tradition in the Malay World' in Anthony Reid (ed), *The Making of an Islamic Political Discourse in Southeast Asia* (Monash University Press 1993) 41, fn 12. For a comprehensive discussion of the work and its authorship, see VI Braginsky, '*Tajus Salatin* ("The Crown of Sultans") of Bukhari al-Jahauri as a Canonical Work and an Attempt to Create a Malay Literary Canon' in David Smyth (ed), *The Canon in Southeast Asian Literatures: Literatures of Burma, Cambodia, Indonesia, Laos, Malaysia, the Philippines, Thailand and Vietnam* (Curzon Press 2000). Cf as well the superficial analysis in Ingrid Saroda Mitrasing, 'The Age of Aceh and the Evolution of Kingship, 1599–1641' (PhD dissertation, Leiden University 2011) 35–38.

[12] Bukhari al-Jauhari, *De kroon aller koningen van Bocharie van Djohor* (PP Roorda van Eysinga ed and tr, Landsdrukkerij 1827). A French translation was made by Aristide Marre: *Makôta radja-râdja ou la couronne des rois* (Maisonneuve 1878). One manuscript is in the Leiden University Library, catalogued as LUB.D 625, Codex Orientalis 3053. Another manuscript, copied in 1824, is in the British Library, digitally available at <http://www.bl.uk/manuscripts/FullDisplay.aspx?ref=Or_13295> accessed 10 December 2014. For a Malay romanized edition of the Leiden manuscript, see Khalid M Hussain (ed), *Taj us-Salatin* (2nd edn, Dewan Bahasa dan Pustaka 1992).

[13] Cf Abdullah, 'The Formation of a Political Tradition' (n 11) 42; Bertrand, *L'histoire à parts égales* (n 7) 365.

[14] Bukhari, *De kroon aller koningen* (n 12) 14. Translations are from the Dutch. For the reference to Hippocrates, Galen, and Aristotle, see Bukhari, *De kroon aller koningen* (n 12) 12.

define the ambivalent human condition, characterized by the desire to pursue detrimental deeds and the aversion of actions that are wholesome. Man, therefore, is
essentially powerless, regardless of his social status: at the moment of death, the differences 'between sultan and subject, between ruler and slave, between the rich and
the poor' will turn out to be non-existent. All are equal on Judgment Day; 'all kings
who are haughty in this world and consider none of their fellow humans equal to
themselves, will be raised like ants'.[15] Consequently, man should be humble and
consider himself nothing but a servant of Allah, without looking down at others
and oppressing his fellow servants. Allah, by contrast, is eternal and perfect, self-
originating and hence without extension or bodily attributes; man should realize
that his existence 'in the knowledge and providence of Allah is like the existence of
a fish in the water'—there is no life possible outside, even though the fish does not
know what water is.[16] The worldly life of man is generally spent in equal ignorance
and insignificance, being nothing but a short rest on the way towards eternity.

On the basis of this exposition of human nature and self-knowledge, Bukhari
built the central tenets of his political counsels, which make up the main part of the
treatise. Evidently, a crucial concern for Bukhari was how to ensure stability and
the maintenance of royal power. The Sultanate of Aceh had recently experienced
a period of intense internal turmoil, with five consecutive kings being murdered
and a sixth dethroned by his own son;[17] it is likely that Bukhari's intention was to
reach a stable political order by compounding a range of traditional teachings. To
that end, he gave a series of advices on how to rule, each one of which is illustrated
by *exempla* taken from scriptural and historical writings. The result is clearly in line
with the genre of Islamic *adab* literature, treatises that defined rules of princely
'civility' following the decrees of the Qur'an and the models of pagan ancient history, in particular Alexander the Great.[18]

A pivotal concept advanced by Bukhari in this context is the one of sovereignty,
kerajaan, which is divided into two separate but complementary elements of royal
obligation: *hukumah*, the responsibility for the juridical regulation of society, and
nubuwwah, the prophetic duty to guard over religious orthodoxy.[19] The obvious
ideal is the perfect amalgamation of these two elements in one ruler, personified
by the prophet Moses and his theocratic rule over the Jews. Ever since, the first
element of sovereignty has been subordinate to the second, which means that all
servants of Allah are also bound to obey their worldly rulers. Nonetheless, Bukhari
made a clear and significant distinction between the worldly and the prophetic
realm. As Bertrand shows in his analysis of the treatise, this distinction opens up the

[15] Bukhari, *De kroon aller koningen* (n 12) 25, 27. On the ambiguities in the Islamic creed of the
equality of all believers before God, see Louise Marlow, *Hierarchy and Egalitarianism in Islamic Thought*
(Cambridge University Press 1997).

[16] Bukhari, *De kroon aller koningen* (n 12) 32.

[17] Abdullah, 'The Formation of a Political Tradition' (n 11) 47–48.

[18] Bertrand, *L'histoire à parts égales* (n 7) 348–49. For Alexander the Great as *exemplum*, see Bukhari,
De kroon aller koningen (n 12), eg 147–50, 163–64, 176.

[19] See Bertrand, *L'histoire à parts égales* (n 7) 349 and Jajat Burhanudin, '*Kerajaan*-Oriented
Islam: The Experience of Pre-Colonial Indonesia' (2006) 13 Studia Islamika 45, 45–47.

possibility of civil disobedience (or even rebellion), for what to do with a ruler who does not follow the precepts of Allah and his Prophet? Bukhari's answer is that the words of such an evil ruler should be obeyed, but not his deeds; the reason for such compliance is not the majesty of the ruler, but rather to avoid social discord. If there is no risk of disorder, 'we do not have to obey his words nor his deeds. We should even not turn our eyes to his face. For those who deviate from the commandments of Allah and his Prophet are his enemies, and it is our duty to treat the enemies of Allah as our enemies'. Rulers, then, are the caliphs or delegates of Allah on the earth, but they should not 'believe out of ignorance and naivety to be Gods themselves, who alone should be honoured and obeyed'.[20] The obligation that subjects owe to their ruler is dependent on his devoutness and the preservation of social order. Kings who do not follow the example of the prophets and who do not 'love their subjects as if they were their children', who forget their own nature and become enslaved by the passions, are 'shadows of the Devil and delegates of Satan' who will be duly punished at Judgment Day.[21]

The way to avoid such tyranny is by practising *keadilan*, justice, which in turn follows from the *ihsan* or virtue of the ruler.[22] Justice, then, is not an abstract ideal but a practice, and the treatise correspondingly highlights the practical aspects of virtuous rule: kings should be generous, courageous, and sober (as well as male and good-looking), they should choose their delegates wisely and keep company of learned men, and they are to keep all heresy at bay. Most importantly, a king should 'consider himself as one of his subjects, for the ruler of subjects is nothing else than another person who judges among them and over them in truth'.[23] Such truth and honesty are the tokens of justice, which implies that open communication and the choice of trustworthy advisors and delegates are essential. Here the importance of rhetoric emerges: rulers should surround themselves with tactful but candid servants and shun those who 'with lovely words and various compliments entertain the king's mind'. Such flatterers have a disastrous effect, 'calling evil deeds virtues, even though because of their actions the king is brought day and night to Hell'.[24] True speech and trustworthiness, therefore, are necessary prerequisites of good government, for the king and his advisors alike; this also explains Bukhari's long digression on how to attain knowledge of gestures and facial expressions. It is such practical intelligence, *akal*, which steers rulers to do good and avoid evil. Numerous *exempla* of Muslim rulers serve to illustrate the argument, many taken from the eleventh-century Persian mirror of princes *Siyasatnama*.[25] Yet the practical characteristics of

---

[20] Bukhari, *De kroon aller koningen* (n 12) 50. Cf the analysis in Bertrand, *L'histoire à parts égales* (n 7) 352–53, and Abdullah, 'The Formation of a Political Tradition' (n 11) 45–46.

[21] Bukhari, *De kroon aller koningen* (n 12) 60.

[22] Cf Bertrand, *L'histoire à parts égales* (n 7) 350.

[23] Bukhari, *De kroon aller koningen* (n 12) 66.

[24] Bukhari, *De kroon aller koningen* (n 12) 74, 84.

[25] Nizam al-Mulk, *Siyasatnama: The Book of Government or Rules for Kings* (Hubert Darke ed and tr, Curzon Press 2002). For analysis, see Marta Simidchieva, 'Kingship and Legitimacy in Nizam al-Mulk's *Siyasatnama*, Fifth/Eleventh Century' in Beatrice Gruendler and Louise Marlow (eds), *Writers and Rulers: Perspectives on Their Relationship from Abassid to Safavid Times* (Reichert 2004).

justice imply that true faith is not indispensable for good government: justice can equally be found under non-Muslim rulers, such as the sixth-century Persian king Khosrau I. Such infidel kings may not end up in heaven (purgatory is reserved for them), but they understand the principles of maintaining power by ruling justly and making the people prosper: 'justice bars all mischief from the infidel king and it removes all dangers from his entire kingdom, for through his justice the life of the ruler is lengthened and his rule persists'. Tyrants, by contrast, also when they are Islamic, will never be able to escape divine wrath.[26]

The aim of government, then, is to establish a perfect harmony between rulers and ruled. The intrinsic equality and weakness of all entails a model of social and political concord where all share in reciprocal duties and obligations and all fulfil their corresponding functions. Following the Islamic tradition, the personal qualities of the ruler and his officials are thus considered more important than details of legislation or the impersonal organization of the state.[27] Government is 'like an elevated palace that rests on four pillars', constituted by servants, generals, treasurers, and ambassadors, who have to be obedient to Allah and their ruler and trustworthy in their actions and advices. Rulers, at the same time, should be humble and magnanimous; all have to seek honour by striving for what is 'good, fair and honest in the world'.[28] Yet the bottom line of good government is equity and mutual trust. The ruler should speak justice in such a way 'as if every one of his subjects … is equal to him', following the maxim that he passes the sentence he would like to be passed for himself. Moreover, the ruler should always be trustworthy and reliable, for 'the act of keeping one's promises is the nature of all noble, benevolent, wise and religious men'. This practice of *wafa ahad*, keeping one's promises, is the glue that keeps society together and therefore the essence of humanity. 'He who does not keep his word and treats his master treacherously cannot be called a human being among other humans.'[29]

In the conclusion of the treatise, Bukhari presented his work as being a 'companion' and 'roadmap' for all rulers, officials and subjects through the labyrinth of politics, 'unfolding the nature of the master and the servant'. Its professed aim was to establish a 'mutual love between the king and his subjects', a love that was exemplified by the book itself. After the Qur'an, Bukhari claimed, his treatise came next in significance, bringing its readers and listeners 'temporal and eternal blessing'. Rulers should thus read the book daily right after morning's prayer; and prosperity should 'treasure the book by preserving it as pearls for the ears of the mind, and by preserving its aims as gems for the ring of the heart, because it contains revealed and secret adornments'.[30]

---

[26] Bukhari, *De kroon aller koningen* (n 12) 101.
[27] Abdullah, 'The Formation of a Political Tradition' (n 11) 44. See also Ann KS Lambton, *State and Government in Medieval Islam: An Introduction to the Study of Islamic Political Theory: The Jurists* (Oxford University Press 1981).
[28] Bukhari, *De kroon aller koningen* (n 12) 115, 164.
[29] Bukhari, *De kroon aller koningen* (n 12) 178, 214, 219.
[30] Bukhari, *De kroon aller koningen* (n 12) 220–23, 226.

A Tale of Two Parrots: Readers and Envoys
between South East Asia and the Dutch Republic

Taj al-Salatin was a highly popular text throughout South East Asia. Copies of the treatise circulated widely in the region, not only in Sumatra and the Malay Peninsula but also on Java. Yasadipura I, a famous poet at the eighteenth-century Surakarta court, translated the work into Javanese; Hamengkuwono I, the founder of the Yogyakarta dynasty who ruled from 1755 to 1792, used it allegedly as a guide. At the beginning of the nineteenth century, Hussein Shah, Sultan of Johor and Singapore, was said to have relied on the work in his dealings with the English East India Company.[31] Until today, the treatise continues to exercise political influence in the Malay-speaking world.[32]

Moreover, *Taj al-Salatin* was also read by Dutch colonial actors in the area. In 1603, the year of its composition, the first European manual for learning Malay was published in Amsterdam by Frederick de Houtman, one of the protagonists in the first Dutch explorations of South East Asia who had just spent two years in a prison in Aceh.[33] With the gradual expansion of Dutch colonial rule throughout the seventeenth and eighteenth centuries, mastering Malay became an instrument of understanding, controlling, and evangelizing the indigenous populations. One of the most important colonial actors in this context was François Valentijn, a minister long based at the island of Ambon in the Moluccas, who published towards the end of his life an extensive description of what he called the 'Dutch empire' in South East Asia. In the part on Malacca, Valentijn mentioned that he was the proud owner of a few 'very rare books written in Arabic script' which had taught him all he knew about the area. One of these works was *Taj al-Salatin*. The book was a 'juwel', he said, which, 'although being filled with many fantasies and useless matters', was not only very helpful to learn Malay, but it also revealed 'many useful matters concerning Javanese, Malay and other Kings, which we could not learn from other writers'.[34] Valentijn actually owned two copies of the treatise, which

---

[31] Bertrand, *L'histoire à parts égales* (n 7) 363; Abdullah, 'The Formation of a Political Tradition' (n 11) 41, fn 12; Marcinkowski, 'Taj al-Salatin' (n 11).

[32] See eg Farish A Noor, 'Blind Loyalty? Re-Reading the *Taj-us Salatin* of Buchara al-Jahauri' (2009) <http://blog.limkitsiang.com/2009/02/11/blind-loyalty-re-reading-the-taj-us-salatin-of-buchara-al-jauhari/> accessed 10 December 2014; and Muhd Norizam Jamian and Shaiful Bahri Md Radzi, 'In Search of a Just Leader in Islamic Perspective: An Analysis of Traditional Malay Literature from the Perspective of *Adab*' (2013) 9(6) Asian Social Science 22.

[33] Frederick de Houtman, *Spraeck ende woord-boeck, inde Maleysche ende Madagaskirsche talen, met vele Arabische ende Turcsche woorden* (Jan Evertsz Cloppenburgh 1603). On De Houtman's period in prison, see Frederick de Houtman, 'Cort verhael vant gene wedervaren is Frederick de Houtman tot Atchein' in Willem S Unger (ed), *De oudste reizen van de Zeeuwen naar Oost-Indië, 1598–1604* (Martinus Nijhoff 1948). For analysis, see Bertrand, *L'histoire à parts égales* (n 7) 95–97, 252–54.

[34] François Valentijn, *Beschryving van Oud en Nieuw Oost-Indien, bevattende een naauwkeurige en uitvoerige verhandeling van Nederlands Mogentheid in die gewesten* (Johannes van Braam 1724–26) vol 5, 316.

were auctioned off after his death in 1728.[35] Another colonial actor, the Swiss-born George Henrik Werndly who authored a long-used teaching method of Malay in 1736, mentioned *Taj al-Salatin* as an essential part of the ideal Malay library.[36] This 'orientalist' interest in the treatise eventually culminated in the 1827 edition and translation by Roorda van Eysinga. He equally praised the style of the work and explicitly aimed to preserve it for the Malay-speaking world and to divulge its contents among a European audience. *Taj al-Salatin*, then, had enjoyed long and lasting popularity even before Grotius' *De iure praedae* was rediscovered and integrally published in 1864. What would have happened if *De iure praedae* had been published straight away, and if it had circulated at the royal courts in South East Asia during the seventeenth century?

It may be pertinent to emphasize that this particular hypothesis of if-history is not as unlikely as it might seem. Indeed, in 1602, a year before *Taj al-Salatin* was composed in Aceh, a delegation of representatives of the sultan of Aceh, Alau'd-din Ri'ayat Syah, travelled to the Dutch Republic. This embassy followed from earlier contact in Aceh, where two Dutch merchants had enjoyed an audience with the sultan, bringing a missive from stadholder Maurice of Orange (ironically written in Spanish) that suggested establishing a common front against the King of Spain.[37] To show his appreciation and interest, the sultan sent a delegation of his own to the Dutch Republic on board of two Dutch vessels. On their way west, the Dutch seized the Portuguese carrack *Sao Tiago* at Saint Helena in the Atlantic, and after having abandoned the Portuguese crew at an island off the coast of Brazil, the *Sao Tiago* was taken to the Dutch Republic and auctioned off together with its valuable cargo. The episode, witnessed by the Aceh delegation, was comparable to the seizure of the *Santa Catarina* the next year. Grotius commented upon it in *De iure praedae* as being entirely legitimate, since the Dutch 'had been provoked by a hostile response to their overtures and by previous recourse to armed attack on the part of the Portuguese'. Indeed, according to Grotius, the Dutch remained 'mindful in victory of their own humanity rather than of the injuries for which others were responsible'.[38]

The Aceh embassy eventually arrived in the Dutch Republic in July 1602, in the city of Middelburg. One of the delegates, the elderly Abdul Zamat, died within a few days upon arrival on the damp northern soil; he received a stately burial in the presence of representatives of the local government and the directors of the recently established VOC. The other two delegates, Sri Muhamad and Mir Hasan, went on to the frontline of the war against the Spanish troops, where Maurice of Orange had established his military camp. With much ceremony, the delegates presented

---

[35] Vladimir Braginsky, 'Newly Found Manuscripts That Were Never Lost' (2010) 38 Indonesia and the Malay World 419.

[36] George Henrik Werndly, *Maleische Spraakkunst uit de eige schriften der Maleiers opgemaakt* (Wetstein 1736) 344. See Michael Laffan, *The Makings of Indonesian Islam: Orientalism and the Narration of a Sufi Past* (Princeton University Press 2011) 80–81.

[37] The letter is published in Unger (ed), *De oudste reizen* (n 33) 132–34.

[38] Hugo Grotius, *Commentary on the Law of Prize and Booty*, (Martine van Ittersum ed, Liberty Fund 2006) 299. See also van Ittersum, *Profit and Principle* (n 1) 123–51.

the stadholder two missives from the Sultan of Aceh together with a series of gifts. They then visited the camp, dined with the stadholder and discussed with him the seizure of the *Sao Tiago*. After a tour through the country, they left again for Aceh. There are no sources recounting their own experience, but the delegates apparently hoped the diplomatic ties with the Dutch would last: they brought two parrots with them to Holland that reportedly spoke Malay.[39]

Consequently, in the period that *Taj al-Salatin* was composed in Aceh, the sultan's court had first-hand knowledge of the Dutch Republic and eyewitness experience of the Dutch-Portuguese naval antagonism, which culminated in the seizures of the *Sao Tiago* and the *Santa Catarina*. Moreover, the diplomatic relations between Aceh and the Dutch soon became a pattern in the area: in 1603, the King of Johor alleg-edly asked the Dutch for military assistance against the Portuguese, which led to a Dutch-Johorese alliance, the ensuing attack on the *Santa Catarina*, and an embassy of representatives of Johor sent to the Dutch Republic that same year.[40] Within a few years, the Sultan of Aceh and the King of Johor entered into official treaties with the Dutch that stipulated military collaboration against the Portuguese and a local trading monopoly for the Dutch.[41] Grotius was deeply involved in this pro-cess of diplomatic rapprochement, drafting on behalf of the VOC a series of letters to South East Asian rulers, including to the King of Johor.[42] Indeed, this pattern of cooperation and commerce, formalized in equal treaties with sovereign rulers in South East Asia, forms the essence of Grotius' claims in *De iure praedae* for the legitimacy of Dutch conduct overseas on the basis of natural law and the law of nations. This is the pattern that characterized Dutch colonial policies throughout the region, leading to the gradual establishment of a Dutch empire by law in South East Asia. Although the Dutch initially were mere 'flies in the milk', they intruded in existing diplomatic networks to formalize and justify their presence overseas through treaties with local rulers, and subsequently used these treaties to claim colonial authority upon the basis of obligation by consent.[43]

The few existing contemporary Malay sources that mention the VOC presence in the area highlight this Dutch propensity to make (and manipulate) treaties.[44]

---

[39] See the translation of their missives in Unger (ed), *De oudste reizen* (n 33) 136–37, and the con-temporary account in Emanuel van Meteren, *Commentarien ofte memorien van den Nederlandtschen staet, handel, oorloghen ende geschiedenissen van onsen tyden* (1608), folios 60–61. The Aceh embassy is discussed in detail in Bertrand, *L'histoire à parts égales* (n 7) 196–211.

[40] Borschberg, 'The Seizure of the *Santa Catarina* Revisited' (n 8) 52, 59–60. See also E Netscher, *De Nederlanders in Djohor en Siak, 1602 tot 1865* (Bruining & Wijt 1870) 7–28.

[41] See JE Heeres (ed), *Corpus diplomaticum Neerlando-Indicum. Verzameling van politieke contracten en verdere verdragen door de Nederlanders in het Oosten gesloten* (Martinus Nijhoff 1907–38), vol 1, 41–45, 48–50.

[42] A draft of Grotius' letter to the King of Johor is reproduced in Borschberg, *Hugo Grotius* (n 1) 155. For the text of a similar letter, written to the Sultan of Tidore in the Moluccas, see Grotius, *Commentary* (n 38) appendix II.9, 553–55.

[43] See Arthur Weststeijn, '"Love Alone is Not Enough": Treaties in Seventeenth-Century Dutch Colonial Expansion' in Belmessous (ed), *Empire by Treaty* (n 4).

[44] GL Koster, 'Of Treaties and Unbelievers: Images of the Dutch in Seventeenth- and Eighteenth-Century Malay Historiography' (2005) 78 (1) Journal of the Malayan Branch of the Royal Asiatic Society 59.

Indeed, the various diplomatic exchanges with the VOC must have made the royal courts of Aceh, Johor, and elsewhere in the region sufficiently aware of the Dutch perspective as it was presented by Grotius—in some cases they actually read Grotius through his letters for the VOC. So granted that *De iure praedae* was published in its day, and granted it circulated at those royal courts, brought east by envoys or merchants, how would it have been received in seventeenth-century South East Asia? The only way to answer that question is by taking the perspective of *Taj al-Salatin*: the only source we know of that, given its popularity, can be said to represent the dominant political outlook at the royal courts in the area.

(Un) Common Ground: Mutual Trust, Conflicting Personalities

It goes without saying that *Taj al-Salatin* and *De iure praedae* are highly dissimilar in composition, contents, and scope. The first is a mirror of princes, giving counsel on the art of good government within a religious framework; the second is basically the legitimation of an act of piracy, founded on a secularizing exposition of natural law and the law of nations.[45] The main difference, arguably, is that *Taj al-Salatin* discusses politics in a highly personalized way, starting from its discussion of human nature and weakness, being explicitly directed at rulers that are considered the embodiment of the state, and using *exempla* of individual anecdotes as illustration to its precepts. *De iure praedae*, by contrast, is what might be called a depersonalizing treatise that seeks to legitimize a particular political episode by formulating universally valid norms of human behaviour, the foundation of society, and the workings of international politics.

Yet if we zoom in on a couple of specific themes present in both works, there seems to be more common ground. For example, the notion of a harmony between rulers and ruled that dominates *Taj al-Salatin* might have made its readers receptive to Grotius' prolegomena on the formation and essence of a political society. Bukhari's partly Sufi, partly Galenic elaboration of man's passions and virtues is not incongruent with the stoic view on human nature in *De iure praedae*. Likewise, the emphasis on the importance of trust, equity, and obligation that we find in *Taj al-Salatin* is mirrored in the centrality of keeping agreements in Grotius' exposition of society and international law. A just ruler administers justice as he would like it to be administered if he were the defendant, *Taj al-Salatin* claims. Moreover, 'nothing is more detestable to rulers than deviating from their promises'.[46] Can this be considered the South East Asian alternative to *pacta sunt servanda*?

The significance of this theme of trust, equity and obligation becomes particularly pertinent in the practical context of the diplomatic relations between the Dutch

---

[45] On the secularizing aspects of *De iure praedae*, see Mark Somos, *Secularisation and the Leiden Circle* (Brill 2011) 383–437.

[46] Bukhari, *De kroon aller koningen* (n 12) 196.

Republic and the South East Asian royal courts. *Taj al-Salatin* makes emphatically clear that envoys are expected to be absolutely reliable, being the voice of their ruler. 'It is the envoy's duty to speak the truth, not to fear people and not to worry about dangers.'[47] Using the metaphor of the body politic, the treatise comments that 'the nature of man is like the nature of a populous country: the king is the mind, his administrator is the judgment, his envoy the tongue and his writing the language. The nature of the king and his government can be seen in the manners of the envoy and the nature of his conversation'.[48] Given these statements, it is likely that the rulers of Aceh, Johor, and elsewhere expected the diplomatic relations they developed with the Dutch to be utterly sincere and the treaties they signed to be mutually binding.[49] Indeed, as Bertrand shows, juridical guarantees of contractual obligation were common practice in South East Asia, as attested by their codification in the mid-fifteenth-century Laws of Malacca.[50]

An ensuing important issue is the legitimacy of entering into an alliance with unbelievers. As is well known, one of Grotius' crucial and ground-breaking claims was his allegation that treaties with infidels are compatible with natural as well as divine law.[51] Significantly, *Taj al-Salatin* also dedicates an entire chapter to the issue of how to deal with infidels—perhaps a reflection of the increasing contact with Europeans, be it Catholic Portuguese or Protestant Dutchmen, in the area around Aceh. Citing the seventh-century instructions of Umar, Bukhari listed all the criteria infidels had to fulfil in order to live in a Muslim country, emphasizing the separation between believers and unbelievers; if 'the pagans meet with these conditions they are relieved from all evil, for then a righteous ruler cannot harm them'.[52] Accordingly, the social contract between rulers and ruled also applied to non-Muslim subjects, albeit under strict conditions. It is telling that many of the treaties signed with the Dutch throughout the seventeenth century explicitly codified such permissive toleration, stipulating that both parties would not interfere in each other's religious affairs.[53] In some cases at least, the Dutch and their South East Asian counterparts seemed to understand each other pretty well.

Nonetheless, the encounter between East and West also gave rise to substantial incongruities, which expose the oddities of Grotius' theory from a 'peripheral' perspective. A case in point is the issue of sovereignty. As *Taj al-Salatin* reveals, sovereignty was in South East Asia entirely associated with the person of the ruler. One of the fundamental tenets of Grotius' work, however, followed the claim that

---

[47] Bukhari, *De kroon aller koningen* (n 12) 146.

[48] Bukhari, *De kroon aller koningen* (n 12) 177.

[49] This is corroborated by a Johorese source from the end of the seventeenth century, the *Hikayat Hang Tuah*, which emphasized the significance of the treaty between Johor and the VOC from 1641. See Koster, 'Of Treaties and Unbelievers' (n 44) 67.

[50] Bertrand, *L'histoire à parts égales* (n 7) 362–63. The Laws of Malacca are published in Liaw Yock Fang (ed), *Undang-Undang Melaka: The Laws of Melaka* (Martinus Nijhoff 1976).

[51] See Richard Tuck, 'Alliances with Infidels in the European Imperial Expansion' in Sankar Muthu (ed), *Empire and Modern Political Thought* (Cambridge University Press 2012) 61–83.

[52] Bukhari, *De kroon aller koningen* (n 12) 203.

[53] See Heeres (ed), *Corpus diplomaticum Neerlando-Indicum* (n 41) vol 1, eg 37, 60, 64, 77, 93, 108–09.

private entities like the VOC could behave like a public *persona* in the international legal constellation, for example signing treaties. Grotius thus invested the VOC as a private trading company with a public mark of sovereignty, enabling it to enforce international legal rights, such as the freedom of trade. This reasoning resulted in turning the VOC into what might be called a 'corporate sovereign' that performed the rights and duties of an international legal personality.[54]

Taj al-Salatin shows that this practice of 'corporate sovereignty' would have made no sense to South East Asian readers and rulers. For them, there simply could be no distinction between public and private sovereign actors, for the sovereignty of the ruler, his *kerajaan*, was entirely dependent on his public personality and strongly associated with his individual behaviour and virtue. How could a company of merchants that did not even have a single leader possibly perform the same rights and obligations as a sovereign prince? It is not surprising that the Aceh delegation visiting the Dutch Republic in the summer of 1602 rushed to the military camp of Maurice of Orange, the only one under the Dutch grey skies that seemed to be worthy of the pomp and circumstance befitting a sovereign ruler.

Likewise, the discussion of sovereignty or *kerajaan* in *Taj al-Salatin* reveals the oddity of Grotius' distinction between the political, the religious, and the legal realm. Bukhari separated the juridical aspect of sovereignty (*hukumah*) from its prophetic aspect (*nubuwwah*), arguing for a perfect amalgamation between the two and a clear hierarchy of the second over the first. Grotius, however, postulated the legal realm as entirely distinct from the political and the religious—which is why international law could become for him a specific category of analysis in the first place. Yet how to perceive of international law as being totally unrelated to politics or religion? For those familiar with the teachings of *Taj al-Salatin*, such a distinction would have been simply nonsensical.

Overall, the common ground as well as the possible misunderstandings between East and West are well illustrated by the treaty that the Sultanate of Aceh signed with the Dutch vice-admiral Olivier de Vivere in January 1607, four years after the capture of *Santa Catarina* and the composition of *Taj al-Salatin*. The treaty formalized a reciprocal agreement whereby the Dutch would obtain a rendezvous post in Aceh for storage of supplies and ammunition, as well as trading privileges such as exemption from import and export duties; in turn, Aceh was to receive military support against the Portuguese, the common enemy of the two contracting parties. The treaty followed what was becoming a general pattern of treaty-making between the Dutch and indigenous rulers in the area, based on cooperation and commerce. It also stipulated that those responsible for 'any scandal in any religious affairs' would be punished by their respective governments, a clause that, paradoxically, confirmed two different viewpoints: on the one hand it corroborated the separation between believers and unbelievers that is central to the Islamic perspective of

---

[54] This interpretation of Grotius is elaborated in much detail in Wilson (n 1). On the conceptualization of international legal personality, starting from Leibniz, see Janne Nijman, *The Concept of International Legal Personality: An Inquiry into the History and Theory of International Law* (TMC Asser Press 2004).

Taj al-Salatin, on the other it also illustrated the Grotian theorem that international law and religion are distinct realms. Finally, the treaty meant to uphold the monopoly of the VOC in the area by explicitly forbidding other Dutchmen and Europeans to trade in the Sultan's lands. Vice-admiral De Vivere signed this treaty in the name of the Dutch States-General, even though the treaty clearly served the interests of the VOC as a trading corporation with an elusive international legal personality. To complicate matters more, the treaty said that only European traders who possessed a 'missive of our king' would be allowed in the area. The Sultan of Aceh was thus declared to have entered a treaty with a non-existent Dutch king, in whose name vice-admiral De Vivere sought to obtain important privileges for the corporate sovereign he truly served, the VOC.[55]

Conclusion: A Strange Creature in the Mirror

The realm of diplomacy and the practical politics of treaty-making, then, show that there was much possible common ground between the Dutch and indigenous regimes in South East Asia, but that the legal personalities involved in this exchange between East and West were largely incompatible. Some of the abstract themes discussed in *Taj al-Salatin* as well as in *De iure praedae*, such as obligation and agreement (even when concerning infidels), materialized in this political praxis, opening room for mutual understanding and cooperation. Nonetheless, the foundational premises of *Taj al-Salatin* and *De iure praedae* largely diverged, with on the one hand a highly personified elaboration of good government where the sovereign ruler is the caliph of Allah, on the other a depersonalized exposition of natural and international law that maintains validity also without divine sanction.

In his stimulating analysis of *Taj al-Salatin*, Romain Bertrand engages in a comparable quest for commensurability between East and West, which he finds in the mystical tendencies that dominated European political thought around 1600. Referring to the esoteric treatises of Jean Bodin, Giordano Bruno, and Tommaso Campanella, other contemporaries of Bukhari, Bertrand concludes that 'the location of exoticism is not the Malay or Javanese world, but that particular moment in time that was, from one side of Eurasia to the other, the end of the sixteenth century'.[56] The opposing position is exemplified by the work of Antony Black on medieval political thought. Black forcefully maintains that Islamic and European political philosophy and culture developed along deviating roads in the late Middle Ages, and that there is little convergence between the two ever since.[57]

Any exercise in such a comparison between different worldviews in far-away areas risks taking the West as the template—and this current exercise in 'if-history'

---

[55] Heeres (ed), *Corpus diplomaticum Neerlando-Indicum* (n 41) vol 1, 48–50.
[56] Bertrand, *L'histoire à parts égales* (n 7) 374.
[57] See Antony Black, 'Classical Islam and Medieval Europe: A Comparison of Political Philosophies and Cultures' (1993) 41 Political Studies 58; and more recently Antony Black, *The West and Islam: Religion and Political Thought in World History* (Oxford University Press 2008).

is surely not immune to that risk. Nonetheless, the hypothetical question how the South East Asian readers of *Taj al-Salatin* might have approached Grotius' *De iure praedae*, makes it possible to open up a 'peripheral' perspective on the conflated history of international law and empire, 'provincializing' the paramount figure of Grotius. It is a perspective that reveals how certain crucial aspects of Grotius' theory, particularly the theme of recognition and obligation, were also dominant features of political thought in the Malay region. Here the readers of *Taj al-Salatin* would not have had much difficulty in making sense of *De iure praedae*. More importantly, however, the South East Asian perspective also shows that Grotius' proposition of the VOC as a sovereign actor with international legal personality, as well as his distinction between the legal, the religious, and the political realm, must have been absolutely alien to those readers. The development of Dutch colonial rule throughout the seventeenth century and beyond betrays to what extent this combination of understanding and misunderstanding facilitated the gradual rise of VOC power in the area: the mutually cherished notions of trust and equity gave rise to an extensive practice of treaty-making, but the Dutch managed to employ these treaties for progressively infringing the authority of local rulers. They did so by upholding the sovereign claims of the VOC, Grotius' employer as well as his brainchild, a private trading company that behaved like a public legal persona without political or religious features. Seen in the Malay mirror, it was a strange creature indeed.

Bibliography

Abdullah, Taufik, 'The Formation of a Political Tradition in the Malay World' in Anthony Reid (ed), *The Making of an Islamic Political Discourse in Southeast Asia* (Monash University Press 1993)

Alexandrowicz, Charles H, *An Introduction to the History of the Law of Nations in the East Indies* (Clarendon Press 1967)

al-Jauhari, Bukhari, *De kroon aller koningen van Bocharie van Djohor* (PP Roorda van Eysinga ed and tr, Landsdrukkerij 1827)

al-Mulk, Nizam, *Siyasatnama: The Book of Government or Rules for Kings* (Hubert Darke ed and tr, Curzon Press 2002)

Anand, Ram Prakash, *Origin and Development of the Law of the Sea: History of International Law Revisited* (Martinus Nijhoff 1983)

Bertrand, Romain, *L'histoire à parts égales: Récits d'une rencontre Orient-Occident (XVIe–XVIIe siècle)* (Seuil 2011)

Black, Antony, 'Classical Islam and Medieval Europe: A Comparison of Political Philosophies and Cultures' (1993) 41 Political Studies 58

Black, Antony, *The West and Islam: Religion and Political Thought in World History* (Oxford University Press 2008)

Blom, Hans W (ed), *Property, Piracy and Punishment: Hugo Grotius on War and Booty in De Iure Praedae: Concepts and Contexts* (Brill 2009)

Borschberg, Peter, 'The Seizure of the *Santa Catarina* Revisited: The Portuguese Empire in Asia, VOC Politics and the Origins of the Dutch-Johor Alliance (*c.*1602–1616)' (2002) 33 Journal of Southeast Asian Studies 31

Borschberg, Peter, *Hugo Grotius, the Portuguese and Free Trade in the East Indies* (NUS Press 2011)

Braginsky, VI, '*Tajus Salatin* ("The Crown of Sultans") of Bukkhari al-Jahauri as a Canonical Work and an Attempt to Create a Malay Literary Canon' in David Smyth (ed), *The Canon in Southeast Asian Literatures: Literatures of Burma, Cambodia, Indonesia, Laos, Malaysia, the Philippines, Thailand and Vietnam* (Curzon Press 2000)

Braginsky, Vladimir, 'Newly Found Manuscripts That Were Never Lost' (2010) 38 Indonesia and the Malay World 419

Burhanudin, Jajat, '*Kerajaan*-Oriented Islam: The Experience of Pre-Colonial Indonesia' (2006) 13 Studia Islamika 45

Chakrabarty, Dipesh, *Provincializing Europe: Postcolonial Thought and Historical Difference* (Princeton University Press 2000)

Fang, Liaw Yock (ed), *Undang-Undang Melaka: The Laws of Melaka* (Martinus Nijhoff 1976).

Grotius, Hugo, *Commentary on the Law of Prize and Booty* (Martine van Ittersum ed, Liberty Fund 2006)

Heeres, JE (ed), *Corpus diplomaticum Neerlando-Indicum: Verzameling van politieke contracten en verdere verdragen door de Nederlanders in het Oosten gesloten* (Martinus Nijhoff 1907–38) vol 1

Houtman, Frederick de, *Spraeck ende woord-boeck, inde Maleysche ende Madagaskirsche talen, met vele Arabische ende Turcsche woorden* (Jan Evertsz Cloppenburgh 1603)

Houtman, Frederick de, 'Cort verhael vant gene wedervaren is Frederick de Houtman tot Atchein' in Willem S Unger (ed), *De oudste reizen van de Zeeuwen naar Oost-Indië, 1598–1604* (Martinus Nijhoff 1948)

Hussain, Khalid M (ed), *Taj us-Salatin* (2nd edn, Dewan Bahasa dan Pustaka 1992)

Ittersum, Martine van, *Profit and Principle: Hugo Grotius, Natural Rights Theories and the Rise of Dutch Power in the East Indies (1595–1615)* (Brill 2006)

Jamian, Muhd Norizam and Radzi, Shaiful Bahri Md, 'In Search of a Just Leader in Islamic Perspective: An Analysis of Traditional Malay Literature from the Perspective of *Adab*' (2013) 9(6) Asian Social Science 22

Keene, Edward, *Beyond the Anarchical Society: Grotius, Colonialism and Order in World Politics* (Cambridge University Press 2002)

Koster, GL, 'Of Treaties and Unbelievers: Images of the Dutch in Seventeenth- and Eighteenth-Century Malay Historiography' (2005) 78 (1) Journal of the Malayan Branch of the Royal Asiatic Society 59

Laffan, Michael, *The Makings of Indonesian Islam: Orientalism and the Narration of a Sufi Past* (Princeton University Press 2011)

Lambton, Ann KS, *State and Government in Medieval Islam: An Introduction to the Study of Islamic Political Theory: the Jurists* (Oxford University Press 1981)

Marcinkowski, M Ismail, 'Taj al-Salatin' *Encyclopaedia Iranica* (2009) <http://www.iranicaonline.org/articles/taj-al-salatin> accessed 10 December 2014

Marlow, Louise, *Hierarchy and Egalitarianism in Islamic Thought* (Cambridge University Press 1997)

Marre, Aristide, *Makôta radja-râdja ou la couronne des rois* (Maisonneuve 1878)

Meteren, Emanuel van, *Commentarien ofte memorien van den Nederlandtschen staet, handel, oorloghen ende geschiedenissen van onsen tyden* (1608)

Mitrasing, Ingrid Saroda, 'The Age of Aceh and the Evolution of Kingship, 1599–1641' (PhD dissertation, Leiden University 2011)

Moyn, Samuel and Sartori, Andrew (eds), *Global Intellectual History* (Columbia University Press 2013)

Moyn, Samuel and Sartori, Andrew, 'Approaches to Global Intellectual History' in Moyn, Samuel and Sartori, Andrew (eds), *Global Intellectual History* (Columbia University Press 2013)

Netscher, E, *De Nederlanders in Djohor en Siak, 1602 tot 1865* (Bruining & Wijt 1870)

Nijman, Janne, *The Concept of International Legal Personality: An Inquiry into the History and Theory of International Law* (TMC Asser Press 2004)

Noor, Farish A, 'Blind Loyalty? Re-Reading the *Taj-us Salatin* of Buchara al-Jahauri' (2009) <http://blog.limkitsiang.com/2009/02/11/blind-loyalty-re-reading-the-taj-us-salatin-of-buchara-al-jauhari/> accessed 10 December 2014

Roelofsen, Cornelis G, 'The Sources of *Mare Liberum*: The Contested Origins of the Doctrine of the Freedom of the Sea' in WP Heere (ed), *International Law and its Sources* (Kluwer 1988)

Ronkel, Philippus Samuel van, 'De Kroon der Koningen' (1899) 41 Tijdschrift voor Indische taal-, land- en volkenkunde van het Koninklijk Bataviaasch Genootschap van Kunsten en Wetenschapen 55

Shogimen, Takashi and Nederman, Cary J (eds), *Western Political Thought in Dialogue with Asia* (Lexington 2009)

Simidchieva, Marta, 'Kingship and Legitimacy in Nizam al-Mulk's *Siyasatnama*, Fifth/ Eleventh Century' in Beatrice Gruendler and Louise Marlow (eds), *Writers and Rulers: Perspectives on Their Relationship from Abassid to Safavid Times* (Reichert 2004)

Somos, Mark, *Secularisation and the Leiden Circle* (Brill 2011)

Stumpf, Christoph, 'Völkerrecht unter Kreuz und Halbmond: Muhammad al-Shaybani und Hugo Grotius als Exponenten religiöser Völkerrechtstraditionen' (2003) 41 Archiv des Völkerrechts 83

Travers, Robert, 'A British Empire by Treaty in Eighteenth Century India' in Saliha Belmessous (ed), *Empire by Treaty: Negotiating European Expansion, 1600–1900* (Oxford University Press 2014)

Tuck, Richard, 'Alliances with Infidels in the European Imperial Expansion' in Sankar Muthu (ed), *Empire and Modern Political Thought* (Cambridge University Press 2012)

Valentijn, François, *Beschryving van Oud en Nieuw Oost-Indien, bevattende een naauwkeurige en uitvoerige verhandeling van Nederlands Mogentheid in die gewesten* (Johannes van Braam 1724–26) vol 5

Werndly, George Henrik, *Maleische Spraakkunst uit de eige schriften der Maleiers opgemaakt* (Wetstein 1736)

Weststeijn, Arthur, '"Love Alone is Not Enough": Treaties in Seventeenth-Century Dutch Colonial Expansion' in Saliha Belmessous (ed), *Empire by Treaty: Negotiating European Expansion, 1600–1900* (Oxford University Press 2014)

Wilson, Eric, *The Savage Republic: De Indis of Hugo Grotius, Republicanism, and Dutch Hegemony in the Early Modern World System (c.1600–1619)* (Martinus Nijhoff 2008)

2

Indirect Hegemonies in International Legal Relations: The Debate of Religious Tolerance in Early Republican China

Stefan Kroll*

In early republican China, intellectuals, diplomats, and political authorities argued over the introduction of religious freedom and/or Confucianism as a state religion into the new constitution. The controversy unfolded against the background that China's international treaties of the nineteenth century already contained (unequal) regulations regarding religious tolerance and that also the Provisional Constitution of 1912 granted religious freedom. While all the parties made references to other constitutions in Europe and the Western world, which included either religious freedom and/or a state religion, it was at the same time absolutely unclear to much of the Chinese population what the meaning of the concept of religion actually entailed.

Was it more than just another word for Christianity? If so, was the concept applicable to the particular doctrine and the special rites of Confucianism? This chapter examines this debate and studies it as a case of normative transformation, which was largely characterized by a tension between local and global normative expectations. The overall aim to make China a self-determined nation was directly connected to the need to adapt foreign knowledge and technology, even though antipathy against foreigners was widespread.

The chapter presents a form of 'European control' which is described as indirect hegemony. While no direct mechanisms of coercive leadership were exercised, dominant external expectations shaped the domestic transformation of normative order. Chinese political and intellectual elites were not directly forced to adapt foreign ideas and norms but were convinced that the adaptation of external knowledge

* The research for this chapter was conducted during fellowships in the Max Planck Fellow Group 'Governance of Cultural Diversity' in Göttingen and at the LOEWE-Research Focus 'Extrajudicial and Judicial Conflict Resolution' at Goethe University. I thank Sara Dezalay, the members of the 'Working Group Empire and International Law' in Helsinki, and the members of *RiesiKo*—a joint research colloquium of the chairs for International Relations and Theories of global Orders as well as International Organizations—in Frankfurt for comments on earlier versions of the manuscript.

International Law and Empire: Historical Explorations. First Edition. Martti Koskenniemi, Walter Rech, and Manuel Jiménez Fonseca. © Martti Koskenniemi, Walter Rech, and Manuel Jiménez Fonseca 2016. Published 2016 by Oxford University Press.

was the only way to reform the country. This was so because of the general feeling of inferiority vis-à-vis Western countries that afflicted Chinese elites at the time. As a means to oppose foreign pressure, foreign normative patterns were internalized and implemented. The internalization of external expectations meant a situation where the direct control of external actors or institutions was substituted by internal processes of self-control.

The chapter is organized in three sections. Section one presents the concept of hegemony which is applied in this article. Using the case of China and informal empire in the nineteenth and early twentieth centuries, the complex relation between hegemony and freedom is established. Section two describes the changing pattern of religious tolerance in the unequal treaty regime. The section shows how regulations of religious tolerance were exercised in China via international legal agreements. Section three examines, against this background of unequal legal relations and foreign presence, the conflicts around the introduction of religious freedom and/or Confucianism as a state religion within the constitution in the early Republican phase. References to international legal principles as well as to constitutions in the Western world were made especially by Christian and Confucian associations as well as by intellectuals and foreign-trained politicians and influenced the constitutional debate. The chapter is completed by a short concluding section.

Hegemony and Freedom in Semi-Colonial China

China was never a colony in a formal sense. From the middle of the nineteenth century until the middle of the twentieth century, Chinese governments were forced to sign unequal treaties, which regulated the presence of foreigners in certain areas (treaty ports, international settlements, and protectorates).[1] The treaties regulated extraterritorial jurisdiction as well as the control over tariffs and the presence of foreign diplomats and merchants and their families in those areas. The rights of Christians and Christian Missions were also part of most of the treaties. All this constituted a situation which historians have dubbed 'informal empire' or 'semi-colony'.[2] With regard to international law, China was not yet considered as a full member of the international law community by many Western international legal scholars. China was, as Woolsey put it in a comment on the unequal treaties of 1858, 'in a degree within the sphere of the law of nations',[3] rather than being considered as a full part of it. The quote is a striking example for how legal theorists ended up bending and stretching legal terms and categories in order to be able to classify the vague legal status of countries like China at the end of the century. The

---

[1] Dong Wang, *China's Unequal Treaties—Narrating National History* (Lexington Books 2005).

[2] Jürgen Osterhammel, 'Semi-Colonialism and Informal Empire in Twentieth-Century China: Towards a Framework of Analysis' in Wolfgang J Mommsen and Jürgen Osterhammel (eds), *Imperialism and After: Continuities and Discontinuities* (Allen & Unwin 1986) 290.

[3] Theodore Dwight Woolsey, *Introduction to the Study of International Law* (3rd edn, C Scribner & Company 1871) 420.

unequal treaty regime created a tension of virtual equality and actual inequality which was difficult to reformulate in international legal terms.[4]

The Chinese case of informal empire forms a situation of the encounter of empire and hegemony. According to Heinrich Triepel's theory of hegemony this is when 'imperialism consciously abstains from the incorporation of foreign territories in the formation of an existing state'.[5] While hegemony is the extension of state authority beyond territorial borders, only the incorporation of new territories into an existing administration forms an empire. China was independent, though not in the sense of real autonomy, but in the sense of the absence of measures which would have finally led to an absolute alleviation of her international legal personality.[6] In other words, there was still a will by foreign powers to uphold a virtual residue of sovereign equality in China.[7] The Chinese case has been studied, predominantly, with regard to its mechanisms, or processes, of empire. I take the virtual residue of equality to shed light also on the mechanisms of hegemony. The perspective of hegemony indeed provides useful explanatory models of the mechanism of foreign influence in China. The subtle mechanisms of hegemony, which are discussed in this chapter, go beyond the rather simplifying explanation of direct domination and violence which are not capable of grasping the complex process of normative transformation. As Peter Zarrow has noted, 'the paradox of the foreign presence in China was that it was simultaneously overwhelming and inconspicuous'.[8] While the overwhelming parts have been studied widely, this chapter focuses on the inconspicuous mechanisms.

The reference on Triepel, as an analytical link in this section, has to be contextualized and reflected. Triepel is known for his anti-democratic thinking and his support of monarchy as the ideal state model.[9] Furthermore, as he wrote on 'leaders', 'leading groups', and 'leading states' during the 1930s in Germany, the question of his relationship to Nazism has to be addressed. Triepel was a fierce conservative, but had not adopted racist or anti-Semitic ideologies. In 1935 he was retired against his will.[10] Triepel's work on hegemony was, according to Michael Stolleis, not a book of National Socialism even though it provided 'dangerous keywords'.[11] Triepel's work could rather be described as a comparative socio-legal work on the world

---

[4] Stefan Kroll, *Normgenese durch Re-Interpretation: China und das europäische Völkerrecht im 19. und 20. Jahrhundert* (Nomos 2012) 40–41.

[5] Heinrich Triepel, *Die Hegemonie: Ein Buch von führenden Staaten* (Verlag von W Kohlhammer 1938) 187 (author's translation).

[6] Ibid, 309.

[7] Herfried Münkler describes empires, in contrast to hegemonies, as situations where the asymmetry of power is too big for the fiction of equality to still mask it. Herfried Münkler, *Imperien: Die Logik der Weltherrschaft—Vom alten Rom bis zu den Vereinigten Staaten* (2nd edn, Rowohlt 2005) 77.

[8] Peter Zarrow, *China in War and Revolution, 1895–1949* (Routledge 2005) 10.

[9] Christian Tomuschat, 'Heinrich Triepel (1868–1946)' in Stefan Grundmann et al (eds), *Festschrift 200 Jahre Juristische Fakultät der Humboldt-Universität zu Berlin: Geschichte, Gegenwart und Zukunft* (De Gruyter 2010) 497, 516.

[10] Ibid, 501.

[11] Michael Stolleis, *Staats- und Verwaltungsrechtswissenschaft in Republik und Diktatur: Geschichte des öffentlichen Rechts in Deutschland*, vol 3 (Beck 1999) 388.

historical scale whose concept had been developed decades before.[12] The difference to fascist ideologies of leadership can be illustrated by a review by Carl Schmitt. Carl Schmitt, as is well known, supported through his work the legal foundations of the dictatorship. Against this background it is interesting that Schmitt in his review on Triepel's book does not reveal it as contributing to Nazi-thinking. On the contrary, Schmitt criticized the work, because some of its aspects stood in opposition to contemporary notions of the '*Führer*'.[13]

However, in this chapter Triepel's ideas on hegemony are used not as a historical point of reference but for conceptual reasons. Triepel conceptualized hegemony as a structural element of law.[14] This perspective, that hegemony is part of the law rather than standing in opposition to it, is one of the key assumptions which are discussed in this chapter: How does law shape international equality and inequality? In which sense is law an integral part of what is described here as indirect forms of hegemony?

Hegemony, basically, describes the unequal relations of formally equal entities. Within an international system which is based on the legal equality of all of its members, the concept of hegemony signifies that one state or a small group of states is, in fact, in a leading position. The international legal system is particularly amenable to hegemony due to its special institutional structure. Triepel pointed out that—other than in federal systems, which are characterized by the existence of state law, which in many ways hold up barriers against hegemonic structures— rather loosely structured normative systems leave room for the establishment of unequal regimes.[15] Nico Krisch, in a similar fashion, observed with the expression of 'softer international law' that 'softer rules favour powerful actors because they usually benefit more from a wider freedom of action than weaker states'.[16] Even though nineteenth century international law was guided by a principle of equality, the softness of international legal institutions opened the space for legalized inequality.

Hegemonic leadership is a form of international power which stands between influence and authority.[17] This is only conceivable if there is a minimum of allegiance to the hegemon. In other words, hegemony establishes, to a certain degree, an accepted form of inequality. The determination of allegiance seems to be the weak point of the concept, however. If allegiance is triggered just by force it is not real, and thus cannot be considered as constituting an honest consent, which is constitutive of a 'real hegemony'.[18] Furthermore, even the self-determined adaptation of cultural patterns from a hegemon (law, science, technology) cannot be

---

[12] Ibid, 389.

[13] Tomuschat, 'Heinrich Triepel' (n 9) 507; Carl Schmitt, 'Führung und Hegemonie' (1939) 63 Schmollers Jahrbuch für Gesetzgebung, Verwaltung und Volkswirtschaft im Deutschen Reiche 513.

[14] Stolleis, *Staats- und Verwaltungsrechtswissenschaft* (n 11) 389.

[15] Triepel, *Die Hegemonie* (n 5) 289.

[16] Nico Krisch, 'International Law in Times of Hegemony: Unequal Power and the Shaping of International Legal Order' (2005) 16 The European Journal of International Law 369, 396. Krisch also points out that, paradoxically, dominant states are at the same time interested in the legalization of inequality, mostly through bilateral treaty agreements.

[17] Triepel, *Die Hegemonie* (n 5) 140.   [18] Ibid, 204.

understood simply as expressions of cultural hegemony. On the contrary, the case of China shows that this process of adaptation can be driven also by a strategy of opposition rather than by a desire for assimilation. Chinese elites were not just passive consumers of foreign norms and cultural patterns but active agents of processes of internalization and translation which were motivated by instrumental strategies to check and oppose external influences.[19] That this, however, had the effect of gradual assimilation in the long term, is one of the puzzles this chapter has to deal with.

This hinges also on the productive potential of authority. Even though this constitutes another debate, which goes beyond the scope of this chapter, the case study shows progressive side-effects of the practices of inequality in so-called legal 'peripheries'. The essay aims not at modifying the research results which mark international law as discriminatory,[20] but is an endeavour to draw a more differentiated picture of the exercise of international authority. While the exercise of international authority often takes the form of suppression, paternalism, and inequality, it is, however, also a frame within which new concepts of international order emerge, which, at some point in a contingent historical process, decoupled from its initial asymmetric founding conditions. This could be understood as an expression of power which is not only a repressive but also a productive force.[21] The protection of religious minorities, though introduced in an unequal context, was, as we will see, dedicated to protecting individuals from violence and exclusion. However, an in-depth historical analysis of productive forces of hegemony would have to answer the question why in some cases hegemonic pressure turned into emancipatory developments, while in other cases the repressive elements remained the main characteristic. Why did China and Japan turn hegemonic structures into progressive, reform-oriented developmental paths, while other places of European colonialism continued to suffer from it?

This chapter uses the case of the discourses surrounding religious freedom and/or Confucianism as a state religion in the early Republican phase in China to examine what is described as hegemonic freedom, or freedom under hegemonic conditions. The debates on religious freedom were not directly influenced by the unequal treaty regime. While the presence of foreigners was still important, however, the underlying mechanism of hegemony corresponded no longer to the classical category of imperial or hegemonic intervention. More important was the intervention of non-state actors such as Christian and Confucian associations in China and abroad as well as the activism of public intellectuals and political commentators. Especially, references to international law and Western constitutions served as a narrative frame to substantiate the positions of all parties to the controversy in the debate. Hereby, external normative expectations became an important factor of internal

---

[19] Kroll, *Normgenese durch Re-Interpretation* (n 4).

[20] Antony Anghie, *Imperialism, Sovereignty and the Making of International Law* (Cambridge University Press 2005); Gerrit W Gong, *The Standard of 'Civilization' in International Society* (Clarendon Press 1984).

[21] Michel Foucault, *Dispositive der Macht: Michel Foucault über Sexualität, Wissen und Wahrheit* (Merve Verlag 1978) 35.

policy making. Yet, this still establishes a form of hegemony, not the kind which is the result from direct coercion, but a hegemony which consists in the adaptation to normative expectations. In other words, this forms a situation of confined freedom which is characterized by an extensively narrowed reservoir of normative possibilities. Reform options, between which the Chinese intellectuals and politicians assumed that they could choose, were restrained by the perceived international normative framework. Normative decisions are not made with regard to local requirements but with reference to what 'strong', 'leading', and 'successful' states—according to the adjectives used in the sources which I present below—perform.[22]

Historical writings interpret confined freedom as a situation in which power and freedom become indistinct and where it becomes difficult to differentiate whether a normative decision was triggered by external or internal reasons.[23] Furthermore, in these situations control is not performed by rules and orders, but by a 'strategy of subjectification' which means that individuals substitute external control for self-control.[24] This mechanism of self-control was first coined by Michel Foucault and refers to a form of governance which 'is not a way to force people to do what the governor wants; it is always a versatile equilibrium, with complementarity and conflicts between techniques which assure coercion and processes through which the self is constructed and modified by himself'.[25] Against this background one could argue that China was still governed from the outside, not by means of obvious domination but by mechanisms which led Chinese elites to transform their society from within and with recourse to both external and local sources of knowledge.[26] While religious freedom was an important element of the unequal treaties of the nineteenth century (domination) it turned into an issue internal to the making of the first Chinese Constitution (technology of the self). International law played an important role in setting up the normative framework which was a precondition for this mechanism of self-transformation. Furthermore, international law helped to uphold this kind of hegemony, as it functioned as a medium in which control and self-control, desire and compulsion, freedom and hegemony converged. Hegemony, understood in this sense, is an expression of international law rather than its antithesis. Or, in an adaptation of Martti Koskenniemi's words—who described international law as a hegemonic technique which has the potential to turn political interests into legal claims—hegemony is an international legal technique.[27]

---

[22] This is the core argument of neo-institutional theories of world society to explain why nation states adopt world cultural principles even though there is no visible functional requirement for it. See John W Meyer and others, 'World Society and the Nation-State' (1997) 103 American Journal of Sociology 144.

[23] Christoph Lau and Andrea Maurer, 'Herrschaft' (*Docupedia-Zeitgeschichte. Begriffe, Methoden und Debatten der zeithistorischen Forschung*, February 2010) 11 http://docupedia.de/zg/Herrschaft accessed 3 December 2014.

[24] Ibid.

[25] Michel Foucault, 'About the Beginning of the Hermeneutics of the Self: Two Lectures at Dartmouth' (1993) 21 Political Theory 198, 204.

[26] Ibid, 203–04.

[27] Martti Koskenniemi, 'International Law and Hegemony: A Reconfiguration' in Martti Koskenniemi, *The Politics of International Law* (Hart Publishing 2011) 221.

Religious Tolerance in International Law
and within the Unequal Treaties

International treaties are important for the justification of hegemony as a legal concept. International treaties have the effect of formalizing international inequality.[28] The consent to hegemonic processes in international treaties has the effect of legalizing the hegemonic order.[29] In international law, legalized hegemony sometimes appears under the headline of friendship. So-called 'Treaties of Friendship, Commerce, and Navigation' were widely used during the nineteenth century to 'facilitate commerce, navigation, and investment between the States Parties and reciprocally to protect individuals and businesses'.[30] Even though these treaties in general are not considered as triggering hegemonic processes, because of their reciprocal structure,[31] this observation is only half true for the treaties between Western and non-Western powers. In the case of China the format of these treaties was used to legalize unequal relations, inter alia the unequal regulation of religious tolerance. Friendship was a euphemism for foreign control.

During the nineteenth century, religious tolerance was a routine in the treaties between Western and non-Western powers. According to Franz von Liszt, while the regulation of religious freedom disappeared from treaties between European states during this period, it remained an important aspect of treaties between Christian states in Europe and non-Christian states in Asia and Latin America.[32] Elsewhere, I have discussed to what degree the protection of religious liberty in those treaties could be construed as an instrument to protect Christian minorities in non-Christian environments, while the protection of non-Christian religions in Western countries was not considered.[33] In the following I will follow up on this research and debate how the understanding of religious tolerance in the treaties with China developed over a longer period and how it influenced the discourse on religious freedom and/or Confucianism as a state religion by means of subtle hegemony.

The treaties of Tianjin (1858), between China on the one side and Russia, the US, the UK, and France on the other, are central documents for the research on religious tolerance in China. All four treaties were instruments for the protection of

---

[28] See also Krisch, 'International Law in Times of Hegemony' (n 16) 389ff.

[29] Triepel, *Die Hegemonie* (n 5) 203. The legalization of inequality is important, for it means the determination of power vis-à-vis third parties (ibid, 202). However, the legalization of hegemony is generally limited, for the majority of the European states were not willing to give up the 'axiom of legal equality of all states' (ibid, 205) (author's translation).

[30] Andreas Paulus, 'Treaties of Friendship, Commerce and Navigation' in Rüdiger Wolfrum (ed), *Max Planck Encyclopedia of Public International Law* (online edn, Oxford University Press 2011) <http://opil.ouplaw.com/home/EPIL> accessed 3 December 2014.

[31] Triepel, *Die Hegemonie* (n 5) 257.

[32] Franz von Liszt, *Das Völkerrecht systematisch dargestellt* (Verlag von O Haering 1902); Stefan Kroll, 'The Legal Justification of International Intervention: Theories of Community and Admissibility' in Fabian Klose (ed), *The Emergence of Humanitarian Intervention. Ideas and Practices from the Nineteenth Century to the Present* (Cambridge University Press 2016) 81–82.

[33] Kroll 'The Legal Justification of International Intervention' (n 32) 79–84.

Christian traders, diplomats, and missionaries. By these treaties, Chinese authorities' pledge was that no individual that professes or teaches Christian faith shall be hindered or persecuted: 'All that was written and proclaimed against Christianity in the past by the Chinese Government, or approved by it, is completely abrogated, and is now without value in all provinces of the Empire.'[34] The treaties prioritized the Christian religion over other beliefs. The Christian faith was presented as 'peaceful', and as a means to 'bring man to virtue' and 'teach the man to do good'.[35]

In the beginning, the treaties referred only to the protection of Christians in China; no inverse protection of Chinese beliefs in Western countries was included. This is not surprising, since, as underlined in the abstract by Franz von Liszt, the protection of religious freedom of Christians was a normative standard in Europe and among European powers during that period. However, it clearly forms an element of inequality. Even more important with regard to inequality is, nevertheless, the prioritization of Christianity vis-à-vis other religions within the multi-religious Chinese society. There was no common rule of universal religious tolerance in the agreements. A first step in the direction of equalizing religious tolerance was the application of the treaty rules on Chinese Christians. Western commentators of the treaties remarked already in the late 1850s that the 'new freedoms' from the treaties were incomplete if not granted to the Chinese population as well:

Greater freedom in traversing the country in every direction in order to preach the doctrines of Christianity will be unserviceable if religious liberty to accept those doctrines and observe the corresponding rites and ceremonies be denied to the Chinese. In commerce, in arts and in religion, therefore, Western nations must, in self-defence, insist that the Chinese Government shall confer upon this people great benefits in the most direct and immediate manner. Especially will this be the case with religious liberty.[36]

Even though the main motivation to grant these freedoms to the Chinese population at large was described as an issue of 'self-defence', it certainly was a step towards an extended application of the treaty rules. The first treaty which contained a common rule of religious tolerance was an agreement between the US and China of 1868:

The 29th article of the treaty of the 18th of June, 1858, having stipulated for the exemption of Christian citizens of the United States and Chinese converts from persecution in China on account of their faith, it is further agreed that citizens of the United States in China, of every religious persuasion, and Chinese subjects in the United States, shall enjoy entire liberty of conscience and shall be exempt from all disability or persecution on account of their religious faith or worship in either country. Cemeteries for sepulture of the dead of whatever nativity or nationality, shall be held in respect and free from disturbance or profanation.[37]

---

[34] Article XIII, Treaty of Amity, Commerce and Navigation between China and France (signed 27 June 1858) (1858) 119 CTS 180.

[35] Ibid; Article XXIX, Treaty of Peace, Amity and Commerce between China and the United States (signed 26 June 1858) (1858) 119 CTS 123.

[36] 'Fifty Years Ago. From the "North China Herald" of April 18, 1857. From the Leading Article' *The North China Herald* (Shanghai, 19 April 1907) 148.

[37] Article IV, 'Additional Articles to the Treaty between the United States of America and the Ta Tsing Empire of 18th of June, 1858, signed, in the English and Chinese language, at Washington,

This illustrates how the understanding of religious tolerance changed on the Western side. As we will see in the next section, it took another forty years until the Chinese political elites interpreted the concept of religious tolerance not only as a synonym for the protection of Christianity, but openly discussed under which conditions a rule of common religious tolerance should be considered in the emerging constitutional law in China.

Religious Tolerance and State Religion in the Chinese Constitution

In 1912, after the revolution, the newly established Republic of China adopted a Provisional Constitution. Article 6(7) stipulated that all 'citizens shall have the freedom of religion'.[38] The constitution was provisional; therefore in the following years a Drafting Committee was tasked with the elaboration of a permanent constitutional text. The process was very complicated due to the unstable political situation during the republican phase:

> Struggles over building a new kind of government were thus concerned with *how* the members of the political community were to behave ... War stalked these decades, leaving no city, village, or family untouched ... Foreign imperialism and outright invasion, civil war, regional and clan violence, and banditry all played roles in destroying the old social structure and opening the way for new contenders for power to emerge.[39]

A final version of the constitution was promulgated in 1923, but never fully implemented, for the government was overthrown soon after. This section examines the debates that surrounded the elaboration of the constitution with regard to the issue of religious freedom and/or Confucianism as a state religion. The amendment of the regulation of religious freedom within the provisional constitution was one of the most complicated matters during the whole drafting process.[40]

The unequal treaties and the debates that surrounded them were still important in that context. At least some voices expressed the hope that the new constitution could supersede treaty regulations with regard to religion. The drafting process was generally shaped by references to global normative standards and other constitutions in Europe. This is not surprising, for the whole idea of constitution making was a foreign import. Recent scholarship has illustrated how this process of adoption of normative patterns has led to a process of adaptation or reinterpretation

---

28th July, 1868' in William F Mayers (ed), *Treaties between the Empire of China and Foreign Powers* (J Broadhurst Total 1877) 94.

[38] 'The Provisional Constitution of the Republic of China' (1912) 6 The American Journal of International Law—Supplement: Official Documents 149.

[39] Zarrow, *China in War* (n 8) xvi.

[40] For an overview of the historical events regarding this debate see Hsi-yuan Chen, 'Confucianism Encounters Religion: The Formation of Religious Discourse and the Confucian Movement in the Modern Era' (DPhil thesis, Harvard University 1999) 145.

of those legal concepts and rules within the new cultural, social, and normative environment.[41] The story this chapter tells in what follows is, however, focused more on the problem of how to fit traditional normative views into the corset of a foreign legal format. How to formulate a rule of religious freedom when no concept of, and not even a Chinese term for, religion existed? Why consider the doctrine of Confucianism as a religion when its key characteristics are so different from European religions? The main pattern of the debate will be reconstructed and analysed within the frame of indirect hegemony. Even though the constitutional debate was an autonomous internal process it was shaped by normative expectations from the outside. These normative expectations were, nevertheless, introduced into the debate by Chinese political and intellectual elites themselves. Transnational religious associations played an important role as channels for the transmission of information and as organizations that carried out direct lobbying activities. The process as a whole can be seen as an example of indirect hegemony by way of 'subjectification' that was introduced in the opening section.

To substantiate this, I would like to underline again the transformation of the foreigner's perspective on the unequal treaty regulations in the early twentieth century. As has been already shown in the previous section, Christian privileges in the regulation of religious freedom have been defended as an issue of self-defence in the middle of the nineteenth century. Sixty years later, the unequal treaties were viewed more critically. In 1926, the *National Christian Council* (NCC), a nongovernmental organization of protestant Christian groups and missions in China remarked that:

Christianity in China 'is seriously complicated and embarrassed, if not definitely hindered, by the fact that special privileges were granted to missionaries and religious freedom guaranteed to Chinese Christians in China's treaties with Western nations.' ... 'the time has arrived, when Christians whether nationals of China or of other lands, in propagating the Christian faith should no longer rely on or claim for themselves any special privileges granted in Chinese treaties, but upon the provision for religious toleration in the Chinese constitution.' It was also explicitly stated ... 'that Western nations should revise their treaties with China, and that in the revision no special provision should be included in regard to missionary work.'[42]

Just a few years after the international community of states had rejected the Chinese efforts to achieve the termination of the unequal treaty regime at conferences in Paris (1919) and Washington (1921–22), a religious organization of foreigners and Chinese individuals asked for revision of the treaties. This quote is remarkable because it illustrates the existence of transnational social interests which were not congruent with that of the various national governments or ethnicities involved.

---

[41] Arnulf Becker Lorca, 'Universal International Law: Nineteenth-Century Histories of Imposition and Appropriation' (2010) 51 Harvard International Law Journal 475; Kroll, *Normgenese durch Re-Interpretation* (n 4).

[42] Quoted from 'National Christian Council' *The North China Herald* (Shanghai, 23 October 1926) 161.

And this is, as we will see in more detail below, a significant aspect of the mechanisms of indirect hegemony.

The religious associations were composed of, at least in the case of the Christian associations, foreigners and Chinese citizens. They were located in China but also in other countries and therefore part of a movement that was wider than China. In the US, for example, a *United Society of Chinese Protestants in America* was active and sent a petition to visiting Qing officials in 1906 making a claim for religious freedom to be consecrated by the constitution—according to Liu Yi 'this can be regarded as the first petition for religious freedom in Chinese history'.[43] In China, groups like the NCC or the 1894-founded *International Institute of China* provided places to meet for Christians of various nationalities. It is important to see that the associations in China were embedded in global networks of religious interest groups. With regard to the NCC a commentator observed in 1928 that 'it is quite evident that much of the thinking of the delegates of the National Christian Council is based on the previous thinking of these worldwide Christian gatherings [the Jerusalem Meeting of the International Missionary Council and the Lausanne Conference on Christian Unity]'.[44] This illustrates that these groups served not only as meeting places for Christians of any nationality in China but also as channels for the diffusion of global views on Christian communities in general and religious freedom in particular. Against this background it is not surprising that one argument, which was repeatedly presented in the debate over religious tolerance, was a civilizational one. According to it, China should grant religious liberties because it 'is done by all the leading nations of the world'.[45] In 1904, Yuan Shikai and his government issued a decree which even called 'Religious freedom ... the general principle of the contemporary world'.[46]

It is very important to note that all the parties to the debate, during the drafting of the constitution, included global references in their argumentation. Even conservative voices who tried to avoid a general rule of religious tolerance in favour of Confucianism as a state religion substantiated this claim by pointing to the model of European constitutions. While Protestants, for example, founded the Beijing Association for Religious Freedom and against State Religion and argued that there was 'no strong country with a state religion in the world',[47] other groups, such as the Confucian Religion Association, fought for the introduction of Confucianism as the state religion in the constitution. One of their high representatives, Chen Huanzhang, who held a PhD from Columbia University, argued in a lecture that religious freedom and state religion were not opposites but compatible. In a petition to the Drafting Committee Chen and other representatives of the Confucian

---

[43] Yi Liu, 'Confucianism, Christianity, and Religious Freedom: Debates in the Transformation Period of Modern China (1900–1920s)' in Fenggang Yang and Joseph B Tamney (eds), *Confucianism and Spiritual Traditions in Modern China and Beyond* (Brill 2012) 251.

[44] 'National Christian Council' *The North China Herald* (Shanghai, 20 October 1928) 104.

[45] 'Religion and Civilization' *The North China Herald* (Shanghai, 13 January 1912) 81.

[46] Quoted from Liu, 'Confucianism, Christianity, and Religious Freedom' (n 43) 261.

[47] Ibid, 259.

Religious Association referred, in order to support his claim, to the constitutions of eleven European states which recognized both religious freedom and state religion.[48]

Chen is a good example that not only the embeddedness within transnational networks was an important factor that informed individual perspectives in the debate, but also foreign education. The following anecdote strikingly underlines the importance of foreign references during that period on a more general level. In the context of educational reforms at the turn of the century, thousands of Chinese students had been sent to foreign universities (in Japan, Europe, and the US). Furthermore, the traditional imperial examination system had been interrupted in 1905 and as a consequence this opened a path for returning students to start a civil service career.[49] Nevertheless, the returning students had to prove their qualification in their respective subjects of specialization. In 1907, therefore, 'for the first time in the history of literary examinations in China, the highest degree in the land ... was conferred on eight men, whose chief claim for the honour was that they had graduated from some Western university'.[50] This alone is already very important for the establishment of indirect hegemony; however, it was not the most remarkable. Really striking was that 'nearly all the returned students from Europe and America employed English as their vehicle of expression' instead of Chinese.[51] This is as unexpected as it is surprising. This does not mean that the returning students came home with something like a cosmopolitan identity. On the contrary, these new elites were still heavy patriots, but saw in Western science and technology the only way to restore the country.[52] The use of a foreign language in an official exam thus basically symbolizes the turn away from the older generation of literati. Furthermore, the examinations entered a new path not only with regard to language but also with regard to religion. The comment on the exam in *The North China Herald* concluded with a note that in the examinations 'not the slightest distinction was made between Christian and non-Christian candidates', and that, therefore, 'in a few years religious liberty will become one of the possessions of the Chinese people'.[53]

Thus, in light of the lobbying of non-governmental networks and the hopes of political commentators: what were the obstacles that led to the debates around the introduction of religious liberty and/or Confucianism as state religion in the constitution? According to Chen Hsi-yuan, 'China had no "religion" until the end of the 19th century'.[54] What is meant by this? Chen argues that the notion and concept of 'religion' was a Western import which could not grasp the traditional cults and

---

[48] Chen, 'Confucianism Encounters Religion' (n 40) 149–51; Liu, 'Confucianism, Christianity, and Religious Freedom' (n 43) 254.

[49] Kroll, *Normgenese durch Re-Interpretation* (n 4) 148.

[50] WW Yen, 'The Recent Imperial Metropolitan Examinations' *The North China Herald* (Shanghai, 18 January 1907) 125.

[51] Ibid.

[52] Stephen G Craft, *V K Wellington Koo and the Emergence of Modern China* (University Press of Kentucky 2004) 1–30.

[53] Yen, 'The Recent Imperial Metropolitan Examinations' (n 50) 126.

[54] Chen, 'Confucianism Encounters Religion' (n 40) 1.

forms of worship practised in the manifold regions of China.[55] For many Chinese, religion was, initially, just another word for Christianity and Christianity was very different from the various Chinese practices of belief. China was a multi-ethnic and multi-religious community in which various beliefs were practised simultaneously and faith did not have the character of exclusiveness.[56] However, 'once the term "religion" was introduced into China and became prevalent in Chinese discourse at the turn of the twentieth century, answering the "alien" question of whether "Confucianism [as the most important system of morality in China] is a religion" had become imperative for the Chinese'.[57]

Traditionally, Confucianism was seen as a doctrine rather than a belief. Even though it is still disputed whether Confucianism should be considered as a religion or not, during the early republican phase there was a visible tendency to treat Confucianism as a religion. This tendency can be traced back to the debates around religious freedom and state religion. Even the anti-foreign and anti-Christian forces in China seemed to have realized that for the conservation of Confucian tradition it might be a good strategy to either put Confucianism under the constitutional protection of religious freedom or, even better, to constitute it as the state religion of China which would secure its special status and subordinate other beliefs.

Against this background, in particular four positions were put forward in the debates around religious freedom and/or state religion. A first perspective was to argue against religious freedom but in favour of Confucianism as a state religion. This position was substantiated by the argument that China had always been a multi-religious society, and this was—in contrast to Europe—without having religious wars with thousands of dead but instead a long tradition of religious tolerance. Intellectual leaders, like the influential Kang Youwei, deduced from this that Confucianism in fact had been the state religion for a long time and that religious tolerance was never affected.[58] Also, in this view, a recognition of Confucianism in the constitution would not damage the unwritten rule of religious tolerance in China. Furthermore, for the conservation of Confucian tradition it would be a good strategy to constitute Confucianism as the state religion because this would secure its special status and subordinate other beliefs—interestingly this also served as a strategic position for those who actually did not consider Confucianism as a religion.

We thus find a second position, closely related to the previous one and represented by those who rejected both religious freedom and Confucianism as a state religion. Even though this group remained rather invisible in the sources studied above, it is possible and indeed necessary to address them here as well. Basically, this second position was represented by Confucian conservatives who generally refused foreign influences and did not consider Confucianism as a religion. Some of them argued for Confucianism as a state religion for strategic reasons,

---

[55] Ibid.
[56] Wilhelm Grube, *Religion und Kultus der Chinesen* (Verlag von Rudolf Haupt 1910).
[57] Chen, 'Confucianism Encounters Religion' (n 40) 12.   [58] Ibid, 147.

as described in the previous paragraph. But others upheld their rejection of this strategic position and reclaimed a non-religious and even anti-religious perspective. The position against a common rule of religious freedom was driven by anti-Christian and anti-foreign motivations. The anti-Christian movements of the 1920s are well-known; nevertheless they also played a role in the early Republic anti-Christianism constitutional debate. As I have already mentioned, religion in the beginning was a synonym for Christianity and therefore the protection of religious freedom was mainly understood as the protection of Christians—we have seen by the example of the unequal treaties that this was largely true for the nineteenth century. Even though there were an increasing number of Chinese Christians in the republican period, for many of the conservatives Chinese Christians were first of all foreigners or, at least, representatives of foreign ideas. Karl Grube, a German specialist on religion in China at the beginning of the twentieth century, observed that it was not Christianity that was refused by the Chinese, but the foreign element in it.[59]

How does this anti-foreignism go together with the global orientation of the political and intellectual elites which have been described above? The answer is that the existing anti-foreignism did not affect the elites in a way that would have influenced the constitution-making process substantially. Even Kang Youwei who 'has been regarded as the chief advocate of Confucianism as the "state religion"'[60] was not in principle against the adoption of foreign ideas. On the contrary, Kang was one of the most important reformers in China at the turn of the century and it was his ambition not to substitute the old with the new but to combine both.[61] So, the advocates of the state religion shared points of agreement with anti-foreign groups; however, altogether the new elites were in search of more serious reform strategies than simply to avoid the foreign, in that period.

This leads to the third perspective, which argued in favour of religious freedom and state religion. As has been shown already, influential representatives of the Confucian Religion Association did not see a general incompatibility in the rules of religious freedom and state religion. This position was also held by Christian groups in China. Gilbert Reid, the founder of the International Institute, in a letter to the editor of *The North China Herald* directly referred to Chen and the position of the Confucian Religion Association that religious freedom and state religion should be combined and came to the conclusion: 'The memorial is signed by men who are progressively conservative, and who, while strongly Confucian, are by no means antagonistic to the spread of Christianity … Let as many individuals as possible become Christian, but let the State for the time being remain Confucian.'[62] This was the compromise position of Confucian and Christian groups and missionaries: namely that the special role of Confucianism should be reflected by the

---

[59] Grube, *Religion und Kultus* (n 56) 11: '*Das Christentum als solches, ist den Chinesen überhaupt höchst gleichgültig, und nicht als fremde Lehre ist es bei ihnen verpönt, sondern als fremde Lehre.*'

[60] Chen, 'Confucianism Encounters Religion' (n 40) 94.

[61] Kroll, *Normgenese durch Re-Interpretation* (n 4) 139.

[62] Gilbert Reid, 'A State Religion' *The North China Herald* (Shanghai, 6 September 1913) 732.

constitution but that religious freedom should be granted for other religious groups as well.

The fourth position was to claim religious freedom and to refuse a state religion. It was held by various groups and individuals, foreign and Chinese. In a direct answer to Gilbert Reid's letter, which was just quoted, Wong Pah-wei pointed out, for example, that 'the Republic is composed of five races and the Mohamedans, the Tibetans, and the Mongols have each their own religion ... China cannot make one of the religions of the Han race compulsory on the other races which form the Republic. If she did this, she would destroy equality of race and by so doing destroy the Republic itself'.[63] Other comments asked for 'concerted actions' of Christians against the state religion plans, for it was seen in particular as a threat to the spread of Christianity in China.[64] Yet others argued with regard to the alleged alliance of Christianity and Western progress as well as to the positive experiences in Japan and concluded 'it is only the ignorant, it is only the uninformed who propose a state religion in these days of universal intercourse'.[65] The incompatibility of religious freedom and a state religion was eventually represented by other Christian voices such as the Society for Religious Freedom which was founded in 1916 in Beijing.[66] This last position can be seen as the radical position of the Christians who wanted to avoid any superior treatment of Confucianism in the constitution.

Conclusion and Future Prospects

Eventually, the constitution of 1923 contained the following article: 'A citizen of the Republic of China shall be free to honor Confucius and to profess any religion ...'.[67] Confucianism was not named a state religion and was not even represented as a religion. This reflected on the one hand the view that Confucianism was not a religion and thus could not be a state religion, and, on the other, that a rule of state religion would stand in opposition to religious freedom.[68]

So in the end the views which pointed to the special role of Confucianism as well as to the common principle of equal freedom for all religions succeeded. Confucianism occupied a distinctive place in the constitution in the sense that Confucianism's non-religious character was addressed, as well as its predominant social role in China's past and present. This outcome is interesting, for it shows that both distinct local views of the religious as well as global normative expectations were introduced in the final version of the constitution. As this chapter illustrated, the process was influenced by transnational religious interest groups

---

[63] Pah-wei Wong, 'A State Religion' *The North China Herald* (Shanghai, 6 September 1913) 732.
[64] 'A State Religion for China?' *The North China Herald* (Shanghai, 30 August 1913) 633.
[65] 'Confucianism and China' *The North China Herald* (Shanghai, 24 January 1914) 240.
[66] Liu, 'Confucianism, Christianity, and Religious Freedom' (n 43) 262–65.
[67] Translated and published by the Commission on Extraterritoriality, *Constitution of the Republic of China* (Trinity College Library—Moore Collection Relating to the Far East 1924) Article 12.
[68] Liu, 'Confucianism, Christianity, and Religious Freedom' (n 43) 272.

and intellectuals rather than by direct hegemonic mechanisms of foreign governments. It is striking, by the way, that only Christians and Confucians took part in the debates as organized associations. It would be very important for further research to examine the role of the other religious minorities in that context. The various actors used their freedom within a confined frame of external normative expectations. The dynamic which led to the conversion of these expectations in China was, however, the desire to make China a self-determined nation. Altogether, the use of confined freedom led into a spiral which meant a gradual assimilation over a longer time span. This was theorized as a mechanism of governance which in political philosophy is discussed as 'subjectification'. The assimilation was not all-encompassing, however. Distinctive aspects of Chinese morality survived in the constitution. Confucianism was not re-conceptualized as a religion, even though this could have meant practical advantages, as was argued by some of the reformist forces. This shows that global references formed strong influences during the whole period of constitution drafting, but the final version of the rule for religious tolerance in the constitution was unique.[69]

Finally, the question has to be raised to what degree the pattern of indirect hegemony in early republican China can be generalized. The role of academic and diplomatic elites in the identification and adaptation of external expectations, the function of transnational associations as mediators and advocacy groups in normative debates, the activity of foreign experts as missionaries of foreign ideas, all these are patterns which can be observed in other regional and historical contexts too. Even though the case study cannot be generalized in principle, it, nevertheless, presents a set of mechanisms and processes which are relevant for further comparisons of different forms of hegemony and asymmetrical relations in international law and international relations. The strategy of Chinese elites to use global knowledge for furthering domestic development—and becoming autonomous of external interference in the end—is representative also of reform strategies in other parts of the world during the nineteenth century like the Ottoman Empire or Japan. Processes of indirect hegemony can help to explain why, in the long term, these opposition strategies led to convergence of normative institutions.

In the long term, China seems to have reproduced foreign pattern not only domestically but also in its international relations. While at the end of the nineteenth century Japan was the country which successfully renegotiated its unequal treaties and then itself acted as a hegemon in East Asia, China wanted to end the unequal treaty regime without having own expansionist plans. Today, however, China has reproduced many of the techniques associated with Western imperialism, for instance, in Africa or Latin America. This kind of comparison would also deserve further attention in future projects.

---

[69] Shmuel Eisenstadt, 'Multiple Modernities' in Shmuel Eisenstadt (ed), *Multiple Modernities* (Transaction Publishers 2002), 1–29.

Bibliography

'Additional Articles to the Treaty between the United States of America and the Ta Tsing Empire of 18th of June, 1858, signed, in the English and Chinese language, at Washington, 28th July, 1868' in William F Mayers (ed), *Treaties between the Empire of China and Foreign Powers* (J Broadhurst Total 1877)

'Fifty Years Ago. From the "North China Herald' of April 18, 1857. From the Leading Article' *The North China Herald* (Shanghai, 19 April 1907) 148

'A State Religion for China?' *The North China Herald* (Shanghai, 30 August 1913) 633

'Confucianism and China' *The North China Herald* (Shanghai, 24 January 1914) 240

'Religion and Civilization' *The North China Herald* (Shanghai, 13 January 1912) 81

'National Christian Council' *The North China Herald* (Shanghai, 23 October 1926) 161

'National Christian Council' *The North China Herald* (Shanghai, 20 October 1928) 104

'The Provisional Constitution of the Republic of China' (1912) 6 The American Journal of International Law—Supplement: Official Documents 149

Anghie, Antony, *Sovereignty, Imperialism and the Making of International Law* (Cambridge University Press 2003)

Chen, Hsi-yuan, 'Confucianism Encounters Religion: The Formation of Religious Discourse and the Confucian Movement in the Modern Era' (DPhil thesis, Harvard University 1999)

Commission on Extraterritoriality, *Constitution of the Republic of China* (Trinity College Library—Moore Collection Relating to the Far East 1924)

Craft, Stephen G, *V K Wellington Koo and the Emergence of Modern China* (University Press of Kentucky 2004)

Eisenstadt, Shmuel, 'Multiple Modernities' in Shmuel Eisenstadt (ed), *Multiple Modernities* (Transaction Publishers 2002)

Foucault, Michel, *Dispositive der Macht. Michel Foucault über Sexualität, Wissen und Wahrheit* (Merve Verlag 1978)

Foucault, Michel, 'About the Beginning of the Hermeneutics of the Self: Two Lectures at Dartmouth' (1993) 21 Political Theory 198

Gong, Gerrit W, *The Standard of 'Civilization' in International Society* (Oxford University Press 1984)

Grube, Wilhelm G, *Religion und Kultus der Chinesen* (Verlag von Rudolf Haupt 1910)

Koskenniemi, Martti, 'International Law and Hegemony: A Reconfiguration' in Martti Koskenniemi, *The Politics of International Law* (Hart Publishing 2011)

Krisch, Nico, 'International Law in Times of Hegemony: Unequal Power and the Shaping of International Legal Order' (2005) 16 The European Journal of International Law 369

Kroll, Stefan, *Normgenese durch Re-Interpretation: China und das europäische Völkerrecht im 19. und 20. Jahrhundert* (Nomos 2012)

Kroll, Stefan, 'The Legal Justification of International Intervention: Theories of Community and Admissibility' in Fabian Klose (ed), *The Emergence of Humanitarian Intervention: Ideas and Practices from the Nineteenth Century to the Present* (Cambridge University Press 2015)

Lau, Christoph and Maurer, Andrea, 'Herrschaft' (*Docupedia-Zeitgeschichte. Begriffe, Methoden und Debatten der zeithistorischen Forschung*, February 2010) 11 <http://docupedia.de/zg/Herrschaft> accessed 3 December 2014

Liszt, Franz von, *Das Völkerrecht systematisch dargestellt* (Verlag von O Haering 1902)

Liu, Yi, 'Confucianism, Christianity, and Religious Freedom: Debates in the Transformation Period of Modern China (1900–1920s)' in Fenggang Yang and Joseph B Tamney (eds) *Confucianism and Spiritual Traditions in Modern China and Beyond* (Brill 2012)

Lorca, Arnulf Becker, 'Universal International Law: Nineteenth-Century Histories of Imposition and Appropriation' (2010) 51 Harvard International Law Journal 475

Meyer, John W and others, 'World Society and the Nation-State' (1997) 103 American Journal of Sociology 144

Münkler, Herfried, *Imperien. Die Logik der Weltherrschaft—Vom alten Rom bis zu den Vereinigten Staaten* (2nd edn, Rowohlt 2005)

Osterhammel, Jürgen, 'Semi-Colonialism and Informal Empire in Twentieth-Century China: Towards a Framework of Analysis' in Wolfgang J Mommsen and Jürgen Osterhammel (eds), *Imperialism and After: Continuities and Discontinuities* (Ellen & Unwin 1986)

Paulus, Andreas, 'Treaties of Friendship, Commerce and Navigation' in Rüdiger Wolfrum (ed), *Max Planck Encyclopedia of Public International Law* (online edn, Oxford University Press 2011) <http://opil.ouplaw.com/home/EPIL> accessed 3 December 2014.

Reid, Gilbert, 'A State Religion' *The North China Herald* (Shanghai, 6 September 1913)

Schmitt, Carl, 'Führung und Hegemonie' (1939) 63 Schmollers Jahrbuch für Gesetzgebung, Verwaltung und Volkswirtschaft im Deutschen Reiche 513

Stolleis, Michael, *Staats- und Verwaltungsrechtswissenschaft in Republik und Diktatur: Geschichte des öffentlichen Rechts in Deutschland*, vol 3 (Beck 1999)

Tomuschat, Christian, 'Heinrich Triepel (1868–1946)' in Stefan Grundmann et al (eds), *Festschrift 200 Jahre Juristische Fakultät der Humboldt-Universität zu Berlin: Geschichte, Gegenwart und Zukunft* (De Gruyter 2010)

Treaty of Amity, Commerce and Navigation between China and France (signed 27 June 1858) (1858) 119 CTS 180

Treaty of Peace, Amity and Commerce between China and the United States (signed 26 June 1858) (1858) 119 CTS 123

Triepel, Heinrich, *Die Hegemonie. Ein Buch von führenden Staaten* (Verlag von W Kohlhammer 1938)

Wang, Dong, *China's Unequal Treaties—Narrating National History* (Lexington Books 2005)

Wong, Pah-wei, 'A State Religion' *The North China Herald* (Shanghai, 6 September 1913)

Woolsey, Theodore Dwight, *Introduction to the Study of International Law* (3rd edn, C Scribner & Company 1871)

Yen, WW, 'The Recent Imperial Metropolitan Examinations' *The North China Herald* (Shanghai, 18 January 1907)

Zarrow, Peter, *China in War and Revolution, 1895–1949* (Routledge 2005)

3

International Law, Empire, and the Relative Indeterminacy of Narrative

Walter Rech

Introduction

Since the early sixteenth century international lawyers have constantly employed history in diverse and prominent ways, for instance, as a repository of precedents and customary norms, as a proof of an overarching moral and divine order legitimizing particular legal claims, and also as a tool for raising the status and prestige of their field. From the mid-nineteenth century onward, lawyers have additionally appealed to historical narratives to turn their discipline from a mere regulator of diplomatic exchange and international disputes into a holistic and purportedly universal enterprise addressing all fundamental needs and challenges of mankind. International lawyer Henry Wheaton thus boasted that although in its ancient infancy the law of nations was a weak body of rules easily manipulated for backing dissimulation, crime, and corruption, it had meanwhile progressed and now embodied one of 'the most valuable products' of civilization.[1] Among the major achievements of the modern law of nations Wheaton proudly listed the mitigation of war, the abolition of the slave trade, and the principles of neutrality and freedom of the seas.

Yet, as postcolonial and critical scholars have noticed, there were downsides to this progressive discourse. It legitimized the rule of the civilized over the uncivilized and the establishment of colonies and empires, thus furnishing one of the most powerful ideological justifications for Western expansion throughout modern history.[2] Today still, the ideologies of progress, evolution, modernity, and development

---

[1] Henry Wheaton, *History of the Law of Nations in Europe and America from the Earliest Times to the Treaty of Washington* (Gould, Banks & Co 1845) 54, 760.

[2] That the argument of progress and civilization served imperialist purposes was recognized by a few European international lawyers too, but this recognition was still accompanied by an endorsement of 'acceptable' forms of colonialism. As Martti Koskenniemi recalls, international lawyers who were critical of civilizatory narratives still 'advocated the formal extension of European sovereignty into colonial territory' as a means 'to check the excesses of purely commercial colonization': Martti Koskenniemi, *The Gentle Civilizer of Nations: The Rise and Fall of International Law 1870–1960* (Cambridge University Press 2001) 107.

International Law and Empire: Historical Explorations. First Edition. Martti Koskenniemi, Walter Rech, and Manuel Jiménez Fonseca. © Martti Koskenniemi, Walter Rech, and Manuel Jiménez Fonseca 2016. Published 2016 by Oxford University Press.

provide the default mode of thinking about law, politics, and economics. Current humanity still lives under the belief that modern expertise, science, and technology supply the standards of a higher form of existence domestically, internationally, and globally.[3] It is on the basis of this interiorized dogma that many both in the West and beyond came to believe in the project of 'law and development', in the idea that democracy and the rule of law should be exported to non-Western countries, and that free trade invariably 'drives growth, generates jobs, improves living standards and reduces poverty'.[4] All of these particular beliefs rely on the broader faith in progress which has spread across Western science, politics, and economics in the past two centuries, and which persists as a mainstream public discourse in the face of much intellectual and scholarly critique.[5]

Progress and Empire

The narrative of progress established itself as a defining component of international legal argument around the mid-nineteenth century, as philosophical and scientific discourses were spreading progressive and evolutionary ideas across law and the social sciences. By 1885 Thomas Joseph Lawrence, then Deputy Whewell Professor of international law at Cambridge, could firmly rely on Darwin's discoveries in the field of natural science to argue that '[l]aw has grown, like everything else on earth, and there is no reason to suppose that its period of development is ended'.[6] Lawrence posited that every age is characterized by a particular conception of justice, and that recent historical developments fully justified the current 'primacy of the great powers' and their colonial ambitions.[7] He thus noted that the doctrine of sovereign equality represented a remnant of obsolete conceptions of international law,[8] and it was Europe's 'duty to aid in the development of the most backward quarters of the globe, and to exercise police authority over barbarous races'.[9] He believed that while human history was advancing towards universal peace and order, it did so by harsh natural mechanisms such as the 'struggle for existence' and the 'survival of the fittest'.[10]

---

[3] Luc Ferry, *L'innovation destructrice* (Plon 2014) 76. Ferry makes this point very clearly, though he is less convincing when he tries to separate his critique of modernity from a critique of the West (ibid, 68).

[4] This is the opinion of the Australian opposition trade spokeswoman Penny Wong (Labor Party), as reported by Sarah Martin, 'China, Australia seal landmark free trade agreement' (*The Australian*, 17 November 2014) <http://www.theaustralian.com.au/business/in-depth/china-australia-seal-landmark-free-trade-agreement/story-fnpebfcn-1227126102864> accessed on 19 November 2014. The opinion was given after China and Australia finalized a sweeping free trade deal at the 2014 G20 summit.

[5] Thomas Skouteris, *The Notion of Progress in International Law Discourse* (TMC Asser Press 2010) ch 4; Rebecca M Bratspies and Russell A Miller, 'Progress in International Law—An Explanation of the Project' in Rebecca M Bratspies and Russell A Miller (eds), *Progress in International Law* (Nijhoff 2008).

[6] Thomas Joseph Lawrence, *Essays on Some Disputed Questions in Modern International Law* (2nd edn revised and enlarged, Deighton, Bell and Co 1885) 6.

[7] Ibid, 208.   [8] Ibid, 209.   [9] Ibid, 277.   [10] Ibid, 255.

Lawrence hereby offered a simplified and popularized picture of Darwin's thought, a kind of social Darwinism with international legal flavour.[11] However, Darwin himself gave plenty of reasons for commentators to apply his naturalist theory to human society, and might expect some of his ideas to be interpreted with broad discretion. He frequently suggested a parallel between the natural and human world by using the vocabulary of social and political sciences, especially economics, and took inspiration, among other sources, from Malthus' essay on population.[12] *The Origin of Species* featured notions such as 'the polity of nature', 'the economy of nature', the organic 'division of labour', and the 'economising' drive of natural selection.[13] There emerged a utilitarian picture of nature as ever-evolving towards higher stages of efficiency and perfection, and of man as an incessantly advancing and superior species.

A competitive conception of society and politics could especially be drawn from chapter 10 of *The Origin of Species*, devoted to the 'geological succession of organic beings'. Here Darwin discussed the gap between lower, primitive forms of life and the highest, most developed ones, whose superiority was based on the acquisition of 'some advantage in the struggle for life' through evolution.[14] In the eyes of Lawrence and other Darwinians, such ideas might well be applied to human society, both domestic and international,[15] to vindicate the pre-eminence of the bourgeois over the proletariat, of the civilized over the barbarians. Internationally, this would entail the Western right to occupy and colonize foreign lands for the sake of promoting higher evolution. As Darwin in chapter 10 of his masterpiece delved into a scientific analysis of the worldwide spread of dominant, European living species over foreign continents, he seemed to rehearse the history of colonialism, and perhaps prophesize the tragic fate looming over indigenous populations:

From the extraordinary manner in which European productions have recently spread over New Zealand, and have seized on places which must have been previously occupied, we may believe, if all the animals and plants of Great Britain were set free in New Zealand, that in the course of time a multitude of British forms would become thoroughly naturalized there, and would exterminate many of the natives.[16]

For those who, like Lawrence, wished to read *The Origin of Species* as a sociological and political text, Darwin might additionally offer an apology of nationalism and of the modern state as an organism vital for the nation's survival and affirmation in the global struggle for existence. This would serve as a set of arguments in defence of the national interest and against cosmopolitanism, precisely the kind of argument that Lawrence aimed at making. While investigating the natural selection of organisms, Darwin maintained that if a country were 'open on its borders new forms would certainly immigrate, and this also would seriously disturb the relations

---

[11] On the ambivalence and the various possible readings of *The Origin of Species*, see Peter J Bowler, *Evolution: The History of an Idea* (University of California Press 1984) 266.
[12] Charles Darwin, *The Origin of Species* (first published 1859, Wordsworth 1998) 51.
[13] Ibid, 49, 84, 89, 114.   [14] Ibid, 254.   [15] Bowler, *Evolution* (n 11) 272.
[16] Darwin, *The Origin of Species* (n 12) 255.

of some of the former inhabitants'.[17] This held even more as regards an island (such as, presumably, Britain), in which gradual internal evolution might be disrupted by the arrival of foreign species.[18]

Yet Darwin at the same time provided arguments that could be read as universalist and cosmopolitan, arguments that Lawrence entirely overlooked. For instance, Darwin admitted that even in islands a cross with foreign species is 'occasionally—perhaps at very long intervals—indispensable' to give 'vigour and fertility to the offspring'.[19] If the reader wished to read this statement with reference to English political history, they could identify the occasional and providential crosses with the waves of invasion and immigration by Romans, Anglo-Saxons, Normans, or the Irish. Darwin reckoned that the increasing diversification of species in one country improves the local division of labour and thus yields evolutionary advantages, an argument potentially supporting (controlled) immigration, plausibly, indeed, Irish immigration to England.[20] So construed, *The Origin of Species* might inspire solidarity, not only competition, and demystify the fear of otherness.

Still, the prevalent tone of Darwin's text suggested to Lawrence and other Darwinians[21] that the struggle for existence would remain harsh and merciless, as only 'the vigorous, the healthy, and the happy survive and multiply'.[22] At the international level, Lawrence assumed that the law of the survival of the fittest implied the inevitable, progressive subjection of indigenous populations to the West or to other major world civilizations. Darwin himself seemed to imply that smaller native tribes deemed incapable of self-government and disconnected from major civilizations, especially in Africa and Australia, would fall victim to this process. In the final pages of *The Origin of Species* Darwin predicted that 'it will be the common and wide-spread species, belonging to the larger and dominant groups, which will ultimately prevail and procreate new and dominant species'.[23]

Providence and Empire

Darwin expressed a programmatic scepticism about any (Christian) providential 'plan of creation' or 'unity of design', since no scientific evidence could be cited in support of the existence of a divine cosmic order.[24] Yet he retained a historical metanarrative of a theological kind. As Vico, Kant, and Hegel had earlier done, Darwin filled the vacuum left by the Christian theology of history with an equally providential, if secular, philosophy of history. He asserted that 'as natural selection works solely by and for the good of each being, all corporeal and mental endowments will tend to progress towards perfection'.[25] He thus exalted this progressive, self-organized natural system, and the 'beauty and infinite complexity of the

---

[17] Ibid, 64.   [18] Ibid, 64.   [19] Ibid, 75.   [20] Ibid, 89.
[21] David Burton, 'Theodore Roosevelt's Darwinism and Views on Imperialism' (1965) 26 Journal of the History of Ideas 103.
[22] Darwin, *The Origin of Species* (n 12) 62.   [23] Ibid, 368.   [24] Ibid, 363.
[25] Ibid, 368.

coadaptations between all organic beings'.[26] There were some important analogies between Darwin's discourse and the theology he wished to combat: his idea of a teleological cosmic order calls to mind the medieval philosophies of Bonaventure or Aquinas, and his glorification of nature's beauty strikingly resonates with Christian eulogies of God's creation, notably Saint Francis of Assisi's *Laudes creaturarum*.[27]

A further commonality between Darwinian and Christian worldviews is that they operated in similar ways as means to justify empire. Just as Lawrence resorted to ideas of progress and evolution to shore up British imperialism, Spanish Scholastic theologians had appealed to divine providence and the Christian view of history to legitimize Spain's and ecclesiastical interests on the American continent. A set of paradigmatic Christian arguments for empire were famously formulated by Francisco de Vitoria, for instance in his *Relectio de Indis*, Question 3, Article 2, in which he suggested that the lawfulness of the Spaniards' imperial power might derive from their duty and right to spread the Christian religion.[28] This point rested on a theological view of history according to which it was the mission of all Christian believers, in particular of the church ministers, to preach the message of Christ and thus prepare themselves and all nations for His second coming. In support of this argument Vitoria quoted Christ's requiring the apostles to go 'into all the world and preach the gospel to every creature', as well as the universalist statement that 'the word of God is not bound', contained in the Second Epistle to Timothy.[29] Vitoria concluded that:

... if the barbarians, either in the person of their masters or as a multitude, obstruct the Spaniards in their free propagation of the Gospel, the Spaniards, after first reasoning with them to remove any cause of provocation, *may preach and work for the conversion of that people even against their will*, and may if necessary take up arms and declare war on them, insofar as this provides the safety and opportunity to preach the Gospel.[30]

A few decades later the same argument was reaffirmed by theologian Juan Ginés de Sepúlveda as he endorsed his sovereign's and the church's power in the Americas in the treatise *Democrates secundus, sive de iustis belli causis apud Indios*.[31] In Sepúlveda's opinion, natural law and Christian charity obliged (and therefore also entitled, since *ad impossibilia nemo tenetur*) the Spaniards to evangelize the natives. In his view it was God, the source of all law, who wished that all peoples be saved and who called on the devout to guide the pagans on the right path.[32] This mission, Sepúlveda argued, should be accomplished even against the natives' will. To prove

---

[26] Ibid, 84.   [27] Ibid, 369.

[28] Francisco de Vitoria, 'On the American Indians' in Francisco de Vitoria, *Political Writings* (Anthony Pagden and Jeremy Lawrance eds, Cambridge University Press 1991). For an analysis of Vitoria's doctrine and its implications see Anthony Pagden, *The Burdens of Empire: 1539 to the Present* (Cambridge University Press 2015) 45–74.

[29] Mark 16:15; 2 Tim 2:9.   [30] Vitoria, 'On the American Indians' (n 28) 285.

[31] Juan Ginés de Sepúlveda, *Democrates secundus, sive de iustis belli causis apud Indios* (1544), translated into Spanish in Marcelino Menéndez y Pelayo and Manuel García-Pelayo (eds), *Tratado sobre las justas causas de la guerra contra los indios* (Fondo de Cultura Económica 1986).

[32] Ibid, 137.

this he referred to Augustine of Hippo's comment on Psalm 72:11, a verse which read '[m]ay all kings bow down to him and all nations serve him'. In Sepúlveda's reading, Augustine relied on the psalm to encourage Christians' firmness in their evangelizing mission and reassert the *compelle intrare* statement in Jesus' Parable of the Great Banquet.[33]

Alongside providential history, Sepúlveda provided an alternative argument for the justice of the Spanish empire. This was the idea of the Americans as irrational barbarians, hence slaves by nature in the sense described by Aristotle in the first book of *Politics*.[34] For their own good, Sepúlveda argued, the natives should be ruled by the Spaniards who would put some civilized restraints on their quasi-animal conduct. Yet this sounded like a problematic argument to his Christian audience as it seemed to entail that, on ground of their alleged irrationality, the natives could not grasp the truth of the gospel and be converted, which would undermine the authority and mission of the church in the Americas. It was for this reason, among more humanitarian ones, that the Dominican Bartolomé de Las Casas, engaged in a famous dispute with Sepúlveda, denied the Americans' barbarism and characterized them as civilized and virtuous instead.[35] Las Casas argued that Americans 'are of such gentleness and decency that they are, more than the other nations of the entire world, prepared to abandon the worship of idols and to accept, province by province and people by people, the word of God and the preaching of the truth'.[36]

With hindsight, however, Las Casas' argument looks largely incongruent, at least in the particular way he articulated it. He construed Sepúlveda's position as contradictory because it proclaimed the necessity of converting the natives while simultaneously defining them as hopelessly irrational barbarians. Yet Sepúlveda actually conceded that if the barbarians yield to the Spaniards they will be able to relinquish their 'feral' existence and turn to humanity and virtue.[37] This was in line with the teachings of Aristotle, who had maintained that while barbarians by nature lack reason they can still receive and learn it from their masters.[38] Las Casas thus misconstrued Sepúlveda's position as based on a fixist anthropology to which he opposed his providential theology of history. For him, Sepúlveda remained stuck to a Greek image of history as a purposeless cyclical struggle in which the strongest rule over the weak and love has no place. Las Casas defied it through an optimistic vision of the world, one in which the spirit of the gospel would be followed and the Christian community would continue expanding by means of charity, not war. However, his

[33] Luke 14:23. While Augustine referred to the *compelle intrare* argument in his polemical writings, he actually did not rely on or hint at it in the particular comment quoted by Sepúlveda, who thus cited wrongly on this occasion. See Augustine of Hippo, 'Expositions of the Psalms' in *The Works of Saint Augustine*, vol III/7 (Maria Boulding tr, New City Press 2001) 464.

[34] Aristotle, *Politics* (Ernest Barker tr, Oxford University Press 1998) 15 (Book I, ch 5, 1254a).

[35] On the controversy between Sepúlveda and Las Casas see Anthony Pagden, *The Fall of Natural Man: The American Indian and the Origins of Comparative Ethnology* (Cambridge University Press 1982) chs 5 and 6.

[36] Bartolomé de Las Casas, *In Defense of the Indians* (Stafford Poole tr, Northern Illinois University Press 1992) 28.

[37] Sepúlveda, *Democrates secundus* (n 31) 85.

[38] Aristotle, *Politics* (n 34) 16 (Book I, ch 5, 1254b).

legal and theological argument might still be regarded as imperial for the proselytizing intent underpinning it.

Combining Individuality and Universality: The Rhetorical Power of Progressivism and Providentialism

It is hardly surprising that providential and progressive narratives have served as powerful rhetorical weapons in Western hands for advancing an imperialist under-standing of international law. Firstly, from the perspective of rhetorical strategy and social communication, it is nearly a tautology to say that Western scholars simply had to explain imperialism in terms of providence or progress if they wanted to be heard within a society largely consisting of (religious or secular) believers, regard-less of whether these scholars actually shared such beliefs. If the audience speaks the language of religion and progress, the author has to write in that language too.

Yet from an international legal perspective the narratives of providence and pro-gress were not rhetorical languages like any other. They offered a particularly suit-able jargon for describing fundamental issues of world peace, justice, and order.[39] For the early modern public as for today's observers, every war, every major trade deal, every pandemic, and every change in the world order almost naturally invites a reflection on the destiny of humanity and, perhaps, on the possibility for mankind to be redeemed at last, be it through grace or through man's own Faustian effort. In early modern times, when modern international law emerged, this eschatological sensibility was awakened even more powerfully by geographic explorations and the colonial encounter. Otherness was then perceived as most radical, and theologies and philosophies of history were employed to bridge the gap between Europeans and natives,[40] sometimes for reconciliatory purposes yet more often for the sake of empire. By including overseas peoples into purportedly universal yet in fact Eurocentric plots, European historians both plead for cosmopolitanism and justi-fied the imposition of European modes of existence on indigenous populations.[41]

At the level of individual psychology, a further reason for the success of provi-dentialist and progressivist narratives was their capability of explaining the human condition and providing an existentially meaningful account of social life. In addition to allowing Europeans to understand (more or less accurately) the other, providentialism and progressivism also helped Europeans understand themselves. Religious and philosophical narratives fulfilled this latter function by combining the sense of individuality, especially the intuition of moral and legal obligation,

---

[39] Martti Koskenniemi, 'Law, Teleology and International Relations: An Essay in Counterdisciplinarity' (2012) 26 International Relations 3.

[40] Giuliano Gliozzi, *Adamo e il nuovo mondo: La nascita dell'antropologia come ideologia coloni-ale: dalle genealogie bibliche alle teorie razziali (1500–1700)* (Franco Angeli 1977).

[41] On this exclusion/inclusion mechanism see Koskenniemi, *The Gentle Civilizer* (n 2) 127, and Antony Anghie, *Imperialism, Sovereignty and the Making of International Law* (Cambridge University Press 2007) 21.

with a world-historical view of human community. They posed normative demands on individuals while assuring them that providence or Reason would intervene and grant the orderly development of human history, as well as the possibility of grace and 'improvement', despite these individuals' lack of goodwill and human sinfulness or self-interest more generally. Providence and progress endowed man with individual freedom and responsibility while limiting the nefarious consequences of the inevitable misuse of such divine gifts.

Christianity, in particular, put forward a fairly optimistic view of history in this respect.[42] In Christians' view, Christ had established a New Covenant between God and man which, unlike the covenants of the Old Testament, could not be jeopardized by impious humanity. While in the Old Testament divine wrath visited the peoples of the earth in response to immoral and irreligious conduct by these peoples or some of their members, in the new covenant God would no longer castigate nations directly and collectively, but only indirectly through political authorities punishing crimes under law.[43] Further, it is particularly significant in eschatological terms that the New Covenant resulted from God's unconditional love and compassion. In the Old Testament God promised treasures to Moses and the people of Israel only conditionally, provided they obeyed Him fully and kept the covenant,[44] whereas, according to Christians, Christ redeemed the whole of humanity from the original sin without posing any condition (though Christians should obviously expect chastisement as a result of their individual faults). This optimistic view of history, grounded on the idea of unconditional redemption, proved a decisive aspect for the propagation of early Christianity in competition with pagan religions and with 'impious' and pessimistic philosophical worldviews such as the doctrine of cyclical history and the idea of the eternal return.[45] In modern times, the same promise of redemption and happiness (supplemented with economic wealth) would constitute a fundamental factor facilitating the popularization of a secularized philosophy of progress.

To be sure, within Christianity there emerged confessional and denominational differences as to how to conceive the relationship between individual morality and the course of history, between free will and grace, faith and works. According to the Spanish Catholic theologians involved in debates over overseas empire, for instance, the spread of Christian faith in the Americas was clearly meant as a cooperative endeavour of God and His pious messengers on earth. It was actualized by the works of believers under the supervision of divine wisdom. As theologians' professional task was to demonstrate the meaningfulness of history and human existence, they reassured believers that acts of charity impacted on the world and that,

---

[42] On the concept of history in ancient times and the Bible, see Arnaldo Momigliano, 'Time in Ancient Historiography' in Arnaldo Momigliano, *Essays in Ancient and Modern Historiography* (Blackwell 1977). See also Marc Zvi Brettler, *The Creation of History in Ancient Israel* (Routledge 1998) 48.

[43] Rom. 13:1.   [44] Exod. 19:5.

[45] Augustine, *The City of God Against the Pagans*, vol IV (Philip Levine tr, Harvard University Press 1966) 53–65 (Book XII, chs 12–14). See also Johannes van Oort, 'The End is Now: Augustine on History and Eschatology' (2012) 68 (1) HTS Teologiese Studies/Theological Studies 4.

although the greater part of mankind (including the greedy colonizers rebuked by Las Casas) was short of good intentions, a transcendent scheme would guide historical transactions for the better. The success of theological and progressive histories thus lay in their categorical affirmation of a promise, be it eternal salvation or indefinite progress, a promise assuring the meaningfulness of human history and existence altogether.

Both subjective and transcendent elements of historical development were still at work in eighteenth- and nineteenth-century philosophies. While in the writings of this age there emerged a growing sense of the necessity of the historical process, especially due to the established analogy between the regularities of social life and the laws governing the physical world, human agency was never fully delegitimized, and came back in many Christian and lay versions from Kierkegaard through to Dostoyevsky and Nietzsche. Historicism too remained aware of the relevance of individual human agency despite social conditioning, even when this agency was seen from the perspective of an overarching universal process à la Hegel. To be sure, one might argue that the only agency that Hegel ever emphasized was his own, or at most that of Napoleon, but he still accorded individuality and particularity an indispensable role in the development of universal Reason.[46] In a similar vein, for Darwin, evolution was a largely unforeseeable process that could be barely steered by man, yet he conceded that evolution materially resulted from attempts made by competitive individuals to improve their own condition and thereby the species.[47]

Both Hegelianism and Darwinism were once admired as meaningful frameworks for understanding the human condition and the historical and social world. For the present readership, however, the problem is that they have been put to use for purposes that would now be regarded as objectionable and disgraceful, such as radical nationalistic policies and eugenical practices. Perhaps worryingly, parts of those nineteenth-century modes of thinking survive in today's public discourse in cloaked forms, for instance in ideologies of growth, free trade, and development. Through these refurbished vocabularies, old progressivism and providentialism continue to operate as tools for backing imperial policies in the Global South.

On the other hand, progressive and providential narratives have furnished arguments to resist empire, too. In the past three centuries, the philosophy of progress has sometimes functioned as an emancipatory political resource, stimulating institutional transformation and reforms in legal areas from criminal and labour law through to family and environmental law. Similarly, on the providentialist side, Francis of Assisi's revolution against mundane opulence, the Liberation Theology movement's fight for the empowerment of the weakest, and the social and political

---

[46] This is most clearly visible in Georg Wilhelm Friedrich Hegel, *Phenomenology of Spirit* (AV Miller tr, Oxford University Press 1977); Georg Wilhelm Friedrich Hegel, *Elements of the Philosophy of Right* (HB Nisbet tr, Cambridge University Press 1991). To be sure, the Hegelian question would remain whether there will still be room for truly active human agency after Napoleon and the completion of modernity. For a classical reading on the end of agency (and of political history altogether), see Alexandre Kojève, *Introduction à la lecture de Hegel* (Gallimard 1968) 385, 413.

[47] Darwin, *The Origin of Species* (n 12) 49.

engagement of Protestant denominations in Afro-American communities all attest to theology being capable of advocating (if not always successfully or consequently) for societal change. This would seem to confirm that nearly any philosophico-historical narrative can be used for emancipatory and counter-emancipatory purposes alike.

Cyclical History: A Weak Tool for Empire?

Prior to providentialism and progressivism, Western scholarship had already resorted to other historical theories to advance or contest empire. One of these was cyclical history. Since its classical formulations in Plato, Aristotle, and Polybius, this theory argued that the history of nations follows a regular pattern of birth, development, and decline, and is characterized by the succession of standard forms of government, typically monarchy, aristocracy, and democracy, each of which tends to pass into a degenerative form, that is, tyranny, oligarchy, and anarchy, respectively. This kind of history was premised on specific assumptions about law and politics, and writers tended to design the history of a polity around an idealized golden age that they identified with a given political system, often a 'mixed constitution'. Commonly, for classical writers from antiquity until early modern times, this golden age was characterized by internal cohesion, wealth, external influence, and imperial power.

Cyclical historians, like all other historians, happened to make parochial and apologetic statements in their works. They were prone to justifying current hegemony, as Polybius did with Rome in his *Histories*,[48] or they announced the dawn of an age of splendour for their nation to the detriment of other powers, as sixteenth-century French humanists did as they advocated for France's military and cultural supremacy against former Italian predominance;[49] or yet, in times of crisis, they lamented their country's weakness and called for a revival of ancient belligerent virtues and a fresh start into an eon of prosperity, much as Machiavelli did in *The Prince*.[50] Cyclical historians typically situated themselves in one particular age and pleaded for stability or change depending on the needs of the time.

Yet cyclical history came with a feeling of fatalism and evanescence that fundamentally undermined its own normative claims, including imperial claims. Why should political leaders and military commanders wish to take the trouble of creating an empire if this endeavour would inexorably crumble, perhaps already in their lifetimes? They would surely commit to imperial policies for the sake of both

---

[48] Polybius, *The Histories* (WR Paton tr, revised by FW Walbank and Christian Habicht, Harvard University Press 2011) 295 (Book VI, ch 2).

[49] Julian H Franklin, *Jean Bodin and the Sixteenth-Century Revolution in the Methodology of Law and History* (Columbia University Press 1963) 48; Donald R Kelley, *Foundations of Modern Historical Scholarship: Language, Law and History in the French Renaissance* (Columbia University Press 1970) 242ff.

[50] Niccolò Machiavelli, *The Prince* (Peter Bondanella tr, Oxford University Press 2005) 87.

personal and their families' and clients' benefit, but they would not need to buy into Machiavelli's or others' cyclical history for this reason alone.[51] As to realist scholars, they have often been fascinated by cyclical history as an antidote to naïve providentialism and progressivism, but cyclical history is certainly not a necessary precondition for political realism; quite the contrary, the perpetual historical regularities asserted by the cyclical doctrine may turn into dogmatic and metaphysical obstacles to a genuinely 'realist' examination of political 'facts' in their particularity and contingency.[52]

That cyclical history appeared as scarcely persuasive as an imperial argument is also signalled by the fact that Greek writers, who sketched the first theories of cyclicity in the West, did not rely on it to legitimize empire. In Plato's and Aristotle's seminal accounts, cyclical history took the shape of internal constitutional history, and bore no immediate relevance to the question of empire. Both Plato and Aristotle described the imperial struggle between Greeks and barbarians as a virtually atemporal conflict, not as an instance of cyclical history. They aprioristically defined the Greeks as civilized and the 'barbarous' Persians as uncivilized (though the latter might potentially learn civilization from the Greeks, as Aristotle seemed to concede).[53] Within this anthropological framework, Greeks and barbarians were characterized as mutual enemies by nature, and they would retain this qualification regardless of any changes and revolutions in their respective forms of government and economic systems. This dichotomic and ahistorical conception of Greek/barbarian relations was paradigmatically stated in Book 5 of Plato's *Republic*, in which Socrates, featuring as the main character, theorized a two-tiered law of war. Socrates argued that Greek combatants were permitted to carry on an all-out fight against barbarian enemies but, when waging war against other Greeks, they should maintain a sense of fraternity and keep on sharing in the same religious rituals:

Then being Greeks they will not ravage Greece, nor set their buildings alight. They will not accept that everyone, men women and children, in every city is an enemy, but that a few who are at any time hostile are responsible for the dispute. And it's for all these reasons they will be unwilling to ravage their land, and destroy their houses, as most of them are friends, but will pursue their dispute to the point where those responsible are compelled to be punished by those who are not, but who are nevertheless suffering.[54]

To be sure this was meant as a normative point, not a description of actual politics. In the *Laws* Plato, personified by the 'Athenian', stated that internal infightings

---

[51] Actually, regardless of any philosophico-historical speculations, Italian leaders even failed to pay attention to Machiavelli's more elementary warning about the imminent threat of foreign troops occupying Italy, a threat painfully materialized by the Sack of Rome in 1527. See Maurizio Viroli, *Niccolò's Smile: A Biography of Machiavelli* (Antony Shugaar tr, Farrar, Straus and Giroux 2000) 249.

[52] This is in theory. Obviously political realism has never truly managed to carry out the analysis of empirical facts without some implicit reference to a philosophico-historical framework. This was already openly recognized by EH Carr, *The Twenty Years' Crisis 1919–1939: An Introduction to the Study of International Relations* (MacMillan 1983) 10.

[53] Aristotle, *Politics* (n 34) 16 (Book I, ch 5, 1254 b).

[54] Plato, *Republic*, vol 1 (Chris Emlyn-Jones and William Preddy trs, Harvard University Press 2013) 531 (Book V, 471b).

among Hellenes tended to be more brutal than combats between Hellenes and bar-barians.[55] He thus admitted that the cruellest acts of violence are those perpetrated against the brother within the family and in civil wars, not against the foreigner and in interstate conflict. Around the same time, an analogous admission was being made in the biblical book of Genesis, in which the origin of human violence was traced back to Cain's murder of Abel. Here, violent death precisely resulted from family dynamics, not alien threats.[56]

In the imperial doctrines of Plato and Aristotle cyclical history did not feature prominently. It rather possessed the supplementary function of exemplifying how 'natural' struggles for empire came about. It was deliberately framed as a specula-tive, conjectural philosophy of history rather than as 'history proper', or as mytho-logical and religious history. It was in this conjectural manner that Plato described the evolution of human society and the surfacing of war in Book 2 of the *Republic*. By borrowing Socrates' voice, Plato suggested that nascent polities expand freely and peacefully until they reach a point when they need to acquire external resources and goods that neighbours may not be willing to trade.[57] At that stage war is inevi-table, but this was not something that Plato bemoaned. In a statement worthy of a political realist, Socrates/Plato claimed that once conflict has broken out 'the state must become bigger, not by some small unit, but by a whole army which can go out and fight the assailants to defend all our property'.[58]

For Plato, as for Greek thinkers generally, antagonism qualified as a fundamen-tally natural and biological, not merely historical, phenomenon. It was charac-terized as a principle permeating all levels of human existence, from individuals through to families and states. War was even waged within the human soul itself—in a delicate balance between reason, spirit, and appetite—and, analogously, by social bodies and classes within the same polity. In the views of Plato, Aristotle, or Thucydides, history was meant to illustrate contingent and contextual reasons for specific conflicts and imperial enterprises, not explain away the drive to conquest as such.

In Machiavelli's writings, too, what allowed the logic of empire to prevail over religion, law, and morals was not the notion of historical cyclicity, but the political realism and anthropological 'pessimism'[59] that underpinned that history. Therein lay the strength (and the weakness) of Machiavelli's argument. Centuries later, real-ists in international relations still buy into his political doctrine because they trust his political acumen and share his anthropological understanding, not because they believe in his historiographical approach. Thus, for the likes of Hans Morgenthau

---

[55] Plato, *Laws* (RG Bury tr, Harvard University Press 1926) 19 (Book I, 629d).

[56] Michele Nicoletti, *La politica e il male* (Morcelliana 2000).

[57] Plato, *Republic* (n 54) 179 (Book II, 373e).

[58] Ibid. In the *Laws* Plato actually argued that good politicians should aim at external peace, but this was meant as a prudential rather than pacifist or humanitarian statement: Plato, *Laws* (n 55) 15 (Book I, 628c).

[59] Carl Schmitt, *The Concept of the Political: Expanded Edition* (George Schwab tr, The University of Chicago Press 2007).

and Henry Kissinger the drive to power and empire is inherently human, and the regularities of history merely attest to it a posteriori.[60]

Obviously this does not mean that cyclical history *cannot* be used to legitimize empire, only that it is rhetorically less effective than progressivism and providentialism for that purpose. The idea itself of cyclicity is accompanied by the spectres of fatalism and ineluctable decline that would loom over any imperial project. When empire is already in place, the assumption of cyclicity announces its eventual collapse, and when empire is yet to be grounded, the same cyclical view predicts that the glory of empire might be ephemeral and vain.

'History Proper' v. Philosophy of History

No study of past historiography would be accomplished if it did not take into account 'history proper'; that is, what professional historians—and not lawyers, theologians, and philosophers—actually do. In a way, however, it is not so sure what should count as 'history proper' and who the 'proper historians' are. Should the canon include Greek and Roman authors, Renaissance writers, and nineteenth-century 'scientific' historicists, or only contemporary contextualists? The superiority of the moderns over the ancients has been powerfully contested by postmodern literary critique, according to which there are no such things as objectivity and neutrality in history writing, hence the conventional distinction between historiography and philosophy of history is virtually worthless. If this holds, between historical and philosophical or theological narratives there only remains a programmatic distinction of form.[61] Whilst the structures of the philosophy and theology of history are conditioned by speculative assumptions, historiographical writing is rather meant to be restrained by rhetorical imperatives and techniques. To be sure, such imperatives should be viewed less as outright limits that historical discourse has to suffer than as its conditions of possibility, as deliberate and artificial self-limitations strengthening historiography's claim to neutrality and impartiality. It is by stepping back as narrators and letting 'facts' speak that professional historians since Thucydides have endeavoured to increase the credibility of historical plots.[62] And it is on the basis of such reported evidence—as purportedly distinct from religious beliefs and philosophical conjectures—that 'history proper' since Thucydides has proved an irreplaceable instrument for analysing, and often justifying, empire.

---

[60] Hans Morgenthau, *Politics among Nations: The Struggle for Power and Peace* (McGraw-Hill Higher Education 2006); Henry Kissinger, *Diplomacy* (Simon & Schuster 1994). For a critique of Morgenthau's anthropological assumptions see BS Chimni, *International Law and World Order: A Critique of Contemporary Approaches* (Sage Publications 1993) 26.

[61] Hayden White, 'Historicism, History, and the Figurative Imagination' (1975) 14(4) History and Theory 48, 49.

[62] John Marincola, *Greek Historians* (Oxford University Press 2001) 73.

'History Proper' and Empire

One of the first attempts at writing a thorough history of international law, encompassing both doctrine and practice, was that made by English jurist Robert Plumer Ward (1745–1846) with his *Enquiry into the Foundation and History of the Law of Nations* of 1795.[63] The book was actually written in a style that many perceived as novelistic and entertaining, and indeed Ward was destined to be acclaimed more for his novels than for his legal writings. As noted by a biographer, one of Ward's novel, *De Vere, or, The Man of Independence*, 'may have prompted [George] Canning's quip that Ward's law books were as interesting as novels and his novels as dull as law books'.[64] Though literary in style, and underpinned by strong normative assumptions, Ward's *Enquiry* still embodied one of the first serious attempts by a European writer to lay down a 'proper' history of the law of nations. Partly echoing the historicist discourse of coeval authors like Vico, Montesquieu, and the Scottish Enlightenment historians, Ward conveyed a strong sense of the law's historical and geographical relativity. The preface argued that any international legal issue might lead to endless disputes, and there was no evident reason why all nations of the earth ought to acknowledge and obey the same law.[65] Building on this relativist intuition he came to endorse a regionalist understanding of the law of nations, which he epitomized as follows:

Under all these points, it appeared to me, that we expected too much when we contended of the *universality* of the duties laid down by the Codes of the Law of Nations; that, however desirable such universality might be, the whole world were not susceptible of that intimacy and closeness of union, which many philosophers of high name are willing to suppose; that it falls under different divisions and *sets* of nations, connected together under particular religions, moral systems, and local institutions, to the exclusion of other divisions or sets of nations; that these various divisions may indeed preserve an intimacy among one another, and obey the same law; but that they may be contra-distinguished from others who may have different religions, and moral systems, operated upon by very different local circumstances: in fine, that what is commonly called the Law of Nations, falls very short of *universality*; and that, therefore, the law is not the law of *all* nations, but only of particular classes of them; and thus there may be a *different* law of nations for *different* parts of the globe. Not only this, but even, in the same part of the globe, there may have been very different sorts of Law of Nations, according as revolutions have taken place in the religion, system of morality, and local institutions of the nations which compose it.[66]

In a historicist and sociological spirit, Ward set out to study the manners, customs, arms, and politics of Europe's peoples with a view to grasp the principles and rules

---

[63] Robert Plumer Ward, *An Enquiry into the Foundation and History of the Law of Nations, from the Time of the Greeks and Romans to the Age of Grotius*, 2 vols (Strahan and Woodfall 1795).

[64] Clive Towse, 'Ward, Robert Plumer (1765–1846)' in *Oxford Dictionary of National Biography* (Oxford University Press 2004) <http://www.oxforddnb.com/view/article/28703> accessed on 17 November 2014.

[65] Ward, *An Enquiry* (n 63) vol 1, Preface , VIII.

[66] Ibid, XIII, emphasis in the original.

of their particular law of nations. For him, law was not an autonomous normative field but a social phenomenon that ought to be understood historically and in context.

Yet the choice of the relevant context to study is precisely one of the main points at which 'history proper' creaks.[67] In the preface of his *Enquiry* Ward conveys the impression of being a sceptical historian of the modern kind, acknowledging the relativity of knowledge, the impossibility of universal normativity, and the priority of local, contextual analysis over grand narratives. But Ward only resorts to this relativism and contextualism as a rhetorical strategy, in particular as a weapon in his counterrevolutionary political struggle as the French Revolution was raging. A few years before writing the *Enquiry*, as a law student, Ward had travelled in France and returned to England appalled, with the images of the early phases of the revolution in mind. In 1794 he made himself known for his loyalty to the Pitt government by providing information to unmask a republican plot, and was then invited to produce a work on the law of nations by Lord Stowell.[68] It was in this context that Ward set out to write a historical book on the law of nations. It was supposed to disprove the French revolutionaries' understanding of politics and international affairs and to back counterrevolutionary claims. For Ward, as for Edmund Burke,[69] the thesis about the relativity and historicity of law served as a tool for disproving revolutionary natural law thinking, and the argument for the existence of 'very different sorts of Law of Nations' within the same (European) region was meant to set France apart from the majority of European countries that purportedly preserved the healthy core of the law of nations, which went back to the Greek and Roman civilizations as well as Christianity and medieval chivalry. With France ideologically isolated, its revolution would not become a legal precedent but rather remain a transitory anomaly that could not affect the established principles of the public law of Europe.

To today's readers, Ward's normative overtones make it appear a highly hybridized and ambiguous work, oddly mixing potentially relativist historiographical analyses of past laws with claims about historical progress and the persisting relevance of religion in the law of nations. It simultaneously recognized divine law, natural law, positive law, and empirical reality as sources of the law of nations.[70] This eclectic edifice could only stand as long as Ward renounced outright relativism to construct a hierarchy of legal sources or at least privileged one among them, and so he did. While going over the *Enquiry* it slowly becomes clear that Ward sees religion as the actual foundation of the law of nations, and one religion—the Christian—as superior to others.[71] Indeed what matters to Ward are only European nations, the real protagonists of his history, whereas other peoples are left out. Since

---

[67] Martti Koskenniemi, 'Histories of International Law: Significance and Problems for a Critical View' (2013) 27 Temple International & Comparative Law Journal 215, 231.

[68] Towse, 'Ward' (n 64).

[69] Edmund Burke, *Reflections on the Revolution in France* (JGA Pocock ed, Hackett 1987).

[70] Ward, *An Enquiry* (n 63) vol 1, Preface, XXII–XXIV, 24, 61.

[71] Ibid, vol 1, 123, 129.

in Ward's narrative Christianity is the **truest religion**, and any law of nations stems from religious principles, only Europeans can practically build and enjoy a 'finally certain' historical progress.[72]

This did not prevent Ward from equating the history of the (European) law of nations with the (ideal) history of humanity,[73] thereby universalizing and rationalizing Europe's law in a way typical of earlier natural law scholarship.[74] If on the one hand Ward took a regionalist perspective to posit that 'the law of nations is not the law of the world',[75] on the other hand he pictured this very law of nations as a subject that 'must for ever be of consequence to mankind'.[76] He literally saw his book as contributing to increasing understanding about the nature of the human species.[77] *Enquiry* thus qualified as 'history proper' and philosophy of history at once. It made a twofold statement about the necessity of both examining historical instances of international legal principles and rules in context as well as sketching the broader role of the law of nations in the path of mankind, a statement that might still speak to many international lawyers at present. And yet in Ward's work the history of mankind and international law was reduced to the history of the West as attesting to the ideal pattern of legal evolution. Not unlike some present narratives of progress, it was a history that could be read as putting constraints on the way the future might be shaped in non-Western countries.

Like any international legal scholar of the time, though, Ward made a few cosmopolitan moves. When addressing, in passing, the issue of colonization, he contested older European claims to overseas sovereignty on the basis of discovery and royal patents. He wondered 'who among us but would be filled with indignation were a fleet of ships from some part of the Globe, hitherto unknown, (if such there be) to arrive to Europe on discoveries, and pretend to spoil us of our goods, or take possession of our territories upon the authority of similar patents?'[78] Here Ward put his relativist and regionalist view of law and politics at the service of an apparently universalist cause. He continued noticing, with some relief, that the right of discovery was no longer acknowledged by the time of his writing; it was an obsolete right 'upon which our ancestors proceeded, at the close of the fifteenth century'.[79] But such a statement is exactly what makes Ward's anti-imperialism suspect. By attributing the right to discovery and unlawful colonization to 'our ancestors', he seemed implicitly to justify later European techniques for legalizing overseas occupation. The latter might include the labour theory of appropriation, especially as expounded by Grotius, under whose wise guide the law of nations after many centuries of uncertainty was 'to be found at last resting upon sure ground'.[80] Regardless

---

[72] Ibid, vol 2, 6.

[73] On this equation, see Koskenniemi, 'Histories of International Law: Significance and Problems' (n 67) 220.

[74] Walter Rech, *Enemies of Mankind: Vattel's Theory of Collective Security* (Nijhoff 2013) 105.

[75] Ward, *An Enquiry* (n 63) vol 1, 131.   [76] Ibid, vol 2, 628.   [77] Ibid, vol 2, 628.

[78] Ibid, vol 1, 116.   [79] Ibid, vol 1, 116.

[80] Ibid, vol 2, 628. Hugo Grotius linked labour and land occupation in *De iure belli ac pacis (The Rights of War and Peace)* II (first published 1625, Richard Tuck ed, Liberty Fund 2005) 447–49 (Book II, ch 2, §§16–17).

of what Ward might have meant in writing these passages, they could be interpreted both ways, in favour of or against colonialism.

Enquiry opened the new field of international legal history with an attitude that we still encounter in today's international law, parochial and cosmopolitan in the same breath. The book started off with a methodological regionalist approach potentially critical of despotic universalism, but ended by picturing Europe's regional law of nations as a universal model grounded on a universal religion. There resulted an ambivalent work that could be cited as endorsing or criticizing empire depending on the eyes of the beholder.

Contextual History and Existentialism

The ambivalence of 'history proper' is still visible in twentieth century 'contextualism'. The latter term refers to two dominant prongs in intellectual history, the *Begriffsgeschichte* or 'conceptual history' primarily associated to the name of Reinhardt Koselleck, and the Cambridge School led by Quentin Skinner. These streams share the fundamental assumption that political concepts, far from being timeless entities in the sense of the traditional history of ideas, take on diverse meanings depending on the context in which they are employed and the purpose they serve, often as rhetorical weapons within power struggles. In Skinner's opinion, historical texts should be studied with a view to grasp not only their literal sense, but also their performative function within a given political context.[81]

According to Skinner this contextualist project possesses a profound civic relevance. It can unveil the contingency of beliefs, practices, and institutions in one's society, as well as the hidden logics of foreign value systems. By unveiling the relativity of societal phenomena in space and time, Skinner argues, contextualism can become a tool for developing a self-critical attitude and a greater tolerance for cultural diversity.[82] Skinner's counter-hegemonic intentions are beyond any doubt, yet one might wonder whether the contextualist approach necessarily operates in a counter-hegemonic and emancipatory way. As the discussion of Ward's work has shown, contextualizing histories may sometimes be read as endorsing, not criticizing, imperial projects. One might reply that Ward was 'not yet' a true contextualist, and that his highly ideologized work would not qualify as history proper under current standards. Yet this argument would be predicated on a twofold scientific illusion: that we can reconstruct some original intention and meaning in past events and documents, and that the more we take distance from historical objects the more we understand them. It is unlikely that this detachment can actually occur, and that it could ever allow a deeper insight into the context, since the scholar is already always in a relationship with contexts and objects in the world before setting

---

[81] Quentin Skinner, *Visions of Politics, Volume I: Regarding Method* (Cambridge University Press 2002) VII.
[82] Ibid, 125.

out to study them.[83] Skinner is, of course, entirely aware of these issues, and he acknowledges that '[n]o historian can hope to bracket his own beliefs' or recover any truthful original meaning of a text.[84]

Even if the historian could succeed in accurately reconstructing the meaning of a text, it might still be asked whether her restraining herself to contextual research were a desirable endeavour in ethical and political terms. As Anne Orford has recently noted, some historians' quest for historiographical purity might express a problematic refusal to engage with contemporary politics.[85] Orford, as well as Martti Koskenniemi, are putting forward a critical understanding of international legal history that draws attention to international law's complicity in colonialist and imperialist phenomena, thereby endeavouring to make contextual research fruitful without relapsing into political disengagement.[86]

Similarly dissatisfied with the alternative between a potentially nihilistic contextualism and naïve progressivism, international lawyers such as Fleur Johns, Richard Joyce, and Sundhya Pahuja have lately elaborated on contemporary philosophical debates on the concept of 'event' to advance an existentialist version of international legal history.[87] Existentialism in fact appears to combine the positive aspects of both contextualism and progressivism. Much like investigating 'contexts', exploring 'events' allows for a liberating understanding of past occurrences outside the box of historical and normative continuity; just as imagining progress, evoking historical events calls forth the possibility of freedom, propitious change, and development. These aspects clearly come to light in the recent formulations of evental philosophy by Alain Badiou, whose work has inspired Johns, Joyce, and Pahuja.[88] Badiou's theory indeed provides international lawyers with renewed hope in radical change and in the possibility, remote as it may be, to curb the power of empire and global capital. It is a theory that enables today's scholars to appreciate the persisting meaningfulness of human agency and political contestation in opposition to the prevailing dogma that under conditions of complexity it is no longer possible to steer the evolution of law or other social systems.[89]

Yet Badiou's theory is affected by various limits, most patently its tendency to equate Badiou's own political belief, Maoist socialism, with universal truth.[90]

---

[83] Martin Heidegger, *Being and Time* (John Macquarrie and Edward Robinson trs, Blackwell 1978); Hans-Georg Gadamer, *Truth and Method* (William Glen-Doepel tr, Sheed and Ward 1979) 340.

[84] Skinner, *Visions of Politics, Volume 1* (n 81) 27.

[85] Anne Orford, 'On International Legal Method' (2013) 1 London Review of International Law 166, 174.

[86] Martti Koskenniemi, 'Vitoria and Us: Thoughts on Critical Histories of International Law' (2014) 22 Rechtsgeschichte—Legal History 119.

[87] Fleur Johns, Richard Joyce, and Sundhya Pahuja (eds), *Events: The Force of International Law* (Routledge 2011).

[88] See especially Alain Badiou, *Being and Event* (first published 1988, Oliver Feltham tr, Continuum 2005); Alain Badiou, *Ethics: An Essay on the Understanding of Evil* (first published 1993, Peter Hallward tr, Verso 2001); Alain Badiou, *Logics of Worlds* (first published 2006, Alberto Toscano tr, Continuum 2008).

[89] Niklas Luhmann, *Law as a Social System* (Klaus Ziegert tr, Oxford University Press 2004).

[90] Ernesto Laclau, 'An Ethics of Militant Engagement' in Peter Hallward (ed), *Think Again: Alain Badiou and the Future of Philosophy* (Continuum 2004), 127; Guilherme Vasconcelos Vilaça, 'Badiou's Ethics: A Return to Ideal Theory' (2014) 3 Badiou Studies 271, 273.

Despite Badiou's own admonition that a well-understood version of Maoism would not allow for despicable drifts towards brutality as occurred in the case of *Sendero luminoso* in Peru, the reader inevitably has the feeling that his philosophy has no internal critical resources for preventing such drifts. Badiou's existentialism, like any existentialism, inevitably carries in itself a normative void that can be exploited for purposes that are not always emancipatory and transformative.[91] Tellingly, twentieth-century existentialist philosophy has been first spearheaded by such controversial figures as Martin Heidegger and Carl Schmitt, both of whom came to be supporters of the Nazi regime in the early 1930s. While both authors developed their existentialist approach before the Nazis came to power, their philosophies of 'event' and 'exception'[92] could be, and for a while were, read as legitimizing Nazi policies, and neither author took the trouble of denying this possible interpretation in any straightforward way.[93] Regardless of the vexed question of whether Heidegger and Schmitt ever truly believed in the Nazi project or merely supported it strategically and opportunistically, their existential visions of philosophy and politics were fully compatible with totalitarianism and lacked a critical standpoint from which to question the authoritarian use of political violence. And this is not only a problem affecting right-wing ideology. In the post-war period, another existentialist scholar on the opposite end of the political spectrum, Jean-Paul Sartre, came to advocate violence as a means of advancing a political cause.[94]

As ideological struggles have become a distant memory, today's scholars might not see any complication in promoting the philosophy of the event, but it should be kept in mind that this philosophy has not always been as emancipatory as it seems. This results from the very concept of the event as expounded by existentialists. Because they assume that the event is unforeseeable, inexplicable, and undefinable—therein lying its revolutionary power—any historical occurrence, including the most atrocious acts of violence, can be pointed to as 'evental'. The question then would be, as so often is in politics, who decides what the event is and when it occurs? To answer this question the existentialist has to go back to individual political beliefs based on which they recognize some occurrences as genuine historical events and deny others as mere accidents or, worse yet, as acts worthy of repression. This interpretative arbitrariness is visible, for instance, in Badiou's mythologies of the French Revolution and the Paris Commune as well as in Schmitt's existentialist account of

---

[91] The ambivalence of this 'evental' reading of history has been noted by Martti Koskenniemi in his foreword to Johns, Joyce, and Pahuja (eds), *Events* (n 87) XVIII–XX, XX.

[92] Carl Schmitt, *Political Theology: Four Chapters on the Concept of Sovereignty* (George Schwab tr, University of Chicago Press 2005); Martin Heidegger, *Beiträge zur Philosophie (Vom Ereignis)* (Vittorio Klostermann 1989).

[93] Heidegger somehow accounted for his political position under the Nazi dictatorship in 'Aufklärung meines Falles' (*Der Spiegel*, no 23, 1976) 193–219. On the Schmittian case, see Reinhard Mehring, *Carl Schmitt: Aufstieg und Fall. Eine Biografie* (CH Beck 2009). On Schmitt's ideological ambivalence and opportunism, see Michele Nicoletti, *Trascendenza e potere: la teologia politica di Carl Schmitt* (Morcelliana 1990); Michael Stolleis, *Geschichte des öffentlichen Rechts in Deutschland: Weimarer Republik und Nationalsozialismus* (Beck 2002).

[94] Jean-Paul Sartre, 'Préface' in Frantz Fanon, *Les damnés de la terre* (La Découverte 2002) 36.

the history of international law in the *Nomos der Erde*. In the latter work Schmitt idealized the historical meaningfulness of a few order-creating episodes, especially those contributing to the *jus publicum Europaeum* such as the Treaty of Tordesillas and the Congress of Vienna, and he lashed out against other political events for which he felt no ideological sympathy, notably the rise of superpower dualism after World War Two.[95]

It is precisely the political character of historical narrative that largely explains the blurriness of the borders between historiographical methodologies, such as contextualism, existentialism, and the teleological philosophy of history. Schmitt's *Nomos der Erde* certainly appears as a contextualist book, at least according to the standards of the time. It depicted international legal history as a succession of fragmented and separate ages characterized by autonomous and context-dependent legal structures, not, as had been common in previous literature,[96] as a cumulative and progressive evolution of principles and institutions.[97] In this sense, the *Nomos* developed contextualist intuitions already contained in Schmitt's work since *Political Theology*, and also resonated with recent contextualist writings by legal historians, notably Otto Brunner, who in his celebrated *Land und Herrschaft* (inspired by readings of Schmitt) attacked scholars' tendency anachronistically to apply the concepts of modern political and legal theory to earlier epochs.[98] Yet Schmitt's account was not purely contextualist. His *Nomos* featured one major metanarrative and overarching constant, the idea that all law stems from an original act of land occupation and distribution. This assumption in turn gave an existential flavour to Schmitt's story. Constructed around exceptional acts of violence and spatial revolution, his history no longer appeared as a mere assortment of autonomous eons but as the showcase for the representation of events that would testify to the existential meaningfulness of political and legal 'order'.

Hybridity and Politics

There is nothing inherently imperial or counter-imperial in contextualism, progressivism, cyclical history, or the theology of history. Any of these approaches can be used for disparate and sometimes contradictory ends. The choice of one or the other depends on the social and intellectual milieu in which the author is situated. In times in which empire legitimizes itself through the theology of history,

---

[95] On Schmitt's existentialist view of international law see Walter Rech, 'Eschatology and Existentialism: Carl Schmitt's Historical Understanding of International Law and Politics' in Matilda Arvidsson, Leila Brännström, and Panu Minkkinen (eds), *The Contemporary Relevance of Carl Schmitt: Law, Politics, Theology* (Routledge 2015) 147–64.

[96] Martti Koskenniemi, 'Histories of International Law: Dealing with Eurocentrism' (2011) 19 Rechtsgeschichte—Legal History 152, 155–56.

[97] Schmitt's approach would be followed and expanded by Wilhelm Grewe in *The Epochs of International Law* (1984) (revised by Michael Byers, De Gruyter 2000).

[98] Otto Brunner, *Land und Herrschaft. Grundfragen der territorialen Verfassungsgeschichte Südostdeutschlands im Mittelalter* (2nd edn, Rudolf M Rohrer Verlag 1942) XV.

outsiders will seek to replace 'providence' with 'Reason' and 'progress' for emancipatory purposes; but when progressivism itself becomes a mainstream ideological tool, theology might reacquire a revolutionary potential.[99] The same would apply to contextualism, which equally contains imperial and anti-imperial tendencies at the same time.

Eventually, any historical methodology looks hybrid despite programmatic statements to the contrary. While each historical approach has its own, unmistakable leitmotif, historians tend to integrate it with themes from competing streams.[100] This can be viewed as a rhetorical strategy as well as a naked constraint of history writing, which requires the historian to use a plurality of methods simultaneously. Every providential or progressive history *qua* history must describe past contexts, and thereby merge with contextualism, though it is supposed to move on to 'explain' the context by recourse to metanarratives. Contextualism is equally impure from a methodological perspective. Among right-wing scholars, it is accompanied by apologies of 'order' and nostalgic references to past golden ages, as in Schmitt's *jus publicum Europaeum*, whereas in left-wing scholarship it is often blended with notions of emancipation and transformation ultimately resting on a philosophy of history for which the historian cannot provide any further justification.

Given this persistent ambivalence some may fear that discussing historiographical methodologies might lead us once more into a speculative world in which every single text and utterance can be reread and reassessed, and differences are meticulously detected just to be dismantled, a pantheistic yet nominalistic world in which everything looks the same although, or precisely because, everything is unique. Yet in many regards methodological differences 'exist'—as shaped and reinforced by authors and audiences—and are politically relevant. This chapter has shown, for instance, that approaches such as providentialism and progressivism have proved extremely powerful rhetorical tools for legitimizing empire, whereas other strands, such as cyclical history, entailed a fatalist worldview that appealed much less to those interested in justifying an offensive and muscular imperialism. From this angle, the relentless replacement and repetition of historiographical forms in Western history, from Plato through to Las Casas, Ward, and Lawrence, can be regarded as expressing the persistent centrality of political fights and the possibility, and perhaps necessity, for international lawyers to make commitments within these contests. What counts as meaningful behind the despairing open-endedness and reiteration of methodological disputes may be the ethical and political struggles of which they represent a sublimated form.

---

[99] David Kennedy has similarly expounded a cyclical understanding of the doctrinal history of international law in 'When Renewal Repeats: Thinking Against the Box' (1999–2000) 32 New York Journal of International Law and Politics 335.

[100] With reference to international law, this eclectic mechanism has been described by Martti Koskenniemi in *From Apology to Utopia: The Structure of International Legal Argument* (Reissue with a new epilogue, Cambridge University Press 2005).

Bibliography

Anghie, Antony, *Imperialism, Sovereignty, and the Making of International Law* (Cambridge University Press 2007)

Aristotle, *Politics* (Ernest Barker tr, Oxford University Press 1998)

Augustine, *The City of God Against the Pagans*, vol IV (Philip Levine tr, Harvard University Press 1966)

Augustine of Hippo, 'Expositions of the Psalms' in *The Works of Saint Augustine*, vol III/7 (Maria Boulding tr, New City Press 2001)

Badiou, Alain, *Ethics: An Essay on the Understanding of Evil* (Peter Hallward tr, Verso 2001)

Badiou, Alain, *Being and Event* (Oliver Feltham tr, Continuum 2005)

Badiou, Alain, *Logics of Worlds* (Alberto Toscano tr, Continuum 2008)

Bowler, Peter J, *Evolution: The History of an Idea* (University of California Press 1984)

Bratspies, Rebecca M and Miller, Russell A, 'Progress in International Law—An Explanation of the Project' in Rebecca M Bratspies and Russell A Miller (eds), *Progress in International Law* (Nijhoff 2008)

Brettler, Marc Zvi, *The Creation of History in Ancient Israel* (Routledge 1998)

Brunner, Otto, *Land und Herrschaft. Grundfragen der territorialen Verfassungsgeschichte Südostdeutschlands im Mittelalter* (2nd edn, Rudolf M Rohrer Verlag 1942)

BS Chimni, *International Law and World Order: A Critique of Contemporary Approaches* (Sage Publications 1993)

Burke, Edmund, *Reflections on the Revolution in France* (JGA Pocock ed, Hackett 1987)

Burton, David, 'Theodore Roosevelt's Darwinism and Views on Imperialism' (1965) 26 Journal of the History of Ideas 103

Carr, EH, *The Twenty Years' Crisis 1919–1939: An Introduction to the Study of International Relations* (MacMillan 1983)

Darwin, Charles, *The Origin of Species* (first published 1859, Wordsworth 1998)

Ferry, Luc, *L'innovation destructrice* (Plon 2014)

Franklin, Julian H, *Jean Bodin and the Sixteenth-Century Revolution in the Methodology of Law and History* (Columbia University Press 1963)

Gadamer, Hans-Georg, *Truth and Method* (William Glen-Doepel tr, Sheed and Ward 1979)

Gliozzi, Giuliano, *Adamo e il nuovo mondo. La nascita dell'antropologia come ideologia coloniale: dalle genealogie bibliche alle teorie razziali (1500–1700)* (Franco Angeli 1977)

Grewe, Wilhelm G, *The Epochs of International Law* (1984) (revised by Michael Byers, De Gruyter 2000)

Grotius, Hugo, *De iure belli ac pacis (The Rights of War and Peace)* II (first published 1625, Richard Tuck ed, Liberty Fund 2005)

Hegel, Georg Wilhelm Friedrich, *Phenomenology of Spirit* (AV Miller tr, Oxford University Press 1977)

Hegel, Georg Wilhelm Friedrich, *Elements of the Philosophy of Right* (HB Nisbet tr, Cambridge University Press 1991)

Heidegger, Martin, 'Aufklärung meines Falles' (*Der Spiegel*, no 23, 1976) 193–219

Heidegger, Martin, *Being and Time* (John Macquarrie and Edward Robinson trs, Blackwell 1978)

Heidegger, Martin, *Beiträge zur Philosophie (Vom Ereignis)* (Vittorio Klostermann 1989)

Johns, Fleur, Joyce, Richard, and Pahuja, Sundhya (eds), *Events: The Force of International Law* (Routledge 2011)

Kelley, Donald R, *Foundations of Modern Historical Scholarship: Language, Law and History in the French Renaissance* (Columbia University Press 1970)

Kennedy, David, 'When Renewal Repeats: Thinking Against the Box' (1999–2000) 32 New York Journal of International Law and Politics 335

Kissinger, Henry, *Diplomacy* (Simon & Schuster 1994)

Kojève, Alexandre, *Introduction à la lecture de Hegel* (Gallimard 1968)

Koskenniemi, Martti, *The Gentle Civilizer of Nations: The Rise and Fall of International Law 1870–1960* (Cambridge University Press 2001)

Koskenniemi, Martti, *From Apology to Utopia: The Structure of International Legal Argument* (Reissue with a new epilogue, Cambridge University Press 2005)

Koskenniemi, Martti, 'Foreword' in Fleur Johns, Richard Joyce, and Sundhya Pahuja (eds), *Events: The Force of International Law* (Routledge 2011)

Koskenniemi, Martti, 'Histories of International Law: Dealing with Eurocentrism' (2011) 19 Rechtsgeschichte—Legal History 152

Koskenniemi, Martti, 'Law, Teleology and International Relations: An Essay in Counterdisciplinarity' (2012) 26 International Relations 3

Koskenniemi, Martti, 'Histories of International Law: Significance and Problems for a Critical View' (2013) 27 Temple International & Comparative Law Journal 215

Koskenniemi, Martti, 'Vitoria and Us: Thoughts on Critical Histories of International Law' (2014) 22 Rechtsgeschichte—Legal History 119

Laclau, Ernesto, 'An Ethics of Militant Engagement' in Peter Hallward (ed), *Think Again: Alain Badiou and the Future of Philosophy* (Continuum 2004)

Las Casas, Bartolomé de, *In Defense of the Indians* (Stafford Poole tr, Northern Illinois University Press 1992) 28.

Lawrence, Thomas Joseph, *Essays on Some Disputed Questions in Modern International Law* (2nd edn revised and enlarged, Deighton, Bell and Co 1885)

Luhmann, Niklas, *Law as a Social System* (Klaus Ziegert tr, Oxford University Press 2004)

Machiavelli, Niccolò, *The Prince* (Peter Bondanella tr, Oxford University Press 2005)

Marincola, John, *Greek Historians* (Oxford University Press 2001)

Martin, Sarah, 'China, Australia seal landmark free trade agreement' (*The Australian*, 17 November 2014) <http://www.theaustralian.com.au/business/in-depth/china-australia-seal-landmark-free-trade-agreement/story-fnpebfcn-1227126102864> accessed on 19 November 2014

Mehring, Reinhard, *Carl Schmitt: Aufstieg und Fall: Eine Biografie* (CH Beck 2009)

Momigliano, Arnaldo, 'Time in Ancient Historiography' in Arnaldo Momigliano, *Essays in Ancient and Modern Historiography* (Blackwell 1977)

Morgenthau, Hans, *Politics among Nations: The Struggle for Power and Peace* (McGraw-Hill Higher Education 2006)

Nicoletti, Michele, *Trascendenza e potere: la teologia politica di Carl Schmitt* (Morcelliana 1990)

Nicoletti, Michele, *La politica e il male* (Morcelliana 2000)

Oort, Johannes van, 'The End is Now: Augustine on History and Eschatology' (2012) 68(1) HTS Teologiese Studies/Theological Studies 4

Orford, Anne, 'On International Legal Method' (2013) 1 London Review of International Law 166

Pagden, Anthony, *The Fall of Natural Man: The American Indian and the Origins of Comparative Ethnology* (Cambridge University Press 1982)

Pagden, Anthony, *The Burdens of Empire: 1539 to the Present* (Cambridge University Press 2015)

Plato, *Laws* (RG Bury tr, Harvard University Press 1926)

Plato, *Republic*, vol 1 (Chris Emlyn-Jones and William Preddy tr, Harvard University Press 2013)

Polybius, *The Histories* (WR Paton tr, revised by FW Walbank, Christian Habicht, Harvard University Press 2011)

Rech, Walter, *Enemies of Mankind: Vattel's Theory of Collective Security* (Nijhoff 2013)

Rech, Walter, 'Eschatology and Existentialism: Carl Schmitt's Historical Understanding of International Law and Politics' in Matilda Arvidsson, Leila Brännström, and Panu Minkkinen (eds), *The Contemporary Relevance of Carl Schmitt: Law, Politics, Theology* (Routledge 2015)

Sartre, Jean-Paul, 'Préface' in Frantz Fanon, *Les damnés de la terre* (La Découverte 2002)

Schmitt, Carl, *Political Theology: Four Chapters on the Concept of Sovereignty* (George Schwab tr, University of Chicago Press 2005)

Schmitt, Carl, *The Concept of the Political: Expanded Edition* (George Schwab tr, The University of Chicago Press 2007)

Sepúlveda, Juan Ginés de, *Democrates secundus, sive de iustis belli causis apud Indios* (1544) translated into Spanish in Marcelino Menéndez y Pelayo and Manuel García-Pelayo (eds), *Tratado sobre las justas causas de la guerra contra los indios* (Fondo de Cultura Económica 1986)

Skinner, Quentin, *Visions of Politics, Volume I: Regarding Method* (Cambridge University Press 2002)

Skouteris, Thomas, *The Notion of Progress in International Law Discourse* (TMC Asser Press 2010)

Stolleis, Michael, *Geschichte des öffentlichen Rechts in Deutschland: Weimarer Republik und Nationalsozialismus* (Beck 2002)

Towse, Clive, 'Ward, Robert Plumer (1765–1846)' in *Oxford Dictionary of National Biography* (Oxford University Press 2004) <http://www.oxforddnb.com/view/article/ 28703> accessed on 17 November 2014

Vilaça, Guilherme Vasconcelos, 'Badiou's Ethics: A Return to Ideal Theory' (2014) 3 Badiou Studies 271

Viroli, Maurizio, *Niccolò's Smile: A Biography of Machiavelli* (Antony Shugaar tr, Farrar, Straus and Giroux 2000)

Vitoria, Francisco de, 'On the American Indians' in Francisco de Vitoria, *Political Writings* (Anthony Pagden and Jeremy Lawrance eds, Cambridge University Press 1991)

Ward, Robert Plumer, *An Enquiry into the Foundation and History of the Law of Nations, from the Time of the Greeks and Romans to the Age of Grotius*, 2 vols (Strahan and Woodfall 1795)

Wheaton, Henry, *History of the Law of Nations in Europe and America from the Earliest Times to the Treaty of Washington* (Gould, Banks & Co 1845)

White, Hayden, 'Historicism, History, and the Figurative Imagination' (1975) 14 (4) History and Theory 48

PART II

LEGAL DISCOURSES OF EMPIRE

4

The Concepts of Universal Monarchy and Balance of Power in the First Half of the Seventeenth Century—A Case Study

Peter Schröder

The struggle for political hegemony in early modern Europe was not solely pursued by military means. The many layered antagonistic claims—often motivated by religious and political ambitions, within Europe and beyond its borders—led to a variety of theories which aimed to foster claims for political influence and hegemony. Universal monarchy and balance of power are the two main concepts which can be discerned as the principal strategies employed in the strife, if not for Empire, at least for hegemony. The study of religion and Empire is closely related to the claims to universal monarchy, as it was this concept which not only claimed legitimate dominion over the world, but in doing so, commanding the role of purveyor of order and peace. Catholicism was used to reinforce the claim to empire. However, during the process of state building in the late sixteenth and seventeenth centuries, universal monarchy was increasingly challenged and eventually superseded by the alternative idea of a balance of power, as a means of organizing the emerging European state system.[1] Indeed, among most political thinkers of the seventeenth century the idea of universal monarchy had lost its constructive political value and was mostly used polemically.[2] Theories which attempted to found

---

[1] Hume famously argued that the ancient Greeks had organized their interstate relations by using a balance of power by all but its name: David Hume, 'Of the Balance of Power' in David Hume, *Political Essays* (Knud Haakonssen ed, Cambridge University Press 1994). See also John Robertson, 'Universal Monarchy and the Liberties of Europe: David Hume's Critique of an English Whig Doctrine' in Nicholas Phillipson and Quentin Skinner (eds), *Political Discourse in Early Modern Britain* (Cambridge University Press 1993).

[2] See Arno Strohmeyer, 'Ideas of Peace in Early Modern Models of International Order: Universal Monarchy and Balance of Power in Comparison' in Jost Dülffer and Robert Frank (eds), *Peace, War and Gender from Antiquity to the Present. Cross-cultural Perspectives* (Klartext Verlag 2009). The classical study on the concept of universal monarchy is still Franz Bosbach, *Monarchia Universalis: Ein politischer Leitbegriff der Frühen Neuzeit* (Vandenhoeck & Ruprecht 1988). In contrast to Strohmeyer's assertion Bosbach shows how the use of universal monarchy was still present up to the age of Louis XIV in political pamphlets. His study is, however, less concerned with the history of political thought: see ibid, 13.

International Law and Empire: Historical Explorations. First Edition. Martti Koskenniemi, Walter Rech, and Manuel Jiménez Fonseca. © Martti Koskenniemi, Walter Rech, and Manuel Jiménez Fonseca 2016. Published 2016 by Oxford University Press.

interstate relations and peace in Europe upon the concepts of universal monarchy or the universal supremacy of the Catholic Church played a minor part in international political thought. Instead the idea of a balance of power as the best means to organize the European state system gained traction among political thinkers in this period.[3]

The aim of this chapter is to contrast these two concepts by way of a brief case study, looking at *A Discourse Touching the Spanish Monarchy: Laying Down Directions and Practices Whereby the King of Spain May Attain to an Universal Monarchy* by Tommaso Campanella (1568–1639), first composed in Latin around 1600 and published in English in 1654. Campanella's proposal is one of the most accomplished and far-reaching accounts of universal monarchy in the early seventeenth century.[4] He draws as much on Botero's reason of state arguments as on Dante and the idea of a Catholic universal Church. I will contrast Campanella's proposal with the *Grand Design* by the Duke of Sully (1559–1641). What Sully puts forward in his *Memoirs*[5] is a plan for how best to conduct French foreign policies with the aim of forming an alliance against the Habsburgs.[6] Dynastic and confessional allegiances remained to play their part in the ensuing European state system, as can be seen in Sully's proposal. However, the Westphalian settlement of 1648 was multi-polar and power relations were increasingly complex. This was reflected in Samuel Pufendorf's work and a brief outlook at Pufendorf will highlight how political thought developed further in the attempt to understand and organize the increasingly complex European state system.

Universal Monarchy—Campanella's International Thought

The relationship between papacy and empire was the central subject of political debate in the later Middle Ages and Dante succinctly summarized the debate in

---

[3] See Bruno Arcidiacono, *Cinq Types de Paix: Une Histoire des Plans de Pacification perpétuelle* (Presses Universitaires de France 2011) 75–112, and the brief overview in Martin van Gelderen, 'Universal Monarchy, the Rights of War and Peace and the Balance of Power: Europe's Quest for Civil Order' in Hans-Åke Persson and Bo Stråth (eds), *Reflections on Europe: Defining a Political Order in Time and Space* (Peter Lang Publishing 2007).

[4] But see also Prudencio de Sandoval, *La vida y hechos del Emperador Carlos Quinto Max. Fortissimo. Rey de Espana, y de las Indias, Islas, y Tierrafirme del mar Oceano* (Valladolid 1604). For further references of Spanish writings vindicating Spanish claims to world hegemony see Xavier Gil, 'Spain and Portugal' in Howell A Lloyd, Glenn Burgess, and Simon Hodson (eds), *European Political Thought 1450–1700: Religion, Law and Philosophy* (Yale University Press 2007) 442.

[5] I will quote from *The Memoirs of the Duke of Sully during his Residence at the English Court; to which he was sent Ambassador from Henry IV of France, upon the Accession of King James the First. Containing An Account of his Negotiations ... Also A Relation of the Political Scheme, commonly called the Great Design of Henry IV ...* (Dublin 1751).

[6] See Etienne Thuau, *Raison d'Etat et pensée politique à l'époque de Richelieu* (Albin Michel 2000) 287: 'Henri IV semble avoir un instant envisagé de faire valoir ses droits sur le trône impérial [ie of the German Holy Roman Empire]. Ce projet, Sully en nie l'existence ... Or Sully avait été en 1600 partisan de la candidature royal. Mais l'opinion n'était pas favorable et il semble avoir voulu dans ces *Mémoires* effacer ce souvenir.' See also Gaston Zeller, 'Les rois de France candidats à l'Empire' (1934) 173 Revue historique 237–311, 457–534.

the three books of his *Monarchy*. Dante is a staunch advocate of universal monarchy, and argued that 'it was by right, and not by usurping, that the Roman people took on the office of the monarch (which is called empire) over all man'.[7] In the third book he discussed the well-trodden question of the relationship between the papacy and the emperor and firmly sided with the imperial camp: 'the ... imperial authority derives directly from ... God ... the authority of the church is not the cause of imperial authority'.[8] Campanella refers repeatedly to Dante and his views on imperial power. In contrast to Dante, Campanella suggested that the King of Spain ought to make use of the Catholic faith so that 'the Kingdom of Spain may be the more firmly incorporated into the Church, by having both Cardinals, and Popes themselves always true to their [Spain's] Faction'.[9] The Catholic Church is thus to be used in support of Spanish universal monarchy. Indeed, according to Campanella, 'it is not sufficient that we have the Clergy on our side; but we are further to labour that at length we may get a *Spaniard* to be elected *Pope*, or rather, one of the house of *Austria*'.[10]

Campanella's aspirations do not end there. Just as Alexander the Great or Julius Caesar had used legislation on religious matters for their own political ends, the Spanish King should also 'make a Law, to be observed by all Christians; ... that whensoever any People or Country shall forsake the *Roman* Religion, all Princes shall be bound, upon pain of forfeiting their Estates, to root out, and extirpate the same'.[11] Dynastic and religious politics should go hand-in-hand in order to achieve the ambitious objective of universal monarchy. All means necessary ought to be employed in this endeavour. Thus ultimately the Spanish King would also be in a position to defend and promote the Catholic faith. Campanella leaves no doubt that for him, Catholicism and universality are aspects of the same enterprise. Therefore, the Spanish Monarch must promote the Catholic faith within Europe against the heretical Protestants, at the frontiers of Europe against the infidel Turks[12] and beyond the frontiers of the known world towards the New

[7] Dante, *Monarchy* (P Shaw ed, Cambridge University Press 1996) 33.

[8] Dante, *Monarchy* (n 7) 86ff.

[9] Tommaso Campanella, *A Discourse Touching the Spanish Monarchy: Laying Down Directions and Practices Whereby the King of Spain May Attain to an Universal Monarchy* (London 1658) 42. On Campanella see also John M Headley, 'Tommaso Campanella and the End of the Renaissance' (1990) 20 The Journal of Medieval and Renaissance Studies 157; Anthony Pagden, *Spanish Imperialism and the Political Imagination* (Yale University Press 1990) 37–63; Beate Gabriele Lüsse, *Formen der humanistischen Utopie* (Schöningh 1998) 95–119.

[10] Campanella, *A Discourse* (n 9) 25. In his concept of universal monarchy Dante had separated imperial and Church authority as these were in his view the main reasons for the antagonistic factions within Italy at the time of his writing. In this respect Campanella pursued a different strategy and emphasized the importance of the Catholic Church for the Spanish project of universal monarchy. In any case it should be noted that 'the universal Empire had never been anything but a dream; the universal Church had to admit that the defense of the individual state took precedence over the liberties of the Church or the claims of the Christian commonwealth': Joseph R Strayer, *On the Medieval Origins of the Modern State* (Princeton University Press 1970) 57.

[11] Campanella, *A Discourse* (n 9) 46.

[12] Campanella, *A Discourse* (n 9) 22: 'He [the King of Spain] is the Chief *Defender of Christian Religion* ... calling together also the Christian Princes, to consult about the recovery of those Countreys they have lost, and are at this day in the hands of *Hereticks*, and *Turks*.'

World.[13] Catholicism simultaneously reinforces the Spanish claim to universal monarchy and, if the Spanish were to succeed in attaining this claim, it would profit. The Spanish King would not only rule over the world, but he would also be 'dignified with the Title of the Catholick or Universal King', which according to Campanella shows 'plainly, that this is the will of the Holy Spirit'.[14] Interestingly Campanella avoided discussion of the fact that the Spanish monarchy was a composite monarchy, thus suggesting uniformity where it could only be identified in the plurality of a composite structure.[15]

The rise of Spain also inherently explains her decline, as the wheel of fortune is unreliable and subject to constant change. 'There was an Occasion ... offered to *Charles* the V who ... might have been able to have made himself Lord of the whole Earth',[16] but he failed to seize the chance *fortuna* offered. This is a familiar argument in Machiavelli's *Principe*.[17] According to Campanella, this failure occurred, fundamentally, because the Spanish rulers neglected to take possession of their conquests in the way Machiavelli had called for in chapter three of his *Principe*.[18] The fundamental strategic mistake of the Spanish monarchy was her misguided policy and constant conflict in the Low Countries, which was the principal reason for the decline of Spain.[19]

---

[13] Campanella, *A Discourse* (n 9) 27: 'the *Indians* had violated the *Law of Nature*, the King of *Spain* invading them upon the Interest of the *Christian Religion*, (whose Handmaid the *Law of Nature* is) their Country is his lawful possession'.

[14] Campanella, *A Discourse* (n 9) 25. Despite Campanella's emphasis on strengthening the power of the Spanish king, his main concern might have been the Catholic Church and its spiritual world dominance. Since the Spanish Monarchy was the leading Catholic power of Campanella's time, he might have wanted to position the Spanish monarchy as the political and military instrument for the Catholic Church's dominance.

[15] See JH Elliott, *Imperial Spain 1469–1716* (Penguin Books 1976), 167ff; Henry Kamen, *Spain's Road to Empire: The Making of a World Power 1492–1763* (Penguin Books 2003), 153ff; Xavier Gil, 'The Good Law of a Vassal: Fidelity, Obedience and Obligation in Habsburg Spain' (2009) 5 Revista Internacional de los Estudios Vascos 92; and more generally JH Elliott, 'A Europe of Composite Monarchies' in JH Elliott, *Spain, Europe & the Wider World 1500–1800* (Yale University Press 2009) 3–24.

[16] See Campanella, *A Discourse* (n 9) 81ff.

[17] Niccolò Machiavelli, *The Prince* (Quentin Skinner and Russell Price eds, Cambridge 2008) 85: 'fortune is the arbiter of half of our actions'. And a little further, towards the end of this chapter Machiavelli states (87): 'I conclude ... that since circumstances vary and men when acting lack flexibility, they are successful if their methods match the circumstances and unsuccessful if they do not.' See also Peter Schröder, *Niccolò Machiavelli* (Campus Einführungen 2004) 107–20. Despite the fact that Campanella mentioned Machiavelli only once and in the most negative terms, it is clear that he was influenced by Machiavelli. There can be no doubt that even whole chapters in his writing on universal monarchy are inspired by Machiavelli. See notably Campanella, *A Discourse* (n 9), ch XVII 'Of the Peoples Love and Hate', as well as his discussion on fortune and prudence in chs VI and VII.

[18] Machiavelli, *The Prince* (n 17) 8: 'considerable problems arise if territories are annexed in a country that differs in language, customs and institutions, and great luck [bisogna avere gran fortuna] and great ability are needed to hold them'. Machiavelli is, obviously, not criticizing Charles V here, but he singles out the French king Louis XII as a negative example of a ruler who did not understand how to hold his conquests. See Peter Schröder, 'Die Kunst der Staatserhaltung' in Otfried Höffe (ed), *Machiavelli: Der Fürst* (De Gruyter 2012). But see also Anthony Pagden, who argued that 'the *De Monarchia hispanica* was clearly not ... a "Machiavellian" strategy for extending the power of the papacy and the Spanish Monarchy': Pagden, *Spanish Imperialism and the Political Imagination* (n 9) 62.

[19] This is repeatedly claimed by Campanella. See Campanella, *A Discourse* (n 9) 174, 186.

Although Charles V and Philip II failed to achieve universal monarchy, the Spanish dominions certainly provided formidable foundations for universal monarchy. This was the gist of Campanella's writing, in his claim that 'the Universal Monarchy of the world ... is at length come down to the Spaniard'.[20] Given this brief sketch of Campanella's vision for Spanish monarchy, his model could hardly claim to be an acceptable attempt to pacify warring Europe.[21] Universal monarchy had to be achieved against the resistance and claims of other powers both within and outside of Europe. The time had clearly passed for the assertion that peace could be achieved through universal monarchy.[22] Already by the beginning of the seventeenth century, with the remarkable exception of Campanella, the concept of universal monarchy had lost any positive connotations for leading political thinkers, especially with regards to its ability to provide a stable, peaceful political order.[23]

Balance of Power—Sully's Challenge of Spanish Universal Monarchy

Let us turn to Sully and the *Grand Design* in order to compare his argument with that of Campanella. The *Grand Design* is known as the plan of the French King Henry IV, though it is only through the writings of the Duke of Sully that we know about this scheme.[24] The driving force behind it, as Sully stated himself, was:

the Hatred against *Spain* ... which is the great and common Motive by which these Powers [i.e. the monarchies of France, England, Denmark, and Sweden] are animated ... it only remains to examine, by what Means the House of *Austria* [i.e. Habsburg] may be reduced to the sole Monarchy of *Spain*; and the Monarchy of *Spain* to Spain only. These Means consist either in Address or Force.[25]

From the textual evidence of the *Memoirs* the key motive for Sully's plan was to secure French power, which in turn would bring about security and peace in Europe. Therefore, the interpretation that he tried to create some kind of European federation, inspired by a 'European conscience',[26] needs to be questioned. These

---

[20] Campanella, *A Discourse* (n 9) preface.

[21] See also Arcidiacono, *Cinq Types de Paix* (n 3) 30ff.

[22] To the best of my knowledge, a study is still lacking which situates and analyses Campanella's ideas about universal monarchy in the context of the seventeenth century or indeed the ensuing debates during the Thirty Years War. See, however, the brief account in Bruno Arcidiacono, '*Contra Pluralitatem Principatuum*: Trois Critiques du Système dit Westphalien (formulées avant la Paix de Westphalie)' in Pierre-Marie Dupuy and Vincent Chetail (eds), *The Roots of International Law/Les fondements droit international: Liber Amicorum Peter Haggenmacher* (Brill 2014), 470–73.

[23] Bosbach, *Monarchia Universalis* (n 2) 87.

[24] Moriz Ritter, 'Die Memoiren Sullys und der grosse Plan Heinrichs IV' (1870) 11 Abhandlungen der Historischen Klasse der Königlichen Bayrischen Akademie der Wissenschaften 1; Anja Victorine Hartmann, *Rêveurs de Paix? Friedenspläne bei Crucé, Richelieu und Sully* (Hamburg 1995).

[25] Sully, *Memoirs* (n 5) 182.

[26] Klaus Malettke, 'Europabewußtsein und Europäische Friedenspläne im 17 und 18 Jahrhundert' (1994) 21 Francia 92.

plans for a powerful alliance, which would allow the French to match the superior military might of the Spanish monarchy, depended, according to Sully, largely on the English Crown.

Campanella on the other hand believed that the largest threat to the Spanish claim to universal monarchy would come from France and Henry IV. For Campanella there could be no doubt 'that there is no Christian Kingdome, that is more able to oppose, and put a stop to the growing of the *Spanish Monarchy*, then *France*'.[27] It was for this reason that Campanella argued that an alliance between the French and the English needed to be avoided at all costs. Indeed, using Henry IV's conversion to Catholicism,[28] Campanella is able to use religious politics to further his goals of Spanish dominance, suggesting that the Pope should be persuaded to 'interdict the King of *France* the contracting of any League, or Friendship, either with the Queen of England, or with any other Hereticks'.[29] Sully's plans for a French alliance with England were thus, unsurprisingly, perceived by the Habsburg camp as the most dangerous threat to their political ambitions and claims.

It is in this context that James I's succession to the English throne was of the utmost importance, as:

the Death of Elizabeth … gave so violent a Shock to Henry's grand Design, as had like to have made him abandon all Hopes of its Success. He nevertheless attempted to rem-edy the fatal Effects apprehended from it, by endeavouring to inspire her successor, King James, with all her Sentiments in regard to it. And for this Purpose he resolved to send me Ambassador to the English Court.[30]

Sully relates in great detail the precautions taken in deciding how to proceed so as not to raise the suspicions of the newly crowned English King. He stresses that 'the principal Object of these Instructions [given to Sully by Henry IV for his ambassa-dorship to England] had always been a close Alliance between France and England, against Spain'.[31] Again, the contrast with Campanella is illuminating here. The lat-ter was writing at a time when Elizabeth was still alive and the succession of James to the English throne was still only an event to be anticipated upon the Queen's death. Campanella argues that the Spanish should endeavour to sow discord between the English and Scots, as well as among the English nobility and between the Parliament

---

[27] Campanella, *A Discourse* (n 9) 144. On the conflict between France and Spain see also Randall Lesaffer, 'Between Faith and Empire: The Justification of the Spanish Intervention in the French Wars of Religion in the 1590s', Chapter 5 in this volume.

[28] Campanella urges the Spanish king to 'perswade the Pope, that the King of France hath a purpose of Assisting the Hereticks': Campanella, *A Discourse* (n 9) 151.

[29] Ibid.

[30] Sully, *Memoirs* (n 5) 74. See notably GE Aylmer, *The Struggle for the Constitution 1603–1689* (Blandford Press 1963) 11: 'The most important fact about the succession of King James I on the death of Queen Elizabeth in the spring of 1603 is that it was peaceful.'

[31] Sully, *Memoirs* (n 5) 87. On Henry IV see notably Saint-René Taillandier, *Henri IV avant la messe* (Grasset 1934) and Saint-René Taillandier, *Le cœur du roi: Henri IV après la messe* (Grasset 1934). A new comparative study on Henry IV and Elizabeth is still a desideratum—E Paranque is preparing a PhD thesis on *The Rhetoric of Monarchy: A Comparison of France and England (1567–1603)*. But see also JB Black, *Elizabeth and Henry IV* (University of Michigan Library 1914).

and the Court. He claims that 'the time now draweth on, that after the death of the said Queen *Elizabeth*, who is now very old, the Kingdom of *England* must fall into the hand of their Ancient and continual Rivals, the Scots'.[32] The Spanish monarch should promise the different interested parties in England:

(no one of them knowing anything what is said to the other) all the possible aids that can be from Spain, for the restoring of them to their Inheritances, Legally descending down to them from their Ancestours; and undertake to effect this for them, if not as to the whole Kingdome, yet at least to some part of it.[33]

Campanella stresses over and over again, that the aim ought to be 'that the seeds of a continual War betwixt England and Scotland will be sown; in so much that neither Kingdome shall have any leisure to work any disturbance to the *Spanish* Affaires'.[34] In order to achieve Spanish aims, Campanella suggests thwarting French and English plans against Spain. He urges the Spanish king to:

send privately to King *James* of *Scotland*, and promise him, that He [the Spanish king] will assist him to the utmost of his Power in his getting possession of the Kingdome of England, upon this condition; viz, that he shall either restore there again the Catholick Religion;[35] ... or at least, that he shall not annoy, or in anyway disturbe the said Spanish Fleet.[36]

The competitive courting of the English as part of the struggle for hegemony between the French and Habsburgs can be seen in Campanella, advocating the Spanish interest, as much as in Sully, advocating the French interest. False promises played as large a role in these endeavours as straightforward bribery did.

Sully's frustration with France's inability to make headway in forming an alliance with the English against the Habsburgs under the reign of King James repeatedly comes to the fore in his *Memoirs*. Sully relates, for instance, how he had to find his way through the labyrinth of competing interests pursued by the various factions at the English court, which 'was full of Suspicion, Mistrust, Jealousy, secret and even public Discontent'.[37] He does not shy away from employing contemporary French prejudices against the English:

It is certain the *English* hate us; and this Hatred is so general and inveterate, that one would almost be tempted to number it among their natural Dispositions. It is undoubtedly an Effect of their Arrogance and Pride; for no Nation in Europe is more haughty and disdainful, nor more conceited in an Opinion of its superior Excellence.[38]

According to Sully, in light of such English stubbornness, it is in the French interest to achieve a position of independent power and thus avoid the necessity of relying on an ally who 'if we examine what they call Maxims of State, we shall discover in them only the Laws of Pride itself, adopted by Arrogance and Indolence'.[39] To be absolutely clear, what he advocates in his *Memoirs* most prominently is not a

---

[32] Campanella, *A Discourse* (n 9) 158.   [33] Ibid, 159.   [34] Ibid, 160.
[35] On the religious conflicts in England see Aylmer, *The Struggle for the Constitution* (n 30) 40–48.
[36] Campanella, *A Discourse* (n 9) 159.   [37] Sully, *Memoirs* (n 5) 110.
[38] Ibid, 107.   [39] Ibid, 108.

proposal for some kind of a European federation, but a policy which is informed by France's self-interest.[40] When his ideas are contrasted with those of Campanella, this becomes even more evident.

The *Grand Design* was part of the diplomatic and political struggle for influence and power. England seemed to be in an advantageous position, because she had not yet committed herself formally to an alliance in the struggle between the Habsburg branches of Austria and Spain on the one hand and France, some German estates (such as the Prince Elector of the Palatinate), and the Low Countries on the other. As dynastic alliances still formed an essential part of European interstate policy, Sully considers the various marriage projects.[41] He also makes clear how Barnevelt, one of the leaders of the Dutch revolt against the Spanish,[42] tried to push him and Henry IV into a formal alliance.

The Spanish were also lobbying strongly for the English to either join an alliance with them or, at the very least, grant assurances of their neutrality, as well as the Northern powers and several German princes were also seeking English assistance. Sully summarized this situation in unambiguous terms: 'Upon the whole; it appeared as though all the Princes of *Europe* considered the gaining of *England* in their Interest, as of the utmost Consequence.'[43] This suggests that Sully's concerns, as expressed in his writing, were influenced by contemporary diplomatic and political manoeuvring and various endeavours to form alliances in interstate politics. The broad underlying principle of the *Grand Design* was the assumption that 'peace is the great and common Interest in *Europe*. Its petty Princes ought to be continually employed in preserving it between the greater Powers … and the greater Powers should force the lesser into it, if necessary, by assisting the weak and oppressed.'[44] The implication of such a claim was that the Habsburgs threatened peace in Europe and were oppressing the smaller states. In order to counter this aggressive Habsburg attitude and their alleged claim to universal monarchy, a balance of power had to be established in Europe, which would guarantee the peace and security of all European states.

Sully's employment of the idea of an equilibrium or balance of power is original in many ways—though he could have found this idea in Mornay's *Discours au Roy Henry III sur les moyens de diminuer l'Espagnol*.[45] As far as I can see Sully's

---

[40] See also Henri Carré, *Sully. Sa vie et son oeuvre 1559–1641* (Payot 1932).

[41] Cf Sully, *Memoirs* (n 5) 121. Campanella also stresses the importance of dynastic politics. Campanella, *A Discourse* (n 9) 139. For the importance of marriage and dynastic politics in interstate relations see Richard Bonney, *The European Dynastic States 1494–1660* (Oxford University Press 1991) 79–301; William Doyle, *The Old European Order 1660–1800* (Oxford University Press 1992) 73–80; Hermann Weber, 'Die Bedeutung der Dynastien für die europäische Geschichte in der frühen Neuzeit' (1981) 44 Zeitschrift für bayerische Landesgeschichte 5; Johannes Kunisch and Helmut Neuhaus (eds), *Der dynastische Fürstenstaat. Zur Bedeutung der Sukzessionsordnungen für die Entstehung des frühmodernen Staates* (Duncker & Humblot 1982).

[42] See John Lothrop Motley, *The Life and Death of John of Barneveld, Advocate of Holland: with a View of the primary Causes and Movements of the Thirty Years War* (Harper & Brothers 1874).

[43] Sully, *Memoirs* (n 5) 116.   [44] Ibid, 109ff.

[45] A systematic comparison between Mornay and Sully is still lacking. According to Philippe de Mornay, 'Discours au Roy Henry III sur les moyens de diminuer l'Espagnol' in *Memoires de Messire Philippes de Mornay* (Paris 1624), the question of whether there is peace or war among

contribution to the development of the idea of a balance of power in Europe has not been noted by those who studied its history.[46] He uses the balance of power as a decisive tool to achieve a new, peaceful European order, which at the same time would strengthen the French position: 'The Steps taken by the House of *Austria* to arrive at Universal Monarchy, which evidently appears from the whole Conduct of *Charles Quint* and his Son', Sully asserts, 'have rendered this Severity as just as it is necessary.'[47] Political pamphleteers increasingly employed the idea of a balance of power to rhetorical ends, especially when it could be connected to the looming threat of a universal monarchy.[48]

The balance of power was thus intended to provide peace and security while at the same time advancing France's position of power and influence within this system.[49] Quite clearly France's self-styled image as defender of a European equilibrium was much more acceptable to the other European powers than French pretensions to hegemony would have been.[50] But given the power of France, the image of balance meant that France was seen to be the counterweight to the Habsburgs on the other side of the scale. This aspect was emphasized by the English historian William Camden, who asserts in his *History of ... Elizabeth* that it was England which could tip the balance on either side, depending on which side of the scales she put her weight:

Thus sate she [Queen Elizabeth] as an heroical Princess and Umpire betwixt the *Spaniards*, the *French* and the Estates; so as she might well have used that Saying of her Father, *Cui adhaero, praest*, that is, *The Party to which I adhere getteth the upper hand*. And true it was

the Christian states depends on the two great powers of France and Spain. If the equilibrium is unsettled to France's disadvantage, she will no longer be in a position to defend her legitimate interests. Mornay uses the word 'balance' here (271) to describe the desirable political equilibrium. At the same time weakening the Habsburgs was also intended to re-establish the imperial dignity of the French Crown: 'Ce seroit un preparatif pour remettre un jour l'Empire en la Maison de France' (275).

[46] See notably Michael Sheehan, *The Balance of Power: History & Theory* (Routledge 1996) and Moorhead Wright (ed), *Theory and Practice of the Balance of Power 1486–1914* (Littlehampton Book Services Ltd 1975). Both mention briefly only the younger brother of Sully, Philippe de Béthune. Nor is the balance of power analysed in any detail in the few and already mentioned existing studies on Sully.

[47] Sully, *Memoirs* (n 5) 45.

[48] Ernst Kaeber, *Die Idee des europäischen Gleichgewichts* (Alexander Duncker 1907) is still invaluable, but unfortunately he does not consider Sully's *Grand Design* in his study. See his dismissive remarks, 30. (The *Grand Design* is later mentioned in a different context, 150).

[49] Rohan and Béthune also made similar points. On these thinkers see the discussion in Peter Schröder, 'Überlegungen zum Problem der Staatsräson im Anschluss an Machiavelli' in Rüdiger Voigt (ed), *Staatsräson. Steht die Macht über dem Recht?* (Nomos 2012).

[50] Interesting, though beyond the scope of this chapter, is the shift of argument among the great European powers. English semi-official writers styled Great Britain in the eighteenth century as defender of the balance of power, whereas French and Habsburg polemicists accused Britain of ambitions towards universal monarchy. A good overview of these changes can be found in Kaeber, *Die Idee des europäischen Gleichgewichts* (n 48) 124–37; Sheehan, *The Balance of Power* (n 46) 97–120. One of the early English sources mentioning England as defender of the balance of power is William Camden, *The History of the most renowned and victorious Princess Elizabeth late Queen of England* (4th edn, London 1688).

which one hath written, that France and Spain are as it were the Scales in the Balance of Europe, and England the Tongue or the Holder of the Balance.[51]

When Sully relates the negotiations he held with King James in London during his ambassadorship he writes that:

... the King of *England* ... described the present political Affairs of Europe: In which, he said, it was necessary to preserve an Equilibrium between three of its Powers ... of these three Powers [the Habsburgs, Bourbons, and Stuarts], the House of *Austria* in *Spain*, from the Spirit of Dominion with which she was possessed, was the only one who sought to make the Balance incline in her favour.[52]

The *Grand Design* is thus presented by Sully as part of Henry IV's foreign policy. In this respect, Sully's advice and the *Grand Design* amounted to what was, above all, a piece of propaganda aimed against the dominance of the House of Habsburg. The belief that, following the *Grand Design*, 'a universal Cry from all Parts of Christendom would have been raised against the House of *Austria*' is reiterated repeatedly.[53] The Habsburg dynasty is thus presented as the only obstacle to European peace and security, because its aspirations to universal monarchy undermines the equilibrium of the European state system.

Not surprisingly Campanella—writing in the interest of Spanish universal monarchy—perceived the French as the main threat to peace and stability in Europe. He maintained 'that He [the Spanish King] hath no body to stand to fear of, but only the King of *France*, and the King of *England*; which two Princes, by reason of being of different Religions, can never agree together'.[54] Campanella's assertion that the different religious confessions of the two crowns would rule out any potential alliance between them was a serious miscalculation.[55] Their political interests were plainly not determined by religious allegiance alone. Interestingly, in a rare example, Campanella also employs the concept of the balance of power when he considers the French challenge to the Spanish position in Italy. Campanella holds that the French:

... cannot overcome them [the Spanish]: for, in this case, the very Princes, and States of Italy, who have to this day alwaies held with the *French*, would go over to the *Spaniard*: for it is their Design, to keep the balance alwaies so even betwixt these two Nations, as that neither of them may preponderate, and bear down the Scales, and so make a Prey of the Other.[56]

The balance of power is, for him, a political tool employed by the Italians. Sully is forced to argue for his proposal from a much weaker position and accordingly:

... the Purport of the Design may be perceived ... to divide *Europe* equally among a certain Number of Powers, in such a Manner, that none of them might have Cause, either of

---

[51] Camden, *The History of the most renowned and victorious Princess Elizabeth* (n 50) 223.
[52] Sully, *Memoirs* (n 5) 148.   [53] Ibid, 68.   [54] Campanella, *A Discourse* (n 9) 119.
[55] This might be explained by the fact that for the Habsburg's alliances were determined by religious confession. Campanella stresses that 'we are to understand, that the house of *Austria* is in league with none, save only Catholick Princes': Campanella, *A Discourse* (n 9) 139.
[56] Campanella, *A Discourse* (n 9) 119.

Envy or Fear, from the Possessions or Power of others. The Number of them was reduced to Fifteen; and they were of three Kinds: *viz.* six great hereditary Monarchies; five elective Monarchies; and four sovereign Republicks.[57]

The consistency of his appeals for his plan on the basis of equality, balancing of power, and a disinterested French politics indicates that he had to argue much more carefully than Campanella, who unabashedly argued for the Spanish Crown's dominion over the world. But Sully was far less neutral in his design than he presents himself to his readers. His proposal to counterbalance Habsburg power in Europe and beyond appears to be based on the resulting balance taking the form of a simple bipolar construction. It seemed:

difficult for French writers to move beyond a simple bipolar image of the balance. Since France clearly was one of the two 'poles', she could seek support to balance Spain or Austria, but was unconvincing when she aspired to any more subtle balance role.[58]

However, the *Grand Design* tried to address exactly this difficulty. It played an essential part in the propaganda efforts to convince the European Protestant powers of France's genuine interest in the balance and of her disinterest in a hegemonic position of power. Part of what the *Grand Design* had to achieve was thus to demonstrate that France had no such ambitions and did not harbour self-interested desires for a powerful position. As Sully repeatedly claimed: 'Among all these different Dismemberings, we may observe, that *France* reserved nothing for itself but the Glory of distributing them with Equity. Henry had declared this to be his Intention long before.'[59]

To what extent this strategy would be able to convince those invited to join the alliance is difficult to assess. However, it is more likely that it displayed 'Sully's scarcely disguised intention of confirming the primacy of France'.[60] Sully tries hard to counteract such an impression by stressing the fact that:

though *England*, and the *United Provinces*, should use their utmost Efforts of which they are capable against the House of *Austria*, unless they were assisted even by the whole Force of the *French* Monarchy, on whom the chief Management of such a War must fall for many Reasons; the House of *Austria* by uniting the Forces of its two Branches, would with ease ... sustain itself against them.[61]

When Sully deals with Europe as a whole in order to discuss how to arrange a new order in view of the existing different Christian confessions, his proposals remain fairly general and superficial. His leading conviction is, however, that Europe should not be divided by confessional differences, but by the political interests of the Habsburgs and her allies on the one hand, and the counterweight formed around France and her allies on the other. He makes this explicit in a later part of

---

[57] Sully, *Memoirs* (n 5) 52.   [58] Sheehan, *The Balance of Power* (n 46) 39.
[59] Sully, *Memoirs* (n 5) 50.
[60] FH Hinsley, *Power and the Pursuit of Peace: Theory and Practice in the History of Relations between States* (Cambridge University Press 1963) 28.
[61] Sully, *Memoirs* (n 5) 32.

the *Memoirs*, where he again presents the *Grand Design* in some detail: 'Europe', he asserts, 'is divided into two Factions, which are not so justly distinguished by their different Religions, because the Catholicks and Protestants are confounded together in almost all Places, as they are by their Political Interests'.[62] Sully's statements on the subject in the *Memoirs* are contradictory. The argument presented here serves to suggest that Calvinists and Lutherans are indeed to be seen on an equal footing with the Catholics.[63]

From here, Sully quickly moves on to present an outline of his envisaged plan. Despite the fact that Russia, the Armenians, and the Greeks are 'ranked ... among the Christian Powers',[64] he excludes them from any further consideration. Interestingly, he does so on the grounds that the cultural and religious differences between them and the European states are too great to consider them as potential elements of his proposed European federation. For him these countries 'belong to *Asia* at least as much as to *Europe*. We indeed may almost consider them as a barbarous Country, and place them in the same Class with *Turkey*.'[65] This exclusion was fairly conventional in the early seventeenth century. Given the centuries long struggle between the Habsburg's and the Ottomans, it is hardly surprising that Campanella had also argued against:

the *Turk* [who] endeavours to make himself Lord of the whole World ... He will also at this time already be called, *The Universal Lord*; as the King of *Spain* is called, *The Catholick King*: so that these two Princes seem now to strive, which of them shall attain to the Universal Monarchy of the Whole World.[66]

Campanella was much more concerned about the Ottoman Empire than Sully, because it posed a real threat to Spanish claims for universal monarchy:

... seeing that ... the *Turk* stretcheth forth his hand against All Men ... all whom yet he is frequently wont to delude by his Cessations from Armes, and Truces, (for He keeps his faith with none of them:) it would be a businisse worth our serious consideration, how this Practise of his might be turned against Himself.[67]

Campanella argued from a geopolitical perspective that the King of Spain should endeavour to form alliances among the powers of the Middle East against their 'common enemies, the Turk's country'.[68] Again the struggle for empire and religion go hand-in-hand in this argument, culminating in the claim that Jerusalem should

---

[62] Ibid, 178.

[63] Note that the issue of religion was perceived as particularly problematic and divisive by Sully, as is evident from other remarks in his *Memoirs*. See eg ibid, 26.

[64] Ibid, 40.   [65] Ibid, 40. This point is almost expressis verbis reiterated in ibid, 179.

[66] Campanella, *A Discourse* (n 9) 197.

[67] Ibid, 204. Cf. Colin Imber, *The Ottoman Empire 1300–1650: The Structure of Power* (Palgrave Macmillan 2002) 71: 'In 1606 peace negotiations began ... between the Habsburg and Ottoman Empires ... When Habsburg negotiators travelled to Istanbul in 1608 to ratify the text [of the peace treaty], they rejected it since the clause on the equality of the Emperors had been dropped.' See also Winfried Schulze, *Reich und Türkengefahr im späten 16 Jahrhundert: Studien zu den politischen und gesellschaftlichen Auswirkungen einer äußeren Bedrohung* (Beck 1978) and Dorothy M Vaughan, *Europe and the Turk: A Pattern of Alliances, 1350–1700* (Liverpool University Press 1954).

[68] Campanella, *A Discourse* (n 9) 205.

be recovered, 'which should be reserved for the King of Spain'.[69] This military crusade was supported by an intellectual offensive, and Campanella advocated that:

the King should erect certain Schools in all the Principal Cities, wherein the *Arabick* Tongue should be taught; that so by this meanes there may be such among his subjects as shall be able to dispute with the *Turks, Moors,* and *Persians,* who by the use of that Tongue spread their *Mahumetanisme,* as We do *Christianity,* by the *Latine* Tongue.[70]

Whereas Campanella stressed the conflict with the Turks, Sully was keen to concentrate on the heartland of Europe and the rearrangements he considers necessary for establishing a new lasting order.[71]

The *Grand Design* was, therefore, much less aggressive than Campanella's vision of Spanish universal monarchy, and one of its key aspects consisted in the project to create a 'general Council, representing all the States of Europe'.[72] This general council is envisaged as a representative body of all European states. It should have the competence to moderate and, if necessary, arbitrate conflicts within the state system. However, the originality of this project, with an arbiter formed on a representative basis, should not be over-emphasized, as it was in many ways simply a reformulation of contemporary ideas about the institution of arbitration.[73] Nevertheless, Sully claims that its 'Establishment ... was certainly the happiest Invention that could have been conceived'.[74] In order to establish this type of representative body of European states, sweeping changes of territorial possessions were envisaged, with the establishment of the council signifying only the ultimate step and conclusion of these radical alterations of the European map. Sully was aware that 'to divest the House of *Austria* of the Empire; and all its Possessions in *Germany, Italy* and all the *Low Countries*; in a Word, to reduce it to the sole Kingdom of *Spain*' posed a fundamental challenge.[75] It was not conceivable that the Habsburg monarchy could be persuaded to such revolutionary and disadvantageous measures, even if Sully emphasized that the aim was an equilibrium of the European powers, and that therefore the Habsburg branches should remain 'nevertheless ... equally powerful with the other Sovereignties of *Europe*'.[76] Sully had no doubt himself that such a dramatic change could only be achieved by war.

War thus represented not the *ultima ratio* but the necessary means to break Habsburg hegemony. Sully is clear from the outset of his *Memoirs* that conquest

---

[69] Ibid, 205.   [70] Ibid, 182.

[71] This was a rather typical attitude among European political writers. See Kaeber, *Die Idee des europäischen Gleichgewichts* (n 48) 78.

[72] Sully, *Memoirs* (n 5) 53.

[73] See, for instance, the ideas about arbitration developed by Bodin: Jean Bodin, *Les Six Livres de la République* (Paris 1583) 799: 'Qui est le plus haut poinct d'honneur qu'un Prince peut gainer, à sçavoir d'estre esleu arbitre de paix entre les autres.' Regarding Sully, Klaus Malettke, *Frankreich, Deutschland und Europa im 17 und 18 Jahrhundert: Beiträge zum Einfluß französischer politischer Theorie, Verfassung und Außenpolitik in der Frühen Neuzeit* (Marburg 1994) 273ff stresses Sully's innovative idea of the federal character of the council and its underlying idea of a system of collective security. With a slightly more cautious judgement regarding such a system, see also Hartmann, *Rêveurs de Paix?* (n 24) 90ff.

[74] Sully, *Memoirs* (n 5) 53.   [75] Ibid, 44.   [76] Ibid, 44.

is a perfectly acceptable way to acquire rights of dominion in the international sphere.[77] But his assessment of war is at times contradictory, as he also asserts that he is 'from repeated Experience, convinced, that the Happiness of Mankind can never arise from War'.[78] Nevertheless, the changes he considered necessary for the establishment of the representative body of the European states were a preliminary step which posed the greatest obstacle to the realization of the *Grand Design*. Given that at the time of this work Europe had already been at war for almost two decades, the prospect of using war to reorganize the European state system at the end of the current war may have been seen as much more acceptable, as it meant that a new war need not be launched to achieve the goals of the *Grand Design*. War aims, after all, could be formulated in the context of the ongoing war. The constitution of the Holy Roman Empire, with its contradictory division of sovereign rights and obligations, meant that France would find allies in Germany against the Habsburgs. With the Emperor's edict of restitution of 1629[79] and again, after the Swedish intervention, with the Peace of Prague of 1635, the Habsburgs had managed to impose their claims on the German estates.[80] Sully suggested, therefore, that:

France would … endeavour to gain the neighbouring Princes and States to join with them in their Design; especially the Princes of *Germany*, who were most immediately and dangerously menaced with being subjected to the Tyranny of the House of Austria.[81]

In the context of the period 1629–35, Sully's suggestion can thus be read as an almost immediate reaction to the unfolding scenes of the theatre of the Thirty Years War. These far-reaching war aims could become more acceptable for the other states at war with the Habsburgs, as the underlying aim was reformulated as the establishment of the balance of power, at the price of Habsburg territories and to the benefit of the smaller states.

Both Sully and Campanella argued that the balance of power and universal monarchy respectively were the best means to avoid conflict and to achieve peace in Europe. However, not surprisingly, both men foremost pursued the interest of their king. Both concepts were used to advance the interest of France and Spain respectively, and both concepts aimed to make these interests more palatable to the other European powers within the state system. Not only were the interests of France and Spain pitched against each other, but so were also the theoretical arguments which underscored them.[82] However, the concept of *interest* itself was

---

[77] Cf eg ibid, 9.   [78] Ibid, 16.

[79] The text of the edict can be found in Peter H Wilson, *The Thirty Years War: A Sourcebook* (Palgrave Macmillan 2010) 114–17. See also Marc R Forster, 'The Edict of Restitution (1629) and the Failure of Catholic Restoration' in Olaf Asbach and Peter Schröder (eds), *The Ashgate Research Companion to the Thirty Years War* (Routledge 2014).

[80] See Adam Wandruszka, *Reichspatriotismus und Reichspolitik zur Zeit des Prager Friedens von 1635* (Graz, H Böhlaus Nachf 1955) and Martin Espenhorst, 'The Peace of Prague—A Failed Settlement?' in Asbach and Schröder (eds), *The Ashgate Research Companion* (n 79).

[81] Sully, *Memoirs* (n 5) 32.

[82] As a consequence of this juxtaposition, the moment France gained power and influence to the detriment of Habsburg Spain, Louis XIV was now accused of pursuing universal monarchy. The struggle for empire is thus reflected in the—changing—references to balance of power politics and universal monarchy.

increasingly analysed by political thinkers. This facilitated a more sophisticated and critical analysis of interstate relations.

Conclusion and Outlook: Rethinking the European State System

Writing after the Peace of Westphalia, Samuel Pufendorf is the one who deserves recognition for advancing the reflection on the theoretical tools of international political thought. Pufendorf argued that to conceive of the various competing interests of states within a system of states allowed consideration of these interests in a different framework.[83] For him the strict notion of absolute sovereignty was applicable neither to the Holy Roman Empire nor to interstate relations. On the former, he famously concluded that 'the best account we can possibly give of the Present State of Germany, is to say, That it comes very near a System of States, in which one Prince or General of the League excells the rest of the Confederation'.[84] What he effectively argued for was a system-based concept of sovereignty which would allow states to enter into agreements without giving up their sovereignty entirely:

A system results when several neighbouring states are so connected by perpetual alliance that they renounce the intention of exercising some portions of their sovereign power, above all those which concern external defence, except with the consent of all, but apart from this the liberty and independence of the individual states remain intact.[85]

The state is meant to understand and pursue the long-term interest. Pufendorf distinguishes between the office and the person holding the office, which means that 'a certain Method of governing' is prescribed to the person of the ruler.[86]

---

[83] This in turn allowed natural law to be meaningful for regulating interstate relations in this specific context. But this is not the place to pursue this question further. Meinecke and Dufour over-emphasize the importance of interest for Pufendorf's international thought. See Friedrich Meinecke, *Die Idee der Staatsräson in der neueren Geschichte* (R Oldenbourg 1960) 264–86; Alfred Dufour, 'Pufendorfs föderalistisches Denken und die Staatsräsonlehre' in Fiammetta Palladini and Gerald Hartung (eds), *Samuel von Pufendorf und die europäische Frühaufklärung* (Akademie Verlag GmbH 1996) 122. More nuanced is the argument by David Boucher, *Political Theories of International Relations* (Oxford University Press 1998) 246: 'It is certainly the case that in trying to accommodate self-interest with the universal standards of conduct expressed in the Natural Law, the ethical constraint often appears to be extremely weak, and even subordinate to the Reason of State.'

[84] Samuel Pufendorf, *The Present State of Germany* (Michael J Seidler ed, Liberty Fund 2007) 178. See also Peter Schröder, 'The Constitution of the Holy Roman Empire after 1648: Samuel Pufendorf's Assessment in his *Monzambano*' (1999) 42 Historical Journal 961; Michael Seidler, '"Monstrous" Pufendorf: Sovereignty and System in the *Dissertations*' in Cesare Cuttica and Glenn Burgess (eds), *Monarchism and Absolutism in Early Modern Europe* (Routledge 2011) 159–75.

[85] Samuel Pufendorf, *On the Duty of Man and Citizen* (J Tully ed, Cambridge University Press 1991) II-8-15 145. On the innovative and modern character of Pufendorf's position, also in relation to discussions about the European Union and human rights see David Boucher, 'Resurrecting Pufendorf and Capturing the Westphalian Moment' and more generally Werner Maihofer, 'Schlußwort: Was uns Pufendorf noch Heute zu sagen hat' in Bodo Geyer and Helmut Goerlich (eds), *Samuel Pufendorf und seine Wirkungen bis auf die heutige Zeit* (Nomos 1996).

[86] Samuel Pufendorf, *Of the Law of Nature and Nations* (Basil Kennet ed and tr, London 1717) VII-VI-9 695.

Pufendorf thus reformulates the concept of interest, which in his account becomes less subjective, because it needs to be perceived within the framework of a system of states. In his criticism of the balance of power doctrine the Abbé Saint Pierre developed this argument further. We can, therefore, discern an important shift in the way interstate relations are discussed in the middle of the seventeenth century. The concepts of universal monarchy and balance of power were not sufficiently able to reflect the increasing complexities of European interstate relations.

Bibliography

Sully, Duke of, *The Memoirs of the Duke of Sully during his Residence at the English Court; to which he was sent Ambassador from Henry IV of France, upon the Accession of King James the First. Containing An Account of his Negotiations … Also A Relation of the Political Scheme, commonly called the Great Design of Henry IV …* (Dublin 1751)

Alighieri, Dante, *Monarchy* (P Shaw ed, Cambridge University Press 1996)

Arcidiacono, Bruno, *Cinq Types de Paix: Une Histoire des Plans de Pacification perpétuelle* (Presses Universitaires de France 2011)

Arcidiacono, Bruno, '*Contra Pluralitatem Principatuum*: Trois Critiques du Système dit Westphalien (formulées avant la Paix de Westphalie)' in Pierre-Marie Dupuy and Vincent Chetail (eds), *The Roots of International Law/Les fondements droit international: Liber Amicorum Peter Haggenmacher* (Brill 2014)

Aylmer, GE, *The Struggle for the Constitution 1603–1689* (Blandford Press 1963)

Black, JB, *Elizabeth and Henry IV* (University of Michigan Library 1914)

Bodin, Jean, *Les Six Livres de la République* (Paris 1583)

Bonney, Richard, *The European Dynastic States 1494–1660* (Oxford University Press 1991)

Bosbach, Franz, *Monarchia Universalis: Ein politischer Leitbegriff der Frühen Neuzeit* (Vandenhoeck & Ruprecht 1988)

Boucher, David, 'Resurrecting Pufendorf and Capturing the Westphalian Moment' in Bodo Geyer and Helmut Goerlich (eds), *Samuel Pufendorf und seine Wirkungen bis auf die heutige Zeit* (Nomos 1996)

Boucher, David, *Political Theories of International Relations* (Oxford University Press 1998)

Camden, William, *The History of the most renowned and victorious Princess Elizabeth late Queen of England* (4th edn, London 1688)

Campanella, Tommaso, *A Discourse Touching the Spanish Monarchy: Laying Down Directions and Practices Whereby the King of Spain May Attain to an Universal Monarchy* (London 1658)

Carré, Henri, *Sully: Sa vie et son oeuvre 1559–1641* (Payot 1932)

Doyle, William, *The Old European Order 1660–1800* (Oxford University Press 1992)

Dufour, Alfred, 'Pufendorfs föderalistisches Denken und die Staatsräsonlehre' in Fiammetta Palladini and Gerald Hartung (eds), *Samuel von Pufendorf und die europäische Frühaufklärung* (Akademie Verlag GmbH 1996)

Elliott, JH, *Imperial Spain 1469–1716* (Penguin Books 1976)

Elliott, JH, 'A Europe of Composite Monarchies' in JH Elliott, *Spain, Europe & the Wider World 1500–1800* (Yale University Press 2009)

Espenhorst, Martin, 'The Peace of Prague—A Failed Settlement?' in Olaf Asbach and Peter Schröder (eds), *The Ashgate Research Companion to the Thirty Years War* (Routledge 2014)

Forster, Marc R, 'The Edict of Restitution (1629) and the Failure of Catholic Restoration' in Olaf Asbach and Peter Schröder (eds), *The Ashgate Research Companion to the Thirty Years War* (Routledge 2014)

Gelderen, Martin van, 'Universal Monarchy, the Rights of War and Peace and the Balance of Power: Europe's Quest for Civil Order' in Hans-Åke Persson and Bo Stråth (eds), *Reflections on Europe: Defining a Political Order in Time and Space* (Peter Lang Publishing 2007)

Gil, Xavier, 'Spain and Portugal' in Howell A Lloyd, Glenn Burgess, and Simon Hodson (eds), *European Political Thought 1450–1700: Religion, Law and Philosophy* (Yale University Press 2007)

Gil, Xavier, 'The Good Law of a Vassal: Fidelity, Obedience and Obligation in Habsburg Spain' (2009) 5 Revista Internacional de los Estudios Vascos 92

Hartmann, Anja Victorine, *Rêveurs de Paix? Friedenspläne bei Crucé, Richelieu und Sully* (Hamburg 1995)

Headley, John M, 'Tommaso Campanella and the End of the Renaissance' (1990) 20 The Journal of Medieval and Renaissance Studies 157

Hinsley, FH, *Power and the Pursuit of Peace: Theory and Practice in the History of Relations between States* (Cambridge University Press 1963)

Hume, David, 'Of the Balance of Power' in David Hume, *Political Essays* (Knud Haakonssen ed, Cambridge University Press 1994)

Imber, Colin, *The Ottoman Empire 1300–1650: The Structure of Power* (Palgrave Macmillan 2002)

Kaeber, Ernst, *Die Idee des europäischen Gleichgewichts* (University of Michigan Library 1907)

Kamen, Henry, *Spain's Road to Empire. The Making of a World Power 1492–1763* (Penguin Books 2003)

Kunisch, Johannes and Neuhaus, Helmut (eds), *Der dynastische Fürstenstaat: Zur Bedeutung der Sukzessionsordnungen für die Entstehung des frühmodernen Staates* (Duncker & Humblot 1982)

Lesaffer, Randall, 'Between Faith and Empire: The Justification of the Spanish Intervention in the French Wars of Religion in the 1590s' Chapter 5 in this volume

Lüsse, Beate Gabriele, *Formen der humanistischen Utopie* (Schöningh 1998)

Machiavelli, Niccolò, *The Prince* (Quentin Skinner and Russell Price eds, Cambridge 2008)

Maihofer, Werner, 'Schlußwort: Was uns Pufendorf noch Heute zu sagen hat' in Bodo Geyer and Helmut Goerlich (eds), *Samuel Pufendorf und seine Wirkungen bis auf die heutige Zeit* (Nomos 1996)

Malettke, Klaus, 'Europabewußtsein und Europäische Friedenspläne im 17 und 18 Jahrhundert' (1994) 21 Francia 92

Malettke, Klaus, *Frankreich, Deutschland und Europa im 17 und 18 Jahrhundert. Beiträge zum Einfluß französischer politischer Theorie, Verfassung und Außenpolitik in der Frühen Neuzeit* (Marburg 1994)

Meinecke, Friedrich, *Die Idee der Staatsräson in der neueren Geschichte* (R Oldenbourg 1960)

Mornay, Philippes de, 'Discours au Roy Henry III sur les moyens de diminuer l'Espagnol' in *Memoires de Messire Philippes de Mornay* (Paris 1624)

Motley, John Lothrop, *The Life and Death of John of Barneveld, Advocate of Holland: with a View of the primary Causes and Movements of the Thirty Years War* (Harper & Brothers 1874)

Pagden, Anthony, *Spanish Imperialism and the Political Imagination* (Yale University Press 1990)

Pufendorf, Samuel, *Of the Law of Nature and Nations* (Basil Kennet ed and tr, London 1717)

Pufendorf, Samuel, *On the Duty of Man and Citizen* (J Tully ed, Cambridge University Press 1991)

Pufendorf, Samuel, *The Present State of Germany* (Michael J Seidler ed, Liberty Fund 2007)

Ritter, Moriz, 'Die Memoiren Sullys und der grosse Plan Heinrichs IV' (1870) 11 Abhandlungen der Historischen Klasse der Königlichen Bayrischen Akademie der Wissenschaften 1

Robertson, John, 'Universal Monarchy and the Liberties of Europe: David Hume's Critique of an English Whig Doctrine' in Nicholas Phillipson and Quentin Skinner (eds), *Political Discourse in Early Modern Britain* (Cambridge University Press 1993)

Sandoval, Prudencio de, *La vida y hechos del Emperador Carlos Quinto Max. Fortissimo. Rey de Espana, y de las Indias, Islas, y Tierrafirme del mar Oceano* (Valladolid 1604)

Schröder, Peter, 'The Constitution of the Holy Roman Empire after 1648: Samuel Pufendorf's Assessment in his *Monzambano*' (1999) 42 Historical Journal 961

Schröder, Peter, *Niccolò Machiavelli* (Campus Einführungen 2004)

Schröder, Peter, 'Die Kunst der Staatserhaltung' in Otfried Höffe (ed), *Machiavelli: Der Fürst* (De Gruyter 2012)

Schröder, Peter, 'Überlegungen zum Problem der Staatsräson im Anschluss an Machiavelli' in Rüdiger Voigt (ed), *Staatsräson: Steht die Macht über dem Recht?* (Nomos 2012)

Schulze, Winfried, *Reich und Türkengefahr im späten 16 Jahrhundert: Studien zu den politischen und gesellschaftlichen Auswirkungen einer äußeren Bedrohung* (Beck 1978)

Seidler, Michael, '"Monstrous" Pufendorf: Sovereignty and System in the *Dissertations*' in Cesare Cuttica and Glenn Burgess (eds), *Monarchism and Absolutism in Early Modern Europe* (Routledge 2011)

Sheehan, Michael, *The Balance of Power: History & Theory* (Routledge 1996)

Strayer, Joseph R, *On the Medieval Origins of the Modern State* (Princeton University Press 1970)

Strohmeyer, Arno, 'Ideas of Peace in Early Modern Models of International Order: Universal Monarchy and Balance of Power in Comparison' in Jost Dülffer and Robert Frank (eds), *Peace, War and Gender from Antiquity to the Present. Cross-cultural Perspectives* (Klartext Verlag 2009)

Taillandier, Saint-René, *Henri IV avant la messe* (Grasset 1934)

Taillandier, Saint-René, *Le cœur du roi. Henri IV après la messe* (Grasset 1934)

Thuau, Etienne, *Raison d'Etat et pensée politique à l'époque de Richelieu* (Albin Michel 2000)

Vaughan, Dorothy M, *Europe and the Turk: A Pattern of Alliances, 1350–1700* (Liverpool University Press 1954)

Wandruszka, Adam, *Reichspatriotismus und Reichspolitik zur Zeit des Prager Friedens von 1635* (Graz, H Böhlaus Nachf 1955)

Weber, Hermann, 'Die Bedeutung der Dynastien für die europäische Geschichte in der frühen Neuzeit' (1981) 44 Zeitschrift für bayerische Landesgeschichte 5

Wilson, Peter H, *The Thirty Years War: A Sourcebook* (Palgrave Macmillan 2010)

Wright, Moorhead (ed), *Theory and Practice of the Balance of Power 1486–1914* (Littlehampton Book Services Ltd 1975)

Zeller, Gaston, 'Les rois de France candidats à l'Empire' (1934) 173 Revue historique 237–311, 457–534

5

Between Faith and Empire: The Justification of the Spanish Intervention in the French Wars of Religion in the 1590s

Randall Lesaffer

Introduction

On 17 January 1595, the French King Henry IV (1589–1610) issued a declaration of war against the Spanish King Philip II (1555–1598). The declaration argued in great detail why the French king saw himself forced to resort to open war, listing the many offences the Spanish had inflicted upon him and the French over the years.[1] Seven weeks later, on 7 March 1595, Philip II reacted by issuing a counter-declaration. The Spanish government did, however, not declare war upon 'Henry de Béarn', whom it refused to recognize as King of France, thus denying him the sovereignty needed to wage war upon Spain. It declared him and his allies and adherents public enemies and defended the justice of its support of the French Catholic League and its intervention in the affairs of France.[2]

With its declaration, Henry IV chose to transform the French religious war into an overt, international war between his country and the leading power of the time, the Spanish monarchy. With its counter-declaration, Spain declined to take the bait and chose to continue the conflict in terms of an intervention at the side of the oppressed Catholics of France against the heretic usurper Henry.

As a declaration of war and a counter-declaration of non-war, the two texts of 1595 offer an interesting insight into the *jus ad bellum* of the late sixteenth century, but there is more to them. The French declaration initiated the final phase of the series of religious wars that had ravished France since 1562 and in which Spain had intervened throughout. The declaration of war of 1595 elicited one of the few

---

[1] *Déclaration de la volonté du Roy sur l'ouverture de la guerre contre le Roy d'Espagne* (Iamet Mettayer and Pierre L'Huillier 1595).

[2] *Edict du Roy nostre Syre en forme de declaration contre la publication de guerre, faicte par le Prince de Bearne, soy disant roy de France, par lequel sa Majesté declare, sa volonté estre d'entretenir la Saincte Ligue en faveur des Catholicques de France* (Rutger Velpius 1595), also in Jean Dumont, *Corps universel diplomatique du droit des gens* (Brunel and Husson 1726–1731) vol V.1, 515–56.

International Law and Empire: Historical Explorations. First Edition. Martti Koskenniemi, Walter Rech, and Manuel Jiménez Fonseca. © Martti Koskenniemi, Walter Rech, and Manuel Jiménez Fonseca 2016. Published 2016 by Oxford University Press.

official justifications ever rendered by the Spanish government for its intervention. The French Wars of Religion in turn were part of a drawn-out string of interconnected civil, religious, and international conflicts that had started in the 1560s and sucked in Spain, France, the Low Countries, parts of the Holy Roman Empire, and the British Isles. These probed different legal questions in relation to war, rebellion, religion, intervention, and empire.

Present-day scholars have looked to the religious wars of the sixteenth and early seventeenth centuries for antecedents to the current doctrine of humanitarian intervention.[3] Indeed, the period produced numerous writings by lawyers, theologians, and political thinkers from both sides of the religious divide addressing the question whether and under what conditions a prince might or ought to use force for the benefit of the subjects of another prince. These theories of intervention emerged in two different contexts. First, they arose in the context of the justification of conquest and empire in the American Indies. The School of Salamanca acted as trailblazer but its thought was picked up by Protestant writers, such as the civilian Alberico Gentili (1552–1608).[4] Second, the question of intervention also arose in the Calvinist as well as Catholic literature from the wars of religion on resistance against tyranny and religious oppression.[5]

This chapter delves into the discourse of the justification by Spain of its intervention in the French Wars of Religion to tease out the legal doctrines which were applied to it. This is not done through an engagement with the legal and political literature from the period, but through the analysis of the two main official justifications which Spain offered for its intervention in France. Apart from the 1595 counter-declaration, this is the declaration issued in March 1590 after the decision was made by Spain to send two armies to France in aid of the Catholic League.[6]

The Spanish justifications for its actions in France provide occasion to study intervention in the context of empire as they tied the discourse of religious

---

[3] Simon Chesterman, *Just War or Just Peace? Humanitarian Intervention and International Law* (Oxford University Press 2001) 9–16; Terry D Gill, 'Just War Doctrine in Modern Context' in Terry D Gill and Wilco Heere (eds), *Reflections on Principles and Practice of International Law: Essays in Honour of Leo J. Bouchez* (Martinus Nijhoff 2000) 17–64; Alexis Heraclides, 'Humanitarian Intervention in International Law 1830–1939: The Debate' (2014) 16 Journal of the History of International Law 26, 26; Nicholas J Wheeler, *Saving Strangers: Humanitarian Intervention in International Society* (Oxford University Press 2000).

[4] JA Fernandez-Santamaria, *The State, War and Peace: Spanish Political Thought in the Renaissance 1516–1559* (Cambridge University Press 1977); Anthony Pagden, *Lords of All the World: Ideologies of Empire in Spain, Britain and France c.1500–c.1800* (Yale University Press 1995); Robert A Williams Jr, *The American Indian in Western Legal Thought: The Discourse of Conquest* (Oxford University Press 1990).

[5] Robert M Kingdom, 'Calvinism and Resistance Theory, 1550–1580' and JHM Salmon, 'Catholic Resistance Theory, Ultramontanism, and the Royalist Response, 1580–1620' in JH Burns and Mark Goldie (eds), *The Cambridge History of Political Thought 1450–1700* (Cambridge University Press 1991); Quentin Skinner, *The Foundations of Modern Political Thought* (Cambridge University Press 1978) vol II, 302–48.

[6] *Declaration du roy d'Espaigne sur les troubles, misères, & Calamitez qui affligent la Chrestienté, & notamment le Royaume de France: Avec les lettres de sa Maiesté au Clergé pour fournir de leurs moyens aux fraiz de la guerre. Sur la copie imprimee a Douay. Par Iean Bogard Imprimeur de sa Maiesté Catholique* (Loys Tantillon 1590).

intervention to the policies of empire. To Madrid, the bedrock of the justice of its actions was the defence of the true faith of Europe, Catholicism. Spain itself linked this to the defence of its empire and its factual hegemony over Europe, as it equated Protestantism to rebellion and perceived an international Protestant conspiracy to destroy the Spanish monarchy at work everywhere. Spain's enemies used the same connection in reverse as they considered the Catholic oppression of Protestantism one among many proofs of the Spanish desire to *monarchia universalis*, the subjection of the whole of Christianity to its will.

Justifications of War in Early Modern Europe

Modern scholarship has largely overlooked declarations and manifestos of war as textual sources for the study of the law of nations of Early Modern Europe. Two explanations spring readily to mind. First, since the nineteenth century, the historiography of international law has focused lopsidedly on the intellectual history of the field, to the detriment of legal practice. Second, the Early Modern Age is traditionally considered in terms of the rise of the sovereign State towards its triumph in the nineteenth century. In the grand narrative of the history of the *jus ad bellum* (use of force law), it figures as the period of the demise of the just war doctrine—which asserted material conditions restricting the right to wage war—and the rise of the doctrine of legal or formal war—which did not.[7] But as more recent research has shown, reality was more nuanced as the doctrine of just war proved resilient all through the Early Modern Age.

Under the just war doctrine, war is a substitute for law enforcement action. It is the forcible execution of a pre-existing right. In the classical rendering by Saint Thomas Aquinas (1225–1274), for a war to be just, a belligerent needs to have authority (sovereignty), just cause, and righteous intention. Whereas over time, writers would forward different lists of just causes, the cause of war always came down to a reaction against a prior—or at least imminent—wrongful action committed by the enemy. A just war could be either defensive or offensive, in the sense that the just belligerent was the second or first to use force. But on a more conceptual level, the just belligerent always acted defensively as he reacted against a prior violation of his right. Righteous intention referred to the mental and moral disposition with which a belligerent entered and fought the war. A just belligerent had to wage war not out of greed, ambition, or vengeance, but to do justice. Righteous intention pointed at the goal of the war, which had to be the achievement of an equitable and lasting peace. Under the latter two conditions lurked two additional conditions. The war had to be proportional and necessary. It had to be waged with measure in function of the injury and its goals, and it was a solution of last resort.

---

[7] See the classical rendering by Joachim von Elbe, 'The Evolution of the Concept of Just War in International Law' (1939) 33 American Journal of International Law 665; also, although with more nuance, Stephen C Neff, *War and the Law of Nations: A General History* (Cambridge University Press 2005).

The just war was discriminatory in that it opposed a just against an unjust belligerent. Only the just belligerent could benefit from the protection of the *jus in bello* (laws of war). At the end of the war stood a just peace whereby the object of contention would fall to the just side.[8]

Under the doctrine of formal war, war was a substitute for civil trial. In the absence of a higher authority to settle the claims of justice of both sides, war became an instrument of judgement. Whereas a just war was the execution of a pre-existing right, victory in a formal war constituted title to a right. For a war to be legal, it sufficed that it was waged by a sovereign holding the necessary authority to wage war, and that it was formally declared. Formal war was non-discriminatory: both sides had a right to wage war and thus benefited equally from the laws of war; at the end of the war the object of contention would go to the victor of the war, or of the peace negotiations.[9]

Mainstream literature on the law of nations from the late sixteenth to the eighteenth century was inherently dualist as it operated both concepts of war side by side. This caused no undue conceptual difficulties as they functioned on separate levels. According to Hugo Grotius (1583–1645), and mainstream authors after him including Emer de Vattel (1714–1767), the just war pertained to the natural law of nations, whereas formal war fell within the remit of the voluntary—positive—law of nations. The natural law of nations was only enforceable in conscience, whereas the voluntary law of nations created rights and obligations which were externally enforceable.[10]

The Grotian scheme was the novel systematization of the old distinction between the spiritual and temporal from medieval thought. Although it was adopted by the medieval civilians, the just war doctrine was first and foremost the product of theologians and canonists. It addressed the question of what waging war would do to the eternal soul; concerns about its practical effects in the here and the now were a distant second. The concept of formal war found its earlier full statements in the works of the late sixteenth-century civilians Baltasar de Ayala (1548–1584) and Gentili, but it rooted back to the writings of the late-medieval Roman lawyers. To the medieval and early modern writers, just war and formal war were not mutually exclusive. They resulted in different effects at different levels. Most authors indicated a logical link between the two. Because human fallibility more often than not made an objective judgement on the opposing claims of justice of sovereigns impossible, the effects of claiming the enemy to be unjust had to be limited in the here and now.[11] But this did not prevent princes from having to take utmost care not to lightly engage in an unjust war; this could still damn their soul for all eternity.

---

[8] Peter Haggenmacher, *Grotius et la doctrine de la guerre juste* (Presses Universitaires de France 1983); Neff, *War and the Law of Nations* (n 7) 45–68; Frederick H Russell, *The Just War in the Middle Ages* (Cambridge University Press 1975).

[9] James Q Whitman, *The Verdict of Battle; The Law of Victory and the Making of Modern War* (Harvard University Press 2012).

[10] Stephen C Neff, *Justice among Nations: A History of International Law* (Harvard University Press 2014) 158–201.

[11] Already noted by Raphael Fulgosius (1367–1424), ad Digestum 1.1.5.

Also, at a more mundane level, the just war retained its relevance for those cases of 'imperfect' war in which the conditions of formal war were not fulfilled, such as self-defence, reprisal, or intervention.[12]

This duality of early modern doctrine mirrored the duplicity which existed in practice. During the Early Modern Age, the princes and republics of Christian Europe adhered to a non-discriminatory conception of war when waging war and making peace. At the level of the application of the *jus in bello* and in peace treaties, no discriminations were made on the basis of claims to justice. But in the propagandistic exercises to justify war at its inception, the concept of just war loomed large. Throughout the Early Modern Age, belligerents went to a lot of trouble to justify their actions when they resorted to force or war. It was customary at the beginning of a war not only to indicate the war to the enemy but to publish an extensive justification for it. This could be included in the text of the declaration to the enemy itself, and/or in a separate manifesto. In both cases, the text was usually printed and distributed in large numbers, and translated in several languages. Its audiences were multiple. These included one's own armed forces, officials, and elites, but also those of allies, third powers, and even enemies. Trying to convince the enemy's subjects of the justice—and thus divine sanction—of one's cause was not a futile exercise and could have a real destabilizing effect upon the enemy. Many members of the elites of the European powers, especially those living in border areas where much of the military action would take place, had ties, interests, and property in different countries. Moreover, with regards to religious conflicts, it has to be remembered that many countries, and most noteworthy the majority of countries ruled by Protestants, had sizable religious minorities.

In recent years, several extensive studies by diplomatic historians on declarations and manifestos of war have appeared. These survey studies indicate that these declarations and manifestos used a standard reasoning and outline, which were based on the just war doctrine. The justification for war commonly rested on three arguments. First, the declarations and manifestos opened with an extensive, historical narrative which listed the injustices committed by the enemy over a—preferably—long period of time. These served as the just causes for war. Second, this was opposed to the good will and the desire for peace of their own prince which was substantiated by listing his benevolent actions towards the enemy. This, together with the longevity of the opponent's enmity, showed that war was really the last resort. Third, the goals of war were mentioned, whereby the desire for a lasting, just peace was given centre stage. All in all, declarations and manifestos of war laid great emphasis on the absolute necessity to resort to force, or to full and open war, in order to achieve a lasting, just peace.[13]

---

[12] Neff, *War and the Law of Nations* (n 7) 119–30.

[13] Frederic J Baumgartner, *Declaring War in Early Modern Europe* (Palgrave Macmillan 2011); Bernd Klesmann, *Bellum Solemne: Formen und Funktionen europäischer Kriegserklärungen des 17. Jahrhunderts* (Philipp von Zabern 2007); Anuscha Tischer, *Offizielle Kriegsbegründungen in der frühen Neuzeit: Herrscherkommunikation in Europa zwischen Souveränität und korporativem Selbstverständnis* (LIT 2012).

These conclusions do not exhaust the potential of declarations and manifestos of war as sources for our comprehension of the early modern *jus ad bellum*. The just war doctrine, as applied in these texts, offered a highly flexible framework for belligerents to translate their policies into a language of law and morality. Into this mould belligerents could pour different arguments about war and force which reflected the concrete rules and categories that were commonly recognized and which made up the *jus ad bellum*.[14]

As declarations and manifestos often put great emphasis on the necessity to resort to full and open war, they betrayed a keen awareness of the distinction between war and lesser forms of use of force. This prompts the question whether, at the end of the sixteenth century, there emerged a doctrine of religious intervention in the wider structure of the just war doctrine, and if so, what it implied. As was mentioned above, the question whether a prince could or should intervene to the benefit of the subjects of another prince was actively debated in the scholarly and political literature of the sixteenth century. Two major doctrinal approaches can be distinguished from these writings. These approaches were distinct but not mutually exclusive. First, some authors claimed a right, and sometimes a duty, for princes to protect innocent people against severe violations of natural law or against tyranny. Protection against religious oppression could come under both categories. Second, authors also based the right to intervention on the fact that the peoples involved belonged to the same international community. This could be common ethnicity or religion, or reference to the universal community of mankind. In relation to religion, it meant that an attack on co-religionists in another State was an attack on the whole religion, and thus constituted an attack on any foreign people of the same denomination. The underlying reasoning was that in the absence of a superior authority, sovereign princes who were part of this community were its highest authority and as such had a right or duty to enforce its laws. Whereas the first tradition argued primarily in terms of the protection of private individuals' natural rights, the second argued in terms of the public enforcement of common order and the laws it was vested on, harking back to medieval ideas about the *jus gladii*.[15]

---

[14] Recent case studies include Randall Lesaffer, 'Defensive Warfare, Prevention and Hegemony. The Justifications for the Franco-Spanish War of 1635' (2006) 7 Journal of the History of International Law 91–123, 141–79; Pärtel Piirimäe, 'Just War Theory in Theory and Practice: The Legitimation of Swedish Intervention in the Thirty Years War' (2002) 45 Historical Journal 499.

[15] Martti Koskenniemi, 'Empire and International Law: The Real Spanish Contribution' (2011) 61 University of Toronto Law Journal 1; Raymond Kubben, 'We Should Not Stand Beside … International Legal Doctrine on Domestic Revolts and Foreign Intervention Throughout the Early Stages of the Dutch Revolt' in Paul Brood and Raymond Kubben (eds), *The Act of Abjuration: Inspired and Inspirational* (Wolf Legal Publishers 2011); Anthony Pagden, 'Gentili, Vitoria, and the Fabrication of a Natural Law of Nations' in Benedict Kingsbury and Benjamin Straumann (eds), *The Roman Foundations of the Law of Nations. Alberico Gentili and the Justice of Empire* (Oxford University Press 2010); Richard Tuck, *The Rights of War and Peace: Political Thought and the International Order from Grotius to Kant* (Oxford University Press 1999) 16–77; DJB Trim, 'If a Prince Use Tyrannie Towards his People: Interventions on Behalf of Foreign Populations in Early Modern Europe' in Brendan Simms and DJB Trim (eds), *Humanitarian Intervention: A History* (Cambridge University Press 2011); Guus van Nifterik, 'Religious and Humanitarian Intervention in Sixteenth- and Seventeenth-Century Legal Thought' in Randall Lesaffer and Georges Macours (eds), *Sovereignty and the Law of Nations*

The French Wars of Religion

The French Wars of Religion are a series of eight civil wars which ravaged France between 1562 and 1598.[16] They opposed the Calvinist minority, which was never more than ten per cent of the French population, to the Catholic majority. At stake was control over the public sphere. Whereas the Huguenots—as the French Calvinists were known—wanted the right to exercise their religion in public and a share in the government, the Catholics denied this in the name of the unity of Church and State. From the beginning, the wars were a three-way contest with the French monarchy contriving to steer a middle course. During the reign of Charles IX (1560–1574), his regent the Queen Mother Catherine de Medici (1519–1589) tried to restore peace by making concessions to the Huguenots. This split the Catholic majority into those who were willing to compromise for the sake of national unity and rallied around the king, and the radicals led by the House of Guise, who equated heresy to sedition. Two more fault lines that run through the Catholic constituency exacerbated tensions. First, there was the contention between Gallicans and Ultramontanes. Whereas the first stressed the national identity of the French Church and its close alliance to the king who acted as its main protector, the others put obedience to Rome first and demanded the immediate implementation of the conclusions of the Council of Trent in France. Second, Catholics were also divided on the issue of foreign policy. Radical Catholics proposed to give precedence to the prosecution of Protestantism over geopolitical concerns, and therefore supported cooperation with Spain, the self-acclaimed champion of the Catholic faith. This had been one of the bases under the Peace of Cateau-Cambrésis between France and Spain (1559) at the end of the reign of Henry II (1547–1559). The moderate faction, often in alliance with the Huguenots, gave priority to geopolitical concerns and proposed to return to the policies of Francis I (1515–1547) and Henry II from before the peace, which had made France into the centre of a multi-religious coalition—including German protestant princes and the Ottoman sultan—against France's historic enemy, Spain.

For the first ten years, the French monarchy managed to keep a somewhat independent course, but in 1572 this radically changed. The alleged collusion of the royal government with the Guise family in plotting the Saint Bartholomew massacre destroyed the confidence of the Huguenots in the monarchy.[17] The massacres

(16th–18th Centuries): Proceedings of the Colloquium Organised at the Palace of the Academy, Brussels, 26 April 2002 (Koninklijke Vlaamse Akademie van België 2006).

[16] For the French Wars of Religion: Mack P Holt, *The French Wars of Religion, 1562–1629* (2nd edn, Cambridge University Press 2005); Robert J Knecht, *The Rise and Fall of Renaissance France 1483–1610* (Fontana Press 1996); JHM Salmon, *Society in Crisis: France in the Sixteenth Century* (Routledge 1975); NM Sutherland, *The Huguenot Struggle for Recognition* (Yale University Press 1980); Geoffrey Treasure, *The Huguenots* (Yale University Press 2013).

[17] NM Sutherland, *The Massacre of St. Bartholomew and the European Conflict* (Barnes & Noble 1972).

drove Charles IX and his successor **Henry III** (1574–1589) into the arms of the radical Catholic faction. The ensuing wars, wherein the Huguenots fought for their survival as a political force, provided the context for the most vocal expressions of Calvinist resistance theories aimed at the king. Leadings writers such as Theodor Beza (1519–1605), François Hotman (1524–1590), and the author of *Vindiciae contra tyrannos* (1579) stressed the elective and consensual character of kingship. They argued that through his tyrannical behaviour the French king had broken his compacts with the people and with God and could be deposed or even killed.[18]

Relations between Henry III and the Catholic faction were uneasy from the beginning, but after 1576 they gradually broke down, in part due to the behaviour of Henry's heir, his younger brother François (1555–1584), Duke of Alençon, later of Anjou. Seeking to enhance his position at court and to put pressure on his brother, Anjou at times allied himself to the Huguenot cause. He pleaded for a French intervention on the side of the Dutch rebels in their fight against Spain in the Low Countries and eventually accepted the sovereignty over the Netherlands from the hands of the Dutch.[19] But it was his death rather than his actions in life which destroyed Henry's position with the Catholics.

Anjou's demise in June 1584 raised the spectre of a Huguenot king on the throne of France. Next in line was Henry of the House of Bourbon, King of Navarre and Prince of Béarn. Duke Henry of Guise (1550–1588) reacted by forming a coalition to support the rival claim of another Bourbon, the elderly Cardinal Charles of Bourbon (1523–1590). After having secured financial support from Spain, the Catholic League raised its banner to oppose Navarre's succession and exterminate Protestantism. The widespread fear of a Protestant king, combined with Spanish subsidies, gave the League the leverage to force the king's hand. Henry III had little choice but to put himself at its head.[20]

The radicalization of the League and the power struggle between Henry III and Guise led to disaster. In October 1588, during the meeting of the Estates General at Blois, the King had the Duke and his brother, Cardinal Louis of Guise (1555–1588), arrested and murdered. The desperate attempt of the king to restore his authority backfired. The League, now a coalition of nobles under the leadership of Charles of Guise, Duke of Mayenne (1554–1611), the radical regime of the Sixteen at Paris, and associations of city notables in the provinces, turned upon the King. The Faculty of Theology of the Sorbonne declared him deposed from the throne and the Pope excommunicated Henry III and dispensed his subjects from their

---

[18] See the sources cited in n 5; see also Stephanus Junius Brutus, *Vindiciae, Contra Tyrannos, or, Concerning the Legitimate Power of a Prince over the People and of the People over a Prince* (George Garnett ed, Cambridge University Press 1994); Donald R Kelley, *François Hotman: A Revolutionary Ordeal* (Princeton University Press 1973) 227–91.

[19] Mack P Holt, *The Duke of Anjou and the Politique Struggle During the Wars of Religion* (Cambridge University Press 1986).

[20] On the Catholic League: JHM Salmon, 'The Paris Sixteen, 1584–1594: The Social Analysis of a Revolutionary Movement' in JHM Salmon, *Renaissance and Revolt: Essays in the Intellectual and Social History of Early Modern France* (Cambridge University Press 1987).

obedience. The clash between Henry III and the Catholic League produced some of the most sweeping literature on resistance against tyranny of the period.[21]

Henry III was left with no alternative but to ally himself with Navarre. Both kings marched upon Paris and laid a siege around the city. Henry III paid the highest price for his betrayal of the Catholic League. On 1 August 1589, he was stabbed by a monk. Before he died, he recognized Henry of Navarre as his legitimate successor.

The death of the last Valois king changed the character of the war of religion into a contest for the throne of France. On one side stood Henry IV, supported by the Huguenots and a gradually expanding number of moderate Catholics; on the other side, the Catholic League. As its support among Gallicans dwindled, it became increasingly dependent upon Spain. The political discourse of the League now centred on the right of succession. Whereas some concentrated their argument on the claim that Charles of Bourbon—Charles X—was a generation closer to the former incumbents than Henry IV, the majority based themselves on the paramountcy of the so-called 'Law of Catholicity'—which demanded that the king be Catholic—over the Salic Law—which stipulated that the throne only passed through the male line. After the death of Charles X in May 1590, the defenders of the League moved to underscore the elective character of the monarchy.[22]

The Justification for Intervention of 1590

Just like the Dutch Revolt (1567–1648), the French Wars of Religion were internationalized from their inception. On the Huguenot side, German Protestant princes, the English Queen Elizabeth (1558–1603), and the Dutch rebels rendered diplomatic, financial, and military assistance. On the Catholic side, Spain and the Pope were the main, albeit not the only, foreign supporters.[23]

All through the decades of its involvement, the Spanish monarchy chose not to enter into an open war with France, but tried to keep its commitment as low as possible. As long as the war was a three-way conflict, Spain had leeway to pressure the French monarchy to do its bidding through the leverage of its support to radical Catholics, thus being able to manage its commitment. At no time before 1590 had France stood very high on the lists of priorities of Madrid. In the 1560s and 1570s, the focus was on the war in the Mediterranean against the Ottoman Turks.[24] After an effective truce had been reached in 1577–78, Philip II had to divert the resources of his empire to fighting the Dutch rebels, while in 1580 he invaded Portugal to

[21] eg Jean Boucher, *De Iusta Henrici Tertii Abdicatione e Francorum Regno* (Nivellius 1589).

[22] On the political thought of the League: Frederic J Baumgartner, *Radical Reactionaries: The Political Thought of the French Catholic League* (Droz 1975).

[23] Geoffrey Parker, 'Spain, her Enemies and the Revolt of the Netherlands, 1559–1648' (1970) 49 Past and Present 72.

[24] Norman Housley, *The Later Crusades: From Lyons to Alcazar 1274–1580* (Oxford University Press 1992) 137–50.

enforce his claim on the throne of the Braganzas.[25] The intervention by Queen Elizabeth in the Netherlands in 1585 and the raids by English privateers on Spanish shipping and bases in the Caribbean in 1585–86 led to an overhaul of Spanish strategy. England was now indicated as the linchpin of the international, Protestant coalition.[26] It became the maxim of imperial strategy that England needed to be taken out first by a regime change which would bring a Catholic monarch on the English throne as in the days of Mary Tudor (1553–58) and her husband Philip II. Once England was returned to the Catholic fold, its support to the Dutch and French Calvinists would stop and Spain would be able to successfully end the Dutch rebellion and help the French Catholics to victory. The failed invasion attempt with the Armada of 1588 was the direct result of this strategic review.[27]

Whereas Spain's enemies accused Philip II of wanting to subject Europe to its domination and seeking *monarchia universalis*, the Spanish king and his advisers saw their strategy in defensive terms.[28] They perceived the hand of an international conspiracy of Protestant and some Catholic powers, even involving the Turks, to dismantle the Spanish monarchy and destroy the Catholic Church. Philip II held a Messianic view of his kingship, seeing himself as the divinely appointed champion of the Church against the onslaught of heretics and the Turks. As the Spanish empire was the instrument to do this, its defence was tied in with the cause of Catholicism.[29]

Spanish involvement in France was greatly stepped up through the Treaty of Joinville of 31 December 1584, which Spain made with the Duke of Guise and Charles of Bourbon after the death of Anjou. Since the late 1570s, the Spanish embassy in France had gradually developed stronger ties with Henry of Guise, but now it committed itself and its French strategy completely to him. Thereby it tied its lot to the success of one player, and lost the freedom to manage its commitments. In exchange for some future territorial concessions and the promise to apply the decisions of the Council of Trent, Spain promised a generous subsidy and effectively recognized the claim of Charles of Bourbon to the throne.[30]

---

[25] Roland Cueto, '1580 and All That … Philip II and the Politics of Portuguese Succession' (1992) 8 Portuguese Studies 150.

[26] RB Wernham, *Before the Armada: The Growth of English Foreign Policy* (Jonathan Cape 1966) 355–405.

[27] Colin Martin and Geoffrey Parker, *The Spanish Armada* (Mandolin 1999); Henry Kamen, *Philip of Spain* (Yale University Press 1997) 242–300; Geoffrey Parker, *The Grand Strategy of Philip II* (Yale University Press 1998) 111–203; Geoffrey Parker, 'David or Goliath? Philip II and His World in the 1580s' in Geoffrey Parker, *Empire, War and Faith in Early Modern Europe* (Allen Lane 2002); Valentin Vazquez de Prada, 'Philippe II et la France. De Cateau-Cambrésis à Vervins. Quelques réflexions. Quelques précisions' in Jean-François Labourdette, Jean-Pierre Poissou, and Marie-Catherine Vignal (eds), *Le Traité de Vervins* (Presses de l'Université Paris-Sorbonne 2000).

[28] Franz Bosbach, *Monarchia Universalis. Ein politischer Leitbegriff der frühen Neuzeit* (Vandenhoeck & Ruprecht 1988) 64–86.

[29] Geoffrey Parker, 'The Place of Tudor England in the Messianic Vision of Philip II of Spain' (2002) 12 Transactions of the Royal Historical Society 167.

[30] Dumont, *Corps universel diplomatique* (n 2) vol V.1, 441–43; PP de Törne, 'Philippe II et Henri de Guise: Le début de leurs relations (1578)' (1931) 167 Revue Historique 323; De Lamar Jensen, *Diplomacy and Dogmatism: Bernardino de Mendoza and the French Catholic League* (Harvard University Press 1964) 51–92.

The murder of Henry III and the succession by Henry IV further forced Philip's hand. In the autumn of 1589, the Castilian Council of State debated shifting the priority from the English enterprise and the war in the Netherlands to the French theatre. Even a generous offer of truce to the Dutch rebels was entertained, but came to nothing. In February 1590, before the start of the new campaigning season, the Council advised a two-pronged attack on France. Alessandro Farnese (1545–92), the Duke of Parma and Governor-General of the Spanish Netherlands, would enter from the North with the Army of Flanders, while the fleet which was prepared for England would be diverted to land a force in Brittany.[31]

On 8 March 1590, the government of Philip II issued a justification for its planned military intervention in the form of a public declaration. The French edition was accompanied by a letter to Spain's primate, Cardinal Gaspar de Quiroga y Vela, Archbishop of Toledo (1512–94). This betrayed its main purpose. It was to mobilize money from the Church for the enterprise.

The declaration was not a declaration of war, but a statement of intention to fight the French Protestants and an exhortation to all Catholic princes to join the cause. If there was no intention to declare a formal war, the declaration wanted to justify Spain's action under the doctrine of just war. It followed the standard outline of a declaration of just war opposing the injustices committed by the enemy to their own record of acting justly and benevolently. The historical narrative, which was kept brief and was without chronological order, reached back to the Peace of Câteau-Cambrésis. What distinguished the declaration most from a normal declaration of war were the targeted enemy and the victims of its actions.

The enemy the declaration was aimed at was not a single foreign sovereign; it was the international coalition of Lutherans and Calvinists.[32] This placed the Spanish intervention in France into the wider framework of its grand strategy to defend the Church and its empire. But express reference was only made to the defence of faith and Church.

The declaration listed four major acts of injustice the enemy had committed. These fulfilled the condition of just cause, while at the same time indicating the unrelenting desire of the enemy to do harm and the absolute necessity to stop him by force. Only two of the enemy's perpetrations concerned Spanish interests. These were the Dutch rebellion and the opposition against the legitimate claims of Philip II to the Portuguese throne. The other two had harmed third parties. First, there was the fact that the Protestants had spread heresy through France, thereby causing sedition and civil strife, and brought destruction upon France. Great emphasis was put on the sufferings of Church and clerics.[33] This was contrasted

---

[31] Geoffrey Parker, *The Army of Flanders and the Spanish Road 1567–1659* (2nd edn, Cambridge University Press 1990) 244–45; Parker, *Grand Strategy* (n 27) 274–75; Geoffrey Parker, *Felipe II: La Biografía Definitiva* (Planeta 2010) 879–80.

[32] 'par les destables hereticques de la secte de Luther & de Calvin': *Declaration du roy d'Espaigne* (n 6) 4.

[33] 's'estans les guerres civiles allumees audict Royaume par le moyen des pestiferes heresies, appuyees de ceux qui les devoyent estraindre des premiers: s'estans la France remplie de meurtres, brigandages, volleries, rasementz, & desmolitions d'Eglises, Monasteres, & saincts lieux, carnages, & boucheries des religieux, violemens de Nonnains, & mille autres impietez commisez': ibid, 4.

to the aid the Spanish king had given his brother-in-law Charles IX with money and men to uphold peace and order. Second, the heretics held the legitimate King Charles X, the Cardinal of Bourbon, in unjust captivity.[34]

It was these two last reproaches, and particularly the former one of those, that served as the main cause for Spain's intervention. The others were accessory, but brought the intervention under the just war doctrine on the basis of the more traditional argumentation of defending and enforcing Spanish rights. That leaves the question why Spain thought it could use force to counter harm done to French Catholics.

The declaration did not elaborate on the captivity of Charles X, beyond stating that his liberation was a goal of the Spanish and their allies. But it amounted to a just cause. By referring to Charles X's unjust captivity, Spain implied that it acted in defence of an ally. It recognized Charles to be the legitimate sovereign of France, and it had an alliance treaty with him, that of Joinville. Under the classic interpretation of just war, the defence of a sovereign ally was an accepted cause.

The text and context of the declaration construed Spain's justification around the damage inflicted upon the French kingdom, its people, and the Church. The declaration did not provide an express argument why this was thought to legitimate Spain's intervention, but the whole build-up of the text made the underlying reasoning clear. This reasoning consisted of three logical steps. First, the attack on the French Church was an attack on the whole Church. Second, heresy equated sedition, civil strife, and the utter ruin of kingdoms. Putting the two together meant that the Protestant attack on the French Church would lead to the ruin of Europe. The latter conclusion was expressed where the text stated that heresy had led to the division of Europe and that this would allow the Turks to destroy Christianity.[35] Third, the Spanish king like all true Christian princes had a right, or even a duty, to defend the Church and Christianity from this attack. Intervention was thus justified on the basis of the unity of the Church and of Christianity, and of the responsibility of the Spanish king as one of the highest officials of Christianity to protect them.

All this was corroborated by the expressed goals of the intervention. These were the liberation of Charles X and the extermination of heresy in France. The latter was said to be a first, necessary step for the wider extermination of heresy in Europe and the salvation of Christianity. Once this was achieved, Europe would be reunited and would be able to divert its resources against the Turks and reconquer the Holy Land. By naming the intervention in France as a precondition to Christian unity, the text expressed the strategic shift from England to France, which Madrid had decided on and implemented by redirecting the fleet from England to Brittany.

---

[34] 'Tres-chrestien Roy de France Charles dixiesme iniustement detenu en captivité par les hereticques': ibid, 7.

[35] 'ont mis tel desordre en la Chrestienté que les Turcz se promettent d'emporter ce qui reste d'entier en icelle par la division qu'on y voit de tous costez': ibid, 6.

The Justification for Intervention of 1595

Despite the decisions taken in February 1590, Spain proved hesitant to execute them. Parma was especially reluctant as he feared that the Dutch would profit from the redirection of the Army of Flanders to the south.[36] But the siege of Paris by Henry IV left Spain with no choice. In July 1590, Parma invaded France with 20,000 men and, after some brilliant manoeuvring, lured Henry IV into lifting the siege. Spanish troops entered Paris. In 1592, Parma had to repeat this invasion, this time to break the siege of Rouen. By late 1592, the war was dragging into a stalemate and negotiations between the two sides intensified. The gradual erosion of support for the League made the continuation of the war effort ever more dependent on Spanish support.[37] More than two years after the death of the Catholic pretender, Charles X, Philip II wanted to solve the matter of succession. At the meeting of the Estates General in Paris in the spring of 1593, his envoy pushed for the election of Philip II's oldest daughter—Isabella Clara Eugenia (1566–1633), who through her mother was the granddaughter of Henry II—to the French throne.[38] Hereby, Philip II overplayed his hand and triggered a backlash of French feelings against this attempt to put a foreign princess on the throne of France.[39] In the face of Henry IV's expected conversion, support for the League further crumbled. On 25 July, Henry IV converted to Catholicism. In February 1594, he was anointed king at Chartres and, one month later, entered Paris. Before the campaign of 1595, he declared open war upon Spain. Hereby, Henry IV wanted to underscore that the war was now an international conflict between two sovereign powers, thus hoping to rally Protestants and Gallican Catholics around his flag. Moreover, through this declaration, Henry IV catered to the wishes of his Dutch and English allies as he was now fully committing to the fight against the common enemy.[40]

The French declaration of war of 17 January adhered to the traditional structure of justifications of war. The war was said to be a final resort against the incessant attacks and injustices committed by Philip II. These forced the king to turn to war in order to defend his honour and his subjects. Apart from the attacks on France, lands, property, subjects, and religion, the declaration mentioned Spain's ambition

---

[36] Parker, *Army of Flanders* (n 31) 244–46.
[37] Holt, *French Wars of Religion* (n 16) 141–51; Vincent J Pitts, *Henri IV of France: His Reign and Age* (John Hopkins University Press 2009) 155–69.
[38] *Harague faicte en l'assemblee generale des trois Estatz de France le second iour d'Avril, par les tres-illustre, & tres-excellent Duc de Ferie, au nom du Roy Catholique, pour l'election d'un Roy Tres-Chrestien* (Iean Pillehotte 1593). The text did not mention her name but the implication was clear. Later, the Spanish envoy became more assertive.
[39] Gustave Baguenault de Puchesse, 'La politique de Philippe II dans les affaires de France, 1559–1598' (1879) 13 Revue des questions historiques 5, 51–7; Luc Duerloo, *Dynasty and Piety: Archduke Albert (1598–1621) and Habsburg Political Culture in an Age of Religious Wars* (Ashgate 2012) 39–41; Albert Mousset, 'Les droits de l'infante Isabelle-Claire-Eugenie à la couronne de France' (1914) 16 Revue Hispanique 46.
[40] Holt, *French Wars of Religion* (n 16) 151–65; Jensen, *Diplomacy and Dogmatism* (n 30) 190–210; Pitts, *Henri IV* (n 37) 169–96.

as a cause of the disturbance of Christianity.[41] In this way, the declaration coupled the defence of France to the wider interest of the liberty of the whole of Europe and brought it under the traditional discourse of the Protestant coalition to ward off Spain's desire for *monarchia universalis*. Lastly, the text singled out the assassination attempts against Henry IV among the just causes for war.

Remarkably, the Madrid government chose not to address these accusations in its counter-declaration of 7 March 1595, but provided its own justification for its actions. As was mentioned above, the statement was not a declaration of war, but named Henry IV and his adherents public enemies. The declaration gave all French Catholics who had separated themselves from the League two months to return into its fold. The declaration denied Henry de Béarn, as he was consistently called, the right to wage war upon Spain because he was not the sovereign king of France. It mentioned the papal refutation of Henry's claim to the throne in this context. Thereby, the French declaration was summarily set aside.

From a legal perspective, the indication of Henry IV and his adherents as 'public enemies' is as problematic as it is striking. As a legal term, it seems to imply that Henry IV and his adherents, not being lawful belligerents, did not fall under the protection of the laws of war but were rebels who could be punished under criminal law. The declaration also suggested that the French pretender's faction was considered the public enemy of Christianity, and that the Spanish king could act as its protector. But it did not clearly spell out these things, while in reality, the Spanish applied the laws of war as they would in case of a regular war—just as they did by and large in the conflict against the Dutch rebels.[42] The truth of the matter was that the Spanish government did not deny Henry IV the status of belligerent in order to be allowed not the treat him as one. Its only purpose was to avoid an accusation of having violated French sovereignty; it did so by denying him sovereignty altogether. Even in this case of non-war, the Spanish declaration, as so many during the Early Modern Age, only reflected their position with regards the *jus ad bellum*, and was pushed aside the moment the matter of the application of *jus in bello* arose.

The main thrust of the Spanish declaration was to offer a justification for the Spanish intervention in France and its continued aid to the Catholic League. The same fundamental line of argument from the declaration of 1590 was reiterated, and this time more explicitly: the ruin of the French Church which was threatened through the actions of the enemy spelled the ruin of the French Kingdom and of Christianity.[43] The basic legitimation for intervention was the unity of the

---

[41] 'la discorde & iuste ialousie, que l'ambition dudit Roy d'Espagne a excitée en [la Chrestienté]': *Déclaration de la volonté du Roy*, (n 1) 5.

[42] Geoffrey Parker, 'Early Modern Europe' in Michael Howard, George J Andeopoulos, and Mark R Shulman (eds), *The Laws of War: Constraints on Warfare in the Western World* (Yale University Press 1994).

[43] 'de ruiner & extirper entierement la susdite Religion, en un Royaume où elle a toûjours fleuri, ce qui est la chose la plus lamentable qu'on pourroit imaginer, non seulement pour ledit Royaume, mais aussi pour toute la Chrestienté': *Declaration de Philippe II*, in Dumont, *Corps universel diplomatique* (n 2) vol V.1, 515.

Church and of Christianity and the responsibility of the Spanish king to act as their protector.

The declaration followed the standard scheme for declaring just war by opposing the malevolence of the enemy to the benevolence of Spain, bringing the historical narrative back to 1559. The indicated enemy was more narrowly circumscribed than had been the case in 1590: Henry of Béarn and his supporters. Although the declaration refuted the idea that this was an international war between two foreign powers, in the historical narration some of that seeped through. Whereas the injustices committed against Spain were ultimately laid at the doorstep of the Protestants and their allies, the text stressed the indulgence of Spain in not having resorted to war against the French throne. The implication towards Anjou's and Henry III's betrayal of Spanish interests was clear from the narration. The text also implicated the ingratitude of the French monarchy in the face of the many good deeds Spain had bestowed upon it. In this respect, the declaration pitched the Spanish justification more as a traditional defence of its own rights against injustices committed than the 1590 declaration had done. Nevertheless, the focus was on intervention.

The sole stated goal of the intervention was the preservation of the Catholic religion and Church in France and to aid the Catholics. The stress was such as to exclude any reference to a Spanish claim on the throne.

Religious Intervention as an Instance of Imperial Defence

The French declaration of war against Spain and the Spanish counter-declaration marked the final escalation of the French wars of religion and Spain's involvement therein. Regardless of the Spanish legal position, it was now first and foremost a war between two sovereign kings and it was fought as regular war. As an increasing number of radical Catholic leaders and towns made their peace with Henry IV, especially after Pope Clement VIII (1592–1605) granted him absolution and lifted his excommunication in August 1595, the persuasive force of the Spanish position that it interfered in an internal conflict rapidly dissipated. The war quickly petered out as the two sides were war weary from the very start of the 'official' war. The French reconquest of the northern town of Amiens in September 1597 and the submission of the last of the great radical nobles in January 1598 convinced Philip II, who under the anticipation of approaching death wanted to disengage from the different armed conflicts the Spanish monarchy was involved in, that it was time to make peace. On 2 May 1598, just days after Henry IV had reached a new settlement with the Huguenots with the Edict of Nantes, the Peace of Vervins was concluded between France and Spain.[44] Legally speaking, it was a real peace treaty which ended an actual war, in the sense of a formal war, between two sovereign

---

[44] Annette Finley-Croswhite, *Henry IV and the Towns: The Pursuit of Legitimacy in French Urban Society, 1589–1610* (Cambridge University Press 1999); Holt, *French Wars of Religion* (n 16) 164–77; Parker, *Felipe II* (n 31) 929–30.

powers. The argument of intervention had served its purpose out, and was silently surrendered.[45]

To Philip II and his counsellors, the interventions in France were part of the overall grand strategy of the Spanish Empire, which they considered inherently defensive. The American historian Paul Kennedy has erected Habsburg Spain as the classic case for imperial overstretch. In his analysis, the vastness of the commitments for the imperial defence of Spain ultimately outweighed its resources and doomed it to collapse.[46] Whatever the limitations of such historic determinism, it is correct that the sheer weight of Spanish power instilled fear in the minds of the other princes of Europe for their survival as independent powers and that the multitude of the Spanish king's lands, titles, and claims constantly put him in the way of conflict. Whereas the mere will to hold the empire together was enough for other princes to interpret this as an ambition to *monarchia universalis*, Spain considered the defence of every land, title, or claim an essential condition to the survival of its empire. Spain feared that the loss of one territory or the concession of one claim would trigger a chain reaction and invite Spain's multiple enemies to fall upon it. It was this 'domino theory' that made Spain blind to the diplomatic fallout of the aggressive way in which it reacted to the revolt in the Netherlands in the 1560s or the way in which it enforced Philip's claim to the Portuguese throne in 1580. It also caused Spain to equate the survival of the Spanish monarchy to the perseverance of its factual hegemony over much of Christian Europe. It was this rationale that made Spain's grand strategy in its own eyes into one of imperial defence. In Philip's mind, this was strongly linked to the defence of the Catholic Church and faith, which he believed God had bestowed upon him.

The justification under the *jus ad bellum* Spain offered in its declarations of 1590 and 1595 for its intervention in France was designed to fit this grand strategy of imperial defence. For this, the full potential of the just war doctrine was exploited in two manners. First, in the declarations, religious intervention was not erected as a distinct category of use of force but squared with the just war doctrine and its conditions of just cause, righteous intention, and necessity. The major distinction with a regular declaration of war lay not in the way the just war doctrine operated, but only in the claim that this 'just war' did not amount to a formal war, but something else. As such, the declarations indicated a clear understanding of a distinction between perfect and imperfect war, or in nineteenth-century terms, between war and measures short of war.

The two Spanish declarations followed the standard outline of regular declarations of just war by offering a historical narrative which opposed the incessant injustices of the enemy to the just and benevolent behaviour of one's own side and by putting one's own actions at the service of the higher common goal of a just peace for Christianity. As in regular declarations, the enemy's historical and recent

---

[45] Dumont, *Corps universel diplomatique* (n 2) vol V.1, 561–64.
[46] Paul Kennedy, *The Rise and Fall of Great Powers: Economic Change and Military Conflict from 1500 and 2000* (Fontana Press 1988) 39–93.

perpetrations served as so many just causes for war, while their longevity indicated the absolute necessity to use force to stop this and to have a true and just peace.

While this structure was fixed, the concrete just causes and the definition of what constituted a just peace, not to mention the common values and interests that would be sustained under it, were variable. In the Spanish declarations, three just causes were forwarded: defence of Spain's own rights, defence of an ally, and defence of the common Church and faith as a condition for the preservation and unity of Europe in the face of the Turkish threat.

The emphasis was with the latter cause. Through it, the Spanish declarations presented religious intervention as a form of just war. Its legitimation was on the basis that an attack against one part of the Church was an attack on the whole, while an attack on the Church spelled rebellion, sedition, and ultimately the ruin of the whole of Christianity through its division. In combination with the under-lying reason that the king of Spain, as any Christian prince, held a responsibility to protect the common faith and the order of Europe, this justified Spain's interven-tion. In short, Spain's justification of its intervention was based on the idea of com-mon community, order, values, and laws rather than on the protection of innocent victims. Religious intervention was an act of 'collective defence', rather than inter-vention on behalf of a third party. Remarkably but coincidentally, on this point, the Spanish declarations came close to the theory of the Protestant Gentili.[47] The declarations stayed far from an appeal to a right to resistance. This was unneces-sary as Henry IV was not recognized to be the legitimate king by Spain, and would probably have been unwanted, as it undercut the sacred respect for monarchical power and would have offered too close a parallel with the justifications the Dutch deployed for their rebellion against the Spanish king.[48]

Second, religious intervention was expressly connected to the grand strategy of imperial defence through the language and logic of just war. Because Spain con-sidered its empire the divine instrument for the salvation of Church and religion, its defence was implicitly linked to the higher goal of protecting the Church. The combining of the cause of religious intervention to the defence of Spain's own rights and interests in the causal narrative added another link between faith and empire. Lastly, the references to the unity of Christianity in the face of the Turkish threat were traditional to the discourse of war and peace in Europe since the mid-fifteenth century. At the time of Philip's father, the Emperor Charles V (1519–1558), the claim to lead the Christian West in a crusade against the Turks had been used to claim the secular overlordship over the Christian West, next to the pope, its spir-itual leader. The external defence against the common enemy was the first duty of the secular head of Christianity. The discourse of a crusade against the Turks in the two declarations was a reminder of that tradition of imperial overlordship, or *monarchia universalis* as Philip's enemies would have it. It also harked back to the

---

[47] Alberico Gentili, *De iure belli libri tres* (text of 1612, Clarendon Press 1933) 1.15.116.
[48] Martin van Gelderen, *The Political Thought of the Dutch Revolt 1555–1590* (Cambridge University Press 1992).

old conception of the *respublica Christiana* as a community of Christian princes and republics under the supreme authority of the pope and emperor and the supreme aegis of the *jus commune* of Roman and canon law.[49] It was remarkable that the Spanish declarations singled out Spain's role in defending the common Church and the interest of Christianity over the defence of its own interests or the defence of an ally. Herein, the English justification of its intervention in the Low Countries in 1585 was radically different as its line of argument preferred the defence of English interests in the Low Countries and its moral obligations to the people of the Low Countries because of the longstanding bonds of trade and kingship rather than the defence of a common religion.[50] The Spanish king emphasized his responsibility as a leading monarch within Christianity and expressed his sense of the duty imposed upon him by God. Even in choosing the discourse of religious intervention, Spain could not stop from styling itself like the European hegemonic power it was. By linking faith and empire, Spain made any attack on its interests an attack on the common faith, and cloaked the defence of its empire with the additional moral weight of doing God's bidding and defending the faith. In terms of the just war doctrine, the defence of faith and empire were joined into one single just cause. Moreover, whereas the violation of a Spanish right might suffice to give Spain just cause, it was in this connection of its empire to the common purpose of safeguarding religion that provided the necessity to use force and of its righteous intentions. In sum, while the declarations stressed that the empire stood at the service of religion, in fact religious intervention stood as much at the service of empire.

Whereas religious intervention would not survive long into the seventeenth century as an argument for use of force among the princes of Europe, the 1590 and 1595 declarations in one way preconfigured a legal strategy for justification of war under the just war doctrine that Spain and other great powers would further develop and use in the seventeenth century outside the context of religious warfare. This strategy operated a vague notion of what can be called 'imperial' or 'hegemonic defence' as a concept. It was based on the equation of the interests of the actual— Spain—or would-be hegemonic power—France—with the existing or desired order of Europe considered to be inherently just. Every attack on a right or interest of the hegemonic power hence automatically became an attack which jeopardized the survival or realization of European order, eliciting a just reaction. This connection between one's own and the common interest was not essential to argue a just cause—claiming an attack on one's own interest sufficed for this—but it was to argue the necessity of the war as an instrument to attain a just peace and a just order. The attack on one's own interest, or preferably a series of attacks, exposed the stubborn determination of the enemy to overhaul the legitimate order of Europe.

---

[49] John M Headley, *The Emperor and his Chancellor. A Study of the Imperial Chancellery under Gattinara* (Cambridge University Press 1983); James Muldoon, *Empire and Order: The Concept of Empire, 800–1800* (Macmillan 1999); Randall Lesaffer, 'Charles V, *Monarchia Universalis* and the Law of Nations' (2003) 71 Legal History Review 79.

[50] *A Declaration of the Causes Mooving the Queene of England to give aide to the Defence of the People Afflicted and Oppressed in the Lowe Countries* (Christopher Barker 1585).

By consequence, so the underlying reasoning went, war was necessary to stop this and preserve the order of Europe. The French declaration of war against Spain of May 1635, and the Spanish counter-declaration that followed this, illustrate this well as both sides applied the same strategy of 'hegemonic defence'. In the case of Spain, Catholicism and religious unity formed the foundation of that order. For France, it was the preservation of the liberty of all European princes and republics against Spain's desire for *monarchia universalis*, a liberty France considered itself the foremost protector of and on which it based its moral right to be the leading power of Europe.[51]

The argumentative strategy of 1635, just as that of religious intervention used by Spain in 1590 and 1595, bore testimony to the malleability of the just war doctrine. Whereas to the modern, secular mind, this is enough to undercut its authority, to the deeply religious majority of the elites from the times of the wars of religion and the ensuing century of confessionalization, its foothold in moral theology went a long way to preserve it. This, as much as its flexibility, helps to explain its resilience in the diplomatic practice throughout the Early Modern Age.[52]

Bibliography

A Declaration of the Causes Mooving the Queene of England to give aide to the Defence of the People Afflicted and Oppressed in the Lowe Countries (Christopher Barker 1585)

Baumgartner, Frederic J, *Radical Reactionaries: The Political Thought of the French Catholic League* (Droz 1975)

Baumgartner, Frederic J, *Declaring War in Early Modern Europe* (Palgrave Macmillan 2011)

Bosbach, Franz, *Monarchia Universalis: Ein politischer Leitbegriff der frühen Neuzeit* (Vandenhoeck & Ruprecht 1988)

Boucher, Jean, *De Iusta Henrici Tertii Abdicatione e Francorum Regno* (Nivellius 1589)

Brutus, Stephanus Junius, *Vindiciae, Contra Tyrannos, or, Concerning the Legitimate Power of a Prince over the People and of the People over a Prince* (George Garnett ed, Cambridge University Press 1994)

Chesterman, Simon, *Just War or Just Peace? Humanitarian Intervention and International Law* (Oxford University Press 2001)

Cueto, Roland, '1580 and All That ... Philip II and the Politics of Portuguese Succession' (1992) 8 Portuguese Studies 150

De Lamar Jensen, *Diplomacy and Dogmatism: Bernardino de Mendoza and the French Catholic League* (Harvard University Press 1964)

Déclaration de la volonté du Roy sur l'ouverture de la guerre contre le Roy d'Espagne (Iamet Mettayer and Pierre L'Huillier 1595)

---

[51] Lesaffer, 'Defensive Warfare' (n 14) 174–79. On the intellectual background of these two visions on European order, see Peter Schröder, 'The Concepts of Universal Monarchy and Balance of Power in the First Half of the Seventeenth Century—A Case Study', Chapter 4 in this volume.

[52] See Randall Lesaffer, 'Too Much History: From War as Sanction to the Sanctioning of War' in Marc Weller and Alexia Solomou (eds), *The Oxford Handbook of the Use of Force in International Law* (Oxford University Press 2015).

Declaration du roy d'Espaigne sur les troubles, misères, & Calamitez qui affligent la Chrestienté, & notamment le Royaume de France. Avec les lettres de sa Maiesté au Clergé pour fournir de leurs moyens aux fraiz de la guerre. Sur la copie imprimee a Douay. Par Iean Bogard Imprimeur de sa Maiesté Catholique (Loys Tantillon 1590)

Duerloo, Luc, *Dynasty and Piety: Archduke Albert (1598–1621) and Habsburg Political Culture in an Age of Religious Wars* (Ashgate 2012)

Dumont, Jean, *Corps universel diplomatique du droit des gens* (Brunel and Husson 1726–1731) vol V.1

Edict du Roy nostre Syre en forme de declaration contre la publication de guerre, faicte par le Prince de Bearne, soy disant roy de France, par lequel sa Majesté declaire, sa volonté estre d'entretenir la Saincte Ligue en faveur des Catholicques de France (Rutger Velpius 1595)

Elbe, Joachim von, 'The Evolution of the Concept of Just War in International Law' (1939) 33 American Journal of International Law 665

Fernandez-Santamaria, JA, *The State, War and Peace: Spanish Political Thought in the Renaissance 1516–1559* (Cambridge University Press 1977)

Finley-Croswhite, Annette, *Henry IV and the Towns: The Pursuit of Legitimacy in French Urban Society, 1589–1610* (Cambridge University Press 1999)

Gelderen, Martin van, *The Political Thought of the Dutch Revolt 1555–1590*

Gentili, Alberico, *De iure belli libri tres* (text of 1612, Clarendon Press 1933)

Gill, Terry D, 'Just War Doctrine in Modern Context' in Terry D Gill and Wilco Heere (eds), *Reflections on Principles and Practice of International Law: Essays in Honour of Leo J. Bouchez* (Martinus Nijhoff 2000)

Haggenmacher, Peter, *Grotius et la doctrine de la guerre juste* (Presses Universitaires de France 1983)

Harague faicte en l'assemblee generale des trois Estatz de France le second iour d'Avril, par les tres-illustre, & tres-excellent Duc de Ferie, au nom du Roy Catholique, pour l'election d'un Roy Tres-Chrestien (Iean Pillehotte 1593)

Headley, John M, *The Emperor and his Chancellor: A Study of the Imperial Chancellery under Gattinara* (Cambridge University Press 1983)

Heraclides, Alexis, 'Humanitarian Intervention in International Law 1830–1939: The Debate' (2014) 16 Journal of the History of International Law 26

Holt, Mack P, *The Duke of Anjou and the Politique Struggle During the Wars of Religion* (Cambridge University Press 1986)

Holt, Mack P, *The French Wars of Religion, 1562–1629* (2nd edn, Cambridge University Press 2005)

Housley, Norman, *The Later Crusades: From Lyons to Alcazar 1274–1580* (Oxford University Press 1992)

Kamen, Henry, *Philip of Spain* (Yale University Press 1997)

Kelley, Donald R, *François Hotman: A Revolutionary Ordeal* (Princeton University Press 1973)

Kennedy, Paul, *The Rise and Fall of Great Powers: Economic Change and Military Conflict from 1500 and 2000* (Fontana Press 1988)

Kingdom, Robert M, 'Calvinism and Resistance Theory, 1550–1580' in JH Burns and Mark Goldie (eds), *The Cambridge History of Political Thought 1450–1700* (Cambridge University Press 1991)

Klesmann, Bernd, *Bellum Solemne: Formen und Funktionen europäischer Kriegserklärungen des 17. Jahrhunderts* (Philipp von Zabern 2007)

Knecht, Robert J, *The Rise and Fall of Renaissance France 1483–1610* (Fontana Press 1996)

Koskenniemi, Martti, 'Empire and International Law: The Real Spanish Contribution' (2011) 61 University of Toronto Law Journal 1

Kubben, Raymond, 'We Should not Stand Beside ... International Legal Doctrine on Domestic Revolts and Foreign Intervention Throughout the Early Stages of the Dutch Revolt' in Paul Brood and Raymond Kubben (eds), *The Act of Abjuration: Inspired and Inspirational* (Wolf Legal Publishers 2011)

Lesaffer, Randall, 'Charles V, *Monarchia Universalis* and the Law of Nations' (2003) 71 Legal History Review 79

Lesaffer, Randall, 'Defensive Warfare, Prevention and Hegemony: The Justifications for the Franco-Spanish War of 1635' (2006) 7 Journal of the History of International Law 91–123, 141–79

Lesaffer, Randall, 'Too Much History: From War as Sanction to the Sanctioning of War' in Marc Weller and Alexia Solomou (eds), *The Oxford Handbook of the Use of Force in International Law* (Oxford University Press 2015)

Martin, Colin, and Parker, Geoffrey, *The Spanish Armada* (Mandolin 1999)

Mousset, Albert, 'Les droits de l'infante Isabelle-Claire-Eugenie à la couronne de France' (1914) 16 Revue Hispanique 46

Muldoon, James, *Empire and Order: The Concept of Empire, 800–1800* (Macmillan 1999)

Neff, Stephen C, *War and the Law of Nations: A General History* (Cambridge University Press 2005)

Neff, Stephen C, *Justice among Nations: A History of International Law* (Harvard University Press 2014)

Nifterik, Guus van, 'Religious and Humanitarian Intervention in Sixteenth- and Seventeenth-Century Legal Thought' in Randall Lesaffer and Georges Macours (eds), *Sovereignty and the Law of Nations (16th–18th Centuries): Proceedings of the Colloquium Organised at the Palace of the Academy, Brussels, 26 April 2002* (Koninklijke Vlaamse Akademie van België 2006)

Pagden, Anthony, *Lords of All the World: Ideologies of Empire in Spain, Britain and France c.1500–c.1800* (Yale University Press 1995)

Pagden, Anthony, 'Gentili, Vitoria, and the Fabrication of a Natural Law of Nations' in Benedict Kingsbury and Benjamin Straumann (eds), *The Roman Foundations of the Law of Nations: Alberico Gentili and the Justice of Empire* (Oxford University Press 2010)

Parker, Geoffrey, 'Spain, her Enemies and the Revolt of the Netherlands, 1559–1648' (1970) 49 Past and Present 72

Parker, Geoffrey, *The Army of Flanders and the Spanish Road 1567–1659* (2nd edn, Cambridge University Press 1990)

Parker, Geoffrey, 'Early Modern Europe' in Michael Howard, George J Andeopoulos, and Mark R Shulman (eds), *The Laws of War: Constraints on Warfare in the Western World* (Yale University Press 1994) 40–58

Parker, Geoffrey, *The Grand Strategy of Philip II* (Yale University Press 1998)

Parker, Geoffrey, 'David or Goliath? Philip II and His World in the 1580s' in Geoffrey Parker, *Empire, War and Faith in Early Modern Europe* (Allen Lane 2002)

Parker, Geoffrey, 'The Place of Tudor England in the Messianic Vision of Philip II of Spain' (2002) 12 Transactions of the Royal Historical Society 167

Parker, Geoffrey, *Felipe II: La Biografía Definitiva* (Planeta 2010)

Piirimäe, Pärtel, 'Just War Theory in Theory and Practice: The Legitimation of Swedish Intervention in the Thirty Years War' (2002) 45 Historical Journal 499

Pitts, Vincent J, *Henri IV of France: His Reign and Age* (John Hopkins University Press 2009)

Prada, Valentin Vazquez de, 'Philippe II et la France. De Cateau-Cambrésis à Vervins. Quelques réflexions. Quelques précisions' in Jean-François Labourdette, Jean-Pierre Poissou, and Marie-Catherine Vignal (eds), *Le Traité de Vervins* (Presses de l'Université Paris-Sorbonne 2000)

Puchesse, Gustave Baguenault de, 'La politique de Philippe II dans les affaires de France, 1559–1598' (1879) 13 Revue des questions historiques 5

Russell, H, *The Just War in the Middle Ages* (Cambridge University Press 1975)

Salmon, JHM, *Society in Crisis: France in the Sixteenth Century* (Routledge 1975)

Salmon, JHM, 'The Paris Sixteen, 1584–1594: The Social Analysis of a Revolutionary Movement' in JHM Salmon, *Renaissance and Revolt: Essays in the Intellectual and Social History of Early Modern France* (Cambridge University Press 1987)

Salmon, JHM, 'Catholic Resistance Theory, Ultramontanism, and the Royalist Response, 1580–1620' in JH Burns and Mark Goldie (eds), *The Cambridge History of Political Thought 1450–1700* (Cambridge University Press 1991)

Schröder, Peter, 'The Concepts of Universal Monarchy and Balance of Power in the First Half of the Seventeenth Century—A Case Study' Chapter 4 in this volume

Skinner, Quentin, *The Foundations of Modern Political Thought* (Cambridge University Press 1978) vol II

Sutherland, NM, *The Massacre of St. Bartholomew and the European Conflict* (Barnes & Noble 1972)

Sutherland, NM, *The Huguenot Struggle for Recognition* (Yale University Press 1980)

Tischer, Anuscha, *Offizielle Kriegsbegründungen in der frühen Neuzeit: Herrscherkommunikation in Europa zwischen Souveränität und korporativem Selbstverständnis* (LIT 2012)

Törne, PP de, 'Philippe II et Henri de Guise: Le début de leurs relations (1578)' (1931) 167 Revue Historique 323

Treasure, Geoffrey, *The Huguenots* (Yale University Press 2013)

Trim, DJB, 'If a Prince Use Tyrannie Towards his People: Interventions on Behalf of Foreign Populations in Early Modern Europe' in Brendan Simms and DJB Trim (eds), *Humanitarian Intervention: A History* (Cambridge University Press 2011)

Tuck, Richard, *The Rights of War and Peace: Political Thought and the International Order from Grotius to Kant* (Oxford University Press 1999)

Wernham, RB, *Before the Armada: The Growth of English Foreign Policy* (Jonathan Cape 1966)

Wheeler, Nicholas J, *Saving Strangers: Humanitarian Intervention in International Society* (Oxford University Press 2000)

Whitman, James Q, *The Verdict of Battle: The Law of Victory and the Making of Modern War* (Harvard University Press 2012)

Williams Jr, Robert A, *The American Indian in Western Legal Thought: The Discourse of Conquest* (Oxford University Press 1990)

6

Jus gentium and the Transformation of Latin American Nature: One More Reading of Vitoria?

Manuel Jiménez Fonseca

Introduction

Francisco de Vitoria (1483–1546) is one of the main points of reference for studies of modern international thought and international legal historiography. This privileged place stems from the fact that his scholarship was a response to some of the most important transformations of the early modern world, providing sixteenth-century Christianity with a road map to navigate the turbulent waters of an expanding and changing orb.[1]

The figure of Vitoria has been particularly relevant for recent critical studies on the history of international law.[2] Placing Vitoria in a colonial context, these works have shed light on how his legal doctrines facilitated Spanish political and economic power in Latin America. My intention is to continue this line of inquiry, albeit from a novel perspective, by exploring the other side of the coin of Spanish economic hegemony in Latin America: its power to redefine Latin American nature and transform its use. Adopting an environmental perspective to the study of the intellectual history of international law seems rather relevant at a time of deep environmental anxiety.

Christopher Columbus' arrival at Latin America inaugurated a series of momentous transformations in world history. It has, for instance, been related to the emergence of a capitalist world-economy,[3] the beginning of the scientific

---

[1] See Martti Koskenniemi, 'Empire and International Law: The Real Spanish Contribution' (2011) 61 University of Toronto Law Journal 1, 12.

[2] See eg Antony Anghie, *Imperialism, Sovereignty and the Making of International Law* (Cambridge University Press 2004) 13–31; Brett Bowden, 'The Colonial Origins of International Law: European Expansion and the Classical Standard of Civilization' (2005) 7 Journal of the History of International Law 1, 9–13; China Miéville, *Between Equal Rights: A Marxist Theory of International Law* (Brill 2005) 173–78, 184–90.

[3] Anibal Quijano and Immanuel Wallerstein, 'Latin Americanity as a Concept or the Latin Americas in the Modern World System' (1992) 134 International Journal of Social Science 549, 549–54.

International Law and Empire: Historical Explorations. First Edition. Martti Koskenniemi, Walter Rech, and Manuel Jiménez Fonseca. © Martti Koskenniemi, Walter Rech, and Manuel Jiménez Fonseca 2016. Published 2016 by Oxford University Press.

revolution,[4] and even to the origins of modernity[5]. The environment is one of the realms in which the enormous implications of the conquest of Latin America are more visible. Contemporary historians have, for instance, shed light on how it transformed the world's trade and ecology,[6] how it affected Latin American nature and environmental relations within the continent,[7] and the way in which it set in motion a process of biological homogenization of planetary dimensions[8].

Before the Spanish caravels appeared on the horizon, Latin America had been mostly hidden to and protected from the intrusion of outsiders. For centuries, its ecological, political, social, economic, and cultural reality evolved at a pace in step with the complex internal dynamics of the continent. That was to be radically changed.

Latin American nature was already described in Columbus' diaries with an eye to the possibility of finding tradable commodities.[9] The urgent need to make sense of Latin America, its nature, and peoples, stemmed mainly from a desire to exploit its natural wealth. It was also and to a large degree influenced by the self-appointed universal mission of the Crown of Spain of integrating 'the Latin American reality' within a Catholic understanding of the world. For a long time though, the *conquistadores* had the upper hand in defining the actual approach to the recently acquired overseas territories, hence shaping Latin American life. In their fervent zeal to acquire natural resources which could yield surpluses and a labour force to make them productive, the conquest of the continent became a two-edged sword which entailed the subjugation of its inhabitants on the one hand and the appropriation and commodification of nature on the other.[10]

---

[4] Antonio Barrera-Osorio, *Experiencing Nature: The Spanish Latin American Empire and the Early Scientific Revolution* (University of Texas Press 2006).

[5] See Matthew J Lauzon, 'Modernity' in Jerry H Bently (ed), *The Oxford Handbook of World History* (Oxford University Press 2011) 72.

[6] See Charles C Mann, *1493: How Europe's Discovery of the Latin Americas Revolutionised Trade, Ecology and Life on the Earth* (Granta Publications 2011).

[7] Shawn William Miller, *An Environmental History of Latin America* (Cambridge University Press 2007).

[8] Alfred W Crosby Jr, *The Columbian Exchange: Biological and Cultural Consequences of 1942* (Duke University Press 2003).

[9] See John Cummins, *The Voyage of Christopher Columbus: Columbus Own Journal of Discovery Newly Restored and Translated* (Weidenfeld and Nicolson 1992) 103. Descriptions of the Latin American physical environment abound: some can be found in pages 100, 105, 125, 127, 139.

[10] The definition of nature and the conceptualization of the relationship between humans and nature have been the focus of uncountable scholarly works, such as Michael P Nelson and J Baird Callicott (eds), *The Wilderness Debate Rages On: Continuing the Great New Wilderness Debate* (University of Georgia Press 2008). Both of these endeavours are far beyond the scope of the present work. When I use 'nature' in this chapter I am not referring to a romanticized idea of a pristine realm untouched by humans. Nature is continuously undergoing change, even without human intervention. In this article, nature refers to the phenomena of the physical world taken together, excluding humans and human creation. I will use interchangeably words such as nature, environment, the physical world, ecosystems, natural habitats, and non-human nature to refer to the same phenomena. Even though humans are part of nature, I will make an artificial separation for the sake of conceptual analysis. This understanding of nature sits comfortably with the general focus of this work on the human impact upon ecosystems and, specifically, on the ideological repertoire which served to legitimize the historical appropriation of nature that went hand-in-hand with European imperialism.

It was not long before the rapid disappearance of the colonized population drew some members of the Dominican order to question the ideological basis of the colonial enterprise and to denounce the ignominy of Spanish rule in Latin America. They explored in depth the nature of the relationship between the peoples of Latin America[11] and their new Spanish masters. Ever conscious of the harshness of the *conquistadores*, they tried to protect the former from the latter.

One consequence of the search for a more legitimate and humane vision of the Spanish empire in Latin America was the development of a vocabulary of universal rights. Some of those rights had an economic nature. Articulated by Francisco Vitoria in his famous *Relectio de Indis*, they have been presented by critical scholars as having contributed to Spanish economic hegemony in Latin America. That being true, there is still a less obvious but equally important dimension of the economic rights that Vitoria recognized, which so far have been neglected.

Apart from enhancing the economic power of the Spanish Crown the rights to private property and trade entailed a novel understanding of the relationship between humans and nature in Latin America derived from a specific conception of the boundary between the natural and social spheres. The enjoyment of those rights in the context of a growing intercontinental trade fostered the privatization and commodification of natural resources, contributing to the exploitation of Latin American ecosystems. Accordingly, there is an environmental aspect of the theories of the Spanish scholastics that needs to be explored. In order to do that, it seems pertinent to examine the colonial arguments of one of the most distinguished intellectual Spanish figures of the period, Francisco de Vitoria, and to complement them to a certain extent with the ideas of his pupil Domingo de Soto (1494–1560).

The universalization of hegemonic economic practices and cultural categories during the age of Spanish imperialism is of foremost significance not only for its historical relevance but also because of important continuities with modern globalization. Private property and free trade are still the corner stone of a neo-liberal global order. Notwithstanding the great divergences between these periods, it is still possible to affirm that embedded in particular international legal doctrines, both have naturalized rather contested visions of the good life with detrimental effects on the environment. The process of global ideological and legal homogenization, which started with the conquest of Latin America and continues in a rather different guise in our times, has created as many opportunities for cooperation as exclusion

---

[11] Finding the right term to refer to the societies that came under Spanish sway is not easy. I have avoided the use of words such as 'Indians', 'aborigines', and 'natives' due to their colonial ring. I have also rejected the term 'indigenous people' because it places colonized societies worldwide in one and the same abstract category. Referring to the colonizers as Europeans, despite the fact that this denomination is somewhat anachronistic, I have decided to refer to the colonized as 'Latin Americans' 'the population of Latin America', 'the peoples of Latin America', etc. My aim is to place both colonizer and colonized on an equal conceptual level. The terms I have chosen have their own conundrums. First, 'Latin Americans' is also anachronistic as the term 'Latin America' was only used from the nineteenth century onward. Second, the Spanish extended their power too over regions of North America. Third, not all the societies that inhabited Latin America were colonized by the Spaniards during the period to which this article refers. Finally, the term Latin America was also a colonial creation as a whole continent was named in honour of a single individual: Americo Vespuccio.

and coercion. In this regard, knowledge of the past can be useful for understanding the historical roots of oppressive agendas that had contributed—if inadvertently at times—to great human suffering and environmental damage.

The Environmental Impact of Spanish Colonization in a Nutshell

Colonization set in motion a process of environmental change. In the new milieu of imperial expansion, Latin America's natural resources were of utmost importance. Latin American and African labour extracted gold and silver at a high human cost. These precious metals gave European merchants the resources they needed to trade in Asian markets, fostering Asian economies as a result.[12] As Latin American riches were being drained, their monetary value went to the hands of the newcomers, their Latin American allies, or economic elites located in distant centres of power.[13] At the same time, colonists' demand for certain European commodities that could not be found in Latin America increased European exports. New needs on both sides of the Atlantic fostered the development of a transatlantic commercial chain controlled by an influential European merchant class.[14]

The geographical expansion and intensification of trade had important environmental consequences. Spaniards were far more plunderous than Latin Americans when they decided to exploit a specific natural resource. The search for elements of the environment that could be turned into tradable commodities was a colonists' obsession.[15] The importance of two of these goods for the Latin American colonial enterprise, namely silver and sugar, overran that of any other product. The impact of their extraction and production on Latin American nature was deep and lasting.

The mining industry was one of the main engines of social and ecological transformation in colonial Latin America. Mines entailed the establishment of complex settlements and large populations, which attracted other economic activities, stimulating at the same time the growth of colonial agriculture and pastoralism.[16] Trees were cut for timber to support shafts and tunnels in the mines. In addition, land was deforested in order to make room for cattle and cultivation. This produced

---

[12] John F Richards, 'Early Modern India and World History' (1997) 8 Journal of World History 197, 206.

[13] Elinor GK Melville, 'Global Developments and Latin American Environments' in Tom Griffiths and Libby Robin (eds), *Ecology and Empire: Environmental History of Settler Societies* (Keele University Press 1997).

[14] John H Elliott, *Empires of the Atlantic World: Britain and Spain in Latin America 1492–1830* (Yale University Press 2007) 108.

[15] See Murdo J MacLeod, *Spanish Central Latin America: A Socioeconomic History 1520–1720* (University of Texas Press 2008) 47. See also Carole Shammas, 'The Origins of the Transatlantic Colonization' in Daniel Vikers (ed), *A Companion to Colonial Latin America* (Blackwell Publishing 2003) 25, 33; and Angus Mackay, *Spain in the Middles Ages: From Frontier towards Empire 1350–1500* (McMillan 1977) 173.

[16] See John F Richards, *The Unending Frontier: An Environmental History of the Early Modern World* (University of California Press 2003) 368.

severe localized impacts. In the mining town of Potosí in the Viceroyalty of Peru not a single tree grew around the city at the end of the sixteenth century.[17] The tentacles of the mines reached as far as Chile, Paraguay, and Argentina, which were inserted in a provisioning network staggering in its size and complexity.[18] Caribbean islands also lost a sizable part of their forest cover in order to provide wood for the construction of the ships that carried silver to Spain.[19]

Notwithstanding deforestation, the most adverse impact of mines on humans was neither the consequence of axes nor burning, but mercury instead. It is quite likely that mercury pollution from silver mines in Mexico and Peru was the largest source of industrial pollution in the early modern era (1500–1800).[20] As mercury accumulated in animal and plant tissue its effects spread far from the receiving source, creating long-lasting circles of toxicity.[21] Unlike deforestation, the impact of mercury surpassed the continental reach. Nriagu claims that 'it would seem likely that the Latin American silver mines were partly responsible for the high background concentration of mercury now being reported in the global environment'.[22]

Sugar plantations reduced soil fertility and caused deforestation, having a harmful effect on the environment.[23] Before sugarcane was planted, large portions of land had to be cleared. Therefore, sugar plantations became a rival to other uses of the land, including woodland. Furthermore, as the processing of sugar required large quantities of fuelwood, producers cleared forests that would otherwise have been left intact.[24] The environmental consequences of sugar plantations were severe in the smaller Caribbean islands.[25] In the Brazil coastal area the victim of sugar plantations and other activities associated with settlement was the 1.3 million square kilometres Atlantic forest, one of the most diverse and delicate ecosystems on earth, home to more than 60 per cent of all terrestrial living species.[26]

Paradoxically and in spite of the clear ecological costs of mining and plantation agriculture, a process of environmental recovery followed the Spanish and Portuguese conquest. The lethal impact of colonization on the pre-colonial population of Latin America reduced the human pressure on the regions' landscapes.[27]

---

[17] John C Super, *Food, Conquest and Colonization in Sixteenth-Century Spanish Latin America* (University of New Mexico Press 1988) 19.

[18] Ibid.

[19] Elisabeth Dore, 'Environment and Society: Long-Term Trends in Latin America Mining' (2000) 6 Environment and History 1, 9.

[20] Richards, *The Unending Frontier* (n 16) 369.

[21] Dore, 'Environment and Society' (n 19) 9.

[22] Jerome O Nriagu, 'Mercury Pollution from the Past Mining of Gold and Silver in the Latin Americas' (1994) 149 The Science of the Total Environment 167, 179.

[23] See Stuart B Schwartz, *Sugar Plantations in the Formation of Brazilian Society: Bahia, 1550–1835* (Cambridge University Press 1985) 3; and Richards, *The Unending Frontier* (n 16) 388.

[24] Richards, *The Unending Frontier* (n 16) 413.

[25] See David Watts, 'Ecological Responses to Ecosystem Shock in the Island Caribbean: The Aftermath of Columbus, 1492–1992' in Robin A Butlin and Neil Roberts (eds), *Ecological Relations in Historical Times* (Blackwell 1995) 268, 272–77.

[26] Carlos Galindo-Leal and Ibsen de Gusmão Câmara (eds), *The Atlantic Forest of South Latin America: Biodiversity Status, Threats and Outlook* (Island Press 2003) 3.

[27] Dore, 'Environment and Society' (n 19) 7.

One and a half centuries after Columbus' first voyage, the initial population of the continent of around 70 million[28] was reduced to a tenth of its original figure. In other words, tens of millions of individuals perished.[29] As a result of deforestation, soils, forests, water, and wild life, which had been under intensive use by the peoples of Latin America for millennia, were suddenly given some centuries to regenerate.[30]

Taking into account the great environmental changes that followed Spanish conquest, Vitoria's theories need to be re-examined in order to determine their environmental ramifications. An often overlooked but important consequence of Vitoria's arguments in his *Relectio de Indis* was the possibility of appropriating Latin American nature for colonial ends. The Spanish right to war indirectly led to this result, as in the case of defeat it was legitimate to dispossess Latin Americans of their land and natural resources.[31] This notwithstanding, the appropriation of Latin American natural resources and their transformation into exchangeable commodities was legitimized by the universal rights discourse that Vitoria recognized as part of *jus gentium*.

Dominium rerum and Trade in Vitoria and Soto: The Privatization and Commodification of Latin American Nature

Vitoria opened his *Relectio* by enquiring whether before the arrival of the Spaniards 'these barbarians ... had true dominion, public and private'.[32] His purpose was to determine 'whether they were true masters of their private chattels and possessions, and whether there existed among them any men who were true princes and masters of the others'.[33] Vitoria took into account the economic and political aspects of Latin Americans' power. It was not only important to ascertain whether the peoples of Latin America enjoyed private property rights but also whether they were the true lords of their own domains.[34]

---

[28] Schewering, for example, suggested more than 80 million. See Karl H Schewering, 'The Indian Populations of Latin America' in Jan Knippers Black (ed) *Latin America, its Problems and its Promise: A Multidisciplinary Introduction* (Westview Press 2005) 39–53. Dobyns proposed a number between 90 and 112 million in Henry F Dobyns, 'Estimating Aboriginal Latin American Population: An Appraisal of Techniques with a New Hemispheric Estimate' (1966) 7 Current Anthropologist 395. For a good overview of current debates see Charles C Mann, *Ancient Latin Americans: Rewriting the History of the New World* (Granta Books 2005) 92–6.

[29] Matthew Restall, *Seven Myths of the Spanish Conquest* (Oxford University Press 2003) 141. Importantly, germs travelled faster than conquerors, so in many areas the population of Latin America was declining even before direct contact with the Spaniards.

[30] Miller, *An Environmental History* (n 7) 56.

[31] Francisco de Vitoria, 'On the Latin American Indians' in Francisco de Vitoria, *Political Writings* (Anthony Pagden and Jeremy Lawrance eds, Cambridge University Press 1991) 231, 3.1 s8 283.

[32] Ibid, 1.1 s4 239.   [33] Ibid.

[34] See Patricio J López Díaz-Valentín, 'Relación de Dominio y Ley en la Situación Latin Americana dentro del Pensamiento Vitoriano' in Juan Cruz Cruz (ed), *Ley y Dominio en Francisco Vitoria* (Eunsa 2008) 302.

With regard to ownership, Vitoria's query established from the outset the legal foundations for all the ulterior discussion on the possible just titles whereby 'we Christians were empowered to take possession of their territory'.[35] So, while formulating the problematic he wanted to resolve, he already chose the legal angle from which to look at the matter. He could have alternatively posed the question of how Latin Americans related to their possessions. Did they, for instance, have a legal regime of common or private property or a mixed system? This may sound anachronistic, but we know that in Columbus' first letter from Latin America the Admiral had stated that 'he could not well understand whether' the inhabitants of Latin America 'had private property, or not'.[36] Palacios Rubios had also written that they had no private property and that they farmed in common the few lands they cultivated.[37] But Vitoria's query assumed from the outset that *dominium rerum* was the institutional arrangement that represented the way in which the inhabitants of Latin America related to their territories.

With a simple question Vitoria had fit Latin Americans' commonwealths in the legal mould that was in line with his and his contemporaries' conception of the human relationship to the material world. His understanding of *dominium rerum* as a private power over material reality was based on a particular notion of ownership and use of land[38] that (once universalized) was applied to the Latin American continent in disregard of the alternative ways in which its inhabitants may have related to nature.[39] Regardless of Vitoria's intent and political project, this neglect can largely be explained by contextual and structural conditions, such as the Eurocentric perspective from which the debate about the rights of the peoples of Latin America was conducted.

The increase of human power over the environment that the universalization of private property entailed is illustrated by Soto's definition of *dominium* in his *De iustitia et iure* in contraposition to other types of power over nature. '*Dominium*', he asserted, 'is to be distinguished from possession, use or usufruct ... for *dominium* is not simply the ability to use something and take its produce, but to alienate it, give it away, sell it or neglect it'.[40] The law was the only limitation to the amplified power

---

[35] Vitoria, 'On the Latin American Indians' (n 31) 2. 251–52.

[36] *The First Letter of Christopher Columbus to the Noble Lord Raphael Sanchez Announcing the Discovery of Latin America* (Reproduced in facsimile from the copy of the Latin Version of 1493 with a new introduction, Published by the Trustees 1891) 13.

[37] Juan López de Palacios Rubios, *Libellus de insulanis oceanis quas vulgus Indias appellat per Ioannem Lopez de Palacios Rubios decretorum doctorem regiumque consiliarum editus* (BNM 1513) f 4r [p.9] as cited in Anthony Pagden, *The Fall of Natural Man: The Latin American Indian and the Origins of Comparative Ethnology (Cambridge University Press 1982)* 51.

[38] See Woodrow Wilson Borah, *Justice by Insurance: The General Indian Court of Colonial Mexico and the Legal Aides of the Half-real* (University of California Press 1983) 38.

[39] For an overview of Middle Latin American systems of property see Thomas M Whitmore and BL Turner II, *Cultivated Landscapes of Middle Latin America on the Eve of Conquest* (Oxford University Press 2001) 41–44.

[40] Domingo de Soto, *De iustitia et iure libri decem* (Marcelino Gonzalez Ordoñez tr, Instituto de Estudios Políticos 1967) Book IV, 1.1, 280.

that the owner had over his/her property.[41] Similarly, Vitoria maintained that 'wild beasts and all irrational beings are subject to the power of man'.[42]

Vitoria's and Soto's understanding of the process of formation of private property rights was related to their religious beliefs. According to Vitoria, God had conferred the world to humanity as a whole.[43] Soto cited Genesis 1 to prove the original regime of common property.[44] Under natural law, things remained common during the 'natural state', the historical period that span from the creation to the original sin.[45] After the fall and due to the fact that natural law did not prescribe but just recommended common ownership, things were privately divided through human law[46] and by consensus.[47] This type of agreement had three important features. First, it could be imposed on a minority because, according to natural law, what the majority decided was the rule.[48] Second, it was virtual, in the sense that everyone could take for their own use what had not been already taken.[49] Finally, in order to have universal validity this virtual consensus was recognized as part of *jus gentium*.[50] So, *jus gentium* was of foremost importance for the process of division and privatization of the world's natural resources that had remained common before the fall.[51]

For the Spanish scholastics this religious narrative was not a metaphor, but a description of reality. The expulsion from paradise marked the beginning of the world as they understood it. Once Vitoria accepted the institution of private property as the way of dividing the world that God had given to humanity in common, and once it became universally applicable by virtue of *jus gentium*, it acquired a providential historical force and a totalizing geographical ambit difficult to resist.

Vitoria's and Soto's treatment of *dominium* as control and power over material reality was at odds with Latin Americans' complex and diverse conceptions of nature.[52] This concept transformed their bond with their environment—with the lands they cultivated, the minerals with which they crafted handicrafts and jewellery, the trees they used for timber and construction, the animals they hunted,

---

[41] Ibid.   [42] Vitoria, 'On the Latin American Indians' (n 31) 1.4 s20, 248.

[43] Francisco de Vitoria, *De iustitia*, q62, a1, n10, 69, as quoted in Teodoro López, 'Propiedad y Dominio en Francisco Vitoria' in Cruz Cruz, *Ley y Dominio en Francisco de Vitoria* (n 34) 71.

[44] Soto, *De iustitia* (n 40) Book IV, 3.1, 295.

[45] 'A principio mundi omnia erant communia' ('at the beginning of the World everything was common') in Vitoria, *De iustita* (n 43), q62, a1, n9, 67 as quoted in López, 'Propiedad y Dominio' (n 43) 83. [translated by author].

[46] Vitoria, *De iustita* (n 43) q62, a1, n20, 75.

[47] Koskenniemi has noted that by 'a distinction between binding and merely recommendatory provisions of natural law' Vitoria presented the character of the *divisio rerum* 'in terms of private property'. See Koskenniemi, 'Empire and International Law' (n 1) 14.

[48] For Vitoria, this was a way of maintaining peace: Vitoria, *De iustita* (n 43) q62, a1, n22, 79.

[49] Ibid, q62, a1, n23, 79.

[50] Ibid, q62, a1, n23, 79. See also Soto, *De iustitia* (n 40) Book IV, 3.1, 297.

[51] Brett contends that the division of *dominia* was for Vitoria and Soto the main distinction between *jus gentium* and natural law. See Annabel S Brett, *Changes of State: Nature and the Limits of the City in Early Modern Natural Law* (Princeton University Press 2011) 197.

[52] Vitoria argues that 'we do not speak of anyone being the 'owner' of a thing (*dominum esse*) unless that thing lies within his control'. Vitoria, 'On the Latin American Indians' (n 31) 1.4 s20 248. For Soto's view see *De iustitia* (n 40).

and so forth—into a material relationship between subject and object, owner and owned. The former term of these two opposites was active and related to the latter in terms of superiority.[53] 'Nature', as expressed through the specific vocabulary of the *jus gentium*, became a material entity to be possessed. This stripped 'nature' of religious and cultural readings that were significant to Latin Americans.[54] The idea of ownership reduced the content of Latin Americans' relationship to their territories to a simplified economic version of what had previously been, while the institution of private property altered the form of that relationship to suit private interests. This paradigmatic shift towards the privatization of natural resources did not per se lead to environmental exploitation, but it furnished the legal apparatus that made it possible.

In his inquisition on possible grounds for denying Latin Americans the status of proprietors, Vitoria first dismissed allegations of sinfulness and their condition status as non-believers.[55] Likewise, he then rebutted accusations of irrationality as unfounded.[56] The proof was that their cultures were somehow developed.[57] Accordingly, he concluded that 'the barbarians undoubtedly possessed as true dominion, both public and private, as any Christians'.[58] Soto was of the same opinion, namely, that the peoples of Latin America had rights of jurisdiction and property over their territories.[59] Vitoria was well aware of the threat that a contrary conclusion would have posed to the well-being of the Latin Americans and the survival of the very population his Dominican order so fervently wanted to convert. His conclusion prevented Latin American colonization to be conducted in an unruly fashion. Anarchy suited the avid *conquistadores* but hindered peaceful evangelization. The legal certitude of Latin Americans' right to property was a guarantee against the despoliation of the greedy conquerors', which Vitoria deplored. As far as he was concerned, Spanish 'men' were no longer to operate in a legal vacuum of impunity in Latin America.

Besides, Vitoria was aware of the theoretical correlation between Latin Americans' rationality, their having *dominium*, and the applicability of *jus gentium*. After all, property was one of the institutions that 'learned men' and royal lawyers for that matter most commonly associated with the presence of a civil society.[60] Had he found Latin Americans irrational, they could not have had *dominium*.[61] And without the capacity to hold property there was no chance of a political life and,

[53] See López, 'Propiedad y Dominio' (n 43) 82.

[54] The literature on pre-colonial Latin American beliefs and views of nature is rather large. For an introduction see Lee M Penyak and Walter J Petry (eds), *Religion in Latin America: A Documentary History* (Orbis Books 2006). See also Lawrence E Sullivan (ed), *Native Religions and Cultures of Central and South Latin America* (The Continuum International Publishing Group Inc 2002).

[55] See Vitoria, 'On the Latin American Indians' (n 31) 1.2–1.3 240–46.

[56] Ibid, 1.4 s20 247–48.   [57] Ibid, 1.6 s22 250.   [58] Ibid, 1.6–concl. s23 250.

[59] Domingo de Soto, *Relección 'De dominio'* (Jaime Brufau Prats ed, Universidad de Granada 1964) s34 164.

[60] Elvira Vilches, *New World Gold: Cultural Anxiety and Monetary Disorder in Early Modern Spain* (The University of Chicago Press 2010) 96.

[61] Vitoria adhered to Aquinas' postulate that only those who can govern their acts could own property. Vitoria, 'On the Latin American Indians' (n 31) 1.4 s20, 248.

hence, legal protection against 'invaders attempting to seize their lands'.[62] If that was the case Vitoria could not have resolved the 'Indian question' by recourse to *jus gentium*, which in the face of the Lutheran challenge to the power of the Pope and the Emperor provided a timely and universally valid legitimization of Spanish presence in Latin America.[63] It offered as well the possibility of peaceful evangelization, avoiding Lutheran charges against a corrupted and decadent imperialist Catholicism imposed by force.

Rationality and private property were the lynchpins over which Vitoria would later in his lecture build his arguments regarding *jus gentium*. Sanctioned by *jus gentium*, private property acquired universality and retrospectively defined the way Latin Americans related to their territories before the arrival of the Spaniards.[64]

Having found that Latin Americans owned their territories, Vitoria maintained (in the third part of his *Relectio*) that their right to private property was not absolute. The rights that nations enjoyed under *jus gentium* could limit it. By reference to *jus gentium* he managed to reconcile an initial respect for Latin Americans' property with the introduction of a series of legal entitlements that would eventually bolster Spanish economic/environmental power in Latin America.

The exceptions to Latin Americans' ownership that Vitoria recognized were part of a series of rights that governed relations between different commonwealths. Some of those rights, like the rights to travel and sojourn, seemed a priori neutral.[65] As important as these entitlements were, there was still the need for a further right—the right to trade—that would give the Spanish Crown access to Latin America's wealth. The huge military and administrative expenses of keeping afloat the Spanish empire could only be covered by the revenues that were expected to derive from the 'trips of discovery'. Vitoria's right to trade nicely suited Spanish imperial ambitions.

Vitoria elaborated various arguments in order to justify trade. First, he looked at bilateral relations between the Spaniards and the Latin Americans. Based on reciprocity, he held that commerce benefited them both. The latter could import commodities they did not have in exchange for gold and silver.[66] Mutual gain represented a reasonable foundation for international trade. But could Latin Americans understand the value that gold had for the Europeans? Columbus affirmed that gold was a treasure, the possessor of which could impose his will on the whole

[62] Anthony Pagden, 'Dispossessing the Barbarian: The Language of Spanish Thomism and the Debate over the Property Rights of the Latin American Indians' in David Armitage (ed), *Theories of Empire 1450–1800* (Ashgate 1998) 159, 161.

[63] Pagden suggests that 'Vitoria and his successors were far less concerned with the particulars of the Latin American case than they were with the opportunities it provided for the refutation of Lutheran and, later, Calvinist theories of sovereignty': ibid, 163.

[64] See Alejandro Auat, 'Soberanía en Vitoria: Claves Transmodernas para un Principio Cuestionado' in Cruz Cruz (ed), *Ley y Dominio en Francisco de Vitoria* (n 34) 233.

[65] Samuel Pufendorf would cast a critical eye on these rights. See Samuel Pufendorf, *De jure naturae et gentium libri octo*, vol II (James Brown Scott ed, CH Oldfather and WA Oldfather trs, Clarendon Press 1934) Book III Ch III s9 364–65. A similar type of criticism can be found in Alberico Gentili, *De Jure Belli Libri Tres* (Vol II, John C Rolfe tr of the 1612 edn, Clarendon Press 1933) Book I ch XIX 89.

[66] Vitoria, 'On the Latin American Indians' (n 31) 3.1 s3, 279.

world.[67] Acknowledging the exaggeration of this claim, it is true that gold had a great value in European and Asian markets during the sixteenth century. Because the Spanish and not the Latin Americans were commercially operating on both sides of the Atlantic, only they could know and capture the value that concrete commodities had for different commonwealths. This information asymmetry was obscured by a language of rights that presumed the parity of both sides.

As a result of the introduction of the right to trade in Vitoria's *jus gentium* European merchants' profitable preponderant place as intermediaries between Latin American and European markets received legal sanction. Vitoria was in principle opposed to profits derived from unequal trade because they amounted to the sin of avarice.[68] However, the merchant's personal enrichment could be acceptable as a way of compensating transportation costs.[69] In other words, personal enrichment was justifiable if it enabled the development of commerce in cases in which it would have otherwise not been possible. Accordingly, it is unlikely that Vitoria would have condemned capital accumulation, as it was in fact European merchants and their ships that made that intercontinental trade possible in the first place.[70]

Moving from bilateralism to cosmopolitanism, Vitoria invoked the fellowship of mankind as a further defence of trade.[71] In the naturalist tradition trade was considered as one of the channels through which human knowledge could be shared between different communities.[72] The absence of trade hampered the establishment of political, economic, and cultural ties between different polities. For this reason, Vitoria concluded that 'the barbarians can no more prohibit Spaniards from carrying on trade with them, than Christians can prohibit other Christians from doing the same'.[73] In addition, Latin American rulers were compelled by the law of nature to love the Spaniards and, hence, they could not 'prevent them without due cause from furthering their own interests'.[74] This justification of trade encapsulates perhaps, better than any other, the irony of the Spanish conquest. As Martti Koskenniemi has put it, love was 'often difficult to distinguish from a desire to

[67] Cecil Jane (ed), *Select Documents Illustrating the Four Voyages of Columbus* (Vol II Hakluyt Society 1930–1933) as quoted in Urs Bitterli, *Cultures in Conflict: Encounters Between European and Non-European Cultures, 1492–1800* (Polity Press 1989) 75.

[68] See the discussion in Koskenniemi, 'Empire and International Law' (n 1) 19–20.

[69] Ibid.

[70] For a similar opinion regarding Vitoria's positive attitudes towards profitable trade see Ileana Porras, 'Appropriating Nature: Commerce, Property, and the Commodification of Nature in the Law of Nations' (2014) 27 Leiden Journal of International Law 641, 649.

[71] Vitoria was convinced that the fellowship of men was in consonance with natural law. Vitoria, 'On the Latin American Indians' (n 31) 3.1 s3, 280.

[72] Pagden, *The Fall of Natural Man* (n 37) 77. The social and political value of commercial ties was something that Latin American societies did also recognize. See Karen Olsen Bruhns, *Ancient South Latin America* (Cambridge University Press 1994) 278.

[73] Vitoria, 'On the Latin American Indians' (n 31) 3.1 s3, 280.

[74] Ibid. In the Carnegie Series of Classics of International Law the expression 'furthering their interest' is translated as 'making their profit'. See Francisco de Vitoria, *De indis et de iure belli relectiones* (Ernest Nys ed, John Pawley Bate tr, Carnegie Institution of Washington 1917) Sect III s3 152–53. This is also the understanding of Ileana Porras: see Porras, 'Appropriating Nature' (n 70) 649.

dominate'.[75] Linked to sentiments of love and fraternity, commerce was internationalized, acquiring a positive cosmopolitan character that would be preserved in
the law of nations in the following centuries. Coercion, the fact that it was imposed
on the peoples of Latin America through the threat or the actual use of force by way
of the right to war, remained invisible in Vitoria's legal theories.

Vitoria's right to trade exemplifies the shortcomings of the humanitarianism
that often permeates cosmopolitan justifications of universal rules. The general
interests of an abstract humanity were invoked as the basis of a right that ignored
the particular interests of the concrete millions of humans that inhabited Latin
America, whose opinion on this matter became irrelevant as a source of law.
Cosmopolitanism cloaked the unequal colonial setting in which economic domination came about.[76] But it would be misleading to think that cosmopolitanism
displaced the individual rights of the peoples of Latin America. It was actually
Spanish economic rights—dressed as universal—and their monetized market
economy that had that effect.[77]

At the very least Vitoria's defence of free trade seemed to offer a choice of trading
partners. According to him, Christian kings could not deter their subjects (turned
merchants) from trading with other nations. However, this small niche of liberty
within which Latin Americans could have freely manoeuvred clashed with the interest of the Spanish Crown in developing a trade monopoly in Latin America. This
forced Vitoria to limit the freedom of commerce he had so firmly upheld before
when later in the text he defended Spanish commercial monopoly stating that:

> … And since it is the pope's special business to promote the Gospel throughout the world,
> if the princes of Spain are in the best position to see to the preaching of the Gospel in those
> provinces, the pope may entrust the task to them, and deny it to all others. He may restrict
> not only the right to preach, but also the right to trade there, if this is convenient for the
> spreading of the Christian religion … Besides, the princes of Spain were the first to under-
> take the voyages of discovery, at their own expense and under their own banners; and as since
> they were so fortunate as to discover the New World, it is just that this voyage should be
> denied, and that they alone should enjoy the fruits of their discovery.[78]

The authority of the Pope was enough to limit Latin American trade only if it
was established that a monopoly on commerce was conductive to evangelization.

---

[75] Koskenniemi, 'Empire and International Law' (n 1) 11.

[76] A similar point is made in Emmerich de Vattel, *The Law of Nations or The Principles of Natural
Law Applied to the Conduct and to the Affairs of Nations and of Sovereigns* (Vol III, Charles G Fenwick tr
of the 1758 edn, Carnegie Institution 1916) Book II Ch II s25, 122.

[77] For Brown, 'One of the great changes of the Conquest, particularly within the former Inka
Empire, was the introduction of the market system. Previously, the economy had been based on redistribution and reciprocity … the coming of the Spaniards, however, imposed the rule of an external
social group with a totally alien economic culture in the form of monetised markets': Jonathan C
Brown, *Latin America: A Social History of the Colonial Period* (Thomson Wadsworth 2005) 205. For an
overview of South Latin American systems of exchange before Spanish conquest see Bruhns, *Ancient
South Latin America* (n 72) 278–89.

[78] Vitoria, 'On the Latin American Indians' (n 31) 3.2 s10, 284–85. This contradiction is analysed
in Brett Bowden, *The Empire of Civilization: The Evolution of an Imperial Idea* (The University of
Chicago Press 2009) 139–40.

Vitoria knew, of course, that it was in the interest of the Pope to limit the presence in Latin America of those nations that had embraced the Reformation. This could play to the advantage of the Spanish Crown. A trade monopoly authorized by the Pope could be used not only against Protestant nations but also against Catholic rivals. But Vitoria was also aware that the Pope's power was of no use against nations that no longer recognized his authority. Hence, he complemented the possibility of an exclusive Papal trade concession with the allegation that the burden of colonization had to be compensated by the exclusive enjoyment of eventual benefits. Here, Vitoria was reasoning like an investor. He understood that it was risky to advance financial resources without the security of returns. Yet, he presented the question of Spanish trade monopoly in cosmopolitan terms. It is ironic that he used one of the supreme cosmopolitan ideals—love—to justify free trade, whereas another—justice—served the contrary function of restricting it.

Vitoria's right to trade was detached from the reality of the Spanish occupation of Latin American territories. From the outset, Spanish violence was a pervasive feature of conquest. Since Columbus and his 'men' landed in Hispaniola, they acquired and used the land and its fruits for their own gain and did so by all necessary means. The forceful apprehension of Latin American riches continued unabated as colonization intensified with the full involvement of the Spanish Crown soon afterwards and the defeat of the prosperous Empires of Anahuac and Tawantinsuyu.

Although the peoples of Latin America were allowed to carry on internal trade, the exchange of the main commodities—spices, gold, silver, and sugar—was under the absolute control of Spain. These goods were exchanged between Spain, which forcefully appropriated them in Latin America, and Spain, which gladly received them at home. Consequently, trade entered *jus gentium* hiding a theft of continental proportions because it was predicated on the exchange between two theoretically equal trading partners.[79] In practice, profitability derived from violent conquest and forceful imposition of Spanish terms. While apparently an exception to the general rule of Latin Americans' ownership, trade became in reality an instrument for the enrichment of the Spanish and European merchant class.

The right to carry on commerce did not exhaust the Spanish economic entitlements sanctioned by *jus gentium*. According to Vitoria, in case the Latin Americans had allowed other foreigners to extract natural resources (like gold inside the earth or pearls in the sea) from their lands, they were automatically compelled to offer the Spanish the same advantage.[80] This sounded paradoxical considering Vitoria's defence of a trade monopoly. How could Spain justly deny other nations what Latin Americans could not, namely participation in the exploitation of their own wealth? Without the capacity to decide with whom they were going to negotiate the use of their natural resources, Latin Americans' sovereignty was considerably eroded. What is more, the limitation of Latin Americans' alternatives operated under the dubious premise that they had willingly opened their resources to foreign

---

[79] See Anghie, *Imperialism* (n 2) 21.
[80] Vitoria, 'On the Latin American Indians' (n 31) 3.1 s4 280.

exploitation to begin with. Again, the context in which Latin Americans' consent was obtained did not matter.

In spite of its undeniable economic value, the right of participation in the commons assured the Spanish Crown and conquerors only a meagre part of Latin American mineral resources. Even if the Portuguese or the French enjoyed certain rights of extraction in Latin Americans' territories, their value paled in comparison with what—so the Spanish rightly thought—lay unexplored and unoccupied.[81] So, Vitoria complemented the right of participating in the commons with a right over unoccupied things. He affirmed that goods without owner (here he again mentioned gold and pearls) could be acquired by their first occupant whatever their location.[82] The virtual consensus, from which private property stemmed, meant that the whole world had not yet been divided and many natural resources were still vacant waiting to be occupied. For Spain this right had a strategic economic value as it gave access to Latin America's gold and silver with which to finance the costs of Empire.

Soto differed from Vitoria in this point affirming that the Spaniards had no right over Latin American unoccupied gold.[83] The human race was geographically divided in regions so that the inhabitants of each region had a right over the common things that were within the confines of their particular realm.[84] Moreover, in his lecture *De dominio* he asserted that ownerless goods belonged to the first occupant only in regard to their use but not their *dominium*.[85] This meant that even in the case that some of the world's lands had not yet been divided they could be used but not owned by the first occupant.[86]

When in his lecture Vitoria introduced the right over unoccupied things he made a reference to the law of wild beasts or *ferae bestiae* of the Roman *Institutiones* of Justinian, according to which: 'Wild animals, birds, and fish, that is to say all the creatures which the land, the sea, and the sky produce, as soon as they are caught by any one become at once the property of their captor by the law of nations.'[87] Based on the examples of the *Institutiones* and Vitoria's own examples (gold, pearls, fish) it seems that the Dominican scholastic was referring only to movable things. However, at the end of his lecture he mentioned again the right of occupation stating that: '*Item multa etiam sunt, quae ipsi pro desertis habent velt sunt communia omnibus volentibus occupare.*'[88] In this passage it is less clear that he is solely referring to movables.[89] In principle, there is nothing to suggest that

---

[81] El Dorado was the idealized incarnation of that certitude. See Jorge Magasich-Airola and Jean-Marc de Beer, *America Magica: When Renaissance Europe Thought it had Conquered Paradise* (Anthem Press 2007) 69–98.

[82] Vitoria, 'On the Latin American Indians' (n 31) 3.1 s4, 280.

[83] See Brett, *Changes of State* (n 51) 25.   [84] Ibid.

[85] Soto, *Relección* (n 59) s21, 121.   [86] Ibid, s23, 127.

[87] Justinian, *Institutes*, II. 1. 12.

[88] Vitoria, *De indis* (n 74) Sect III s18, 268. 'Also there are many commodities which the natives treat as ownerless or as common to all who like to take them': ibid, Sect III s18, 162.

[89] Whereas the English translation of *multa* in the Carnegie Series of Classics of International Law is 'commodities' (referring only to movable things), the Spanish translation of the same word is *muchas tierras* (lot of land) that are clearly immovable things. See respectively, Vitoria, *De indis* (n 74) Sect III s18, 162, and Francisco de Vitoria, *Sobre el Poder Civil; Sobre los Indios; Sobre el Derecho de la Guerra* (Estudio preliminar, traducción y notas de Luis Frayle Delgado, Tecnos 2007) 149–50. In Pagden and

multa could not be interpreted as including immovables in general and (deserted) land in particular.

On the one hand, Vitoria could just be referring to movables as earlier in his lecture he had restricted the Spanish right of occupation to that type of thing. Moreover, in his treatise *De iustitia* Vitoria explained that after the *divisio rerum* many things remained undivided and, therefore, belonged to the first who occupied them.[90] And then he illustrates this statement by giving concrete examples and mentioning only movables such as animals, birds, and fish.[91] In addition, in his commentary on Aquinas' *Secunda Secundae* Vitoria stated that once the world was divided 'those lands belong to those infidels, and ... since therefore they are true owners, if they do not want to donate them, it follows that we cannot now retain or capture them. Just as, in the matter of the Indians, certainly no one can capture land from them'.[92] But this conclusion was similar to his affirmation in the first part of his *Relectio de indis* that the peoples of Latin America were the owners of their territories, a conclusion that did not prevent the applicability of the law *ferae bestiae* and the appropriation of unoccupied goods.

On the other hand, in the second part of his lecture Vitoria makes clear in his dismissal of the right of discovery as legitimate title of Spanish power in Latin America that the territories or countries of the peoples of Latin America were within the scope of application of the law *ferae bestiae*.[93] In other words, occupation could theoretically be applied to unoccupied lands. Again, Vitoria's argumentation closed the possibility of applying the law *ferae bestiae* to the whole of Latin America's natural products, movables and immovables. But as he later drew an exception related to unoccupied movables, it would be plausible that exceptionally deserted places would also fall within the scope of the right of occupation.

Vitoria's doctrine created the possibility of seizing Latin America's natural resources as long as they had not been previously exploited, creating an umbrella of legal possibility for the activities of Spanish conquerors and merchants who exploited every natural product of marketable value (animals, trees, plants with medical properties, minerals, fruits, fish, food plants, etc). Putting it simply, through this right the Spanish greatly expanded their power over Latin American natural habitats.[94]

The ecological implications of the right to occupy were far reaching. Nature was placed under a logic of appropriation whereby its value was measured in relation to the commodities it offered and their economic value. Land, resources, and other natural elements of economic significance were potentially capable of being

---

Lawrance *multa* is translated as 'possessions which they regard as uninhabited'. According to this interpretation, uninhabited places, and thus immovables, were included among the unoccupied things that the Spanish could seize. See Vitoria, 'On the Latin American Indians' (n 31) 3.8 s18, 291.

[90] Vitoria, *De iustitia*, q62, a1, n25, 80 as quoted in López, 'Propiedad y Dominio' (n 43) 77.
[91] Ibid, 81.
[92] Vitoria, *Comentarios a la Secunda Secundae*, vol III, q. 62, a. 1, n. 28 as cited in Brett, *Changes of State* (n 51) 198.
[93] Vitoria, 'On the Latin American Indians' (n 31) 2.3 s31 264–65.
[94] Borah, *Justice by Insurance* (n 38) 38.

privately owned. This was not an inconsequential possibility on account of the huge profits to be made from the trade in Latin American goods. In theory, if Latin Americans did not rush to exploit vacant natural resources as intensively as the colonizers, they risked losing economic control over their environment. Independently of who was going to be its new owner and due to the possibility of appropriation, nature was to be exploited more than ever before.

Two factors contributed to increase the impact of the right of occupation. The Spaniards' perception of Latin American nature was conditioned by their idea of wilderness. Portions of forest opened to attract game or certain agro-forestry systems[95] to collect different kinds of nuts might have looked to their eyes as unoccupied grasslands for cattle, and idle trees waiting to be transformed into timber. Even if Latin Americans were actually using particular landscapes, Spaniards logically tended to presume lack of occupation in places where they could not detect the environmental impact of human activities. In this context, the Spaniards, who could impose their standard when judging the occupation or lack of occupation of a particular environment, enjoyed the upper hand in deciding how far their private property rights could encroach upon Latin American nature.

Another element that amplified the influence of the right of occupation was the fact that it entered the law of nations at precisely the historical moment in which Latin America became more depopulated and, hence, more unoccupied.[96] Even if Vitoria was aware of this phenomenon when he formulated the doctrine of occupancy, he could not have fully comprehended its environmental implications. Following his reasoning, once nature bounced back, extending over places that had previously been cultivated or deforested, the only way Latin Americans could retain their historical rights of ownership over the environment was to occupy back those landscapes. This was a burdensome task for a rapidly shrinking population, whose freedom of movement became quite restricted as a result of conquest.

As a consequence of these two factors, wilderness enormously expanded both conceptually through the Spanish appropriation of its meaning and factually due to its application to particular geographical locations and the depopulation of the continent. As Latin Americans died land and commodities were plentiful for the taking.[97] Nature blossomed and so did the economic possibilities of Spanish adventurers and those Latin Americans who rapidly adapted to and benefited from Spanish institutions.[98] Moreover, the new conception of private property allowed neglect of one's possessions.[99] In consequence, there was actually no limit to the amount of land that the Crown could grant to the newcomers or that they could seize.[100]

---

[95] See Whitmore and Turner (n 39) 21. For Amazonian agroforestry systems see William M Denevan, *Cultivated Landscapes of Native Amazonia and the Andes* (Oxford University Press 2001) 69–70.

[96] See Robert G Keith (ed), *Haciendas and Plantations in Latin America History* (Holmes & Meier Publishers Inc 1977) 16.

[97] Miller, *An Environmental History* (n 7) 101.   [98] Borah, *Justice by Insurance* (n 38) 38.

[99] See Soto, *De iustitia* (n 40) 280.

[100] Borah, *Justice by Insurance* (n 38) 38. In fact the Crown tried with little success to limit the seizure of new landholdings threatening to take the land if it was not productive. See JH Elliott, *Spain, Europe & the Wider World 1500–1800* (Yale University Press 2009) 120.

One of the results of these changes in the conception of *dominium* once it was applied to the land was the formation and slow but steady consolidation of a new institution: the *latifundia* and a sort of land nobility that were to shape Latin American political, economic, and social life for centuries to come. But 'land grabbing' became only noticeable at the end of the sixteenth century and during the seventeenth century.[101] At the time of Vitoria the economic value of land was minimal, not only because gold or silver were more profitable but also because there was just too much of it.[102]

The importance of the rights to trade and to acquire common or unoccupied natural resources can hardly be exaggerated. As far as movables are concerned, and for reasons not attributable to Vitoria, these rights transformed what seemed to be the rule at the beginning of Vitoria's disquisition—Latin Americans' ownership—in the exception. Most of the continent's abundant natural resources were opened for European—mainly Spanish and Portuguese—acquisition. Besides, both rights were intertwined, reinforcing one another. The right of occupation was the basis of Spanish trade. Without the property of Latin American commodities, Spanish colonists would have had to buy timber, sugar, gold, or silver from the Latin Americans, considerably reducing their returns. Conversely, trade gave purpose and incentive to the right of occupation. The demand of Latin American commodities in international markets made the apprehension of natural resources extremely profitable.

The *jus gentium* legitimized the exercise of a very subtle form of environmental hegemony and economic violence of dispossession over the peoples of Latin America. Military force was the final guarantor and closure of the system. For Vitoria, the Spanish could only resort to war in order to protect themselves against Latin Americans' desire to destroy them.[103] This characterization of war as self-defence concealed the fact that the exercise of private economic rights by an external social group already constituted a sort of violence, less manifest than military confrontation, perhaps, but as destructive in the long run. The Spanish control of trade and encroachment on Latin American natural resources worked to the material disadvantage of the Latin Americans, imperiling their well-being. But this sort of structural economic violence was an invisible component of Vitoria's system. Resistance against economic oppression was transformed by the law of nations into an attack that triggered the Spanish right to war.[104]

Due to the fact that the economic rights of the Spaniards were part of the law of nations, any interference with their collective or individual[105] enjoyment could be interpreted as a wrong, the only reason that according to Vitoria justified the

---

[101] Keith, *Haciendas and Plantations* (n 96) 20.

[102] MacLeod, *Spanish Central Latin America* (n 15) 96. See also Miller, *An Environmental History* (n 7) 101. For a good account of land tenure in colonial Latin America see Magnus Mörner, 'The Rural Economy and Society in of Colonial Spanish South Latin America' in Leslie Bethell (ed), *The Cambridge History of Latin America Volume II* (Cambridge University Press 1984) 189, 190–204.

[103] Vitoria, 'On the Latin American Indians' (n 31) 3.1 s8, 283.

[104] See Anghie, *Imperialism* (n 2) 21–22.

[105] Vitoria affirms that men can wage war not only for personal protection, but also for the defence of 'their property'. Vitoria, 'On the law of war' in Vitoria, *Political Writings* (n 31) 1.1 s1, 297–98.

waging of war.[106] Moreover, once a wrong was committed the right to war legitimized an offensive use of force against one's enemies.[107] This type of war expanded
Spanish economic power immensely. As Vitoria affirmed, it was 'a universal rule
of the law of nations that whatever is captured in war becomes the property of the
conqueror'.[108] By virtue of war the *conquistadores* acquired Latin Americans' goods,
territories, and even control of their bodies (by making them slaves).[109] It was
logical that as the Spanish carved a sphere of power which allowed them to move
freely within the continent (right to travel) and control and exploit the economic
resources of Latin America (right of trade and occupation), the Latin Americans
would try even forcefully to oppose Spanish presence in their territories. But challenging Spanish economic power by all means created precisely the legal grounds
to increase Spanish economic hegemony. Vitoria's system justified a vicious circle
of destitution and violence, which actually came about due to the *conquistadores'*
rapacious behaviour and the Crown's economic interests in the mineral resources
of Latin America.

The Religious Conception of Nature in Vitoria and Soto: A Counterbalance to Exploitation?

It is important from the outset to bear in mind that the way we look at nature today
and the way Vitoria and Soto did are radically different. Our world and that of the
Spanish scholastics are incommensurable. As Ileana Porras reminds us, concepts like
ecosystems and wilderness are of novel currency and affect our perceptions and the
implications we draw from the world.[110] Vitoria and Soto looked at nature through
their religious lenses. Today we wear different ones. So again, the point of analysis
of Vitoria's and Soto's ideas is not to pass judgement on them, but rather to examine
the kind of glasses they wear in order to ascertain the historical implications that the
power attached to their ideas and worldview has had on the actual world.

Vitoria's legal doctrines legitimized the introduction of economic practices that in
the hands of the Spanish *conquistadores* had an adverse effect on the Latin American
environment. First, under the right to private property nature became an object of
privatization. Every natural element could be seized in order to serve the particular
interests of its owner. For Soto, the distinctive feature of *dominium* was that the
power of the proprietor over its property could be exercised solely for its own benefit.[111] Second, the rights to participate in the commons and occupy vacant resources
defined who was to be the main owner of Latin American natural resources. Both
rights transferred innumerable natural resources—even though Latin Americans

---

[106] Vitoria, 'On the Latin American Indians' (n 31) 3.1 s6 281–82 in combination with Vitoria 3.1 s13, 303.
[107] Vitoria, 'On the Latin American Indians' (n 31) 3.1 s8, 283.   [108] Ibid.
[109] Ibid.   [110] Porras, 'Appropriating Nature' (n 70) 645.
[111] Soto, *De iustitia* (n 40) Book IV, 1.1, 279–80 and Book IV, 1.2, 284.

still retained a fair amount of land for a long time—to the Spaniards, placing them under the control of those who most profited from their exploitation. Finally, the right to trade gave nature a new function. It served the purpose of satisfying individual consumption at the one end of the spectrum and the accumulation of capital at the other end. Whereas nature's commercial value increased in the *jus gentium,* the religious and cultural values that it had before became irrelevant.

All this notwithstanding, the economic rights that Vitoria acknowledged created the possibility of environmental exploitation in Latin America but not its necessity. They operated in a larger ideological context which could have offered a counter ideology that prevented the destruction of nature. After all, and despite the strong economic incentive to commercialize nature, nothing impeded the private owner to preserve it and use it sustainably. So, in order to ascertain whether there was a counterbalance to the exclusive economic value that nature acquired in the *jus gentium* it is important to consider the way in which Vitoria and Soto conceived nature and the human relationship with it.

There are few explicit references to nature in *De indis*. The first can be found in the discussion of whether sin was a reason for denying Latin Americans *dominium* over their lands. Vitoria's ideas about nature were influenced by his condition of religious 'man'. So, he cited Genesis in order to explain that *dominium* was founded in the image of God: 'Let us make man in our own image, after our likeness; and let them have dominion over the fish of the sea and over the fowl of the air, and over the cattle, and over all the earth ...'[112] This assertion was part of a larger argument, to wit, that sinners did not have *dominium*, which he rejected.

Vitoria's views were common among the Spanish scholastics, and particularly within the Thomist tradition.[113] In the *History of the Indies*,[114] Las Casas gave a similar explanation of the creation of the natural world and humanity's position in it. Explaining the topics he was going to cover in chapter 1 of the first book he stated: 'This chapter deals with the creation of heaven and earth—How God gave it, with all its lower creatures for human mastery—How this mastery diminished as a consequence of the original sin ...'[115] Similarly, he stated that God had created nature for the health and utility of human beings, describing it as a 'world machine' dedicated to mankind.[116] For Soto, men's resemblance to God stemmed from the fact that they too had power over the worlds' irrational creatures.[117]

At the time of Vitoria, the Christian interpretation of humanity, nature, and their mutual relationship was based on the creation of the world as narrated in Genesis.

---

[112] Vitoria, 'On the Latin American Indians' (n 31) Sect I s5 121.

[113] For Aquinas' anthropocentric views on nature see Clarence J Glacken, *Traces on the Rhodian Shore: Nature and Culture in Western Thought from Ancient Times to the End of the Eighteenth Century* (University of California Press 1967) 229–37. See also Gary Steiner, *Anthropocentrism and its Discontents: The Moral Status of Animals in the History of Western Philosophy* (University of Pittsburgh Press 2005) 126–31.

[114] See Bartolome de Las Casas, *Historia de Las Indias,* Vol I (Fondo de Cultura Económica 1951).

[115] Ibid, Vol I Book I Ch I, 23.   [116] Ibid, 25.

[117] Soto, *De iustitia* (n 40) Book IV, 1.2, 284. The control of human power over nature was extended by Soto to the four natural elements, namely air, water, land, and fire: ibid, Book IV, 2.1, 288.

At this seminal moment of human history, God's mandate was clear: be fertile and increase, fill the earth and master it. The difficulty in deciphering the meaning of God's will in this passage and, for that matter, in the Bible at large is that there is no fixed meaning attached to biblical words, which makes permanent interpretation necessary.[118] So the biblical implications of human mastery over nature remained unclear. How should humanity relate to the environment?

There are two main interpretations of the way in which Christianity understood and fulfilled God's mandate. According to one position, dominion over nature facilitated its actual domination and eventual exploitation, because the power conferred to humanity was unlimited.[119] A more lenient view of Christianity holds that identifying dominion with domination misrepresents the function assigned to humans in the divine scheme. In reality, dominion over non-human nature could be interpreted as a responsible and restricted mandate, enshrined in the notion of stewardship.[120] Humanity was assigned a superior position in regard to natural order to care and protect it and not to spoil it.

Vitoria did not explain his interpretation of the purpose of human *dominium*. He was silent as to the type of power that it entailed. Therefore, we cannot judge Vitoria's ideas about humanity's relationship to nature based solely on this statement. We can only know that his ideas were inspired by religious beliefs as later in the text he reiterated that *dominium* was based on man's resemblance to God.[121] Unlike Vitoria, Soto explicitly explained that the objective of human *dominium* was to create a right to subjugate the Earth and dominate animals and the natural elements.[122]

Later in Vitoria's lecture there is a more revealing reference to nature. He refuted the argument that even irrational creatures might have dominion, asserting that '… wild animals have no rights over their own bodies (*dominium sui*); still less can they have rights over other things. The major premise is proved by the fact that it is lawful to kill them with impunity, even for sport.'[123]

Vitoria started his disquisition about animals claiming that they, as the rest of irrational creatures, could not be proprietors. In the Thomist tradition human resemblance to God implied that animals were 'objects of human *dominium* rather than subjects of *dominium* themselves'.[124] His position reflects the common anthropocentric theological assumptions of his time and the doctrinal legacy of Saint Thomas[125] and Aristotle.[126]

---

[118] Jeremy Cohen, '*Be Fertile and Increase, Fill the Earth and Master It*': *The Ancient and Medieval Career of a Biblical Text* (Cornell University Press 1989) 8.

[119] See Lynn White Jr, 'The Historical Roots of Our Ecological Crisis' (1967) 155 Science 1203. A critic of Christianity from the perspective of a descendant of North Latin American peoples can be found in Vine Deloria Jr, *God is Red: A Native View of Religion* (Fulcrum Publishing 1992).

[120] Robin Attfield, 'Christian Attitudes to Nature' (1983) 44 Journal of the History of Ideas 369, 374. See John Passmore, *Man's Responsibility for Nature: Ecological Problems and Western Traditions* (Duckworth 1974).

[121] Vitoria, 'On the Latin American Indians' (n 31) Sect I s6, 122.

[122] Soto, *De iustitia* (n 40) Book IV, 2.1, 287–88.

[123] Vitoria, 'On the Latin American Indians' (n 31) 1.4 s20, 248.

[124] Brett, *Changes of State* (n 51) 47.

[125] See Steiner, *Anthropocentrism and its Discontents* (n 113) 130.   [126] Ibid, 57–76.

Vitoria granted humans a broad power over nature based on the opposition of proprietor/property and the right of possession, with the former over the latter. It is worth noticing that Vitoria included both domesticated and undomesticated animals within the same category. None escaped humanity's reach. The Dominican scholar understood human ownership in absolute terms. Humans could resort to the ultimate way of controlling another entity: its destruction.[127] In Soto we find the same right to kill animals as a prerogative of *dominium*.[128] Even though both scholastics only referred to animals, the same treatment was extensible to the rest of non-human nature considering that animals occupied a higher place than flora or inanimate nature in the chain of being.[129]

Vitoria's and Soto's views on human ascendancy over animals make clear the kind of power that these authors derived from human *dominium*. For most authors of Second Scholasticism, human superiority over non-human nature was a necessary consequence of humans having been created in the image of God.[130] Contrastingly, based on the same Christian premises, Las Casas arrived at the contrary conclusion. Humans could not use animals and other natural life as they pleased. They had to realize God's plan for the fulfilment of nature's perfection. For him, human superiority over the environment was limited by God's programme, the content of which was, nonetheless, left undefined.[131] These kind of limits are absent from Vitoria's and Soto's texts. In principle, humans did not need to justify unsustainable practices because the most extreme of them, the destruction of nature, could be freely performed—even for pleasure (according to Vitoria). *Dominium* demarcated a personal space of absolute power over one's property. As far as human power over nature was concerned, being a proprietor was like being a semi-God.

Still we should be cautious when interpreting the views of Vitoria and Soto on human *dominium* as well as their environmental implications. Even if from a contemporary environmental sensitivity their views appear distinctly anthropocentric, there was still a clear limit to this anthropocentrism. For them the purpose of the absolute power that humans had over nature was not personal enrichment. The School of Salamanca was in principle opposed to the accumulation of capital.[132] Human power over God's creation resulted from the need of human

---

[127] For Soto as for Vitoria, *dominium* is the power over the very nature of the thing possessed. This entails destroying one's property, as for example, killing an animal. Soto, *De iustitia* (n 40) Book IV, 1.1, 281.

[128] Soto, *De iustitia* (n 40) Book IV, 1.1, 279.

[129] This expression refers to a Christian belief whereby all creatures were ordered in a scale of perfection from the lowest to the most noble: God. Reference to the Chain of Being was common at the time of Vitoria. Las Casas, for instance, stated that: 'Rational nature, after the angelic, is nobler and more perfect than any other created thing, and thus is the best and noblest part of the whole universe, to the extent that it has a greater resemblance to God.' See Las Casas, *Historia de Las Indias* (n 114) Vol I Book I Ch I, 23. Soto refers to the Chain of Being without explicitly mentioning it in Soto, *De iustitia* (n 40) Book IV, 1.2, 284.

[130] See also López, 'Propiedad y Dominio' (n 43) 82.

[131] Las Casas (n 114) Book I Ch I, 24–25.

[132] Angel García Sanz, 'El Contexto Económico del Pensamiento Escolástico: El Florecimiento del Capital Mercantul en la Espana del Siglo XVI' in F Gómez Camacho and Ricardo Robledo (eds), *Pensamiento Económico de la Escuela de Salamanca* (Ediciones Universidad de Salamanca 1998) 17, 19.

preservation.[133] The satisfaction of basic human needs had become severely compromised after the fall because nature no longer spontaneously supplied humanity with its bounty.[134] Therefore, the natural corollary of the need to transform nature more thoroughly in order to subsist was to grant humans the power to do so. It was the task of the Spanish scholastics to develop the legal institutions conductive to that end.

It is true that for Spanish scholastics there was no constraint to human power over nature and that, as Vitoria affirmed, it could even be exercised for mere pleasure. In this sense their views seem compatible and even conductive to the exploitation of nature. But still there was a limit to the scope of applicability of human environmental power based on the necessity of securing sustenance. But this limit—derived from a particular religious notion of human history—which could have acted as a counterbalance of the profit motive was never incorporated into the secular *jus gentium*.

Concluding Remarks

It is likely that without the Spanish obsession for fast wealth and the enormous dividends that Latin American natural resources gave to the Crown, the Latin American environment would have fared better. Unluckily, the *conquistadores* and the Spanish Crown had different ambitions regarding Latin American natural habitats. In the context of increasing material ambitions, the Spanish economic rights that Vitoria sanctioned were used to legitimize economic domination and environmental exploitation in Latin America. Ideas about nature provided the ideological background in which concrete economic practices flourished. At the same time, those practices and their value for empire shaped ideas, which eventually tended to conform more and more to the economic ethos of imperialism. In the context of an incipient but vibrant global economy, in which considerable power was accumulated, albeit in few hands, by the appropriation, extraction, and exchange of natural products, it was just a matter of time that the fragile non-legal limits that Vitoria and Soto had established to the exploitation of nature were once and for all transcended. In fact, following centuries would witness the ascent of other European powers and economic operators with similar dreams of wealth. In order to satisfy their ambitions they seized innumerable natural resources in Latin America, Asia, the Pacific, and Africa. The history of colonialism is also a history of economic elites (mostly of European origin) and their ascending power over nature worldwide.

[133] In his *relectio De Dominio* Soto distinguish between natural, divine, and human *dominium*, explaining that natural *dominium* is given by nature so that humans can eat and drink: Soto, *Relección* (n 59) s9 99. He then added that by nature humanity has a right over everything that is needed for its conservation: ibid, s13, 107.

[134] Soto, *De iustitia* (n 40) Book IV, 3.1, 296.

Latin Americans had occupied, consumed, used, and traded natural resources for centuries.[135] They had also shaped nature significantly and not always sustainably. However, the legal infrastructure provided by Vitoria allowed the privatization and exchange of nature-as-commodity on a continental scale and the use of that power to apprehend and exploit Latin American ecosystems entailed a substantial intensification of that pattern. In the absence of any limit to the materialization of Spanish economic rights, the fact that, for instance, the exploitation of timber or the establishment of mines and plantation agriculture displaced more sustainable uses of the same lands seemed not only legal but also progressive. Legitimized by the economic rights of *jus gentium*, the exchange economy of the sixteenth and seventeenth centuries (in which Latin American resources played a pivotal role) took shape, becoming one of the main factors of some the most significant and deleterious environmental changes of the Early Modern era.[136]

Despite being aware of the novelty and importance of the moment in which he was writing, it would be disingenuous to make Vitoria responsible for the historical and ongoing human and environmental tragedy that has resulted from centuries of global wealth accumulation. Perhaps more striking than the historical construction of this drama at a time in which the world's natural habitats seemed almost infinite is the continuation of human and environmental suffering in the face of today's awareness of the dreadful impact on both people and landscapes of our global economic system. No intellectual endeavour seems to help humans wake up from the dream of owning nature and prizing what is freely (though not necessarily unlimitedly) at our disposal (air, water, food). It may be that it is not the brain but an organ situated in the chest of our persona that this message has not yet reached.

Bibliography

Anghie, Antony, *Imperialism, Sovereignty and the Making of International Law* (Cambridge University Press 2004)

Attfield, Robin, 'Christian Attitudes to Nature' (1983) 44 Journal of the History of Ideas 369

Auat, Alejandro, 'Soberanía en Vitoria: Claves Transmodernas para un Principio Cuestionado' in Juan Cruz Cruz (ed), *Ley y Dominio en Francisco de Vitoria* (Eunsa 2008)

Barrera-Osorio, Antonio, *Experiencing Nature: The Spanish Latin American Empire and the Early Scientific Revolution* (University of Texas Press 2006)

Bitterli, Urs, *Cultures in Conflict: Encounters Between European and Non-European Cultures, 1492–1800* (Polity Press 1989)

Borah, Woodrow Wilson, *Justice by Insurance: The General Indian Court of Colonial Mexico and the Legal Aides of the Half-real* (University of California Press 1983)

---

[135] See Neal Salisbury, 'The Indian's Old World: Native Latin Americans and the Coming of Europeans' in Peter C Mancall and James H Merrell (eds), *Latin American Encounters: Natives and Newcomers from European Contact to Indian Removal, 1500–1850* (Routledge 2000) 4, 6.

[136] See in general Richards, *The Unending Frontier* (n 16).

Bowden, Brett, 'The Colonial Origins of International Law. European Expansion and the Classical Standard of Civilization' (2005) 7 Journal of the History of International Law 1

Bowden, Brett, *The Empire of Civilization: The Evolution of an Imperial Idea* (The University of Chicago Press 2009)

Brett, Annabel S, *Changes of State: Nature and the Limits of the City in Early Modern Natural Law* (Princeton University Press 2011)

Brown, Jonathan C, *Latin America: A Social History of the Colonial Period* (Thomson Wadsworth 2005)

Bruhns, Karen Olsen, *Ancient South Latin America* (Cambridge University Press 1994)

Cohen, Jeremy, '*Be Fertile and Increase, Fill the Earth and Master It*': The Ancient and Medieval Career of a Biblical Text (Cornell University Press 1989)

Crosby Jr, Alfred W, *The Columbian Exchange: Biological and Cultural Consequences of 1942* (Duke University Press 2003)

Cummins, John, *The Voyage of Christopher Columbus: Columbus Own Journal of Discovery Newly Restored and Translated* (Weidenfeld and Nicolson 1992)

Deloria Jr, Vine, *God is Red: A Native View of Religion* (Fulcrum Publishing 1992)

Denevan, William M, *Cultivated Landscapes of Native Amazonia and the Andes* (Oxford University Press 2001)

Díaz-Valentín, Patricio J López, 'Relación de Dominio y Ley en la Situación Latin Americana dentro del Pensamiento Vitoriano' in Juan Cruz Cruz (ed), *Ley y Dominio en Francisco Vitoria* (Eunsa 2008)

Dobyns, Henry F, 'Estimating Aboriginal Latin American Population: An Appraisal of Techniques with a New Hemispheric Estimate' (1966) 7 Current Anthropologist 395

Dore, Elisabeth, 'Environment and Society: Long-Term Trends in Latin America Mining' (2000) 6 Environment and History 1

Elliott, John H, *Empires of the Atlantic World: Britain and Spain in Latin America 1492–1830* (Yale University Press 2007)

Elliott, JH, *Spain, Europe & the Wider World 1500–1800* (Yale University Press 2009)

Galindo-Leal, Carlos and Câmara, Ibsen de Gusmão (eds), *The Atlantic Forest of South Latin America: Biodiversity Status, Threats and Outlook* (Island Press 2003)

Gentili, Alberico, *De iure belli libri tres* (Vol II, John C Rolfe tr of the 1612 edn, Clarendon Press 1933)

Glacken, Clarence J, *Traces on the Rhodian Shore: Nature and Culture in Western Thought from Ancient Times to the End of the Eighteenth Century* (University of California Press 1967)

Jane, Cecil (ed), *Select Documents Illustrating the Four Voyages of Columbus* (Vol II Hakluyt Society 1930–1933)

Justinian, *Institutes* http://thelatinlibrary.com/law/institutes.html

Keith, Robert G (ed), *Haciendas and Plantations in Latin America History* (Holmes & Meier Publishers Inc 1977)

Koskenniemi, Martti, 'Empire and International Law: The Real Spanish Contribution' (2011) 61 University of Toronto Law Journal 1

Las Casas, Bartolome de, *Historia de Las Indias*, Vol I (Fondo de Cultura Económica 1951)

Lauzon, Matthew J, 'Modernity' in Jerry H Bently (ed), *The Oxford Handbook of World History* (Oxford University Press 2011)

López, Teodoro, 'Propiedad y Dominio en Francisco Vitoria' in Juan Cruz Cruz, *Ley y Dominio en Francisco de Vitoria* (Eunsa 2008)

Mackay, Angus, *Spain in the Middles Ages: From Frontier towards Empire 1350–1500* (McMillan 1977)

MacLeod, Murdo J, *Spanish Central Latin America: A Socioeconomic History 1520–1720* (University of Texas Press 2008)

Magasich-Airola, Jorge and de Beer, Jean-Marc, *America Magica: When Renaissance Europe Thought it had Conquered Paradise* (Anthem Press 2007)

Mann, Charles C, *Ancient Latin Americans: Rewriting the History of the New World* (Granta Books 2005)

Mann, Charles C, *1493: How Europe's Discovery of the Latin Americas Revolutionised Trade, Ecology and Life on the Earth* (Granta Publications 2011)

Melville, Elinor G K, 'Global Developments and Latin American Environments' in Tom Griffiths and Libby Robin (eds), *Ecology and Empire: Environmental History of Settler Societies* (Keele University Press 1997)

Miéville, China, *Between Equal Rights: A Marxist Theory of International Law* (Brill 2005)

Miller, Shawn William, *An Environmental History of Latin America* (Cambridge University Press 2007)

Mörner, Magnus, 'The Rural Economy and Society in of Colonial Spanish South Latin America' in Leslie Bethell (ed), *The Cambridge History of Latin America Volume II* (Cambridge University Press 1984)

Nelson, Michael P and Callicott, J Baird (eds), *The Wilderness Debate Rages On: Continuing the Great New Wilderness Debate* (University of Georgia Press 2008)

Nriagu, Jerome O, 'Mercury Pollution from the Past Mining of Gold and Silver in the Latin Americas' (1994) 149 The Science of the Total Environment 167

Pagden, Anthony, *The Fall of Natural Man: The Latin American Indian and the Origins of Comparative Ethnology (Cambridge University Press 1982)*

Pagden, Anthony, 'Dispossessing the Barbarian: The Language of Spanish Thomism and the Debate over the Property Rights of the Latin American Indians' in David Armitage (ed), *Theories of Empire 1450–1800* (Ashgate 1998)

Passmore, John, *Man's Responsibility for Nature: Ecological Problems and Western Traditions* (Duckworth 1974)

Penyak, Lee M and Petry, Walter J (eds), *Religion in Latin America: A Documentary History* (Orbis Books 2006)

Porras, Ileana, 'Appropriating Nature: Commerce, Property, and the Commodification of Nature in the Law of Nations' (2014) 27 Leiden Journal of International Law 641

Pufendorf, Samuel, *De jure naturae et gentium libri octo*, vol II (James Brown Scott ed, CH Oldfather and WA Oldfather trs, Clarendon Press 1934)

Quijano, Anibal and Wallerstein, Immanuel, 'Latin Americanity as a Concept or the Latin Americas in the Modern World System' (1992) 134 International Journal of Social Science 549

Restall, Matthew, *Seven Myths of the Spanish Conquest* (Oxford University Press 2003)

Richards, John F, 'Early Modern India and World History' (1997) 8 Journal of World History 197

Richards, John F, *The Unending Frontier: An Environmental History of the Early Modern World* (University of California Press 2003)

Rubios, Juan López de Palacios, *Libellus de insulanis oceanis quas vulgus Indias appellat per Ioannem Lopez de Palacios Rubios decretorum doctorem regiumque consiliarum editus* (BNM 1513)

Salisbury, Neal, 'The Indian's Old World: Native Latin Americans and the Coming of Europeans' in Peter C Mancall and James H Merrell (eds), *Latin American Encounters: Natives and Newcomers from European Contact to Indian Removal, 1500–1850* (Routledge 2000)

Sanz, Angel García, 'El Contexto Económico del Pensamiento Escolástico: El Florecimiento del Capital Mercantul en la Espana del Siglo XVI' in F Gómez Camacho and Ricardo Robledo (eds), *Pensamiento Económico de la Escuela de Salamanca* (Ediciones Universidad de Salamanca 1998)

Schewering, Karl H, 'The Indian Populations of Latin America' in Jan Knippers Black (ed), *Latin America, its Problems and its Promise: A Multidisciplinary Introduction* (Westview Press 2005)

Schwartz, Stuart B, *Sugar Plantations in the Formation of Brazilian Society: Bahia, 1550–1835* (Cambridge University Press 1985)

Shammas, Carole, 'The Origins of the Transatlantic Colonization' in Daniel Vikers (ed), *A Companion to Colonial Latin America* (Blackwell Publishing 2003)

Soto, Domingo de, *Relección 'De dominio'* (Jaime Brufau Prats ed, Universidad de Granada 1964)

Soto, Domingo de, *De iustitia et iure libri decem* (Marcelino Gonzalez Ordoñez tr, Instituto de Estudios Políticos 1967)

Steiner, Gary, *Anthropocentrism and its Discontents: The Moral Status of Animals in the History of Western Philosophy* (University of Pittsburgh Press 2005)

Sullivan, Lawrence E (ed), *Native Religions and Cultures of Central and South Latin America* (The Continuum International Publishing Group Inc 2002)

Super, John C, *Food, Conquest and Colonization in Sixteenth-Century Spanish Latin America* (University of New Mexico Press 1988)

The First Letter of Christopher Columbus to the Noble Lord Raphael Sanchez Announcing the Discovery of Latin America (Reproduced in facsimile from the copy of the Latin Version of 1493 with a new introduction, Published by the Trustees 1891)

Vattel, Emmerich de, *The Law of Nations or The Principles of Natural Law Applied to the Conduct and to the Affairs of Nations and of Sovereigns* (Vol III, Charles G Fenwick tr of the 1758 edn, Carnegie Institution 1916)

Vilches, Elvira, *New World Gold: Cultural Anxiety and Monetary Disorder in Early Modern Spain* (The University of Chicago Press 2010)

Vitoria, Francisco de, *De indis et de iure belli relectiones* (Ernest Nys ed, John Pawley Bate tr, Carnegie Institution of Washington 1917)

Vitoria, Francisco de, 'On the Latin American Indians' in Francisco de Vitoria, *Political Writings* (Anthony Pagden and Jeremy Lawrance eds, Cambridge University Press 1991)

Vitoria, Francisco de, *Sobre el Poder Civil; Sobre los Indios; Sobre el Derecho de la Guerra* (Estudio preliminar, traducción y notas de Luis Frayle Delgado, Tecnos 2007)

Watts, David, 'Ecological Responses to Ecosystem Shock in the Island Caribbean: The Aftermath of Columbus, 1492–1992' in Robin A Butlin and Neil Roberts (eds), *Ecological Relations in Historical Times* (Blackwell 1995)

White Jr, Lynn, 'The Historical Roots of Our Ecological Crisis' (1967) 155 Science 1203

Whitmore, Thomas M and Turner II, BL, *Cultivated Landscapes of Middle Latin America on the Eve of Conquest* (Oxford University Press 2001)

7

Cerberus: Rethinking Grotius and the Westphalian System

*José-Manuel Barreto**

This chapter answers the question about the relationship between international law and imperialism by challenging the state-centred doctrine of the modern law of nations. One of the key tenets in the conventional understanding of the modern international order is the principle according to which only the state can be admitted as a full subject of international law; that the state is the sole entity able to convey in itself the 'marks of sovereignty', such as exclusive authority, non-intervention, and territorial integrity. The status of full subject of international law is made dependent on the possession of sovereignty, and the contemporary international legal order—usually characterized as the 'Westphalian system'—is defined as one of equally sovereign states,[1] as an interstate system, or as the state system. Relying on a re-interpretation of Grotius and the analysis of the material—political and economic—history of international law at the time of the events of the Peace of Westphalia, the thesis of this chapter is that not only the state but also the empire and the company are full subjects of international law. The resulting three-headed structure looks like a *Cerberus* (Figure 7.1) and makes evident that international law does not only regulate the relations between nation states. Since its very inception, modern international law has regulated the dealings between states, empires, and companies.[2] In other words, international law is not only a law inter-nations.

* I would like to thank Martii Koskenniemi and Manuel Jiménez Fonesca for inviting me to be part of the working group on 'Imperialism and International Law', as well as the other scholars of the group for their criticisms; Dan Danielsen and Illeana Porras for their encouragement when I began working on this topic; Nora Markard for expressing to me her doubts about the very sense of this idea; and Paul Ursell for helping me with my English.

[1] Gerry Simpson, 'Westphalian System' in Peter Cane and Joanne Conaghan (eds), *The New Oxford Companion to Law* (Oxford University Press 2008) 1243–44. Individuals and international organizations were admitted as subjects of international law in the twentieth century, but they are not regarded as full subjects that enjoy sovereign status and prerogatives.

[2] The idea of the subjectivity of the present day corporation has some advocates. Thus, Dan Danielsen suggests '[i]t would be interesting to explore some of the possible implications for public international law doctrine of treating corporations as quasi-public regulatory institutions': Dan Danielsen, 'Corporate Power and Global Order' in Ann Orford (ed), *International Law and Its Others* (Cambridge University Press 2009) 99. Considering the problem of the lack of accountability of transnationals, Claire Cutler wrote: 'One solution is the recognition of the transnational corporation as a

International Law and Empire: Historical Explorations. First Edition. Martti Koskenniemi, Walter Rech, and Manuel Jiménez Fonseca. © Martti Koskenniemi, Walter Rech, and Manuel Jiménez Fonseca 2016. Published 2016 by Oxford University Press.

Figure 7.1 Hercules capturing *Cerberus* by Sebald Beham, 1545.

This acknowledgement has significant consequences for the very architecture of the international legal system as it concerns its pillars—the subjects of international law—and its very structure—the framework sustaining the edifice of international law which is constructed on the basis of its subjects[3]—a theme central to the theory and practice of international law, and which is found in typical handbooks and syllabuses on the subject.

This conceptualization advances against the grain. The metaphor of *Cerberus* plainly contradicts the entrenched conception with its predicate that only the state—as public entity and exclusive holder of sovereignty—decides on international legal affairs. The introduction of two new subjects into the structure of international law meets a resistance in the status quo position. According to the established theory and the law as we have it, companies are exclusively commercial enterprises and private entities, and therefore cannot be holders of political and public characteristics, let alone sovereignty. Moreover, it is only lately that, despite its catastrophic presence in modern world history, the empire has been introduced as a factor in the debate and theoretical consideration of international law. But reticence remains,

legal subject': Claire Cutler, 'Critical Reflections on the Westphalian Assumptions of International Law and Organization: A Crisis of Legitimacy' (2001) 27 Review of International Studies 133, 146.

[3] The concept of 'structure of international law' in this legal and 'architectonic' connotation is commonly used in the established literature, as is the case throughout in Wilhelm Grewe, *The Epochs of International Law* (De Gruyter 2000).

and if empires are present in contemporary mainstream theories and histories of international law they are cast in a secondary or supporting role within the drama, or even as extras or ghosts.

By way of clarification as to the scope of the thesis presented here, it is necessary to make evident what is at stake. This text claims that the proposed three-headed structure of international law does not only reflect recent transformations of the world order prompted by contemporary globalization—commonly described as the weakening of sovereignty in nation states, and the accumulation of economic and political power in transnational corporations. The thesis of this chapter is rather that there have been three actors or subjects of international law since early modernity, and that the underlying situation has existed all along from the Renaissance until our present days. A centuries-long crisis undermines the Westphalian system. To illuminate the matter I propose to focus on the period when the Netherlands emerged as a sovereign state and as an empire in its own right in the historical context of gaining independence from the Spanish Empire at the end of the Eighty Years War—an event sealed by the Peace of Westphalia. Crucially, the transition that led the Low Countries to a sovereign political constitution was greatly aided by the vast accumulation of capital achieved by the Dutch empire mainly through the Dutch East and West India companies—the VOC and the WIC respectively.

Moreover, it is understood widely in legal disciplines and the social sciences that a strong link exists between modern international law and both the work of Grotius and the Peace of Westphalia. The latter has been generally quoted as the founding historical event of modern international law conceived as a system of equal and sovereign states, or as the law of interstate relationships. Grotius, on his part, has been addressed as its intellectual progenitor. To examine these deep-rooted assumptions this text will take into account critiques which have been advanced separately over the last decades both of Grotius and of the Westphalian doctrine. These critiques point to the one-sidedness of the longstanding interpretation of the theory of Grotius in the historical context of the time, and to the state-centric character of the Westphalian doctrine due to the idealist interpretation of the historical event of the Peace of Westphalia.

The re-contextualization of international law in the history and geography of modern colonialism made by Antony Anghie[4] allows us to look for the colonial settings of international law in the times of Dutch imperialism. At the root of this chapter there is a desire to offer some insights about how international law, both as legal normativity and political discourse, has been used in the past—and can be used in the present and the future—for justifying, as well as for resisting, the violence of imperialism. The construction of this different and more complex description of the legal and material[5] structure of modern international law relies on two sets

---

[4] Antony Anghie, *Imperialism, Sovereignty and the Making of International Law* (Cambridge University Press 2005).

[5] Apart from the legal or architectonic structure of international law, the material structure of international law refers to the political and economic conditions that gave rise and orientation to modern international law, among them, the 'colonial accumulation of capital'. In other words, material structure refers here to the historical process that creates and organizes international law, as a materialist

of arguments—a dual approach that has been present in modern theory of inter-national law since its beginnings.[6] Thus, Section 1 develops a rereading of Grotius' theory that looks for the place occupied by the figure of the company in his theory of international law. Section 2 elaborates a different interpretation of the Peace of Westphalia, tracing the connections between states, empires, and companies, and this historical event. A reformulation of these two classical sites of hegemonic dis-course should allow us to gaze at a different conception of both the subjects and the structure of modern international law, and their connection with imperialism.

The Company and the Colonial Origins of Grotius' Theory of International Law

The first strategy of argumentation of this chapter is to mobilize the critical rein-terpretation of the Grotius' work that has been elaborated in recent years—which points to his involvement with Dutch imperialism—and to develop it in the con-text of exploring the role of the company as a subject of international law. Grotius' life (born in Delf 1583, died in Rostock 1645) is coeval with the Eighty Years War between the Netherlands and Habsburg Spain (commencing in 1568) and with the Thirty Years War (beginning in 1618), and ended only shortly before the Peace of Westphalia (which put an end to both wars in 1648). More pertinently Grotius was an actor himself in the historical drama of the wars. He provided legal advice and doctrinal justification to those involved in these conflicts. He represented the Dutch States General in the truce negotiations convened in the midst of the Eighty Years War. It was famously said that Gustavus Adolphus, King of Sweden and head of one of the belligerent parties in the Thirty Years War, actually took into the bat-tlefield with him a copy of Grotius' *De iure belli ac pacis*.[7] Grotius has also been thought to be an architect of the Peace of Westphalia, since the principles which frame it have been traced to him.[8]

The idea of Grotius as the forerunner of the modern theory of international law is quite old. Already in the early eighteenth century Gianbattista Vico set the tone by calling Grotius the 'jurist of the human race'.[9] Adam Smith followed suit: 'Grotius seems to have been the first who attempted to give the world any-thing like a system of those principles which ought to run through, and be the

---

interpretation would have it, and in a similar sense to that present in Schmitt when he speaks of 'Land-appropriation as a constitutive process of international law': Carl Schmitt, *The Nomos of the Earth in the International Law of the Jus Publicum Europaeum* (Telos Press 2003) 80.

[6] This is already the case in Grotius' dual discourse of *Pars Theoretica* and *Pars Historica* of his *Commentarius in Theses XI*: see Peter Borschberg, *Hugo Grotius: Commentarius in Theses XI. An Early Treatise on Sovereignty, the Just War, and the Legitimacy of the Dutch Revolt* (Peter Lang 1994) 113.

[7] Martine Julia van Ittersum, *Profit and Principle: Hugo Grotius, Natural Rights Theories and the Rise of Dutch Power in the East Indies 1595–1615* (Brill 2006) xxvii.

[8] Edward Keene, 'The Reception of Hugo Grotius in International Relations Theory' (1999/2000) 20/21 Grotiana 135, 140–47.

[9] Quoted in Arthur Nussbaum, *A Concise History of the Law of Nations* (McMillan 1954) 114.

foundation of the laws of all nations'.[10] Some decades later in two of the earliest examples of works that attempted to develop a full narrative of the modern history of international law, Grotius figures prominently. First, Joachín Marín's *Historia del Derecho Natural, y de Gentes*, published in Spain in 1776, commences from Grotius, lauding him as the most important modern authority who applied to the discipline the greatest level of generalization and systematization while anchoring the law of nations to the theory of justice.[11] Second, in 1795 Robert Plumer Ward gave Grotius central place in the pantheon of the legal international tradition, asserting that Grotius 'was universally established in Christendom as the true fountain-head of the European Law of Nations' and called the period that followed his work the 'Age of Grotius'.[12]

In the nineteenth century, after most countries in Latin America achieved independence, scholars like Andrés Bello legitimized the recently secured sovereignty in terms of the European canon of international law. Already in 1832, Bello saw in Grotius' work a synthesis of the theory of international law and the founding block of the discipline as an independent area of scholarship, although he did point to Francisco Suárez as the first modern author.[13] Decades later Wilhelm Heffter described Grotius' theory as a truthful European *Völkercodex*.[14] By the end of the century, Ernest Nys had set the narrative that became standard in the handbooks of international law in the twentieth century: allowing to the School of Salamanca significance as the precursors of the modern tradition—but relegating their contribution to a preliminary and imperfect stage of its development—while Grotius clearly had to be recognized as the founder that made the discipline a secular and humanist 'science'.[15]

In the first half of the twentieth century the prominence of Grotius remained unchallenged, apart from the studies by James Brown Scott and Carl Schmitt, who found in Francisco de Vitoria another forefather of the modern law of nations. But on the whole this was not allowed and Grotius remained at the pinnacle of the canon. For example, Arthur Nussbaum named him 'the founder or the father' of modern international law since Grotius, he claimed, had secured the formation and secularization of international law as a 'unified whole', as well as articulating a number of special areas of the discipline such as the law of the seas and the theory of treaties.[16] Just before and after the Second World War, Cornelis van Vollenhoven

---

[10] Adam Smith, *The Theory of Moral Sentiments* (Millar, Kinkaid & Bell 1767) 436.

[11] Joachín Marín, *Historia del Derecho Natural, y de Gentes* (Manuel Martín 1776) 16, 26.

[12] Robert Plumer Ward, *An Enquiry into the Foundation and History of the Law of Nations in Europe: From the Time of the Greeks and Romans, to the Age of Grotius* (Strahan & Woodfall 1795) xlvi–xlvii, 620–21.

[13] Andrés Bello, *Principios de Derecho de Gentes* (Librería de la Señora Viuda de Calleja é Hijos & Casa de Calleja 1844) 25.

[14] Quoted in Martti Koskenniemi, 'A History of International Law Histories' in Bardo Fassbender and Anne Peters (eds), *The Oxford Handbook of the History of International Law* (Oxford University Press 2012) 953.

[15] Ernest Nys, *Les Origines du Droit Internationale* (Bohn 1894) 11.

[16] Nussbaum, *A Concise History* (n 9) 108, 110, 113. In post-war Germany, Grotius ascendance receded, and Vitoria and Suárez came to prominence in the writings of Soder, Höffner, Stadtmüller,

and Hersch Lauterpacht developed in their work a synthesis and formalization of the 'Grotian Tradition'.[17] It was not until the 1990s that Grotius' pre-eminence was challenged. Antony Anghie questioned the storyline of the Grotian genealogy and, recalling James Brown Scott and Carl Schmitt, sought to redirect attention to Vitoria, whose work would provide scenario and the contents for his thesis about the colonial origins of modern international law.[18]

Not only was Grotius' centrality as progenitor challenged. Most importantly for the purposes of my argument, there has been a shift in the way his legacy is interpreted. The classical reading of Grotius' conception of international law links him to the best of European culture. Thus, Nussbaum identified the Grotian theory with the ideals and values of humanism—tolerance, conciliation, truth, humanity—and credited his work with being part of 'the conscience of the civilised world'.[19] In the Grotian tradition, states are situated within constraints established by moral and legal rules, and this web of norms plays a constitutive or constitutional role defining the relations between sovereigns.[20] The theory of Grotius has also been inveterately identified with a conception of international law as a body of norms that set limits to war, and as a venue or a fortress for peace.

Recently, a different approach has begun to take hold in international theory, portraying Grotius' work as responding to interests attached to the modern colonization of the world, and orientated to the purpose of justifying Dutch imperialism. This line of reflection reads Grotius not as the mythical father of modern international law, but as the advocate for or the lawyer in the service of the VOC.[21] Peace would not be the main goal of Grotius' endeavour. On the contrary, his elaboration of international law may be seen as orientated chiefly to the justification of piracy, imperial violence, and war making. Additionally, when one recognizes the connection with colonialism, the assumed exclusivity of European origin and scope comes into question. It is plain that Grotius' work grew out of problems emerging outside Europe and in the context of the history of the colonization of the world.[22]

---

von der Heydte, and Hadrossek, and of Grewe himself, who developed a devastating critique of the standing of Grotius in the tradition. See Grewe, *The Epochs* (n 3) 188 fn 5, 191–95.

[17] C van Vollenhoven, 'Grotius and the Study of Law' (1925) 19 American Journal of International Law 1; Hersch Lauterpacht, 'The Grotian Tradition of International Law' (1946) 23 British Yearbook of International Law 1.

[18] Anghie, *Imperialism* (n 4).   [19] Nussbaum, *A Concise History* (n 9) 109, 110, 113–14.

[20] A Claire Cutler, 'The "Grotian Tradition" in International Relations' (1991) 17 Review of International Studies 41.

[21] This is the critical work developed mainly by Peter Borschberg, Martine Julia Van Ittersum, Edward Keene, Richard Tuck, and Eric Wilson. In this line of research see also Benjamin Straumann, ' "Ancient Caesarean Lawyers" in a State of Nature: Roman Tradition and Natural Rights in Hugo Grotius's "De iure praedae" ' (2006) 34 Political Theory 328; Renee Jeffery, *Hugo Grotius in International Thought* (Palgrave Macmillan 2006) 6–7; Tarik Kochi, *The Other's War. Recognition and the Violence of Ethics* (Birkbeck Law Press 2009) 59–60.

[22] This is also evident if for a moment we put aside the established title given by the nineteenth-century publishers to the treatise dedicated to justify the VOC's act of piracy—'*De iure praedae*' or '*Commentary on the Laws of Prize and Booty*'—and have in mind Grotius' own way of referring to it as '*De Indis*', in the lineage of Vitoria's important work.

The consequences of this revision of Grotius scholarship coincide with those of the characteristic postcolonial interpretative gesture of tracing the links of a subject to the history of colonialism. We are travelling the path for reflection opened by Antony Anghie when he pointed to the colonial origins of international law. Thus, this investigation is aimed at highlighting the imperial roots of Grotius' theory, and describing the consequences for the theory of the subjects and the structure of international law.[23]

The intellectual work of Grotius in the field of international law was initially constituted and guided by his engagement with the VOC. With *De iure prae-dae* Grotius fulfilled a commission given to him by the directors of the VOC to write a memorandum justifying the violent appropriation of the cargo of the *Santa Catarina*, a Portuguese merchant carrack that was sailing off the coast of Sumatra on February 1603. Actually, *De iure praedae* was never considered by the Amsterdam Admiralty Board—the Dutch authority in charge of deciding on the legality of the treasure—which in 1604 ruled in favour of the seizure of the *Santa Catarina* as legitimate booty anyway. The decision was based on considerations related to the applicability of the doctrine of the just war, among others. Personal motives and patriotism seem to have played a part in the composition of the memorandum. Jakob van Heermskerk, the captain of a Dutch ship that seized the *Santa Catarina*, was a cousin of Grotius.[24] Crucially, in his own words Grotius was 'struck with amazement' at the sight of the 'wealth' displayed when the shipment of musk, silk, clothes, gold, sugar, spices, wooden furniture, and porcelain was auctioned in Amsterdam.[25] To the wonder of all, the value of the loot was equivalent to half of the capital with which the VOC had been created in 1602, and to twice that with which the British East India Company was established just two years before.[26] At the tender age of 21, Grotius was well aware of what was at stake when justifying the plunder of the *Santa Catarina*.

The writing of *De iure praedae* and the declaration of legality of the plunder of the *Santa Catarina* were accompanied by the deterioration of the relations between the Dutch and the Portuguese.[27] Significantly there was also a change in the guidance

[23] A similar interpretation of Grotius from the perspective of Anghie's thesis has already been developed in Ileana Porras, 'Constructing International Law in the East Indian Seas: Property, Sovereignty, Commerce and War in Hugo Grotius' De Iure Praedae—The Law of Prize and Booty, or "On How to Distinguish Merchant from Pirates"' (2006) 31 Brooklyn Journal of International Law 741, 743–44.

[24] Anthony Pagden, 'Occupying the Ocean. Hugo Grotius and Serafim de Freitas on the Rights of Discovery and Occupation' in Anthony Pagden, *The Burdens of Empire: 1539 to the Present* (Cambridge University Press 2015) 159.

[25] Quoted in Peter Borschberg, 'The Seizure of the Santa Catarina Revisited: The Portuguese Empire in Asia, VOC Politics and the Origins of the Dutch-Johor Alliance (c.1602–1616)' (2002) 33 Journal of Southeast Asian Studies 31, 31, 38.

[26] Peter Borschberg, 'The Santa Catarina Incident of 1603: Dutch Freebooting, the Portuguese Estado da Índia and Intra-Asian Trade at the Dawn of the 17th Century' (2004) 11 Revista de Cultura 13.

[27] The animosity between the two was also prompted by the fact that between 1580 and 1640 the Habsburg King of Spain was also the ruler of Portugal, a political arrangement that has been referred to as the Iberian Union or the Iberian Empire.

given to the VOC's ships henceforth. Captains of the vessels sailing to the East Indies had been instructed to 'defend themselves' and to seek compensation for any damage suffered. However, after November 1603, the VOC turned to a policy of full scale piracy. Thus the way was paved for a Dutch 'enterprise' to grow and flourish as vast amounts of capital entered the coffers of the VOC. Piracy became a cornerstone of the economic growth of the VOC,[28] and of the WIC, which captured 547 Spanish ships full of American treasure and African slaves between just 1623 and 1636.[29] The impetus for the establishment and consolidation of the Dutch Empire had been created.

A defence for the 'adventures' undertaken by the VOC is not restricted to *De iure praedae*, with its rationale reverberating throughout Grotius' entire work. *De iure praedae* was his first work, but it was also the source of his *Mare liberum*, the latter being a chapter derived from the earlier work.[30] It has also been said that the argument advanced in *De iure praedae* bears a strong resemblance to the 'objective and the programme' of his *Commentarius in Thesis XI*,[31] and that it contains in an embryonic form Grotius' most important work, *De iure belli ac pacis*.[32] As we will see, just war and sovereignty, two of the principal notions within international law—as well as those of the freedom of the seas, the right to trade, the right to navigation, humanity, reason, God, natural law, and the universality and immutability of the principles of international law themselves—were all elaborated and mobilized in order to defend the interests of the VOC and the Dutch empire.

In what terms did Grotius support the VOC's piracy, and what are the consequences of his engagement with imperialism for his definition of the subjects of international law? Before Grotius, the *jus gentium* contemplated the idea of just war only as a public enterprise, as in the cases of Augustine, Aquinas, and Vitoria, for whom a war could be just only if it was waged by the sovereign. The notion of a just private war did not exist, or could be admitted only in very exceptional circumstances. Grotius justified the legality of the VOC's acts of piracy by creating the distinction between public and private war, while suggesting at the same time the idea of the divisibility of sovereignty. Grotius had to accomplish a 'revolution'[33] in order to uncouple the prerogative to declare and wage war from the Crown or the monarch so as to give legitimacy to a war waged by private individuals, or by associations of individuals and capital as in the case of the VOC.[34] What used to be disallowed or be exceptional became the norm.

[28] Peter Borschberg, 'From Self-Defense to an Instrument of War: Dutch Privateering Around the Malay Peninsula in the Early Seventeenth Century' (2013) 17 Journal of Early Modern History 35, 35.

[29] Barbara Lewis Solow and Stanley L Engerman (eds), *British Capitalism and Caribbean Slavery: The Legacy of Eric Williams* (Cambridge University Press 1987) 43.

[30] HW Blom, 'Introduction' (2005–2007) 26–28 Grotiana 1, 3.

[31] Borschberg, *Hugo Grotius* (n 6) 110.

[32] Porras, 'Constructing International Law' (n 23) 747.

[33] Martine Julia van Ittersum's introduction to Hugo Grotius, *Commentary on the Law of Prize and Booty* (Martine van Ittersum ed, Liberty Fund 2006) xvii.

[34] Richard Tuck, *The Rights of War and Peace: Political Thought and International Order from Grotius to Kant* (Oxford University Press 1999) 85.

The doctrine of natural law, which Grotius develops in Chapter XII of *De iure praedae* from notions of God and reason, foregrounds his theory of private just war.[35] A private war becomes just as a consequence of the existence of a right to wage war that resides in individuals. From this it is possible to infer that groups of individuals, including those associated in the VOC, have a right to wage war.[36] The justice of a private war can also be the indirect outcome of the prerogative to re-establish, even by force, rights that have been violated. These rights are specified as those to navigate and to trade freely, which are understood to be both individual and collective—inasmuch as they are possessed by the 'human fellowship' or by 'all mankind'. A private war becomes a just war also when it is waged to secure compensation for losses, including loss of profit.[37] The VOC was also entitled to use violence against the crew of the *Santa Catarina* as punishment or revenge for the previous execution of seventeen Dutch sailors,[38] as well as for a list of other offences of 'grave nature' committed previously by the Portuguese in the East Indies, including 'savage calumny', 'perfidy', and 'rapine'.[39] In short, a private war is just if 'the true end of war is the attainment of one's right'.[40] Crucially the justice of grabbing cargo as prize or booty, immediately follows the declaration of the justice of a private war. In short the legitimation of private wars entails the creation of another type of just war, and the welcoming of others forms of violence into the sanctuary of international law.

The significance of this 'revolution' performed in the centuries-old doctrine of the just war resides not just in the legitimation of the VOC's piracy readiness. The notion of the legality of private war has also fundamental consequences for the definition of sovereignty and the prospect of its division. The States General or the United Provinces are not the only holders of sovereignty. As Eric Wilson points out, 'by attempting to legitimate the VOC's natural right to wage just war, Grotius invests a private entity with a public mark of sovereignty'.[41] The privilege and responsibility of deciding on whether or not to declare or go to war—a grave one since the integrity or even the existence of a people or a kingdom are at stake—is one that had resided only in the sovereign and is a conspicuous mark of sovereignty: he who holds the capacity to decide on the war is the sovereign.[42] By giving the VOC

---

[35] Straumann finds in Roman private law an antecedent of Grotius' distinction between public and private war, which is instrumental to the doctrine of the just war with which, in turn, he justifies Dutch imperialism: Straumann, 'Ancient Caesarean Lawyers' (n 21) 331, 336.

[36] Grotius, *The Law of Prize and Booty* (n 33) 302.   [37] Ibid, 363–67, 381.

[38] Ibid, xix.

[39] Ibid, 372–76, 381. While Grotius makes the case against the Portuguese, because of the wickedness of their inclination for slander and piracy, he makes evident the true nature of the Dutch: 'the people of these countries [the Low Countries] are extremely zealous in the cultivation not of piracy but of commerce, being moreover free from every rapacious inclination, superior to all others in sexual temperance and in their whole way of life, and characterized by the most profound reverence for the laws, for the magistrates, and above all for religion'; ibid, 369.

[40] Ibid, 384.

[41] Eric Wilson, 'The VOC, Corporate Sovereignty and the Republican Sub-Text of *De iure praedae*' (2005–2007) 26–28 Grotiana 310, 310.

[42] This reasoning is similar to Schmitt's idea according to which the sovereign is the one who decides on the state of emergency, which is the concept used to identify the sovereign in the constitutional

legal capacity to wage war, Grotius transfers sovereignty to a private actor. A new sovereign has been conjured into existence—a private company has become a sovereign because it may go to war on its own volition, or without the express backing of any established public holder of sovereignty. On this basis Wilson concludes: 'the VOC may be accurately denoted a "corporate sovereign".'[43] By becoming a sovereign the company acquires subjectivity or personality in the international legal framework. In other words, Wilson again, 'this [is an] investiture of a non-state actor with public international legal personality'.[44] The company has been established as a sovereign subject of international law.

Paradoxically, Grotius emerges here as illuminating to the thinking of the structure of international law—not the state-centred structure as it has been described in an non-realistic and Eurocentric fashion on the basis of the Westphalian doctrine—but the structure of international law in which the company occupies a central place and is legitimized to wage war.[45] Grotius has not lost his place between the founding fathers of modern international law. He remains inhabiting such an Olympus, yet in another sense or for different reasons. It has been made clear that Grotius is not the founder of international law defined as a system that regulates the affairs between equal and sovereign states. Together with Vitoria, Grotius remains in the selected group of the 'early parents of modern international law',[46] a legal regime that is understood as emerging out of imperialism's needs for legitimation, and that regulated the relations between its subjects, including early modern companies.

sphere, and as a definition of internal sovereignty: Carl Schmitt, *Political Theology: Four Chapters on the Concept of Sovereignty* (Chicago University Press 2005) 5.

[43] Wilson, 'The VOC' (n 41) 310. The same conceptualization has been elaborated regarding the question of the sovereignty of the British East India Company. Against the backdrop of the tradition that exclusively associates 'the Company' with a trading venture, Philip Stern considers among its multiple instantiations those of 'a corporation, a jurisdiction and a colonial proprietor', and describes its constitutional identity as 'a form of government, state, and sovereign'. The company is, Stern concludes citing Edmund Burke, 'a State in the disguise of a merchant'. Stern also refers to the company as 'a nation state and empire', and describes the company as a 'merchant-empire'. Philip J Stern, *The State-Company: Corporate Sovereignty and the Early Modern Foundations of the British Empire in India* (Oxford University Press 2011) viii, 3.

[44] Wilson, 'The VOC' (n 41) 310. Above all, this chapter objects to Wilson's crucial contribution in that the Grotian legal structure of the VOC can resemble more the principles of an empire than those of a republic or a state. In the public status acquired by the VOC in Grotius' 'pamphlet' Wilson only sees a republican feature, and does not pay much attention to the imperialist nature of the VOC. However the *De iure praedae* corresponds more to Grotius' colonial moment than to the republican one, which is embedded in the struggle for independence from Spain.

[45] Regarding this matter, I agree with Peter Haggenmacher when he thinks of Grotius' theory as a continuation of the theory of the School of Salamanca and as a doctrine that justifies war. But I disagree when he concludes that, precisely for this reason, Grotius did not address the question of the structure of international law. See Benedict Kingsbury, 'A Grotian Tradition of Theory and Practice? Grotius, Law and Moral Skepticism in the Thought of Hedley Bull' (1997) 17 Quinnipiac Law Review 3, 8.

[46] A multiple fatherhood extended over centuries could be more appropriate to trace the founding or key figures of modern international law, avoiding the rather subjective and inaccurate pinpointing of a single father—and no mothers, whose contribution is still to be reconstructed.

Cerberus and the History of Dutch Imperialism: An Alternative Interpretation of the Peace of Westphalia

Over the last two decades there has been a chorus of critical interventions in the field of the theory and history of International Law, and in International Relations, that have sought to unveil the mythical origins of the so-called Westphalian theory of modern international law. According to this critique, the Westphalian doctrine does not correspond to the historical facts of the Peace of Westphalia as the treaties signed in Münster and Osnabruck did not create a European-wide state system. Nor did they sanction the principles of sovereignty, equality among states, and non-intervention—which were to form the core of modern international law as it is known and applied today. And sovereignty was not granted to the 'estates', landers, or principalities of the Holy Roman German Empire because they were still subjected to the Emperor. Equality could not be predicated as characterizing the relations between the empire and the principalities, and intervention in the affairs of the landers by the emperor was the rule rather than respect for self-government.[47] This chapter is aware of this body of scholarship but develops a different critique of the Westphalian doctrine.

The Westphalian theory was not born at the time of the peace agreements of 1648 but was elaborated later on. There are various opinions about the date of origin with some scholars placing it as late as the end of the nineteenth and the beginning of the twentieth centuries.[48] Some locate it earlier at the time of the emergence of professional international law at the end of the nineteenth century and with the works of Ernest Nys.[49] Nevertheless, the trajectory of the classical Westphalian doctrine appears to be longer if we take into consideration works like those by Henry Wheaton, who in 1845 adopted the Peace of Westphalia as the historical background of his *History of the Law of Nations*.[50]

Above all, it seems that the first steps in the construction of the Westphalian doctrine occurred not long after the signing of the Peace of Westphalia. Already in the second half of the seventeenth century Samuel Pufendorf interpreted the Peace of Westphalia as a set of treaties devoted to guaranteeing the freedom of the electoral princes of the Holy Roman German Empire—who were his employers—with the aim of avoiding a repetition of previous intrusions into their territories made by foreign powers during the Thirty Years War.[51] With the same autonomist purpose, a

---

[47] Andreas Osiander, 'Sovereignty, International Relations, and the Westphalian Myth' (2001) 55 International Organization 251.

[48] Ibid, 251.

[49] Martti Koskenniemi, *Histories of International Law: Dealing with Eurocentrism* (University of Utrecht 2011) 5–7.

[50] Henry Wheaton, *History of the Law of Nations in Europe and America* (Gould, Banks & Co 1845) 69. The title of the original text in French is very telling: '*Histoire de progrès de droit des gens depuis la Paix de Westphalie jusqu'au congrès de Vienne: avec un précis historique du droit des gens Européens avant la Paix de Westphalie*'.

[51] Tuck, *The Rights of War and Peace* (n 34) 160; van Ittersum, *Profit and Principle* (n 7) xxix–xxx.

cluster of German scholars straddled in between the seventeenth and the eighteenth centuries including Leibniz and Vattel—who had professional attachments to different German princes and 'estates'—contributed to the elaboration of a common conception of the law of nations as interstate law—or as a law that orders the relation between states.[52] On his part, Christian Wolff, in the middle of the eighteenth century, interpreted the treaties of Westphalia as shields protecting the independence of the landers of the Holy Roman German Empire, and defended the principle of equality among states.[53] Thus, his statist conception of international law was in tune with, and can be counted among the sources of, the Westphalian doctrine.

In the early nineteenth century, and again in the historical scenario of the affairs between France and the German 'estates', a second layer of the Westphalian doctrine was established. Indeed, France's imperial expansion to the East had brought most of the German landers into the Confederation of the Rhine, a protectorate under the rule of Napoleon. In this context, the Westphalian theory was a doctrinal apparatus developing from the need to repel the advance of revolutionary and imperialist France and Napoleon—the 'Emperor' of the French, or the 'Spirit' riding a horse in the streets of Jena as Hegel put it—on the dissolved Holy Roman German Empire. A group of German historians, among them AHL Herren, CW Koch, and F Schoell, embraced Kant's project of a society of nations made up of independent states, and interpreted the Peace of Westphalia as the 'inauguration' of a European states-system—a society of sovereign states free from the menace of foreign intervention.[54]

It has to be said that the lack of historical soundness—its mythical character—did not deprive the Westphalian doctrine of having a function in history,[55] mainly that of keeping the autonomy of the German principalities in front of the French kings and the French emperor. Later on, the spreading of the European international law and the Westphalian doctrine to all the corners of the Earth was the consequence of the recognition of new sovereign states emerging following the wars of independence that took place in the Americas mainly in the nineteenth century, as well as the process of decolonization of Africa, Asia, Oceania, the Middle East, and the Caribbean in the twentieth century. In this way the Westphalian doctrine came to be adopted in the course of the nineteenth and twentieth centuries as the proper understanding of the international order, first in Europe and then throughout the world, becoming the dominant criteria guiding international politics and legal practice.

The main concern of this text is rather about the Westphalian conception of the single-subject structure of international law, which comes from an idealist and

---

[52] van Ittersum, *Profit and Principle* (n 7) xxix–xxx; Tetsuya Toyoda, *Theory and Politics of the Law of Nations: Political Bias in International Law Discourse of Seven German Court Councillors in the Seventeenth and Eighteenth Centuries* (Martinus Nijhoff 2011) 12–13.

[53] Toyoda, *Theory and Politics of the Law of Nations* (n 52) 17.

[54] Edward Keene, *Beyond the Anarchical Society: Grotius, Colonialism and Order in World Politics* (Cambridge University Press 2002) 13, 20–22. See also van Ittersum, *Profit and Principle* (n 7) xxx.

[55] See Richard Joyce, 'Westphalia: Event, Memory, Myth' in Fleur Johns, Richard Joyce, and Sundhya Pahuja (eds), *Events: The Force of International Law* (Routledge 2011).

ideological interpretation of the historical event of the Peace of Westphalia. As idealist, it does not pay enough attention to the complexity of the world political and economic scenario in which the peace agreements were signed, focusing exclusively on the geography of Europe and the figure of the state. It also becomes an ideological doctrine when it makes invisible the crucial role empires and companies have accomplished in the construction and evolution of the international legal order since early modernity, granting them freedom and impunity for their destructive designs.[56]

Most critiques of the Westphalian theory looking at it as a myth focus chiefly on analysing two of the three treaties that were part of the Peace of Westphalia: the (second) Treaty of Münster and the Treaty of Osnabruck, both signed on 24 October 1648. Aimed at ending the war of religion that had decimated the population and transformed the German 'estates' into a waste land, the treaties put an end to the Thirty Years War between Catholic and Protestant 'estates' that were part of the Holy Roman German Empire, and between France and the Habsburg powers comprising the Holy Roman German Empire and the Spanish empire.[57] These treaties applied mainly to the territory of the Holy Roman German Empire. A key outcome of the treaties was the definition of the relations between the Holy Roman German Emperor and its more than 300 'estates', princes, and free cities mostly situated in what today is Germany.[58]

This reflection examines the other treaty of Münster (hereinafter the First Treaty of Münster), that perhaps has received less scrutiny. It was signed earlier on 30th January and ratified on 15 May 1648. Charles V, the grandson of Mary of Burgundy, inherited from her the Low Countries, which together with the Spanish Empire and the Holy Roman German Empire formed his own realm, one in 'which the sun never sets'. However, the Dutch Revolt for independence started already in 1566, a mere eleven years after the abdication of Charles V. The First Treaty of Münster put an end to the Eighty Years War between the United Provinces of the Netherlands and Spain, with King Philip IV losing his dominions in the Low Countries, and the Dutch Republic securing independence.[59]

Set in the context of the analysis of the First Treaty of Münster, the purpose of this interpretation is to show how the hegemonic theory of international

---

[56] 'Transnational corporations (TNCs) benefit from their international nonstatus. Nonstatus immunizes them from direct accountability to international legal norms': Jonathan I Charney, 'Transnational Corporations and Developing Public International Law' (1983) Duke Law Journal 748, 767.

[57] The Peace of Westphalia is an event of great importance in European history because it put an end to two of the longest wars that devastated the continent, and because it involved almost all the great European powers of the time, including the Holy Roman Empire, France, Sweden, Spain, the Netherlands, the Old Swiss Confederation, Denmark-Norway, Russia, England, the Ottoman Empire, and Poland-Lithuania.

[58] The political nature of the Holy Roman German Empire was complex and changed over the millennia it lasted. Some date it from the coronation of Charlemagne by Pope Leo III in 800 until its dissolution by Napoleon in 1806.

[59] The exclusive reliance of the analysis of the Peace of Westphalia on the study of these two treaties is such that this side of the peace agreements has been called by some 'the Peace of Westphalia proper'. See Keene, 'The Reception of Hugo Grotius' (n 8) 142.

law—frequently called Westphalian—does not give an account of how empires and companies already historically constituted and operated the international legal system in early modernity. In other words this investigation puts into evidence the crisis of legitimacy of the single-subject structure or statist framework of the mainstream conception of modern international law. In order to fulfil this objective, this chapter outlines an alternative interpretation of the Peace of Westphalia or, to be precise, of the events surrounding the First Treaty of Münster.

In order to trace the contours of the state as a subject of international law, and to bring to light the way in which the empire and the company also acted in the historical milieu of early modernity with analogous status, this chapter relies on the historical analysis of the global—and not only European—factors involved in the Peace of Westphalia. Going beyond a positivistic reading of the treaties, this section engages in the analysis of the material, or political and economic, conditions in which the peace between the Netherlands and Spain was reached. For Giovanni Arrighi, the accumulation of capital accomplished by Dutch imperialism translated into the capacity of the Netherlands to manipulate the European political system.[60] Did the power over the political configuration of Europe include the ability to set or define fundamental features of the system of international law? Was the process of colonial accumulation of capital constitutive of international law?

The State as Subject of International Law

Let's bring back into consideration the critique of the mythical character of the origins of the Westphalian doctrine. It has been said correctly that it is not sound to describe the more than 300 'estates' that at the time of the peace deals were under the jurisdiction of the Holy Roman Emperor as states or as nation states in the modern early sense of the term, and much less in contemporary usage. This is the main reason why those who argue that finding the origins of the Westphalian doctrine in this situation is a myth are correct. However, this critique is valid only regarding the political status of the above-mentioned 300 plus 'estates', and the consequences for them of the peace agreements that ended the Thirty Years War. The same cannot be said regarding the other protagonists of the Conference of Westphalia—the European 'states' signing the treaties.[61]

---

[60] Giovanni Arrighi, *The Long Twentieth Century: Money, Power and the Origins of Our Times* (Verso 2010) 141.

[61] In this chapter the term 'state' is used only to refer to the general figure of the nation state. On their part, the terms 'estate' or 'estate of the Empire' (from the German *Reichsstand*), 'lander', and 'principality' are used to refer to the particular historical communities that were part of the Holy Roman German Empire. These were more than 300 federal or semi-autonomous but non-sovereign German polities, which had different constitutions, such as feudal principalities, free cities, and bishoprics, most of whom had a vote in the Imperial Diet, the parliamentary institution of the Empire. Usually seven of them, the Electors, were entitled to participate in the appointment or confirmation of the Holy Roman Emperor. See Grewe, *The Epochs* (n 3) 185.

It would be counter-evident to deny that most of the European powers that participated in the negotiations that were conducted to terminate the Eighty and the Thirty Years Wars were already early modern nation states: for instance, Spain, France, England, Sweden, and Portugal, as Cassese maintains.[62] Other authors working in the field agree. It is precisely in the 'Spanish Age' of international law—between 1494 and 1648—the period in which Grewe locates the formation of early modern states in Europe.[63] Nussbaum wrote that 'the growth of international law in the new era … must be attributed … to the rise of national states, especially of Spain, England, and France',[64] a group of forerunners to which Toyoda adds the Netherlands.[65] Thus, it appears that for some time there has been a consensus among international legal historians about the idea of placing the end of the medieval order and the origins of the modern state system in the first half of the sixteenth century, while the seventeenth century would be the consolidation of 'the modern law of nations, based on the idea of state sovereignty'.[66] On their part, political historians like Perry Anderson coincide with this assessment about the initial stages of state formation in early modern Europe. He argues that the emergence of 'territorial states'—including Spain and France—and of the 'state-system' in Western Europe occurred at the time of the Renaissance, a process that was connected to the rise of absolutism.[67] In a similar direction and from a sociological perspective, Immanuel Wallerstein also points to the 'long 16th century'—1450 until 1640—as the historical period in which the modern world-system is originated.[68]

Spain went to the peace negotiations as an early nation state which, already for more than a century, had consolidated its dominium over the territory of the Iberian Peninsula—with the marriage of the Queen and King of Castilla and Aragon, and the expulsion of the Muslims and the Jews in 1492—except for the territory of another early nation state, Portugal. The Spanish state was already a case of state-construction at the time of the positioning of Habsburg Spain as the more powerful political actor in Europe in the wake of its imperial conquests and the resultant vast 'colonial' accumulation of capital.[69]

The status of the Netherlands as a nation state at the moment of signing the First Treaty of Westphalia involves a double political and legal move. The Dutch Republic had already been constitutionally established with the Union of Utrecht in 1579, in which the Northern provinces of the Netherlands came together to form a nation,

---

[62] Antonio Cassese, 'States: Rise and Decline of the Primary Subjects of the International Community' in Fassbender and Peters (eds), *The Oxford Handbook of the History of International Law* (n 14) 49.

[63] Grewe, *The Epochs* (n 3) 163–77.   [64] Nussbaum, *A Concise History* (n 9) 61.

[65] Toyoda, *Theory and Politics of the Law of Nations* (n 52) xi fn 3.

[66] Randall Lesaffer, 'Charles V, *Monarchia Universalis* and the Law of Nations (1515–1530)' (2003) 71 Tijdschrift voor Rechtsgeschiedenis 79, 79. To the consensus among legal historians about the time of the origins and formation of the state system Lessaffer adds Truyol y Serra and Ziegler.

[67] Perry Anderson, *Lineages of the Absolutist State* (Verso 1979) 60.

[68] Immanuel Wallerstein, *The Capitalist World-Economy* (Cambridge University Press 2002) 37.

[69] Anderson, *Lineages* (n 67) 60–61.

the Republic of the Seven United Provinces. The Netherlands had also proclaimed independence with the Act of Abjuration in 1581. However, the consequences of the First Treaty of Westphalia are not fully taken into account when thinking of the state as a subject of international law. As Wilson writes: 'Perhaps the most common under-appreciated fact of the Grotian era is that the Eighty Years War, the Dutch war of national liberation, was a revolutionary event.'[70] It is the struggle for independence and sovereignty that makes the Dutch Revolt meaningful for the question of the state as a subject of international law. With the signing of the First Treaty of Westphalia, Spain recognized the Netherlands as a sovereign among the European sovereigns and welcomed a new member to the international community of the time. Thus, this treaty actualized in the international sphere the political and constitutional features of statehood and sovereignty: that is, it gave recognition to the Dutch Republic as independent and sovereign, and in doing so promoted the Netherlands to the category of state in the international arena.[71] On this basis it is possible to say that the Congress of Westphalia, and in particular the First Treaty of Westphalia, established the state as a subject of the law governing the relations between Spain and the Netherlands.

The Empire as Subject of International Law

It is said that the transitional moment of the Peace of Westphalia contributed to the decline of the Holy Roman German Empire and led to an international system in which empires were dissolved—the states being the only holders of sovereignty from then on.[72] It is true that the Westphalian arrangements opposed the notion of 'universal monarchy' attached to the figures of the Habsburg powers of the time—the Holy Roman Empire and the Spanish Empire—and restrained the power that threatened their European neighbours. The treaties that put an end to the Thirty Years War did enact a capacity for the German princes and 'estates' to act in international affairs without prior consent of the Empire. However, neither such an enabling competence, nor the attenuation of imperial powers, led to the acute weakening or collapse of the Holy Roman Empire.

An analogous conclusion can be reached if, for different reasons, when examining the First Treaty of Münsterwe give emphasis to the historical and political circumstances of the signatories. The question of who were the subjects of international law at the time can be equated to that of who had a right to sign international treaties—or be the creators of order in international affairs. From historical evidence it is manifest that at the time of the peace accord Spain and the Netherlands were both fully fledged empires. For more than one and a half centuries the Spanish Empire had been the key player in the formation of the

---

[70] Wilson, 'The VOC' (n 41) 338.   [71] Grewe, *The Epochs* (n 3) 183.
[72] Simpson, 'Westphalian System' (n 1) 1243.

'already global' 'new international law—the *jus publicum Europaeum*', in the terms of Carl Schmitt.[73] But the role of Spain in this historical juncture did not only consist of setting the general outline of early modern international law; Spain also acted as an empire in a sense that pertains directly to the analysis of the Peace of Westphalia. In fact, as Grewe maintains, the colonies and 'the treasure from the Americas' Spain had amassed through conquest and plunder 'underpinned' its capacity to act in the international context.[74] In other words, the standing of Spain in the European political landscape substantially rested on the power and capital accumulated as a result of its imperial expansion. And although Spain lost its dominions in the Netherlands, Spanish colonies continued to thrive in America, Africa, and Asia until the early or late nineteenth century. So, while the peace agreements checked supranational authority, they did not preclude the fact that the Spanish Empire continued to act as such beyond the European scenario.

By the same token, in 1648 the Netherlands was already an empire, having been engaged in trading, waging war, creating ports, and establishing colonies in the Far East, South East Asia, South and North America—including New Amsterdam—the West Indies, and West Africa, from the very beginning of the seventeenth century. The ascendency of the Netherlands did not stop at the moment of gaining independence and sovereignty. The centre of capitalist accumulation and imperial power moved from Spain in the South to the Netherlands in the North of Europe over the decades that preceded and followed the Westphalian treaties, and there was a change in the location of hegemony—the Netherlands becoming the new hegemon.[75] At stake here is not only the fact that the Netherlands acted in Westphalia in the dual personality of a state and an empire. The condition of already being an empire was an enabling cause for the Netherlands to succeed in the war of independence and to obtain recognition as a sovereign. Although he refers to the Netherlands as a nation, Marx had no doubts about the imperial character of Dutch expansion into the East—nor about their hegemony in the Europe of the time, nor about the colonial accumulation of capital in the process—when he described the deeds and the horrors of Dutch colonialism as follows:

The history of the colonial administration of Holland—and Holland was the head capitalistic nation of the seventeenth century—'is one of the most extraordinary relations of treachery, bribery, massacre, and meanness'. Nothing is more characteristic than their system of stealing men, to get slaves for Java … The young people stolen, were thrown into the secret dungeons of Celebes, until they were ready for sending to the slave-ships … The treasures captured outside Europe by undisguised looting, enslavement, and murder, floated back to the mother-country and were there turned into capital.[76]

---

[73] Schmitt, *The Nomos of the Earth* (n 5) 80–139.
[74] Grewe, *The Epochs* (n 3) 137.
[75] Immanuel Wallerstein, 'Dutch Hegemony in the Seventeenth-Century World-Economy' in M Aymard (ed), *Dutch Capitalism and World Capitalism* (Cambridge University Press 1982) 95.
[76] Karl Marx, *Capital, Volume One: A Critique of Political Economy* (The Modern Library 1906) 824.

The Company as Subject of International Law

The VOC was founded as a joint stock company and, enjoying the monopoly of the trade, operated between the Netherlands and Asia—today's South East Asia, China, India, Japan, and Iran. It traded in spices, tea, porcelain, textiles, metals, and even elephants. No contemporary scruple apparently got in the way of the opium traffic conducted by the VOC from India to China, and to Europe. In 1670 the company had 50,000 employees, 30,000 fighting men, and 200 ships, many of them armed.[77] Established in 1602, the VOC surpassed by far the size and turnover of the more famous British East India Company, and calculations of today put the VOC at the top of the list of the richest private companies in modern history.[78] On its part, the WIC operated between Africa and the Americas, including Brazil and New Amsterdam, and traded in sugar, gold, and ivory, among other commodities. It was also one of the biggest traffickers of slaves of the time.[79]

Against common assumptions and long-established doctrine, the VOC was not only a private profit-making enterprise but also held a plethora of political privileges, both state-making and empire-like. From its creation the company was dotted with powers to settle colonies, build fortifications, form a fleet of commercial and war ships, as well as to conscript a military force.[80] It also had state-making capacities akin to judicial functions including administering justice, keeping people in prison, and executing convicts, sometimes by decapitation.[81] The VOC was in possession of the authority to celebrate treaties with the heads of local kingdoms on commercial matters but also on issues involving peace and war. It could capture entrepôts and plantations and exercise territorial control over towns and ports to enforce the monopoly, fending off Asian competitors, including Indian, Malay, and Javanese, and those from Europe like the Portuguese and the English fleets.[82] In fact, when the company collapsed in 1800 its overseas territories were absorbed into the Dutch Empire, and became the Dutch East Indies.

Its economic activities were not limited to trade, but it also had the state-like capacity of intervening in the economy itself by creating money, fixing prices, and—by enforcing 'a firm territorial base'—controlling the production of spices, protecting its own crops, and uprooting or not allowing the cultivation of them in other places, all in order to keep the smooth running of the monopoly in place.[83]

---

[77] Jo Monroe, *Star of India: The Spicy Adventures of Curry* (John Wiley & Sons 2005) 24.

[78] Peter N Stearns, *Globalization in World History* (Routledge 2010) 71.

[79] Hugh Thomas, *The Slave Trade: The Story of the Atlantic Slave Trade: 1440–1870* (Simon & Schuster 1997) 169–72.

[80] Jane Burbank and Frederick Cooper, *Empires in World History* (Princeton University Press 2010) 160–61.

[81] George Miller (ed), *To the Spice Islands and Beyond: Travels in Eastern Indonesia* (Oxford University Press 1996) xvi.

[82] James D Tracy (ed), *The Political Economy of Merchant Empires: State Power and World Trade 1350–1750* (Cambridge University Press 1991), 7.

[83] MN Pearson, 'Merchants and States' in ibid, 107.

The possession of state-like capacities, as well as the need for securing the territorial base and the right levels of production, translated into the VOC's willingness to use the means at its disposal to exert violence, and it did so in a quite characteristically imperial fashion. A short passage of an idiosyncratic case of colonial history can give an idea of how the VOC conducted and successfully enriched itself, and should leave no doubt about the capacity of the VOC to terrorize and commit mass murder. As the commentator says 'the secret of this success was simple. They had no scruples whatsoever':

> The purchase of Run demonstrates the VOC's persistence; it does not do justice to the company's cruelty (normally, but not exclusively, meted out to non-Europeans). Its most successful head, Jan Pieterszoon Coen, had earlier convinced the reluctant Bandanese of his firm's God-given right to monopolise the nutmeg trade in a more typical style: he had had every single male over the age of fifteen that he could get his hands on butchered. Coen brought in Japanese mercenaries to torture, quarter and decapitate village leaders, displaying their heads on long poles. The population of the isles was 15,000 before the VOC arrived; 15 years later it was 600.[84]

Contemporaries saw already in the VOC a truthful sovereign, as when the 'Universal Dictionary of Trade and Commerce', published in 1757, noted how in its majestic figure the VOC was 'absolute, and invested with a kind of sovereignty and dominion ... it makes peace and war at pleasure, and by its own authority'.[85] Historians have also described such powers as those proper of a sovereign. Thus, Niels Steensgaard writes that '[t]he VOC integrated functions of a sovereign power with the functions of business partnership. Political decisions and business decisions were made within the same hierarchy of company managers and officials.'[86] More recently, Burbank and Cooper arrived at the same conclusion after confirming how from its inception the VOC was given functions such as those of using violence, enforcing 'territorial control', and 'governing and policing those territories' in the colonies, as well as dealing with local sovereigns.[87]

For Grewe there is no doubt as to the fact that, from its very incorporation, the VOC was endowed with 'sovereign rights'.[88] Such a belief is echoed in the more recent theories of international law. It is the concentration of such an array of state and empire-making capabilities in this corporation which has led Eric Wilson to speak of the existence at the time of a 'corporate sovereign'.[89] 'The radical, if not subversive, potential of this argument for future scholarship is tremendous,' Wilson maintains.[90] Nevertheless, he circumscribes the impact of this insight to the scholarship

---

[84] 'A Taste of Adventure: The History of Spices is the History of Trade' (*The Economist*, 17 December 1998) <http://www.economist.com/node/179810> accessed on 29 May 2015. This had been already told by Rickfels: 'In the 1620s almost the entire native population of the Banda Islands was driven away, starved to death, or killed in an attempt to replace them with Dutch plantations'. MC Rickfels, *A History of Modern Indonesia Since c.1300* (MacMillan 1991) 30.

[85] Quoted in Burbank and Cooper, *Empires in World History* (n 80) 161.

[86] Quoted in Eric Wilson, *The Savage Republic: De Indis of Hugo Grotius, Republicanism and Dutch Hegemony within the Early Modern World-System (c.1600–1619)* (Martinus Nijhoff 2008) 233.

[87] Burbank and Cooper, *Empires in World History* (n 80) 160.

[88] Grewe, *The Epochs* (n 3) 299.   [89] Wilson, 'The VOC' (n 41) 310–40.

[90] Ibid, 340.

on Grotius and to the understanding of the historical context of Grotius' doctrine in the seventeenth century. The import of the conception of the company and the empire as sovereigns and subjects of international law, as they are thematized in this chapter, has similar prospects. Still, it extends beyond Grotian scholarship and early modernity to encompass international law in general in the context of the five hundred years of the history of the modern/colonial system that commenced with the Conquest of America. It is in this historical horizon that the consequences of the idea of the private corporation as a public entity should be examined.

The VOC did not only hold sovereign powers but also contributed to the formation and consolidation of both the Dutch state and empire. The accumulation of capital achieved by the VOC ensured the Netherlands were capable of waging a protracted and successful war of independence against Spain and, as a consequence, allowed the Low Countries to sit at the table of negotiations as a constitutional sovereign, and to gain recognition from Spain—and from all the states concurring at Münster—as sovereign in the international realm with the signing of the treaty. The VOC propped up the Dutch state or the United Provinces by different avenues as it was expected from its very creation. The appeal of establishing the VOC came from the possibility of having another force that could attack Spanish and Portuguese vessels, as well as holdings in the East. Thus, in the fatigue of the Dutch Revolt the VOC lent money and warships to the States General when it was necessary. And every time the VOC renewed its charter and monopoly, a huge fiscal benefit increased the national treasury. All of this was made in the context of mutual assistance and reciprocity. The creation of a unitary company out of a number of them managed by distinct provinces was promoted by the States General, which not only chartered the VOC and deposited in its officials extensive powers, but also invested public money and lent warships to form the initial flotilla of the VOC.[91]

And how did the Low Countries accumulate sufficient capital and power to force the European and global hegemon of the time, the Spanish Kingdom and Empire, to recognize them as an equal at Münster? For Arrighi two strategies of accumulation allowed the Dutch provinces to become a global empire: the regional consolidation of the Netherlands as a centre of trade and finance in Europe, and the expansion in the world market mainly made possible by the creation of 'large-scale joint-stock companies' which were granted monopolistic trading by the state.[92] It is not only that the companies were 'the principal engines of colonial enterprise and organisers of overseas settlements',[93] but also that both the VOC and the WIC established and consolidated the Dutch Empire in Asia and in the Atlantic world. No representative of the VOC signed the First Treaty of Münster. But if for a moment we put aside positivistic approaches that hide the actual actors and forces pulling the threads in the scenario of international law and look at its material constitutive conditions, we will discover the sheer scale of its sovereign powers and the capital the VOC accumulated throughout the Dutch colonies. For the trained eye

---

[91] Pearson, 'Merchants and States' (n 83) 85–86.
[92] Arrighi, *The Long Twentieth Century* (n 60) 135.   [93] Grewe, *The Epochs* (n 3) 298.

of historians like Burbank and Cooper there is no doubt: 'the VOC, not the state of the Netherlands, made an empire, and it did so by combining the joint-stock company's capacity to accumulate capital with the mechanism of armed, coercive commerce pioneered by the Portuguese.'[94]

Conclusion: *Cerberus*, Imperialism, and the Structure of International Law

The theory and the history of modern international law have been constructed almost entirely around the figure of the nation state. If we dare to take seriously into account the evidence offered by a rereading of the theory of international law and by historical studies about how the company and the empire have been key actors in the formation and evolution of the modern world, international law theory and history should be rewritten—and international law transformed. As Grewe warns, 'the history of the trading companies in respect of their role in the law of nations has not yet been written'.[95] The same caveat can be made regarding the role of the empire, or the empire state, in the development and actual life of international law since early modernity.

An argumentative strategy that can put us in the right direction to advance these projects is the recontextualization of Grotius' theory in the history of colonialism, and the reconstruction of the links of his work with the Dutch Republic, the Dutch Empire, and the VOC. The personal inclination to, and the professional obligation of, justifying an act of piracy and war performed by the crew of a ship that ended up belonging to the VOC led Grotius to develop a theory of just war in which a private company was entitled to decide on the question of war, and to wage war, once he provided the VOC with sovereignty. Above all, although the international legal theory of Grotius reflected the historical arrangements of the time, such an interpretation was lost and is not present in the longstanding dominant doctrine.

Currently there is a battle over the image of Grotius. The portrayal of him as the father of international law as a guarantor of peace among nations is being put into question by those who associate Grotius with the rise of Dutch imperialism and the VOC. However, the solution of this contradiction does not appear to be that of a 'middle' ground that excludes both extremes of the spectrum of interpretations— 'neither war-prone nor hard-core pacifist'.[96] This approach looks rather artificial as it denies historical and textual evidence. A more complex and productive elucidation could be one that, in the Janus-faced tradition of the interpretation of law, includes both aspects present in Grotius' theory. This has been already suggested by Anghie, who stresses that while Grotius' theory 'was directed at creating the

---

[94] Burbank and Cooper, *Empires in World History* (n 80) 159.
[95] Grewe, *The Epochs* (n 3) 298.
[96] Janne E Nijman, 'Images of Grotius, or the International Rule of Law beyond Historiographical Oscillation' (2015) 17 Journal of the History of International Law 83, 135–37.

peace within Europe was simultaneously articulating the doctrines that legitimized European expansion into the East Indies'.[97]

Another starting point for the project of rethinking the formal and material structure of modern international law is that of revising the state-centric Westphalian doctrine, perhaps the more influential interpretation of the principles sustaining the international legal system. This conception has operated over the last centuries as a legitimation of both imperialism and self-determination. In relation to the first function, corporations benefit still today from not having international subjectivity, which renders them invisible. Despite its weight in legal and political international history since early modernity, and despite Grotius' endowment of the company with sovereignty in legal theory, it has continued to act free from international legal obligations. The same is true of empires—or empires disguised as states—which remain unaccountable.

The construction of the Westphalian doctrine also obeys the logic of self-determination. Initially, the rationale for elaborating such a theory was that of containing the advances of the great powers on the autonomy and the territory of less powerful European neighbours. History testifies as to the rise of such an interpretation in different moments and places in the period between the late seventeenth and the early nineteenth centuries. The efforts made by German intellectuals—lawyers, historians, and philosophers—to withstand and delegitimize the threat or the real force of France led to the characterization of the international order as one of independent and equal states, or as a society of states.

However, rendering the state as the only subject of international law meant that the figures of the empire and the 'universal monarchy'—at different times incarnated by the Holy Roman Empire, the Spanish Empire, and Imperial or Revolutionary France—were no longer recognized in modern times as subjects of international law, despite their continued thriving existence—largely to the detriment of the colonized Non-European peoples. The negation of subjectivity to the empire, which sought first of all to dispose the empire of legal privileges and rights, ended up fortifying it by making it invisible and completely free of responsibilities.

It is evident that the Westphalian state-centred doctrine ultimately served, and continues today to aid and abet, the interests of imperialism by concealing the actual agents driving international law—empires and companies—and the involvement of states in the imperialist enterprise. Despite the acute intensification and extension of interactions across borders, the erosion of the state and the diffusion of power that has brought globalization, and notwithstanding the central role played in world affairs by non-state actors such as transnational corporations, the Westphalian conception of international law as interstate law still today underpins the regulation of the contemporary international order. It also

---

[97] Antony Anghie, 'Towards a Postcolonial International Law' in Prabhakar Singh and Benoît Mayer (eds), *Critical International Law: Postrealism, Postcolonialism, and Transnationalism* (Oxford University Press 2014) 141–42. In the same sense Tarik Kochi states that while Grotius longs for peace inside Europe, his theory of just war is 'more expansive' than Vitoria's doctrine, and it is used to justify 'colonial conquest': Kochi, *The Other's War* (n 21) 59–60.

remains alive and well in scholarly work.[98] Above all, challenging the Westphalian state-centric system of international law and giving centre stage to non-state actors,[99] the theory of transnational law can contribute to transform, decolonize, or supersede international law in its current configuration.[100] However, in as much as it remains silent about the part played by empires and companies in seventeenth-century international law, and in the contemporary global order, the state-centric Westphalian theory is immersed in a crisis of legitimacy.[101] Resisting neoliberal globalization or neo-colonialism today requires elaborating a theory of international law in which empires, companies, and states have a role, and are under the law, with no prerogatives but, above all, with responsibilities derived from general international law, human rights law,[102] humanitarian law, international economic law, international criminal law, and environmental law, at least to start with.

Finally, this endeavour to reconfigure the whole gestalt of international law by evincing the complexity of international legal subjectivity—the architectonic legal structure of international law—makes also evident the intrinsic involvement of imperialism and the colonial accumulation of capital—the material structure—in the history of modern international law. The colonial accumulation of capital rendered the VOC capable of contributing to the constitution of the Dutch polity as both state and empire. This, in turn, allowed the United Provinces to fight the Eighty Years War and to secure independence from the Spanish Empire—sealed in the First Treaty of Münster. If significant causality is established between the political and economic forces mobilized by imperialism on the one hand, and international law as we have it on the other, then one can say definitely that imperialism has materially constituted international law. In this constellation of concepts it is also possible to see how the subjects of international law are proxies for modern imperialism. Through the political achievements and the colonial accumulation of capital, as well as throughout the universal history of infamy[103] accomplished by nation states, empires, and companies, imperialism became the main historical force founding, developing, and orienting modern international law.

But *Cerberus* not only incarnates international law with its three heads or subjects. The insight according to which the state, the empire, and the company have inveterately operated as the idiosyncratic agents of modern imperialism suggests a second version of the metaphor of the dog with three heads—*Cerberus* is also the avatar of imperialism itself. In this second embodiment, *Cerberus*, the monster,

---

[98] Justin Rosenberg, *The Follies of Globalisation Theory: Polemical Essays* (Verso 2000) 27–28.

[99] Peer Zumbansen, 'Transnational Law' in J Smits (ed), *Encyclopedia of Comparative Law* (Edward Elgar 2006) 742–44.

[100] José-Manuel Barreto, 'Strategies for Decolonization and Dialogue in the Human Rights Field: A Manifesto' (2012) 3 Transnational Legal Theory 1, 14–15.

[101] Cutler, 'Critical Reflections' (n 2) 147–50.

[102] Robert McCorquodale, 'Pluralism, Global Law and Human Rights: Strengthening Corporate Accountability for Human Rights Violations' (2013) 2 Global Constitutionalism 287.

[103] José-Manuel Barreto, 'A Universal History of Infamy: Human Rights, Eurocentrism and Modernity as Crisis' in Singh and Mayer (eds), *Critical International Law* (n 97) 161–63.

is the image or the symbol that represents imperialism.[104] For centuries, political theory has found in Hobbes' *Leviathan* the beast that embodies the terror absolutist and totalitarian states are capable of inspiring. No such image exists in the annals of political and legal philosophy to epitomize the destruction and horror mobilized by imperialism throughout modern history. Looked at from the perspective of the colonized there could scarcely be a more apt trope to sum up imperialist violence. *Cerberus* can stand now next to *Leviathan* to characterize imperialism and totalitarianism respectively, the two utmost modern actualizations of absolute political violence. In a street corner of Buenos Aires it is possible to hear people talking about imperialism as 'the monster with three heads'—*Cerberus* indeed—the dog that devours all those who attempt to escape from hell, as it is revealed or retold in the 'Manual de Zoología Fantástica' written by Jorge Luis Borges and Margarita Guerrero:

Si el Infierno es una casa, la casa de Hades, es natural que un perro la guarde; también es natural que a ese perro lo imaginen atroz … Sacar el cancerbero a la luz del día fue el último de los trabajos de Hércules. Un escritor inglés del siglo XVIII, Zachary Grey, interpreta así la aventura: 'Este perro con tres cabezas denota el pasado, el presente y el porvenir, que reciben y, como quien dice, devoran todas las cosas. Que fuera vencido por Hércules prueba que las Acciones heroicas son victoriosas sobre el Tiempo y subsisten en la Memoria de la Posteridad'.[105]

Bonn, North Rhine-Westphalia, Carnival of 2015.

Bibliography

'A Taste of Adventure: The History of Spices is the History of Trade' (*The Economist*, 17 December 1998) <http://www.economist.com/node/179810> accessed on 29 May 2015

Anderson, Perry, *Lineages of the Absolutist State* (Verso 1979)

Anghie, Antony, *Imperialism, Sovereignty and the Making of International Law* (Cambridge University Press 2005)

Anghie, Antony, 'Towards a Postcolonial International Law' in Prabhakar Singh and Benoît Mayer (eds), *Critical International Law: Postrealism, Postcolonialism, and Transnationalism* (Oxford University Press 2014)

Arrighi, Giovanni, *The Long Twentieth Century: Money, Power and the Origins of Our Times* (Verso 2010)

Barreto, José-Manuel, 'Strategies for Decolonization and Dialogue in the Human Rights Field: A Manifesto' (2012) 3 Transnational Legal Theory 1

---

[104] In the capacity of *Cerberus* to incarnate in itself these two historical phenomena, a form of identity between modern international law and imperialism is again suggested. Not leaving aside the Janus face character of international law—of law itself, as a force for both domination and emancipation—this identification does not exclude other identities international law can adopt, including those of the international rule of law, agent of peace, and possibility for resistance.

[105] Jorge Luis Borges and Margarita Guerrero, *El Libro de los Seres Imaginarios* (Kier 1967) 15.

Barreto, José-Manuel, 'A Universal History of Infamy: Human Rights, Eurocentrism and Modernity as Crisis' in Prabhakar Singh and Benoît Mayer (eds), *Critical International Law: Postrealism, Postcolonialism, and Transnationalism* (Oxford University Press 2014)

Bello, Andrés, *Principios de Derecho de Gentes* (Librería de la Señora Viuda de Calleja é Hijos & Casa de Calleja 1844)

Blom, HW, 'Introduction' (2005–2007) 26–28 Grotiana 1

Borges, Jorge Luis and Guerrero, Margarita, *El Libro de los Seres Imaginarios* (Kier 1967)

Borschberg, Peter, *Hugo Grotius: Commentarius in Theses XI: An Early Treatise on Sovereignty, the Just War, and the Legitimacy of the Dutch Revolt* (Peter Lang 1994)

Borschberg, Peter, 'The Seizure of the Santa Catarina Revisited: The Portuguese Empire in Asia, VOC Politics and the Origins of the Dutch-Johor Alliance (c.1602–1616)' (2002) 33 Journal of Southeast Asian Studies 31

Borschberg, Peter, 'The Santa Catarina Incident of 1603: Dutch Freebooting, the Portuguese Estado da Índia and Intra-Asian Trade at the Dawn of the 17th Century' (2004) 11 Revista de Cultura 13

Borschberg, Peter, 'From Self-Defense to an Instrument of War: Dutch Privateering Around the Malay Peninsula in the Early Seventeenth Century' (2013) 17 Journal of Early Modern History 35

Burbank, Jane and Cooper, Frederick, *Empires in World History* (Princeton University Press 2010)

Cassese, Antonio, 'States: Rise and Decline of the Primary Subjects of the International Community' in Bardo Fassbender and Anne Peters (eds), *The Oxford Handbook of the History of International Law* (Oxford University Press 2012)

Charney, Jonathan I, 'Transnational Corporations and Developing Public International Law' (1983) Duke Law Journal 748

Cutler, Claire, 'The "Grotian Tradition" in International Relations' (1991) 17 Review of International Studies 41

Cutler, Claire, 'Critical Reflections on the Westphalian Assumptions of International Law and Organization: A Crisis of Legitimacy' (2001) 27 Review of International Studies 133

Danielsen, Dan, 'Corporate Power and Global Order' in Ann Orford (ed), *International Law and Its Others* (Cambridge University Press 2009)

Grewe, Wilhelm G, *The Epochs of International Law* (De Gruyter 2000)

Ittersum, Martine Julia van, 'Introduction' in Hugo Grotius, *Commentary on the Law of Prize and Booty* (Martine van Ittersum ed, Liberty Fund 2006)

Ittersum, Martine Julia van, *Profit and Principle: Hugo Grotius, Natural Rights Theories and the Rise of Dutch Power in the East Indies 1595–1615* (Brill 2006)

Jeffery, Renee, *Hugo Grotius in International Thought* (Palgrave Macmillan 2006)

Joyce, Richard, 'Westphalia: Event, Memory, Myth' in Fleur Johns, Richard Joyce, and Sundhya Pahuja (eds), *Events: The Force of International Law* (Routledge 2011)

Keene, Edward, 'The Reception of Hugo Grotius in International Relations Theory' (1999/2000) 20/21 Grotiana 135

Keene, Edward, *Beyond the Anarchical Society: Grotius, Colonialism and Order in World Politics* (Cambridge University Press 2002)

Kingsbury, Benedict, 'A Grotian Tradition of Theory and Practice? Grotius, Law and Moral Skepticism in the Thought of Hedley Bull' (1997) 17 Quinnipiac Law Review 3

Kochi, Tarik, *The Other's War: Recognition and the Violence of Ethics* (Birkbeck Law Press 2009)

Koskenniemi, Martti, *Histories of International Law: Dealing with Eurocentrism* (University of Utrecht 2011)

Koskenniemi, Martti, 'A History of International Law Histories' in Bardo Fassbender and Anne Peters (eds), *The Oxford Handbook of the History of International Law* (Oxford University Press 2012)

Lauterpacht, Hersch, 'The Grotian Tradition of International Law' (1946) 23 British Yearbook of International Law 1

Lesaffer, Randall, 'Charles V, *Monarchia Universalis* and the Law of Nations (1515–1530)' (2003) 71 Tijdschrift voor Rechtsgeschiedenis 79

Marín, Joachín, *Historia del Derecho Natural, y de Gentes* (Manuel Martín 1776)

Marx, Karl, *Capital, Volume One: A Critique of Political Economy* (The Modern Library 1906)

McCorquodale, Robert, 'Pluralism, Global Law and Human Rights: Strengthening Corporate Accountability for Human Rights Violations' (2013) 2 Global Constitutionalism 287

Miller, George (ed), *To the Spice Islands and Beyond: Travels in Eastern Indonesia* (Oxford University Press 1996)

Monroe, Jo, *Star of India: The Spicy Adventures of Curry* (John Wiley & Sons 2005)

Nijman, Janne E, 'Images of Grotius, or the International Rule of Law beyond Historiographical Oscillation' (2015) 17 Journal of the History of International Law 83

Nussbaum, Arthur, *A Concise History of the Law of Nations* (McMillan 1954)

Nys, Ernest, *Les Origines du Droit Internationale* (Bohn 1894)

Osiander, Andreas, 'Sovereignty, International Relations, and the Westphalian Myth' (2001) 55 International Organization 251

Pagden, Anthony, 'Occupying the Ocean: Hugo Grotius and Serafim de Freitas on the Rights of Discovery and Occupation' in Anthony Pagden, *The Burdens of Empire: 1539 to the Present* (Cambridge University Press 2015)

Pearson, MN, 'Merchants and States' in James D Tracy (ed), *The Political Economy of Merchant Empires: State Power and World Tarde 1350–1750* (Cambridge University Press 1991)

Porras, Ileana, 'Constructing International Law in the East Indian Seas: Property, Sovereignty, Commerce and War in Hugo Grotius' De Iure Praedae—The Law of Prize and Booty, or "On How to Distinguish Merchant from Pirates"' (2006) 31 Brooklyn Journal of International Law 741

Rickfels, MC, *A History of Modern Indonesia Since c.1300* (MacMillan 1991)

Rosenberg, Justin, *The Follies of Globalisation Theory: Polemical Essays* (Verso 2000)

Schmitt, Carl, *The Nomos of the Earth in the International Law of the Jus Publicum Europaeum* (Telos Press 2003)

Schmitt, Carl, *Political Theology: Four Chapters on the Concept of Sovereignty* (Chicago University Press 2005)

Simpson, Gerry, 'Westphalian System' in Peter Cane and Joanne Conaghan (eds), *The New Oxford Companion to Law* (Oxford University Press 2008)

Smith, Adam, *The Theory of Moral Sentiments* (Millar, Kinkaid & Bell 1767)

Solow, Barbara Lewis and Engerman, Stanley L (eds), *British Capitalism and Caribbean Slavery: The Legacy of Eric Williams* (Cambridge University Press 1987)

Stearns, Peter N, *Globalization in World History* (Routledge 2010)

Stern, Philip J, *The State-Company: Corporate Sovereignty and the Early Modern Foundations of the British Empire in India* (Oxford University Press 2011)

Straumann, Benjamin, ' "Ancient Caesarean Lawyers" in a State of Nature: Roman Tradition and Natural Rights in Hugo Grotius's *De iure praedae*' (2006) 34 Political Theory 328

Thomas, Hugh, *The Slave Trade: The Story of the Atlantic Slave Trade: 1440–1870* (Simon & Schuster 1997)

Toyoda, Tetsuya, *Theory and Politics of the Law of Nations: Political Bias in International Law Discourse of Seven German Court Councillors in the Seventeenth and Eighteenth Centuries* (Martinus Nijhoff 2011)

Tuck, Richard, *The Rights of War and Peace: Political Thought and International Order from Grotius to Kant* (Oxford University Press 1999)

Vollenhoven, C van, 'Grotius and the Study of Law' (1925) 19 American Journal of International Law 1

Wallerstein, Immanuel, 'Dutch Hegemony in the Seventeenth-Century World-Economy' in M Aymard (ed), *Dutch Capitalism and World Capitalism* (Cambridge University Press 1982)

Wallerstein, Immanuel, *The Capitalist World-Economy* (Cambridge University Press 2002)

Ward, Robert, *An Enquiry into the Foundation and History of the Law of Nations in Europe: From the Time of the Greeks and Romans, to the Age of Grotius* (Strahan & Woodfall 1795)

Wheaton, Henry, *History of the Law of Nations in Europe and America* (Gould, Banks & Co 1845)

Wilson, Eric, 'The VOC, Corporate Sovereignty and the Republican Sub-Text of *De iure praedae*' (2005–2007) 26–28 Grotiana 310

Wilson, Eric, *The Savage Republic: De Indis of Hugo Grotius, Republicanism and Dutch Hegemony within the Early Modern World-System (c.1600–1619)* (Martinus Nijhoff 2008)

Zumbansen, Peer, 'Transnational Law' in J Smits (ed), Encyclopedia of Comparative Law (Edward Elgar 2006)

8

Revolution, Empire, and Utopia: Tocqueville and the Intellectual Background of International Law

Julie Saada

Our age is achieving something vaster and more extraordinary than anything since the establishment of the Roman Empire. I mean the subjection of four-fifths of the world by the remaining fifth. Let us not scorn ourselves and our age, the men may be small, but the events are great.[1]

The relations between imperialism and liberalism are highly ambivalent in the histories of international law. Some of them insist that liberalism has always been linked to imperialism, claiming that the progress involved in liberal doctrines necessarily leads to the 'civilizing mission' which sustains colonialism, or at least the conquest of foreign countries by European states in order to develop international trade and spread liberalism worldwide.[2] Others assert the opposite, namely that liberalism is anti-imperialist since it promotes the universal equality of rights and every people's right to self-governance. If many other kinds of histories have been written[3]—even the history of the ambivalences between imperialism and liberalism in international law[4]—any history focused on one perspective against the others would be

---

[1] Alexis de Tocqueville, 'Letter to Henry Reeve, April 12, 1840' in Alexis de Tocqueville, *Œuvres complètes, Correspondance Anglaise* (Gallimard 1954) vol VI, tome I, 58. See Melvin Richter, 'Tocqueville on Algeria' (1963) 25 The Review of Politics 362, 385.

[2] For example, Antony Anghie focuses on the colonial origins of international law and shows how these origins created a set of structures that continually repeat themselves at various stages in the history of international law: see Antony Anghie, *Imperialism, Sovereignty and the Making of International Law* (Cambridge University Press 2004). See also Uday Singh Mehta, *Liberalism and Empire* (University of Chicago Press 1999); Matthew Craven, 'Colonialism and Domination' in Bardo Fassbender and Anne Peters (eds), *The Oxford Handbook of the History of International Law* (Oxford University Press 2012); Anthony Brewer, *Marxist Theories of Imperialism: A Critical Survey* (Routledge 1980).

[3] Martti Koskenniemi, 'A History of International Law Histories' in Fassbender and Peters (eds), *The Oxford Handbook of the History of International Law* (n 2).

[4] Nathaniel Berman, *Passion and Ambivalence: Colonialism, Nationalism and International Law* (Martinus Nijhoff Publishers 2012); Emmanuelle Tourme-Jouannet, *The Liberal-Welfarist Law of Nations: A History of International Law* (Cambridge University Press 2012).

International Law and Empire: Historical Explorations. First Edition. Martti Koskenniemi, Walter Rech, and Manuel Jiménez Fonseca. © Martti Koskenniemi, Walter Rech, and Manuel Jiménez Fonseca 2016. Published 2016 by Oxford University Press.

oversimplified. Indeed, sustaining that liberalism is *in se* linked to imperialism over-looks the fact that liberals have been criticizing European imperialism since at least the eighteenth century. The opposite perspective—liberalism considered as a guarantee against imperialism—ignores the ways in which liberal concepts have indeed been used to promote European imperial enterprises. The concept of empire and the justifications that uphold it are extremely flexible, so that there does not exist any intrinsic or necessary link between liberalism and imperialism.[5] Nevertheless, both of these concepts were simultaneously and strategically mobilized by thinkers and political actors who wanted to support one of the most important international developments of the nineteenth century—the expansion of European colonial empires. 'Liberal imperialism' offered an intellectual background that fostered, by the 1870s, the development of international law as 'the legal conscience of the civilized world'[6] and supported European colonization in the name of its 'civilizing mission'. In this piece, my point is not to sustain that there is a contradiction in the liberal doctrines, nor to give a new interpretation of them in order to make them more consistent, but to show that imperialism stemmed from liberalism, given that the very ambivalence of the latter involves very ambivalent trends. Characterized by individual freedom, the equal protection of rights, the rule of law, and, for some thinkers, liberty understood as a social state, political liberalism therefore offered a basis for the colonial project not only as a way to enrich the European states and develop international commerce, or to give them strategic bases worldwide, but also because imperial expansion was a way—especially for France—to stabilize its new liberal regime. The opposite trends that formed liberalism were opened to strategic arguments in favour of European expansion during the nineteenth century—even if the same doctrine had led to opposite views a few decades earlier.[7] I will thus examine how the ambivalent relationship between liberal arguments and the justifications of empire played out on an international stage by looking at the work of Alexis de Tocqueville who wrote contemporaneously to France's colonization of Algeria. The choice to focus on a French context is motivated by the fact that comparatively little work has as yet been done by historians of international law on French (as opposed to British) colonization, and by the critical reception that this author has received. I will then compare Tocqueville and Edgar Quinet's arguments that supported French colonization, and the role played by their conception of the French Revolution and the empire as the achievement of a Christian utopia. Both supported a democratic regime for France, one from a liberal point of view (Tocqueville), the other from a point of view that was republican (Quinet).[8] Both

---

[5] Hannah Arendt contends, in a different manner, that imperialism is less the ultimate phase of capitalism than the prequel to totalitarianism: see Hannah Arendt, *Imperialism: Part Two of the Origins of Totalitarianism* (Schocken Books 2004).

[6] Martti Koskenniemi, *The Gentle Civilizer of Nations: The Rise and Fall of International Law 1870–1960* (Cambridge University Press 2001) 11–97.

[7] Jennifer Pitts, *A Turn to Empire: The Rise of Imperial Liberalism in Britain and France* (Princeton University Press 2005).

[8] 'Liberal' and 'republican' are to be understood in their French meaning at this time. See Serge Berstein and Michel Winock (eds), *Histoire de la France politique: Tome 3, L'invention de la démocratie. 1789–1914* (Le Seuil 2002).

were men of action as well as political theorists, and this permits us to fill in a part of the intellectual milieu in which both the justifications of colonialization and the growth of international law were formed some years after the end of the conquest of Algeria (1830–48). Their writings bring together theories of war and the right of conquest, observations on Algeria that helped to fuel the birth of sociology,[9] and theologico-political reflections—the colonial encounter in Algeria being also an encounter with Islam—all framed within a broader context influenced by the emergence of philosophies of history from Hegel to Comte. Before being justified for its 'civilizing mission', international law had been thought of in terms of theories about the hierarchy of races and cultures, by authors who nevertheless saw themselves as enlightened, and for whom the support of the egalitarian ideals of the French Revolution in no way hindered a simultaneous defence of imperial expansionism. These thinkers thus allow us not only to explore the ambivalent relations between liberalism and imperialism, but also to analyse the ways in which the context of the colonial encounter led these authors to call upon arguments that are themselves highly ambivalent. I will mostly focus on Tocqueville since he wrote several works on colonization and empire. Tocqueville's defence of empire is paradoxical for a thinker attached to political liberty and the rule of law, and sensitive to new forms of despotism, as is clear from the last chapters of *Democracy in America*. How can one reconcile Tocqueville's celebration of both the rights of the citizen in America in 1840 and the subjection of the natives in Algeria in 1837 and 1846, particularly given that his initial project for Algeria had been to create a new democratic people out of French and Algerians? Why did a democratic theorist (and one celebrated as such by his French readers[10]), without even depending on arguments based on race,[11] become an apologist for imperialism by conquest, especially when the latter is violent and lawless? How can one reconcile a commitment to the moral equality of all human beings with a defence of the subordination of non-Europeans? If the French colonization of Algeria was also a religious encounter between Christianity and Islam, the little attention that Tocqueville paid to this topic is striking when we compare to Quinet's writings. Quinet—a historian close to Jules Michelet as well as a political thinker and a republican deputy from 1848 onward—defended the egalitarian principles issued from the Revolution as constituting an accomplishment of Christian ideals, but also those of an Islam that he admired, while at the same time supporting the colonization of Algeria. By situating the ambivalent thesis of Tocqueville within the context of the growth of French imperialism, the support of the post-revolutionary regime and a theological approach to this

---

[9] Jon Elster, *Alexis de Tocqueville: The First Social Scientist* (Cambridge University Press 2009).

[10] In France, there have been a significant number of recent studies on Tocqueville with work by Raymond Aron, Francois Furet, Claude Lefort, Raymond Boudon, Michel Crozier, and Pierre Manent, all of whom attach Tocqueville to the liberal tradition. On Tocqueville's reception in France, see: Jean-Louis Benoit, *Tocqueville: Un destin paradoxal* (Bayard 2005); Serge Audier, *Tocqueville retrouvé: Genèse et enjeux du renouveau tocquevillien en France* (Vrin-EHESS, 2004); Françoise Mélonio, *Tocqueville and the French* (Beth G Raps tr, University Press of Virginia 1998). Unlike in the Anglo-Saxon world, there exists almost no work in France on Tocqueville's support of the colonization of Algeria.

[11] Mehta, *Liberalism and Empire* (n 2) 46–76.

historical moment understood through a philosophy of history, this contribution will explore the intertwined liberal, republican, and imperialist arguments that sustained European expansion during the first half of the nineteenth century, and the ways in which they formed the intellectual background of international law as it developed in the 1870s.

Tocqueville's Liberal Imperialism

Tocqueville mobilized contradictory and evolving arguments towards the question of colonization. Let us keep in mind that the period in which France conquered Algeria, between the taking of Algiers (1830) to the Abd-el Khader surrender (1847) followed by the annexation of Algeria as a French department (1848), was a moment in which France attempted to maintain its rank amidst European empires after having lost the majority of its North American and Asian possessions, first to the profit of Great Britain and then to the United States following the expansionist fervour that manifested itself under Napoleon, extinguished by his defeat in 1815. In the domestic affairs of the country, the Algerian conquest exactly coincided with the return of the Bourbons to power in July 1830 and lasted up until the revolution of 1848. It is thus hardly surprising that Tocqueville, who in 1837 was running for a seat in the French Chamber of Deputies, aligned domestic politics with conquest. In two letters that he published in 1837 he proposed the joining of Arab and French cultures into a new civilization in North Africa. While criticizing the recourse to war and military conquest alone, he articulated a sociological analysis[12] of Algeria in the name of a political project aimed at forming a 'great monument to our country's glory',[13] a 'newborn' democratic people formed 'from the two races' but merged into one 'single people'[14] and ruled by institutions that would guarantee individual liberty, the respect for private property and all rights[15]—a new people[16] that he felt must inevitably arrive because 'by the mere fact of the superiority of its knowledge, a powerful and civilized people such as ours exercises an almost invincible influence on small and fairly barbarous people'.[17] Deputy of the left opposition party under the July Monarchy from 1839 onward, Tocqueville's analysis of the conquest of Algeria was altered when, accompanied by his friend Christophe de Beaumont, he first travelled there in May and June of 1841.[18] He composed his *Essay on Algeria* in

---

[12] In his 1837 letters, Tocqueville relied on travel narratives. He made his own observations from 1841 onward. All my references to Tocqueville's writings on Algeria are quoted from *Writings on Empire and Slavery* (Jennifer Pitts tr, The Johns Hopkins University Press 2000): 'Some Ideas that Prevent French from Having Good Colonies' (1833); 'First Letter on Algeria' (23 June 1837); 'Second Letter on Algeria' (22 August 1837); 'Notes on the Koran' (March 1838); 'Notes on the Voyage to Algeria in 1841'; 'Essay on Algeria' (October 1841); 'First Report on Algeria' (1847); 'Second Report on Algeria' (1847). This book also includes 'The Emancipation of Slaves' (1843).

[13] 'Second Letter on Algeria' (n 12) 24.   [14] Ibid, 18, 25.

[15] Ibid, 24, 26; 'Essay on Algeria' (n 12) 63, 115, 116; 'First Report on Algeria' (n 12) 143, 144, 163; 'Second Report on Algeria' (n 12) 193.

[16] 'Second Letter on Algeria' (n 12) 26.   [17] Ibid, 22.

[18] André Jardin, *Tocqueville: A Biography* (Farrar Straus Giroux 1988).

which he insisted that no peace will be possible with an Arab Prince in Algeria[19] and that domination without colonization is unproductive and precarious, while colonization without domination is incomplete and precarious.[20] He thus deduced that a 'partial colonization' made by the installation of Frenchmen on Algerian lands—'a conquering race' analogous to the Romans[21]—ought to amount to a total domination for which warfare, raids (*razzias*),[22] and 'all of the means of displacing the tribes ought to be employed'.[23] Colonization here is neither the civilizing mission that it would be justified as in the 1880s, nor is it, as it had been in 1837, aimed towards the establishment of a new people.[24] Elected at the Chamber between 1842 and 1849, Tocqueville participated in the work of various committees that had been formed to examine the Algerian situation. In 1846 he gave a noteworthy speech on Algeria and, in 1847, he composed several reports on it.[25] Over the same period, in the summer of 1843, he began writing a work (never completed) on the British Empire in India. His second voyage to Algeria, from October to December of 1846, was undertaken as a reporter for a parliamentary commission. This led him to compose two more reports examining the question of how to consolidate the French conquest. He recommended judicial and administrative reforms (notably with regards to property) with the aim of better installing colonization and remedying the arbitrariness and inefficiency of the institutions put in place by France. After 1847, he ceased commenting on affairs in Algeria in both his public and private correspondence.

Tocqueville's ambivalence on domination in context: The condemnation of slavery and the apology for colonization

When Tocqueville criticized the effects of colonization on colonizers in 1837[26] he was in part inspired by the conception of humanity that had been developed by the French *Lumières*, who in the eighteenth century imagined humankind as a unified whole. The Enlightenment criticized slavery and fought for emancipation through rights,[27] including the French military conquest and political

---

[19] 'Essay on Algeria' (n 12) 61, 63, 65.   [20] Ibid, 63.   [21] Ibid, 61.
[22] Ibid, 70.   [23] Ibid, 83, 85, 87.
[24] Ibid, 111; 'Notes on the Voyage to Algeria in 1841' (n 12) 50. Cheryl B Welch, 'Tocqueville on Fraternity and Fratricide' in Cheryl B Welch (ed), *The Cambridge Companion to Tocqueville* (Cambridge University Press 2006) explains that there are two Tocquevillian models for the outcome of collisions between 'civilized' and 'less-civilized' peoples in the democratic age: the first—fratricide—was morally repugnant; the second—fraternity from above—empirically implausible (322). The third alternative is domination without fellowship, a society characterized by 'tranquil possession' in which two peoples live 'side by side', held together by an outside power that restrains its own nationals from lawless brutality and governs the subjugated population without creating a common political life.
[25] Mary Lawlor, *Alexis de Tocqueville in the Chamber of Deputies: His Views on Foreign and Colonial Policy* (Catholic University of America Press 1959).
[26] 'Essay on Algeria' (n 12) 97–99, 101. To compare with the British context, see Hans Joas and Wolfgang Knöbl, *War in Social Thought. Hobbes to the Present* (Alex Skinner tr, Princeton University Press 2013) 25–42, 65–74.
[27] Gilles Manceron, *Marianne et les colonies. Une introduction à l'histoire coloniale de la France* (La Découverte 2003) 35–44. Kant's writings on perpetual peace were greeted with enthusiasm well beyond Germany, see Marc Belissa, *Repenser l'ordre européen (1795–1802): De la société des rois aux*

colonialization of the Antilles.[28] This criticism was based not only on the idea that conquest and colonization were racist and unjust, but also in the name of the idea that civilization and progress cannot be violently imposed from the exterior. Many liberal arguments condemned wars of conquest.[29] For instance, Benjamin Constant's analysis of conquest focuses on its effects upon conquerors: according to him, the politics of aggression destroy the liberal societies that adhere to it; imperialism destroys liberalism insofar as liberal societies must lie to their citizens in order to justify their non-liberal enterprises, and this is a gangrene and corruption for liberal regimes[30]—an idea that later became very familiar to Tocqueville. When the latter opposed slavery, it was in the name of the principle of equality and natural right,[31] an idea that had been developing since the eighteenth century through the narrative of human progress towards equality and the idea of a common humanity.

But the conception of humanity considered as a whole was highly ambivalent during the Enlightenment and gave birth to arguments in favour of colonization in the name of the struggle against slavery. Condorcet, for instance, hierarchized societies, and if he opposed imperial domination he had in mind the forms that it had previously taken (the conquest of the New World, the trade routes towards Asia and Africa), which in no way hindered him from advancing the idea that European societies have the obligation to civilize less-advanced civilizations by implanting themselves in their midst. Condorcet developed an ideology of the civilizing mission of the enlightened European countries and formulated a very influential theory of progress based upon a conception of the linear development of humanity.[32] If he elaborated, like Turgot, the idea of humanity as a homogenous historical

---

droits des nations (Kimé 2006) 390–97. In the eighteenth century, there existed also conceptions of international law in which the objectives of colonizing or dominating the world were entirely marginal, see Emmanuelle Tourme-Jouannet, 'On The Colonial Origins of International Law: About the Modern Law of Nations in the Eighteen Century' in Pierre-Marie Dupuy and Vincent Chetail (eds), *The Roots of International Law/Les fondements droit international: Liber Amicorum Peter Haggenmacher* (Brill 2014).

[28] Comte's conception of the three ages (theological, metaphysical, and positive) gave war a functional signification within the first two epochs, only to abolish and replace it with the scientific analysis of history and society, simultaneously with a call—highly ambivalent in reality—for the emancipation of the colonies. See Joas and Knöbl, *War in Social Thought* (n 26) 90; Auguste Comte, *56ème Leçon du Cours de philosophie positive; Catéchisme positiviste (1852)* (Garnier 1909) 378; Auguste Comte, *Système de politique positive*, IV (Carillian-Goeury et Dalmont 1854) ch V, 419.

[29] Joas and Knöbl, *War in Social Thought* (n 26) 89.

[30] Benjamin Constant, 'The Spirit of Conquest and Usurpation and their Relation to European Civilization' in *Constant, Political Writings* (Biancamaria Fontana tr and ed, Cambridge University Press 1988). On conquest, see Marc Belissa, *Fraternité universelle et intérêt national (1713–1795): Les cosmopolitiques du droit des gens* (Kimé 1998) 69ff. On the critique of war of conquest, see Richard Tuck, *The Rights of War and Peace: Political Thought and the International Order from Grotius to Kant* (Oxford University Press 1999).

[31] Alexis de Tocqueville, *Oeuvres complètes, tome 3, vol 1, Ecrits et discours politiques* (Gallimard 1962) 54, 330; Alexis de Tocqueville, *Democracy in America* (Arthur Goldhammer tr, The Library of America 2004) 199, 207.

[32] Condorcet, *Outlines of an Historical View of the Progress of the Human Mind* (Lang and Ustick 1796); Alice L Conklin, *A Mission to Civilize: The Republican Idea of Empire in France and West Africa, 1895–1939* (Stanford University Press 1997).

subject,[33] this idea in no way hindered its advocates from claiming that Europe was more advanced than the rest of the world, nor did it keep them from supporting European conquests in the name of civilization,[34] assigning Christianity a special role in the process of civilization—an idea that would later (from Michelet and Comte to Tocqueville and Quinet) give birth to the idea that the French Revolution resulted from the realization of the ideals of primitive Christianity in historical time. The separation of arguments against slavery from those supporting colonization testifies to the ambivalences at the core of liberal doctrines and practices. While the slave trade and then slavery itself were abolished in Europe, their persistence in Africa became an argument in favour of colonial conquest as part of the white man's burden.[35] The European perception of race affected non-European societies since they emphasized the differences between humans rather than the similarities that had been proclaimed by the Enlightenment.[36] In the nineteenth century, this same vision of progress came to justify imperialism in the name of the inequality among races. With this came a growing insistence upon the differences in human capabilities, which was ultimately to serve as justification for various imperialist enterprises. The liberal arguments drawn from Enlightenment criticisms of European expansionism nevertheless justified expansion in the name of Enlightenment[37] to the degree that, by the end of the nineteenth century, international law was liberal in Europe and anti-liberal outside of Europe.[38] Tocqueville, for his part, refused this racial hierarchy.[39] He opposed the theses of his friend Gobineau,[40] the author of the *Essay on the Inequality amongst the Human Races* (1853), and argued for the abolition of slavery everywhere, including in the colonized Antilles.[41] Indeed,

---

[33] Anne Robert Jacques Turgot, *Turgot on Progress: Sociology and Economics* (Ronald L Meek tr, Cambridge University Press 1973) 41, 64. He argues that history has a subject and elaborates a parallel between individual development and that of humankind, thus concluding that different degrees of progress among nations are observable (41–42). The same narrative structure is to be found in Condorcet, *Outlines of an Historical View of the Progress of the Human Mind* (n 32) 4.

[34] Condorcet, *Outlines of an Historical View of the Progress of the Human Mind* (n 32) *Dixième époque*, (for a more recent translation: Condorcet, 'Sketch for a Historical Picture of the Progress of the Human Mind: Tenth Epoch' (Keith Michael Baker tr) (2004) 133 Daedalus 65–82).

[35] John Stewart Mill, *On Liberty, Collected Works* (JM Robson ed, University of Toronto Press/ Routledge & Kegan Paul 1977) vol 18, 224.

[36] Roxann Wheeler, *The Complexion of Race: Categories of Difference in Eighteenth-Century British Culture* (University of Pennsylvania Press 2000).

[37] In the 1830s, pro-Imperialist Liberalism developed very elaborate arguments in favor of the conquest of non-European peoples and territories. At the same time, pluralist and nuanced theories of progress disappeared, being replaced by certain notions of backwardness and a strict dichotomy between barbarism and civilization. Pitts, *A Turn to Empire* (n 7). In international law, see Charles Henry Alexandrowicz, *An Introduction to the Law of Nations in the East Indies* (Clarendon Press 1967).

[38] For a general analysis of the history of empires, see Anthony Pagden, *Lords of all the World: Ideologies of Empire in Spain, Britain and France 1500–1850* (Yale University Press 1995).

[39] Tocqueville, *Democracy in America* (n 31) 394–97, 403, 411, 414, 416, 418–19.

[40] Alexis de Tocqueville, 'Letter to Gobineau (17 November 1853)' in Alexis de Tocqueville, *Oeuvres complètes, Tome IX, Correspondance d'Alexis de Tocqueville et d'Arthur de Gobineau* (Maurice Degros ed, Gallimard 1959) 202.

[41] Ibid, 12–13, 363, 394–97, 402, 404–10, 412, 416, 490. Tocqueville thought that slavery was attacked by Christianity ('The Emancipation of Slaves' (n 12) 207) as unjust and by political economy as disastrous, that it could not endure in an age of democratic liberty and enlightenment (ibid, 201; Tocqueville, *Democracy in America* (n 31) 419), and that slavery 'is contrary to the natural rights of

Tocqueville considered that the abolition of slavery formed an indispensable condition for the maintenance of French power over its colonies.[42] He remained ambivalent, however, concerning the relations that ought to be maintained between different human communities. On the one hand, he affirmed that there exists a universal human community and humanity common to all mankind,[43] founded on a principle of equality that ought to be translated into domestic politics via the coming of democracy. This democracy must be immunized against the risk of degenerating into a new form of despotism that would result from both a form of depoliticization[44] issued from egalitarian uniformity itself[45] and from the direction of citizens' attention uniquely towards their private and material interests.[46] On the other hand, Tocqueville supported the emergence of European hegemony in foreign policy, and—in a more general manner—the idea (adopted from Guizot[47]) that there exist degrees of civilization. In addition to this ambivalence, there is an asymmetry between what he supported in domestic—even European—politics (liberalism and the renunciation of war[48]) and what he supported in foreign politics (imperialism via colonization instituted with a war waged in contradiction to the right of peoples)—so much so that the combination of the two results in a new form of 'liberal imperialism'.

Various theses have been advanced in order to explain how Tocqueville was capable, on the one hand, of supporting a liberalism founded on democratic equality—the one found in *Democracy in America*—while on the other hand supporting colonial imperialism. Some have insisted that Tocqueville made compromises with colonial violence and that his judgements were inconsistent.[49] Another reading claims that he justified conquest and colonization in the name of the power and glory of France. According to this interpretation, Tocqueville projected the classical and liberal notion of sovereignty onto the international arena and so incoherently pursued national interests—which is another way of saying that his imperialist nationalism was merely an application of liberalism to individual states.[50] Yet another reading,

---

humanity' ('First Report on Algeria' (n 12) 146). But he supported the emancipation of the slaves in the French Caribbean for economic and political—but not moral—reasons ('The Emancipation of Slaves' (n 12) 222). Cheryl B Welch explains that his argument is strategical ('Tocqueville on Fraternity and Fratricide' (n 24) 318–19).

[42] 'The Emancipation of Slaves' (n 12) 200–01. See also Seymour Drescher, *Dilemmas of Democracy: Tocqueville and Modernization* (University of Pittsburgh Press 1968) 181.

[43] Tocqueville, *Democracy in America* (n 31) 723.

[44] Sheldon Wolin, *Tocqueville between Two Worlds: The Making of a Political and Theoretical Life* (Princeton University Press 2001) 341.

[45] Tocqueville, *Democracy in America* (n 31) 720; Alexis de Tocqueville, *The Old Regime and the Revolution* (Alan S Kahan tr, University of Chicago Press 1998–2001) vol 2, 262.

[46] Tocqueville, *Democracy in America* (n 31) 749ff.

[47] On Guizot and Tocqueville, see Cheryl B Welch, 'Tocqueville resistance to the Social' (2004) 30 History of European Ideas 83, 96–106.

[48] Tocqueville, *Democracy in America* (n 31) 761, 763–67, 782.

[49] Richter, 'Tocqueville on Algeria' (n 1).

[50] Tzvetan Todorov, 'Tocqueville et la doctrine coloniale' in Alexis de Tocqueville, *De la colonie en Algérie* (Editions Complexes 1988) 24–27. See also Richard Boyd, 'Tocqueville and the Napoleonic Legend' in Ewa Atanassov and Richard Boyd (eds), *Tocqueville and the Frontiers of Democracy* (Cambridge University Press 2013); Stephane Dion, 'Durham et Tocqueville sur la colonisation libérale' (1990)

inversely, emphasizes the opposition between nationalism and liberalism: the position of Tocqueville on Algeria was in contradiction with the views expressed in *Democracy in America*, he put his nationalism before liberalism, and the interests of progressive Christian nations before those of non-Christian ones.[51] From this perspective, it has also been emphasized that if Tocqueville's views on imperialism are contradictory, this is not because he adapts a different theoretical framework for thinking about America, the Indies, or North Africa, but because he fails to consistently apply his own views on the potential for state despotism, the instability of interests, and the power of resentment.[52] One final recent interpretation emphasizes Tocqueville's concern for perpetuating his political engagement in a moment in which France was being rapidly democratized, a situation that prompted him to approve the perpetuation of French power in Algeria—Tocqueville being, among some other French and British liberal thinkers, in a historical moment characterized by 'pressures' and 'anxieties' about the expansion of European colonial empires.[53] One of the virtues of the first of these readings is that it foregrounds the opposed positions taken up by Tocqueville. As for the last reading—which is rather close to my own insofar as the role of republicanism in the defence of the colonization of Algeria is concerned—it demonstrates the specific interest of the colonial empire in Algeria for Tocqueville, namely its direct relationship to domestic politics. Most of these readings are limited insofar as they see Tocqueville's position as incoherent, either insofar as they see it as resulting from his desire to salvage a part of his views at the expense of some others, a 'good liberalism' versus a 'bad imperialism', the defence of human rights against the justification of total war, or criminal ambitions seemingly advanced in concealment as liberal ideas. By maintaining, to the contrary, that Tocqueville supported neither incoherent perspectives, nor that there is continuity between his domestic liberalism and his defence of foreign imperialism, but that his theory is fraught with a play of ambivalences[54] that makes him adopt both liberalism and imperialism, liberalism and republicanism, I intend to show how he himself constructed the ambivalent aspects of liberalism which can be understood at once as both humanist and imperialist. Thus we can better understand why Tocqueville defended democracy in 1835 and 1840 (*Democracy*

---

25 Revue d'études canadiennes/Review of Canadian Studies 60; Nouredine Saadi, 'Tocqueville et l'Algérie: le libéral et le colonial' (2004) 35 The Tocqueville Review/La Revue Tocqueville 123; Olivier Le Cour Grandmaison, *Coloniser. Exterminer: sur la guerre et l'Etat colonial* (Fayard 2005) 98–114.

[51] Richter, 'Tocqueville on Algeria' (n 1) 362–99.

[52] Welch, 'Tocqueville on Fraternity and Fratricide' (n 12) 305; Cheryl B Welch, 'Colonial Violence and the Rhetoric of Evasion: Tocqueville on Algeria' (2003) 31 Political Theory 235.

[53] Pitts, *A Turn to Empire* (n 7) 168, 196, 297; Jennifer Pitts, 'Empire and Democracy: Tocqueville and the Algeria Question' (2000) 8 Journal of Political Philosophy 295; Jennifer Pitts, 'Democracy and Domination: Empire, Slavery, and Democratic Corruption in Tocqueville's Thought' in Atanassov and Boyd (eds), *Tocqueville and the Frontiers of Democracy* (n 50). For a discussion of Jennifer Pitts and Melvin Richter's thesis, see Demin Duan, 'Reconsidering Tocqueville's Imperialism' (2010) 17 Ethical Perspectives 415.

[54] It is for this reason that I have chosen to employ the word 'ambivalence' in its psychoanalytic usage, in a way similar to how Berman used it in order to understand certain moments in the history of international law: Berman, *Passion and Ambivalence* (n 4).

in America) while justifying imperialism in 1837 and 1841–46 (*Letters on Algeria, Work on Algeria*). This double face of liberalism can only be grasped if we confront liberalism as a global theory within a certain context—or, put otherwise, if we grasp it in such a manner that a global theory is diffracted through the contextualized positions of situated actors.[55]

Liberal imperialism, or international politics as a patriotic project

Tocqueville's liberalism is ambivalent not only because it is bound up in colonial imperialism, but also because it sustains this imperialism via recourse to arguments derived from another political tradition—the one that Quentin Skinner has done so much to resuscitate[56]—classical republicanism, even when Tocqueville himself virulently criticized the French Republican Party in six letters that he published in 1843.[57] He indeed did not support colonization only in the name of the material interests of the colonizers.[58] Maintaining France's rank compared to Great Britain in European and international relations was clearly decisive for him, as was the possession of Algeria's large ports in the name of fostering commerce in the Mediterranean.[59] But above all it was the reinvigoration of French democracy that interested Tocqueville, for he had even analysed, in the last chapters of *Democracy in America*, the risk of despotism derived from individualism and the retraction of citizenship into the private sphere. Because the French nation was the product of a violent revolution followed by the Terror and political instability, the liberty it enjoyed was more fragile than that found in Great Britain and America. Thus it was the French, far more so than the Americans, who were turned towards their personal affairs, and this in spite of the attachment to the principles of liberty and equality that they had proclaimed at the time of the Revolution. The French people's patriotic links were weakened, on the one hand, because in democracy it is not only the individuals that become similar but also the nations, to the extent that the attachment to the specificities of a homeland in particular tends to dissolve in light of its similarities with other nations,[60] and on the other because the individuals turn towards their personal interests and pursue their private passions.[61] In an 1841 letter addressed to John Stuart Mill,[62] then in the *Six Letters on the Domestic Situation*

---

[55] I am using Luc Boltanski's term: *On Critique* (Polity 2011). My approach on this point is quite different from the one taken by Mehta, *Liberalism and Empire* (n 2), who defends a historical approach against conceptual abstractions.

[56] Quentin Skinner, *Liberty before Liberalism* (Cambridge University Press 1998); John Greville Agard Pocock, *The Machiavellian Moment* (Princeton University Press 1975).

[57] Alexis de Tocqueville, 'Lettres sur la situation intérieure de la France' in Alexis de Tocqueville, *Oeuvres*, vol 1 (André Jardin, Françoise Mélonio, and Lise Queffélec eds, Gallimard 1991).

[58] Material interests, and more generally national interest, count for Tocqueville, as is indicated by the principle question examined in his 'First Report on Algeria' (n 12) 131: 'Is the domination we exercise in the territory of the old regency of Algiers useful for France?' He does not ask if colonization is in conformity with the interests of humanity or of the inhabitants of Algeria.

[59] 'Essay on Algeria' (n 12) 60.   [60] Tocqueville, *Democracy in America* (n 31) 723–24.

[61] Ibid, 269, 270, 76, 105–07.

[62] Alexis de Tocqueville, 'Letter to John Stuart Mill (18 March 1841)' in *Œuvres complètes, Correspondance Anglaise (Gallimard 1954)*, (Gallimard 1954) tome VI, 1, 335.

in France written in 1843, Tocqueville described a situation of 'decadence' in France where the 'people become more and more indifferent', a state in which individuals, having attached themselves excessively to private interests,[63] had forgotten to love the liberty that they had so dearly acquired in 1789. His analysis of the situation in France is very close to his discussion of the risk of democracy sliding into despotism in *Democracy in America*[64] where he wrote that the principle of equality could produce effects incompatible with liberty and deepens his discussion of his claim that the weakening of civic virtues leads to the dissolution of the social bond.[65] Furthermore, as in the classical republicanism of Machiavelli in particular, but also that of Rousseau, Tocqueville emphasizes that the principle of equality contained in the republican ideal depends upon a conception of humanity that risks dissolving citizens' attachments to their homeland.[66] Citizens must love not only humanity and the principles of liberty and equality from a universal viewpoint but also, and especially, their homeland, for the liberty of the moderns demands a territory, a limited state, a specific community that will make possible mutual confidence and common action. Tocqueville's hope was that individuals, led by well-directed reason and morality, might be able to serve humanity while at the same time loving one fragment of humanity, their particular homeland.[67] If he rejected honour and distinguished individualism from egoism,[68] Tocqueville also showed that the transformation of individualism into egoism is a menace to democracy.[69] He therefore thought that it was necessary to reinforce the civic virtues and patriotism, including the willingness to 'sacrifice private interests to the general good',[70] and he compared American patriotism to the sacrifice of self-interest in religion,[71] opposing it to the indifference that citizens in some European nations feel for the places they live in.[72] Nevertheless, according to Tocqueville the conquest and colonization of Algeria might have been able to revive French patriotism, thereby revitalizing the democratic project.[73] It is for this reason that he directly opposed detractors of colonization who, like Desjobert,[74] saw an opposition between democracy and war,[75] as well as those who, like Mill, saw an opposition between democracy and

[63] Alexis de Tocqueville, 'Etat social et politique de la France avant et depuis 1789' in *Œuvres III* (François Furet & Françoise Mélonio (eds), Gallimard 2004) 62–63.
[64] Tocqueville, *Democracy in America* (n 31) 816ff.			[65] Ibid, 105, 270–71.
[66] Ibid, 585–87, 590–94, 816ff.
[67] Tocqueville, *The Old Regime and the Revolution* (n 45) vol 2, 262.
[68] Tocqueville, *Democracy in America* (n 31) 585–87.			[69] Ibid, 270–71, 720.
[70] Ibid, 590–94.
[71] Ibid, 106. Tocqueville distinguishes two forms of patriotism: the first one is emotional and religious (ibid, 76, 106–07, 189, 269, 339), the second one is more rational (ibid, 106, 270–71).
[72] Ibid, 105.			[73] 'Essay on Algeria' (n 12) 63.
[74] Amédée Desjobert, *La question d'Alger: politique, colonisation, commerce* (P Dufart 1837) 63–65. He contested the anti-slavery argument that defended colonization in order to liberate slaves and control piracy. For him, the honour of France is not to colonize but to civilize by developing an egalitarian relation with a sovereign Algeria. See ibid, 8–9; Amédée Desjobert, *L'Algérie en 1838* (Guillaumin 1838) and, by the same editor: Amédée Desjobert, *L'Algérie en 1844; L'Algérie en 1846*. See also Henri Baudet, 'Tocqueville et la pensée coloniale au 19e siècle' in Alexis de Tocqueville, *Tocqueville, Livre du Centenaire* (Editions du CNRS 1960).
[75] Tocqueville, *Democracy in America* (n 31) 761ff, 779ff.

colonial violence. Nor did Tocqueville, like Comte, support the idea that war is incompatible with economic growth. Rather, he believed that the expenses linked to conquests could be rationalized in terms of the future economic benefits accrued through colonization. Even if he sustained the opposition between aristocratic glory and democratic interest,[76] he thought that a colony generated by warfare could serve a democratic project (forging a new people in 1837) or might bring national glory back to life by proposing a great political project to the citizenry. Inversely, if Tocqueville did criticize the manner in which the French waged the Algerian war, he did so neither in the name of a people's right to self-government nor with reference to the *jus in bello*, but because this brutality destroyed all moral limitations within the perpetrators;[77] that is to say because this war produced anti-democratic effects among an already weakly democratic people—the French.

If Tocqueville is generally thought of as a liberal thinker, it remains true that he, no less than the classical republicans, admired the Roman virtue defeated by liberalism and its conception of negative liberty. By comparing the project to conquer Algeria to the Roman conquests,[78] he thus did more than merely exalt imperialism and expansionist politics carried out in order to affirm national power in international affairs. He found in the model of Roman virtue a way of drawing individuals away from the egoism generated by modern liberty by attaching them to a larger patriotic project, and heroism in conquest provided an antidote to the weakening brought about by material interests.[79] Because democratic liberty requires disinterested patriotism, the colonization of Algeria offered a means of generating actions that would awake in the people a feeling of national greatness, bringing back patriotism and the attachment of citizens to the homeland.[80] Tocqueville thus saw conquest and colonization as solutions to the difficulties encountered by the new French regime, problems that if treated on a purely domestic level seemed irresolvable. It remained to be seen how France could accomplish the transition from an ancient monarchical regime to a democracy without finding itself engulfed in anarchy and state terror, and the solution proposed by Tocqueville involved joining democratic process on the domestic front, within the *metropole*, with an imperialistic foreign politics. From this point of view, there is no contradiction between his domestic politics (liberalism) and his foreign politics (imperialism), nor is there any contradiction between the democratic ideas expressed in *Democracy in America* and the texts on Algeria. Liberal theory can thus become imperialist when it integrates elements drawn from classical republicanism.

---

[76] Joshua Mitchell, *The Fragility of Freedom: Tocqueville on Religion, Democracy, and the American Future* (The University of Chicago Press 1995) 149.

[77] 'Notes on the Voyage to Algeria' (n 12) 43, 44, 57; 'Essay on Algeria' (n 12) 78. Tocqueville also fears that the notion of total war might be diffused in France, bringing back the Terror that followed the Revolution.

[78] See footnote 1.

[79] Alexis de Tocqueville, 'Letter to John Stuart Mill (March 18th 1841)' in Alexis de Tocqueville, *Selected Letters on Politics and Society* (Roger Boesche ed, James Toupain and Roger Boesche trs, University of California Press 1985).

[80] Lawlor, *Alexis de Tocqueville in the Chamber of Deputies* (n 25) 43–66, 173–74. It is also Pitts's thesis in *A Turn to Empire* (n 7) 192–96.

Tocqueville's views on empire and imperialism are not, in any case, univocal. He aimed to promote a French colonial empire in Algeria against another kind of empire that had been built by a war of conquest: the conquest of America. But he described the latter in a greatly ambivalent way. On the one hand, Tocqueville criticized the expropriation and extermination of the natives by the settlers, the violation of their rights and their refusal to recognize the natives as a nation. More generally, he denounced the violence of conquest and the contradictoriness of a government that pretended to be democratic while simultaneously denying the equality of human beings.[81] On the other hand, he considered the gap separating the settlers, the Amerindians, and the slaves in America (especially in the South) as so large that the 'three races' couldn't be assimilated into the same and unique political community. Since Amerindians were considered as 'savage nations' characterized by their extreme love of liberty and the corruption of their society,[82] Tocqueville thought that they were destined, like the slaves, to remain excluded from the democratic citizenry. Tocqueville's ambivalence towards empire is also noticeable when he rejects the Napoleonic Empire that was created by the French conquests of Europe in the aftermath of the French Revolution's wars, while approving and supporting the French conquest of Algeria. As I have shown, his commitment to the liberal regime in France was compatible with republican arguments in favour of the development of the public virtue. And, like the French republicans, he rejected the Napoleonic conquests because of their association with monarchical and imperial regimes, while supporting, like them, the project of colonizing Algeria.[83] The same kind of ambivalence is also striking when we consider his writings on the British Empire. On the one hand, he admired the British domestic political traditions but, on the other hand, he rejected as hypocritical the British imperial model as it existed in India. As Jennifer Pitts noticed, Tocqueville was sceptical about the dichotomy between civilized and barbarous people that Mill and some British thinkers formulated—a part of their argument that colonization benefitted non-European subjects.[84] He thought that the British Empire was corrupted by a 'spirit of caste' which infected the mentality of the settlers, preventing the creation of a new people that would include both the colonists and the natives. Nevertheless, his criticism of the British Empire in India is not very far from the one he made of Algeria, where settlers are described as brutal and corrupted, especially when they did not respect the right of property.[85] But if he aimed to establish stable institutions in Algeria, it was not because he wanted to protect the rights of the natives—it was in order to avoid the corruption of the settlers.[86] The latter were citizens of a

---

[81] See Pitts, *A Turn to Empire* (n 7) 197, 325.

[82] Tocqueville, *Democracy in America* (n 31) 365ff.

[83] Before 1848, a large part of the republican opposition already supported colonization. Tocqueville's point of view in his 1847 report is thus indicative of an emergent transformation in Republican thought. See Manceron, *Marianne et les colonies* (n 27) 93.

[84] Pitts, *A Turn to Empire* (n 7) 222.   [85] 'First Report on Algeria' (n 12) 140.

[86] 'Notes on the Voyage to Algeria in 1841' (n 12) 44, 51; 'Essay on Algeria' (n 12) 88, 101, 103, 114. Tocqueville explained that impeding the settlers from private ownership was an obstacle for them identifying themselves with the country: 'Essay on Algeria' (n 12) 48, 87, 112. Therefore, the settlers'

new democratic regime—the regime of the *metropole*—that needed to be protected even in the colonies.

From Tocqueville to Quinet: French Colonization as a Religious Encounter, or the Religious Side of Liberal Imperialism

Tocqueville's justification of the colonization of Algeria was not supported by political ideals alone. His justifications also mobilized arguments bearing on the material interests of the colonizers and their symbolic interests, and among these are to be found religious arguments that express a certain theologico-political conception and a philosophy of history, two themes very much discussed not only in the German but also in the French thought of the period.

Political ideas and Christian ideals

The taking into account of the religious dimension of the conquest and colonization allows us to better characterize liberal imperialism and to show, once again, how general theories like liberalism were modified by the actors that put them to work, as well as by the ambivalent ways in which they conscripted arguments derived from competing theories. Just as the justification of colonialism led Tocqueville, a proponent of liberalism, to deploy republican arguments, Quinet[87] was led to defend Christian ideals and to propose a new reading of the history of Islam and the religious revolutions, and to justify the colonization of Algeria by theological arguments apparently distant from his Republican anticlerical position. The ambivalent character of the arguments that he mobilized in favour of colonization is to be found among the Socialists as well. Among the Saint-Simonians,[88] their theorist Prosper Enfantin (1796–1864) was indignant with respect to the violence of conquest, but that in no way kept him from defending colonization: Algeria, for him, could serve as a laboratory for social experiments that might be useful for the French people.[89] The idea of creating a new people via the colonization of Algeria was also shared by certain Socialists (even if their political aims were quite different from Tocqueville's). The socialist utopian Charles Fourier (1772–1837) denounced the savagery of colonization while simultaneously regretting that the Princes of Europe were unable to agree amongst themselves well enough to collectively embark on conquests that might surpass in glory those accomplished by Napoleon. The only exception to this was the anarchist

---

right to property must be guaranteed by stable institutions: ibid, 115, 116; 'First Report on Algeria' (n 12) 143, 144, 163; 'Second Report on Algeria' (n 12) 193.

[87] As a Republican, close to Jules Michelet, he was elected to the Constituante in 1848, then went into exile under Bonaparte in 1851. In 1870, he was elected as a Republican in Paris, at the same time as Victor Hugo, Gambetta, and Garibaldi.

[88] They are followers of the utopian philosopher Claude de Saint-Simon (1760–1825).

[89] Barthélemy Prosper Enfantin, *Colonisation de l'Algérie* (P Bertrand Libraire 1843).

Pierre-Joseph Proudhon, who held that the emancipation of the colonies was ine-luctable.[90] For Tocqueville, as for historians like Michelet or Quinet, regardless of their other intellectual disagreements about the Revolution, the democratic ideas that they promoted were understood as an accomplishment of Christian Ideals. Even if many French revolutionaries had been anticlerical, denouncing the confis-cation of power by the Catholic Church within the *Ancien Regime*, they perceived the Revolution as an accomplishment of an originally Christian spirit. Thus, if Tocqueville criticized slavery and contested the inequality of the races, he did so in the name of an equality that was affirmed by Christianity.[91] This Christian ideal, having fallen into disuse over the course of history, was brought back to life and realized in history via the French Revolution.[92] Tocqueville thereby added not only a sociology of religion to his reflections on democracy, as he did in *Democracy in America*, nor did he, in 1838, merely content himself with reading the Koran in order to better understand Algeria.[93] He developed a philosophy of history, or a revolutionary political theology, which gave to the Revolution the significance of accomplishing the original Christian ideals within historical times. Tocqueville's analysis of colonization, as constitutive of his liberal imperialism, must be under-stood within this framework: one is not yet speaking of the 'civilizing mission' that would emerge in the 1880s to justify colonization, but about a patriotic project aimed at defending the accomplishments of a revolution understood as a 'political revolution that transpired in the manner of a religious revolution'.[94] The Revolution was thus inscribed within a political theology, insofar as it was seen as the secularization of Christian ideals transposed into a non-religious—or at least non-clerical—sphere.[95]

Political revolutions and religious utopias: Colonization seen through the prism of philosophy of history

Edgar Quinet presented a similar vision of Christianity, but the colonial encounter led him to inscribe Islam within a totally different vision of the history of human-kind. Quinet produced a political theology of the Revolution, giving French

---

[90] Pierre-Joseph Proudhon, *La Guerre et la Paix, recherches sur le principe et la constitution du droit des gens*, in *Oeuvres complètes*, vol 13 (Librairie internationale 1869). On the positions of the first Socialists, see Manceron, *Marianne et les colonies* (n 27) 184–86; Philippe Darriulat, 'La gauche républicaine et la conquête de l'Algérie, de la prise d'Alger à la reddition d'Abd-el-Kader (1830–1847)' (1995) 82 Revue française d'histoire d'outre-mer 129.

[91] Tocqueville, *Democracy in America* (n 31) 207, 393, 402, 419. This in no way kept him from criti-cizing historical Christianity, perceived by Tocqueville as dangerous because of its proselytizing char-acter: see 'Letter to Gobineau (22 October 1843)' in Tocqueville, *Oeuvres complètes, Tome IX* (n 40).

[92] Tocqueville, *Democracy in America* (n 31) 12, 332, 335.

[93] 'Notes on the Koran' (n 12) 27–35.

[94] Tocqueville, *The Old Regime and the Revolution* (n 45), title of chapter 3: 'How the French Revolution was a Political Revolution Which Acted Like a Religious Revolution, and Why.'

[95] In the letter that he addressed to Gobineau in 1843, Tocqueville judged that modern morality was a laicized reprise of the values of humanity and universality that were revealed by the Gospels and the Pauline message. See Tocqueville, *Oeuvres complètes, Tome IX* (n 40) 46, 47.

imperialism a very specific role within this history.[96] His work, *Christianity and the Revolution*,[97] tried to show 'the ascension of the life of humanity within the moral sphere'[98] by describing its different ages, with each period marked by different religious revolutions. The French Revolution is the 'abridgment and the seal upon all of those that preceded it',[99] marking a point of reconciliation within humankind. In the fifth lesson, Quinet insisted that the Revolution was already present in primitive Christianity. His vision differs from that of classical Pauline Christianity insofar as this latter would separate the spheres of politics and religion[100] while he, to the contrary, believed that the egalitarian utopia of Christianity is accomplished in the political institutions created by the Revolution, which broke away from the corruptions inherent in previous institutions while nevertheless according an important role to the institution of the church and the theory of predestination.[101] The Revolution demonstrated that utopia is of this world and that its bearers are the people. Because 'all that the evangelists include in the spirit, the ideal law, the sacred legislation, must be translated into positive law',[102] it depends upon the people themselves to force utopia into historical time by achieving the gospels in social life.

Quinet consecrated the seventh lesson to Islam, insisting that the colonization of Algeria demands an understanding of the Koran.[103] His great innovation was to affirm that it had been necessary to wait until the eighteenth century to accomplish these ideals in Europe while Islam had immediately accomplished them. Quinet was fascinated by Islam. According to him it had, since its very beginnings, promoted social rights thanks to an 'egalitarian god'. He described it as 'the other universal religion', disseminated by conquest but capable of installing peace and progress domestically in 'a world of terror that surrounds a world of delights'.[104] Unlike Tocqueville, Quinet admired Islam and Mohammad, who he described as a combination of 'Christ and Napoleon',[105] the founder of a religion and a politics that has spread because of the social rights that it promises, namely unity and equality. In a highly lyrical style, Quinet insisted that 'Islam was the first to begin to realize the egalitarian spirit' by erasing privileges, essentially putting into practice the French Civil Code from the seventh century onward. Thus the 'Orient brought together in a single moment that which took us centuries ... It experienced all at once, in the same epoch, its messiah and its social contract, the preaching of its apostles and its Revolution of 1789 ... its primitive church and its constituent assembly'. While Christianity was obliged to wait eighteen centuries for its promise to be realized historically, an egalitarian utopia was first introduced into the world with the coming of Islam, a religion that from the beginning was marked by a 'striking simultaneity of idea and fact'.[106] According to Quinet, however, the source of Islam does not renew

---

[96] Quinet's interest in the philosophy of history was so marked that in 1827–1828 he translated Herder's *Idées sur la philosophie de l'histoire de l'humanité*. He also criticized many historians of his time in *Philosophie de l'histoire de France* [1857] (Payot 2009).

[97] Edgar Quinet, *Le christianisme et la Révolution* (Au comptoir des imprimeurs unis 1845).

[98] Ibid, 10.   [99] Ibid, 12.   [100] Ibid, 108.   [101] Ibid, 120–53.

[102] Ibid, 115.   [103] Ibid, 161.   [104] Ibid, 167.   [105] Ibid, 178.

[106] Ibid, 179.

itself, since all was already accomplished at the outset. The colonial empire that France was establishing in Algeria thus constituted a means of achieving these ideals. His goal was thus to 'reconcile Mohamadism with Christian humanity's great association', the means to this goal being 'the miracle of a people, of a society, that would at last illustrate the agreement of religious ideals with social rights, of the church and the state, in a spirit that is even higher than that of the Koran'.[107] He thus saw colonization as a new kind of crusade, a 'holy war',[108] which aimed at accomplishing 'France's secret instinct' in Algeria, namely the moral emancipation of the colonized thanks to a war that would bring greater benefits to the conquered than to the conquerors[109] by bringing them into a reconciliation with a higher principle—Christian ideals. What could bring these ideals to life was the instauration of a democratic regime via colonization. Quinet distinguished this from the imperialism of conquest issued from the crusades or the conquest of the Americas, because here he is speaking about 'Republican Crusaders' seeking the liberation and moral elevation of their adversaries by reconciling themselves with them over their common unification around a higher principle. Quinet thus justified the colonization of Algeria in the name of an egalitarian political utopia that was also a revolutionary religious utopia, whereas the Socialists envisioned the conquest of Algeria as a means to give birth to a new and egalitarian people—an idea shared by Tocqueville until 1841, although in a non-utopian mode. Tocqueville, of course, was more interested in fostering democracy in France than in the utopian realization of a new people. He wanted to support the French nation in the construction of its democratic regime by making foreign politics into a means of serving domestic politics. Put otherwise, he wanted to rebuild the French nation by co-articulating internationalism and nationalism, and by distinguishing the internationalism that links European nations from that which links these nations to their imperial possessions.

Conclusion

Few studies have analysed the circulation of liberal, republican, and utopian ideas, the role played by nationalism in internationalist ideas and the theologico-political background of these ideas. But if we wish to understand the links between international law and empire, we need to analyse the circulation of ideas between distant, and even opposed, doctrines, in particular during the second great wave of European colonization. The need for this becomes strikingly clear as soon as we consider the ways in which situated political actors built and put into practice the general doctrines: if Enlightenment ideas led to the condemnation of slavery, this same condemnation was in part developed in support of a new form of imperial domination, sometimes justified in the name of the struggle against slavery, at other times upheld as the realization of the promises of the French Revolution. Before being developed in international law via the notion of the 'civilizing mission', the

---

[107] Ibid, 182.   [108] Ibid, 201.   [109] Ibid, 204.

ideals of democracy and equality were paradoxically repurposed by liberals in the name of republican arguments (Tocqueville) and by anti-clerical republicans in the name of Christian theology (Quinet). Both of these actors and political thinkers distinguished between varying kinds of domination, different conceptions of politics and religion. Both underwent changes in their position relative to the French conquest of Algeria. In both cases, the categories that they employed were taken over from their adversaries. Tocqueville the liberal-conservative—member of the Parti de l'Ordre—became republican-progressive when he was forced to defend the empire; Quinet the anticlerical republican adopted a Christian messianic stance when he sought to redefine the French imperial mission in Algeria. Neither of the two presented a simple version of imperialism. In the first case, imperialism was justified via a post-revolutionary, hence non-revolutionary, liberalism. In the second case, imperialism (in the form of colonialism) was based upon a utopian and revolutionary French republicanism.

The background of political and religious ideals, even utopias, was thus formed, before giving birth to international law and to the civilizing mission of which the historiography of international law has not begun to plumb the theologico-political dimension, if all the while emphasizing the importance of Christian ideals among the internationalists of the second half of the nineteenth century.[110] The idea of a civilizing mission did not impose itself all at once, and it emerged—at least according to the testimony of the French sources—within varying intellectual and political frameworks: Quinet's ideal of universal equality, which was also developed by the Socialists, made colonization a mission (the idea was to accomplish primitive ideals in order to bring about a larger historical plan), but this was not supported—as was later to be the case—by any claims about racial hierarchy.

If this intellectual background has been described by Pitts as a volte-face among liberal thinkers who changed their minds between the 1780s and 1830s by transforming their liberal ideas into imperialist ones, this shift is less a volte-face than the development of different and opposed tendencies that were latent in the liberal ideas from the beginning. To put it in another way, liberal ideas were used in strategic arguments by the theorists and politicians who built 'liberal imperialism'. Having to face a context of political instability in the domestic sphere, and with imperial expansion and political competition beyond Europe at an international scale, French liberals like Tocqueville were also confronted by different models of empire, the question of race (in America) and a new religious encounter (in Algeria) that obliged them to articulate opposed trends within liberalism. They thus elaborated a liberal imperialism characterized by its ambivalences: its promotion of equal freedom and imperial conquest as a way to spread the European Enlightenment, its criticism of empires (Napoleonic, British, and also French when they consider the corruption of the settlers) and the support of European expansion as a way to stabilize domestic politics, to get the benefits of an involved citizenry by promoting a sense of national greatness, and to consolidate the rank of their country among European states.

---

[110] Koskenniemi, *The Gentle Civilizer* (n 6) 53, 69–146.

Bibliography

Alexandrowicz, Charles Henry, *An Introduction to the Law of Nations in the East Indies* (Clarendon Press 1967)

Anghie, Anthony, *Imperialism, Sovereignty and the Making of International Law* (Cambridge University Press 2004)

Arendt, Hannah, *Imperialism: Part Two of the Origins of Totalitarianism* (Schocken Books 2004)

Audier, Serge, *Tocqueville retrouvé: Genèse et enjeux du renouveau tocquevillien en France* (Vrin-EHESS, 2004)

Baudet, Henri, 'Tocqueville et la pensée coloniale au 19e siècle' in Alexis de Tocqueville, *Tocqueville, Livre du Centenaire* (Editions du CNRS, 1960)

Belissa, Marc, *Fraternité universelle et intérêt national (1713–1795): Les cosmopolitiques du droit des gens* (Kimé 1998)

Belissa, Marc, *Repenser l'ordre européen (1795–1802): De la société des rois aux droits des nations* (Kimé 2006)

Benoit, Jean-Louis, *Tocqueville: Un destin paradoxal* (Bayard 2005)

Berman, Nathaniel, *Passion and Ambivalence: Colonialism, Nationalism and International Law* (Martinus Nijhoff Publishers 2012)

Berstein, Serge and Winock, Michel (eds), *Histoire de la France politique: Tome 3, L'invention de la démocratie: 1789–1914* (Le Seuil 2002)

Boyd, Richard, 'Tocqueville and the Napoleonic Legend' in Ewa Atanassov and Richard Boyd (eds), *Tocqueville and the Frontiers of Democracy* (Cambridge University Press 2013)

Brewer, Anthony, *Marxist Theories of Imperialism: A Critical Survey* (Routledge 1980)

Comte, Auguste, *56ème Leçon du Cours de philosophie positive; Catéchisme positiviste (1852)* (Garnier 1909)

Comte, Auguste, *Système de politique positive*, IV (Carillian-Goeury et Dalmont 1854)

Condorcet, *Outlines of an Historical View of the Progress of the Human Mind* (Lang and Ustick 1796)

Condorcet, 'Sketch for a Historical Picture of the Progress of the Human Mind: Tenth Epoch' (Keith Michael Baker tr) (2004) 133 *Daedalus* 65–82

Conklin, Alice L, *A Mission to Civilize: The Republican Idea of Empire in France and West Africa, 1895–1939* (Stanford University Press 1997).

Constant, Benjamin, 'The Spirit of Conquest and Usurpation and their Relation to European Civilization' in *Constant, Political Writings* (Biancamaria Fontana tr and ed, Cambridge University Press 1988)

Craven, Matthew, 'Colonialism and Domination' in Bardo Fassbender and Anne Peters (eds), *The Oxford Handbook of the History of International Law* (Oxford University Press 2012)

Darriulat, Philippe, 'La gauche républicaine et la conquête de l'Algérie, de la prise d'Alger à la reddition d'Abd-el-Kader (1830–1847)' (1995) 82 Revue française d'histoire d'outre-mer 129

Desjobert, Amédée, *La question d'Alger: politique, colonisation, commerce* (P Dufart 1837)

Desjobert, Amédée, *L'Algérie en 1838* (Guillaumin 1838)

Desjobert, Amédée, *L'Algérie en 1844* (Guillaumin 1844)

Desjobert, Amédée, *L'Algérie en 1846* (Guillaumin 1846)

Dion, Stephane, 'Durham et Tocqueville sur la colonisation libérale' (1990) 25 Revue d'études canadiennes/Review of Canadian Studies 60

Drescher, Seymour, *Dilemmas of Democracy: Tocqueville and Modernization* (University of Pittsburgh Press 1968)

Duan, Demin, 'Reconsidering Tocqueville's Imperialism' (2010) 17 Ethical Perspectives 415

Elster, Jon, *Alexis de Tocqueville: The First Social Scientist* (Cambridge University Press 2009)

Enfantin, Barthélemy Prosper, *Colonisation de l'Algérie* (P Bertrand Libraire 1843)

Grandmaison, Olivier Le Cour, *Coloniser: Exterminer: sur la guerre et l'Etat colonial* (Fayard 2005)

Jardin, André, *Tocqueville: A Biography* (Farrar Straus Giroux 1988)

Joas, Hans and Knöbl, Wolfgang, *War in Social Thought: Hobbes to the Present* (Alex Skinner tr, Princeton University Press 2013)

Koskenniemi, Martti, *The Gentle Civilizer of Nations: The Rise and Fall of International Law 1870–1960* (Cambridge University Press 2001)

Koskenniemi, Martti, 'A History of International Law Histories' in Bardo Fassbender and Anne Peters (eds), *The Oxford Handbook of the History of International Law* (Oxford University Press 2012)

Lawlor, Mary, *Alexis de Tocqueville in the Chamber of Deputies: His Views on Foreign and Colonial Policy* (Catholic University of America Press 1959)

Manceron, Gilles, *Marianne et les colonies: Une introduction à l'histoire coloniale de la France* (La Découverte 2003)

Mehta, Uday Singh, *Liberalism and Empire* (University of Chicago Press 1999)

Mélonio, Françoise, *Tocqueville and the French* (Beth G Raps tr, University Press of Virginia 1998)

Mill, John Stewart, *On Liberty, Collected Works* (JM Robson ed, University of Toronto Press/ Routledge & Kegan Paul 1977)

Mitchell, Joshua, *The Fragility of Freedom: Tocqueville on Religion, Democracy, and the American Future* (The University of Chicago Press 1995)

Pagden, Anthony, *Lords of all the World: Ideologies of Empire in Spain, Britain and France 1500–1850* (Yale University Press 1995)

Pitts, Jennifer, 'Empire and Democracy: Tocqueville and the Algeria Question' (2000) 8 Journal of Political Philosophy 295

Pitts, Jennifer, *A Turn to Empire: The Rise of Imperial Liberalism in Britain and France* (Princeton University Press 2005)

Pitts, Jennifer, 'Democracy and Domination: Empire, Slavery, and Democratic Corruption in Tocqueville's Thought' in Ewa Atanassov and Richard Boyd (eds), *Tocqueville and the Frontiers of Democracy* (Cambridge University Press 2013)

Pocock, JGA, *The Machiavellian Moment* (Princeton University Press 1975)

Proudhon, Pierre-Joseph, *La Guerre et la Paix, recherches sur le principe et la constitution du droit des gens*, in *Oeuvres complètes*, vol 13 (Librairie internationale 1869)

Quinet, Edgar, *Le christianisme et la Révolution* (Au comptoir des imprimeurs unis 1845)

Quinet, Edgar, *Philosophie de l'histoire de France* (First published 1857, Payot 2009)

Richter, Melvin, 'Tocqueville on Algeria' (1963) 25 The Review of Politics 362

Saadi, Nouredine, 'Tocqueville et l'Algérie: le libéral et le colonial' (2004) 35 The Tocqueville Review/La Revue Tocqueville 123

Skinner, Quentin, *Liberty before Liberalism* (Cambridge University Press 1998)

Tocqueville, Alexis de, 'Letter to John Stuart Mill (March 18th 1841)' in Alexis de Tocqueville, *Selected Letters on Politics and Society* (Roger Boesche ed, James Toupain and Roger Boesche trs, University of California Press 1985)

Tocqueville, Alexis de, 'Letter to Gobineau (17 November 1853)' in Alexis de Tocqueville, *Oeuvres complètes, Tome IX, Correspondance d'Alexis de Tocqueville et d'Arthur de Gobineau* (M Degros (ed), Gallimard 1959)

Tocqueville, Alexis de, *Œuvres complètes, Correspondance Anglaise* (Gallimard 1954)

Tocqueville, Alexis de, *Oeuvres complètes, tome 3, vol 1, Ecrits et discours politiques* (Gallimard 1962)

Tocqueville, Alexis de, 'Lettres sur la situation intérieure de la France' in Alexis de Tocqueville, *Oeuvres*, vol 1 (André Jardin, Françoise Mélonio, and Lise Queffélec eds, Gallimard 1991)

Tocqueville, Alexis de, *The Old Regime and the Revolution* (Alan S Kahan tr, University of Chicago Press 1998–2001)

Tocqueville, Alexis de, *Writings on Empire and Slavery* (Jennifer Pitts tr, The Johns Hopkins University Press 2000)

Tocqueville, Alexis de, *Democracy in America* (Arthur Goldhammer tr, The Library of America 2004)

Tocqueville, Alexis de, 'Etat social et politique de la France avant et depuis 1789' in *Œuvres III* (François Furet & Françoise Mélonio (eds), Gallimard 2004)

Todorov, Tzvetan, 'Tocqueville et la doctrine coloniale' in Alexis de Tocqueville, *De la colonie en Algérie* (Editions Complexes 1988)

Tourme-Jouannet, Emmanuelle, *The Liberal-Welfarist Law of Nations: A History of International Law* (Christopher Sutcliffe tr, Cambridge University Press 2012)

Tourme-Jouannet, Emmanuelle, 'On The Colonial Origins of International Law: About the Modern Law of Nations in the Eighteen Century' in Pierre-Marie Dupuy and Vincent Chetail (eds), *The Roots of International Law/Les fondements droit international: Liber Amicorum Peter Haggenmacher* (Brill 2014)

Tuck, Richard, *The Rights of War and Peace: Political Thought and the International Order from Grotius to Kant* (Oxford University Press 1999)

Turgot, Anne Robert Jacques, *Turgot on Progress: Sociology and Economics* (Ronald L Meek tr, Cambridge University Press 1973)

Welch, Cheryl B, 'Colonial Violence and the Rhetoric of Evasion: Tocqueville on Algeria' (2003) 31 Political Theory 235

Welch, Cheryl B, 'Tocqueville resistance to the Social' (2004) 30 History of European Ideas 83

Welch, Cheryl B, 'Tocqueville on Fraternity and Fratricide' in Cheryl B Welch (ed), *The Cambridge Companion to Tocqueville* (Cambridge University Press 2006)

Wheeler, Roxann, *The Complexion of Race: Categories of Difference in Eighteenth-Century British Culture* (University of Pennsylvania Press 2000)

Wolin, Sheldon, *Tocqueville between Two Worlds: The Making of a Political and Theoretical Life* (Princeton University Press 2001)

PART III

MANAGING EMPIRE: IMPERIAL ADMINISTRATION AND DIPLOMACY

9

Towards the Empire of a 'Civilizing Nation': The French Revolution and Its Impact on Relations with the Ottoman Regencies in the Maghreb

Christian Windler

Both the American and the French Revolution promoted the programme of a new international order ideally directed towards the pursuit of prosperity and peace—essentially replacing an order based on the balance of power. Both were rooted in Enlightenment ideas, the impact of which was not limited to the internal order of states but extended to relations between different states and nations. Foreign relations were expected to be modelled on the new internal relationship between emancipated, free citizens and those elected to lead in political affairs. Like the internal order of the nation, foreign relations were conceived as governed by a 'system of liberty' ('système de liberté', as put by Mirabeau the Elder at the beginning of the French Revolution).[1]

[1] Quoted in Jean Belin, *La logique d'une idée-force: L'idée d'utilité sociale et la Révolution française (1789–1792)* (Hermann 1939) 188. On the theory and practice of foreign relations during the French Revolution: Marc Belissa, *Fraternité universelle et intérêt national (1713–1795): Les cosmopolites du droit des gens* (Kimé 1998); Marc Belissa, *Repenser l'ordre européen (1795–1802): De la société des rois aux droits des Nations* (Kimé 2006); Linda Frey and Marsha Frey, ' "The Reign of the Charlatans Is Over": The French Revolutionary Attack on Diplomatic Practice' (1993) 65 Journal of Modern History 706. On the foreign relations of the early American Republic: Jonathan R Dull, *A Diplomatic History of the American Revolution* (Yale University Press 1985); Reginald Horsman, *The Diplomacy of the New Republic, 1776–1815* (Harlan Davidson 1985); Lawrence S Kaplan, *Colonies into Nation: American Diplomacy, 1763–1801* (MacMillan Publishing Company 1972); Lawrence S Kaplan, *Entangling Alliance with None: American Foreign Policy in the Age of Jefferson* (Kent State University Press 1987); Matthias Köhler, 'No Punctilios of Ceremony? Völkerrechtliche Anerkennung, diplomatisches Zeremoniell und symbolische Kommunikation im Amerikanischen Unabhängigkeitskonflikt' in Hillard von Thiessen and Christian Windler (eds), *Akteure der Außenbeziehungen: Netzwerke und Interkulturalität im historischen Wandel* (Böhlau Köln 2010); Mlada Bukovansky, *Legitimacy and Power Politics: The American and French Revolutions in International Political Culture* (Princeton University Press 2002). This contribution contains important elements of earlier unpublished papers translated into English by James Turpin (then EUI, Florence) and Andreas Affolter (Berne); these papers were based on material of the habilitation thesis of the author, whose results were published in French as Christian Windler, *La diplomatie comme expérience de l'Autre. Consuls français au Maghreb (1700–1840)* (Librairie Droz 2002). The author wishes to thank James Turpin and Andreas Affolter for their

International Law and Empire: Historical Explorations. First Edition. Martti Koskenniemi, Walter Rech, and Manuel Jiménez Fonseca. © Martti Koskenniemi, Walter Rech, and Manuel Jiménez Fonseca 2016. Published 2016 by Oxford University Press.

Both the American and the French Revolution waged 'a war in favour of the theory and against the practice of the eighteenth century', and in both cases, this 'war' on behalf of 'humanity' laid the ideological foundations for the more or less successful affirmation of universal political ambitions.[2] In an analysis of relations between Europe and Asian empires between 1790 and 1830, the German historian Jürgen Osterhammel has pointed out that the universal civilization theory of the Enlightenment morphed into 'the general idea of a civilizing mission'; according to this new idea, it was thought to be the right and duty of any civilized European 'to enforce the universal values of progress'.[3] From the 1780s forward, 'the shift from an inclusive Eurocentrism considering Europe's superiority as a working hypothesis which could be corrected from case to case, towards an exclusive Eurocentrism positing European superiority as an axiom' was 'linked with the real exclusion' of non-European populations and their governments. Among these exclusionary practices, Osterhammel mentions the 'Orientalization of the Ottoman Empire in diplomatic practice' which meant that from that point on the empire was to be treated as part of the *Oriental question*.[4,5]

This chapter focuses on the more immediate effects of the new revolutionary approach to intercultural foreign relations by examining the relations between France and the Ottoman regencies in the Maghreb, with a particular emphasis on Tunis. Within the categorization of non-European peoples established from the sixteenth century onward, the regencies in North Africa were, as part of the Ottoman Empire, more closely associated with the Asian context than with Africa. During the eighteenth century, the (traditionally very difficult) relations between France and the regencies were marked by a strong tendency towards peaceful regulation on the basis of treaties and shared customary norms. This established an increasing degree of legal security in those fields where Christian and Muslim societies interacted; that is, commerce and shipping. This intercultural context begs questions about the impact that the new approach to foreign relations based on natural law had on these relations. The case proves interesting since it concerns relations that remained strained both in the revolutionary period and, in a more general European and Atlantic context, during the Restoration. Maghrebi 'piracy' and 'slavery' were denounced during the French Revolution and were discussed from 1814 at the Congresses of Vienna and Aix-la-Chapelle. In the early nineteenth century, these 'abuses' prompted naval actions, which this won broad support in Europe as well as in the United States.[6]

---

translations and Samuel Weber (Berne), Manuel Jiménez Fonseca, and Walter Rech (both Helsinki) for their useful critical remarks on the manuscript.

[2] James A Field, *America and the Mediterranean World, 1776–1882* (Princeton University Press 1969) 4.

[3] Jürgen Osterhammel, *Die Entzauberung Asiens: Europa und die asiatischen Reiche im 18. Jahrhundert* (CH Beck 1998) 400.

[4] Ibid, 380.   [5] Ibid, 380.

[6] On the relations of the early American Republic with the Muslim powers in the Mediterranean, see Ray Irwin, *The Diplomatic Relations of the United States with the Barbary Powers, 1776–1816* (University of North Carolina Press 1931); Field, *America and the Mediterranean World, 1776–1882*

The first part of this chapter examines the regulation of relations between European powers and the Ottoman regencies, as it had been established through treaties and practice in the eighteenth century. It shows how the regencies, in spite of their subordination to the Sublime Porte, were regarded and acknowledged by the European powers as able to act in an autonomous fashion, by following a specific set of contractual and customary laws shared by Muslims and Christians. The second and third parts illustrate a number of shifts which, beginning with the American and French Revolutions, were supported especially by the British Crown. These processes would alter, fundamentally, European relations with the regencies. While in the eighteenth century, 'corsairs' had been clearly distinguished from 'pirates', the battle against 'Barbary piracy' became a common goal of all 'civilized nations' during the Restoration period. The final part shows that this new approach was not received with unmitigated enthusiasm by those who had been cultivating the relations between Europe and the Maghreb on the ground.

The Regulation of Relations in the Eighteenth Century

From the sixteenth century onward, the regencies of Algiers, Tunis, and Tripoli were formal provinces of the Ottoman Empire, but the real authority of the Sultan in these remote territories was limited. Because of this, and despite receiving their investiture from the Sublime Porte, from the seventeenth century onward, the rulers of Algiers, Tunis, and Tripoli cultivated independent contractual relations with Christian rulers.

Since the end of the great military conflicts between the Ottoman Empire and the Habsburgs in the Mediterranean, at the end of the sixteenth century, the regencies of Algiers, Tunis, and Tripoli were at the centre of a low-level military conflict between Muslims and Christians. On both sides, this conflict was fought by corsairs who ran regular businesses as military entrepreneurs.[7] As members of a foreign elite, which, unlike the Ottoman or Moroccan Sultans, could not claim

---

(n 2); Robert J Allison, *The Crescent Obscured: The United States and the Muslim World, 1776–1815* (University of Chicago Press 1995).

[7] For an overview, the work of Salvatore Bono is still quite useful: Salvatore Bono, *Corsari nel Mediterraneo. Cristiani e musulmani fra guerra, schiavitù e commercio* (A Mondadori 1993). On the economy of corsairing and the redemption of captives in the wider Mediterranean context, see Wolfgang Kaiser (ed), *Le commerce des captifs: Les intermédiaires dans l'échange et le rachat des prisonniers en Méditerranée, xve–xviie siècles* (École française de Rome 2008). On the enslavement of Christian captives in the Maghreb, see Robert C Davis, *Christian Slaves, Muslim Masters: White Slavery in the Mediterranean, the Barbary Coast, and Italy, 1500–1800* (Palgrave Macmillan 2003). For the chronological context treated in this contribution, see Daniel Panzac, *Les corsaires barbaresques: La fin d'une épopée, 1800–1820* (Centre national de la recherche scientifique 1999). The following works remind us that corsairing was a business of Christians as well: Anne Brogini, *Malte, frontière de Chrétienté (1530–1670)* (École française de Rome 2006); Godfrey Wettinger, *Slavery in the Islands of Malta and Gozo, ca. 1000–1812* (Publishers Enterprises Group 2002). On the more general legal context of corsairing, see Michael Kempe, *Fluch der Weltmeere. Piraterie, Völkerrecht und internationale Beziehungen, 1500–1900* (Campus Verlag 2010).

descent from the Prophet, the rulers of Algiers, Tunis, and Tripoli legitimized themselves mainly as champions of *Djihād*. The coastal cities were presented as border strongholds of Islam; corsair activity was justified as a form of holy war against the infidel.[8] However, this did not mean that relations with Christians were conceived in exclusively religious terms. In addition to, for example, comparisons of the French monarchy with flattering but pagan models (including the kings of Persia, Alexander the Great, or Solomon), Maghrebi rulers employed titles that were suitable for both Muslim and Christian rulers.[9] The title *pādishāh*, which in Ottoman terminology was used for both the Sultan and the king of France, marked the imperial precedence of this king vis-à-vis other European rulers, including the Habsburg Emperors.

Whether the Maghrebi corsairs were to be considered as such, or as pirates, was a question that European jurists answered in different and contradictory ways. The answer depended very much on the context in which it was formulated. At the beginning of the seventeenth century, the Italian jurist Gentili, pleading two different cases at the High Court of Admiralty in London, qualified the Barbaresques simultaneously as 'pirates' and 'corsairs'. As a result, property bought from them by English traders had to be returned to its former owner or could, on the contrary, be considered as legitimately acquired.[10] The legal and political recognition of the regencies in the decades before the French Revolution was the result of a long process of regulation through the conclusion of agreements and formal treaties and the everyday practice of norms that eventually became a sort of customary law.

In 1605, the rulers of Tunis and the French Crown agreed on their first treaty. They confirmed the applicability of the Ottoman capitulations with regard to the French Crown, and committed the Tunisian corsairs to observe these regulations. The Franco-Tunisian treaties would be based on the capitulations of the Sublime Porte until the nineteenth century. At the same time, however, a contract law was developed which differed in form and content from the capitulations.[11] The *ahdname* or *imtiyāzāt* of the Sublime Porte, termed as capitulations by Western Europeans, were unilateral, temporary, and revocable collective promises of security conceded by the Sultan. They contained privileges concerning jurisdiction, security guarantees for persons and goods, as well as tax exemptions for certain groups. According to the Ottoman interpretation, the validity of the capitulations was bound to the person of the Sultan who conceded them and of the Christian ruler who received them.[12] While the Ottoman capitulations in favour of Christian princes and their subjects were rooted primarily in Muslim law, the contractual and customary law regulating the relations between the European powers and the Ottoman regencies in the

---

[8] Houari Touati, *Entre Dieu et les hommes. Lettrés, saints et sorciers au Maghreb (XVIIe siècle)* (Éditions de l'École des Hautes Études en Sciences Sociales 1994) 161–91.

[9] The line of argument developed here follows the work of Jocelyne Dakhlia, *Le divan des rois: Le politique et le religieux dans l'Islam* (Aubier 1998) 52–55.

[10] See Kempe, *Fluch der Weltmeere* (n 7) 250–52.

[11] On these questions, see Windler, *La diplomatie* (n 1), especially 220–45.

[12] See Halil İnalcık, 'imtiyāzāt' in B Lewis, VL Ménage, Ch Pellat, and J Schacht (eds), *Encyclopédie de l'Islam. Nouvelle édition*, vol 3 (Brill 1971).

Maghreb was an amalgam of Muslim and European-Christian legal provisions. The treaties that the French court reached with the regencies since the seventeenth century were formally based on the principle of reciprocity. Unlike the capitulations, they were sealed and ratified by both parties. The validity of these treaties was not bound to the person concluding them; in the case of the treaties with the king of France, for example, it was stipulated that they should last 100 years. The influence of the European Law of Nations ideas stemmed primarily from the fact that treaties were often the result of displays of military might by the European powers.

In the course of the codification of the relations between the regencies and the European courts, which was to reach its climax in the eighteenth century, a kind of legal syncretism was established: whereas the treaties concluded under European military pressure were heavily influenced by European ideas of the Law of Nations, the customary law or usage established through the local daily practice was often characterized by Islamic legal conceptions. The ceremonial events in which the European consuls in the Maghreb participated, or the practices of tributes and gifts, counter-balanced, symbolically, the European dominance in shaping contract law.[13]

As bilateral agreements were concluded and several European powers established consuls in the port towns of the Maghreb from the seventeenth century onward, European legal theory began to reflect the changing status of the regencies. Hugo Grotius admitted implicitly that Algiers exercised the *ius ad bellum* of a sovereign power through its corsairs.[14] In his *De iure Maritimo et Navali* (1676), the English jurist Charles Molloy went a decisive step further, by pointing out that legally Tunis, Tripoli, and Algiers could not be considered as pirates, but as enemies, because with the conclusion of the treaties they had obtained the right of legation: '… Tunis and Tripoli, and their Sister Algiers do at this day (though nests of Pirates) obtain the right of Legation … So that now (though indeed Pirates) yet having acquired the reputation of a Government, they cannot properly be esteemed Pirates but Enemies.'[15] So, in a seemingly contradictory argument, Charles Molloy adopted the widespread opinion that the Barbaresques were indeed pirates and, at the same time, denied this idea from a legal point of view.

In the eighteenth century, reports of former captives and travellers continued to perpetuate the image of the Maghrebi 'pirate'. However, European legal doctrine became increasingly explicit in its recognition of the regencies as sovereign powers. The Dutch jurist Cornelius van Bynkershoek argued in his *Questionum juris publici libri duo* (1737) that the people of Algiers, Tripoli, Tunis, and Sale were not pirates, but formed a community with its own territory on which they had established their dominion and with whom, like with other peoples, peace was concluded and war was fought; they had thus the same rights as other peoples.[16] This became codified in maritime law. In the *Codice Ferdinando o Codice marittimo* (1781) (compiled by order of King Ferdinand IV of Naples), the author (Michele de Jorio) adopted

[13] Windler, *La diplomatie* (n 1) 405–75, 485–548.
[14] See Kempe, *Fluch der Weltmeere* (n 7) 256–57.   [15] Quoted in ibid, 258, cf 257.
[16] Ibid, 259–60.

Cornelius van Bynkershoek's opinion, even though his own sovereign was among the very few who had not yet concluded any treaty with the regencies.[17]

French consuls and other practitioners of diplomacy were equally willing to consider the regencies as partners in a network of trans-Mediterranean legal relations. This network was not fully part of the legal community constituted by the Christian European powers; it was a network of norms that only regulated those issues that were of equal concern to both involved parties. Understandably, maritime law was of particular interest. Compared to the Russians and the Spanish (who only later barely participated in this normative system), French diplomatic agents defended the specific norms concerning maritime law that applied to relations between Muslims and Christians. In 1773, Barthélémy de Saizieu, consul in Tunis, complained that during the Russian-Ottoman war, the Russians refused to release the cargo of a French ship belonging to Tunisians and Algerians. The Russians had acted that way 'even though they were not in a state of war with the rulers of the Maghreb, whom they should know to be independent from the Sublime Porte and to be subject to the rules which sovereign and well-policed states have established among themselves and to which they adhere'.[18] In the correspondence between the French secretaries of state, the 'Barbaresques' maritime law' was evoked also, and the Maghrebi corsairs were recognized as respecting these norms. Therefore, they were not to be labelled as 'pirates'.[19]

Quantitative research shows that subjects of European rulers entertaining contractual relations with the regencies did indeed enjoy extensive protection from corsair raids. Already from 1681 to 1700, only 0.5 per cent of the 420 European slaves who used the services of the chancellery of the French consulate in Tunis for their redemption from captivity were of French origin. Like the French, the English captured under hostile flags were set free with speed upon inspection of their passports or after the intervention of their consuls.[20]

Although the principle that contracts should be honoured was common to European and Islamic legal theory, military power (in this case especially the French naval resources) and shared economic interests contributed to ensure in practice the

---

[17] Ibid, 260–61.

[18] Barthélémy de Saizieu, consul, to Bourgeois de Boynes, secrétaire d'État de la Marine, Tunis, 15 Jan 1773: '… malgré qu'ils n'aient pas d'action ni de guerre déclarée avec les princes de Barbarie, qu'ils savent être indépendants de la Porte, et susceptibles comme elle des règles que les États souverains et policés ont établis, et observant entre eux.' Archives Nationales (hereafter AN) AE BI 1145, fo 15v.

[19] Sartine, secrétaire d'Etat de la Marine, to Vergennes, secrétaire d'Etat des affaires étrangères, Versailles, 28 Nov 1774: 'Vous n'ignorez pas, Monsieur, les principes qui constituent le droit maritime des Barbaresques. Ils ne contestent point au Pavillon neutre le droit de couvrir la marchandise non contrebande, et ils n'inquiètent point les navires amis et neutres sur la propriété de leurs cargaisons. Ils reconnaissent que le Pavillon ami sauve la marchandise ennemie. Mais en même temps ils ont pour maxime ancienne et constante que le Pavillon français doit leur répondre de tout ce qui est embarqué pour leur compte. Ils regardent la garantie du Pavillon comme un droit d'autant plus incontestable, qu'ils le respectent eux-mêmes, et qu'ils n'enlèvent point sur les vaisseaux français, les effets de leurs ennemis, soit Italiens, Espagnols, ou même Maltais.' AN, AE, BI 1145, fos 311r–312r.

[20] Godfrey Fisher, *Barbary Legend: War, Trade and Piracy in North Africa 1415–1830* (Clarendon Press 1957); Michel Fontenay, 'Le Maghreb barbaresque et l'esclavage méditerranéen aux XVIe–XVIIe siècles' (1991) 44 Les Cahiers de Tunisie 7, 18–20.

effectiveness of legal norms, in ways quite similar to that which occurred between European powers. In this sense, it was no accident that out of the three Ottoman regencies, the regency of Tunis was least likely to provoke complaints. This regency was much more integrated into the Mediterranean trading networks than Algiers or Tripoli. While French factories along the Algerian coast ran coral-catching operations with European manpower as a kind of off-shore business, in Tunis, local elites and European traders shared significant economic interests. In addition to the export of agrarian products which was carried out by French factories along the Algerian shore, the Tunisians depended on raw wool and dyestuff deliveries from Spain and the New World, as well as on shipping services for the local textile business, which had a quasi-monopoly on the provision of felt hats to the Ottoman Empire. In the case of Tunis, the economic diversification and the weight of export-oriented activities stood against the predominance of the Mediterranean corsair economy.

In the eighteenth century, conflicts between the consuls and the court in Tunis were mainly fought out in legal terms. Treaties and usage regulated the distribution of the prizes, that is, the maritime booty. Before the establishment of mixed courts in the nineteenth century, forms of consultation and mediation were used from the second half of the eighteenth century forward. They did not yet limit the exclusive jurisdictional power of the Bey as ruler of Tunis, but the consuls would at least be heard. Peaceful relations with Christian powers thus evolved from an exception based upon limited promises of security to something considered as the norm.

The descriptions of the regency of Tunis as they appeared in diplomatic practice also show increasing closeness and trust.[21] In the course of the eighteenth century, republican terminology denoting, under the *ancien regime*, the irregular exercise of power was replaced, increasingly, by monarchic categories: although in the letters addressed to the Bey, the court of Versailles avoided designating the regency as a 'kingdom' ('*royaume*'), the consuls themselves did not adhere to this official terminology and spoke of a '*royaume*' in their correspondence with the responsible secretary of state of the navy. Eventually Jean-Michel Venture de Paradis, chancellor of the French consulate in Tunis, followed completely the pattern of Eurocentric inclusion of the regency, as evidenced in his *Observations sur le gouvernement de Tunis* (1788). Adopting European models, he characterized the rulers as enlightened princes. According to Venture, the Tunisian Beys differed from the 'Turkish government', that is 'Oriental despotism', in the humane exercise of their jurisdiction, in their respect for property rights and in the promotion of agriculture and trade.[22] Like the *princes* of royal blood, the cousins of the governing Bey lived in

---

[21] On Enlightenment discourse on the Maghreb see Ann Thomson, *Barbary and Enlightenment: European Attitudes towards the Maghreb in the 18th Century* (Brill Academic Publishers 1987). Ann Thomson does not take into account the diplomatic and consular correspondences.

[22] 'Rien ne sent moins la Barbarie que la cour du bey de Tunis. Il y règne un ton de politesse, d'urbanité et de douceur capable d'étonner tout Européen: on n'y voit ni les principes ni la conduite du gouvernement turc. Les présents et l'argent n'y terminent aucune affaire et on y suit scrupuleusement les règles, les usages et les lois.' Jean Michel Venture de Paradis, 'Observations sur le gouvernement de Tunis, 1788' in Jean Michel Venture de Paradis, *Tunis et Alger au XVIIIe siècle, mémoires et observations rassemblés et présentés par Joseph Cuoq* (Sindbad 1983) 82.

freedom, which was 'the most convincing proof of the civility of this government', as opposed to 'a Turkish government'.[23]

Between 'Civilizing Mission' and Pragmatism: An Ambiguous Exclusion during the French Revolution

In 1758, Émer de Vattel stressed that religious differences had no influence whatsoever on the validity of treaties, as these were defined exclusively by natural law, according to which, men established contacts 'as human beings and not as Christians or Muslims'.[24] Did, then, the American and French Revolutions herald a new age of relations with non-Western societies (including the regencies in the Maghreb), based on mutual respect among mankind? I would argue that in fact the opposite was the case. The self-conception of the revolutionary societies implied an aggressive rejection of the plurality of norms that had been constitutive of intercultural relations and which had shaped the process of legal regulation of relations with the regencies throughout the eighteenth century. As Jürgen Osterhammel has pointed out, Europe 'primarily fashioned itself as the culture establishing a universal order'.[25]

However, in the beginning, the French diplomatic agents feared that the Revolution would endanger their country's position in the Mediterranean. The emergence of new enemies of France had to be avoided; at the same time, given the difficulties of supply, the possibility for importing wheat from the Maghreb to Southern France had to remain open. In the meantime, new divergences resulting from the Revolution were discussed from a weakened position, with the redefinition of the relations between State and Church believed to be one of the sources of new differences.

The Sublime Porte,[26] as well as the regencies in the Maghreb, disapproved of the anti-religious orientation of the Revolution. In the Maghreb, the relation between Church and Crown had been symbolized through the French king's patronage of the Catholic missions; in the aftermath of the revolutionary events in France, the closure of the Consular Chapels became a distinct possibility. In 1793, Foreign Minister Lebrun warned the *Comité d'Aliénation* of the Convention Nationale not to sell Church property belonging to the French system of patronage in the Ottoman Empire and in the Maghreb: according to Lebrun, the Ottoman people

---

[23] Ibid: 'preuve la plus convaincante de la civilisation de ce gouvernement'.

[24] 'en qualité d'hommes, et non en qualité de chrétiens, ou de musulmans': Émer de Vattel, *Le droit des gens, ou principes de la loi naturelle appliqués à la conduite et aux affaires des nations et des souverains* (Albert de Lapradelle ed, Carnegie Institution of Washington 1916), vol 1, book II, chapter XII, § 162, 373–74, also see § 230, 441.

[25] Osterhammel, *Die Entzauberung Asiens* (n 3) 381.

[26] Faruk Bilici, 'La Révolution française dans l'historiographie turque 1789–1927' in Hédia Khadhar (ed), *La Révolution française et le monde arabo-musulman: Colloque international, Tunis 9–11 novembre 1989* (Tunis 1991) 157.

displayed a 'frenetic disdain' towards all those suspected of atheism. The sale of the churches would confirm the accusations of the enemies of the Revolution, according to whom there was no longer any religion in France. If this opinion became predominant, the Sublime Porte could no longer be an ally of France.[27] Using a similar line of argument, Jacques-Philippe Devoize, Consul-General in Tunis, opposed the secularization of the Consular Chapel by a Commissioner dispatched by the Public Welfare Committee. According to Devoize, secularizing the Chapel would not only mean the loss of an important privilege, but also the destruction of an important base of the French presence in Tunis. Devoize stressed that all agreements between Paris and Tunis were based upon the fidelity of everyone involved to their respective religion:

Here, Religion serves politics in complaints often resulting from the depredations by the corsairs. The Bey requires that the captain swear an oath in the presence of the chaplain of the [French] *nation* that the accounts of losses he presents are honest, and then full payment is ordered ... I could mention whole cargoes that have been compensated for according to this oath.[28]

The suspicion of atheism cast doubt on the relations whose bases derived, in the Muslims' point of view, from Muslim legal practice protecting Christian minorities.

At the same time, from the early 1790s forward, there was a manifest paradigm shift in French foreign policy, which would provide completely new legitimacy to French expansion in the Mediterranean. 'Oriental despotism' was considered increasingly as a decisive obstacle to civilization. These thoughts can also be traced in the correspondence of the consuls in the Maghreb, especially when they had to prove their compliance with their superiors' policy. When asked, in 1795, to give useful information for the expansion of French art, science, and industry, Devoize already knew about intrigues to withdraw him from his post as the Consul-General in Tunis, because of doubts about his loyalty to the Republic. He answered following the dominant French discourse on the 'Orient':

... science and arts in Tunis are in the saddest state: as despotism can only survive by the ignorance of man, its implementation in this part of Africa has led to the disappearance of the former, which vanished together with the free men who had cultivated them in the brighter days of Rome and Carthage. They left behind some precious monuments, it is true, but if the stupid Muslim, slave of Barbarian preconceptions, encounters those monuments in the ruins of the latter city, he hurries to damage those masterpieces of art. Thus they are

---

[27] See Lebrun, ministre des Relations extérieures, to Delacroix, vice-président du Comité d'Aliénation of the National Convention, 28 May 1793 AN, AE BI 38, fo 170r/v: 'une antipathie frénétique', fo 170v.

[28] Devoize to Delacroix, ministre des Relations extérieures, Tunis, 24 ventôse an IV, [14 Mar 1796]: 'La religion sert ici la politique dans les réclamations qu'amènent souvent les déprédations des corsaires. Le bey exige du capitaine le serment entre les mains du chapelain de la nation que les notes d'effets qu'il présente sont fidèles, et le paiement en est ordonné sans déduction.... Je pourrais citer des cargaisons entières qui ont été payées d'après ce serment.' Archives du Ministère des Affaires étrangères (hereafter MAE), Correspondance consulaire et commerciales (hereafter CCC). Tunis, vol 34, fos 74v–75v, 75v.

lost for future generations that might have admired them, for which they might indeed have been models.[29]

Similar to reports about the Eastern Mediterranean, ancient ruins became a symbol of decadence caused by despotic governments.

At least if one looks at diplomacy through the ideological foundations on which it rested, the 1790s led to revolutionary innovations in the full sense of the word. The question of whether the political relations of France with Algiers and Tunis could be modified 'according to the law of nations of Europe and have as a rule different principles to those that had been in use until this day' was posed with renewed vigour.[30] While under the Old Regime, the plurality of norms regulating the relations between Christians and Muslims corresponded in a structural sense to the plurality of statuses and jurisdictions within the European social order, the revolutionary universalism based on natural law stood in sharp contrast to existing diplomatic practices. In the Mediterranean, the pluralistic normative order of the European Old Regime had favoured compromises and tacit consensus around common positive norms, thus enabling the continuity of friendly relations. While up to that point disputes had revolved around the interpretation of, and compliance with, contractual and customary norms, the consuls of the revolutionary period made the case that the principles of humanity were ridiculed by 'despotic' governments. Thus, in 1792, Devoize wrote to the Navy minister, Monge, that it was the French republic's duty 'to be the first to shake off the yoke the Barbaresques impose on all powers ...' Accordingly, he believed 'that a free people will not any longer tolerate slavery on its doorstep'.[31] Whereas slavery had until this period been accepted as a side effect of corsair activities practiced by Muslims and Christians alike, the enslavement of prisoners of war now became the symbol of a political order that stood in opposition to the founding principles of the French Republic.[32] Similar arguments were advanced in the young American republic, before it entered the established system by concluding treaties with the regencies following the pattern of those signed by the Old Regime European powers.[33]

[29] Devoize to the Comité de Salut Public, Tunis, 30 nivôse an III [19 Jan 1795]: '... les sciences et les arts n'offrent à Tunis qu'une triste observation à faire, c'est qu'à mesure que le despotisme qui ne peut subsister que par l'ignorance des peuples, s'est établi dans cette partie de l'Afrique, ils ont disparu avec les hommes libres qui les cultivaient dans les beaux jours de Rome et de Carthage. Ils ont bien laissé après eux des monuments précieux, mais en les découvrant parmi les ruines de cette dernière ville, le stupide musulman esclave d'un préjugé barbare, se hâte de mutiler ces chefs-d'œuvre de l'art qui sont perdus pour la postérité dont ils auraient fait l'admiration, en lui servant de modèles.' MAE, CCC, Tunis, vol 33, fo 76r/v. Cf Vallière, consul general in Algiers, to the Comité de Salut Public, Algiers, 14 pluviôse an III [2 Feb. 1795], MAE, CCC, Alger, vol 32, fo 173r.

[30] Memorandum on the Compagnie d'Afrique, 1791, AN, AE BIII 322, pièce 9: 'suivant le droit des gens d'Europe et avoir pour règle des principes différents de ceux qui ont été en usage jusqu'à ce jour'.

[31] Devoize, consul general in Tunis, to Monge, ministre de la Marine, Tunis, 8 Dec 1792, AN, AE BI 1154, fo 168r/v: 'C'est à la République française qu'il appartient de secouer la première le joug que les régences barbaresques imposent à toutes les puissances qui semblent s'être concertées pour le subir; je dois croire qu'un peuple libre ne souffrira pas l'esclavage à sa porte.'

[32] Mémoire pour servir d'instructions aux citoyens Ducher et Lallement, agents extraordinaires allant à Alger et à Tunis, Paris, 4 ventôse an II [22 Feb 1794] MAE, CCC, Tunis, vol 32, fo 115r.

[33] See Kempe, *Fluch der Weltmeere* (n 7) 278–79.

In the 1790s, the religious legitimization of France's supremacy as 'the eldest daughter of the church' was replaced by the claim that France was carrying out a 'civilizing mission', although the term *'mission civilisatrice'* itself was not yet in use. This civilizing claim established an effective ideological foundation for Napoleon's expedition to Egypt, where the military conquest was claimed to be beneficial to the conquered since they could neither free themselves from inherited slavery nor attain civilization and progress on their own.[34] In 1801, Devoize, upon request by Bonaparte, wrote a memorandum on a similar future expedition against Tunis (*Mémoire sur un projet d'expédition contre Tunis*). As the 'leader of a free Nation of warriors',[35] Bonaparte was called upon to proceed in the name of 'Humanity' against these 'barbarians' and to conquer the regency in order 'to destroy the authorities who commit such revolting abuses'.[36] The First Consul was 'to undertake ... the regeneration of this part of Africa'.[37]

The use of such descriptions was highly contextual: until the expedition to Egypt, French politics clashed particularly with neighbouring monarchies; comparisons with the European 'despots' were often more favourable for the princes of the Maghreb who maintained, until 1798, a policy of friendly neutrality towards the Republic. Before the expedition to Egypt and the ensuing disruption of peaceful relations with the Ottoman regencies (as well as after the conclusion of peace treaties with Algiers in 1801 and Tunis in 1802), a sharp contrast formed between the far-reaching projects of a new international order and the diplomatic practices aiming at accommodation.

Until the expedition to Egypt, all revolutionary governments preserved peaceful relations with all Muslim powers; to these the French Republic presented itself as 'the oldest ally'.[38] In 1798, shortly before the declaration of war into which the regencies were forced following the Egyptian expedition, Devoize contrasted their fidelity and loyalty to the Republic with the conspiracy of the kings of Europe against Liberty.[39] These remarks appear in the context of Devoize's close relations with the beylical court, with which the consul conducted financial and commercial affairs, in spite of Marine Ordinance provisions to the contrary. The consul was an integral part of the networks that bound together Muslims, Christians, and Jews in

[34] On the expedition to Egypt, see Henry Laurens (with contributions by Charles C Gillispie, Jean-Claude Golvin, and Claude Traunecker), *L'expédition d'Égypte, 1798–1801* (Éditions Armand Colin 1989). On the civilizing missions, see Boris Barth and Jürgen Osterhammel (eds), *Zivilisierungsmissionen. Imperiale Weltverbesserung seit dem 18. Jahrhundert* (UVK 2005).
[35] Mémoire sur un projet d'expédition contre Tunis, Paris, 6 prairial an IX [26 May 1801]: 'chef d'une Nation libre et guerrière' ; a letter with the same date is signed by Jacques-Philippe Devoize and allows the identification of the author of the *Mémoire* (AN, 327 AP 1).
[36] Ibid: 'détruire des autorités dont l'abus est si révoltant'.
[37] Ibid: 'entreprendre ... la régénération de cette partie de l'Afrique'. In the same context and with the same line of argument, the consul general in Algiers also proposed a war campaign against the Turkish government of Algiers, where the cabyles would receive Napoleon Bonaparte as a 'liberator' (*libérateur*). Quoted in François Charles-Roux, *France et Afrique du Nord avant 1830. Les précurseurs de la conquête* (Félix Alcan 1932) 394.
[38] Rapport sur Tunis, Feb 1793: 'la plus ancienne alliée' (AN, AE BI 38, fo 38v).
[39] Devoize to La Combe Saint-Michel, Tunis, 3 frimaire an VII [23 Nov 1798] (AN, 327 AP 4).

Tunis;[40] his emphasis on the differences of civilizations was an attempt to establish his reputation as an intermediary in the eyes of his superiors. The complexity of close daily interaction and shared personal interests broke the coherence of the discourse on the Maghrebi Other.

A pragmatic approach also characterized the Napoleonic diplomacy after the re-establishment of peaceful relations. Whereas in the French colonies, slavery was legalized anew in 1802, the fight against the enslavement of European prisoners of war in the Maghreb remained an important element of French political discourse. Following the territorial annexations in Europe, this question was raised anew during the first French Empire: since some of the annexed regions in Italy had been at war with the regencies of Algiers, Tunis, and Tripoli, their subjects had often been enslaved by corsairs. Their release was to give French rule over Italian subjects a certain degree of legitimacy. The French consuls in Algiers and Tunis were therefore told to start negotiations. A formal redemption was to be avoided if possible. When, in 1806, Devoize was advised to hand over a sum of money corresponding to the number of released slaves, the Emperor's money was to be given to Ḥammūda Bey 'exclusively as a sign of satisfaction' ('uniquement à titre de satisfaction'), that is, as a gift.[41] It is not clear how effective this case was: in letters to Talleyrand, Devoize himself spoke of the 'price of the enfranchisement' ('*prix de l'affranchissement*') of the slaves.[42]

Ambiguities like these were characteristic of French diplomacy from the 1790s onward. Whereas revolutionary discourse challenged fundamentally the forms of diplomatic relations with Muslim powers as they had been cultivated up to that point, in practice, consuls avoided a clear rupture. The redefinition of practices was a perspective for the future rather than immediate reality.

The Restoration and the Campaign against 'Piracy'

A close look at the Restoration period reveals the full extent of the reorientation of relations to non-Western powers in general, and to the Ottoman regencies in particular. The claim to reorganize the relations with non-European powers according to the rules of 'civilized nations' was advanced with equal vigour by France's European adversaries. As legitimization for exclusion and intervention, the duty to combat 'despotism' and propagate 'civilization' to 'backward' and 'barbarian' peoples was by no means exclusively used by the French. The same concepts justified also the British 'turn to Empire'.[43] The new self-confidence which became

---

[40] See Windler, *La diplomatie* (n 1).

[41] Talleyrand, ministre des Relations extérieures, to Devoize, Paris, 18 Mar 1806 (MAE, CCC, Tunis, vol 38, fos 161r–161bis v).

[42] Devoize to Talleyrand, ministre des Relations extérieures, Tunis, 28 Oct 1806 (MAE, CCC, Tunis, vol 38, fo 196r).

[43] See Jennifer Pitts, *A Turn to Empire: The Rise of Imperial Liberalism in Britain and France* (Princeton University Press 2005) 14–17, 123–62. Cf PG McHugh, 'A Comporting Sovereign, Tribes,

manifest in the narrative about the British Ambassador Macartney's negotiation to avoid kowtowing to the Chinese Emperor in 1793 (which was presented in Europe as a huge diplomatic success),[44] were as much part of the new diplomatic approach as was the British consul's refusal to kiss the Bey's hand during his Tunis audiences (this had been an obligation following the example of the Bey's subjects).[45] The two practices were perceived as humiliating and, therefore, against the background of a changing distribution of military and economic power, rejected. Although diplomatic intermediaries on the ground were in many cases more pragmatic, the narrative about such spectacular episodes was, on the level of symbolic communication, part of the processes of transformation which have been referred to as the 'great divergence', that is, the global shift in the distribution of economic and military resources in favour of Europe in the period around 1800.[46]

Those involved in the 'Restoration' in 1814–15 continued with the transformation of relations to non-Western rulers stemming from the American and French Revolutions. The so-called 'Restoration', which might rather be considered as the consolidation of a new inner-European system of international relations born out of the revolutionary turmoil, was accompanied by an aggressively asserted claim as to the universal validity of the norms on which the new system was based. Relations with the regencies in the Maghreb illustrate that the association of international law with 'Europe', 'Civilization', and 'Christianity' went, in political practice, hand-in-hand with its use in European universalistic discourses. Discrimination and exclusion were based on the universalization of a particular European law of nations, hence the very ambiguity of universalism, during the revolutionary period as well as from 1814–15 onward.[47]

and the Ordering of Imperial Authority in Colonial Upper Canada of the 1830s', Chapter 10 in the present volume.

[44] New research by Henrietta Harrison shows that the importance attached by the emperor to the ceremonial issues related with the kowtow was exaggerated in twentieth-century historiography as a manifestation of a specific Chinese world view and of its incapacity to adapt to (European) modernity. Harrison's interpretation based on extensive research on Chinese documentation is also supported by a close reading of George Staunton's account about the embassy. Although this account, published in 1797 and immediately translated into different European languages, laid the foundations for the British narrative about Macartney's refusal as a highly significant symbolic success, it still showed the Chinese willing and capable to negotiate a solution acceptable to both sides—not precisely the picture popularized in the early twentieth century. In this perspective, Macartney's (and more generally the British diplomacy's) prestige was to be based on the ability to negotiate successfully even in Asia's most respectable court. See George Staunton, *An Authentic Account of an Embassy from the King of Great Britain to the Emperor of China*, vol 2 (London 1797) 129–39, 141–45, 208–15, 218–19, 224–39; French translation: Paris, 1798; German: Berlin and Zurich, 1798–99; Italian: Venice, 1799–1800; Dutch: Amsterdam, 1798–1801. Cf James Hevia, *Cherishing Men from Afar: Qing Guest Ritual and the Macartney Embassy of 1793* (Duke University Press 1995).

[45] Windler, *La diplomatie* (n 1) 435–36.

[46] Kenneth Pomeranz, *The Great Divergence: China, Europe, and the Making of the Modern World Economy* (Princeton University Press 2000).

[47] On the ambiguity of universalization and particularization see Miloš Vec, 'Universalization, Particularization and Discrimination: European Perspectives on a Cultural History of 19th century International Law' (2012) 3(2) InterDisciplines: Journal of History and Sociology 79 <http://www.inter-disciplines.org/index.php/indi/article/viewFile/66/54> accessed 15 April 2016; Luigi Nuzzo, *Origini di una scienza: Diritto internazionale e colonialismo nel XIX secolo* (Vittorio Klostermann 2012).

At the Congresses of Vienna (1814–15) and Aix-La-Chapelle (1818), the inter-diction of North African corsair activities, now declared 'piracy', became the first object of this claim. The denunciation of Maghrebi corsair activities followed the proscription of the Atlantic slave trade mainly pursued by England. It was argued that if the trade with black slaves was to be prohibited, *a fortiori* the trade with 'civilized Christians' in North Africa could not be tolerated.[48] In the summer of 1814, the English Admiral, Sidney Smith, disseminated a memorial calling on European governments to prepare a naval campaign in order to replace the 'pirate states' in the Maghreb with governments that were more open to trade and in accordance with 'civilized nations'. In 1815, the Vienna Congress condemned the enslavement of captives and ordered Lord Exmouth, Commander of the British navy in the Mediterranean, to implement the resolutions of the Congress with military means.[49] After the bombing of Algiers, Lord Exmouth claimed to have defended 'the cause of God and humanity' against 'a horde of fanatics' obeying their 'despots'.[50]

Though the bombing of Algiers destroyed most of the local corsair ships, it failed to bring on the definitive end of corsair activities. Thus, in 1818, the Congress of Aix-La-Chapelle ordered a French and English admiral to call on the Bey of Tunis, the Pasha of Tripoli, and the Dey of Algiers to renounce 'piracy'. The activities of the European powers against corsair activities and the enslavement of prisoners of war were actions as much against the norms legitimizing these practices as against the practices themselves. In 1819, the French Consul-General in Tunis, Devoize, wrote to the Bey's French personal physician that the great powers wanted the regencies to wage war 'like civilized nations'.[51] The answer of the Maghrebi rulers confirmed that these actions were as much about asserting European norms as generally bind-ing rules. According to the Bey of Tunis, the term 'piracy' did not better apply to the principles of his government than to the governments of the Christians; his corsairs had never violated the treaties with, or the immunity of, foreign territories. The Bey emphasized his willingness to observe the treaties as he had already to that point. In practice, he felt impelled to accept the demands of the European powers. In the following years, only a few corsair ships left the harbours of the Maghreb.[52]

The treaties concluded between France and the Bey of Tunis and the Pasha of Tripoli in August 1830 (immediately after the conquest of Algiers) signify the same profound break with the norms that had hitherto been practised by both sides.

Cf Wilhelm G Grewe, 'Vom europäischen zum universellen Völkerrecht: Zur Frage der Revision des "europazentrischen" Bildes der Völkerrechtsgeschichte' (1982) 42 Zeitschrift für ausländisches öffent-liches Recht und Völkerrecht 449.

[48] See Panzac, *Les corsaires* (n 7) 137–226.   [49] Ibid, 227–41.

[50] Exmouth to Croker, Admiralty, Bay of Algiers, 28 Aug 1816, National Archives, Kew, ADM 1/432.

[51] Devoize to [Laurent Gay, 1er médecin du bey], no place [Tunis], no date [Sep 1819], AN, 327 AP 14: 'comme les nations civilisées'.

[52] 'Traduction de la lettre écrite [par Maḥmūd Bey] en idiome arabe au contre-amiral Jurien, com-mandant français, palais du Barde de Tunis, 9 dhū al-ḥidjdja H. 1234 [29 Sep 1819]', MAE, CCC Tunis, vol 43, fos 203r–204r. See Panzac, *Les corsaires* (n 7) 242–43.

Stipulations that were only remotely related to the actual policy of the regencies had to demonstrate the services which France rendered to 'Christian civilization'. The regencies of Tunis and Tripoli had once again to renounce corsair activities and the enslavement of Christian captives. Both of the treaties freed all European powers from the duty to present tributes and gifts to the regencies. Reciprocity in the sense of the European law of nations, however, did not become the basis of the relations between European powers and the two Ottoman regencies. Whereas every European state would be allowed, subsequently, to open consulates in the Maghreb, the regencies were refused the same right on the grounds that their sovereignty was limited by their dependence on the Ottoman sultan. Moreover, the treaties contained significant fiscal and economic concessions for the sole benefit of the Europeans in general and the French in particular. For example, France obtained the exclusive privilege of coral catching on Tunisian shores.[53]

A Culture of Mediation: French Consul-General and Local Political Player

From the Revolution onward, the practice of negotiating specific norms in a shared legal space had been brought back into question. As intermediaries between successive French governments and the regencies, consuls participated in this questioning, but, at the same time, they did not stop cultivating forms of exchange founded on the continuity of treaties and custom. In 1816, the Bey's physician, Louis Frank, in a description of the regency written for a European public, criticized the consuls who accepted a ceremonial unworthy of European state representatives. Of most notable mention is the hand kiss as a ritual of submission to the Bey; if one is to believe Frank, the French Consul-General Devoize was 'ordinarily' reproached for having become 'more Oriental and more African than French'.[54] The case of Devoize, consul to Tunis from the Revolution until 1819, illustrates well the ambiguous position of the intermediary caught between contradictory logics. French consuls depended on the government that they represented for nomination to their posts. But they were also integrated into the local society in which they carried out their duties. While Devoize was bound to French traders he also shared interests with local Muslims and Jews. He was not only a French Consul-General, but a local political

---

[53] Treaty between France and Tunis, signed 8 August 1830, French version in: Eugène Plantet (ed), *Correspondance des beys de Tunis et des consuls de France avec la Cour, 1577–1830*, vol 3 (Felix Alcan 1899); Treaty between France and Tripolis, signed 11 August 1830, French version in Edgard Rouard de Card (ed), *Traités de la France avec les pays de l'Afrique du Nord: Algérie, Tunisie, Tripolitaine, Maroc* (A Pedone 1906).

[54] 'plus Oriental et plus Africain que Français': Louis Frank, 'Tunis, description de cette Régence [1816], par le Dr -, ancien médecin du Bey de Tunis, du Pâcha de Jannina, et de l'armée d'Egypte, revue et accompagnée d'un précis historique et d'éclaircissements tirés des écrivains orientaux, par J[ean] J[oseph] Marcel' in *L'Univers pittoresque: Histoire et description de tous les peuples, de leurs religions, moeurs, coutumes, industries, etc. &. Afrique*, vol 7 (Paris 1862) 94.

player, dealing at the time with competing and conflicting agendas, which stemmed from the multiplicity of his social roles.

After his return from Tunis in 1819, Devoize was charged by Pasquier, the French minister of foreign affairs, with preparing a diplomatic mission aimed at re-establishing French trading rights in Tunis (these were threatened by the reprisals that had followed the controversial regulations of the continental blockade). The nomination of a successor, however, frustrated his hope to crown his career by concluding a new treaty. It still offered him the opportunity to insist on his specific knowledge as an intermediary that his successor, who had until then been posted in the Levant, did not possess. His knowledge and his ability to influence the mind of the prince and his ministers had always allowed him to avoid the resort to military threats: 'I never used threats and I always got what I wanted. This I can say without excessive pride, because I proved it.'[55] At the end of his career, at the age of 80, Devoize postulated the existence of a specific diplomatic culture which was shared by a small number of experienced specialists who defined their rank by the long practice of mediation.

In dispatches to his superiors, Devoize often repeated revolutionary principles, denying all legitimacy of the structures of domination of the regency and the specific norms that governed relations between Europeans and the Maghrebis. 'Piracy' and slavery appeared as symbols of an order that was opposed to the imprescriptible rights of Man and of Nations. However, under the Restoration, he saw the definitive decline of Maghrebi corsairing as the ruin of a system that had assured, when he was younger, French preponderance in the Mediterranean. In 1819 Devoize was required to assist the French and British admirals, Jurien and Freemantle, in their joint mission on behalf of the Congress of Aix-la-Chapelle to obtain from the regencies the renunciation of 'piracy'. Devoize did so against his better judgement, convinced as he was that this decision was contrary to the interests of French trade in the Mediterranean, as he stressed in his unofficial, personal correspondence: 'We once held exclusively all the Mediterranean trade, today we have as rivals all of the states of Italy, and that thanks to the philanthropic treaties of the English with the Barbaresques, whose conclusion is the last mission of the two Anglo-French commissioners.'[56]

When it came to sorting out practical problems in Franco-Maghrebi relations, Devoize defended the shared treaty and customary norms even before his superiors. The legislation of the Revolution and the Empire limited the liberty of trade that Tunisians had, according to treaties, the right to enjoy in Marseilles. Conflicts became even more frequent because the neutrality of the regency in the European wars temporarily encouraged the development of commercial navigation under the

[55] Devoize to Pierre Gay, Voiron, 22 Jan 1825, AN, 327 AP 30: 'Je n'ai jamais employé la menace et j'ai toujours tout obtenu. Je peux le dire sans orgueil, parce que je l'ai prouvé.'

[56] Devoize to Ruffin, Lazareth de Toulon, 30 Nov 1819, AN, 327 AP 13: 'Nous faisions autrefois exclusivement tout le commerce de la Méditerranée, nous y avons aujourd'hui pour rivaux tous les Etats d'Italie, et cela grâces aux traités philanthropiques des Anglais chez les Barbaresques, dont le complément est la dernière mission des deux commissaires anglo-français.'

Tunisian flag. Devoize himself benefited from the advantages offered by the possibility of concealing French ships and cargoes under the flag of the beylik.[57]

Could a French law invalidate a Franco-Tunisian treaty? From the 1790s forward, the priority of treaties and custom was no longer taken for granted. In a political framework based on the principles of a natural law common to all men, put in practice from a French point of view by revolutionary legislation, there could be no differences of principle between internal and international law. During the 1790s, French attempts to enforce national legislation outside the territory of the Republic, in the name of revolutionary universalism, increased. At the origin of the controversies, one finds individual administrative or judicial acts that applied laws or regulations in conflict with treaties and custom. Thus, in 1794, the authorities of Marseilles applied the price regulations on consignments of leather belonging to Tunisian Jews who had rented the beylical leather monopoly.[58]

Numerous infringements of the freedom of trade and the arrangements that limited customs duties were provoked by the continental blockade. Not only were Tunisians obliged to pay higher duties, but some Tunisian ships—though belonging to the Bey himself—were confiscated because they had ventured into harbours under English domination; Malta in particular.[59] As his complaints were not taken into consideration by the French government, the Bey decided on reprisals: he withheld large sums owed to the French and raised in his turn custom duties beyond the threshold fixed by the treaties.[60]

The rigours of imperial customs and their conflict with the treaties disturbed Franco-Tunisian relations long after Napoleon's fall. Two comparative overviews written by Devoize, one in 1811, the other in 1814, show that with regard to customs and other duties raised on shipping, the articles of the treaty concluded in 1742 were respected faithfully by the Regency, whereas the administrations of the Empire were less disposed to allow the Tunisians to benefit from particular treaty and customary rules.[61] One was not able, according to the consul, to make the Bey apply the treaties of 1742 and 1802 literally, if one did not promise him 'as reciprocity' ('à titre de réciprocité') the suppression in France of customs duties that contravened the treaties.[62]

---

[57] Précis des instructions remises au capitaine Montfort (copy adjoined to the letter from Faurrat to Devoize, Marseille, 25 Jun 1808), AN, 327 AP 17.

[58] Devoize to Deforgues, Tunis, 2 pluviôse an II [21 Jan 1794], MAE, CCC. Tunis, vol 32, fos. 72r–73r.

[59] Extraits des articles du traité conclu en 1742 entre la France et Tunis concernant les droits de douane et de tonnage, Paris, 1 Jun 1811, AN, 327 AP 1; Billon to Devoize, Tunis, 19 May and 29 June 1811, AN, 327 AP 15.

[60] Devoize to Talleyrand, Paris, 30 May 1814; Extraits des articles du traité conclu en 1742 entre la France et Tunis concernant les droits de douane et de tonnage, Paris, 30 May 1814, signed: Devoize, MAE, CCC. Tunis, vol 41, fos 297v–298r, 301r–302r.

[61] Extraits des articles du traité conclu en 1742 entre la France et Tunis concernant les droits de douane et de tonnage, Paris, 1 June 1811, AN, 327 AP 1; Extraits des articles du traité conclu en 1742 entre la France et Tunis concernant les droits de douane et de tonnage, Paris, 30 May 1814, signed: Devoize, MAE, CCC, Tunis, vol 41, fos. 301r–302r.

[62] Devoize to Talleyrand, Paris, 30 May 1814, MAE, CCC, Tunis, vol 41, fos 297v–298r.

The negotiation of reciprocal grievances did not take place in 1814–15. Only the most excessive abuses were suppressed, without considering a global solution that would have re-established the treaties and customs. After his retirement, Devoize deplored the consequences of this situation. The relative decline of French trade with Tunis came, according to him, from the dissolution of its former normative setting; the result on the one hand of abuses by the French administration that had entailed reprisals on the part of the Bey—in particular the establishment of a bey-lical monopoly on sales of agricultural products destined for export—and on the other hand of the treaties negotiated by Lord Exmouth that protected the shipping of the Italian powers, who were until then at war with the regencies.[63]

The political circumstances of the Restoration (the decision to oblige, by naval expeditions, the regencies to give up 'piracy' and the enslavement of Christian captives) prevented French diplomacy from looking for a solution to the reciprocal grievances on the basis of the consul's comparative overview, which asked for the respect of treaty and customary law. Malivoire, vice-consul to Tunis, who followed in 1819 as replacement for Devoize as Consul-General, reversed the chronology of abuses and assigned the responsibility for them to the Bey. When in 1821, Ḥasūna al-Mūrālī, interpreter of the regency, asked for the reduction of French customs duties to 3 per cent on several cargoes of oil and wool sent on account of the Bey, Malivoire suggested that the Tunisians' abuses deprived them of the right to ask for the reciprocity granted by Franco-Tunisian treaties: 'If they ask for the rigorous execution of the treaties, it is wholly just that they should begin in setting an example in their strict observation, by agreeing to the suppression of a mass of abuses that have taken place here.'[64] The foreign minister took up this line of argument and pushed for the application of French laws instead of the treaties and rejected reciprocity which was authorized, as was well known, by the letter of the treaties in force.[65] The question of customs duties was resolved by the new treaty of 1824: French consignments of goods would in future pay only 3 per cent. The Consul-General, Guys, refused the demand for an equivalent reduction for Tunisians in France. According to him, reciprocity consisted of granting each the status of most favoured nation. However, this was already the case for Tunisians in France, since they paid the same customs duties as the French.[66]

The efforts of Devoize, which resulted from the multiplicity of social roles stemming from integration in the local social context, defined a culture of mediation that the consul asserted, on occasion, against his own government. Forced to

[63] Devoize to Laurent Gay, Voiron, Dec 1822, AN, 327 AP 13.

[64] Malivoire to Rayneval, Tunis, 14 Mar 1821, MAE, CCC, Tunis, vol 44, fos 22v–23r: 'S'ils réclament l'exécution rigoureuse des traités, il est de toute justice qu'ils commencent par donner l'exemple de leur stricte observation, en consentant à la suppression d'une foule d'abus qui se sont introduits ici.'

[65] Pasquier to Malivoire, Paris, 14 May and 17 July 1821, MAE, CCC, Tunis, vol 44, fos 30v, 43r–44r. See also Malivoire to Pasquier, Tunis, 20 Sep 1821, MAE, CCC, Tunis, vol 44, fos 54r–55r. Instructions particulières pour M Guys, consul général chargé d'affaires à Tunis, Paris, 27 Nov 1823, MAE, CCC, Tunis, vol 44, fo 312r.

[66] Guys to Chateaubriand, Tunis, 31 Jan 1824, MAE, CCC, Tunis, vol 44, fos 354r–355v; Treaty of 15 Nov 1824, French version in Plantet (ed), *Correspondance des beys de Tunis* (n 53).

represent, as Consul-General, policies that denied all legitimacy to the specific local norms, Devoize in other occasions defended Franco-Tunisian treaty and customary law against interference from revolutionary and imperial legislation.

Devoize's attitudes of respect reveal that once pacific relations were established—by necessity (to protect shipping), or by interest (above all commercial)—a space of inter-comprehension developed thanks to the prolonged practice of common norms. The position taken by the consul undermines the received idea of relations determined only by the balance of military force that underlay the imagery of 'Barbary'. Limited and constantly threatened by aggressive attempts at domination, a certain degree of legal security, based on treaties and custom, made possible the permanent stay of Christian bodies of traders (*nations*) in fairly favourable conditions. It also allowed a life that was not deprived of amenities, as Devoize's personal correspondence illustrates. Incoherence between the discourse and the practices of the consuls may be explained by this integration in a 'plurality of worlds of action', which required varied competencies and presented different normative requirements.[67]

Judgements on this diversity were upset by the rise of political cultures that transposed the universalistic rationalism inherited from the Enlightenment into the domain of international relations and the life of Europeans in the Muslim ports. Under the Old Regime, the heterogeneity of the European and Maghrebi laws that interacted in Tunis recalled the plurality of statuses and jurisdictions within European societies. After the Revolution, legal pluralism opposed the society of Tunis—the beylical court, but also French consuls like Devoize—to those who, in Paris, weighed on decisions taken about relations with the Maghreb. At the same time, the bonds that existed between the rulers in the Maghreb and the Ottoman sultan, considered as a limitation of sovereignty, were to become a strong argument against any relation based on reciprocity.[68]

In their relations with European states, the regencies were asked to behave 'like civilized nations'. However, their submission to the norms of the 'civilized' did not turn them into full-fledged subjects of the community of the law of nations as it was defined by Western states. The unilateral redefinition of the normative basis, which, from a Western perspective, was perceived as 'civilization', did not mean the inclusion of the Other. Rather, in the nineteenth century, the unequal treaty became a symbol of the relations with non-Western powers. The European powers' campaign against 'piracy' had created the legal framework for the future colonization of the Maghreb; those who, in the eighteenth century, had been legitimate enemies, following the rules of the law of war, were now deprived of their former sovereign legal status which had gained growing recognition during the eighteenth century.[69]

---

[67] Nicolas Dodier, 'Agir dans plusieurs mondes' (1991) 47 Critique 427, 433 on the approach by Luc Boltanski and Laurent Thévenot, *De la justification. Les économies de la grandeur* (Gallimard 1991).

[68] See Windler, *La diplomatie* (n 1) 307–14 on the French refusal to allow the establishment of Tunisian agents or consuls.

[69] Cf Kempe, *Fluch der Weltmeere* (n 7) 284–86.

Bibliography

'Barthélémy de Saizieu, consul, to Bourgeois de Boynes, secrétaire d'État de la Marine, Tunis, 15 Jan 1773' Archives Nationales AE BI 1145, fo 15v

'Billon to Devoize, Tunis, 19 May and 29 June 1811' Archives Nationales, 327 AP 15

'Devoize, consul general in Tunis, to Monge, ministre de la Marine, Tunis, 8 Dec 1792' Archives Nationales, AE BI 1154, fo 168r/v

'Devoize to Deforgues, Tunis, 2 pluviôse an II [21 Jan 1794]' Archives du Ministère des Affaires étrangères, Correspondance consulaire et commerciales. Tunis, vol 32, fos. 72r–73r

'Devoize to the Comité de Salut Public, Tunis, 30 nivôse an III [19 Jan 1795]' Archives du Ministère des Affaires étrangères, Correspondance consulaire et commerciales, Tunis, vol 33, fo 76r/v

'Devoize to Delacroix, ministre des Relations extérieures, Tunis, 24 ventôse an IV, [14 Mar 1796]' Archives du Ministère des Affaires étrangères, Correspondance consulaire et commerciales. Tunis, vol 34, fos 74v–75v, 75v

'Devoize to La Combe Saint-Michel, Tunis, 3 frimaire an VII [23 Nov 1798]' Archives Nationales, 327 AP 4

'Devoize to Talleyrand, ministre des Relations extérieures, Tunis, 28 Oct 1806' Archives du Ministère des Affaires étrangères, Correspondance consulaire et commerciales, Tunis, vol 38, fo 196r

'Devoize to Talleyrand, Paris, 30 May 1814' Archives du Ministère des Affaires étrangères, Correspondance consulaire et commerciales, Tunis, vol 41, fos 297v–298r

'Devoize to [Laurent Gay, 1er médecin du bey], no place [Tunis], no date [Sep 1819]' Archives Nationales, 327 AP 14

'Devoize to Ruffin, Lazareth de Toulon, 30 Nov 1819' Archives Nationales, 327 AP 13

'Devoize to Laurent Gay, Voiron, Dec 1822' Archives Nationales, 327 AP 13

'Devoize to Pierre Gay, Voiron, 22 Jan 1825' Archives Nationales, 327 AP 30

'Exmouth to Croker, Admiralty, Bay of Algiers, 28 Aug 1816' National Archives, Kew, ADM 1/432

'Extraits des articles du traité conclu en 1742 entre la France et Tunis concernant les droits de douane et de tonnage, Paris, 1 June 1811' Archives Nationales, 327 AP 1

'Extraits des articles du traité conclu en 1742 entre la France et Tunis concernant les droits de douane et de tonnage, Paris, 30 May 1814, signed: Devoize' Archives du Ministère des Affaires étrangères, Correspondance consulaire et commerciales, Tunis, vol 41, fos. 301r–302r

'Guys to Chateaubriand, Tunis, 31 Jan 1824' Archives du Ministère des Affaires étrangères, Correspondance consulaire et commerciales, Tunis, vol 44, fos 354r–355v

'Instructions particulières pour M Guys, consul général chargé d'affaires à Tunis, Paris, 27 Nov 1823' Archives du Ministère des Affaires étrangères, Correspondance consulaire et commerciales, Tunis, vol 44, fo 312r

'Lebrun, ministre des Relations extérieures, to Delacroix, vice-président du Comité d'Aliénation of the National Convention, 28 May 1793' Archives Nationales, AE BI 38, fo 170r/v

'Malivoire to Pasquier, Tunis, 20 Sep 1821' Archives du Ministère des Affaires étrangères, Correspondance consulaire et commerciales, Tunis, vol 44, 54r–55r

'Malivoire to Rayneval, Tunis, 14 Mar 1821' Archives du Ministère des Affaires étrangères, Correspondance consulaire et commerciales, Tunis, vol 44, fos 22v–23r

'Mémoire pour servir d'instructions aux citoyens Ducher et Lallement, agents extraordinaires allant à Alger et à Tunis, Paris, 4 ventôse an II [22 Feb 1794]' Archives du

Ministère des Affaires étrangères, Correspondance consulaire et commerciales, Tunis, vol 32, fo 115r

'Mémoire sur un projet d'expédition contre Tunis, Paris, 6 prairial an IX [26 May 1801]' Archives Nationales, 327 AP 1

'Memorandum on the Compagnie d'Afrique, 1791' Archives Nationales, AE BIII 322

'Pasquier to Malivoire, Paris, 14 May and 17 July 1821' Archives du Ministère des Affaires étrangères, Correspondance consulaire etcommerciales, Tunis, vol 44, fos 30v, 43r–44r.

'Précis des instructions remises au capitaine Montfort (copy adjoined to the letter from Faurrat to Devoize, Marseille, 25 Jun 1808)' Archives Nationales, 327 AP 17

'Rapport sur Tunis, Feb 1793' Archives Nationales, AE BI 38, fo 38v

'Sartine, secrétaire d'Etat de la Marine, to Vergennes, secrétaire d'Etat des affaires étrangères, Versailles, 28 Nov 1774' Archives Nationales, AE, BI 1145, fos 311r–312r

'Talleyrand, ministre des Relations extérieures, to Devoize, Paris, 18 Mar 1806' Archives du Ministère des Affaires étrangères, Correspondance consulaire et commercials, Tunis, vol 38, fos 161r–161bis v

'Traduction de la lettre écrite [par Maḥmūd Bey] en idiome arabe au contre-amiral Jurien, commandant français, palais du Barde de Tunis, 9 dhū al-ḥidjdja H. 1234 [29 Sep 1819]' Archives du Ministère des Affaires étrangères, Correspondance consulaire et commerciales Tunis, vol 43, fos 203r–204r

'Vallière, consul general in Algiers, to the Comité de Salut Public, Algiers, 14 pluviôse an III [2 Feb. 1795]' Archives du Ministère des Affaires étrangères, Correspondance consulaire et commerciales, Alger, vol 32, fo 173r

Allison, Robert J, *The Crescent Obscured: The United States and the Muslim World, 1776–1815* (University of Chicago Press 1995)

Barth, Boris and Osterhammel, Jürgen (eds), *Zivilisierungsmissionen: Imperiale Weltverbesserung seit dem 18. Jahrhundert* (UVK 2005)

Belin, Jean, *La logique d'une idée-force: L'idée d'utilité sociale et la Révolution française (1789–1792)* (Hermann 1939)

Belissa, Marc, *Fraternité universelle et intérêt national (1713–1795): Les cosmopolites du droit des gens* (Kimé 1998)

Belissa, Marc, *Repenser l'ordre européen (1795–1802): De la société des rois aux droits des Nations* (Kimé 2006)

Bilici, Faruk, 'La Révolution française dans l'historiographie turque 1789–1927' in Hédia Khadhar (ed), *La Révolution française et le monde arabo-musulman: Colloque international, Tunis 9–11 novembre 1989* (Tunis 1991)

Boltanski, Luc and Thévenot, Laurent *De la justification: Les économies de la grandeur* (Gallimard 1991)

Bono, Salvatore, *Corsari nel Mediterraneo: Cristiani e musulmani fra guerra, schiavitù e commercio* (A Mondadori 1993)

Brogini, Anne, *Malte, frontière de Chrétienté (1530–1670)* (École française de Rome 2006)

Bukovansky, Mlada, *Legitimacy and Power Politics: The American and French Revolutions in International Political Culture* (Princeton University Press 2002)

Charles-Roux, François, *France et Afrique du Nord avant 1830: Les précurseurs de la conquête* (Félix Alcan 1932)

Dakhlia, Jocelyne, *Le divan des rois: Le politique et le religieux dans l'Islam* (Aubier 1998)

Davis, Robert C, *Christian Slaves, Muslim Masters: White Slavery in the Mediterranean, the Barbary Coast, and Italy, 1500–1800* (Palgrave Macmillan 2003)

Dodier, Nicolas, 'Agir dans plusieurs mondes' (1991) 47 Critique 427

Dull, Jonathan R, *A Diplomatic History of the American Revolution* (Yale University Press 1985)

Field, James A, *America and the Mediterranean World, 1776–1882* (Princeton University Press 1969)

Fisher, Godfrey, *Barbary Legend: War, Trade and Piracy in North Africa 1415–1830* (Clarendon Press 1957)

Fontenay, Michel, 'Le Maghreb barbaresque et l'esclavage méditerranéen aux XVIe–XVIIe siècles' (1991) 44 Les Cahiers de Tunisie 7

Frank, Louis, 'Tunis, description de cette Régence [1816], par le Dr -, ancien médecin du Bey de Tunis, du Pâcha de Jannina, et de l'armée d'Egypte, revue et accompagnée d'un précis historique et d'éclaircissements tirés des écrivains orientaux, par J[ean] J[oseph] Marcel' in *L'Univers pittoresque: Histoire et description de tous les peuples, de leurs religions, moeurs, coutumes, industries, etc. Afrique,* vol 7 (Paris 1862)

Frey, Linda and Frey, Marsha, ' "The Reign of the Charlatans Is Over": The French Revolutionary Attack on Diplomatic Practice' (1993) 65 Journal of Modern History 706

Grewe, Wilhelm G, 'Vom europäischen zum universellen Völkerrecht: Zur Frage der Revision des "europazentrischen" Bildes der Völkerrechtsgeschichte' (1982) 42 Zeitschrift für ausländisches öffentliches Recht und Völkerrecht 449

Hevia, James, *Cherishing Men from Afar: Qing Guest Ritual and the Macartney Embassy of 1793* (Duke University Press 1995)

Horsman, Reginald, *The Diplomacy of the New Republic, 1776–1815* (Harlan Davidson 1985)

Irwin, Ray, *The Diplomatic Relations of the United States with the Barbary Powers, 1776–1816* (University of North Carolina Press 1931)

İnalcık, Halil, 'imtiyāzāt' in B Lewis, VL Ménage, Ch Pellat, and J Schacht (eds), *Encyclopédie de l'Islam,* vol 3 (Nouvelle édition, Brill 1971)

Kaiser, Wolfgang (ed), *Le commerce des captifs: Les intermédiaires dans l'échange et le rachat des prisonniers en Méditerranée, xvᵉ–xviiᵉ siècles* (École française de Rome 2008)

Kaplan, Lawrence S, *Colonies into Nation: American Diplomacy, 1763–1801* (MacMillan Publishing Company 1972)

Kaplan, Lawrence S, *Entangling Alliance with None: American Foreign Policy in the Age of Jefferson* (Kent State University Press 1987)

Kempe, Michael, *Fluch der Weltmeere: Piraterie, Völkerrecht und internationale Beziehungen, 1500–1900* (Campus Verlag 2010)

Köhler, Matthias, 'No Punctilios of Ceremony? Völkerrechtliche Anerkennung, diplomatisches Zeremoniell und symbolische Kommunikation im Amerikanischen Unabhängigkeitskonflikt' in Hillard von Thiessen and Christian Windler (eds), *Akteure der Außenbeziehungen: Netzwerke und Interkulturalität im historischen Wandel* (Böhlau Verlag 2010)

Laurens, Henry, (with contributions by Charles C Gillispie, Jean-Claude Golvin, and Claude Traunecker), *L'expédition d'Égypte, 1798–1801* (Éditions Armand Colin 1989).

McHugh, PG, 'A Comporting Sovereign, Tribes and the Ordering of Imperial Authority in Colonial Upper Canada of the 1830s' Chapter 10 in this volume

Nuzzo, Luigi, *Origini di una scienza: Diritto internazionale e colonialismo nel XIX secolo* (Vittorio Klostermann 2012)

Osterhammel, Jürgen, *Die Entzauberung Asiens: Europa und die asiatischen Reiche im 18. Jahrhundert* (CH Beck 1998)

Panzac, Daniel, *Les corsaires barbaresques: La fin d'une épopée, 1800–1820* (Centre national de la recherche scientifique 1999)

Paradis, Jean Michel Venture de, 'Observations sur le gouvernement de Tunis, 1788' in Jean Michel Venture de Paradis, *Tunis et Alger au XVIIIe siècle, mémoires et observations rassemblés et présentés par Joseph Cuoq* (Sindbad 1983)

Pitts, Jennifer, *A Turn to Empire: The Rise of Imperial Liberalism in Britain and France* (Princeton University Press 2005)

Pomeranz, Kenneth, *The Great Divergence: China, Europe, and the Making of the Modern World Economy* (Princeton University Press 2000)

Staunton, George, *An Authentic Account of an Embassy from the King of Great Britain to the Emperor of China*, vol 2 (London 1797)

Thomson, Ann, *Barbary and Enlightenment: European Attitudes towards the Maghreb in the 18th Century* (Brill Academic Publishers 1987)

Touati, Houari, *Entre Dieu et les hommes: Lettrés, saints et sorciers au Maghreb (XVIIᵉ siècle)* (Éditions de l'École des Hautes Études en Sciences Sociales 1994)

'Treaty of 15 Nov 1824' in Eugène Plantet (ed), *Correspondance des beys de Tunis et des consuls de France avec la Cour, 1577–1830*, vol 3 (Felix Alcan 1899)

'Treaty between France and Tunis, signed 8 August 1830' in Eugène Plantet (ed), *Correspondance des beys de Tunis et des consuls de France avec la Cour, 1577–1830*, vol 3 (Felix Alcan 1899)

'Treaty between France and Tripolis, signed 11 August 1830' in Edgard Rouard de Card (ed), *Traités de la France avec les pays de l'Afrique du Nord: Algérie, Tunisie, Tripolitaine, Maroc* (A Pedone 1906)

Vattel, Émer de, *Le droit des gens, ou principes de la loi naturelle appliqués à la conduite et aux affaires des nations et des souverains* (Albert de Lapradelle ed, Carnegie Institution of Washington 1916)

Vec, Miloš, 'Universalization, Particularization and Discrimination: European Perspectives on a Cultural History of 19th century International Law' (2012) 3(2) InterDisciplines: Journal of History and Sociology 79 <http://www.inter-disciplines.org/index.php/indi/article/viewFile/66/54> accessed 15 April 2016

Wettinger, Godfrey, *Slavery in the Islands of Malta and Gozo, ca. 1000–1812* (Publishers Enterprises Group 2002)

Windler, Christian, *La diplomatie comme expérience de l'Autre: Consuls français au Maghreb (1700–1840)* (Librairie Droz 2002)

10

A Comporting Sovereign, Tribes, and the Ordering of Imperial Authority in Colonial Upper Canada of the 1830s

PG McHugh

Early Winter 1837 on the Canadian Bank of the Niagara River

In the autumn of 1837, rebellion rocked the British provinces of Upper and Lower Canada. In Upper Canada, William Lyon MacKenzie and some 200 of his support-ers had retreated to Navy Island on the Niagara River, a small upstream island on the Canadian side inhabited by a woman and her son. MacKenzie had recently lost an election in which the Lieutenant Governor Sir Francis Bond Head had actively (and, some believed, improperly) campaigned against 'responsible government' (the principle that the Crown's Ministers—the executive—should be members of and responsible to the legislature). Bond Head's intervention in the election endeared him to the conservative element of the province but it was a dangerous and unau-thorized politicization of his office. Governors were meant to be above sectional and populist politics. Bond Head equated responsible government with American republicanism and *demos* unchecked, tapping into loyalist Upper Canadians' anxi-ety about American designs on their territory unfaded from the battling of 1812 and 1815. Historians have pondered over the ideological foundation (if any) of MacKenzie's beliefs,[1] but it is clear he had been drawn into insurrection by events in Lower Canada. After some clashes, including one at Montgomery's Tavern in York (today upper Yonge Street in Toronto), he and his supporters regrouped on Navy Island where American sympathizers supplied them with money, provisions, and arms brought by the steamboat SS *Caroline*. There, MacKenzie, supported by his American 'General' Rensselaer Van Rensselaer,[2] a West Point graduate who had

---

[1] RA MacKay, 'The political ideas of William Lyon MacKenzie' (1937) 3 Canadian Journal of Economics and Political Science 1. Frederick H Armstrong and Ronald J Stagg characterize him as a born contrarian: 'MacKenzie, William Lyon' in *Dictionary of Canadian Biography*, vol 9 (University of Toronto/Université Laval, 2003–) <http://www.biographi.ca/en/bio/mackenzie_william_lyon_9E.html> accessed 16 December 2014.

[2] A nephew of General Stephen Van Rensselaer who had been badly defeated by the British in the Battle of Queenston Heights (1812).

International Law and Empire: Historical Explorations. First Edition. Martti Koskenniemi, Walter Rech, and Manuel Jiménez Fonseca. © Martti Koskenniemi, Walter Rech, and Manuel Jiménez Fonseca 2016. Published 2016 by Oxford University Press.

fought with Bolivar in South America, declared the 'republic of Canada'. As the imperial Army troops had been mostly deployed already in Lower Canada, Head's loyalist ragtag militia gave chase, reaching the Niagara riverbank overlooking Navy Island where it pitched camp. On 29 December Colonel Sir Allan MacNab and Captain Andrew Drew of the Royal Navy crossed the international boundary to destroy the *Caroline*, chasing off the crew, and casting the burning American boat over the Falls. This incursion of British forces in American territory, the destruction of the boat and loss of two American lives sparked one of those international skirmishes that periodically vexed Anglo-American relations and diplomacy during the nineteenth century.

The retreat of MacKenzie's forces to Navy Island also produced a response from the First Nations of Upper Canada whose military support had been an essential and running part of Britain's continental strategizing since the mid-eighteenth century. By the mid-1830s the First Nations of Upper Canada were fragments of their former military might, the Six Nations most especially riven with factionalism, and those that had supported the British against the revolutionary Americans reduced to occupation of the Grand River reserve purchased by the Crown from the Mississaugas in 1784. In the long run, this support of the British had been ruinous for the tribes, its depleting aftermath contributing immensely to the shattering of their power in the region. Still, in 1837 the First Nations of the Great Lakes were proudly committed to their historical alliance with the British Crown.

As Head's militia stood at the edge of the Niagara River a remarkable event occurred. From 'the interior recesses of the Province' a large body of Indians appeared 'painted for war'. After the customary salutations there occurred an exchange between the chiefs and Lieutenant Governor Bond Head which he recounted a few years later:

> ... [T]he senior chief, with that astonishing stillness of manner and native dignity which characterize all Indian orators, briefly told me that he and his brother chiefs had heard that the big knives (the Americans) had invaded the land of their great mother; that, for reasons which they very clearly explained, they did not like the big knives; that they did not desire to leave their great mother, and that they had therefore come to fight the big knives.[3]

Bond Head's account of this episode (as indeed his whole version of the Rebellion) was above all that of a highly disgruntled nature, nursing deep-seated grievance, like that of his fellow 'Patriots', at the imperial government's abandonment of their cause to what they saw as American adventurism and Durham's opportunism.[4] Yet

---

[3] *The Emigrant* (John Murray 1846) a book he published a few years afterwards still fuming at the British Government's pandering to MacKenzie and his ilk. Bond Head took particular exception to the Peel Ministry's placation of the rebels, seeing this as wanton betrayal of loyalist Toryism.

[4] Notably *Report of the Select Committee (Upper Canada) on the State of the Province*, 30 April 1839, Great British Parliamentary Papers (hereafter GBPP) 1839 (289) 8–31, attacking American expansionism and the Durham sideshow. Lord Durham was commissioned from Britain to lead an inquiry into the disturbances. His hastily prepared but bulky Report (1839) was seen as too conciliatory to the 'reformists'. The years that followed the rushed nature of Durham's fact-finding mission, its factual inaccuracies, and author's egotism were being overlooked, as the text was lionized as the iconic statement of settler self-government.

his description of the offer of Indian assistance captured the ambivalence that by then was surrounding official perception of First Nations' status in Upper Canada. On the one hand, the British and their imperial officials were keenly aware of the debt they owed the First Nations who had supported them as allies against the French and Americans. By the late 1820s, however, imperial policy was turning away from militaristic association with the tribes towards a more conscious effort to protect and civilize them. This turn remained very much at an initial and exploratory stage in the 1830s as imperial officialdom spoke less of First Nations as allies (except in the past tense) and more of them as British subjects (the present).

The Lieutenant Governor thought it obvious that Indian help should be used but was aware of 'an unwholesome opinion' held 'in a certain tenement in Downing-street' that it would be 'barbarous' to allow the Indians to assist in repelling an American invasion of Upper Canada.[5] Bond Head was referring to the Colonial Office (then quartered at 14 Downing Street) where Lord Glenelg was the Secretary of State and a prominent evangelical Anglican (as a committee member of the Church Missionary Society). Bond Head accepted that 'philanthropic objections might be raised' to Indians being used to invade the United States but 'nothing would be more just than to allow them, in defending their own territory, to assist in repelling invasion'. In offering military help, the chiefs were evidently unaware of the Lieutenant Governor's uneasiness but sharply aware of why they were offering it (dislike of the 'big knives') and the basis upon which it would be supplied. Before 'they raised the hatchet of war' the chiefs wanted reassurance that 'the wives of their chiefs and young men who should fall would receive the same consideration that in the late war had been granted to the widows of their white brethren'.[6]

The chiefs' anxieties about invasion by the 'big knives' showed awareness of the treatment that their kindred were receiving across the border from the Jackson administration (1829–37).[7] At this time the Canadian-American border was very porous. American Indians crossed freely without regard to boundaries or imperial territoriality to join their Canadian kin and to renew their alliance with the British Crown at annual present-giving ceremonies (which from 1836 had been held for the 'visiting Indians' at Great Manitoulin Island on Lake Huron[8]). They

---

[5] Bond Head, *The Emigrant* (n 3) 168.

[6] The chiefs had plainly absorbed also a long-running issue in the Canadas about discriminatory British practices in the pension and remuneration of those serving the Crown outside of the regular army. This shows the strength of information networks within First Nations and the degree of their political savvy.

[7] R Alder to Glenelg, 14 December 1837, in GBPP 1839 (323) 90–98, at 94; Peter Jones to Glenelg, 6 March 1838: ibid, at 83. Alder was Secretary to the Wesleyan Missionary Society in London: GS French, 'Alder, Robert' in *Dictionary of Canadian Biography*, vol 10 (University of Toronto 2003–) <http://www.biographi.ca/en/bio/alder_robert_10E.html> accessed 8 April 2014. Alder, with his innate conservatism and deference to the Anglican tradition, was to take the English Methodists into schism with the Ryerson (brothers') brand in Upper Canada. English philanthropists like Hodgkin, Bannister, and Buxton referred to the 'fatal difficulties' of American Removal policy. For example, Hodgkin to Ryerson, 27 April 1838, reprinted in *The Christian Guardian* (Toronto, 9 May 1838) (a Methodist newspaper, then being published weekly from Toronto).

[8] Head to Glenelg, 20 August 1836, in GBPP 1839 (323) at 122.

carried with them information about the Indian Wars and Removal policies in the United States. President Andrew Jackson (or 'Old Hickory' as he was popularly known) had been imprisoned (and literally scarred) by the British during the Revolutionary war and had fought them at the Battle of New Orleans (1812). Jackson was also a legendary Indian fighter known and feared for his mercilessness and exacting terms in victory. Given the bellicosity of the early republic (and Old Hickory especially) both Bond Head and the Upper Canadian First Nations had mutual if different reason to worry.[9] Although in this instance the threat was being vastly overblown, American expansionism still worried its northward neighbour.

The chiefs' exchange with Bond Head also showed how they viewed themselves in the scheme of Empire. Plainly they accepted loyalty to the young and freshly enthroned Queen Victoria ('great mother'). They felt themselves able to organize and govern themselves as distinct nations under her, whilst doing so on the basis of equality with her other subjects in the matter of common service. To put their self-depiction another way, they saw themselves both as tribal nations able to negotiate the supply of military service and as subjects entitled to equal treatment in the Crown's recognition of this support. This was perfectly consistent with their history of relations with the British and the customary durability of undertakings signified by the wampum belt, yearly reaffirmed at a present-giving ceremony. It did not strike them as the contradiction in terms that imperial officials were by then seeing it as and which rings through the Bond Head account.

Bond Head's equivocal reply, respectful but ultimately (and paternalistically) firm in its dismissiveness, showed his awareness of this disjuncture. He was indulgent to and respectful of tribal authority. Through praise of the chiefly class, he incorporated First Nations into a classical tradition of pagan virtue and physical prowess but also a modern and romanticizing one where the attributes of the noble savage could no longer suffice.[10] This classical and romantic positioning left the tribes with static impotence. As virtuous pagans they should be left to the exciting but empty meaninglessness of their Godless pursuit of glory for its own sake, and

---

[9] This seems to have been a particular fear of the Christianized Indians, anxiety already being fostered by their missionaries: Chief Joshua Wawanosh, 'Address to the Chippeway Indians' *The Christian Guardian* (Toronto, 5 July 1836).

[10] Theodore Binnema and Kevin Hutchings, 'The Emigrant and the Noble Savage: Sir Francis Bond Head's Romantic Approach to Aboriginal Policy in Upper Canada, 1836–1838' (2005) 39 Journal of Canadian Studies 115. I am grateful to Benjamin Straumann for bringing the theme of pagan virtue to my attention, albeit one that is not pursued here. The noble savage was an established literary figure, of course, most famously in Alexander Pope's 'Essay on Man' (1734):

> Lo, the poor Indian! whose untutor'd mind
> Sees God in clouds, or hears him in the wind …
> To be, contents his natural desire,
> He asks no angel's wing, no seraph's fire:
> But thinks, admitted to that equal sky,
> His faithful dog shall bear him company.

It was typical of Bond Head's rather pompous hortatory literary style (even by early Victorian standards) that he would invoke this classical and hackneyed portrayal of the pagan Amerindian. See also Ter Ellingson, *The Myth of the Noble Savage* (University of California Press 2001).

the eventual, inevitable extinction that will ensue. Bond Head was known for putting Crown paternalism into metaphor-ridden language that resonated masterfully with First Nations sense of their relationship with their great mother.[11] Despite his insistence that he carefully did not mislead the First Nations, there is no indication that they registered his equivocation.[12] This view of Amerindian incorrigibility was one that many of the settlers and backwoodsmen shared though their view was usually expressed in the more cynical, hardened, and negative terms of indolence and social nuisance.

There was also a broader aim in the Bond Head narrative. Soon after his description of the Indians' announcement of availability for military action against the rebels and would-be American invaders, he described the 'sudden arrival' of a small convoy of escaped slaves:

> ... [I]t was evident from the expression of their yellow eyes, red gums, and of many of their clenched ivory white teeth that all they wanted was permission to avenge themselves on the invaders of British soil, where many of them, scarred and mutilated, had sought refuge from the slave States of 'the land of liberty' on the opposite shore.[13]

Here on either side of the Niagara River, Bond Head widened his cast to put tribes and former slaves into a narrative of contrasting constitutional identity. His prose became almost cringingly purple. Across the water lay the acquisitive and lawless American, the emblem of constitutional disorder and rampant opportunism: 'Why, on the one side the citizens of the republic, destitute of respect either for their own laws or for the laws of nations, had invaded and were preparing to massacre and plunder a neighbouring people with whom they were at peace, and who had offered not the slightest cause for offence.' And on the British riverbank there was the law-abiding order of pluralistic British subjecthood under a young Queen and God:

> ... on the other side of the river were to be seen assembled men of various races and colours, Scotch, Irish, English, native Canadians, the red children of the forest, and lastly, the black population of the province ... [Y]et, instead of hailing their 'liberators', they had attacked them, had defeated them, and had driven them from the face of the land they wished to liberate; and now ... they had rushed to the frontier of their country to repel foreigners, whose avowed object was to force them, against their wills, to become republicans.[14]

Though the loyalist gathering, spontaneously assembled, had the power to overwhelm the Island (or so the author claimed), they nonetheless exercised restraint

---

[11] This observation comes from the diary of James Evans, a Methodist missionary who witnessed the Treaties of 9 August 1836 as printed in *The Christian Guardian*, 28 September 1836, 2 November 1836, and 2 January 1837, reprinted Frank A Myers (ed), *1836 Mission Tour of Lake Huron* (Manitoulin Historical Society 1955). Also extracts which circulated amongst London evangelical bodies, enclosure in Memorial to the Colonial Office (not dated, received 10 April 1837) in GBPP 1839 (323) 99–100.
[12] Nor, it seems, that he detected their doubts in the light of Bond Head's forceful extraction of land cessions the year before (in August and September 1836): Aborigines Protection Society, *Report on the Indians of Upper Canada by a Sub-committee of the Aborigines Protection Society* (W Ball, Arnold 1839) 21, indicating that this show of support was not without qualms on the First Nations' part.
[13] Bond Head, *The Emigrant* (n 3) 170.   [14] Ibid, 172.

at his command 'in calm obedience to their laws, and to the administration of their Government'. They did so not because of some 'gaudy transatlantic European theory' about the rights of man but because Crown sovereignty 'was a practical substantial blessing' that 'formed the title-deeds of their lands, the guardian of their liberty, the protector if their lives'. It 'implanted, fostered and encouraged ... gratitude and submission to the Great Author', to civil and religious authority, 'to laws human and divine'.[15] There is here a Tory rhapsodizing of submission, station, and obedience, coupled with a railing against the 'gaudy' Lockean language of rights found in the French Revolution and American Constitution. Bond Head situated this alongside an imperialist celebration of the providential transplantation of British institutions of constitutional stability and loyalism: 'This pervaded the whole province; it was indigenous to British soil.'[16]

Transitional Tribalism and British Subjecthood in the 1830s

The importance and justice of unremitted solicitude[17] for the Indian tribes is deeply felt by His Majesty's Government and warmly avowed by Lord Glenelg [Secretary of State for the Colonies] through whom his late Majesty commended them in the strongest possible terms to the continued care of Your Excellency's predecessor, and signified his express injunction that no measure should be unattempted which might afford a reasonable prospect of reserving the remnant of the aboriginal race from the calamitous fate which had so befallen uncivilized man when brought into immediate contact with the natives of Europe or their descendants.[18]

By the late 1830s the formal allowance of tribal identity (tribal nationhood) and tribe members' status as a full British subject were seen as mutually exclusive categories. Imperial law and practice had reached a stage where Crown sovereignty could not allow both to co-exist. To the extent tribes had any juridical stature as such and in the shaping of British relations with them it occurred in a pre-sovereignty world of *jus gentium* (the law of nature and of nations). In the late 1830s the Maori of New Zealand and frontier Xhosa tribes of the Cape Colony were in that zone in their dealings with Britain but the First Nations of Canada were not. During the years of war with France and America, when First Nations were regarded as separate nations and allies to be cultivated, they might have also been inside a zone where

---

[15] Ibid, 173–74.   [16] Ibid, 173.
[17] This term is taken from Thomas Babington, *A Practical View of Christian Education in its Early Stages: To Which is Added, a Letter to a Son Soon after the Close of His Education, on the Subject of not Conforming to the World* (John Hatchard & Son 1826) 5: 'During education, is the progress of the boy in religion watched with unremitting solicitude, and promoted by all those means that solicitude suggests?' Babington's text was regarded as the classic text on evangelical childrearing: Susan Pedersen, 'Hannah More meets Simple Simon: Tracts, Chapbooks, and Popular Culture in Late Eighteenth-century England' (1986) 25 Journal of British Studies 84. On the heavily religious dimension of sovereign comportment, see text in this article accompanying notes 64–70.
[18] From JB Macaulay, 'Report on Indian Affairs', 1 April 1839, National Archives Canada (hereafter NAC) RG 10, Vol 117, Reel C-11478, 168711–168868, 128–29 (hereafter 'the Macaulay Report').

the *jus gentium* informed Crown dealings. By the 1820s, however, British imperial practice was forming an absolute and more territorialized notion of sovereignty.[19] This meant that the *jus gentium* took a much less prominent role in shaping Crown comportment within its own territories. Indeed, in such settings, the *jus gentium* was consciously discarded as a source bearing upon Crown conduct by some commentators. Settlers, with their acquisitive impatience with the Crown's continuance of wartime ceremonialism and its soft-hearted protestation of a duty of trusteeship over the tribes, could be expected to take this position. The Executive Council of Upper Canada (1839) did that:

The custom of procuring by treaty with barbarous tribes' which probably originated more in the weakness of the discoverers and first settlers and in the relative strength of the original inhabitants, than in any sense of right and justice, was at all events not founded upon any Law in force in Europe, either municipal or national and such Law has never been acknowledged to have existence.[20]

Philanthropical bodies, especially in London, however, cleaved to the continued relevance of the *jus gentium* in shaping Crown dealings with its subject (as well as non-subject) tribal peoples. To them Crown relations with tribal nations remained inside the *jus gentium*. However, at the Colonial Office from this time (under James Stephen) little such talk appeared in correspondence or internal deliberation. Instead the official voice of Empire, in Parliament and the streams of correspondence and commissioning of officers in the field, spoke now in terms of Crown protection of its aboriginal subjects and their amenability to English law. This frequent packaging of sovereign duty was obviously regarded as absorbing and continuing domestically any duties that might previously have pressed from the *jus gentium* as a source for the comportment of Christian princes. In other words, the new policy direction of 'protection and civilization' was implicitly taken as the domesticated British version of the wider European discourse and comportment with what Christian Windler aptly portrays as the 'general idea of a civilizing mission'.[21]

This meant that as a juridical entity, of whatever character might previously have been admitted, the tribe had to disappear. Imperial legal practice technically regarded the tribe as having so disappeared (for else that would countenance *imperium in imperio*). As a matter of imperial law, the juridical tribe was replaced with the tribe members' subjecthood under an essentially interim regime of the 'unremitted solicitude' of Crown protection of their spectral tribalism. Of course, imperial officials did not imagine that legal ceremony and the mere avowal of Crown sovereignty meant that the Crown's tribal subjects immediately shed their customary

---

[19] I describe this in PG McHugh, *Aboriginal Societies and the Common Law* (Oxford University Press 2004) ch 3. For an important recent work likewise see Lisa Ford, *Settler Sovereignty: Jurisdiction and Indigenous People in America and Australia, 1788–1836* (Harvard University Press 2011).

[20] Executive Council (Upper Canada) Report, 1 January 1839, NAC RG 1-E3, Vol 103, Reel C-1204, 50–79, 56.

[21] Cf Chapter 9 in the present volume: Christian Windler, 'Towards the Empire of a "Civilizing Nation": The French Revolution and Its Impact on Relations with the Ottoman Regencies in the Maghreb'.

ways. The imperial theory (or, rather, dogma) of thoroughgoing Crown sovereignty did not ensure its incorporation in practice where continual validation and consolidation on the ground was needed. Bond Head, nodding his head respectfully but condescendingly, appreciated that gap but with a paternal indulgence that did not feel any obligation to deliver First Nations a lesson upon it.

Subjecthood was both an expression of tribe members' present legal status and a description of an eventual idealized destination. Subjecthood embodied imperial law on the technical consequence of Crown sovereignty and amenability of all tribes-people to the jurisdiction of the colonial courts. It also represented the imperial policy of civilizing the tribes by gradually loosening and dissolving the tribal tie so that they became freestanding individuals able to enjoy the full cluster of rights and liberties of their subjecthood. Enmeshed in this also was the Protestant belief in the individual's capacity and responsibility for their own salvation through their own labour. Tribalism was thus a temporary condition under the legal tutelage of the Crown that would disappear as tribe members adopted the ways of Christian civilization.

The awareness of the status of tribal peoples as British subjects under Crown sovereignty sharpened in imperial practice during the 1830s for a number of reasons, and of which Upper Canada is the example in this chapter. Whereas earlier practice was less concerned by *imperium in imperio* after the military victories of 1757 and global expansion of British dominion, the recognition of and accommodation of customary legal systems became a matter of increasing attention. During the seventeenth century and first half of the eighteenth century, imperial and colonial relations with non-Christian communities lacked an overall coherence and tended to be conducted on an ad hoc basis of continual negotiation, renegotiation, and running adjustment.[22] From the military victories of 1757 (Plassey) and 1759 (Plains of Abraham) in the East Indies and North America respectively, British practice necessarily had to take a more deliberate positioning with regard to indigenous legal systems, especially in the circumstances surrounding the impeachment of Warren Hastings.[23] The position of tribal peoples in the Empire of the 1830s was vastly

---

[22] I use the term 'jurisdictionalism' to describe the ad hoc approach to relations between colonial authorities and the independent tribes in McHugh, *Aboriginal Societies and the Common Law* (n 19) ch 3, though this term should not be taken as suggesting that the incremental formatting of relations was a deliberate feature of imperial or colonial practice. See also Daniel Richter, 'Native Peoples of North America and the Eighteenth-Century British Empire' in *The Oxford History of the British Empire 2: The Eighteenth Century* (Oxford University Press 1998) 349: There were 'a host of British people pursuing a variety of interests within parameters se by historical experience, Imperial structures, and finally, basic structures of ... [Amerindian] political culture'. Lisa Ford has given an excellent study of the last vestiges of this jurisdictionalism in *Settler Sovereignty: Jurisdiction and Indigenous People in America and Australia, 1788–1836* (Harvard University Press 2010). See also Damen Ward, 'Constructing British Authority in Australasia: Charles Cooper and the Legal Status of Aborigines in the South Australian Supreme Court, c.1840–60' (2006) 34 Journal of Imperial and Commonwealth History 483. Some underlying principles did appear nonetheless in this ragbag of colonial practice, most notably the early and constant prohibition by American colonial authorities of settlers acquiring land directly from the Indian occupiers.

[23] Mithi Mukherjee, 'Justice, War, and the Imperium: India and Britain in Edmund Burke's Prosecutorial Speeches in the Impeachment Trial of Warren Hastings' (2005) 23 Law and History Review 589.

different to those of British India in the late-eighteenth, but inconclusive debate about the East India Company's government was an early and important marker of how imperial attention was becoming directed increasingly towards the regulation of subject non-Christian peoples. These questions pressed more in the settlement colonies of the early mid-nineteenth century as imperial organization demilitarized and as land-hungry white agrarianism—or what has been termed 'explosive colonization'[24]—took hold. At the same time, the rise of evangelical fervour (in Britain especially, though far from only[25]) accentuated issues of imperial authority and duty towards subject peoples. This intensified religiosity was pervasive in the governing classes not merely in sects and branches of devotional activity, although the Quakers and Wesleyanism had distinct profiles. Initially, evangelical lobbying was directed towards abolition of the slave trade and slavery, but increasingly during the 1830s, and as those achievements were sealed in law, attention turned towards the position of aborigines. As the British Empire sharpened its consciousness of its sovereign authority over non-Christian peoples necessarily it also developed a more conscious sense of the ends to which that should be exercised. There appeared the notion of imperial 'trusteeship'.[26]

As imperial competition exited the forefront of calculation, the civilizing mission came into prominence bringing with it contestation over the disposition and management of sovereign authority. It was one thing to acknowledge very generally and vaguely a sovereign trustee's duty of protection, but the manner of its exercise in particular settings became a matter of considerable debate and disagreement across the Empire and as the colonial reform movement acquired influence during the 1830s. This movement became a kind of counter voice to the philanthropic influence of Exeter Hall, the building (and term) associated with the anti-slavery and aborigines protection groups of this time. The guru of this movement was Edward Gibbon Wakefield, a controversial self-publicist in his time, who developed Adam Smith's general critique of mercantilism into a theory of the management of land supply in settlement colonies. Although historians have long debated the extent of Wakefieldian influence on British colonial practice in the 1830s and 1840s,[27] important transformations in colonial land policy appeared from the early 1830s bearing that sign. The advocates of 'systematic colonization' were not impervious to the position of aboriginal peoples, especially if this could be used against the colonial elites (as in Upper Canada[28]). Their pamphleteering made a necessary concession to the evangelical sentiment,[29] whilst the 'tenths'

---

[24] James Belich, *Replenishing the Earth: The Settler Revolution and the Rise of the Anglo-World, 1783–1939* (Oxford University Press 2009).

[25] eg Randy J Sparks *On Jordan's Stormy Banks: Evangelicalism in Mississippi, 1776–1876* (University of Georgia Press 1994).

[26] George Mellor, *British Imperial Trusteeship, 1783–1850* (Faber & Faber 1951).

[27] For instance, see AGL Shaw, 'British Attitudes towards the Colonies, 1820–1850' (1969) 9 Journal of British Studies 71.

[28] eg the passage from Charles Buller's appendix to the Durham Report cited in Aborigines Protection Society, *Report on the Indians of Upper Canada* (n 12) 30.

[29] See CA Bodelsen, *Studies in Mid-Victorian British Imperialism* (reprint of 1924 edn, Heinemann 1960) 18–22, stressing that the colonial reformers were supporters of Empire, and close Crown

policy of the New Zealand Company (with its clear adaption of the clergy reserves approach in the Canadas) was a careful accommodation of the evangelical creed.[30] Their main concern, however, was with abolishing the old (corrupt) system of free grants with auction sale of land at a minimum upset price. By the early 1830s this influence was occurring in Upper Canada[31] and reformists' attention was also being directed towards Australia[32] and New Zealand. This meant that imperial officials became increasingly caught in the friction between two forms of pressure both with access to political influence and public opinion (in the dawning era of mass print circulation).

Bureaucratic reorganization of 1825, when the colonial wing of the War and Colonial Office obtained its own Under-Secretary, channelled those pressures towards a particular government office. Another sign of imperial demilitarization, the rise of the Colonial Office during the 1830s, put in place the bureaucratic system and, in James Stephen, an Under-Secretary (with legal training) of immense competence and integrity—that was nonetheless soon groaning under the weight of work.[33]

Even without the pressure of the colonial reformers, the Colonial Office still faced disagreement at home and from colonies abroad as to how the trusteeship duty was to be put into operation. There were all kinds of views about the extent and nature of the tolerance of tribalism implicit in Crown protection. Likewise there was much disagreement about land policy in the colonies particularly as this steered a more reformist direction during the 1830s and emigration increased.

By the 1830s, this sensitivity to the plight of aboriginal peoples was not an even one, in that some parts of Empire drew more attention and debate than others. Southern Africa absorbed considerable attention during the 1830s and evidence from it occupied much of the Select Committee on Aborigines hearings 1836–37. Nor was the grasp of the nature of sovereign authority consistent throughout the Empire. During the 1830s and 1840s there recurred colonial episodes in which appeared traces of the jurisdictionalism of an earlier imperial period.[34] The metropolitan view was articulated through the Colonial Office and its legal advisors. It was consistent on the thoroughgoing effect of Crown sovereignty and the

authority distinguishing them from the later Manchester school of free trade. For instance Edward Gibbon Wakefield published a tract *Dandeson Coates and the New Zealand Association* (Henry Hooper 1837) which, with characteristic craftiness, paralleled the prospective systematic colonization of New Zealand and the civilization of Maori with William Penn's Quaker mission in Pennsylvania.

[30] On the 'tenths' system as practised in New Zealand see Native Trust Office (New Zealand), *Native Reserves in Wellington and Nelson under the control of the Native Trustee* (*Appendices to Journal of the House of Representatives*) 1929, Session I, Paper G-01 (Government Printer 1929). Wakefield also explained his approach in evidence to the Select Committee on New Zealand (1840).

[31] Under the 'Bathurst Regulations' on land disposal, 'Copies of the regulations lately adopted in the Canadas for granting waste lands in these provinces' GBPP 1826–27 (254).

[32] On the 'Ripon Land Regulations', see Peter Burroughs, 'Wakefield and the Ripon Land Regulations of 1831' (1965) 11 Historical Studies 452–66, and Peter Burroughs, *Britain and Australia 1831–1855: A Study in Imperial Relations and Crown Land Administration* (Clarendon Press 1967).

[33] DM Young, *The Colonial Office in the Early Nineteenth Century* (Longman Paul 1961); Helen Taft Manning, 'Who Ran the British Empire 1830–1850?' (1965) 5 Journal of British Studies 88.

[34] Ward, 'Constructing British Authority in Australasia' (n 22).

amenability of all inhabitants, tribe members included, to English law. Faced with the reality of tribal organization and political presence some colonial officials, however, were not always so sure of the difference between tolerance and law. All were aware, anyway, that the reality of consolidating imperial authority over the tribes was a gradual and bumpy process especially where the bundled legal powers of protection and the policy of gradual civilization jarred with settlers' pressing and vociferous self-interest.

Under the mantle of Crown protection, this transitionalism allowed the tribes to hold a view of their retained political authority and status within the colony at odds with imperial law and policy goals. Settlers, impatient with what they saw as official indulgence of tribalism and the withholding of their land from gainful use, resisted few opportunities to deride and prick this accommodation. It gave the tribes and their chiefs an inflated sense of importance and stature, or so many settlers and their representatives moaned, that did not square with their subjecthood and technical liability to the same laws as everyone else.

The more regularized insistence upon the status of tribal peoples as British subjects emanating from the metropolitan centre from the 1830s was not only a product of the demilitarization and bureaucratization of imperial organization as well as the influence of evangelical proselytizing, it was also, and more subtly, an expression of the constitutional anxieties of the Reform era. Bond Head was not alone in his condemnation of American republicanism and the demagoguery of MacKenzie, Baldwin, and the supporters of responsible government. Recognition of continued tribal status involved acceptance of the divisibility of sovereignty inconceivable to British constitutional thought of the period (though yet to be articulated in its robust Austinian form[35]). By the early 1830s imperial officials were certainly aware of the judgments of the Marshall Supreme Court in the United States where the independent tribes of the continental interior had been described as 'domestic dependent nations'.[36] In British eyes, this constitutional characterization allowed the American republic to wage war against the tribes as separate nations and to invoke the law of nations as justification for the ensuing destructiveness and dispossession. James Stephen, the influential Under-Secretary at the Colonial Office, was scathing of this self-serving legalism:

Whatever may be the ground occupied by international jurists they never forget the policy and interests of their own Country. Their business is to give to rapacity and injustice, the most decorous veil which legal ingenuity can weave. Selden, in the interest of England maintained the doctrine of what was called mare clausum. Vattel in the interest of Holland laid down the principle of open fisheries. Mr Marshall great as he was, was still an American, and adjudicated against the rights of Indians. All such law is good, just as long as there is power to enforce it, and no longer.[37]

---

[35] See Mark Francis, 'The Nineteenth-Century Theory of Sovereignty and Thomas Hobbes' (1980) 1 History of Political Thought 517.

[36] Mark Hickford, *Lords of the Land: Indigenous Property Rights and the Jurisprudence of Empire* (Oxford University Press 2012), especially chs 3 and 4.

[37] James Stephen, Under-Secretary at the Colonial Office, 'Minute to Vernon Smith, 28 July 1840' CO209/4, 343–44. This passage has been cited extensively by other writers: eg and recently Blake

Here Stephen made clear his belief that protection of aborigines was not a matter of rights so much as an appropriately measured deployment of royal authority; the question of how the Crown performed its obligation towards its tribal subjects. The power to enforce its laws lying with the sovereign authority, these could be used as much negatively as positively, the purpose of Marshall's characterization of the tribes being to draw a 'decorous veil' over that depredation. It was the duty of a civilized Christian sovereign to regard its constitutional authority and the remit of its law with Christian seriousness and to apply it beneficently for all its subjects. If the British took one lesson from the politics of abolition[38] it was a deep belief in the importance of subjecthood. Stephen's position was founded on the prevalent and contemporary imperial principle (or, more accurately, dogma) of tribal peoples' subjecthood rather than a Marshall-like incorporation of the Crown's historical pattern into depiction of the constitutional position of the tribes, an approach that American theories of sovereignty allowed but, by then, the British did not. His minute was a telling observation on the post-Revolutionary divergence of American and British imperial constitutionalism, the former a federalist discourse of multiple sovereign communities, the British a centralizing one of a single, paramount sovereignty.[39]

Further in this revealing minute we see Stephen making a point that will become apparent from the Upper Canada setting of the 1830s. For all the bannering and headlining of a philanthropical concern with the 'rights of aborigines', the imperial and colonial discourses of the 1830s were not primarily rights-based, except to the extent that tribal peoples in the white settlement colonies were seen not as holding hardened collective rights but as potentially holding the individual rights of British subjects once they had advanced sufficiently to civilization.[40]

There were moments where advocates for tribal peoples spoke of aborigines' rights in terms of their being inherent. In January 1838 Buxton wrote to Lord Glenelg

---

Watson, 'The Impact of the American Doctrine of Discovery on Native Land Rights in Australia, Canada, and New Zealand' (2011) 34 Seattle University Law Review 507, 525. Also Sidney Harring, *White Man's Law: Native People in Nineteenth-Century Canadian Jurisprudence* (Osgoode Society for Canadian Legal History 1998) 21.

[38] On abolition as more of a quest for imperial order than a proto-human rights movement see Lauren Benton, 'Abolition and Imperial Law, 1790–1820' (2011) 39 Journal of Imperial and Commonwealth History 355.

[39] For a New Zealand analysis, by former Chief Justice Martin (1863), confirming the Stephen view of the Marshall cases, see Mark Hickford's magisterial *The Lords of the Land: Indigenous Property Rights and the Jurisprudence of Empire* (Oxford University Press 2011) 426–27. In an 1863 pamphlet the New Zealand jurist distinguished the Marshall cases in the same way as Stephen. There were, he said, 'two modes of colonizing: one by which the people of the territory colonized may be locally brought within the dominion of the Crown, yet may remain in nearly everything as independent as before; and a second, by which they may be brought (as far as possible) even from the beginning within the law and political system of the colonizers'.

[40] It is a feature of federal American Indian Law that it never became a rights-discourse as in other areas of American constitutional doctrine, especially with regard to race. Instead federal Indian law remained jurisdictional in orientation, its constant concern being with the nature of governmental authority in Indian country, ie asking the question whether the relevant jurisdictional forum is tribal, federal, or state.

proposing a Bill 'recognising by adoption of some general principle, the rights of aborigines of countries where new British colonies are being formed'. Though associated personally with the philanthropical cause, Glenelg held unquestioningly to the discretionary aspect of his Ministerial office, rejecting peremptorily any suggestion of legal constraint. He did 'not at present perceive what is the specific object with a view to which the interference of the legislature is necessary or desirable'.[41] Another notable instance occurred in the Aboriginal Protection Society's tract by Standish Motte, a barrister, entitled *Outline of a System of Legislation* (1840), which advocated a general statutory framework for the protection of tribal peoples. The foundational principles of such a statute would be:

... the declaration of the indefeasible rights of every people, (not under allegiance to any other power,) to the natural rights of man, comprehending

1. Their rights as an independent nation. That no country or people has a right by force or fraud to assume the sovereignty over any other nation.
2. That such sovereignty can only be justly obtained by fair treaty, and with their consent.
3. That every individual of a nation whether independent or owing allegiance to any other power has a right to personal liberty, and protection of property and life.[42]

This was a paradigmatic instancing of the Lockean principles at the core of American and French constitutionalism of the late-eighteenth century, and of a 'republican' (that is, democratic) hue that made establishment British figures very nervous. These Aboriginal Protection Society's initiatives were but a more secularized version of the egalitarianism that was making the Methodist creed attractive to Upper Canada First Nations, and bringing the Quaker and Methodist groups into political alliance.

There was, then, pressure at this time for the transposition of the discretion-laden Crown protection into harder legal format. The models raised were as an all-encompassing statutory code of inherent rights; through the oversight of an independent inspectorate;[43] or by issue of inalienable Crown grants under trust. Those were pathways down which imperial and colonial officials plainly did not want to turn, and ensured that they did not. Indeed, and as an important example seen more fully below shows, imperial officials consciously refused to issue Crown grants to reserve land in Upper Canada as to put the Christianized Indians' occupation of their cultivated land on a legally cognizable footing. Firmly unwilling

---

[41] James Heartfield, *The Aborigines Protection Society: Humanitarian intervention in Australia, New Zealand, Fiji, Canada, South Africa, and the Congo, 1836–1909* (Hurst & Co 2011) 34.

[42] Standish Motte, *Outline of a System of Legislation, for Securing Protection to the Aboriginal Inhabitants of all the Countries Colonized by Great Britain, Extending to them Political and Social Rights, Ameliorating their Condition, and Promoting their Civilization/Drawn up at the Request of the Committee of the Aborigines Protection Society* (John Murray 1840) 14.

[43] Another approach advocated by evangelical groups, such as Saxe Bannister before the Select Committee on Aborigines, *Report from the Select Committee on Aborigines (British settlements); with the minutes of evidence, appendix and index*, Evidence (Saxe Bannister), GBPP 1837 (425) 15 (hereafter *Select Committee on Aborigines Report*); Motte echoed this call in his *Outline of a System* (n 42).

to transform tribal occupancy of any sort into a type of enforceable right, they cleaved unshakeably to the mantle of Crown protectionism.

In what was still a pre-democratic age, wide sections of the British ruling élite shivered with 'rights-anxiety'. As we saw Bond Head observing in his memoir of the recent disturbances, the language of inherent Lockean rights was 'a gaudy transatlantic European theory'. Such talk had overtones of mob rule and the disappearance of social order and tiering, the Terror, and rootless American chaos and disorder (which anxiety the bloody American Civil War was to confirm for many). The inability of the imperial Crown to shed the high discretion of protection, exemplified below by its unresponsiveness to the Methodist missionaries' request for land deeds, was in some respects also an expression of this deeper anxiety.

Whilst imperial officials were by the 1830s quite sure that imperial sovereignty brought tribes' status as subjects, they were equally and sharply aware of the concomitant sovereign duty of protection. The notion of protection had not by then formed into the juridical mechanism of the 'protectorate' as it appeared in European state practice during the Scramble era of the late-nineteenth century. In the 1830s the notion of protection was not internationalized,[44] so much as a description of a general obligation of the sovereign towards a particular vulnerable class of its subjects. Protection applied as much, and as variably, towards, imbeciles, minors, and Ionian Islanders as towards tribe members. The intense debate over aborigines revolved upon how the Crown comported with its sovereign obligation of protection and civilization. The foundation of the Aborigines Protection Society (1836)—in both the title this early pressure group gave itself as well as the nature of its constant petitioning, pamphleteering, and lobbying of the Colonial Office— showed how public discourse shaped about the exercise of royal authority (under the prerogative). It was not called the 'Aboriginal Rights Society'.

The outcome of this was a gap between tribal nationhood as a legally non-existent status and the strong reality of its everyday continuance in colonial political life. The legal phantom of tribal nationhood materialized very much in the ordering of day-to-day life and Crown relations with the tribes. Yet that gap between an imaginary absence and an intrusive presence—between tribal nationhood *de iure* and nationhood *de facto*—was never regarded as inherently problematic. That gap was bridged by the cluster of powers held by the Crown under the prerogative, and exercised on its behalf through its paramount colonial official, the Governor. To repeat, these powers were seen as there for the Crown to deploy protectively, so that the Crown respected the tribal nationhood and their interests for the interim, even as it was applying policies and practices intended to dissolve them. In this way the Crown maintained continuity in practices that had underpinned relations with tribal peoples, ensuring its own consistency amongst the various tribes whilst seeking also to transform them. To modern eyes the Crown is seen as conniving in a contradiction between recognizing tribal nationhood (or at least in propagating the pretence of what its own imperial law deemed absent) and seeking its destruction. This was not a contradiction that

---

[44] During the 1830s the British had the Ionian Islands under protection.

occurred to imperial and colonial figures who saw tribalism as a temporary condition to be countenanced, tolerated begrudgingly or benignly (though with highly varying degrees of patience), and accepted pragmatically as the process of civilization took root. There were many disagreements within imperial and colonial circles and from one colony to another as to how the Crown's protection was to occur in this meanwhile, but the underlying premise of interim tolerance of tribal nationhood was undisputed. If this was a necessary concession to the reality of tribal political authority within a colony, concession it was nonetheless seen as being.

For those who pulled the levers of imperial power or directed criticism towards them, law did not represent a normative system that generated obligations of a legal kind perceived as operating externally and imperatively on the metropole. Instead law was instrumental, a facilitating rather than a constraining means that worked suggestively and through the self-monitoring, and in many respects self-correcting, internal structures of Empire. It guided rather than limited official conduct as it encountered one contingency after another. As it was, the disposition of these relations was prone to the conduct of the Crown's officials on the ground—its colonial Governors most especially. This necessary reliance upon local imperial officials, with the time-lag in communication back and forth, limited London's capacity to steer the course of relations being conducted in the imperial sovereign's name. In the way law shaped imperial conduct it was seen less as an imperative or stipulative set of rules than as a matter of self-disciplining comportment, of law running internally up and down the structures of authority. It was the means by which the Crown organized itself, commissioned its officers, and through the network of relations of superior and subordinate monitored their operationalization of its authority. In the imperial setting of the early Victorian era, law represented both the means by which the imperial Crown established and retained (without any perception of it limiting) its own authority whilst also disciplining through its pyramids of authority (civil and military), in the sense of checking and attempting to render consistent and orderly, the activity of its officers and subjects. The legal structure of Empire was a series of pyramidical layering of offices. Within this network of structures there continually relayed a pulsating reporting upwards to superiors, with instructions issuing downwards to subordinates. These hierarchies embodied the *auctoritas* exercised through vertically directed channels informed by culturally validated notions of station, social rank, and office.

Observance of *auctoritas* occurred not only in the careful layering and delegating of authority. It had iterative and performative qualities. It could be seen in the formal way officials and gentlemen spoke to and engaged with one another personally and in correspondence (the scrupulous sensitivity to positioning as superior, equal, or subordinate) and in the presentation and bearing of themselves in the settings (formal and informal) of their official role. The legalism of Empire occurred iteratively, inscriptively, and performatively, routinely as well as ornamentally.[45] It was synonymous with office and station, voice, and the performance of role.

---

[45] The allusion is to David Cannadine, *Ornamentalism: How the British Saw their Empire* (Allen Lane 2001). Cannadine draws extensively on Mark Francis' important *Governors and Settlers: Images of*

This fundamental feature of colonial political life in the pre-legislative and pre-democratic gubernatorial period reflected, in legal terms, the centrality of the royal prerogative as a source of authorization. Whilst this chapter considers the several prerogatives shaping Crown relations with the tribes, the prerogative underpinned other important aspects of colonial life such as government employment, the amelioration or pardoning of court sentence, compensation for damages done by or work done for government (that is claims in tort and contract), pensions, and poor relief. Petitions, the right of the subject to petition their sovereign reaffirmed in the Bill of Rights ([Article] 5), were a very common feature of colonial life and took much of the Governor's business time. These petitions involved either a matter claimed as a legal right (petition of right) or asked a favour or privilege (petition of grace). Governors did what they could administratively to discipline this process, some better than others.[46]

Law, being based upon the structured and hierarchical nature of imperial authority in which the fundamental issue of comportment was the continual dynamic, likewise provided a means by which the exercise of that authority was discussed and debated within the early Victorian Empire. It was to the structure of imperial authority and its disposition that controversy at any time or in any place instinctively turned, often irresolutely. Imperial successes, imperial failures, imperial inaction, moments of excitements, or periods of stasis were always being screened in terms of the chain of command warranted from the Crown. Comportment was also a suggestive as well as continual exercise in all the various settings of time and place. In all imperial settings, the management of native policy was controversial and never admitted any consensus other than vague acceptance of an eventual goal of Christianization and tribe members' destined (though never achieved) full incorporation into the imperial economy. Secretaries of State, their officials, Governors, and those commissioned by them were constantly being told the conduct and response that particular situations and issues required. Indeed, at all levels during the imperial era the Crown and its authorities from top dog down in London and the Colonial Office was under constant bombardment.

Protection and Prerogative—the 'Unremitted Solicitude' and 'Spontaneous Liberality' of the Crown

The British Empire was never the premeditating design of its monarch or the pursuit of an elitist oligarchy. It was famously acquired in the (protracted) fit of an absent mind. Yet though the network of formality through which the British Empire conducted itself was usually a response to the initiative and unsolicited

---

Authority in the British Colonies, 1820–60 (Palgrave Macmillan 1992) stressing the performative nature of British imperial authority.

[46] JK Johnson, *In Duty Bound: Men, Women and the State in Upper Canada, 1783–1841* (McGill-Queen's University Press 2014).

enterprise of the Crown's subjects, this royal instrumentation issued under the prerogative was an essential precondition and facilitation of the legality of impe-rial venturing. In the imperial sphere numerous prerogative powers merged into the Crown undisputed authority over its wayfaring subjects. As its adventuring subjects took sojourn overseas, and particularly as this turned into plantation and colonization from the late Tudor period, royal warrant imbued this activ-ity with legality. By the mid-eighteenth century the Crown colony had become the favoured form, a system in which a Governor exercised governmental author-ity through an Executive Council and Legislative Assembly (representative or non-representative).

With (if not from) the Royal Proclamation (1763) issued in the aftermath of Pontiac's Rebellion, we see the conduct of relations with tribes being regarded as an imperial interest and matter of direct royal authority too fragile and vital militarily as well as strategically to be left to land-hungry colonists. From the mid-eighteenth century and certainly by the 1830s, as the notion of Crown trusteeship dug in, this authority was being withheld from settler legislatures as a matter of imperial interest. These relations had been conducted by the American colonies under the loose and situational jurisdictionalism of the seventeenth and early eighteenth cen-tury, but with the Royal Proclamation 1763 the Crown consciously identified and retrieved an authority that anyway had never been packaged as a totality and explic-itly granted as such to the colonial authorities. The American colonists and their belletrists rankled at the Proclamation's calling in of this authority, not least because recourse to the 'Norman Yoke'[47] was aimed at stopping their westward expansion (and land speculation). The overtones of untrammelled executive authority that the American colonists detected in this step became an element—one that the his-toriography tends to ignore or underplay—in the constitutional contestation that combusted in Revolution. From the Proclamation, the management of relations with the tribes came to be recognized as a distinct head of imperial jurisdiction, or 'imperial interest' as it was known. This was a capacity that had been, so to speak, 'called in' by the metropolitan officers of Empire. It derived from a cluster of pre-rogative powers, that British authorities only became willing to pass onto settler authorities from the 1840s, and which in Canada at confederation was vested in the Dominion (1867). The Select Committee on Aborigines (1837) recommended that the Governors of Crown colonies should be specially invested with authority to conduct relations with tribal peoples. This recommendation did not become incorporated into the formality of British practice but remained a matter of infor-mal instruction by dispatch, where Governors were told to conciliate the goodwill of the tribes and to treat them with liberality.

Whilst never being made the matter of specific authorization in Governors' formal instruments of office as the Select Committee had recommended and though it was recognized as a distinct sphere of Crown governance, these relations

---

[47] For discussion see Robert A Williams, *The American Indian in Western Legal Thought: The Discourses of Conquest* (Oxford University Press 1992) 251–86.

encompassed several prerogative powers. These absorbed easily the demilitarization of the Empire in train from the 1820s and the reorientation of relations to the civilizing mission. The deployment of these remained in the hands of the Governor though more in his civil than military capacity and subject now to Colonial Office oversight. In this way contestation over sovereign comportment became focused on a department (the Colonial Office) and its man-on-the-spot, the Governor.

Initially relations with tribes in the New World had occurred under the broad foreign relations power of the Crown and the associated military power conferred in the constituent instruments. Those instruments reflected the more jurisdictional outlook of their times, adverting to tribes but not claiming any inherent authority over them (other than the implicit right to proselytize and wage war if need be). Supplementary informal instructions regularly advised grantees to conciliate their goodwill and control settlers' dealings with them, but in the main and until the Royal Proclamation the colonies controlled Indian policy themselves. Elements of the jurisdictional approach recurred in the Royal Proclamation (1763) where the Indian tribes are spoken of both as allies and subjects of the Crown even as it announced the more centralized turn in the management of those relations. This duality was consistent with the manner in which the chiefs were presenting their military help on the shores of the Niagara River in 1837, unaware that it had been discarded in the imperial theory that was now informing the colonial practice.

The several prerogative powers of Crown protection included the Crown's powers in issuing patents for lands and its formal grant as the source of land title in a colony, its power to regulate the civil service, its powers in the administration of justice (criminal prosecutions especially), and its power to represent vulnerable classes of its subjects in legal proceedings as *parens patriae*. Those various forms of prerogative power knitted into the protective mantle that the Governor was to exercise with discretion and tolerance, and to reinforce the sovereign authority of the Crown, as tribes made the transition to full subjecthood. By the 1830s and in terms of legal authorization, Crown protection of subject tribes had nothing to do with the foreign relations power except in the continuance of practices and ritualism of an earlier era. The continuance of the ceremonialism of a diplomatic age became a performative inscription of sovereign authority rather than the renewal of alliance that the militarism of the War against France had necessitated. Treating aboriginal tribes as though they still had distinct nationhood through an essentially pacifying ritualism was not the same as an actual legal acceptance of it.

In 1834 the British Parliament petitioned the King, showing acute awareness of who held the constitutional wherewithal to enable protection, and the legal foundation of relations with tribes arising from their subjecthood:

That His Majesty's faithful Commons in Parliament assembled, are deeply impressed with the duty of acting upon the principles of justice and humanity in the intercourse and relations of this country with the native inhabitants of its colonial settlements, of affording to them the protection in the enjoyment of their civil rights, and of imparting to them that degree of civilization, and that religion, which Providence has blessed this nation, and humbly prays that His Majesty will take such measures, and give such directions to the governors and officers of His Majesty's colonies, settlements and plantations as shall secure to the natives the due observance of justice and the protection of their rights, promote the spread of civilization amongst them, and lead them to the peaceful and voluntary reception of the Christian religion.[48]

Where issues of land were concerned, imperial officials' management of relations with indigenous peoples as well as the voracious settler communities became particularly touchy. In settler colonies the availability of land presented questions to which only lengthy attention could do justice. Suffice it to say that the turbulent legalism of land availability dominated colonial and imperial politics from the 1820s and well into the early national periods of settler self-government. Yet, to reiterate an earlier point, in the imperial period of concern here—the 1820s through early 1840s—this legalism was not one of land *rights* so much as land *title*. That is to say, the tumultuous legalism of land that engrossed settler society was concerned with the process of getting and endowing the possession of land with legal incontrovertibility. Through its patenting, the Crown was instrumental to that security. Land titling posed the role and responsibility of the Crown in protecting its native subjects beside—and often against—its longstanding willingness to facilitate formally the economic enterprise and ambition of its white subjects. The politics of the white settler colonies in the colonial period were not simply the politics of access to land. They were the politics of the Crown's role in vesting and formal validation of land titles with legal security. These politics spoke simultaneously of the Crown's sovereign authority and the ongoing need for its officers to verify and consolidate that authority with the expeditious patenting of settlers' title. Under constant fire and try as Governors might, meeting settlers' ever-growing demands for land was impossible. Inevitably the colonial clamour always outstripped the constant and often fretful responses by Governors to the unquenchable. Squatting, unlawful leasing from chiefs, unlawful direct purchases, booze-running, and constant encroachment (lumbering, fishing, trapping) were just some of the devices settlers used to force the official hand. The unshakeable perception of imperial under-responsiveness and London's softness on the tribes occupying unused land encouraged settler communities in the belief that they could manage their affairs, as well as those of the indigenous population, much more efficaciously. In that sense, and driven by disgruntlement over the land question, settler self-government became, at least in settlers' rationale, a consequence of the imperial Crown's inability to comport itself persuasively.

From the early 1830s Governors found their disposition of land to settlers increasingly subject to minute regulation and more precise proceduralizing from London even as surging colonization and wilful settler temperament made the sought-after orderliness less rather than more obtainable.[49] Nonetheless and as the unresponsiveness to the Select Committee recommendation (1837) signalled, no attempt

---

[48] *Select Committee on Aborigines Report* (n 43) GBPP 1837 (425) 5.
[49] For an account, John C Weaver, *The Great Land Rush and the Making of the Modern World 1650–1900* (McGill-Queens University Press 2003).

was made to reduce Crown trusteeship to a code, especially with regard to the Governor's dealings with tribes over land. Certainly these dealings were disciplined, in Upper Canada through the procedures embodied in the Royal Proclamation (1763) and Dorchester Regulations to Indian superintendents (1794)[50] as well as the usual monitoring from the Governor and his Indian superintendents (who until 1830 were part of the provincial military rather than civil establishment). This internal disciplining was an exercise of sovereign authority overseen by the imperial hierarchy rather than a limitation of it (as the Proclamation came to be characterized in Canadian legal doctrine of the late-twentieth century). The Proclamation set out the procedures that the Crown would generally follow in obtaining land from tribes and permitting white settlement but implicitly left itself as the 'sole arbiter' of its own justice.

The change of imperial land policy during the early 1830s ran into many obstacles and against vested interests in the colonies. Attempts at the closer regulation of settler acquisitiveness were more attended in the proverbial breach than the observance, not only in Upper Canada but also Australia. Governors had to strategize and mediate on key and very heated questions of access and enforcement, never to the satisfaction of land-hungry settlers in all their hues of wealth, station, and literacy. Testy and uncooperative, settlers were not minded to observe laws preventing their use of land or controlling access when they saw it there for the taking. That this was often Crown land, be it unceded Indian lands, unsurveyed ceded lands or clergy reserves, or land patented to an absentee crony of the local elite under the old system of free grant, only fuelled the colonists' demand for greater autonomy. An appendix to the Durham Report (1839), written by Charles Buller, a leading colonial reformist, demonstrated how land policy, self-sufficiency, and settler autonomy were becoming intertwined. This was an association that became stronger during the 1840s and 1850s as the white settlement colonies boomed. By 1861 the Durham Report, including the appendix, was being celebrated, thinkingly by the likes of John Stuart Mill in press and the hustings[51] but more unthinkingly in the brand of early Victorian populism and boosterism that Belich has termed 'settlerism'.[52] With convenient forgetfulness of the flaws in its preparation and the

---

[50] 'Dorchester to Simcoe, additional instructions, Indian Department, 26 December 1794' in EA Cruickshank (ed), *The Correspondence of Lieutenant-Governor John Graves Simcoe* (5 vols, Ontario Historical Society 1923–31), III, 241–42, 260–61.

[51] John Stuart Mill, *The Collected Works of John Stuart Mill, Volume XIX—Essays on Politics and Society Part II* (John M Robson ed, Toronto: University of Toronto Press, London: Routledge and Kegan Paul 1977) 563. Mill described himself as a major contributor to the change in attitude towards colonies that had come in the previous two decades (in chapter XVIII of *Representative Government*). It was always believed that Buller and Wakefield, who accompanied the prickly and flamboyant Durham, were the authors of the Report, a belief Mill confirmed in referring to the 'intellect and practical sagacity of its joint authors, Mr Wakefield and the lamented Charles Buller'. Mill's views on white colonization began to cool down during this decade: see Katherine Smits, 'John Stuart Mill on the Antipodes: Settler Violence against Indigenous Peoples and the Legitimacy of Colonial Rule' (2008) 54 Australian Journal of Politics and History 1. As to the changes in his view of colonization see also Duncan Bell, 'John Stuart Mill on Colonies' (2010) 38 Political Theory 34.

[52] Belich, *Replenishing the Earth* (n 24) 159–61.

monstrous ego behind it,[53] the Report became a kind of Magna Carta of settler autonomy.

The cost of Empire was a perennial preoccupation in London and the 1830s were no exception. Whilst the Crown had significant authority exercised through its governors, appropriations to support their establishment still needed a Parliamentary vote. Imperial expenditure became more closely monitored at this time. Cost-cutting was a theme as incessant in the Colonial Office as those of trusteeship and land availability for settlers. The change of land policy towards a system more like that advocated by the colonial reformists also became associated with the raising of a local revenue to lessen the burden on the Mother Country, to encourage emigration and set the colony towards financial self-sufficiency. Self-sufficiency and autonomy became an emergent predicate of imperial policy during the 1830s and by the 1840s, and as the legend of the Durham Report grew, it was well on its way to becoming a cardinal principle. The Colonial Land and Emigration Commission was established in 1840, amongst its tasks (passed on from the heavily stretched Colonial Office) being the monitoring of colonial land laws and management. The Colonial Land and Emigration Commissioners were responsible for the management of land sales in the British colonies, and used some of the proceeds to promote and regulate emigration to the colonies.

The 1830s were a transitional decade in the British Empire, as the white settlement colonies of Australasia and British North America took form and the imperial militarism of earlier decades receded in prominence. These transitions were occurring in Upper Canada and run through Bond Head's recollection of his meeting with the chiefs beside the Niagara River.

First Nations in Upper Canada during the 1830s: From Allies to Protection to Civilization

By the late 1820s the orientation of Indian policy in Upper Canada was shifting perceptibly from military alliance towards subjecthood and the associated processes of protection and civilization. As part of the ritualism of alliance there had commenced during the late-eighteenth century a practice of annual present-giving by the British. For the First Nations this present-giving established a tributary relationship of mutual support, ritualistically reaffirmed every year, reflecting what they had duly and honourably rendered for the British across several decades of hostility with the Americans through to the War of 1812 and rumblings after. By 1837 present-giving had been under prolonged review. Indians were increasingly being seen as a social nuisance rather than valuable allies, particularly by the covetous settlers eyeing their fertile but unused land. In ceremonially (but, for the British pointlessly) reaffirming a political relationship founded on military support,

---

[53] Ged Martin, *The Durham Report and British Policy: A Critical Essay* (Cambridge University Press 1972).

present-giving seemed more to impede than promote their civilization. In bringing Indians across the border to partake it also risked the British being accused of breaching international law by encouraging Indian unrest. Arms, as well as blankets, ornaments, and trinkets, had always figured on the gift list. Moreover, present-giving had become costly and fostered the persistence of a view of the relationship with First Nations that the British as well as the headstrong settler communities were no longer minded to take.

A Report in 1828 by Major General HC Darling, military secretary to the Governor General, set out an Indian 'civilization' programme, mostly by establishing Indians in sedentary communities where they could be educated, Christianized, and trained as farmers. Darling's Report caught the mood of imperial economizing by setting the end goal of self-sufficient aboriginal communities.

Soon after this Report the administration of Indian affairs (in both Canadas) was transferred to the civil side and out of the military department (1830).[54] This, along with the adjusting of accounting practice (1832)[55] so that the charge for the Indian Department in Canada was submitted to the imperial Parliament in a separate estimate, had the effect of making more obvious the amount of imperial expenditure on presents.[56] Dominated by supporters of retrenchment like Gladstone, Stanley, and Joseph Hume, the Military Expenditure Select Committee of the British Parliament recommended (1835) that the Indian Department in the Canadas should be reduced or eliminated entirely.[57] By the mid-1830s the practice, both in its cost and ongoing justification, was coming under very close scrutiny.[58]

Lieutenant Governors Colborne and Bond Head, and their officers, defended these ceremonies and the complicated bureaucratic process as necessary for maintenance of civil order. The ritual of present-giving and the busy micro-economy it promoted represented a vital iterative and performative affirmation of Crown sovereignty that encouraged Indian tractability (especially in land cessions). Picking up on London's sensitivity to its sovereign obligation and reluctance to halt immediately this ritualism of allegiance, they argued for the continuance at least in the short term. This subtle repositioning of the justification away from military and strategic to more local purposes showed that whilst the authorities were worried about Indian capacity to cause mayhem they were by this stage confident that an uprising could always be outgunned or over-forced. The possibility of Indian Wars, such as those then afflicting the United States (and known to Canadians and First Nations), were not raised as a serious possibility, although, by the same token, the

[54] Murray to Colborne, 4 December 1828 GBPP 1834 (617) 127; Kempt to Murray, 25 January 1830, ibid, 89; Murray to Kempt, 22 March 1830, ibid, 90 (rejecting Kempt's request for reconsideration of this step).

[55] Howick to Stewart, 4 February 1832, ibid, 137; Goderich to Colborne, 3 April 1832, ibid.

[56] For instance: Return of Indian Presents for years 1830–33, ibid, 125–26; Colborne to Murray, 14 October 1830, ibid, extract at 128; Colborne to Aylmer, 19 February 1831, ibid, 130.

[57] *Report of the Select Committee on Colonial Military Expenditure*, GBPP 1835 (474) iii, 4th Resolution.

[58] Glenelg to Gosford 14 January 1836, ibid, 1–4.

absence of such Wars was used by local imperial officials as justification for the continuance of present-giving.

Reports of abuses of the system reached London and though the allegations drew strong denial from Canadian officials they drew attention not only due to the cost but also to the value of a ritual that did little to advance the vaunted goal of civilization. One report described the presents as being traded in quickly and almost entirely for 'spiritous liquors', characterized the Indian Department as sloppily inept, and those collecting as mostly American Indians from across the border, half-castes with little or no Indian appearance, or children attending a missionary school advocating American republicanism.[59] London, acknowledging the faithful obligation of the Crown not to stop present-giving immediately, began to insist nonetheless that the practice would only be continued in the interim and that the presents should be more oriented towards agricultural implements and the civilizing mission.[60] In August 1837 Lieutenant Governor Bond Head informed London that the Indians had been 'clearly and officially informed' that henceforth presents would be given only to resident Indians.[61] His superintendent Samuel Jarvis had been deputed to deliver this news. Bond Head had left the party travelling to Great Manitoulin Island and returned to Toronto on learning of the King's death. Jarvis returned in the same capacity the next year, Bond Head having left office. He reported a noticeable decline in attendance and tried to placate Indian fears that they would be impressed into Crown service as ordinary soldiers rather than as allies. The message was, however, beginning to reach First Nations that the Crown was disowning them as autonomous allies despite Jarvis 'applauding the alacrity and good conduct of the resident Tribes during the late Rebellion'.[62] The appearance of these resident tribes on the banks of the Niagara was being cast in terms of their loyalist subjecthood rather than as a demonstration of continuing historical alliance.

It was not until 1852 that the British Government unilaterally ended the 'spontaneous liberality' of present-giving over the protest of provincial officials.[63] By the time that this decision was taken and imperial misgivings about seeming to renounce its honour were finally discarded, Indian policy-making in Upper Canada had been through several degrees of reorientation, with two more important ones to come. Soon after, in 1860, full jurisdictional competence over First Nations was transferred to the Province, which had also gained responsible government in 1850. In 1867 the British North America Act confederated the colonies into the Dominion of Canada, with the federal legislature being given competence over 'Indians and lands reserved for Indian' (section 91(24)).

---

[59] Thomas Wilson to RW Hay, 5 January 1832, ibid, 139. See Colborne's testy response to Goderich, 30 November 1832, ibid.

[60] Howick to Stewart, 4 February 1832, (n 55) 137.

[61] Head to Glenelg 22 August 1837, ibid, at 154.

[62] Jarvis, Report of 25 August 1838, as reported in the Macaulay Report (n 18) 9.

[63] David McNab, *Circles of Time: Aboriginal Land Rights and Resistance in Ontario* (Wilfrid Laurier University Press 1999) 52. The term describing present-giving comes from the Macaulay Report (n 18) 4. Speeches of Chiefs in response to hearing the discontinuation of Indian presents, Manitowaning, 1852 (LAC RG 10, vol 198, pt 1, nos 6101–6200, 116405–116408).

Meanwhile through the late 1830s the apparatus of the colonial state tightened in fits and starts around First Nations, even as white colonists and imperial loyalists clashed over responsible government and the gaudy Durham roadshow swept quickly through the Province.[64] Durham had been appointed Governor General of Canada and dispatched with a team (that included Edward Gibbon Wakefield and Charles Buller) to report on the 'recent disturbances'. Having been gently but firmly sent packing with a gracious if not patronizing send-off from Bond Head beside the Niagara River, the 1837 Rebellion was essentially a drama in which the First Nations had no role.[65] There continued the policy of buying land by the established treaty-making procedures[66] but policy towards the First Nations on their remnant land was by then reaching a crossroads. Opinion divided between those who thought the Indians could become civilized agriculturalists and those who thought their condition irredeemable or, at least, vastly less transformable than the evangelical optimistically supposed.[67] Metropolitan officials and missionaries, caught in the fervour of the era of abolition, regarded the salvation of the souls of non-Christian peoples and their adoption of a civilized lifestyle as both feasible and as a duty arising from their common humanity. After all, He hath 'made of *one* blood all nations of men, to dwell on the face of the earth'.[68] Frontiersmen and colonial politicians were more sympathetic with the American policy of removal.

In the summer of 1836 Bond Head proposed removing the Indian population to the Great Manitoulin Island on Lake Huron.[69] In August, at a Great Council on Manitoulin Island, he obtained two cessions of land by treaty (the term used but a misnomer in the sense of the Indians being Crown subjects).[70] To facilitate his vision,

---

[64] Bruce Curtis, 'The "Most Splendid Pageant Ever Seen": Grandeur, the Domestic, and Condescension in Lord Durham's Political Theatre' (2008) 89 Canadian Historical Review 55. Curtis uses a notion of comportment similar to that in this chapter but with less focus on the deployment of legalism.

[65] Glenelg issued Durham 'Instructions relative to the Management of the Indian Tribes', 22 August 1838, NAC RG 10, vol 116, Reel C-1147,168655-77 (hereafter Glenelg, 'Instructions to Durham'); however, these did not figure in the published material or materially in the deliberations of the Report.

[66] By the 1830s there had been some local embellishment of this procedure, including, since 1818, the practice (again, born of cost-cutting) of granting annuities rather than a lump sum. See Head to Glenelg, 18 July 1837, NAC MG 11, Q Series, Vol 397, pt 2, Reel C-12623, 375–76.

[67] A good example of the settler community's impatience with philanthropic accommodation of Indian claims is *Report of the Executive Council (Upper Canada) to Legislative Assembly in response to a petition to the House of Commons, United Kingdom*, 1 January 1839, NAC RG 1-E3, Vol 103, Reel C-1204, 50–79.

[68] *The Christian Guardian* (Toronto, 21 March 1838).

[69] Bond Head to Glenelg, 20 August 1836, GBPP 1839 (323) 122–23. The suggestion of an Indian settlement on Great Manitoulin Island had also been made by James Winniett in 1829: Memorandum, ibid, 145. On Winniett see Douglas Leighton, 'Winniett, James' in *Dictionary of Canadian Biography*, vol 7 (University of Toronto 2003–) <http://www.biographi.ca/en/bio/winniett_james_7E.html> accessed 17 March 2014.

[70] To 'talk of treaties with the Mohawk Indians, residing in the heart of one of the most populous districts of Upper Canada, upon lands purchased for them and given to them by the British Government, is much the same, in my humble opinion, as to talk of making a treaty of alliance with the Jews in Duke street or with the French emigrants who have settled in England': John Beverly Robinson, A-G, to Robert Wilmot Horton, Under-Secretary of State for War and Colonies, 14 March 1824, cited in *Sero v Gault* (1921) 64 DLR 327 (Ont SC) [330] (Riddell, J).

Bond Head obtained Great Manitoulin Island itself by Treaty [45, as it became known] from the Mississauga and Ojibway First Nations and Treaty 45½ for the Saugeen tract south of the Bruce Peninsula from the Saugeen Anishinabe First Nation. Although he failed to complete these cessions by the usual forms or with provision for an annuity, he stressed his careful compliance with the underlying principle and sought Colonial Office endorsement.[71] With uncharacteristic sheepishness Bond Head delayed full explanation of his proposal until mid-November, insisting that it was first 'necessary to refute the Idea which so generally exists in England about the Success which has attended the Christianizing and civilizing of the Indians'.[72] He set out three points that he believed 'every Person of sound Mind in this Country who is disinterested in their Conversion, and acquainted with the Indian Character' would agree:

1. That an attempt to make Farmers of the Red Men has been, generally speaking a complete Failure;
2. That congregating them for the Purpose of Civilization has implanted many more Vices than it has eradicated; and, consequently,
3. That the greatest Kindness we can perform towards these intelligent, simple-minded People, is to remove and fortify them as much as possible from all Communication with the Whites.

Glenelg's initial response deferred very cautiously to Bond Head's proposal as that of the imperial man on the spot but the evangelical in him instinctively railed against the Tory suggestion of the imperfectability of his fellow man.[73] At least, Glenelg mused (echoing a proposal not dissimilar to one that would soon be presented—and quickly rejected—for New Zealand), removing Indians to a safe distance would allow the missionaries a zone beyond the corrupting influence of nearby settlement.

Missionaries at home and abroad as well as the Report of the Lower Canada Executive Council (1837)[74] soon attacked Bond Head's proposal. This coincided with the full swing of the Select Committee on Aborigines and foundation of the Aborigines Protection Society (1836). Glenelg quickly backtracked, clearly happy to have his qualms confirmed. He had been impressed by the Lower Canada Report, which criticized removal both in principle as well as practicability, and advocated sedentary agriculturalism under missionary stewardship.[75] The Bond Head proposal quickly lost what scant traction it had.

---

[71] Head to Glenelg, 20 August 1836, GBPP 1839 (323) 122–23: 'Your Lordship will at once perceive that the Document is not in legal Form, but our dealings with the Indians have been only in Equity; and I was therefore anxious to show that the transaction had been equitably explained to them.' Bond Head sent a document with a Wampum attached.

[72] Bond Head to Glenelg, 20 November 1836, ibid, 124–32, 125.

[73] Glenelg to Bond Head, 5 October 1836 and 20 January 1837 (longer, with the beginnings of unease), ibid, 72–74.

[74] 'Report of a Committee of the Executive Council: the Honourable Mr Smith, Mr De Lacy, Mr Stewart and Mr Cochran on Your Excellency's Reference of the 7 October 1836 respecting the Indian Department', enclosure in Gosford to Glenelg, 13 July 1837, ibid, 27–34.

[75] Glenelg to Arthur, 22 August 1838, ibid, 86–89.

Removal as proposed by Bond Head did not become Upper Canada Indian policy. Thereafter the approach of the imperial government was towards creating 'civilized, Christianized, and self-governing native communities seated securely on reserves protected by the British imperial government'.[76] The Lower Canada Report became the mission statement of this goal of 'compact settlements'. These reserves were to be subject to Crown protection but white squatting was widespread and by the early 1840s worsening considerably. With the large influx of immigrants from Britain and Ireland squatting and its associated practices would have been largely unstoppable even by a better resourced, more vigilant, and less complicit Indian Department. These practices were listed before but the likes of booze-running, illegal leasing, and poaching were so rampant in Upper Canada that repetition underlines the shortfall between the avowal of protection and the actuality. Crown land policy in the province remained disorganized and chaotic, its outcomes rather than its legal avowals seeming to reward the initiative of those white settlers who helped themselves.[77] Inevitably this meant that the reserves became whittled down by surrender, sometimes presented to the First Nations as inevitable else they would simply lose the land by the relentless attrition of white squatting and usurpation.

Through the 1830s and into the early 1840s the colonial legal systems of the Canadas continually re-inscribed the imperial view of the legal incapacity of tribes and the role of the Crown as legal protector of their collective interests. This legalism, in all its variety and episodes, showed the underlying concern with sovereign order rather than any validation of inherent aboriginal rights. The appeal to Crown protection was woven through the Select Committee Report (1837), where it was characterized as an executive obligation too important to be left to self-interested settler authorities and laws. The Committee recommended the establishment of Protectorates in Australia, the function exercised under royal warrant by Indian 'superintendents' in British North America since the mid-eighteenth century when relations bore the hallmark of diplomacy.[78]

Bond Head was an arch-representative of this paternal protectionism. Although he was a self-important and verbose figure whose appointment bewildered his contemporaries as well as historians,[79] the over-parted Lieutenant Governor nonetheless had a strong, perhaps overdeveloped, sense of that protection as vital to imperial order. Peter Jones, the Ojibwa Methodist Minister, known to his people as

---

[76] John S Milloy, 'The Early Indian Acts: Developmental Strategy and Constitutional Change' in Ian L Getty and Antoine S Lussier (eds), *As Long as the Sun Shines and the Water Flows: A Reader in Canadian Native Studies* (University of British Columbia Press 1983) 59. See Glenelg using this term in his instructions to Arthur, 22 August 1838 (n 75) 86–89.

[77] Lillian Gates, *Land Policies of Upper Canada* (University of Toronto Press 1968); John Clarke, *Land, Power, and Economics on the Frontier of Upper Canada* (McGill-Queen's Press 2002).

[78] Dorothy V Jones, *License for Empire: Colonialism by Treaty in Early America* (University of Chicago Press 1982); Richard White, *The Middle Ground: Indians, Empires, and Republics in the Great Lakes Region, 1650–1815* (Cambridge University Press 1991). Also see Daniel J Hulsebosch, '*Imperia in Imperio*: The Multiple Constitutions of Empire in New York, 1750–1777' (1998) 16 Law and History Review 319.

[79] Helen Taft Manning and JS Galbraith, 'The Appointment of Francis Bond Head: A New Insight' (1961) 42 Canadian Historical Review 50.

Kahkewãquonãby, tried with colleagues throughout the 1830s to obtain title deeds to his people's land.[80] He was evidently sceptical of the effectiveness of unvarnished Crown protection but too politic to voice this antagonistically lest that excite the forces of dispossession he sought to parry. The provincial Methodists carefully situated their petitioning within a strong loyalist frame.[81] Nonetheless the Methodists' scepticism of Crown competence chafed Bond Head. He responded sarcastically, asking 'who ever heard of Bodies of Indian Hunters in all directions moaning for legal "Documents"?'[82] The Methodists, who had complained of Treaty 45½, might 'just as well declare, that when wild beasts roar at each other it is to complain of the Want among them of Marriage Licences, for Animals understand these "*Documents*" just as well as Indians understand Title Deeds'. Bond Head's reply stressed that the King would 'never consent to the *Intervention* of any Powers between himself and the Red Aborigines of America; and … [t]hat His Majesty would especially object to the Principle of committing the temporal affairs of the Indians to the Ministers of any Christian Denomination whatsoever'.[83] In London Glenelg's tone was more accommodating and reassuring rather than curtly dismissive but no title deeds were forthcoming to bring the legal guarantee of land retention that Jones and his brethren sought.[84] In London and Upper Canada the pressure for land grants was not directed towards an Indian title at large so much as those lands of Christian Indians actually under cultivation (their Lockean property arising from input of labour) and missionary supervision.[85] That did not signify the end of the Methodist quest, although ultimately it was unsuccessful.

The Methodist Ministers, worried by what had occurred with Treaty 45½, were not the only colonial figures who thought about the lack of enforceability of tribal occupancy in local courts. The so-called 'Macaulay Report' (1839) was a moderate and prolix report on Indian policy, like the Darling Report (and the Bagot one soon after) by a legal member of the 'Family Compact', the elite Tory group whose dominance of provincial government was challenged by the 'recent disturbances'. Macaulay was quite clear that the only form of legal instrument that could bind the Crown with regard to tribal occupancy was an Order in Council (prerogative legislation) or patent under seal.[86] The careful practices attending land cessions were likened to the occupancy they extinguished or reduced to reserves in that they too were regarded as unenforceable. As Glenelg instructed Durham (1838), however 'rigidly the Rules respecting the disposal of lands may be observed in general and

---

[80] These overtures had begun in the early 1830s before the Bond Head proceedings gave them extra momentum: Peter Jones to Goderich, 26 July 1831, GBPP 1834 (617) 135.

[81] See eg Egerton Ryerson's letter to Glenelg, 18 April 1838, reprinted in *The Christian Guardian* (Toronto, 9 May 1838) 105.

[82] Memorial of the President and Ministers of the Weslyan Methodist Church, 24 June 1837, GBPP 1839 (323) 152–53.

[83] Bond Head to Glenelg, 24 June 1837, ibid, 149–52, 153–54 (response to Memorialists). And see David Mills, *The Idea of Loyalty in Upper Canada, 1784–1850* (McGill-Queen's University Press 1998).

[84] Glenelg to Arthur, 28 March 1838, GBPP 1839 (323) 81–82, proposing title deeds to Indian land be drawn up but held by the Crown and not issued to the Indians. This proposal was not acted upon.

[85] Notably Alder to Glenelg, 14 December 1837, ibid, 91–92.

[86] Report of 1 April 1839, NAC, RG 10, Vol 117, Reel C-11478, 168711–168868, 128–29.

it is necessary to observe them with the utmost strictness, yet if in any case it is for the clear advantage of the Indians to depart from those rules, the departure ought without hesitation to be sanctioned'.[87] To reiterate, protection of tribal occupancy was a matter of sovereign comportment and not a matter of cognizable legal right, or of endowing that occupancy with legal security. Thus the occasions upon which the non-justiciability of aboriginal occupancy was addressed explicitly, or variations thereon, became occasions for the revalidation of that principle. Property rights were associated with the capacity for civic participation as well as the input of labour and this required attainment of a level of civilization that First Nations of Upper Canada had yet to reach. Transitional tribalism and legal standing as enfranchised individuals were mutually exclusive categories, stages in the progress towards civic identity that could not coexist. The former (tribalism) was an historical (and historiographical) precursor to the latter (full civil liberty).

Glenelg's last full year in office was 1838.[88] Although he had battled under immensely trying circumstances to accommodate his philanthropical disposition inside Ministerial office, it was his response to the Canadian Rebellion that ultimately necessitated his resignation (although the perception of him as languidly dilatory, indecisive, and—so the colonial reformers' propaganda mischievously had it—under the sway of James Stephen did not help). The plight of non-Christian peoples had absorbed his attention not only in relation to British North America but also the indigenous people of New Zealand, Australia, and Cape Colony as well as the indenturing of emancipated labourers in the sugar colonies. Under pressure from his own people and assisted by the fastidiously neutral but highly acute James Stephen he had attempted to steer British policy along a more humanitarian course. But by the end of that decade the noise from those advocating colonial reform and systematic land policies in the white settlement colonies was becoming as loud as the evangelical. The booming voice as well as the economies of the settler colonies would eventually outmatch the evangelical particularly in the years after the Mutiny (1857).

The account given here of the metropolitan and colonial discourse of Crown protection has focused on the legal dimension of the principle of 'unremitted solicitude' as seen through imperial officialdom's deployment of the prerogative towards a special—the tribal—class of the Crown's subjects. In their different ways, Glenelg and Stephen were two important officials supremely sensitive to the range of sources that informed sovereign comportment.

Nonetheless the *jus gentium* (law of nations or nature) was a source of law that appeared in debate during the 1830s about how the Crown should conduct its relations with tribal peoples. The Aboriginal Protection Society's Report on Upper Canada (1839), for example, opened by stating that the 'rights of the Indians &c

---

[87] Glenelg, 'Instructions to Durham' (n 65) 22–23.
[88] Glenelg resigned on 8 February 1839. His resignation caused more sensation in the press than the rumbling surrounding the publication of the Durham Report, which was laid before Parliament on 11 February, large extracts having already appeared in *The Times*. Glenelg's resignation enabled the Aborigines Protection Society to play to the contemporary caricature of him as vague and languidly aloof: Aborigines Protection Society, *Report on the Indians of Upper Canada* (n 12) 22.

in their relations with Great Britain depend on the law of nature and nations; upon the injunctions of Christianity and upon treaties …' The term *jus gentium* or 'the law of nature and nations' did not mean 'international law' in the modern sense so much as describe the universal laws that applied among peoples and princes. It thus described not only how states dealt with one another but how states dealt with peoples who were not subject to them. By the late 1830s any such sourcing of sovereign comportment was disappearing from the Upper Canada debate, as the movement of talk from alliance to subjecthood signalled. The Report of the Executive Council of Upper Canada (1839) quoted earlier reflected fully the self-interested view of the settler community and their tendentious criticism of Crown solicitude as a matter of self-indulgent softness towards Indians, rather than as comportment shaped by its sensitivity to the *jus gentium*.

It must not be thought that the question of sovereign comportment was shaped predominantly by a secular legal discourse of the deployment of Crown prerogative authority. Though the discourse was about the use (abuse and non-use) of Crown legal authority, the framing of this was not regarded as a primarily, much less predominantly, legal one. It is impossible to over-emphasize the impact of religious thought upon political debate, especially during the surge of religious fervour of the 1830s.[89] This fervour had a pervasive influence on the conduct of imperial affairs both in general terms and in the contestation arising in particular settings where missionary societies took particular interest in the fate of tribal peoples, such as southern Africa, New Zealand, and Upper Canada. The philanthropical turn was most significantly structured by doctrines of atonement (the redeeming sacrifice of Christ), and eschatology (the theology of last things, and more broadly of the course and fulfilment of the historical process).[90] Protestant supposition about the responsibility of man for his own redemption (and the centrality of individual good works) wrapped around the belief in monogenesis—the belief that the human family derived from a common ancestor—and stadial history associated with Scottish Enlightenment thinkers on the historical progress of man from hunter-gatherer, to pasturage, to agriculture, to commercial civilization. Likewise the colonial reformers felt compelled to acknowledge and weave Christian duty into their propaganda in justification of systematic colonization, as well as drawing more foundationally upon the political economy of Adam Smith.[91] These positions could blend into all

---

[89] JGA Pocock, 'A Discourse of Sovereignty' in Nicholas Phillipson and Quentin Skinner (eds), *Political Discourse in Early Modern Britain* (Cambridge University Press 1993) 381: 'The great discovery which we constantly make and remake as historians is that English political debate is recurrently subordinate to English political theology; and few of us know one-tenth of the theology available to competently trained divines and laymen among our predecessors.'

[90] Boyd Hilton, *The Age of Atonement: The Influence of Evangelicalism on Social and Economic Thought, 1785–1865* (Clarendon Press 1991), especially 20–21, 379.

[91] See CA Bodelsen, *Studies in Mid-Victorian British Imperialism* (n 29) 18–22, stressing that the colonial reformers were supporters of Empire and close Crown authority, distinguishing them from the later Manchester school of free trade. For instance Edward Gibbon Wakefield published a tract, *Dandeson Coates and the New Zealand Association* (Henry Hooper 1837), which with characteristic craftiness paralleled the prospective systematic colonization of New Zealand and the civilization of Maori with William Penn's Quaker mission in Pennsylvania.

shades and hues, and did so in vigorous debate of such hot contestation because fundamental questions of belief and Christian duty as well as economic prosperity were felt to be at stake.

Quakers dominated the highly influential Aborigines Protection Society founded in 1837 as a response to the deliberations of the Parliamentary Select Committee. The Aborigines Protection Society lobbying and pamphleteering embodied a repositioning and revisioning of Quaker thought in the realm of political action. The Quakers' movement from studied political passivism towards a consciously activist religiosity, in turn, absorbed elements of the more general politicized turn of Christian thought in this period. Under the Quakers' leadership, the Aborigines Protection Society became a particularly prominent though by no means the only influential missionary society. It petitioned Downing Street (both addresses) and published a tract excoriating the Bond Head removal proposal. The *Report on the Indians of Upper Canada* (1839) was scathing of the policy and the unseemly, pushy manner in which Bond Head had formulated and operationalized it. It was 'difficult to decide whether its impolicy be the more reprehensible, or its injustice the more to be reprobated'.[92]

Dandeson Coates, the self-righteous Secretary of the Church Missionary Society, was as much an irritant at the Colonial Office as Wakefield for the colonial reform movement.[93] Several missionary societies exerted pressure in London and Upper Canada on behalf of tribal peoples, the Bond Head removal policy becoming a particular lightning rod. By this inpouring of religious duty into politics, the regeneration of savagery—in both its aboriginal and British forms—turned on the confessional imperative of Christian doctrine, this being the initial act towards the conversion and rededication of the individual and nation towards a Christian future.[94] As the heat generated by the Bond Head proposal showed constantly, the policy of removal was objectionable because it entailed the abnegation of the fundamental Christian precept to see Christ in their fellow man.

If Quakerism had significant influence on the general orientation of imperial practice through its members' lobbying and access to political levers in Britain, then Wesleyanism likewise had an impact through its proven persuasiveness on the ground in Upper Canada. Bond Head's splenetic rejection of the Methodist missionaries' request for land titles was as much a counter-statement of religious and political belief as the request itself. The egalitarian tenets of the low-church dissenting tradition of Methodism with its envisioning of separate but integrated economic development and retained political community appealed to First Nations[95]

---

[92] Ibid, 17.

[93] E Trevor Williams, 'The Colonial Office in the Thirties' (1943) 2 (7) Historical Studies: Australia and New Zealand 141, 158–59. Glenelg and Stephen sat on the Committee of this body but rarely attended meetings and punctiliously kept their dealings with the Society on a professional basis, notwithstanding the colonial reformers continual allegation and innuendo otherwise.

[94] Mark Murphy, 'The Peaceable Kingdom of Nineteenth Century Humanitarianism: The Aborigines Protection Society and New Zealand' (Master's dissertation in Political Science, University of Canterbury 2002).

[95] Catherine Murton Stoehr, 'Salvation from Empire: The Roots of Anishinabe Christianity in Upper Canada, 1650–1840' (PhD dissertation, Department of History Queen's University 2002) 128–30.

as much as it threatened the more established Christianity that Bond Head saw himself as representing. It was vastly more attractive than the hierarchical and rigidifying views of social station and disabling paternalism associated with the High Anglican Toryism of the Family Compact ruling elite and their ilk running the Indian Department.[96] Bond Head was pilloried as shunning the obligation that all Christians owed their fellow unbelieving man and denying their capacity to progress through the stages towards commercial civilization. Even the Methodist missionaries' argument for title deeds was presented in terms of the Christianized Indians having begun the journey towards civilization. It was not an argument that *all* Indian communities should have the deeds to their reserved land (by way of inalienable trust), but one directed selectively towards the legal recognition of those indigenous communities in missionary tutelage and cultivating land.

Questions of sovereign comportment in the imperial settings of the 1830s thus engaged deep-rooted and highly contested Christian belief about the nature of man and his historical destiny at a time when these were a matter of intense, continual public and confessional attention. The heated disagreement over Bond Head's short-lived removal policy in Upper Canada and the Imperial Crown's backtracking in the face of furious protest (the most powerful of which originated from dissenting religious traditions) signified the imperial sensitivity to the spiritual as well as temporal consequences of the exercise of its authority. This intense debate was concerned with the Crown's performance of its multifaceted sovereign duty, a conception of duty that was culturally rather than jurisprudentially formed as to be counterweighed with a strong sense of rights (under a positivist Hohfeldian dichotomy of duty/rights).[97]

From Imperial Order to Colonialist State

By the early 1840s the legal and administrative machinery of the colonialist state was consolidating what the imperial venture had commenced. The Bagot Report (1844) found problems with squatting rife on Indian lands; poor land records; lacklustre administration of band funds by officials; shrinking game and fish resources; and alcohol abuse. It recommended a more centralized control of Indian affairs, including the organization and filing of correspondence and recording of matters such as band lists. Maintaining the theme of the 1830s, it recommended agricultural training and tools for tribe members to replace present-giving and treaty money (annual payments, a cost-saving device initiated in 1818). It portended the system of individualization of title later to be adopted as land policy in settler New Zealand (1862) and the allotment laws of the American west (1887)

[96] Douglas Leighton, 'The Compact Tory as Bureaucrat: Samuel Peter Jarvis and the Indian Department, 1837–1845' (1981) 73 Ontario History 40.

[97] WN Hohfeld, 'Fundamental Legal Conceptions' (1913) 23 Yale Law Journal 16. On the positivist agenda of classification of law into types see also Arthur Corbin, 'Rights and Duties' (1924) Faculty Scholarship Series Paper 2932 <http://digitalcommons.law.yale.edu/fss_papers/2932> accessed 31 March 2014.

by suggesting that Indians be encouraged to adopt individual ownership of land under a special Indian land registry system, to buy and sell plots of land among themselves (but without sales to non-Indians, an initial feature of the later versions).[98] Individualization was a hallmark of Canadian legislation from the Gradual Civilization Act (Upper Canada, 1857)[99] through the concept of enfranchisement (the process by which aboriginals lost their Indian status and became full British subjects). It operated through civic status rather than land ownership. For that reason, and whilst damaging enough, it never made the devastating inroads that occurred in those other jurisdictions.

Through the 1830s we see other features of the colonialist state forming around First Nations of Upper Canada (today's Ontario) as part of the regime of Crown protection and the more minute, group-by-group detailing of their incorporation into an enveloping paradigm of subjecthood. As well as the avowal of Crown protection[100] and the relentless reporting inside the hierarchical apparatus, the correspondence to London responded more punctiliously to the metropolitan demand for more precise information. Increasingly the content of this correspondence went from epistolatory narrative to appendices of tables, ledger accounts, statistics, capitated costing and projections, and censuses.[101] The days of the epic heroic rituals of alliance that the chiefs re-enacted in council and the large-scale gatherings and ceremonialism of present-giving were passing. From allies of the Crown, First Nations had become a distinct class of protected subject, in legal and administrative enclosure on their reserves, sums and numbers in the ledger-sheets and quotidian reporting of the Indian Department, and occasional official enquiry. As the chiefs turned away from the banks of the Niagara River in 1837, their services so sincerely offered yet so embarrassedly unwanted, they were also turning away from a proud history of alliance and careful balance-of-power diplomacy towards a more numbing future of protection and irrelevance.

---

[98] John Leslie 'The Bagot Commission: Developing a Corporate Memory for the Indian Department' (1982) 17 Historical Papers 31. It was Bond Head the arch-advocate of Crown protection who, contra the Methodist Ministers, condemned giving individual Indians title to their land as certain to lead to its loss: Bond Head to Glenelg, 24 June 1837, GBPP 1839 (323) 153–54.

[99] Province of Canada Statutes 1857, Cap xxvi.

[100] WT Murphy, 'The Oldest Social Science? The Epistemic Properties of the Common Law Tradition' (1991) 54 Modern Law Review 182, 185–86: 'The key to the emergence of modern social science, and to the construction of "society" as an object in a quite distinctive way, is the uneven conjunctural appearance of economic theory and statistics. It is in the combination of the two, stretching from the 1830s through today, that "modern" society is brought into existence ... In economics, a new way of imagining the social was brought into existence. With the emergence of modern statistics, a new way of mapping and measuring the coordinates of "society", so understood, came into being. In combination, these new frameworks and images have, in operational terms, displaced the epistemic privileges once claimed by the common law. What results is a new, modern, positivity of the social, in relation to which the epistemic properties of the common law tradition become increasingly opaque.'

[101] For instance Dean Neu, '"Presents" for the "Indians": Land, Colonialism and Accounting in Canada' (2000) 25 Accounting, Organizations and Society 163.

Bibliography

'Alder to Glenelg, 14 December 1837' Great British Parliamentary Papers 1839 (323) 91–92

'Bond Head to Glenelg, 20 August 1836' Great British Parliamentary Papers 1839 (323) 122–23

'Bond Head to Glenelg, 20 November 1836' Great British Parliamentary Papers 1839 (323) 124–32

'Bond Head to Glenelg, 24 June 1837' Great British Parliamentary Papers 1839 (323) 149–52, 153–54 (response to Memorialists)

'Bond Head to Glenelg, 24 June 1837' Great British Parliamentary Papers 1839 (323) 153–54

'Colborne to Aylmer, 19 February 1831' Great British Parliamentary Papers 1834 (617) 130

'Colborne to Murray, 14 October 1830' Great British Parliamentary Papers 1834 (617) 128

'Copies of the regulations lately adopted in the Canadas for granting waste lands in these provinces' Great British Parliamentary Papers 1826–27 (254)

'Dorchester to Simcoe, additional instructions, Indian Department, 26 December 1794' in EA Cruickshank (ed), *The Correspondence of Lieutenant-Governor John Graves Simcoe* (5 vols, Ontario Historical Society 1923–31)

Glenelg, 'Instructions relative to the Management of the Indian Tribes', 22 August 1838, National Archives Canada RG 10, vol 116, Reel C-1147, 168655–77

'Glenelg to Arthur, 22 August 1838' Great British Parliamentary Papers 1839 (323) 86–89

'Glenelg to Arthur, 28 March 1838' Great British Parliamentary Papers 1839 (323) 81–82

'Glenelg to Bond Head, 5 October 1836 and 20 January 1837' Great British Parliamentary Papers 1839 (323) 72–74

'Glenelg to Gosford 14 January 1836' Great British Parliamentary Papers 1835 (474) 1–4

'Goderich to Colborne, 3 April 1832' Great British Parliamentary Papers 1834 (617) 137

'Head to Glenelg, 18 July 1837' National Archives Canada MG 11, Q Series, Vol 397, pt 2, Reel C-12623, 375–76

'Head to Glenelg, 20 August 1836' Great British Parliamentary Papers 1839 (323) 122

'Head to Glenelg, 22 August 1837' Great British Parliamentary Papers 1835 (474) 154

'Hodgkin to Ryerson, 27 April 1838' reprinted in *The Christian Guardian* (Toronto, 9 May 1838)

'Howick to Stewart, 4 February 1832' Great British Parliamentary Papers 1834 (617) 137

'Jarvis, Report of 25 August 1838' 1 April 1839, National Archives Canada RG 10, Vol 117, Reel C-11478, 168711–168868, 9

'Kempt to Murray, 25 January 1830' Great British Parliamentary Papers 1834 (617) 89

'Memorial of the President and Ministers of the Weslyan Methodist Church, 24 June 1837' Great British Parliamentary Papers 1839 (323) 152–53

'Murray to Colborne, 4 December 1828' Great British Parliamentary Papers 1834 (617) 127

'Murray to Kempt, 22 March 1830' Great British Parliamentary Papers 1834 (617) 90

'Peter Jones to Goderich, 26 July 1831' Great British Parliamentary Papers 1834 (617) 135

'Peter Jones to Glenelg, 6 March 1838' Great British Parliamentary Papers 1839 (323) 83

'R Alder to Glenelg, 14 December 1837' Great British Parliamentary Papers 1839 (323) 90–98

'Report of 1 April 1839' National Archives Canada, RG 10, Vol 117, Reel C-11478, 168711–168868, 128–29

'Report of a Committee of the Executive Council: the Honourable Mr Smith, Mr De Lacy, Mr Stewart and Mr Cochran on Your Excellency's Reference of the 7 October 1836 respecting the Indian Department', enclosure in Gosford to Glenelg, 13 July 1837, Great British Parliamentary Papers 1839 (323) 27–34

'Return of Indian Presents for years 1830–33' Great British Parliamentary Papers 1834 (617) 125–26

'Speeches of Chiefs in response to hearing the discontinuation of Indian presents', Manitowaning, 1852, LAC RG 10, vol 198, pt 1, nos 6101–6200, 116405–116408

'Thomas Wilson to RW Hay' 5 January 1832 Great British Parliamentary Papers 1835 (474) 139

Winniett, James, 'Memorandum', Great British Parliamentary Papers 1839 (323) 145

Aborigines Protection Society, *Report on the Indians of Upper Canada by a sub-committee of the Aborigines Protection Society* (W Ball, Arnold 1839) 21

Armstrong, Frederick H and Stagg, Ronald J, 'MacKenzie, William Lyon' in *Dictionary of Canadian Biography*, vol 9 (University of Toronto/Université Laval, 2003–) <http://www.biographi.ca/en/bio/mackenzie_william_lyon_9E.html> accessed 16 December 2014

Babington, Thomas, *A practical view of Christian education in its early stages: to which is added, a letter to a son soon after the close of his education, on the subject of not conforming to the world* (John Hatchard & Son 1826)

Belich, James, *Replenishing the Earth: The Settler Revolution and the Rise of the Anglo-World, 1783–1939* (Oxford University Press 2009)

Bell, Duncan, 'John Stuart Mill on colonies' (2010) 38 Political Theory 34

Benton, Lauren, 'Abolition and Imperial Law, 1790–1820' (2011) 39 Journal of Imperial and Commonwealth History 355

Binnema, Theodore and Hutchings, Kevin, 'The Emigrant and the Noble Savage: Sir Francis Bond Head's Romantic Approach to Aboriginal Policy in Upper Canada, 1836–1838' (2005) 39 Journal of Canadian Studies 115

Bodelsen, CA, *Studies in Mid-Victorian British Imperialism* (reprint of 1924 edn, Heinemann 1960)

Burroughs, Peter, 'Wakefield and the Ripon Land Regulations of 1831' (1965) 11 Historical Studies 452–66

Burroughs, Peter, *Britain and Australia 1831–1855: A Study in Imperial Relations and Crown Land Administration* (Clarendon Press 1967)

Cannadine, David, *Ornamentalism: How the British Saw their Empire* (Allen Lane 2001)

Clarke, John, *Land, Power, and Economics on the Frontier of Upper Canada* (McGill-Queen's Press 2002)

Corbin, Arthur, 'Rights and Duties' (1924) Faculty Scholarship Series Paper 2932 <http://digitalcommons.law.yale.edu/fss_papers/2932> accessed 31 March 2014

Curtis, Bruce, 'The "Most Splendid Pageant Ever Seen": Grandeur, the Domestic, and Condescension in Lord Durham's Political Theatre' (2008) 89 Canadian Historical Review 55

Ellingson, Ter, *The Myth of the Noble Savage* (University of California Press 2001)

Enclosure in Memorial to the Colonial Office (not dated, received 10 April 1837), Great British Parliamentary Papers 1839 (323) 99–100

Evans, James, 'Diary Entries' in *The Christian Guardian* (Toronto, 28 September 1836)

Evans, James, 'Diary Entries' in *The Christian Guardian* (Toronto, 2 November 1836)

Evans, James, 'Diary Entries' in *The Christian Guardian* (Toronto, 2 January 1837)

Executive Council (Upper Canada) Report, 1 January 1839, National Archives Canada RG 1-E3, Vol 103, Reel C-1204, 50–79, 56

Ford, Lisa, *Settler Sovereignty: Jurisdiction and Indigenous People in America and Australia, 1788–1836* (Harvard University Press 2011)

Ford, Lisa, *Settler Sovereignty: Jurisdiction and Indigenous People in America and Australia, 1788–1836* (Harvard University Press 2010)

Francis, Mark, 'The Nineteenth-Century Theory of Sovereignty and Thomas Hobbes' (1980) 1 History of Political Thought 517

Francis, Mark, *Governors and Settlers: Images of Authority in the British Colonies, 1820–60* (Palgrave Macmillan 1992)

Gates, Lillian, *Land Policies of Upper Canada* (University of Toronto Press 1968)

GS French, 'Alder, Robert' in *Dictionary of Canadian Biography*, vol 10 (University of Toronto 2003–) <http://www.biographi.ca/en/bio/alder_robert_10E.html> accessed 8 April 2014

Harring, Sidney, *White Man's Law: Native People in Nineteenth-Century Canadian Jurisprudence* (Osgoode Society for Canadian Legal History 1998)

Head, Bond, *The Emigrant* (John Murray 1846)

Heartfield, James, *The Aborigines Protection Society: Humanitarian intervention in Australia, New Zealand, Fiji, Canada, South Africa, and the Congo, 1836–1909* (Hurst and Co 2011)

Hickford, Mark, *Lords of the Land: Indigenous Property Rights and the Jurisprudence of Empire* (Oxford University Press 2012)

Hickford, Mark, *The Lords of the Land: Indigenous Property Rights and the Jurisprudence of Empire* (Oxford University Press 2011)

Hilton, Boyd, *The Age of Atonement: The Influence of Evangelicalism on Social and Economic Thought, 1785–1865* (Clarendon Press 1991)

Hohfeld, WN, 'Fundamental Legal Conceptions' (1913) 23 Yale Law Journal 16

Hulsebosch, Daniel J, '*Imperia in Imperio*: The Multiple Constitutions of Empire in New York, 1750–1777' (1998) 16 Law and History Review 319

Johnson, JK, *In Duty Bound: Men, Women and the State in Upper Canada, 1783–1841* (McGill-Queen's University Press 2014)

Jones, Dorothy V, *License for Empire: Colonialism by Treaty in Early America* (University of Chicago Press 1982)

Leighton, Douglas, 'The Compact Tory as Bureaucrat: Samuel Peter Jarvis and the Indian Department, 1837–1845' (1981) 73 Ontario History 40

Leighton, Douglas, 'Winniett, James' in *Dictionary of Canadian Biography*, vol 7 (University of Toronto 2003–) <http://www.biographi.ca/en/bio/winniett_james_7E.html> accessed March 17 2014

Leslie, John, 'The Bagot Commission: Developing a Corporate Memory for the Indian Department' (1982) 17 Historical Papers 31

Macaulay, JB, 'Report on Indian Affairs', 1 April 1839, National Archives Canada RG 10, Vol 117, Reel C-11478, 168711–168868, 128–29

MacKay, RA, 'The political ideas of William Lyon MacKenzie' (1937) 3 Canadian Journal of Economics and Political Science 1

Manning, Helen Taft and Galbraith, JS, 'The Appointment of Francis Bond Head: A New Insight' (1961) 42 Canadian Historical Review 50

Manning, Helen Taft, 'Who Ran the British Empire 1830–1850?' (1965) 5 Journal of British Studies 88

Martin, Ged, *The Durham Report and British Policy: A Critical Essay* (Cambridge University Press 1972)

McHugh, PG, *Aboriginal Societies and the Common Law* (Oxford University Press 2004)

McNab, David, *Circles of Time: Aboriginal Land Rights and Resistance in Ontario* (Wilfrid Laurier University Press 1999)

Mellor, George, *British Imperial Trusteeship, 1783–1850* (Faber & Faber 1951)

Mill, John Stuart, *The Collected Works of John Stuart Mill, Volume XIX—Essays on Politics and Society Part II* (John M Robson ed, Toronto: University of Toronto Press, London: Routledge and Kegan Paul 1977)

Milloy, John S, 'The Early Indian Acts: Developmental Strategy and Constitutional Change' in Ian L Getty and Antoine S Lussier (eds), *As Long as the Sun Shines and the Water Flows: A Reader in Canadian Native Studies* (University of British Columbia Press 1983)

Mills, David, *The Idea of Loyalty in Upper Canada, 1784–1850* (McGill-Queen's University Press 1998)

Motte, Standish, *Outline of a system of legislation, for securing protection to the Aboriginal inhabitants of all the countries colonized by Great Britain, extending to them political and social rights, ameliorating their condition, and promoting their civilization /drawn up at the request of the Committee of The Aborigines Protection Society* (John Murray 1840)

Mukherjee, Mithi, 'Justice, War, and the Imperium: India and Britain in Edmund Burke's Prosecutorial Speeches in the Impeachment Trial of Warren Hastings' (2005) 23 Law and History Review 589

Murphy, Mark, 'The Peaceable Kingdom of Nineteenth Century Humanitarianism: The Aborigines Protection Society and New Zealand' (Master's dissertation in Political Science, University of Canterbury 2002)

Murphy, WT, 'The Oldest Social Science? The Epistemic Properties of the Common Law Tradition' (1991) 54 Modern Law Review 182

Myers, Frank A (ed), *1836 Mission Tour of Lake Huron* (Manitoulin Historical Society 1955)

Native Trust Office (New Zealand), *Native Reserves in Wellington and Nelson under the control of the Native Trustee (Appendices to Journal of the House of Representatives)* 1929, Session I, Paper G-01 (Government Printer 1929)

Neu, Dean, ' "Presents" for the "Indians": Land, Colonialism and Accounting in Canada' (2000) 25 Accounting, Organizations and Society 163

Pedersen, Susan, 'Hannah More Meets Simple Simon: Tracts, Chapbooks, and Popular Culture in Late Eighteenth-century England' (1986) 25 Journal of British Studies 84

Pocock, JGA, 'A Discourse of Sovereignty' in Nicholas Phillipson and Quentin Skinner (eds), *Political Discourse in Early Modern Britain* (Cambridge University Press 1993)

Province of Canada Statutes 1857

Report of the Executive Council (Upper Canada) to Legislative Assembly in response to a petition to the House of Commons, United Kingdom, 1 January 1839, National Archives Canada RG 1-E3, Vol 103, Reel C-1204, 50–79

Report of the Select Committee (Upper Canada) on the State of the Province, 30 April 1839, Great British Parliamentary Papers 1839 (289) 8–31

Report of the Select Committee on Colonial Military Expenditure, Great British Parliamentary Papers 1835 (474)

Richter, Daniel, 'Native Peoples of North America and the Eighteenth-Century British Empire' in *The Oxford History of the British Empire 2: The Eighteenth Century* (Oxford University Press 1998)

Ryerson, Egerton, 'Letter to Glenelg, 18 April 1838', reprinted in *The Christian Guardian* (Toronto, 9 May 1838)

Select Committee on Aborigines, *Report from the Select Committee on Aborigines (British settlements); with the minutes of evidence, appendix and index*, Evidence (Saxe Bannister), Great British Parliamentary Papers 1837 (425) 15

Sero v Gault (1921) 64 DLR 327 (Ont SC)

Shaw, AGL, 'British Attitudes towards the Colonies, 1820–1850' (1969) 9 Journal of British Studies 71

Smits, Katherine, 'John Stuart Mill on the antipodes: settler violence against indigenous peoples and the legitimacy of colonial rule' (2008) 54 Australian Journal of Politics and History 1

Sparks, Randy J, *On Jordan's Stormy Banks: Evangelicalism in Mississippi, 1776–1876* (University of Georgia Press 1994)

Stephen, James, 'Minute to Vernon Smith, 28 July 1840' CO209/4, 343–44

Stoehr, Catherine Murton, 'Salvation from Empire: The Roots of Anishinabe Christianity in Upper Canada, 1650–1840' (PhD dissertation, Department of History Queen's University 2002)

The Christian Guardian (Toronto, 21 March 1838)

Wakefield, Edward Gibbon, *Dandeson Coates and the New Zealand Association* (Henry Hooper 1837)

Ward, Damen, 'Constructing British Authority in Australasia: Charles Cooper and the Legal Status of Aborigines in the South Australian Supreme Court, *c.*1840–60' (2006) 34 Journal of Imperial and Commonwealth History 483

Watson, Blake, 'The Impact of the American Doctrine of Discovery on Native Land Rights in Australia, Canada, and New Zealand' (2011) 34 Seattle University Law Review 507

Wawanosh, Chief Joshua, 'Address to the Chippeway Indians' *The Christian Guardian* (Toronto, 5 July 1836)

Weaver, John C, *The Great Land Rush and the Making of the Modern World 1650–1900* (McGill-Queens University Press 2003)

White, Richard, *The Middle Ground: Indians, Empires, and Republics in the Great Lakes Region, 1650–1815* (Cambridge University Press 1991)

Williams, E Trevor, 'The Colonial Office in the Thirties' (1943) 2 (7) Historical Studies: Australia and New Zealand 141

Williams, Robert A, *The American Indian in Western Legal Thought: The Discourses of Conquest* (Oxford University Press 1992)

Windler, Christian, 'Towards the Empire of a "Civilizing Nation": The French Revolution and Its Impact on Relations with the Ottoman Regencies in the Maghreb', Chapter 9 in this volume

Young, DM, *The Colonial Office in the Early Nineteenth Century* (Longman Paul 1961)

11

Territory, Sovereignty, and the Construction of the Colonial Space

*Luigi Nuzzo**

Defining Sovereignty

Looking at international law from a spatial perspective it is easy to affirm that in the nineteenth century international law was still far from being identified with a universal positive law. As a matter of fact, due to its historical dimension, it could be described as exclusively the law of those populations that shared a common past, had common values, and followed the same Christian religion. On a political and legal level that meant that only the Western states were legitimate producers of international law, and that the 'modern' international law was based on the legal relationships between states recognizing themselves as sovereign legal subjects.[1] On the one hand sovereignty was a necessary element of the state; on the other hand it could be thought of only in connection with a territory and a population based on it. As the German doctrine explained well during the second half of the nineteenth century, the concept of people identified itself with the state. This meant that its institutional existence was possible only within the state and as an object of its *imperium*. At the same time the territory existed only as an element of spatial qualification of state sovereignty. In other words the state could not be conceived without its own territory within which it exercised its power in an absolute and exclusive way.[2]

But, as Bluntschli wrote in his handbook on international law, if sovereignty, once applied to a state territory, could be defined as territorial sovereignty (*Gebiethoheit*),

* This chapter is part of a larger project entitled *Space, Time and Law in a Global City: Tianjin 1900–1945*, that has been developed during the academic year 2014–15 at the Institute of International Law and Justice at the New York University School of Law within the Hauser Global Fellow Program. The project received a grant from the Fondazione Monte dei Paschi di Siena.

[1] Luigi Nuzzo, *Origini di una scienza: Diritto internazionale e colonialismo nel XIX secolo* (Vittorio Klostermann 2012).

[2] Paul Laband, *Das Staatsrecht des Deutschen Reiches* (5th edn, Mohr 1911) vol 1 172; Georg Jellinek, *Allgemeine Staatslehre* (3rd edn, Scientia 1966) 355–58; Maurizio Fioravanti, *Giuristi e costituzione nell'Ottocento tedesco* (Giuffrè 1979); Michael Stolleis, *Geschichte des öffentlichen Rechts in Deutschland* (Beck 1989) vol 2.

International Law and Empire: Historical Explorations. First Edition. Martti Koskenniemi, Walter Rech, and Manuel Jiménez Fonseca. © Martti Koskenniemi, Walter Rech, and Manuel Jiménez Fonseca 2016. Published 2016 by Oxford University Press.

what kind of right had the state to its **own territory**? What legal relationship linked state and territory?

Moving from the realm of private law, influenced by the methodological renewal of Savigny and involved in the great project of legal construction of the German state from an organicist point of view, jurists such as Bluntschli, Gerber, and later Laband had no doubt: the territory was not only an essential element for the life of the state but it was also the object of a *staatsrechtlichen Staatsrechts*.[3] 'The territorial sovereignty belongs to public law, such as the property belongs to private law', and as well as it is fixed by the right of property in the private law, the state had a full and exclusive *dominium* over its territory.[4] Critical voices were not lacking. Just two years after the publication of Gerber's *Grundzüge*, Carl Victor von Fricker, in public discourse held at the University of Tübingen in honour of Karl von Württemberg, affirmed that 'every representation of the national territory as object of the state are false or wrong'.[5] According to Fricker any analogy with private law was no longer possible. The relationship between *res* and owner was completely different from the relationship between territory and state as a deep difference existed between the human relationships required to own a thing and the state relationships concerning a territory. The state *imperium* was not a projection of the concept of *dominium* in the field of public law, and consequently it was no more possible to consider the territory as a thing on which the state had a real right (*ius in re*). As a matter of fact, if territory was correctly qualified as a necessary element of the state, it couldn't contemporaneously be a simple object. The territory was the state. Identifying itself with the state, it spatially qualified the sphere of state sovereignty and worked as medium for the identification between state and *Volk*, and for the exercise of its *imperium* over the people living within. As Fricker wrote, territory was 'ein Moment in Wesen des Staats, seine räumliche Undurchdringlichkeit'.[6]

Fricker's theory was successful. In Germany, despite the criticisms of international lawyers seduced by positivism and intolerant towards the organicism of the old theory of the state, it was taken up and developed by stars of public law such as Preuss and Jellinek, while in Italy it was revived by Santi Romano and used in the process of the transformation of the liberal rule of law into the administrative state.

It is not my aim to reconstruct the rich doctrinal debate in Germany and Italy over the relationship between state and territory and the nature of the state's right over the territory. These short reflections are the starting point for an analysis of the construction process of the non-Western space. Linking sovereignty, territory, and subjects, the European public lawyers were able to represent the state space as a homogeneous and pacified space, and entrusted to international lawyers the hard task of coordinating the different spatialities of the Western states, finding an objective principle that could hold back their will. According to its historical

---

[3] Carl Friedrich Gerber, *Grundzüge eines Systems des deutschen Statsrechts* (Tauchnitz 1865) 66; Laband, *Das Staatsrecht des Deutschen Reiches* (n 2) 164.

[4] Johann Caspar Bluntschli, *Das moderne Völkerrecht der civilisirten Staaten als Rechtsbuch dargestellt* (Beck 1868) 164.

[5] Carl Victor von Fricker, *Vom Staatsgebiet* (Fues 1867) 17.   [6] Ibid.

dimension, at the midway point of the nineteenth century international law, it could not be considered merely an *äussere Staatsrecht* or be reduced to diplomatic practice. On the contrary it was a law ruled by public opinion and subject to the judgement of history. Its origins dated back to the state of necessity that pre-existed states' building and presupposed the existence of an international community that shared the same religion and the same values.[7] This former dimension of necessity from which international law descended made resort to formal sanction useless, and imposed only a few simple rules of civilization as conditions for access and permanence. At the same time, finding in the international community the necessary principle from which it was possible to reconstruct and represent international law in an organic way, international lawyers were compelled to interrogate themselves about the spatial dimension of the international community and the sphere of effectiveness of its law. The international law was a Christian and European law. It originated from the meeting of three different elements: Catholicism, feudalism and the Crusades, and Roman law. Following the Reformation the principle of territorial sovereignty and equality between states provided this law with a new base and allowed the creation of a common legal, moral, and economic space. International law formed and defended its boundaries, referring to a common legal consciousness and to an increasingly strong sense of belonging to a cohesive and affordable community, entrusting the filter of Christianity with the evaluation of the civilization of a nation.

In the following years the selected international lawyers of the *Institut de droit international* reintroduced the image of international law as not directly related to the sovereignty of single states, located its foundation in the legal conscience of the civilized and Christian nations, and claimed the exclusivity of its interpretation. Similarly, the relevance acquired by the concept of civilization did not automatically produce deep changes within the discourse of international law. On the one hand it contributed with its opposite, the concept of savagery, to the process of construction and self-representation of Western identity.[8] On the other hand, towards the end of the century it made new and deeper relations between peoples possible and spread awareness that the satisfaction of national interests meant reinforcement of trade, the creation of a network of mutual dependencies, and, finally, the realization of the economic reasons of the community.[9] The international society of European, civil, and Christian states was now also an *Interessengemeinschaft* based on the objective principle of the solidarity of interests and open to those who recognized or adapted to its moral, religious, legal, political, and economic standards.[10]

---

[7] August W Heffter, *Das europäische Recht der Gegenwart* (8th edn, Schroede 1882) 3.

[8] Jörg Fisch, 'Zivilisation, Kultur' in Otto Brunner, Werner Conze, Reinhart Koselleck (eds), *Geschichtliche Grundbegriffe: Historische Lexikon zur politisch-sozialen Sprache in Deutschland* (Klett Cotta 1992) vol 7 669.

[9] Erich Kaufmann, *Das Wesen des Völkerrechts und die clausola rebus sic stantibus: Eine rechtsphilosophische Studie zum Rechts-, Staats- und Vertragsbegriffe* (Scientia 1964) 190ff; Henry Bonfils, *Manuel de droit international public (droit des gens)* (Rousseau 1894) 4–7.

[10] Frantz von Liszt, *Völkerrecht systematisch dargestellt* (9th edn, Haering 1913) 2.

Oriental Interlude

The state invented by the public lawyers of the nineteenth century was not only the measuring unit of the Western spatiality and the sole legitimized producer of international law, but also the filter through which it was possible to look at non-Western political subjects for evaluating their level of civilization. This process of evaluation was performed on an international level as well as a national one. In the first case it was necessary for the subject to satisfy the principle of reciprocity, conforming its own actions to the laws and practice of the (Western) international community. In the second case a sufficient level of civilization required a full exercise of sovereignty over a subject's territory and population, abolition of slavery, and the guarantee of some fundamental rights (first of all life, liberty, property) to citizens and foreigners.

According to these criteria international lawyers considered non-Western states such as the Ottoman Empire, China, and Japan not fully civilized and refused to recognize them as subjects of international law. Their backwardness, due first of all to historical reasons, was still far from being overcome. Once again, international law was a product of European Christendom whose goals of free trade and the community of nations had been realized thanks to the sense of brotherhood inspired by Christianity.[11]

The lack of any Christian openness in the Eastern peoples towards their neighbours produced isolation and rejection of the Other and consequently the absence of any form of international trade. Legislative 'anomalies', legal processes not able to guarantee legal certainty and the protection of the defendant, as well as different cultural traditions equally distant from Western sensibilities deepened the differences and sharpened the distrust of Europe and the United States towards a world they did not know and could not understand. A general transfer of the whole Western legal system, therefore, not only seemed impractical to international lawyers but could not have been realized in a uniform manner in all the Eastern countries. Because of the deep differences existing between each state the construction of international relations on a plane of perfect equality and reciprocity had to be subjected to a careful examination of the welfare state, the forms of government, the legal and judicial system, and religion.[12]

Thus, what could be done? On a theoretical level international lawyers recovered the old natural law. Based on universal principles of the Christian West, and asking for humanity as a minimum condition for access, it still had a universal dimension that international positive law could not hold, and was able to recompose in a global legal order the differences produced by Christianity and civilization.

---

[11] David Dudley Field, 'De la possibilité d'appliquer le droit international européen aux nations orientales' (1875) 7 Revue du droit international et législation comparée 659.

[12] A Krauel, 'Applicabilité du droit des gens européen à la Chine' (1875) 9 Revue du droit international et de législation comparée 387.

At the same time, with a 'little help' from diplomacy, they found in the consular law the best instrument to protect Western economic interests and re-territorialize the Eastern space without breaking the representation of a positive international law.

As a matter of fact the treaties signed with Eastern states during the nineteenth century and the political debate that was associated with their stipulation required legal doctrine to acknowledge the state of transformation happening in the field of international relations. They also give us important information about the difficulties international lawyers engaged with in the attempt to give form to the system of international law, reconciling diplomatic practice and scientific reflection.

The treaty between the Ottoman Empire and the Western Powers signed in Paris in 1856 is a good example. As is well known, in this agreement the Ottoman Empire was admitted 'to participate in the advantages of the public law and concert of Europe' and the signatories' engaged themselves 'to respect the territorial integrity of the Ottoman Empire'. As recently underlined, this cannot be seen as the first sign of the overcoming of the old Christian international law and the introduction of a universal international law founded on the idea of civilization.[13] The Ottoman Empire was part of the European political system, but the different level of civilization and religious differences excluded it from the select circle of producers of international laws, and thus justified the suspension of fundamental principles of international law towards it. The necessity to protect the Christian minorities inside the Ottoman Empire and the impossibility of leaving Western citizens to the 'arbitrary acts' of its justice system justified the limitation of Ottoman sovereignty and the introduction of a new legal regime that the international lawyers defined as exceptional. It was an incredibly paradoxical situation: a new feeling of universalism and humanitarianism led international lawyers to desire the application of international law beyond the Christian West, but also to limit the internal sovereignty of Eastern states in defence of Western economic interests and the Christian minorities. This legitimated, in the first case, the application of consular law and, in the second, military intervention. In both cases it was an exceptional response and in both cases the victim was the same: the principle of territorial sovereignty. The deficit of Christianity (and therefore of civilization) that marked the legal and political life in the Ottoman Empire required diplomats and international lawyers to break the relationship between sovereignty, subject, and territory, and made possible that spaces and subjects within the Ottoman territory were placed outside its *imperium*. Outside the borders of Western states the efficacy of the principle of the territorial sovereignty of law faded away, allowing that 'the territorial integrity of the Ottoman Empire' as well as its Christian principalities was entrusted to the *guarantee* of the European Concert.[14]

---

[13] Traité de Paix signé à Paris le 30 mars 1856 (Imprimerie Royale 1856) Article 7. See Nuzzo, *Origini* (n 1) 52–66, 61–77; and now broadly Eliana Augusti, *Questioni di Oriente: Europa e impero ottomano nel diritto internazionale dell'Ottocento* (Edizioni Scientifiche Italiane 2013).

[14] One the different meaning of *garantie* see Milan Milosevitch, *Les Traités de garantie au XIX siècle: Étude de droit international et d'histoire diplomatique* (Rousseau 1888) 15–21, 336–42.

This meant a formal recognition of the different ways through which the concept of sovereignty worked in the Ottoman Empire. As is well known, Wallachia, Moldavia, Serbia, Montenegro, and Bulgaria were under the *suzeraineté* of the Porte.[15] According to Loiseau this term, 'aussi étrange comme cette espèce de seigneuire est absurd', came from French feudal law and originally specified only a personal feudal superiority. Yet over time it had become a *puissance publique* that included the exercise of jurisdictional rights and differed from sovereignty merely for having been usurped by vassals against their sovereign.[16] Reconsidered in modern times and within the international order this ambiguous term was used to describe different kinds of relationships of subjection whose common element was a transfer of external sovereignty from the vassal state to the suzerain. The latter, in other words, did not exercise full sovereignty over the subordinate state, but a 'certain supremacy' or a 'limited sovereignty' that normally gave the right to decide foreign policy, to receive an annual tribute, and to exercise military control. The power of interference did not, however, arrive to legitimize the rule of the internal administration that followed to be entrusted to the vassal state.[17]

According to the Western international lawyers, it was a semi-sovereign state.[18] It represented a hybrid form of political subject in which coexisted an *innere Selbständigkeit* that revealed itself as legislative, jurisdictional, and administrative autonomy, and the absence of a full *äussere Unabhängigkeit*. This represented another paradoxical situation and a *vulnus* of modern international law. On the one hand the dualism in the exercise of the sovereignty was not compatible with the unity and the indivisibility of sovereignty. On the other the aspiration of the subjected state to obtain full independence and the will of the suzerain to maintain its control led inevitably to a permanent state of war. 'The bloody wars fought for the independence of the Danubian Principalities and the ruinous consequences that followed the semi-sovereignty of the states subjected to Turkey', Fiore noted, 'are an eloquent instruction.'[19]

Fiore rightly referred to the Christian principalities of the Balkans as an example of semi-sovereign states, demonstrating the exceptionality of any limitation of sovereignty in international law, but, as with his colleagues, he omitted to note that the diplomatic solution adopted at Paris in 1856 produced on a theoretical level a still more paradoxical situation, if possible. The European powers, as a matter of fact, introduced in an official document their obligation to guarantee the

[15] Augusti, *Questioni di Oriente* (n 13) 15–29.

[16] Charles Loiseau, *Traité des seigneurs* (chez Abel l'Angelier 1609) 19.

[17] Conrad Bornhak, *Einseitige Ahängigkeitsverhältnisse unter den modernen Staaten* (Duncker & Humblot 1896); M Boghitchiévitch, *Halbsouveranität: Administrative und politische Autonomie seit dem Pariser Vertrag* (Springer 1903).

[18] Heffter, *Das europäische Recht* (n 7) 48–51; Bluntschli, *Das moderne Völkerrecht* (n 4) 88–89; Fyodor Fyodorovich Martens, *Völkerrecht: Das internationale Recht der civilisirten Nationen systematisch dargestellt* (Carl Bergbohm tr, Weidmann 1883) vol 1 250–52; Bonfils, *Manuel de droit international public* (n 9) 102.

[19] Pasquale Fiore, *Il diritto internazionale codificato e la sua sanzione giuridica* (Unione Tipografico Editrice 1900) 143.

independence and entirety of the Ottoman Empire (Article 7) and simultaneously stated that Wallachia and Moldavia would continue to enjoy the previous privileges and immunities under the suzerainty of Ottoman Empire and their guarantee (Article 22). Through a semantic slide the sovereignty that the treaty of Adrianopolis still recognized to the Ottoman Empire over Moldavia and Wallachia lost intensity and became merely suzerainty.[20] Consequently the territory of the two principalities became the object of three different kinds of power: the internal autonomy of its government, the suzerainty of Ottoman Empire, and the guarantee of the European Concert. On the other hand Moldavia and Wallachia were in substance fully independent states under the international guarantee of European powers.[21]

The territorial entirety of the Ottoman Empire and the non-interference in its internal affairs was not, therefore, an absolute and unilateral obligation. On the contrary, it was an effect of a contract between the Porte and the European powers: a simple guarantee subordinated to the fulfilment of the promise to improve the conditions of Christian subjects. But it was also a guarantee that conferred to the European powers a collective right to claim the fulfilment of the commitment and, otherwise considering the contract concluded, to act directly in the defence of Christians subjects.[22] Turkey was now compelled to observe European public law within its territory and to entrust to that law the governance of its Christian subjects.

Admitted to the advantages of the European public law the Porte had assumed, in front of the civilized world, a heavy task. It was not a 'normal' country and thus could not ask Europe to observe those rules that it was obliged to follow. Humanitarian reasoning pushed the European powers to defend the 'human rights' of Christian minorities and also justified their intervention into the internal affairs of a sovereign state.[23]

In the same way, its admission to the benefits of the *ius publicum europaeum* did not lead to the abrogation of the capitulations' system. Although the Ottoman Empire had submitted an explicit request for its abolition and the same plenipotentiaries of the European powers had recognized that—according to Article 7 of the Treaty—the reasons still able to justify a jurisdiction of the Western consuls failed, the Congress of Paris did not go beyond the assumption of a formal commitment to revise the ancient privileges. The Western Powers entrusted to a future conference, to be held in Istanbul but never to occur, the revision of the capitulations.[24] 'What

---

[20] 'Traité séparé entre la Russie et la Porte relatif aux principautés de Moldavie et de Valachie, (signed 2–14 September 1829)' in Georg Friederich von Martens and Friederich Saalfeld (eds), *Nouveau Recueil de Traites* (Dieterich 1831) vol 8, 151.

[21] Bornhak, *Einseitige Ahängigkeitsverhältnisse* (n 17) 56.

[22] Gustav Rolin-Jaequemyns, 'Le droit international et la phase actuelle de la Question d'Orient' (1876) 8 Revue du droit international et de législation comparée 293.

[23] Bluntschli, *Das moderne Völkerrecht* (n 4) 268; see Eliana Augusti, 'L'intervento europeo in Oriente nel XIX secolo: storia contesa di un istituto controverso' in Luigi Nuzzo and Milos Vec (eds), *Constructing International Law: The Birth of a Discipline* (Vittorio Klostermann 2012) 277.

[24] Protocole no XIV (Séance du 25 mars 1856), attachment to Traité de Paix (n 13) 98–108; see also the observations of Fyodor Fyodorovich Martens, *Das Consularwesen und die Consularjurisdiction im Orient* (Weidmansche Buchhandlung 1874) 503–09.

did the Porte guarantee', Fedozzi asked himself, 'to protect the foreigners and their property on its territory? What did the Turkish government promise in place of the capitulations and treaties signed with the Christian states?'[25]

These were rhetorical questions to which lawyers could not respond positively without questioning both the network privileges of the capitulations built over the past two centuries and the economic reasoning and religious representations on which they were based.[26] In the Ottoman Empire the overlap between the religious level and law and the connection between church and state had allowed the construction of a pluralistic legal system based on a variety of regulatory and jurisdictional levels. Within its boundaries litigations between non-Muslim subjects, pagans, Jews, or Christians (*rayas*) were excluded from the jurisdiction of the Ottoman judicial authorities and from the observance of Muslim law. These were instead entrusted to the leaders and to the legal provisions of the respective communities.

Motivations and interests of economic nature, however, had led European merchants to formalize—in special texts known as capitulations—guarantees, immunities, and privileges which the sultans had granted them since the fifteenth and sixteenth century for the development of commercial activities in the territories of the empire. Three centuries later, not only did the capitulations continue to be in use but, it being impossible to recognize a full international legal subjectivity to Turkey, European powers entrusted the legal relations and protection of Western interests in the East to these merchants. They were acts unilaterally granted by the sultan that ensured to the foreign beneficiaries freedom of religion, commerce, and residence, tax exemptions, the possibility to be judged by their own consuls, the presence of the consul of the defendant during the criminal process, and, finally, imposed upon the Ottoman authorities a requirement to proceed with the search of a domicile of a Western citizen only after giving notice to the consuls.

As an expression of the generosity of the sovereign, the capitulations were spontaneous, temporary, and revocable acts. This, on the one hand, pushed the European powers to ask for continual updates in order to confirm the concessions previously bestowed or to introduce additional privileges. On the other hand it pushed them to transfuse guarantees, immunities, and rights contained in the capitulations into real bilateral treaties able to secure the benefits.[27]

---

[25] Francesco Contuzzi, *Trattato teorico-pratico di diritto consolare e diplomatico nei raffronti coi Codici (civile, commerciale, penale e giudiziario) e con le convenzioni in vigore* (Utet 1910) vol 1 566.

[26] See Gustave Pélissie du Rausas, *Le regime des capitulations dans l'empire ottoman* (Rousseau 1902) vol 1 1; more recently, Herbert J Liebensy, 'The Development of Western Judicial Privileges' in Majid Khadduri and Herbert Liebensy (eds), *Law in the Middle East* (Middle East Institute 1955) vol 1.

[27] The capitulation of 28 May 1740 between Louis XVI and Mahmud I is the archetype to which all agreements between the Porte and the Western powers referred. The text is edited in Jules De Clercq, *Recueil des Traités de la France* (Durand et Pedone Lauriel 1880) vol 1 21. Particularly useful is Louis-Joseph-Delphin Féraud-Giraud, *De la juridiction française dans les échelles du levant et de barbarie: Étude sur la condition légale des étrangers dans le pays hors chrétienté* (Thorin 1866); Louis-Joseph-Delphin

Since the beginning of the nineteenth century it became clear that it was not possible to entrust the defence of Western citizens only to a regime of capitulations. Generous concessions of a 'capricious' sultan had to find a more reliable foundation in the will of the sovereign and the articles of a treaty. It was necessary to rethink the relationship between sovereignty, territory, and subject, and to admit that outside the boundaries of the Christian West the principle of the territoriality of a sovereign state, the modern conquest of the European nations, could not retain its unconditional application.

The impossibility of leaving Western citizens to the abuses of an unreliable judiciary made it necessary to limit the sovereignty of the Eastern states. An old legal fiction, extraterritoriality, enabled the Western diplomacy to achieve this goal. Viewed with suspicion by international lawyers, outside the boundaries of the West it was elevated to the legal principle of a new colonial order. It allowed them to deterritorialize western citizens who found themselves in the Eastern countries, freeing them from the *imperium* of the local authority and entrusting them to their own consular courts.

With the Ottoman Empire partially accepted in the European concert, the different level of civilization and the irreducibility of a different religion legitimized, once again, the suspension of the fundamental principles of international law and the emergence of an exceptional regime founded on consular authority and the principle of extraterritoriality.[28] Outside the borders of Christendom the necessity and 'the force of things' imposed to enlarge the powers and privileges normally accorded to consuls. They were really public ministers and enjoyed all the prerogatives of diplomatic agents: judicial immunity, inviolability, rights provided by the diplomatic ceremonial, tax and customs exemptions, a body of troops, and, mainly, an 'exceptional' jurisdictional competence.[29] As a matter of fact, the exceptional prerogatives enjoyed by the consuls in the East reflected an exceptionality inherent in the very same consular law. In search of a difficult compromise between a universal international law based on morality and a positive international law expressive of a common Christian conscience of the civilized states (and thus only applicable to them), consular law seemed an effective tool to regulate relations with states and political entities considered to be on a lower level of civilization. It seemed able to ensure adequate protection of Western subjects and their economic interests while, at the same time, not breaking the image of the scientific and systematic nature of international law that the European international lawyers had begun laboriously to build during the first half of the nineteenth century.

Féraud-Giraud, *Les justices mixtes dans les pays hors chrétienté: causeries à l'occasion d'un essai de réglementation internationale* (Durand & Pedone Lauriel 1884).

[28] Martens, *Völkerrecht* (n 18) vol 2, 86–87. Recently extraterritoriality has come back to receive the interest of international lawyers: see Turan Kayaoğlu, *Legal Imperialism: Sovereignty and Extraterritoriality in Japan, the Ottoman Empire, and China* (Cambridge University Press 2010).

[29] August von Bulmerincq, 'Consularrecht' in Franz von Holtzendorff (ed), *Handbuch des Völkerrechts* (Richter 1887) vol 4, 723.

Denying Sovereignty

The legal and cultural backwardness of the countries of the Maghreb and the Near and Far East had justified the limitation of their sovereignty, the application of the principle of extraterritoriality, and, consequently, the expansion of consular jurisdiction. However, they were still regarded as states—'semi-civilized' states, but sovereign entities with legal personality. In Africa, on the other hand, from the nineteenth-century Western point of view there were absolutely 'wild' populations that occupied the lowest position on the racial scale of mankind. They did not meet the European standards of statehood and therefore could not in any way be recognized as members of the international community.

What rights could they therefore claim over their territory? Was it possible to find something resembling a sovereign power exercised over a given territory that could exclude any concurrent power? Could Africa be regarded as *res nullius* and therefore freely occupied?[30]

As is well known, Francisco de Vitoria and Alberico Gentili had the merit to recall from Roman law the concept of occupation, a mode of acquisition of property according to *jus gentium*, but also to recognize that, unlike the Roman law, it could be considered within the law of the nations as a way of acquiring public and private ownership over lands without *dominus*.[31] In both cases, however, neither the theologian of Salamanca nor the lawyer of San Ginesio qualified the American lands as *res nullius*.[32]

On the contrary, recalling the medieval canonists, Gentili had admitted that also among the indigenous peoples private properties and public lordships existed. The

---

[30] See Jörg Fisch, *Die europäische Expansion und das Völkerrecht: Die Auseinandersetzungen um den Status der überseeischen Gebiete vom 15. Jahrhundert bis zur Gegenwart* (Steiner 1984); Martti Koskenniemi, *The Gentle Civilizer of Nations: the Rise and Fall of International Law 1870–1960* (Cambridge University Press 2001) 110ff; Nuzzo, *Origini* (n 1) 223ff. It is useful to remember that according to Roman law it was possible to acquire, through occupation, only the property of a *res nullius*—that is, things that had no owner (wild animals, fish, and *res hostilis*), as well as a lost treasure. Land could be the object of occupation only in case of an island rising from the sea, and if it could be considered as *res derelicta* (in this case it had to be abandoned and not in Italy). With special reference to the use of Roman law in international law and imperial practices see Randall Lesaffer, 'Argument from Roman Law in Current International Law: Occupation and Acquisitive Prescription' (2005) 16 European Journal of International Law 25; Lauren Benton and Benjamin Straumann, 'Acquiring Empire by Law: From Roman Law to Early Modern European Practice' (2010) 28 Law and History Review 1; and now Andrew Fizmaurice, *Sovereignty, Property and Empire 1500–2000* (Cambridge University Press 2014) 33ff.

[31] Francisco de Vitoria, *Relectio de indis* (Luciano Pereña and José Manuel Pérez ed, Consejo Superior de Investigaciones Cientificas 1967) I, 2–3; I, 2, 10, 42; 54; Alberico Gentili, *De iure belli libri III* (Clarendon Press 1933) I 17 132.

[32] In the same way as Vitoria (*Relectio de indis* (n 31) I, 2, 10, 54), by virtue of natural law that allowed seizure of relinquished things, Gentili denied that the discovery could be considered a legitimate title for the occupation of American territories. 'Ergo', Gentili wrote in *De iure belli* (n 31) I, 19, 144–45, 'cum hispani fuerint primi, qui invenerint et occupaverint illas provincias, sequitur quod iure possident, sicut solitudinem inhabitatam hactenus invenissent'. But, those lands having their lawful owners, it seemed to him that 'non ideo posset occupare provincias barbarorum et constituere novos dominos et veteres deponere et vectigalia capere'.

concept of *dominium* took root even before the civil law—in the natural law—and therefore also the infidels, as Innocent IV wrote, benefited as rational beings from the gift that God had given to all men to 'occupy everything that had not been occupied yet' once the sin of Adam had destroyed the primitive innocence and forced humanity to abandon the initial state of common and undivided possession.[33] Moreover, despite Gentili's criticism, in the Spanish legal discourse the Indies had also never been qualified as *res nullius*. Donated by Alexander VI to Ferdinand and Isabella, they were considered as a part of the Crown of Castile and under its *imperium*. But this did not exclude the existence of indigenous lordships after recognition of the Hispanic supremacy, as well as the possibility that indigenous populations could also acquire landed properties. As a matter of fact, involved in a net of feudal relationships based on grace and mutual assistance, native people could also join the Spaniards in the process of land distribution by submitting a formal request (*merced*) to the viceroy.[34]

However, in the second half of the nineteenth century, when the international lawyers were called to identify or to invent titles that could legitimize the new European colonialism, the transfer of occupation into the law of nations no longer appeared to be sufficient. The overlap between the American experience and the African one was no longer viable and the arguments of Vitoria and Gentili were useless. The issue was no longer to establish the principle that the land, if not belonging to anyone, was a good that could be occupied, but to identify the legal criteria that made of the concept of *res nullius* a qualifying attribute of the African territories.

Grotius, Locke, and especially Vattel provided the arguments they were looking for. They introduced the distinction between public and private occupation and sanctioned the occupation of all territories with no economic use and not connected to a Western concept of private property, leaving to the doctrine of international law of the nineteenth century only the task of carrying out the last step: transforming occupation into a way of acquisition of sovereignty over a non-sovereign territory.[35] But it was not immediate or easy to identify the premise of the occupation of a territory in a lack of sovereignty and no more than (or not only) the fact that it was not inhabited or economically used. Vattel continued to exert a tremendous

---

[33] Luigi Nuzzo, *Il linguaggio giuridico della Conquista: Strategie di controllo nelle Indie spagnole* (Jovene 2004) 76.

[34] Ibid, 163ff.

[35] Hugo Grotius, *De iure belli ac pacis libri tres* (BJA De Kanter van Hettinga Tromp, R Feenstra, and CE Persenaire eds, Scientia 1993) II 2, 16–17, 201–02; II 3, 1–4, 205–07; II 3, 19, 217–19; John Locke, *Two Treaties of Government* in *The Works of John Locke* (Scientia 1963) vol 5 II 352–67; Emmerich De Vattel, *Le droits des gens ou principe de la loi naturelle appliqués à la conduite et aux affaires des nations et des souverains* (Hein 1995) I 7, 76–78; I 18 191–96; II 7, 86–98 319–27; see also Richard Tuck, *The Rights of War and Peace, Political Thought and the International Order from Grotius to Kant* (Oxford University Press 1999) 102–08, 120–25; 166–96 with reference to Hobbes, Wolff, Pufendorf. On the use of Locke in American colonial politics, see Robert Williams Jr, *The American Indian in Western Legal Thought: The Discourse of Conquest* (Oxford University Press 1990) 246–51; Barbara Arneil, *John Locke and America: The Defence of English Colonialism* (Clarendon Press 1996); see always Jörg Fisch, *Die europäische Expansion* (n 30) 265–83; now also Fitzmaurice, *Sovereignty, Property and Empire* (n 30) 85ff.

influence over the lawyers of that time, and private law was still an inexhaustible reservoir to identify conceptual schemes, categories, and definitions to be used in the construction of the international lawyers' discourse.[36]

It appeared then so difficult for European international lawyers, at least until the middle of the century, to separate the private law level from the public law, to admit that the same area could be subjected to different assessments depending on the chosen point of observation, and to agree in this way that on the same place, at the same time, a right of ownership, but not a right of sovereignty, could be exercised.

Unable to distinguish between private property and territorial sovereignty, lawyers such as Georg Friedrich Martens, Klüber, Schmalz, and Heffter excluded the possibility of occupying a territory on which 'wild' people exercised property rights. On the one hand property was still a natural right and as such it must also be recognized as being held also by barbarian peoples.[37] On the other hand belonging to a superior civilization and the responsibility for its spread did not yet attribute, as Heffter stated, 'any right'. The civilized states could not impose their laws. They only had to try to establish trade relationships and gain territory to colonize through the conclusion of a normal contract of sale.[38] It took a few years, however, and the same reasons that prevented Heffter from justifying the occupation of indigenous territories led Johann Caspar Bluntschli to find in favour of the European states a right of sovereignty over even those territories in order to make them productive and to spread civilization. He was, of course, aware that the 'wild' populations exercised agriculture and breeding, but that did not seem to be sufficient both to recognize their inalienable right to property and, even more so, to admit an indigenous sovereignty over their possessions. The natives only held the right to exist: it was a minimum entitlement enjoyed by all human beings, in the face of which even the right/duty of civilization had to stop. However, Bluntschli attributed to the states involved in the process of diffusion of Western values the fulfilment of specific obligations towards indigenous populations. They could even recognize some 'rights' in their favour. The expulsion of the natives, for example, was not allowed. They had to be granted a right of emigration and fair compensation for the suffered expropriation, and above all it was not possible to occupy a portion of land greater than what could have been civilized or politically organized. Bluntschli clearly distinguished between territories belonging to a state and territories held by barbarian tribes, and firmly stated that 'the colonizer state, in order to protect the settlement and spread civilization, can

---

[36] Elisabetta Fiocchi Malaspina, 'La ricezione e la circolazione di "Le droit des gens" di Emmer de Vattel nel XIX secolo' (2013) 43 Materiali per una storia della cultura giuridica moderna 303.

[37] Georg Friedrich von Martens, *Précis du droit des gens moderne augmenté des notes de Pinheiro-Ferreira: Précédé d'une introduction et complété par l'exposition des doctrines des publicistes contemporains et suivi d'une Bibliographie raisonnée du Droit des gens (1785–1788)* (M Ch Vergé ed, 2nd edn, Guillaumin et Cie Libraries 1864) 129–30.

[38] Heffter, *Das europäische Recht* (n 7) 157–58; Johann Ludwig Klüber, *Droit des gens moderne de l'Europe* (2nd edn, Aillaud 1831) vol 1, 175; Theodor Anton Heinrich Schmalz, *Das europäische Völker-Recht, in acht Büchern* (Duncker & Humblot 1817) 37. Compare on this point Koskenniemi, *The Gentle Civilizer* (n 30) 284ff; Luigi Nuzzo, 'History, Science and Religion: International Law and the Savigny's Paradigm' in Nuzzo and Vec (eds), *Constructing International Law* (n 23); Fitzmaurice, *Sovereignty, Property and Empire* (n 30) 219ff.

extend its sovereignty over the territories occupied by savages'. But at the same time the lack of or limited economic exploitation of the territory continued to play an important role in his discourse about the legitimation of the occupation.[39]

These are ambiguities and persistence themes that can be also found in later works such as the *Treaty of Public International Law* by Pasquale Fiore, for which the right of occupation of the territories belonging to a state, that is, of the territories inhabited by civilized populations and with 'established governments', was excluded. Conversely, however, it admitted the occupation of the regions located outside their territorial limits and inhabited by savage nations, but only if they had not used them.[40] This clarification shows the difficulty in getting rid of the influence of Vattel and the heavy legacy of private law in the construction of international legal discourse on occupation, which significantly disappeared in the German edition of the *Handbook of International Law* by Fyodor Fyodorovich Martens. For the Russian Baltic lawyer the occupation was in fact valid: when it had been done in the name and with the consent of a state, or ratified by a state government if the occupant had been a private person; when it was effective, that is, with the concurrence of *animus possidendi*, a material apprehension and a real control of the occupied territory; and finally, if the occupied territories were 'not belonging to anyone and inhabited by barbarian tribes'.[41] Once he had eliminated reference to non-economic exploitation as a prerequisite for the occupability of indigenous lands, Martens denied the indigenous tribes the exercise of a sovereign power within their territory and excluded, therefore, that they could be considered states. For the Russian international lawyer the indigenous tribes were lacking a stable social organization and lived in spaces without clearly defined borders. It was then not possible to qualify the agreements stipulated with the tribal chief as international treaties, nor to entrust the relationships with this marginal mankind to the positive law. The basis for its applicability— 'the solidarity of interests and the feeling of the need for mutual relationships'—was lacking. The example of civilization that Europe generously offered and the old natural law that 'only' called for the respect of the fundamental values of life, honour, and property was thus enough for the barbarous populations.[42]

The Congress of Berlin enlightened the paradox behind this construction. Through the application of Western standards of evaluation the African tribes could not formally be considered as nations or states; at the same time it was possible to occupy land that was not belonging to any state. The right of occupation stopped only before another state. In all other cases the fact that a land was inhabited did not exclude that right.[43] The existence of a population not politically organized as a

[39] Bluntschli, *Das moderne Völkerrecht* (n 4) 165–67; see also Robert Phillimore, *Commentaries upon International Law* (3rd edn, Butterworths 1879) vol 1, 347–49; Traver Twiss, *The Laws of the Nations considered as Independent Political Communities: On the Right and Duties of Nations in Time of Peace* (Oxford University Press 1884) 217–18.

[40] Pasquale Fiore, *Trattato di diritto internazionale pubblico* (2nd edn, Unione Tipografico Editrice 1882) vol 2, 105–06.

[41] Martens, *Völkerrecht* (n 18) vol 1 , 352–53.   [42] Ibid, 352.

[43] Jörg Fisch, 'Africa as Terra Nullius: The Berlin Conference and International Law' in Stig Förster, Wolfgang J Mommsen, and Ronald Robinson (eds), *Bismarck, Europe, and Africa: The Berlin Africa*

state, as Catellani reminded, could have avoided or limited the exercise of the right of occupation in the matter of the private property, but not in the matter of the state sovereignty.[44]

Anyway, the powers gathered in Berlin did not consider it appropriate to precisely define the object of the occupation, fix the requisites of legitimacy, or finally clarify the relationships between the indigenous populations and their territories. The hypocrisy of the shared 'Rechtsüberzeugung' of the Western states, so strongly expressed in Articles 34 and 35, led the diplomats to avoid any definition.[45] On the one hand, in fact, it was not theoretically acceptable to equate the indigenous populations to real states with international legal subjectivity, and thus to recognize them as full members of the international community. It was not possible to transform any personal sovereignty of the tribal chief over the different families subjected to him into a power of political representation also valid outside. On the other hand it seemed embarrassing to have to accept the natural consequences of these evaluations: where lack of sovereignty was the only requirement to qualify a territory as *nullius*, regardless of whether it was inhabited or not, indigenous populations could be easily stripped of their possessions, and every treaty of cession of territory or protectorate agreement with their tribal chiefs would be worthless for international law.[46]

The silence that followed the proposal of the American plenipotentiary John Kasson therefore seems understandable. It was based on the assumption that 'the modern international law' would have admitted 'the right of indigenous races to freely dispose of themselves and their territory' and that occupations often arose from acts of violence. This led the US diplomat to ask that the validity of the occupation be subordinate to the 'voluntary consent' of the people whose land would

Conference 1884–1885 and the Onset of Partition (Oxford University Press 1988); Koskenniemi, *The Gentle Civilizer* (n 30) 121ff.

[44] Enrico Levi Catellani, *Le colonie e la conferenza di Berlino*, (Unione Tipografica Editrice 1885) 579–80, 588–90. See also Ferdinand Lenter, *Das internationale Colonialrecht* (Manz'sche Hof- Verlags- und Universitäts Buchhandlung 1886) 91–94; Ferdinand von Martitz, 'Das Internationale System zur Unterdrückung des Afrikanischen Sklavenhandels in seinem heutigen Bestande' (1886) 1 Archiv für öffentliches Recht 3.

[45] Karl Heimburger, *Der Erwerb der Gebietshoheit: Eine Staats- und völkerrechtliche Studie* (Braun'schen Hofbuchdruckerei 1888) 4. As is well known, Articles 34 and 35 of the General Act of the Berlin Conference decided how the African soil should be shared: 'any power which henceforth takes possession of a tract of land on the coasts of the African Continent outside of its present possession, or which being hitherto without such possessions shall acquire them, as well as the Power which assume a Protectorate there, shall accompany the respective act with a notification thereof, addressed to the other signatory Power of the present act, in order to enable them, if need be, to make good any claims of their own'; and 'the signatory powers of the present act recognize the obligation to insure the establishment of authority in the regions occupied by them on the coasts on the African Continent sufficient to protect existing rights, and as the case may be, freedom of trade, and transit under the conditions agreed upon': '*Acte général de la Conférence de Berlin*, 26.3.1885' in Wilhelm Grewe (ed), *Fontes Historiae Iuris Gentium* (de Gruyter 1995) vol 3, 1.

[46] Cf Carlo Ghirardini, 'Delle cosidette "occupazioni qualificate" nel diritto internazionale' (1912) 6 Rivista di diritto internazionale 32.

have been occupied, and also to consider this the bare minimum for the recognition of the occupation by the international community.[47]

The proposal was not even voted on. The issues it concerned were too 'delicate', according to the German August Busch, president of the session. The Powers took charge of the need to respect 'to the possible extent' the rights of the indigenous, and did not bring into question the practice hitherto followed in the process of colonization. But it was not legally and politically possible to ascribe to the indigenous a right of veto or to impose mandatory requirements on the activities reserved to the discretionary evaluation of each state.[48]

It was not clear which were the rights of indigenous peoples and what was 'the possible extent' to which the French plenipotentiary De Courcel undertook the Western ministers. Without ever denying European powers a right/duty to civilization, the doctrine had tried, in different periods and ways, to constrain the action, identifying the limits of the occupation and the rights that could be conferred on indigenous peoples. They represented the more miserable part of humanity and certainly could not be considered sovereign entities with international legal personality like the Western civilized states and those half-civilized of the East, but they were not outside the international community. On the contrary, they were included as passive spectators of a legal order produced by others with more refined consciences. They were constrained, as human beings, to respect the principles of natural law, and they were under the beneficial effects of a positive law—the production of which, however, they could never participate in. As we have seen, it had guaranteed them, in different ways according to the different feelings of the commentators, a minimum right to life, the assurance that the occupation was supposed to be peaceful or limited to unused areas, the recognition of the opportunity of a consent, a right of emigration, an adequate compensation for the occupied territory, and the respect for private property.[49] From the 1880s there also began

---

[47] However, Kasson recognized the ability of the signatory Powers to introduce other legal or factual elements in order to subordinate the validity of the occupation, see 'Protocole no 8 (Séance du 31.1.1885)' (1885) 15 Archives diplomatiques 253 (hereafter 'Protocole no 8'). Charles Salomon, *L'occupation des territoires sans maître: Étude de droit international* (Giard 1889) 214–16, defined Kasson as 'le défenseur officieux des indigènes', and commented in this way his proposal: 'Il faut reconnaître du reste qu'une déclaration humanitaire en faveur des droits des indigènes n'aurait pas été à sa place dans l'Acte de Berlin.' Also Eduard Engelhardt, 'Étude sur la déclaration de la Conférence de Berlin relative aux occupation' (1886) 18 Revue du droit international et de législation comparée 573, underlined the inopportuneness of Kasson's proposal. On Kasson's intervention and the answer of Westlake see Matthew Craven, 'The Invention of a Tradition: Westlake, the Berlin Conference and the Historicization of International law' in Nuzzo and Vec (eds), *Constructing International Law* (n 23) 383.

[48] Protocole no 8 (n 47) 254.

[49] The European international lawyers also during the last years of the nineteenth century agreed about the necessity to protect the private property of indigenous people; see Guido Fusinato, 'Le mutazioni territoriali: Il loro fondamento giuridico e le loro conseguenze' in Guido Fusinato, *Scritti giuridici* (Bocca 1921) vol 1, 424; Catellani, *Le Colonie e la conferenza di Berlino* (n 44) 579–84; Fiore, *Il diritto internazionale codificato* (n 19) 37–38, 113; Arndt von Holtzendorff, *Die koloniale Frage und ihre Lösung durch das Reich* (Gaertner's Verlagsbuchhandlung 1889) 15–16; John Westlake, *The Collected Papers of John Westlake on Public International Law* (Lassa Oppenheim ed, Cambridge University Press 1914) 136–57.

the conceptualization of the natives as minors, with no ability to act, and whose intellectual and legal protection would be covered by the commitment of civilized nations.[50] Around the same time Franz Holtzendorff and Paul Heilborn introduced a right of independence for indigenous peoples, but without recognizing their state character or the same rights of any independent states.[51] Some lawyers, then, went so far as to give them a right to something similar to sovereignty, that could therefore prevent occupation when there was a political organization with a resemblance of stability.[52]

Even the lawyers of the Institute, at the request of Laveleye, Holtzendorff, and Moynier, grappled with the problem of the occupation, but for them it was also not an easy task to provide a definition. Ferdinand von Martitz, the rapporteur of a commission appointed in the Brussels session of 1885 with the task of 'developing and completing' the provisions contained in Articles 34 and 35 of the acts of the Berlin Conference, made the first attempt.[53]

The draft, presented in Heidelberg in 1887 and discussed in the next session held in Lausanne the following year, began with the definition of *territorium nullius*: 'It is considered *territorium nullius* [therefore suitable to be occupied] each region that

---

[50] Joseph Hornung, 'Civilisés et barbares' (1885) 17 Revue de droit international et de législation comparée 1, 17: 'Le mond chrétien n'a pas encore pris franchement ce rôle de tuteur qui appartient aux bons et aux forts'; Robert Adam, 'Völkerrechtliche Okkupation und deutsches Kolonialstaatsrecht' (1891) 6 Archiv für öffentliches Rechts 193 233–35; Franz von Holtzendorff, 'Das Landgebiet der Staaten' in Franz von Holtzendorff (ed), *Handbuch des Völkerrechts* (Richter 1887) vol 2, 256. The representation of the native as a pupil became established only at the beginning of the twentieth century; see Carlos Petit, 'Il modello coloniale dello Stato di diritto: La Costituzione africana in Guinea' in Pietro Costa and Danilo Zolo (eds), *Lo stato di diritto: Storia, teoria, critica* (Feltrinelli 2002); Bartolomé Clavero, *Freedom Law and Indigenous Rights: From Europe's Oeconomy to the Constitutionalism of the Americas* (Robbins Collection 2005); Luigi Nuzzo, 'A Dark Side of the West Legal Modernity: The Colonial Law and its Subject' (2011) 33 Zeitschrift für neure Rechtsgeschichte 205.

[51] Franz von Holtzendorff, in 'Der Staat als rechtliche Persönlichkeit' in Holtzendorff (ed), *Handbuch des Völkerrechts* (n 50) vol 2, saw in the indigenous populations a 'quasi rechtliche Persönlichkeit'. 'Höher gebildete Völker', he wrote in 'Das Landgebiet der Staaten' (n 50) 257, 'haben die Grundsätze der internationalen Moral überall zu achten und müssen anerkennen, daß auch Wilde ein naturliches Recht des Daseins, unabhängig von Staatsgesetzen, für sich in Anspruch nehmen dürfen.' Paul Heilborn, *Das völkerrechtliche Protektorat* (Springer 1891) 25, underlined that 'trotzdem gestehen die Staaten den Stämmen durchaus nicht die Rechte von Staaten zu. Diplomatischer Verkehr z. B. wird mit Stämmen nicht unterhalten. Da die Stammeshäuptlinge nur eine Personalhoheit über ihre Stammengenossen, keine Gebietshoheit ausüben, besitzen sie auch keine Iurisdiction über die innerhalb ihrer Stammensitze sich aufhaltenden Europäer.'

[52] See eg Karl Freiherr von Stengel, *Die Rechtsverhältnisse der deutschen Schutzgebiete* (Mohr 1901) 8; Bonfils, *Manuel de droit international public* (n 9) 300; Frantz Despagnet, *Cours de droit international public* (Larose 1894) 425; Salomon, *L'occupation des territoires* (n 47) 206; Gaston Jèze, *Étude théorique et pratique sur l'occupation comme mode d'acquérir les territoires en droit international* (Giard et Briére 1896) 115; Engelhardt, 'Étude sur la déclaration' (n 47) 582. None of these jurists ever recognized that the political organization of the indigenous peoples could be compared to that of the European states, nor ever accepted the idea of considering them to be in a position of equality. For a summary of the different positions taken on the legal doctrine see Mark Frank Lindley, *The Acquisition and Government of Backward Territory in International Law* (Longmans, Green and Co Ltd 1926) 13–20.

[53] The members of the Commission were Asser, Engelhardt, Geffken, de Laveleye, Martens, Martitz, and Twiss, 'Quatrième commision d'études: Examen de la théorie de la conférence de Berlin de 1885, sur l'occupation des territoires' (1888) 9 Annuaire de l'Institut de droit international 247. On the works of the Institute's commissions see also Fitzmaurice, *Sovereignty, Property and Empire* (n 30) 284ff.

is not actually under the sovereignty or the protectorate of any of the states forming the community of the law of nations, it does not matter that this region is or is not inhabited' (Article 1). The natives, it was added to avoid misunderstanding, were not out of the international community 'in the strict sense', but at the same time could be considered as members of it because 'international law does not recognize the rights of independent tribes'. For this reason the draft considered it an 'exaggeration' to confer rights of sovereignty to the 'wild and semi-wild peoples', and that it was 'inconsistent with the history of international law' to recognize the agreements signed with these populations as real treaties of cession. They were 'essential' for settling on occupied territory or to establish a protectorate, but did not transmit a valid claim of acquisition. Occupation was necessary. Only the occupation, in fact, would have made the protectorate effective and would have interdicted, once notified, the action of other colonizing powers on the same territory, or would have been able to refine the agreement, turning a derivative claim of acquisition into an original one.[54]

On the one hand, then, Martitz did not escape the difficulties of providing a definition of *territorium nullius*, and through it addressed the issue of the sovereignty of indigenous peoples. On the other hand, demanding occupation as a condition of effectiveness for the protectorate, he had tried to overcome the problems which led in practice to the vagueness of Article 34, by which the European powers could establish a protectorate through a simple notification. In both cases, Martitz was not isolated in the positions he held.[55] On the contrary, he summarized some theses widely shared by internationalists and diplomats.

That was not enough to save his project. In the session of the Institute held in Lausanne in 1888, thanks to the absence of the German jurist and the existence of an alternative plan signed by another member of the commission, Eduard Engelhardt, the discussion of the text stopped at the examination of Article 3.[56]

The reports of the meeting clearly explain the reasons. Engelhardt, Bar, and Renault criticized the definition of *territorium nullius*.[57] Admitting the occupation of territories not subjected to the sovereignty or protectorate of states that are part of the family of nations required first to ensure what was its meaning and who

---

[54] Ferdinand von Martitz had already addressed this point in his important essay 'Das Internationale System' (n 44).

[55] 'Projet Martitz', Article VI (1888) 9 Annuaire de l'Institut de droit international 249: 'Une occupation à titre de *protectorat*, pour devenir effective, suppose la conclusion d'un accord avec le chef d'un peuple indigène.' In the footnotes he added: 'Ainsi, vis-à-vis de l'étranger, le chef indigène est remplacé par le gouvernement protecteur. Mais les individus appartenant à la tribu indigène ne sont pas *sujets* de celui-ci.' Contradictions and limits of Article VI were also stressed by Frantz Despagnet, *Essai sur les protectorats: Étude de droit international* (Librairie de la société du recueil géneral des lois et des arrêts 1896) 231–33. But also for him it was necessary that the authority over the protected territory was effective; in the same vein see William Edward Hall, *A Treatise on the Foreign Powers and Jurisdiction of the British Crown* (Scientia, 1979) 131; Westlake, *The Collected Papers* (n 49) 185.

[56] Engelhardt submitted his project during the session of Heidelberg, (1888) 9 Annuaire de l'Institut de droit international 251–55. It is a short version of his previous article, 'Étude sur la declaration de la confèrence de Berlin' (n 47), published two years before in the Revue.

[57] 'Extrait du procès-verbal de la séance plénière tenue par l'Institut, à Lausanne, le 7 septembre 1888, sous la présidence de M. Rivier' (1889) 10 Annuaire de l'Institut de droit international 176.

could be admitted to join it. Denying any relevance to the fact that the territory was inhabited seemed, then, to officially consecrate a right to the use of the force and dispossession in favour of the European powers.

Engelhardt then proposed to express in the article the wish that the occupations of 'uncivilized' countries were preceded by agreements with indigenous peoples. It was a proposal already made by Kasson in Berlin and that could adapt the theoretical position to the practice held in Africa. Inevitably, however, it clashed with the insuperable objection, already advanced by the American plenipotentiary, that 'these treaties of cession with more or less real indigenous leaders, more or less legitimate, do not have serious value'.[58]

Guido Fusinato also intervened in the discussion. Author of an important essay on 'territorial mutations' a few years earlier, the Italian jurist believed the assembly could not disregard a definition. The *territorium nullius*, the projection on the public level of *res nullius*, was simply 'that space that was not under the sovereignty or protectorate of a state, regardless of whether it was inhabited or not'.[59] It was an extremely effective definition that had a great success in international legal theory. The assembly, however, rejected the amendment proposed by Fusinato, deciding to entirely suppress the first article of the draft of Martitz.

Even for the Institute, in fact, it was not possible to identify the requirements for the legality of the occupation to provide an official pronouncement. The delicacy, from a political point of view, of the issues addressed and the difficulty of bringing within the traditional legal categories the radical otherness of the African experience made every definition dangerous. Moreover, the jurists of the Institute reminded themselves, as justification for their actions, that their task was to merely clarify and supplement the provisions taken in Berlin. 'Fortunately', therefore, the Institute was not called to examine the existence of indigenous sovereignty, or to establish the conditions under which the indigenous people could be considered as state actors with international legal personality or admitted to the international community. As already happened in Berlin, disputes between civilized states had to be avoided on the issue of the occupation. 'I believe that', said the president of the session in Lausanne, Alphonse Rivier, eliminating any doubt, 'the task of the Commission was defined. It has to study the conditions under which the occupation will be considered a title in front of the other states; therefore, there is no need to take care of the relations between civilized states.'[60]

---

[58] Ibid, 182. Engelhardt too had criticized the proposal of Kasson: Engelhardt, 'Étude sur la déclaration' (n 47) 580.

[59] The intervention of Fusinato is in (1889) 10 Annuaire de l'Institut de droit international 183. In his article on 'Le mutazioni territoriali' (n 49) 442–43, he did not equate indigenous peoples to 'true' states with an international legal personality and thus excluded their 'full political recognition'. Instead he argued that they 'per quanto rozzamente costituite, pure possiedono regolarmente una certa organizzazione che a loro concede il diritto di essere trattate, almeno in tale riguardo, come associazioni politiche indipendenti'. According to this the natives retained a right of property on their own land.

[60] Alphonse Rivier, 'Extrait du procès-verbal de la séance plénière tenue par l'Institut, à Lausanne, le 7 septembre 1888, sous la présidence de M Rivier' (1889) 10 Annuaire de l'Institut de droit international 184.

Once they had rejected the draft of Martitz, the Institute found that the project of Engelhardt corresponded to their duties and objectives. Adopted in Lausanne, 7 September 1888, it did not, however, add much to what was planned in the Berlin Conference. Occupation as a title of sovereignty was effective if the taking of possession had been made on behalf of a government, if it had been notified, and if a 'local power equipped with the means to maintain order and to ensure regular exercise of his authority' had been established on the occupied territory. The same requirements were necessary to form a protectorate. In this case, however, a 'full' sovereignty over the territory would not have been gained and the indigenous peoples would have kept administrative autonomy with 'no restrictions'.[61]

The inability to recognize the indigenous peoples as international legal subjects and the lack of definition of the legal nature of the African territory allowed only minor additions to the requirements for the effectiveness of occupation, and authorized also extending to the protectorates the principle of effectiveness. It was really too little to overcome even in theory—let us not forget that it was only a project—the limits and contradictions of Articles 34 and 35. The two projects, like the acts of Berlin, said nothing on the legal value of the hundreds of treaties with African chiefs on which the European colonial policy was founded. In practice it was difficult to doubt their validity, but how to justify them on a theoretical level? The doctrine gave different answers, but overall these were unsatisfactory.[62]

Lawyers such as Jèze, Bonfils, and Pradier-Fodéré who recognized that the chiefs were entitled to some rights of sovereignty, attributed to the agreements stipulated with the natives the value of international treaties, and therefore considered as possible a derivative purchase of the African territory. For most of the international lawyers, however, this was unthinkable. The territorial acquisitions on the African continent were always with an original title and the only condition to which the transfer of the title was subordinated remained the occupation. About the significance of treaties with the natives, however, the positions were different. Trying to simplify it, it can be said that for some the lack of international subjectivity of the indigenous populations made these agreements ineffective on the legal level, and only allowed some political impact or the provision of a moral title to be attached to them.[63] Others, though starting from the same premise, saw in the agreement a clear indication of the desire to occupy or even the starting point of an occupation that could not be considered as lacking any effect, even if it did not have the strength to transmit—due to the deficit of statehood of the counterpart—sovereign rights in favour of the occupying power. The agreement created an expectation, ensured a '*Vorzugsrecht*' or a '*Präventionsrecht*', 'qualifying' the subsequent occupation. For

---

[61] The entire debate is in ibid, 187–90.

[62] See the works of Fisch, *Die europäische Expansion* (n 30) 332ff; and Koskenniemi, *The Gentle Civilizer* (n 30) 136ff.

[63] Conrad Bornhak, 'Die Anfänge des deutschen Kolonialstaatsrechts' (1887) 2 Archiv für öffentliches Recht 7; Adam, 'Völkerrechtliche Okkupation' (n 50) 193; Alphonse Rivier, *Principes du droit de gens* (Rousseau 1896) vol 1, 188–89; Fiore, *Il diritto internazionale* (n 19) 159; Heilborn, *Das völkerrechtliche Protektorat* (n 51) 23–24; Westlake, *International Law* (Cambridge University Press 1904) vol 1, 121; Westlake, *The Collected Papers* (n 49) 147.

its completion and to define the original acquisition, the effectiveness of the taking of possession was necessary, but it was by itself already able to prevent occupation by third states. This would have solved the paradox of a treaty that was ineffective at an international level, but equally binding for the other civilized states and the indigenous populations.[64]

Even greater problems derived from the new figure of the colonial protectorate. If the acts of the Berlin Conference on the Congo issue made no reference to the consent of indigenous peoples and therefore their agreement, even if desirable, was not a premise for the occupation, the protectorate, on the contrary, assumed their consent as necessary. This produced paradoxical results. The colonial protectorate came from a transfer of the international protectorate, a well-known institution of the law of nations, in Africa. In the overseas transfer, however, it had undergone substantial modification of its fundamental elements. In Africa it was not necessary that the signatories were two independent and sovereign states, one of which, the protected state, had agreed to a limitation of its sovereignty on the international level, entrusting to the protecting state the function of representation but preserving legal personality and full control of its territory. In order to justify the colonization of the African continent, the Western powers granted to the indigenous tribes the opportunity to act as if they were legal entities with full sovereignty, capable of having rights of which they were not even aware. At the same time they continued to deny that the agreements signed with them were authentic international treaties.

The contradictions also concerned the theoretical relationship between occupation and protectorate. Articles 34 and 35 attributed to the European states the possibility to choose between two instruments with different intensity and different conditions for the control of the territory and of the African populations. On the one hand, as we have seen, the absence of state sovereignty qualified the African territory as *territorium nullius* and legitimized its occupation. On the other hand the fact that those territories were occupied by people with whom it was somehow necessary to secure diplomatic relations made it possible to conclude treaties of protectorate.

This meant that the European powers would have from time to time to entrust the choice between occupation and protectorate on the basis of an evaluation of the degree of civilization attained by the indigenous populations. In practice, however, it was not so easy to determine the degree of civilization required to employ one instrument or another, or to define a clear distinction between occupation and protectorate and identify the limits beyond which the limitation of the indigenous sovereignty produced by a protectorate developed into a full transfer of territory. Most of the doctrine was fully conscious of this and defined the protectorate as a 'masked', 'dummy', 'veiled', or 'qualified' occupation, able to confer to the protecting state, on the one hand, the right to acquire a territory, yet formally subjected to the sovereignty of another entity; on the other, to prevent the possibility that a

---

[64] Stengel, *Die Rechtsverhältnisse* (n 52) 43ff; Martitz, 'Das Internationale System' (n 44) 17–18; Salomon, *L'occupation des territoires* (n 47) 232–37; Despagnet, *Essai sur les protectorats* (n 55) 248–51.

third party could make claims on the same territories.[65] The colonial protectorate multiplied the anomalies and the uniqueness of the international protectorate and resolved the contradiction between autonomy and subordination, becoming the 'easiest and least questionable way to occupy the non-civilized countries'.[66]

As a matter of fact it allowed putting into a single category different cases and experiences and to legitimate, on a theoretical plane, the control of an African territory whenever occupation—as a way to obtain the sovereignty—was not a useful instrument. On the one hand occupation could require effectiveness or total assumption of sovereignty over all the controlled territory; on the other hand it could be difficult to qualify as *nullius* the territories where the indigenous chiefs had some powers of direction or managing.

There is another important point. In order to prevent the conflicts between the European powers engaged in the partitioning of Africa and in order to overcome the legal paradoxes linked to the drawing up of treaties with subjects lacking a clear national subjectivity or international legal personality, the European diplomacy thought that the best thing was to determine in a treaty the sphere of influence (or *hinterland*). This would have allowed each power to develop, within defined boundaries, its colonial activity until the point it realized its 'own legitimate' right to occupy a section of Africa, as well as to ban every interference by the others in its colonial space.[67] The agreements between Germany and Great Britain in 1886, 1890, and 1893, between Germany and Portugal in 1886, between France and Great Britain in 1889 and 1890, and the treaties between Great Britain and Italy in 1891 and 1894 are only a few examples of agreements that changed the African geography. They created a new space completely committed to the economic and political decisions of the owner state's influence. It was a new space in which the indigenous people lost their political subjectivity.[68] The sphere of influence was an unknown category of international law. It had an ambiguous nature always on the verge on becoming a fictitious occupation.[69] However, according to most European international lawyers, the contractual assignation of the colonial space was not able to create a sovereignty right on that territory, but only a *ius excludendi alium*. Thanks to the contract, each state saved the right of occupying or creating a protectorate, and at the same time committed itself not to interfere into the sphere

---

[65] Westlake, *International Law* (n 63) 123–24; Westlake, *The Collected Papers* (n 49) 187–88; Catellani, *Le Colonie e la conferenza di Berlino* (n 44) 591; Pasquale Fiore, 'Du Protectorat colonial et de la sphère d'influence (hinterland)' (1907) 14 Revue générale de droit international public 148; Paul Pradier Fodéré, *Traité de droit international public européen et américain, suivant les progrès de la science et de la pratique contemporaines* (Durand et Pedone Lauriel 1885) vol 2 342; Bonfils, *Manuel de droit international public* (n 9) 548.

[66] Fiore, 'Du Protectorat colonial' (n 65) 150.

[67] On the differences between sphere of influence and hinterland see Friedrich Schack, *Das deutsche Kolonialrecht in seiner Entwicklung bis zum Weltkriege: Die allgemeinen Lehren. Eine berichtende Darstellung der Theorie und Praxis nebst kritischen Bemerkungen* (Friederichsen & Co 1923) 70ff.

[68] Fiore, 'Du protectorat colonial' (n 65) 156; Koskenniemi, *The Gentle Civilizer* (n 30) 152–55.

[69] See Salomon, *L'occupation des territoires* (n 47) 255; Frantz Despagnet, 'Les occupations de territoire et le procédé de l'Hinterland' (1894) 1 Revue générale de droit international public 103; Adam, 'Völkerrechtliche Okkupation' (n 50) 285.

of others (*Vorbehaltstheorie*). Lacking a real engagement on the territory, the agreement could have effectiveness only between the parties—indeed, only international courtesy was able to prevent another state, which knew the treaty, from creating a disturbance.[70] In the opinion of a few German authors, the sphere of influence did not mark a territory on which a state reserved only the right to future exploitation, but instead conferred a real right of sovereignty (*Souveränitätstheorie*).[71] In this way every distinction between *Schutzgebiete* and the sphere of influence failed to recognize a right of sovereignty in the possibility, provided by the treaty, to exercise the right of occupation or to constitute a protectorate. It would have been a right that everyone would have to accept once the treaty had been notified and any formal claim was missing.[72] Thus, through notification, a contractual right became an absolute right that was valid *erga omnes*.

In Italy, some years before, Gennaro Mondaini published an interesting essay about *La sfera di influenza nella storia coloniale e nel diritto*. Mondaini was not a lawyer. He was a historian observing the colonial phenomenon, and around 1920 he was the author of an important handbook on colonial history and legislation. This Italian scholar did not only underline the novelty or ambiguity relating to the sphere of influence but, emphasizing also the historical aspects of the sphere of influence, offered a different point of view. According to him, the roots of the sphere of influence were in the history. They were linked to the famous *Bulla Inter Cetera* of Alexander VI, allowing us to see an interesting transfer between the pre-modern age and the colonial experience. The institution mirrored, in a particular way, the exceptional nature of the colonial world, and it clearly indicated the transformations in the old international law produced by that world. According to Mondaini, the sphere of influence revealed that the relations between Western states and 'savage' (or 'semi-savage') populations could be regulated by 'special and more or less juridical principles', as had already happened in the colonial protectorate or the occupation; but also that the relations between civil states, if engaged in colonial questions, could not be regulated by the general principles of international law. On the contrary, they were entrusted to a new autonomous law: colonial law. Settlement, hinterland, sphere of influence, and protectorates as a matter of fact were certainly a *vulnus* regarding international law, but were also the signs of a great energy which was able to carry international law away and to make it conform to necessities of social life. The exceptionality, therefore, was the general principle of colonial law, namely the instrument of its autonomy from international law and of its 'antigiuridicità formale'.[73]

[70] Laband, *Das Staatsrecht des Deutschen Reiches* (n 2) 276–77; Adam, 'Völkerrechtliche Okkupation' (n 50) 283–85; Liszt, *Völkerrecht systematisch dargestellt* (n 10) 83; Stengel, *Die Rechtsverhältnisse* (n 52) 4–5; Despagnet, 'Les occupations' (n 69) 115; Louis Deherpe, *Essai sur le développement de l'occupation en droit international: Etablissement et déformation de l'œuvre de la conférence de Berlin 1885* (Librairie de la Société du recueil général de lois et des arrêts 1903) 175–76; Hall, *A Treatise on International Law* (n 55) 134–36; Westlake, *International Law* (n 63) 128–32.

[71] Schack, *Das deutsche Kolonialrecht* (n 67) 71.

[72] Felice Arcoleo, *Il problema coloniale nel diritto pubblico* (Pierro 1914) 164–67.

[73] Gennaro Mondaini, *La sfera di influenza nella storia coloniale e nel diritto* (Seeber 1902) 15–16, 47, 62; Luigi Nuzzo, 'Kolonialrecht' in Europäische Geschichte Online (EGO) <http://www.ieg-ego.eu/nuzzol-2011-de> accessed 14 April 2016.

The Italian Job: Conclusions

It was not an isolated position. German and Italian jurists between the end of the nineteenth century and the beginning of the next shared the idea that what was happening in the former territories of the Ottoman Empire, in China, and in Sub-Saharan Africa was not simply a violation of international law. They thought that the embarrassment shown by many international lawyers, using words like 'curiosity', 'novelty', 'anomaly', 'absurdity', and 'irregularity' to describe the uniqueness of the political experiences of which they were not able to understand the legal significance should be overcome by a broader legal reading. There was nothing in international life that could be considered an absurd or inadmissible thing, wrote Jellinek in Germany and Cavaglieri in Italy. International lawyers, therefore, had the task of studying the new phenomena to reclassify them within pre-existing legal categories or, if necessary, invent new and more suitable ones.[74]

In this sense the consular law in its Eastern version as well as the colonial law in sub-Saharan Africa constituted an interesting answer. They were two different laws (the first personal and the second territorial) for two different kinds of territories and populations. But both shared the same nature of special or exceptional law. Both were used to absorb the 'otherness' of the non-Christian and 'semi-civilized' populations of North Africa, the East, and the Far East, as well as the 'savagery' of the tribes of Sub-Saharan Africa, and both were used to preserve the identity of international law as a Western interstate positive law by suspending its application to those populations alone.[75]

At the same time, trying to give legal form to what was happening outside the West led first the German lawyers and then the Italian to an important reflection on the limits of the concept of sovereignty in the reading of the relationship between state and territory as well as on the relationship between metropolitan and colonial territory and on the different legal nature of the rights that the state could exercise over them.

Sovereignty, territory, and subjects were still necessary elements of statehood, but the absence of one of them—even the most important, sovereignty—did not necessarily condemn the political formation which was missing it within the administrative authorities.

Sovereignty, Jellinek wrote, was not an essential category of the state, but just a historical category useful to understand the process of the formation of the Western

---

[74] Georg Jellinek, *Ueber Staatsfragmente* (Koester 1896); Arrigo Cavaglieri, *Contributo alla definizione di alcune figure del diritto pubblico contemporaneo* (Tipografia dell'Unione cooperativa editrice 1906).

[75] The similarities between consular and colonial law are well testified by the German *Schutzgebietgesetz* of 16.3.1886 that entrusted in the colonial possessions the Emperor with legislative and executive powers and referred to the *Consulargerichtsbarkeitgesetz* of 10.7.1879 the questions concerning the private, criminal, and processual law. The application of the consular law in the colonies was dependent on a *Verordnung* of the Kaiser. See Georg Meyer, *Die staatsrechtliche Stellung der deutschen Schutzgebiete* (Duncker und Humblot 1888) 121–28.

state.[76] As we have seen, taking examples from the Ottoman Empire, outside the borders of the Western states sovereignty could lose exclusivity and indivisibility, coexisting with the recognition of broad spheres of autonomy. For the Austrian lawyer this meant that only an approach free from 'doctrinal preconceptions' could notice the existence of ambiguous political subjects. Provided with territory, subjects, and a more or less degree of legislative, administrative, and jurisdictional autonomy, they could be defined as fragments of a state, *Staatsfragmente*.

It was an extremely flexible category, able to include the Danubian principalities or other territories of the Ottoman Empire, to explain the particular legal condition of Finland, or to be applied to foreign concessions in China, and finally to the German colonial possessions in Africa.

For the German legal doctrine the African possessions were at the same time inside and outside the Empire, '*völkerrechtlich Inland und staatsrechtlich Ausland*'.[77] They were subjected to territorial sovereignty of the Empire, but were not territories of the Empire. Laband defined them as *Pertinenzen*, Meyer and Köbner, *Nebenlanden*, and Jellinek, as I have said, *Staatsfragmente*.

This approach did not immediately obtain a positive outcome in Italy. Santi Romano, the most prominent Italian jurist of the twentieth century, strongly criticized Jellinek's *Staatsfragmente*, underlining the paradox of a theory in which the colony was out of the Empire but inhabited by imperial subjects who were subjected to imperial sovereignty. On the contrary, Santi Romano conceived territory, sovereignty, and subject as three strictly connected elements of a single concept, imagining the territory as the tool able to ensure the coexistence of metropolitan and colonial legal order.

Only four years later, however, looking for a good answer to the crisis of the liberal Italian state, Romano found it more useful to follow the German doctrine, and he too excluded the possibility that the metropolitan and colonial territory had the same legal nature.[78] If, from the international law point of view, the distinction between the two territories was irrelevant because they both were subjected to the state's exclusive sovereignty, it became a fundamental one according to public law. The right of the state on its own territory, Romano wrote in 1902, could not be described as a public law version of the relationship between an owner and an object liable to be owned; neither could it be simplistically identified with the right of

---

[76] Jellinek, *Ueber Staatsfragmente* (n 74) 11; Georg Jellinek, *Die Lehre von der Staatenverbindungen* (Hölder 1882) 63–68. The *Staatsfragmente* became part of the main work of Jellinek, the *Allgemeine Staatslehre* (n 2) 647–60.

[77] Bornhak, 'Die Anfänge des deutschen Kolonialstaatsrechts' (n 63) 9; see also Paul Erich Hinz, *Die Rechtsbegriffe 'Inland' und 'Ausland' in Anwendung auf die deutschen Schutzgebiete* (Noske 1908) 7–11; Meyer (n 75) 88–104; Laband, *Das Staatsrecht des Deutschen Reiches* (n 2) 285; Stengel, *Die Rechtsverhältnisse* (n 52) 38ff; Otto Köbner, *Die Organisation der Rechtspflege in den Kolonien* (Mittler und Sohn 1903) 9–14; Edler Hoffmann, *Deutsches Kolonialrecht* (Göschen'sche Verlagshandlung 1907) 21–25; Franz Joseph Sassen, *Das Gesetzgebung und Verordnungsrecht in den deutschen Kolonien* (Laupp 1909) 13–25.

[78] Santi Romano, 'Osservazioni sulla natura giuridica del territorio dello Stato' (hereafter Romano, 'Osservazioni') in Santi Romano, *Scritti minori* (Guido Zanobini ed, Giuffrè 1990) vol 1 204–15.

sovereignty that each state boasted over its territory.[79] Going back to what Fricker had written forty years earlier, the territory was in fact an essential, intrinsic element of the state—it founded its existence and identified itself with it. The right exercised by the state over its territory, therefore, could not be simply a right *in rem*, but was rather a 'special right', a subjective right on its own person.[80]

Overseas, however, this identification did not work, and the relationship between state and territory was again, in an analogy with private law, 'an exclusive and complete domain of a subject on a material thing'. The homogeneity, unity, and indivisibility of metropolitan territory was opposed in an insurmountable way to fragmentation, multiplicity, and the diversity of colonial possessions. The profound otherness of places and people prevented the colonies becoming part of the 'national territory', confining them in the elusive category of the 'aggregati', 'appendici', 'frammenti', or 'pertinenze' of the state territory, and made them an object of a 'diritto reale di natura pubblicistica'; that is, a right *in rem* with a public law nature.[81]

The territorial unity between the state and the colony was no longer, therefore, the necessary prerequisite to the exercise of a right of sovereignty; nor was it possible to see in the territory the minimum common denominator of different legal systems. It had become just the object of a state right; a right that could take different forms depending on the space in which the state itself was going to operate. Within the metropolitan borders it acted in accordance with the separation of powers and the rule of law and therefore exercised a personal right over its own territory. In the colony, on the contrary, it assumed the feature of the 'Stato patrimoniale', that is, the form of state that existed before the constitutional state, thus exercising a right *in rem* over that territory.

This did not lead to the exclusion of the colony and its inhabitants from the state order, but 'only' to confine them in a different age—an age in which there was no constitution, no separation of powers, nor the uniqueness of the legal subject. In the colony the state invested itself with administrative powers and acted directly, without the intermediation of the Parliament, through decrees, orders in council, regulations, and the military apparatus.

It was a brilliant solution that solved the problem of the coexistence between metropolis and colony, legitimizing the existence of a multilevel normativity as well as the presence of different subjects with different status. At the same time it offered

---

[79] Obviously Laband and Gerber constituted the main targets of Romano's criticism, but the Italian jurist underlined also the ambiguities of Georg Jellinek, *Allgemeine Staatslehre* (n 2) 401, where he affirmed that 'das Staatsrechtliche Recht am Gebiete ist daher nichts als ein Reflex der personenherrschaft. Es ist ein Reflexrecht, kein Recht im subjektiven sinne'.

[80] Romano, 'Osservazioni' (n 78) 210–12. As we see, the book of Carl Victor von Fricker, *Vom Staatsgebiet* (n 5), was the starting point for this kind of approach. The influence of the German doctrine on Santi Romano has been studied by Alessandra Di Martino, *Il territorio dallo stato-nazione alla globalizzazione. Sfide e prospettive dello stato costituzionale aperto* (Giuffrè 2011) 191–94, 210ff.

[81] Romano, 'Osservazioni' (n 78) 214–15; see also Santi Romano, *Il diritto pubblico italiano* (Giuffrè 1988) 56–57; then Santi Romano, *Corso di diritto coloniale* (Atheneum 1918) 114–23; Santi Romano, *Corso di diritto internazionale* (Cedam 1926) 139–40.

new perspectives on the changes that the colonial expansion had produced in the structures of the European liberal state itself. Thus, assuming the colony as point of observation of Europe, Romano inverted the most obvious approach concerning relationships between centre and periphery, and started to use the colony and its exceptionality to reflect on the limits of the parliamentarian system, on the crisis of the rule of law as a form of modern European state, and on the opportunity to overcome a normativistic approach to law.

Bibliography

'Acte général de la Conférence de Berlin, 26.3.1885' in Wilhelm G Grewe (ed), *Fontes Historiae Iuris Gentium* (de Gruyter 1995)

'Extrait du procès-verbal de la séance plénière tenue par l'Institut, à Lausanne, le 7 septembre 1888, sous la présidence de M. Rivier' (1889) 10 Annuaire de l'Institut de droit international 176

'Projet Martitz', Article VI (1888) 9 Annuaire de l'Institut de droit international 249

'Protocole no 8 (Séance du 31.1.1885)' (1885) 15 Archives diplomatiques 253

'Quatrième commision d'études: Examen de la théorie de la conférence de Berlin de 1885, sur l'occupation des territoires' (1888) 9 Annuaire de l'Institut de droit international 247

'Traité séparé entre la Russie et la Porte relatif aux principautés de Moldavie et de Valachie, (signed 2–14 September 1829)' in Georg Friederich von Martens, Friederich Saalfeld (eds), *Nouveau Recueil de Traites* (Dieterich 1831)

Adam, Robert, 'Völkerrechtliche Okkupation und deutsches Kolonialstaatsrecht' (1891) 6 Archiv für öffentliches Rechts 193 233

Arcoleo, Felice, *Il problema coloniale nel diritto pubblico* (Pierro 1914)

Arneil, Barbara, *John Locke and America: The Defence of English Colonialism* (Clarendon Press 1996)

Augusti, Eliana, 'L'intervento europeo in Oriente nel XIX secolo: storia contesa di un istituto controverso' in Luigi Nuzzo and Milos Vec (eds), *Constructing International Law: The Birth of a Discipline* (Vittorio Klostermann 2012)

Augusti, Eliana, *Questioni di Oriente: Europa e impero ottomano nel diritto internazionale dell'Ottocento* (Edizioni Scientifiche Italiane 2013)

Benton, Lauren and Straumann, Benjamin, 'Acquiring Empire by Law: From Roman Law to Early Modern European Practice' (2010) 28 Law and History Review 1

Bluntschli, Johann Caspar, *Das moderne Völkerrecht der civilisirten Staaten als Rechtsbuch dargestellt* (Beck 1868)

Boghitchiévitch, M, *Halbsouveranität: Administrative und politische Autonomie seit dem Pariser Vertrag* (Springer 1903)

Bonfils, Henry, *Manuel de droit international public (droit des gens)* (Rousseau 1894)

Bornhak, Conrad, 'Die Anfänge des deutschen Kolonialstaatsrechts' (1887) 2 Archiv für öffentliches Recht 7

Bornhak, Conrad, *Einseitige Ahängigkeitsverhältnisse unter den modernen Staaten* (Duncker & Humblot 1896)

Bulmerincq, August von, 'Consularrecht' in Franz von Holtzendorff (ed), *Handbuch des Völkerrechts* (Richter 1887)

Catellani, Enrico Levi, *Le colonie e la conferenza di Berlino*, (Unione Tipografica Editrice 1885)

Cavaglieri, Arrigo, *Contributo alla definizione di alcune figure del diritto pubblico contemporaneo* (Tipografia dell'Unione cooperativa editrice 1906)

Clavero, Bartolomé, *Freedom Law and Indigenous Rights: From Europe's Oeconomy to the Constitutionalism of the Americas* (Robbins Collection 2005)

Clercq, Jules De, *Recueil des Traités de la France* (Durand et Pedone Lauriel 1880)

Contuzzi, Francesco, *Trattato teorico-pratico di diritto consolare e diplomatico nei raffronti coi Codici (civile, commerciale, penale e giudiziario) e con le convenzioni in vigore* (Utet 1910)

Craven, Matthew, 'The Invention of a Tradition: Westlake, the Berlin Conference and the Historicization of International Law' in Luigi Nuzzo and Milos Vec (eds), *Constructing International Law: The Birth of a Discipline* (Vittorio Klostermann 2012)

Deherpe, Louis, *Essai sur le développement de l'occupation en droit international: Etablissement et déformation de l'œuvre de la conférence de Berlin 1885* (Librairie de la Société du recueil général de lois et des arrêts 1903)

Despagnet, Frantz, *Cours de droit international public* (Larose 1894) 425

Despagnet, Frantz, 'Les occupations de territoire et le procédé de l'Hinterland' (1894) 1 Revue générale de droit international public 103

Despagnet, Frantz, *Essai sur les protectorats: Étude de droit international* (Librairie de la société du recueil général des lois et des arrêts 1896)

Di Martino, Alessandra , *Il territorio dallo stato-nazione alla globalizzazione: Sfide e prospettive dello stato costituzionale aperto* (Giuffrè 2011)

Engelhardt, Eduard, 'Étude sur la déclaration de la Conférence de Berlin relative aux occupation' (1886) 18 Revue du droit international et de législation comparée 573

Engelhardt, Eduard, 'Projet de déclaration internationale proposé' (1888) 9 Annuaire de l'Institut de droit international 251

Féraud-Giraud, Louis-Joseph-Delphin, *De la juridiction française dans les échelles du levant et de barbarie: Étude sur la condition légale des étrangers dans le pays hors chrétienté* (Thorin 1866)

Féraud-Giraud, Louis-Joseph-Delphin, *Les justices mixtes dans les pays hors chrétienté: causeries à l'occasion d'un essai de réglementation internationale* (Durand & Pedone Lauriel 1884)

Field, David Dudley, 'De la possibilité d'appliquer le droit international européen aux nations orientales' (1875) 7 Revue du droit international et législation comparée 659

Fiocchi, Malaspina Elisabetta, 'La ricezione e la circolazione di "Le droit des gens" di Emmer de Vattel nel XIX secolo' (2013) 43 Materiali per una storia della cultura giuridica moderna 303

Fioravanti, Maurizio, *Giuristi e costituzione nell'Ottocento tedesco* (Giuffrè 1979)

Fiore, Pasquale, *Trattato di diritto internazionale pubblico* (2nd edn, Unione Tipografico Editrice 1882)

Fiore, Pasquale, *Il diritto internazionale codificato e la sua sanzione giuridica* (Unione Tipografico Editrice 1900)

Fiore, Pasquale, 'Du Protectorat colonial et de la sphère d'influence (hinterland)' (1907) 14 Revue générale de droit international public 148

Fisch, Jörg, *Die europäische Expansion und das Völkerrecht: Die Auseinandersetzungen um den Status der überseeischen Gebiete vom 15. Jahrhundert bis zur Gegenwart* (Steiner 1984)

Fisch, Jörg, 'Africa as terra nullius: The Berlin Conference and International Law' in Stig Förster, Wolfgang J Mommsen, and Ronald Robinson (eds), *Bismarck, Europe, and Africa: The Berlin Africa Conference 1884–1885 and the Onset of Partition* (Oxford University Press 1988)

Fisch, Jörg, 'Zivilisation, Kultur' in Otto Brunner, Werner Conze, Reinhart Koselleck (eds), *Geschichtliche Grundbegriffe: Historische Lexikon zur politisch-sozialen Sprache in Deutschland* (Klett Cotta 1992)

Fizmaurice, Andrew, *Sovereignty, Property and Empire 1500–2000* (Cambridge University Press 2014)

Fusinato, Guido, 'Le mutazioni territoriali: Il loro fondamento giuridico e le loro conseguenze' in Guido Fusinato, *Scritti giuridici* (Bocca 1921)

Gentili, Alberico, *De iure belli libri III* (Clarendon Press 1933)

Gerber, Carl Friedrich, *Grundzüge eines Systems des deutschen Statsrechts* (Tauchnitz 1865)

Ghirardini, Carlo, 'Delle cosidette "occupazioni qualificate" nel diritto internazionale' (1912) 6 Rivista di diritto internazionale 32

Grotius, Hugo, *De iure belli ac pacis libri tres* (BJA De Kanter van Hettinga Tromp, R Feenstra, and CE Persenaire eds, Scientia 1993)

Hall, William Edward, *A Treatise on the Foreign Powers and Jurisdiction of the British Crown* (Scientia, 1979)

Heffter, August W, *Das Europäische Recht der Gegenwart* (8th edn, Schroede 1882)

Heilborn, Paul, *Das völkerrechtliche Protektorat* (Springer 1891)

Heimburger, Karl, *Der Erwerb der Gebietshoheit: Eine Staats- und völkerrechtliche Studie* (Braun'schen Hofbuchdruckerei 1888)

Hinz, Paul Erich, *Die Rechtsbegriffe 'Inland' und 'Ausland' in Anwendung auf die deutschen Schutzgebiete* (Noske 1908)

Hoffmann, Edler, *Deutsches Kolonialrecht* (Göschen'sche Verlagshandlung 1907)

Holtzendorff, Franz von, 'Das Landgebiet der Staaten' in Franz von Holtzendorff (ed), *Handbuch des Völkerrechts* (Richter 1887)

Holtzendorff, Franz von, 'Der Staat als rechtliche Persönlichkeit' in Franz von Holtzendorff (ed), *Handbuch des Völkerrechts* (Richter 1887)

Holtzendorff, Arndt von, *Die koloniale Frage und ihre Lösung durch das Reich* (Gaertner's Verlagsbuchhandlung 1889)

Hornung, Joseph, 'Civilisés et barbares' (1885) 17 Revue de droit international et de législation comparée 1

Jellinek, Georg, *Ueber Staatsfragmente* (Koester 1896)

Jellinek, Georg, *Allgemeine Staatslehre* (3rd edn, Scientia 1966)

Jèze, Gaston, *Étude théorique et pratique sur l'occupation comme mode d'acquérir les territoires en droit international* (Giard et Briére 1896)

Kaufmann, Erich, *Das Wesen des Völkerrechts und die clausola rebus sic stantibus: Eine rechtsphilosophische Studie zum Rechts-, Staats- und Vertragsbegriffe* (Scientia 1964)

Kayaoğlu, Turan, *Legal Imperialism: Sovereignty and Extraterritoriality in Japan, the Ottoman Empire, and China* (Cambridge University Press 2010)

Klüber, Johann Ludwig, *Droit des gens moderne de l'Europe* (2nd edn, Aillaud 1831)

Köbner, Otto, *Die Organisation der Rechtspflege in den Kolonien* (Mittler und Sohn 1903)

Koskenniemi, Martti, *The Gentle Civilizer of Nations: The Rise and Fall of International Law 1870–1960* (Cambridge University Press 2001)

Krauel, A, 'Applicabilité du droit des gens européen à la Chine' (1875) 9 Revue du droit international et de législation comparée 387

Laband, Paul, *Das Staatsrecht des Deutschen Reiches* (5th edn, Mohr 1911)

Lenter, Ferdinand, *Das internationale Colonialrecht* (Manz'sche Hof- Verlags- und Universitäts Buchhandlung 1886)

Lesaffer, Randall, 'Argument from Roman Law in Current International Law: Occupation and Acquisitive Prescription' (2005) 16 European Journal of International Law 25

Liebensy, Herbert J, 'The Development of Western Judicial Privileges' in Majid Khadduri and Herbert Liebensy (eds), *Law in the Middle East* (Middle East Institute 1955)

Lindley, Mark Frank, *The Acquisition and Government of Backward Territory in International Law* (Longmans, Green and Co Ltd 1926)

Liszt, Frantz von, *Völkerrecht systematisch dargestellt* (9th edn, Haering 1913)

Locke, John, *Two Treaties of Government* in *The Works of John Locke* (Scientia 1963)

Loiseau, Charles, *Traité des seigneurs* (chez Abel l'Angelier 1609)

Martens, Fyodor Fyodorovich, *Das Consularwesen und die Consularjurisdiction im Orient* (Weidmansche Buchhandlung 1874)

Martens, Fyodor Fyodorovich, *Völkerrecht: Das internationale Recht der civilisirten Nationen systematisch dargestellt* (Carl Bergbohm tr, Weidmann 1883)

Martens, Georg Friedrich von, *Précis du droit des gens moderne augmenté des notes de Pinheiro-Ferreira: Précédé d'une introduction et complété par l'exposition des doctrines des publicistes contemporains et suivi d'une Bibliographie raisonnée du Droit des gens (1785–1788)* (M Ch Vergé ed, 2nd edn, Guillaumin et Cie Libraries 1864)

Martitz, Ferdinand von, 'Das Internationale System zur Unterdrückung des Afrikanischen Sklavenhandels in seinem heutigen Bestande' (1886) 1 Archiv für öffentliches Recht 3

Meyer, Georg, *Die staatsrechtliche Stellung der deutschen Schutzgebiete* (Duncker und Humblot 1888)

Milosevitch, Milan, *Les Traités de garantie au XIX siècle: Étude de droit international et d'histoire diplomatique* (Rousseau 1888)

Mondaini, Gennaro, *La sfera di influenza nella storia coloniale e nel diritto* (Seeber 1902)

Nuzzo, Luigi, *Il linguaggio giuridico della Conquista: Strategie di controllo nelle Indie spagnole* (Jovene 2004)

Nuzzo, Luigi, 'A Dark Side of the West Legal Modernity: The Colonial Law and its Subject' (2011) 33 Zeitschrift für neure Rechtsgeschichte 205

Nuzzo, Luigi, 'Kolonialrecht' Europäische Geschichte Online (EGO) <http://www.ieg-ego.eu/nuzzol-2011-de> accessed 14 April 2016

Nuzzo, Luigi, 'History, Science and Religion: International Law and the Savigny's Paradigm' in Luigi Nuzzo and Milos Vec (eds), *Constructing International Law: The Birth of a Discipline* (Vittorio Klostermann 2012)

Nuzzo, Luigi, *Origini di una scienza: Diritto internazionale e colonialismo nel XIX secolo* (Vittorio Klostermann 2012)

Pélissie du, Rausas Gustave, *Le regime des capitulations dans l'empire ottoman* (Rousseau 1902)

Petit, Carlos, 'Il modello coloniale dello Stato di diritto: La Costituzione africana in Guinea' in Pietro Costa and Danilo Zolo (eds), *Lo stato di diritto: Storia, teoria, critica* (Feltrinelli 2002)

Phillimore, Robert, *Commentaries upon International Law* (3rd edn, Butterworths 1879)

Pradier, Fodéré Paul, *Traité de droit international public européen et américain, suivant les progrès de la science et de la pratique contemporaines* (Durand et Pedone Lauriel 1885)

Protocole no XIV (Séance du 25 mars 1856), attachment to Traité de Paix signé à Paris le 30 mars 1856 (Imprimerie Royale 1856)

Rivier, Alphonse, *Principes du droit de gens* (Rousseau 1896)

Rolin-Jaequemyns, Gustav, 'Le droit international et la phase actuelle de la Question d'Orient' (1876) 8 Revue du droit international et de législation comparée 293

Romano, Santi, *Corso di diritto coloniale* (Atheneum 1918)

Romano, Santi, *Corso di diritto internazionale* (Cedam 1926)

Romano, Santi, *Il diritto pubblico italiano* (Giuffrè 1988)

Romano, Santi, 'Osservazioni sulla natura giuridica del territorio dello Stato' in Santi Romano, *Scritti minori* (Guido Zanobini ed, Giuffrè 1990)

Salomon, Charles, *L'occupation des territoires sans maître: Étude de droit international* (Giard 1889)

Sassen, Franz Joseph, *Das Gesetzgebung und Verordnungsrecht in den deutschen Kolonien* (Laupp 1909)

Schack, Friedrich, *Das deutsche Kolonialrecht in seiner Entwicklung bis zum Weltkriege: Die allgemeinen Lehren: Eine berichtende Darstellung der Theorie und Praxis nebst kritischen Bemerkungen* (Friederichsen & Co 1923)

Schmalz, Theodor Anton Heinrich, *Das europäische Völker-Recht, in acht Büchern* (Duncker & Humblot 1817)

Stengel, Karl Freiherr von, *Die Rechtsverhältnisse der deutschen Schutzgebiete* (Mohr 1901)

Stolleis, Michael, *Geschichte des öffentlichen Rechts in Deutschland* (Beck 1989)

Traité de Paix signé à Paris le 30 mars 1856 (Imprimerie Royale 1856)

Tuck, Richard, *The Rights of War and Peace, Political Thought and the International Order from Grotius to Kant* (Oxford University Press 1999)

Twiss, Traver, *The Laws of the Nations considered as Independent Political Communities: On the Right and Duties of Nations in Time of Peace* (Oxford University Press 1884)

Vattel, Emmerich De, *Le droits des gens ou principe de la loi naturelle appliqués à la conduite et aux affaires des nations et des souverains* (Hein 1995)

Vitoria, Francisco de, *Relectio de Indis* (Luciano Pereña and José Manuel Pérez ed, Consejo Superior de Investigaciones Científicas 1967)

Westlake, John, *International Law* (Cambridge University Press 1904)

Westlake, John, *The Collected Papers of John Westlake on Public International Law* (Lassa Oppenheim ed, Cambridge University Press 1914)

Williams Jr, Robert, *The American Indian in Western Legal Thought: The Discourse of Conquest* (Oxford University Press 1990)

PART IV

A LEGAL CRITIQUE OF EMPIRE?

12

An Anti-Imperialist Universalism? *Jus Cogens* and the Politics of International Law

Umut Özsu

If international law has long been denounced for its idealism, its insufficient engagement with the concrete materiality of political and economic power, there is arguably no better illustration of the kind of murky generality to which its critics regularly point than *jus cogens*. Indeed, international lawyers have themselves voiced a considerable amount of scepticism about *jus cogens* over the years. Even before the 1969 Vienna Convention on the Law of Treaties, the first and still the most significant attempt to secure formal recognition for *jus cogens*, numerous arguments were mounted against its overt integration into positive international law. Some expressed discomfort at the fact that no authoritative enumeration of *jus cogens* norms was available,[1] while others claimed that they were products of 'fashionably "progressive", if unrealistic, thinking', with the lack of a meta-sovereign superordinate authority rendering the very idea of *jus cogens* something between an 'empty stunt' and a formula that 'can readily be made to serve hidden sectional interests'.[2] These and related sentiments have only gained strength since the Vienna Convention's entry into force in 1980. Positivists have rejected *jus cogens* as a throwback to natural law that has never won approval from a sufficient number of states,[3] feminists have argued that *jus cogens* norms fail to deliver on their universalistic promise by prioritizing the experiences of men,[4] and realists have maintained that

---

[1] Egon Schwelb, 'Some Aspects of International *Jus Cogens* as Formulated by the International Law Commission' (1967) 61 American Journal of International Law 946, 963–64, 973.

[2] Georg Schwarzenberger, 'International *Jus Cogens*?' (1965) 43 Texas Law Review 455, 476–78, 467. See also Georg Schwarzenberger, 'The Problem of International Public Policy' (1965) 18 Current Legal Problems 191.

[3] Michael J Glennon, 'De l'absurdité du droit impératif (*jus cogens*)' (2006) 110 Revue générale de droit international public 529. Natural law appears in different guises in the debate on *jus cogens*. For useful discussion see Jerzy Sztucki, Jus Cogens *and the Vienna Convention on the Law of Treaties: A Critical Appraisal* (Springer-Verlag 1974) 59–66; Antonio Gómez Robledo, 'Le *ius cogens* international: sa genèse, sa nature, ses fonctions' (1981) 172 Recueil des cours 9, 23–32; Mark W Janis, 'The Nature of *Jus Cogens*' (1988) 3 Connecticut Journal of International Law 359, 361–63.

[4] Hilary Charlesworth and Christine Chinkin, 'The Gender of *Jus Cogens*' (1993) 15 Human Rights Quarterly 63.

International Law and Empire: Historical Explorations. First Edition. Martti Koskenniemi, Walter Rech, and Manuel Jiménez Fonseca. © Martti Koskenniemi, Walter Rech, and Manuel Jiménez Fonseca 2016. Published 2016 by Oxford University Press.

jus cogens presupposes an international judiciary equipped to distinguish it from *jus dispositivum*, not to mention a world in which political and economic power does not actually determine its scope and content.[5] Alongside the closely related concept of obligations *erga omnes*,[6] the idea of international *jus cogens* has even been dismissed as a kind of kitsch—an artefact that enjoys no roots in reality but that continues to circulate on the basis of a widely felt desire for ready-made solutions to injustice and inequality.[7]

This study takes its lead from Article 53 of the Vienna Convention, a provision that purports to nullify any treaty which conflicts with a 'peremptory norm of general international law'—that is, 'a norm accepted and recognized by the international community of States as a whole as a norm from which no derogation is permitted'.[8] The *locus classicus* of *jus cogens*, ostensibly the most sacrosanct and foundational of all international legal principles, Article 53 was negotiated against the background of a wide range of disputes relating to the limits of treaty-making. On the one hand were a large number of socialist and Third World states that saw the concept as a means of reforming, if not revolutionizing, international legal relations. Once *jus cogens* gained entry into international law, substantively unjust treaties and concessionary agreements would be regarded with much the same disdain as nineteenth-century unequal treaties, and the principle of self-determination would be accorded the same degree of normative weight as the prohibitions against slavery, genocide, and aggression. Article 53 was for many such states a galvanizing force, a source of solidarity promising to ensure that sovereign rights would not be contravened, at least not with the sort of impunity that had been possible

---

[5] Paul B Stephan, 'The Political Economy of *Jus Cogens*' (2011) 44 Vanderbilt Journal of Transnational Law 1073.

[6] On the complex relation between the two, see Michael Byers, 'Conceptualizing the Relationship between *Jus Cogens* and *Erga Omnes* Rules' (1997) 66 Nordic Journal of International Law 211; Christian J Tams, *Enforcing Obligations* Erga Omnes *in International Law* (Cambridge University Press 2005) 138–57; Christian Tomuschat, 'Reconceptualizing the Debate on *Jus Cogens* and Obligations *Erga Omnes*—Concluding Observations' in Christian Tomuschat and Jean-Marc Thouvenin (eds), *The Fundamental Rules of the International Legal Order:* Jus Cogens *and Obligations* Erga Omnes (Nijhoff 2006); Paolo Picone, 'The Distinction between *Jus Cogens* and Obligations *Erga Omnes*' in Enzo Cannizzaro (ed), *The Law of Treaties Beyond the Vienna Convention* (Oxford University Press 2011); Thomas Weatherhall, Jus Cogens: *International Law and Social Contract* (Cambridge University Press 2015) 8–11, 351–83. See also Alexander Orakhelashvili, *Peremptory Norms in International Law* (Oxford University Press 2006) ch 4.

[7] Martti Koskenniemi, 'International Law in Europe: Between Tradition and Renewal' (2005) 16 European Journal of International Law 113, 122. For a recent attempt to catalogue critiques of *jus cogens*, see Robert Kolb, *Peremptory International Law*—Jus Cogens: *A General Inventory* (Hart 2015) ch 2.

[8] Article 53 operates alongside Article 64, which provides that '[i]f a new peremptory norm of general international law emerges, any existing treaty which is in conflict with that norm becomes void and terminates', as well as Article 71, which requires states parties to '[e]liminate as far as possible the consequences of any act performed in reliance on any provision which conflicts with the peremptory norm of general international law' and to '[b]ring their mutual relations into conformity with the peremptory norm of general international law' if a treaty is held to be void under Article 53. Article 66 provides for recourse to the International Court of Justice in the event of a dispute as to the application or interpretation of Article 53. See Vienna Convention on the Law of Treaties (signed 23 May 1969) 1155 UNTS 331 (hereafter VCLT), 344, 347–49.

under formal colonialism. On the other hand was a group of Western states intent on holding firm to *pacta sunt servanda* and deeply sceptical of inflated notions of 'international community'. For such states, a failure to define and control the application of *jus cogens* jeopardized the putative clarity of international law's sources, introducing something dangerously similar to what Prosper Weil would later dub 'relative normativity', a nebulous spectrum of international authority in which a select group of rules were endowed with quasi-constitutional status at the expense of others.[9] Framed though it was in general terms, the juridical architecture of *jus cogens* was thus home to intense controversy, a patchwork of competing ideological and institutional pressures. How precisely was international *jus cogens* to be understood? Who was authorized to decide which rules of international law counted as *jus cogens*? In accordance with which criteria would these decisions be made? Would such determinations bind states that had opposed Article 53 or that did not agree that a given rule was of a peremptory character? These and other questions rendered *jus cogens* an object of sharp disagreement rather than a catalogue of unquestionable imperatives—a site of contestation upon which turned the entire regime of treaty law enshrined in the Vienna Convention.

I revisit the Vienna Convention's preparatory work with a view to analysing the way in which *jus cogens*—the putative apex of an 'international legal system' that only gains in complexity and heterogeneity with every passing year—was deployed by socialist and non-aligned states, in many cases often newly liberated from colonial rule.[10] This yields two results. First, examining the conditions under which *jus cogens* entered into widespread international legal discourse deepens appreciation of the fact that many elements of international law which are typically deemed to be axiomatic are in fact generated through sustained and acrimonious competition. To worry that international law's unity and integrity will be eroded if different courts, states, and organizations are allowed to designate different rules as *jus cogens*, as many continue to do today,[11] is to miss the point that *jus cogens*, like international law generally, has always been driven by fundamentally divergent projects, responsive to fundamentally different political and economic forces. The push to elaborate and devise enforcement mechanisms for *jus cogens* is rooted in a desire to safeguard international legal order by articulating its most rudimentary

---

[9] Prosper Weil, 'Towards Relative Normativity in International Law?' (1983) 77 American Journal of International Law 413.

[10] For the minutes of the various negotiations, see United Nations Conference on the Law of Treaties, First Session (Vienna 26 March–24 May 1968) UN Doc A/CONF.39/11 (hereafter UNCLOT I); United Nations Conference on the Law of Treaties, Second Session (Vienna 9 April–22 May 1969) UN Doc A/CONF.39/11/Add.1 (hereafter UNCLOT II). For a cross-section of the positions of states on the terms of what ultimately became Article 53, see Ralf Günter Wetzel and Dietrich Rauschning, *The Vienna Convention on the Law of Treaties: Travaux Préparatoires* (Alfred Metzner Verlag 1978) 371–79. A useful précis of the negotiating history can be found in Shabtai Rosenne, *The Law of Treaties: A Guide to the Legislative History of the Vienna Convention* (Sijthoff 1970) 290–93.

[11] See eg Karl Zemanek, 'The Metamorphosis of *Jus Cogens*: From an Institution of Treaty Law to the Bedrock of the International Legal Order?' in Cannizzaro (ed), *The Law of Treaties* (n 6) 409–10 (criticizing the EU Court of First Instance for purporting to pronounce on the compatibility of Security Council resolutions with *jus cogens* norms in its *Kadi* judgment).

'moral' and 'social' preconditions.[12] But if contemporary international law can be characterized as 'universal', this is so only to the extent that *jus cogens*, arguably the strongest and most explicit source of its claim to 'universality', has been constructed on the basis of far-reaching conflict between competing visions of world order. Second, *jus cogens'* contentious history highlights the difficulty of developing a properly emancipatory political programme through lofty appraisals of international law's normative force. The absence of a definitive list of peremptory norms has encouraged advocates to apply the notion to everything from tyrannicide to the Brezhnev Doctrine to the concept of a 'common heritage of mankind',[13] and loose invocations of 'humanity' of the sort issued by *jus cogens'* proponents seem almost designed to invite Schmittian charges of hypocrisy and dissimulation. Moreover, *jus cogens* has contributed only marginally to the effort to consolidate the achievements of decolonization by way of a top-to-bottom reconfiguration of international legal order—the project upon which many of its adherents originally pinned their hopes and in the name of which they were wont to marshal large doses of messianic rhetoric. When all is said and done, *jus cogens*, presented by its advocates (and even by some of its opponents) as the spearhead of international law's 'progressive mission', has proven no more valuable a means of furthering respect for sovereign equality, still less facilitating a global redistribution of wealth, than the rather prosaic formalism it was intended to supplant.

Forging the Universal

Conceptually murky and politically contested though it may be, *jus cogens* boasts an extensive and multifaceted international legal history. For centuries the idea that a particular class of legal norms imposed binding obligations upon all states fed abhorrence of the pirate as the archetypal 'enemy of mankind'. From Roman law to the Permanent Court of International Law's decision in the *Lotus* case, the pirate was characterized as an anti-social enemy of the law of nations, an outlaw against whom action can and should be undertaken by all and sundry.[14] Similarly, in the late nineteenth century, moralistic condemnation of the slave trade resulted in its characterization as a fundamental contravention of international law. The prohibition was reinforced in the early twentieth century, largely by way of the League of Nations Covenant and the 1926 Slavery Convention, both of which

---

[12] To take but one example, Andreas Paulus has sought to defend *jus cogens* in light of US hegemonic power and international law's increased technical disaggregation. See Andreas L Paulus, '*Jus Cogens* in a Time of Hegemony and Fragmentation' (2005) 74 Nordic Journal of International Law 297.

[13] For these and other examples, see Dinah Shelton, 'Normative Hierarchy in International Law' (2006) 100 American Journal of International Law 291, 303.

[14] Thus, Judge Moore's dissenting opinion in the *Lotus* case harkened back to Roman law when branding the pirate 'an outlaw ... the enemy of all mankind—*hostis humani generis*—whom any nation may in the interest of all capture and punish'. *Case of the S.S. 'Lotus'* (*France v. Turkey*) PCIJ Rep Series A No 10 (1927), 70. For a suggestive sweep of the general history see Daniel Heller-Roazen, *The Enemy of All: Piracy and the Law of Nations* (Zone 2009).

instituted duties to prevent and suppress the trade.[15] Juridical opinion responded to these and other developments, such as the drive to ban aggression or cement the distinction between civilians and combatants, by speculating about the legal foundations of international order. In his separate opinion in the *Oscar Chinn* case, Walther Schücking, for instance, wrote that a treaty should be voided if it ran afoul of 'international public policy', making explicit reference to *jus cogens* in the process.[16] Similarly, in one of the earliest attempts to subject the notion of international *jus cogens* to scholarly examination, Alfred Verdross suggested that no treaty can violate the foundational principles of international law, 'the *ethical minimum* recognized by all the states of the international community'.[17] Writing at a time when many lamented the 'social disintegration in the international community' resulting from the deracination of the League project and the apparent inevitability of global war,[18] Verdross approached the question from a standpoint informed by natural law theory but responsive to elements of Kelsenian formalism, dismissing the notion that a legal instrument could stand in the way of 'the universally recognized tasks of a civilized state' by claiming that a treaty which failed to respect the lives, liberties, and proprietary rights of a party's population was in reality no treaty at all.[19] Nevertheless, the real work was left for the mid-twentieth century. Despite the ubiquity of the concept of *ordre public* or *öffentliche Ordnung* in nineteenth- and early twentieth-century treatises on international law, it was only after the Second World War, in the context of a series of reports by the International Law Commission that would culminate in the Vienna Convention, that *jus cogens*, an idea with roots in both the civil law and common law traditions, came to be adopted by international lawyers. Article 53, the product of years of study, debate, and hard bargaining, was to be the cornerstone of a new corpus of 'imperative international law', promising to do away with exclusive forms of consensualism once and for all.

As always, context is crucially important. If the drive to articulate and establish international *jus cogens* came to a head only after the Second World War, it did so in a context marked by deeply stratified models of world order, not least those seeking

---

[15] For a thorough review see Lauri Hannikainen, *Peremptory Norms* (Jus Cogens*) in International Law: Historical Development, Criteria, Present Status* (Lakimiesliiton Kustannus 1988) 75–87, 137–39. See also Jenny S Martinez, *The Slave Trade and the Origins of International Human Rights Law* (Oxford University Press 2012).

[16] The *Oscar Chinn* case (*United Kingdom v. Belgium*) PCIJ Rep Series A/B No 63 (1934), 149–50.

[17] Alfred von Verdross, 'Forbidden Treaties in International Law' (1937) 31 American Journal of International Law 571, 574 (original emphasis). For an even earlier attempt see Friedrich August von der Heydte, 'Die Erscheinungsformen des zwischenstaatlichen Rechts: *jus cogens* und *jus dispositivum* im Völkerrecht' (1932) 16 Zeitschrift für Völkerrecht 461.

[18] Wolfgang Friedmann, 'The Disintegration of European Civilisation and the Future of International Law: Some Observations on the Social Foundations of Law' (1938) 2 Modern Law Review 194, 213.

[19] Verdross, 'Forbidden Treaties' (n 17) 574, 577. Two years earlier Verdross had already provided a sketch of this argument in 'Anfechtbare und nichtige Staatsverträge' (1935) 15 Zeitschrift für öffentliches Recht 289. He would defend the position further thirty years later, taking the opportunity to comment on the ILC's work and respond to criticisms from the likes of Schwarzenberger: see Alfred Verdross, '*Jus Dispositivum* and *Jus Cogens* in International Law' (1966) 60 American Journal of International Law 55, especially 60–63.

to distinguish between a 'First World' of market capitalism, a 'Second World' of 'democratically deficient' socialism, and a 'Third World' of pervasive poverty and uneven development.[20] This and similar frameworks were appropriated and reconfigured by a great many non-Western states, frequently as part of a process of decolonization that saw the emergence of an ambitious Non-Aligned Movement and the expansion of an already powerful socialist bloc. Writing in 1960, only five years after the Bandung Conference, Bert Röling was already taken by the depth of cooperation he saw across Asia and Africa. In his view, '[t]he common experience of the colonial pattern, the comparable struggle for freedom fought by all, and the resented low standard of living produce[d] a common attitude and opinion with which the old countries are forced to reckon'.[21] Rival ambitions and the emergence of competing factions engendered serious difficulties, but solidarity ties between Third World states only gained force in the years that followed. By 1973, only a year before the General Assembly adopted the Declaration and Programme of Action on the Establishment of a New International Economic Order and the closely related Charter of Economic Rights and Duties of States, Georges Abi-Saab, impressed by the Non-Aligned Movement's resilience, was characterizing Article 53 as the Third World's 'greatest triumph' in the Vienna negotiations.[22] Just as the logic of the dominant Cold War vision of a politico-economically segmented international system enjoyed influence among elites in the First World, who tended to view *jus cogens* with suspicion, so too did it find support among jurists and policymakers in the Second and Third Worlds, who agitated to secure formal recognition for *jus cogens*.

All of this exerted a profound influence upon *jus cogens*, feeding directly into the final wording of Article 53. Statements made by delegates at the 1968–69 Vienna Conference on the Law of Treaties were often marked by ambiguity, and it was not uncommon for states to modify their positions in light of ongoing discussions, amendment proposals, and revised drafts of various provisions. Even among states that backed an explicit reference to *jus cogens* in the final treaty, there was significant disagreement as to how such principles ought to be understood and operationalized. Some delegates attempted to frame *jus cogens* as 'an evolutionary, not a revolutionary, juridical concept',[23] or as 'an essential and inherently dynamic ingredient of international law',[24] whereas others were more effusive in their support, branding

---

[20] Such models owed much of their popularity to the modernization theory of the late 1950s and 1960s. For the emergence and development of modernization theory, see Nils Gilman, *Mandarins of the Future: Modernization Theory in Cold War America* (Johns Hopkins University Press 2003); David C Engerman et al (eds), *Staging Growth: Modernization, Development, and the Global Civil War* (University of Massachusetts Press 2003); Nicolas Guilhot, *The Democracy Makers: Human Rights and the Politics of Global Order* (Columbia University Press 2005) ch 3. For the original articulation of the division between the 'First', 'Second', and 'Third' 'Worlds', see Alfred Sauvy, 'Trois mondes, une planète' (14 August 1952) 118 L'Observateur 14.

[21] BVA Röling, *International Law in an Expanded World* (Djambatan 1960) 73.

[22] Georges Abi-Saab, 'The Third World and the Future of the International Legal Order' (1973) 29 Revue égyptienne de droit international 27, 52.

[23] UNCLOT I (n 10) 298 (Nigeria). See also UNCLOT II (n 10) 98 (Cameroon).

[24] UNCLOT I (n 10) 301 (Ghana).

it 'the universal legal conscience of civilized countries',[25] 'the higher interests of the international community as a whole',[26] or the direct or indirect outgrowth of a long and venerable tradition of natural law theory.[27] Nevertheless, it is not difficult to distinguish between two basic perspectives on the draft of what became Article 53, and this distinction was both real and consequential. First World states generally argued that the murkiness of an undefined *jus cogens* would encourage arbitrary violations of international law, and that invalidating treaties on grounds of non-conformity with *jus cogens* was supported neither by existing case law nor by established state practice.[28] For their part, delegates from the socialist bloc and the Third World tended to present *jus cogens* as a 'milestone in the development of the codification of law',[29] not least as they were convinced that '[a] treaty which had been imposed by force was void *ab initio*' and that '[i]t would be contrary to the very concept of justice and to the rules of *jus cogens* to claim otherwise'.[30] Critics expressed concern at the attempt to transfer a concept of domestic private law to the international law of treaties: imposing limits upon the freedom of contract might make sense in the domestic context, as in situations of unconscionability or undue influence, but the will of a sovereign state was not that of an individual rights-bearer and restricting laissez-faire treaty-making was therefore difficult, if not altogether impossible.[31] Enthusiasts countered by pointing out that the kind of normative hierarchy presupposed by *jus cogens* was intrinsic to international law and had little if anything to do with municipal law. International law had its own architecture, and *jus cogens*, whatever its origins and ultimate effects, was an indispensable component of that architecture.[32] References were made to Hersch Lauterpacht, Georg

---

[25] Ibid, 301 (Colombia).   [26] Ibid, 305 (Cyprus).

[27] For variations on this theme see eg UNCLOT I (n 10) 8 (Spain), 258 (Holy See), 294 (Mexico), 311 (Italy), 320 (Ecuador); and also UNCLOT II (n 10) 95 (F.R.G.), 104 (Italy), 105 (Costa Rica), 294 (Monaco). For countervailing considerations and charitable accounts of legal positivism see eg UNCLOT I (n 10) 311 (Hungary), 327 (Humphrey Waldock).

[28] See eg UNCLOT I (n 10) 216 (Australia), 275–76 (Netherlands), 304–05 (UK), 309 (France), 323 (Canada), 323–24 (Switzerland), 324–25 (Norway). See also UNCLOT II (n 10) 94–95 (France), 97–98 (UK), 103 (Switzerland), 105 (Netherlands), 106 (Belgium), 107 (Japan).

[29] UNCLOT I (n 10) 219 (Ceylon). And in a similar tone, see also 296 (Kenya), 296–97 (Cuba), 322–23 (Philippines), 326 (Malaysia), 327 (Mali). See further UNCLOT II (n 10) 95 (Philippines), 98 (Colombia), 103 (Cyprus).

[30] UNCLOT I (n 10) 154 (Bolivia). For related points, see also UNCLOT I (n 10) 220–21 (USSR), 264–65 (Ethiopia), 274–75 (Cuba), 312–13 (Romania), 318 (Czechoslovakia). See further UNCLOT II (n 10) 104 (USSR). The specific issue of 'imposed treaties' would be addressed explicitly in a number of other provisions of the Vienna Convention, particularly Article 52 ('A treaty is void if its conclusion has been procured by the threat or use of force in violation of the principles of international law embodied in the Charter of the United Nations'). See VCLT (n 8) 344. The issue was of serious concern to Western, socialist, and non-aligned states and jurists alike; for a synoptic overview see Stuart S Malawer, *Imposed Treaties and International Law* (William S Hein 1977), especially 79–105, 129–34.

[31] See eg UNCLOT I (n 10) 221, 299–300 (Turkey); UNCLOT II (n 10) 99 (Turkey), 106 (Belgium). For differing approaches to this question, one of the most complex to arise from the debate regarding *jus cogens*, see especially Elsayed Abdel Raouf Elreedy, 'The Main Features of the Concept of Invalidity in the Vienna Convention on Treaties' (1971) 27 Revue égyptienne de droit international 13; Ian Sinclair, *The Vienna Convention on the Law of Treaties* (2nd ed, Manchester University Press 1984) 205–06.

[32] See eg UNCLOT I (n 10) 302 (Poland).

Schwarzenberger, and others in an effort to buttress all manner of positions during the course of these debates.[33]

An especially lucid illustration of this divide is offered by a debate stemming from an amendment proposed by the United States. The amendment was one of many to be floated during the Vienna Conference, but served as something of a lodestone, attracting widespread approbation and denunciation in the process. Anxious that *jus cogens* would be used to circumvent national sovereignty, American delegates suggested that Article 53 contain a reference to norms that were recognized as being of a peremptory character by 'the national and regional legal systems of the world'.[34] Evidently 'ultra-nationalist',[35] the proposal was defended by a number of Western states. France, the most rigorous and trenchant critic of international *jus cogens*,[36] stressed that the question—an 'extremely important' one that lay on the 'ill-defined borderline between morality and law'[37]—needed to be considered with great care. It was necessary to examine the issue in light of the present equality and not the past inequality of states, the French declared, this being the only way to avoid 'confrontation between the upholders of different political, social or economic systems'.[38] It was also necessary to avoid imprecision as to *jus cogens*' creation, scope, and effects,[39] especially by taking steps to control its application, as the contrary would force many states, particularly those subscribing to a monist conception of the relation between domestic and international law, to evaluate the validity of treaties in accordance with a 'supreme, undefined law', eviscerating the 'climate of security and confidence' requisite for smooth interstate relations.[40] The American proposal went some way to stabilizing *jus cogens*, furnishing an 'objective criterion' for ascribing *jus cogens* status to some but not other rules.[41] A variety of other states threw their weight behind this and related initiatives.[42] Australia, for instance, agreed with much of the United States' draft amendment, but went on to lend its support to a rather dubious suggestion to count as peremptory norms only those rules of general international law that were accepted as such by the world's 'principal' legal systems.[43]

---

[33] See eg ibid, 216, 316 (Australia), 298–99 (Chile).
[34] See UN Doc A/CONF.39/C.1/L.302, reproduced in United Nations Conference on the Law of Treaties, First and Second Sessions (Vienna 26 March–24 May 1968 and 9 April–22 May 1969), Documents of the Conference, UN Doc A/CONF.39/11/Add.2, 174. See also UNCLOT I (n 10) 295, 330 (USA).
[35] UNCLOT I (n 10) 315 (Spain).
[36] France was so troubled by the nebulousness of *jus cogens* that it was one of only eight countries to vote against the adoption of what became Article 53 (the others being Australia, Belgium, Liechtenstein, Luxembourg, Monaco, Switzerland, and Turkey). Indeed, concerns about *jus cogens* played a key role in its ultimate decision to vote against the Vienna Convention, the only state to do so. For analysis see Olivier Deleau, 'Les positions françaises à la Conférence de Vienne sur le droit des traités' (1969) 15 Annuaire français de droit international 7, especially 14–17. For recent reconsideration see Hélène Ruiz Fabri, 'La France et la Convention de Vienne sur le droit des traités' in Gérard Cahin, Florence Poirat, and Sandra Szurek (eds), *La France et le droit international*, vol 1 (Pedone 2007).
[37] UNCLOT I (n 10) 309.　　　　[38] Ibid, 309.　　　　[39] UNCLOT II (n 10) 94.
[40] UNCLOT I (n 10) 309; UNCLOT II (n 10) 94.　　　　[41] UNCLOT I (n 10) 309–10.
[42] See eg ibid, 311 (Italy), 320 (Belgium), 323 (Canada), 324 (Switzerland), 326 (Malaysia), 330 (UK).
[43] Ibid, 317.

That said, the American proposal and its various offshoots came in for serious criticism from a majority of states, including nearly all those associated with the socialist bloc and Non-Aligned Movement. Just as Byelorussia opposed the American amendment on the grounds that it 'gave only second place to the principles of the United Nations Charter',[44] so too did Hungary state that 'it was not the internal or regional law of States but their co-ordinated will manifesting itself on the international plane that could become the source of a peremptory norm of international law'.[45] Cuba noted that the American proposal 'would enable a State to thwart any rule of *jus cogens* by invoking its domestic legislation',[46] Uruguay took issue with the fact that it might permit regional organizations to accord *jus cogens* status to aggressive policies,[47] and Tanzania argued that it would simply 'wreck' *jus cogens*, as 'it was well known that there were national systems whose basic principles were entirely contrary to what was believed to be the whole basis of *jus cogens*, namely, human dignity'.[48] Interestingly, Humphrey Waldock, the International Law Commission's fourth rapporteur on the law of treaties and a significant influence on the drafting of what would become Article 53, took the opportunity to respond to the American proposal, explaining that it 'approached the question from the wrong angle', since '[i]t was for the community of States as such to recognize the peremptory character of a norm'.[49] Thus, although the idea of 'regional' *jus cogens* was not without support among legal scholars at the time,[50] the American move was rejected.

Soviet policymakers were no less given to structuring their relations with the Third World in clientelistic terms than their American counterparts. Yet, as noted by jurists like Grigory Tunkin, the Soviet Union and its allies proved more than willing to assist less powerful states in Asia, Africa, and Latin America on the question of international *jus cogens*.[51] This gave rise to a paradox of sorts. In an effort to consolidate their domestic authority and stave off foreign intervention, socialist states had long relied upon strong conceptions of sovereignty, for the main part by

---

[44] Ibid, 307.   [45] Ibid, 311.   [46] Ibid, 297.   [47] Ibid, 303–04.
[48] Ibid, 322.   [49] Ibid, 328.
[50] For thoughts on the matter see eg Michel Virally, 'Réflexions sur le *"jus cogens"*' (1966) 12 Annuaire français de droit international 5, 14–15; Eric Suy, 'The Concept of *Jus Cogens* in Public International Law' in *The Concept of* Jus Cogens *in International Law: Conference on International Law, Lagonissi (Greece), April 3–8, 1966—Papers and Proceedings II* (Carnegie Endowment for International Peace 1967). Interestingly, such support would continue even after the conclusion of the Vienna Convention. See eg Sztucki, Jus Cogens *and the Vienna Convention* (n 3) 106–08; Giorgio Gaja, '*Jus Cogens* Beyond the Vienna Convention' (1981) 172 Recueil des cours 271, 284. But see also Charles de Visscher, 'Positivisme et *jus cogens*' (1971) 75 Revue générale de droit international public 5.
[51] See eg Grigory Tunkin, 'International Law in the International System' (1975) 147 Recueil des cours 1, 90ff; Grigory I Tunkin, *Theory of International Law* (William E Butler tr, Harvard University Press 1974) 154ff. For related claims, see also György Haraszti, *Some Fundamental Problems of the Law of Treaties* (Akadémiai Kiadó 1973) 157–58; Levan Alexidze, 'Legal Nature of *Jus Cogens* in Contemporary International Law' (1981) 172 Recueil des cours 219, 249–51ff. Tunkin was particularly significant in this regard. In addition to being the leading Soviet international lawyer, he had served as a member of the International Law Commission in the years preceding the Vienna Conference. International lawyers from socialist states had long stressed that the treaty-making power is constrained by certain fundamental principles; see eg Manfred Lachs, 'Le développement et les fonctions des traités multilatéraux' (1957) 92 Recueil des cours 229, 253–54.

prioritizing treaty over customary law, adopting a preponderantly dualist model of treaty incorporation, and subscribing to the thesis that socialist states belonged to a different 'camp' than bourgeois states. Even with the re-annexation of the Baltic states in 1944–45, the crushing of the Hungarian Revolution in 1956, and the push into Czechoslovakia in 1968, Soviet policy had made a point of presenting socialist internationalism as a means of forestalling military intervention and policing the boundaries of domestic jurisdiction. Further, despite the reluctance of many early Soviet thinkers to recognize the binding nature of international law, Soviet jurists had also come to position themselves at the forefront of the assault on natural law, arguing that reliance upon a crypto-theological 'international morality' under-mined the consensual foundations of international relations and made it possible for even the crassest imperialism to clothe itself in legal garb. International law was a fundamentally state-driven enterprise, they insisted, and speculating about the overriding authority of this or that class of moral principles would delegitimate and subvert respect for the will of independent states. Both tendencies—the commit-ment to state sovereignty and the strong critique of natural law[52]—posed signifi-cant problems for their espousal of *jus cogens*. After all, how could precisely those states that clung most uncompromisingly to strict interpretations of sovereignty present themselves as leading proponents of a body of normative injunctions with which no treaty could ever fail to conform? In what sense could support for *jus cogens* be reconciled with a stern, unqualified repudiation of the natural law tradi-tion, given that it was on just this tradition that many advocates relied, implicitly if not always explicitly, when developing arguments on behalf of *jus cogens*?

Of course, answers to such questions—to the extent that one can speak of 'answers' here at all—came in social rather than logical form. From a strictly logical standpoint, it was impossible to defend *jus cogens* without agreeing to important constraints upon the treaty-making power. This, in turn, demanded a significant dilution of the hard-nosed legal positivism to which socialist jurists regularly com-mitted themselves. Considered from a sociological perspective, though, the matter

---

[52] Soviet approaches to international law evolved over time and sharp disagreements were not uncommon. However, these two tendencies were nearly always present, and would remain mainstays of Soviet legal theory until the end of the Cold War. See eg Evgeny Pashukanis, 'International Law' in Evgeny Pashukanis, *Selected Writings on Marxism and Law* (Piers Beirne and Robert Sharlet eds, Peter B Maggs tr, Academic Press 1980); TA Taracouzio, *The Soviet Union and International Law: A Study Based on the Legislation, Treaties and Foreign Relations of the Union of Socialist Soviet Republics* (Macmillan 1935), especially chs 2–3; John N Hazard, 'Cleansing Soviet International Law of Anti-Marxist Theories' (1938) 32 American Journal of International Law 244; Ivo Lapenna, *Conceptions soviétiques de droit international public* (Pedone 1954); WW Kulski, 'The Soviet Interpretation of International Law' (1955) 49 American Journal of International Law 518; Jan F Triska and Robert M Slusser, *The Theory, Law, and Policy of Soviet Treaties* (Stanford University Press 1962), especially ch 1; John B Quigley Jr, 'The New Soviet Approach to International Law' (1965) 7 Harvard International Law Club Journal 1; John N Hazard, 'Renewed Emphasis Upon a Socialist International Law' (1971) 65 American Journal of International Law 142; Tunkin, *Theory of International Law* (n 51); Kazimierz Grzybowski, *Soviet International Law and the World Economic Order* (Duke University Press 1987) ch 2. For recent recon-sideration of the Soviet Union's formative influence on international law, see especially John Quigley, *Soviet Legal Innovation and the Law of the Western World* (Cambridge University Press 2007); and Scott Newton, *Law and the Making of the Soviet World: The Red Demiurge* (Routledge 2015).

lent itself to explanation more readily. *Jus cogens* functioned in something remarkably close to a discursive vacuum, capable of furthering a wide variety of different projects. It was therefore deemed possible to combat empire with *jus cogens*, at least insofar as its content was invested with strong conceptions of sovereignty and self-determination. Still, it is clear that *jus cogens* brought with it an inversion of argumentative strategies. States belonging to a First World in which the idea of sovereignty was viewed with increasing suspicion and 'transnational law' was colonizing large chunks of public international law nevertheless found themselves retreating to a rather classical defence of state consent. Such a position seemed unavoidable in the face of far-reaching and dangerously under-specified peremptory norms, capable of being employed for purposes running directly counter to their individual and collective interests. For their part, socialist states set aside their traditional prioritization of treaty law in order to cultivate an effusive rhetoric of 'international community'. While they admitted that *jus cogens* norms were created by state consent, expressly through conventional or impliedly through customary international law, they contended that this did not make *jus cogens* norms weaker or less comprehensive, since such norms were intrinsic to international legal order and had to bind all states, even would-be dissenters, if they were to count for anything at all.[53] Established lines of argumentation were thus turned on their heads in a contest between two models of international law. The utopia of a normatively integrated international order became the apology of state power; the apology of state power produced the utopia of a normatively integrated international order.[54] *Jus cogens'* contested canon was forged in and through this complex conflict, the product of a Cold War rivalry in which even the most entrenched interpretations of international law were disassembled and reconstituted in new combinations.

Ultimately, sheer numbers carried the day: the final wording of Article 53 contained a bald but highly suggestive statement to the effect that treaties conflicting with peremptory norms of general international law must be deemed null and void. No reference was made either to municipal law or to the world's 'principal' legal systems. France had articulated the concerns of a number of states when it had suggested that *jus cogens*, if expressly recognized, might be generated through majoritarian action, creating 'an international source of law subject to no control and lacking all responsibility'.[55] And there was indeed something to this, particularly since lack of agreement on the rules that would count as *jus cogens*, coupled

---

[53] See eg Tunkin, 'International Law in the International System' (n 51) 92–93; Alexidze, 'Legal Nature of *Jus Cogens*' (n 51) 255–58. For conceptual difficulties arising from such claims, see especially Michael Akehurst, 'The Hierarchy of the Sources of International Law' (1975) 47 British Yearbook of International Law 273, 284–85; Christos L Rozakis, *The Concept of* Jus Cogens *in the Law of Treaties* (North-Holland 1976), 73–84; Ronald St John Macdonald, 'Fundamental Norms in Contemporary International Law' (1987) 25 Canadian Yearbook of International Law 115, 130–34; Gennady M Danilenko, 'International *Jus Cogens*: Issues of Law-Making' (1991) 2 European Journal of International Law 42, 48–57; Evan J Criddle and Evan Fox-Decent, 'A Fiduciary Theory of *Jus Cogens*' (2009) 34 Yale Journal of International Law 331, 339–42.

[54] I am, of course, drawing here upon Martti Koskenniemi, *From Apology to Utopia: The Structure of International Legal Argument* (Reissue with a new epilogue, Cambridge University Press 2005).

[55] UNCLOT II (n 10) 94.

with the absence of clarity about the way in which a given rule might come to secure this status, rendered the very idea of peremptory norms problematic.[56] But this too was not permitted to stand in the way of Article 53. The content of *jus cogens*, and of the 'shared philosophy of values' it was often believed to enshrine,[57] may have remained inchoate and indeterminate—so much so that *jus cogens* was deemed by many to display all the classic signs of a floating signifier, an idealist fiction with little or no moorings in concrete political struggle, let alone the procedures and institutions of international dispute settlement. Yet it was just this vagueness—this ability to relay and facilitate disparate claims to sovereignty, self-determination, and non-intervention—that made the vocabulary of *jus cogens* so appealing for those who found themselves on the margins of international life.

Failures of a Contested Concept

Disputes about *jus cogens*, the 'unruly horse' of the law of treaties,[58] ultimately turn on disputes about the nature of international law. Is international law in possession of basic norms or foundational principles? How and where should one draw the line between state power and international authority? To what degree can legal relations between states and other actors be said to comprise an integrated 'order' or 'system'? Is it possible to develop a genuinely defensible hierarchy of international law's constituent formations, so as to taxonomize what might otherwise seem like a hopelessly messy tangle of rules and procedures? For some, *jus cogens* norms would seem to rest atop the international order, surveying treaties, customs, and other sources of legal obligation from a position of untrammelled supremacy, or at least with a symbolic currency that speaks to '[t]he inner moral aspiration of the law',[59] the 'values' that guarantee 'peace and relative well-being in the world for everyone'.[60] For others, the very idea of *jus cogens* is laughably imprecise, untenably distant from the reality of international affairs, rooted in a deeply suspect tradition of natural law theory, and uncomfortably amenable to deployment in the name of radically divergent ideologies, particularly since there has always been a great deal of confusion as to how *jus cogens* can and should be distinguished from the more mundane *jus dispositivum*.

---

[56] For recent reconsideration of the problem, see Jan Klabbers, 'The Validity and Invalidity of Treaties' in Duncan B Hollis (ed), *The Oxford Guide to Treaties* (Oxford University Press 2012) 570–71. Of course, not all lawyers have been as critical in this regard. Roberto Ago, for instance, argued that the lack of an authoritative list of *jus cogens* norms in international law was not especially worrisome, since even *jus cogens* norms in the domestic context developed through practice and precedent. See Roberto Ago, 'Droit des traités à la lumière de la Convention de Vienne' (1971) 134 Recueil des cours 297, 323.

[57] UNCLOT I (n 10) 297 (Lebanon).

[58] TO Elias, *The Modern Law of Treaties* (Sijthoff 1974) 177. See also TO Elias, 'Problems Concerning the Validity of Treaties' (1971) 134 Recueil des cours 333, 388.

[59] Andrea Bianchi, 'Human Rights and the Magic of *Jus Cogens*' (2008) 19 European Journal of International Law 491, 495.

[60] Tomuschat, 'Reconceptualizing the Debate' (n 6) 428.

Brought down from the heights of legal inviolability and moral indubitability, the doctrinal form of *jus cogens* reveals itself to be not the apex of a closed order distinguished by internal coherence and immanent rationality, but what one might, following Pierre Bourdieu, call a fractured, tension-ridden 'juridical field', a site of contestation through which competing assertions of power and legitimacy come to be mediated and refracted.[61] To be sure, *jus cogens* could not have amounted to just anything. Not all rules of international law could be absorbed into the emergent canon of peremptory norms, as international law's existing structures imposed certain limitations upon the range of arguments that could be made on their basis. Yet the fate of *jus cogens* was anything but predetermined. A remarkably high degree of uncertainty has marked the question of *jus cogens*, and multiple, often incommensurable political programmes have found a home in the proposition that certain limits may be drawn on the treaty-making power. As Abi-Saab observed long ago, *jus cogens* may be an 'empty box', but it is one that can be 'filled' with a range of different materials.[62]

But just as *jus cogens'* amorphous character endows it with the ability to translate and formalize competition between different visions of international order, so too does it preclude it from realizing decolonization's vision of a world liberated from all vestiges of domination and exploitation. Admittedly, support among Third World jurists for *jus cogens* and analogous modes of legal universalism continued in the years that followed the Vienna negotiations. Some wrote that *jus cogens* rules ought to be understood neither as *Grundnormen* nor as by-products of natural law, but simply as functional preconditions of an actually effective international order—as 'the necessary ballast to keep the ship of society stable and steady'.[63] Others suggested that the absence of concrete examples of *jus cogens* norms in Article 53 was a benefit rather than a drawback, since it allowed states, particularly those with 'a stake in strengthening the conditions for détente, national independence and self-determination of peoples', to identify and promote *jus cogens* 'in their actual experience of struggle and cooperation'.[64] Even Mohammed Bedjaoui, a leading legal advocate of Third World coordination and development during the 1970s and 1980s, lent support to the view that it was through *jus cogens* that the 'paganism' of classical international law might finally be replaced with a genuinely inclusive and participatory order.[65]

[61] See, famously, Pierre Bourdieu, 'The Force of Law: Toward a Sociology of the Juridical Field', Richard Terdiman (tr), (1987) 38 Hastings Law Journal 814 (sketching a field-analytic method that overcomes the traditional distinction between legal formalism and legal instrumentalism).

[62] Abi-Saab, 'The Third World' (n 22) 53. See also Georges Abi-Saab, 'The Uses of Article 19' (1999) 10 European Journal of International Law 339, 341. On this motif see further Hélène Ruiz Fabri, 'Enhancing the Rhetoric of *Jus Cogens*' (2012) 23 European Journal of International Law 1049, 1053 (arguing that '[t]he box is no longer empty, thanks to those courts and other bodies that have not hesitated to identify some rules as *jus cogens*').

[63] V Nageswar Rao, '*Jus Cogens* and the Vienna Convention on the Law of Treaties' (1974) 14 Indian Journal of International Law 362, 368.

[64] Merlin M Magallona, 'The Concept of *Jus Cogens* in the Vienna Convention on the Law of Treaties' (1976) 51 Philippine Law Journal 521, 523, 542.

[65] For his classic discussion of 'legal paganism' see Mohammed Bedjaoui, *Towards a New International Economic Order* (Holmes & Meier 1979) 98–101.

Key elements of the New International Economic Order project like the right to development, the right to self-determination, and the principle of permanent sovereignty over natural resources possessed the status of *jus cogens* norms, Bedjaoui occasionally suggested, marshalling an astonishing range of material to support a broadly anti-formalist argument on behalf of what he termed 'international solidarity'.[66] Nevertheless, proponents of *jus cogens* have demonstrated little capacity to achieve their original emancipatory objectives—a fact that is due in no small part to the abstract, even speculative, utopianism by which the notion of *jus cogens* (like that of human rights) is ultimately inspired. Consider self-determination, a central concern for many advocates of *jus cogens*. Throughout the 1960s and 1970s, socialist and non-aligned states invested heavily in the concept of self-determination, the principal legal point of reference for the post-1945 wave of decolonization. Article 53 was deemed to be crucially important in this regard, allowing such states to attach even greater normative force to self-determination than they had previously. However, subsequent developments in respect of self-determination have seldom yielded the desired results. Self-determination remains a right (or principle) whose scope is murky, content imprecise, and application inconsistent. It may have been 'successful' for the Eritreans, Kosovars, and East Timorese, for instance, but it has clearly 'failed' the Kurds, Palestinians, and Western Saharans. In many cases, as with the Tamils, Tibetans, and Chechens, this has proven to be the case even when self-determination has been couched in the form of a right to recognition or representative government ('internal self-determination') rather than a full-fledged right of remedial secession ('external self-determination'). What is more, there is no evidence to suggest that self-determination's widespread characterization as a *jus cogens* norm—a tendency which the International Court of Justice has supported to some degree by stating that self-determination is an *erga omnes* principle[67]—has made it any more 'weighty'. As Antonio Cassese pointed out a quarter century after the Vienna Convention was first opened for signature, the World Court has never declared a treaty concerning self-determination to be null and void on the specific ground that it violates a peremptory norm—a fact that might illustrate an exceptionally strong record of compliance with *jus cogens* on the part of states were it not so clearly emblematic of the vacuous generality in which *jus cogens* continues to be enshrouded.[68] If what is at stake in the debate about *jus cogens* is nothing less than the nature and relevance of international law, the extent to which law is equipped

---

[66] See Bedjaoui, *Towards a New International Economic Order* (n 65) 185; Mohammed Bedjaoui, 'The Right to Development and the *Jus Cogens*' (1986) 2 Lesotho Law Journal 93; and also Mohammed Bedjaoui, 'Right to Development and the *Jus Cogens*' in Milan Bulajić, Dimitrije Pindić, and Momirka Marinković (eds), *The Charter of Economic Rights and Duties of States: Ten Years of Implementation* (Institute of International Politics and Economics 1986). For more on Bedjaoui, see Umut Özsu, '"In the interests of mankind as a whole": Mohammed Bedjaoui's New International Economic Order' (2015) 6 Humanity: An International Journal of Human Rights, Humanitarianism, and Development 129.

[67] *Case Concerning East Timor (Portugal v. Australia)* [1995] ICJ Rep 90, 102.

[68] Antonio Cassese, *Self-Determination of Peoples: A Legal Reappraisal* (Cambridge University Press 1995) 173–74. The assessment remains fundamentally valid.

to make 'international relations more human in character by basing them on the equality of men and that of States',[69] it cannot be denied that *jus cogens*, and the kind of abstract universalism it exemplifies, has done precious little to reassure critics of its capacity to effect lasting and concrete change.

To replace the empire of power with the empire of law, as many advocates of *jus cogens* continue to dream of doing, is to ignore the fact that the empire of law, with *jus cogens* as its most 'majestic' centrepiece, is itself an empire of power, at least of a certain variety. Whatever their differences, partisans of *jus cogens* routinely slough off allegations of romanticism, of having become enamoured of an ethereal and purely fictitious construct, in the hope of reaching across the full range of international relations, striving not simply to displace traditional conceptions of international law but also to fix the foundations of world order once and for all. But if asserting *jus cogens* is an act of power, it is also clearly not powerful enough. Lacking the kind of authority needed to transform the messy, all-too-human reality it purports to govern, *jus cogens* fails time and again to deliver on its original promise of a revolutionized international order. The result is a deeply contested concept that consistently falls short of satisfying even the more modest demands of the 'progressive' agenda to which it owes its existence.

Bibliography

Abi-Saab, Georges, 'The Third World and the Future of the International Legal Order' (1973) 29 Revue égyptienne de droit international 27

Abi-Saab, Georges, 'The Uses of Article 19' (1999) 10 European Journal of International Law 339

Ago, Roberto, 'Droit des traités à la lumière de la Convention de Vienne' (1971) 134 Recueil des cours 297

Akehurst, Michael, 'The Hierarchy of the Sources of International Law' (1975) 47 British Yearbook of International Law 273

Alexidze, Levan, 'Legal Nature of *Jus Cogens* in Contemporary International Law' (1981) 172 Recueil des cours 219

Bedjaoui, Mohammed, *Towards a New International Economic Order* (Holmes & Meier 1979)

Bedjaoui, Mohammed, 'Right to Development and the *Jus Cogens*' in Milan Bulajić, Dimitrije Pindić, and Momirka Marinković (eds), *The Charter of Economic Rights and Duties of States: Ten Years of Implementation* (Institute of International Politics and Economics 1986)

Bedjaoui, Mohammed, 'The Right to Development and the *Jus Cogens*' (1986) 2 Lesotho Law Journal 93

Bianchi, Andrea, 'Human Rights and the Magic of *Jus Cogens*' (2008) 19 European Journal of International Law 491

Bourdieu, Pierre, 'The Force of Law: Toward a Sociology of the Juridical Field', Richard Terdiman (tr), (1987) 38 Hastings Law Journal 814

---

[69] UNCLOT I (n 10) 321 (Ivory Coast).

Byers, Michael, 'Conceptualizing the Relationship between *Jus Cogens* and *Erga Omnes* Rules' (1997) 66 Nordic Journal of International Law 211

Case Concerning East Timor (Portugal v. Australia) [1995] ICJ Rep 90

Case of the S.S. 'Lotus' (France v. Turkey) PCIJ Rep Series A No 10 (1927)

Cassese, Antonio, *Self-Determination of Peoples: A Legal Reappraisal* (Cambridge University Press 1995)

Charlesworth, Hilary and Chinkin, Christine, 'The Gender of *Jus Cogens*' (1993) 15 Human Rights Quarterly 63

Criddle, Evan J and Fox-Decent, Evan, 'A Fiduciary Theory of *Jus Cogens*' (2009) 34 Yale Journal of International Law 331

Danilenko, Gennady M, 'International *Jus Cogens*: Issues of Law-Making' (1991) 2 European Journal of International Law 42

Deleau, Olivier, 'Les positions françaises à la Conférence de Vienne sur le droit des traités' (1969) 15 Annuaire français de droit international 7

Elias, TO, 'Problems Concerning the Validity of Treaties' (1971) 134 Recueil des cours 333

Elias, TO, *The Modern Law of Treaties* (Sijthoff 1974)

Elreedy, Elsayed Abdel Raouf, 'The Main Features of the Concept of Invalidity in the Vienna Convention on Treaties' (1971) 27 Revue égyptienne de droit international 13

Engerman, David C, et al (eds), *Staging Growth: Modernization, Development, and the Global Civil War* (University of Massachusetts Press 2003)

Fabri, Hélène Ruiz, 'La France et la Convention de Vienne sur le droit des traités' in Gérard Cahin, Florence Poirat, and Sandra Szurek (eds), *La France et le droit international*, vol 1 (Pedone 2007)

Fabri, Hélène Ruiz, 'Enhancing the Rhetoric of *Jus Cogens*' (2012) 23 European Journal of International Law 1049

Friedmann, Wolfgang, 'The Disintegration of European Civilisation and the Future of International Law: Some Observations on the Social Foundations of Law' (1938) 2 Modern Law Review 194

Gaja, Giorgio, '*Jus Cogens* Beyond the Vienna Convention' (1981) 172 Recueil des cours 271

Gilman, Nils, *Mandarins of the Future: Modernization Theory in Cold War America* (Johns Hopkins University Press 2003)

Glennon, Michael J, 'De l'absurdité du droit impératif (*jus cogens*)' (2006) 110 Revue générale de droit international public 529

Grzybowski, Kazimierz, *Soviet International Law and the World Economic Order* (Duke University Press 1987)

Guilhot, Nicolas, *The Democracy Makers: Human Rights and the Politics of Global Order* (Columbia University Press 2005)

Hannikainen, Lauri, *Peremptory Norms (Jus Cogens) in International Law: Historical Development, Criteria, Present Status* (Lakimiesliiton Kustannus 1988)

Haraszti, György, *Some Fundamental Problems of the Law of Treaties* (Akadémiai Kiadó 1973)

Hazard, John N, 'Cleansing Soviet International Law of Anti-Marxist Theories' (1938) 32 American Journal of International Law 244

Hazard, John N, 'Renewed Emphasis Upon a Socialist International Law' (1971) 65 American Journal of International Law 142

Heller-Roazen, Daniel, *The Enemy of All: Piracy and the Law of Nations* (Zone 2009)

Heydte, Friedrich August von der, 'Die Erscheinungsformen des zwischenstaatlichen Rechts: *jus cogens* und *jus dispositivum* im Völkerrecht' (1932) 16 Zeitschrift für Völkerrecht 461

Janis, Mark W, 'The Nature of *Jus Cogens*' (1988) 3 Connecticut Journal of International Law 359

Klabbers, Jan, 'The Validity and Invalidity of Treaties' in Duncan B Hollis (ed), *The Oxford Guide to Treaties* (Oxford University Press 2012)

Kolb, Robert, *Peremptory International Law*—Jus Cogens: *A General Inventory* (Hart 2015)

Koskenniemi, Martti, *From Apology to Utopia: The Structure of International Legal Argument* (Reissue with a new epilogue, Cambridge University Press 2005)

Koskenniemi, Martti, 'International Law in Europe: Between Tradition and Renewal' (2005) 16 European Journal of International Law 113

Kulski, WW, 'The Soviet Interpretation of International Law' (1955) 49 American Journal of International Law 518

Lachs, Manfred, 'Le développement et les fonctions des traités multilatéraux' (1957) 92 Recueil des cours 229

Lapenna, Ivo, *Conceptions soviétiques de droit international public* (Pedone 1954)

Macdonald, Ronald St John, 'Fundamental Norms in Contemporary International Law' (1987) 25 Canadian Yearbook of International Law 115

Magallona, Merlin M, 'The Concept of *Jus Cogens* in the Vienna Convention on the Law of Treaties' (1976) 51 Philippine Law Journal 521

Malawer, Stuart S, *Imposed Treaties and International Law* (William S Hein 1977)

Martinez, Jenny S, *The Slave Trade and the Origins of International Human Rights Law* (Oxford University Press 2012)

Newton, Scott, *Law and the Making of the Soviet World: The Red Demiurge* (Routledge 2015)

Orakhelashvili, Alexander, *Peremptory Norms in International Law* (Oxford University Press 2006)

The *Oscar Chinn* case (*United Kingdom v. Belgium*) PCIJ Rep Series A/B No 63 (1934)

Özsu, Umut, '"In the interests of mankind as a whole": Mohammed Bedjaoui's New International Economic Order' (2015) 6 Humanity: An International Journal of Human Rights, Humanitarianism, and Development 129

Pashukanis, Evgeny, 'International Law' in Evgeny Pashukanis, *Selected Writings on Marxism and Law* (Piers Beirne and Robert Sharlet eds, Peter B Maggs tr, Academic Press 1980)

Paulus, Andreas L, '*Jus Cogens* in a Time of Hegemony and Fragmentation' (2005) 74 Nordic Journal of International Law 297

Picone, Paolo, 'The Distinction between *Jus Cogens* and Obligations *Erga Omnes*' in Enzo Cannizzaro (ed), *The Law of Treaties Beyond the Vienna Convention* (Oxford University Press 2011)

Quigley Jr, John B, 'The New Soviet Approach to International Law' (1965) 7 Harvard International Law Club Journal 1

Quigley, John, *Soviet Legal Innovation and the Law of the Western World* (Cambridge University Press 2007)

Rao, V Nageswar, '*Jus Cogens* and the Vienna Convention on the Law of Treaties' (1974) 14 Indian Journal of International Law 362

Robledo, Antonio Gómez, 'Le *ius cogens* international: sa genèse, sa nature, ses fonctions' (1981) 172 Recueil des cours 9

Röling, BVA, *International Law in an Expanded World* (Djambatan 1960)

Rosenne, Shabtai, *The Law of Treaties: A Guide to the Legislative History of the Vienna Convention* (Sijthoff 1970)

Rozakis, Christos L, *The Concept of* Jus Cogens *in the Law of Treaties* (North-Holland 1976)

Sauvy, Alfred, 'Trois mondes, une planète' (14 August 1952) 118 L'Observateur 14

Schwarzenberger, Georg, 'International *Jus Cogens*?' (1965) 43 Texas Law Review 455

Schwarzenberger, Georg, 'The Problem of International Public Policy' (1965) 18 Current Legal Problems 191

Schwelb, Egon, 'Some Aspects of International *Jus Cogens* as Formulated by the International Law Commission' (1967) 61 American Journal of International Law 946

Shelton, Dinah, 'Normative Hierarchy in International Law' (2006) 100 American Journal of International Law 291

Sinclair, Ian, *The Vienna Convention on the Law of Treaties* (2nd ed, Manchester University Press 1984)

Stephan, Paul B, 'The Political Economy of *Jus Cogens*' (2011) 44 Vanderbilt Journal of Transnational Law 1073

Suy, Eric, 'The Concept of *Jus Cogens* in Public International Law' in *The Concept of* Jus Cogens *in International Law: Conference on International Law, Lagonissi (Greece), April 3–8, 1966—Papers and Proceedings II* (Carnegie Endowment for International Peace 1967)

Sztucki, Jerzy, Jus Cogens *and the Vienna Convention on the Law of Treaties: A Critical Appraisal* (Springer-Verlag 1974)

Tams, Christian J, *Enforcing Obligations Erga Omnes in International Law* (Cambridge University Press 2005)

Taracouzio, TA, *The Soviet Union and International Law: A Study Based on the Legislation, Treaties and Foreign Relations of the Union of Socialist Soviet Republics* (Macmillan 1935)

Tomuschat, Christian, 'Reconceptualizing the Debate on *Jus Cogens* and Obligations *Erga Omnes*—Concluding Observations' in Christian Tomuschat and Jean-Marc Thouvenin (eds), *The Fundamental Rules of the International Legal Order:* Jus Cogens *and Obligations* Erga Omnes (Nijhoff 2006)

Triska, Jan F and Slusser, Robert M, *The Theory, Law, and Policy of Soviet Treaties* (Stanford University Press 1962)

Tunkin, Grigory I, *Theory of International Law* (William E Butler tr, Harvard University Press 1974)

Tunkin, Grigory, 'International Law in the International System' (1975) 147 Recueil des cours 1

United Nations Conference on the Law of Treaties, First Session (Vienna 26 March–24 May 1968) UN Doc A/CONF.39/11

United Nations Conference on the Law of Treaties, First and Second Sessions (Vienna 26 March–24 May 1968 and 9 April–22 May 1969), Documents of the Conference, UN Doc A/CONF.39/11/Add.2

United Nations Conference on the Law of Treaties, Second Session (Vienna 9 April–22 May 1969) UN Doc A/CONF.39/11/Add.1

Verdross, Alfred von, 'Anfechtbare und nichtige Staatsverträge' (1935) 15 Zeitschrift für öffentliches Recht 289

Verdross, Alfred von, 'Forbidden Treaties in International Law' (1937) 31 American Journal of International Law 571

Verdross, Alfred, '*Jus Dispositivum* and *Jus Cogens* in International Law' (1966) 60 American Journal of International Law 55

Vienna Convention on the Law of Treaties (signed 23 May 1969) 1155 UNTS 331

Virally, Michel, 'Réflexions sur le "*jus cogens*"' (1966) 12 Annuaire français de droit international 5

Visscher, Charles de, 'Positivisme et *jus cogens*' (1971) 75 Revue générale de droit international public 5

Weatherhall, Thomas, Jus Cogens: *International Law and Social Contract* (Cambridge University Press 2015)

Weil, Prosper, 'Towards Relative Normativity in International Law?' (1983) 77 American Journal of International Law 413

Wetzel, Ralf Günter and Rauschning, Dietrich, *The Vienna Convention on the Law of Treaties: Travaux Préparatoires* (Alfred Metzner Verlag 1978)

Zemanek, Karl, 'The Metamorphosis of *Jus Cogens*: From an Institution of Treaty Law to the Bedrock of the International Legal Order?' in Enzo Cannizzaro (ed), *The Law of Treaties Beyond the Vienna Convention* (Oxford University Press 2011)

13

Drift towards an Empire? The Trajectory of American Reformers in the Cold War

Hatsue Shinohara

Prologue

In November 1942, Quincy Wright wrote a rather long letter to Manley O Hudson, his long-time ally in a movement to foster international law. Both of them were devoted scholars of international law who believed that international law could and should embody the notion of international society, and thus contribute to the stability of the world. Wright argued that jurists must fight to change the situation, claiming that Hudson was 'entirely right in declining to float with the stream'. If not, he continued, the present condition would lead to 'an empire established by conquest, which had within itself the seeds of its own destruction' and would degenerate 'toward the collapse of the civilization'. He even contended that 'the temporary success' of empire 'was due to the incapacity of jurists and statesmen to organize the system of states'. If jurists and statesmen did not resolutely oppose the challenge of totalitarian states, then empire would rise and become more powerful. For Wright, their efforts and commitment in the interwar years were to fight against empire, never to foster it. Wright then elaborated what would be necessary to make international law more effective. 'I would not draw quite as sharp a line as you do between juristic activity and political propaganda ... Law like all social institutions depends eventually upon public opinion.' He claimed that if jurists failed to enlist support from the public, 'the law will die'. Thus, he suggested that jurists should collaborate with 'the statesmen if their efforts are to bear fruit' and argued that if the public do not appreciate international law, it would undermine the foundation of law as a 'social institution'.[1]

Contrary to Wright's observation in this letter, in the unfolding development of the Cold War the United States was often depicted as a hegemon, or as the founder of an 'informal' empire. Was there a shift in US policy? If so, was the shift related to international law, and more specifically did academic discourse presented by

[1] Quincy Wright to Manley O Hudson, 13 November 1942, Box 98, Folder 1, Papers of Manley O Hudson, Harvard Law Library, Cambridge, Massachusetts, US.

International Law and Empire: Historical Explorations. First Edition. Martti Koskenniemi, Walter Rech, and Manuel Jiménez Fonseca. © Martti Koskenniemi, Walter Rech, and Manuel Jiménez Fonseca 2016. Published 2016 by Oxford University Press.

international lawyers play a certain role in it? Was the triangle composed of jurists, statesmen, and the public, proposed by Wright as an indispensable and ideal condition for the effectiveness of international law, also changing under the context of Cold War? Or was Wright's assumption that international law was fighting against empire instead a groundless observation? This work will narrate the trajectory of reform-minded scholars' discussions to illustrate an intellectual context, small yet not insignificant, I believe, to an understanding of the issues involving US hegemony and international law.

Defining the Problematics

Before moving onto the examination of lawyers' thoughts and discussions, some preliminary work needs to be done to clarify key concepts as well as to set the framework of this chapter.

First of all, the notion of 'empire' is a problematic one. Given the time-scope and aim of this chapter, which will be articulated later, I would like to note that there are two important facets in the phenomenon of empire. First, a core or centre exists, and second, a core possesses superior power, which in turn produces a hierarchical order between a core and the non-core state(s). Most likely, this order can be depicted as the one between a ruler and the ruled. This unequal distribution of power, or more appropriately the outstanding supremacy of a core, leads to a creation of a hierarchical order which can spread to and encompass several dimensions– political, military, economic, and cultural factors. As the term 'cultural imperialism' epitomizes, unequal and hierarchical order can exist in the specific field of culture. In spite of the complex and multi-faceted nature of an empire, this chapter will focus upon the military dimension of empire, because military supremacy seems to be an indispensable foundation for building and maintaining an empire. More specifically, as a key concept that projects the legal dimension of military supremacy, this work problematizes the notion of collective security and its possible legal implications for empire. That being the case, the regulation of unilateral use of force by a state had been the fundamental aim for scholars like Wright and Hudson in the interwar years. They strove hard to achieve a peaceful international order, in which the use of force was to be regulated. With this system they hoped that empire would be eradicated.

Second, does this work refer to the Roman, British, or Japanese empires? No, we are dealing with the American empire, but this denomination can also be naturally contested. As the above letter from Wright to Hudson in 1942 indicated, at least in his own perception, the United States was not and should not be regarded as an 'empire'. However, one notable American diplomatic historian used the title *Empire without Tears* for a book discussing US foreign relations in the interwar years.[2] Thus, we can label the United States as an empire even in that period. Neil Ferguson, on

---

[2] Warren Cohen, *Empire without Tears: American Foreign Relations, 1921–1933* (Alfred Knopf 1987).

the other hand, argued 'not merely that the United States is an empire but that it always has been an empire'.[3] Other scholars, such as most notably Antonio Negri and Michael Hardt, or Robert Keohane, contend that more or less the United States had and has possessed the features of empire.[4] Following such scholars, this work assumes that the United States was gradually building up its empire, even though it did not take the shape of formal colonialism leading to a territorial empire.

Regarding the topic on international law and empire, recent scholars have produced some interesting and important academic works, but Martti Koskenniemi argues that how and what to write about the issue has not been agreed upon.[5] And when we discuss empire and international law historically, what and how to write is another problem. Wilhelm G Grewe, in turn, who wrote a history of international law based upon the framework of a series of great powers' 'epochs', argued that some legal frameworks inherently contained the element of power relations. He claimed that post-war legal mechanisms possessed the fundamental and insolvable tension between 'the legal equality of States and the actual supremacy of the Great Powers'. The tension was, for instance, formalized in the institution of veto powers granted to five countries in the UN as well as in the Non-Proliferation Treaty signed in 1968.[6]

Other scholars have dealt with the specific issue of US hegemony and international law. An edited volume by Michael Byers and Georg Nolte analyses the issues resulting from US hegemony and the foundation of international law,[7] while Anu Bradford and Eric A Posner contend that United States exceptionalism in international law was not so unique in comparison to the European Union and China.[8] In addition, Chalmers Johnson claimed that the United States established an empire of military bases that was supported by security treaties and Status of Forces Agreements.[9] The latter are usually depicted as powerful manifestations of US hegemonic status. Furthermore, if we emphasize the political aspects of international law, the practice of international law itself can be regarded as a source of power, as Shirley V Scott argued in her recent work.[10]

Thus, whatever we might call it, 'empire', 'hegemon', or 'colossus', this chapter stands upon the premise that the United States occupies a preponderant position in international relations. Furthermore, historicizing the emergence of American

---

[3] Niall Ferguson, *Colossus: The Rise and Fall of the American Empire* (Penguin Books 2004).

[4] Antonio Negri and Michael Hardt, *Multitude: War and Democracy in the Age of an Empire* (The Penguin Press 2004); Robert Keohane, *After Hegemony* (Princeton University Press 2005).

[5] Martti Koskenniemi, 'A History of International Law Histories' in Bardo Fassbender and Anne Peters (eds), *The Oxford Handbook of the History of International Law* (Oxford University Press 2012) 964–65.

[6] Wilhelm G Grewe, *The Epochs of International Law* (Michael Byers tr, De Gruyter 2000) 645–46.

[7] Michael Byers and George Nolte, *United States Hegemony and the Foundation of International Law* (Cambridge University Press 2003).

[8] Anu Bradford and Eric A Posner, 'Universal Exceptionalism in International Law' (2011) 52 Harvard International Law Journal 3.

[9] Chalmers Johnson, *The Sorrows of Empire* (Metropolitan 2004).

[10] Shirley V Scott, *International Law, US Power: The United States' Quest for Legal Security* (Cambridge University Press 2012).

empire, this work also presupposes that the trend came to be more obvious in the post-war years under the milieu of the Cold War. I will examine how prominent liberal scholars in the interwar years[11]–Wright, Hudson, and Charles G Fenwick–grasped the condition and what kind of legal discussions they elaborated. The approach to be taken in this work is that of an intellectual history.[12] The exploration of the thoughts and activities of international jurists might not simply be confined to the parameter of intellectual history, but it can open the way to a focus upon the role of lawyers in setting the agenda and signalling the directions of international law.[13]

In addition, state practice and policy makers' stances towards international law should be briefly touched upon,[14] because lawyers' discourses cannot exist in a vacuum, completely isolated from the context of the time and national policy. If the United States was emerging as an empire, were reform-minded scholars disappointed? Was there any stark difference in post-war discussions from those of the interwar years? To address these questions, I will sketch out the state of discourse on international law in the 1950s and 1960s. An ultimate question to be addressed in this work would be how American reformers sensed and recognized the post-war conditions and if their discussions indicate any propensity to support US imperial position and practice. Also, following Wright's premise of a strategic triangle in which collaboration between lawyers, statesmen, and the public understanding would be constructive and ideal, this work will narrate the state of the teaching of international law because it can be deemed as a necessary introductory process for the general public and non-professionals to learn and understand international law.

An Emerging Gulf in the 1950s

Events shape the context and environment in which the state discusses the direction and implementation of its policy. Perhaps most of us would agree on some basic 'facts': around the same time that the United States won World War II and the United Nations was established, its difficulty with handling the Soviet Union came to be realized. In March 1947, just two years after the end of the war, the Truman Doctrine was

---

[11] See Hatsue Shinohara, *US International Lawyers in the Interwar Years: A Forgotten Crusade* (Cambridge University Press 2014).

[12] See David Kennedy, 'When Renewal Repeats: Thinking against the Box' (2000) 32 Journal of International Law and Politics 335. According to Kennedy, the 1950s and 1960s were the period of confusion and transition in terms of the history of legal discourse in the United States. See also David Kennedy, 'The Discipline of International Law and Policy' (1999) 12 Leiden Journal of International Law 9.

[13] For a brief discussion on the role of international lawyer, see Hedley Bull, *The Anarchical Society: A Study of Order in World Politics* (Columbia University 1977), 152–55: see also Martti Koskenniemi, *The Gentle Civilizer of Nations: The Rise and Fall of International Law 1870–1960* (Cambridge University Press 2001); David Kennedy, 'Thesis about International Law Discourse' (1980) German Yearbook of International Law 353.

[14] See Anthony Carty, 'Doctrine versus State Practice' in Bardo Fassbender and Anne Peters (eds), *The Oxford Handbook of the History of International Law* (Oxford University Press 2012).

proclaimed and in 1949 the North Atlantic Treaty Organization was established. In the Far East, June 1950 saw the outbreak of the Korean War. In this series of developments, George F Kennan, who published the famous 'X Article' in the Foreign Affairs magazine, played an important role in the formative stage of the Cold War. He also published a short but influential book, which argued that too much reliance on legalism and moralism had misled US foreign policy in the interwar years.[15]

Following its pre-war tradition, the American Society of International Law (ASIL) invited high-ranking officials as notable guest speakers to its annual meetings. These speakers usually described the current conditions and directions of US policy. In April 1950, for instance, John Foster Dulles, Consultant to the Secretary of State, read his paper 'New Aspects of American Foreign Policy' before the Society. He stressed that the United States was no longer a small power. Dulles argued that the UN Charter was already 'dated', because during the five years since its establishment 'much has happened'. Then he talked about new developments in Europe and Asia: in particular, in Europe NATO was founded, while in Asia the US policy to support Nationalist China resulted in failure. In his speech he frequently referred to 'the danger of Soviet Communism'.[16]

Two years later, in April 1952, Secretary of State Dean Acheson delivered a speech entitled 'The Development of International Community'. In it, he pointed out that a similarity existed between the Tennessee Valley Authority, which was established as a relief activity under New Deal initiatives, and the task of rehabilitation in post-war Europe through the Marshall Plan. Turning to the issue of defence, he remarked that it 'was an integral part of the function of the community' and mere assurances were not enough. Specifically, the importance of 'a series of community actions by the people of the North Atlantic Area' was highly stressed.[17]

After Charles Cheney Hyde's presidential term of the ASIL (1946–49), the leadership of the ASIL fell onto the shoulders of Manley O Hudson. In his 1950 presidential speech, 'International Law at Mid-Century', he narrated the development of international law in the century, and stated his appraisal that the application of international law had been expanded to a significant degree. He proclaimed that the defining feature of international law in the twentieth century would be 'the conviction that the interests of the international community can be advanced through cooperation centering in a general international organization'. He contended that although the UN membership did not cover all nations, the UN should not be regarded as an 'exclusive club'. Because the UN should be identified with 'the whole community of states', the UN Charter should be regarded as 'a basic constitutional instrument of the whole community of states whose relations are governed by international law'. At the same time he also stated that the US policy had been changing drastically, saying that 'the pendulum has swung to an opposite extreme'.[18]

---

[15] George F Kennan, *American Diplomacy 1900–1950* (University of Chicago Press 1951).
[16] John Foster Dulles, 'New Aspects of American Foreign Policy' (1950) Proceedings of the American Society of International Law (hereafter Proceedings, ASIL) 48.
[17] Dean Acheson, 'The Development of International Community' (1952) Proceedings, ASIL 18.
[18] Manley O Hudson, 'International Law at Mid-Century' (1950) Proceedings, ASIL 38.

At that year's meeting a significant session signalling a future direction on security was held under the chairmanship of Myres S McDougal of Yale Law School. In this session Harold D Laswell of Yale University read his paper and presented a pessimistic outlook on the world condition, arguing that 'the loss of security under present world conditions goes deeper than chronic threat of war'. Using such terms as 'bi-polarity', he continued, 'a free America depends upon a secure world, which implies a free world commonwealth'. He was supportive of and positive about US leadership, because the US aim would be 'to garrison a commonwealth, without being transformed into a garrison-prison state, in order to bring about the disappearance of all garrison-prison systems of power'.[19] As McDougal later recalled, one of his contributions to the ASIL was his initiative to get Lasswell involved in the Society, as this kind of presentation might have a certain impact on its members.[20]

One startling and unanticipated (at least for this author) upshot in this 1950 meeting was a growing gulf between Wright and Fenwick—who had forged such a strong bond to establish new international law during the interwar years—over how to grasp the present condition and future direction.

Wright chaired the session on 'Freedom of Communication across National Boundaries' and read his paper. In it he called for a more careful approach to the Soviet Union, because the Soviet people might feel that their culture and values would be more 'vulnerable', and suggested that 'a variety of cultures' would be 'a condition of human progress'. Even though he understood that the United States had 'a vital interest in the state of world opinion' and that the State Department had been working to influence world opinion, it would be dangerous if these efforts were regarded 'as a manifestation of American imperialism and not of a sincere desire for peace and security, freedom and justice'.[21] As this remark indicated, Wright began to grasp the possibility that US actions could be imperialistic, in particular from the perspective of other countries.

Following Wright's paper, Fenwick delivered his own, stating that: 'I would like to start off by a direct attack upon my friend, Quincy Wright, with whose views I differ radically.' He contended that Wright's view was based upon the perspective of the UN, but that he would like to propose something more fundamental: namely, international law was composed not only of customary laws and treaty laws but also 'of certain broad principles of morality and justice' which represented 'our heritage of Christian civilization'. Furthermore, he highly valued the importance of 'mutual intercourse'. Therefore, if a powerful country started to set up an 'iron curtain', it might hamper the flow of communication, and that itself would constitute 'not an insignificant offense, but a major crime against the international community'.[22]

[19] Harold D Laswell, 'Conditions of Security in a Bi-Polarizing World' (1950) Proceedings, ASIL 8.
[20] Frederic Kirgis, *The American Society of International Law's First Century 1906–2006* (Martinus Nijhoff 2006) 251, fn 139.
[21] Quincy Wright, 'Freedom and Responsibility in respect to Trans-National Communication' (1950) Proceedings, ASIL 95.
[22] Charles Fenwick, 'Freedom of Communication across National Boundaries' (1950) Proceedings, ASIL 107.

In the following discussion, Fenwick went on to argue that there was 'a higher international law', which was the defence against 'the physical coercion and intimidation behind the Communist system'. He even argued that the United States can 'employ persons to penetrate Russia'. In response one member raised the point that what Fenwick presented was the international law of the future, but in the process of reaching that point, 'acceptance of restraints upon ourselves is our great problem as intellectuals'. Fenwick was then asked if Americans were willing to give up atomic weapons. The member claimed it would be 'our great dilemma' and said, 'how far will we go in the international law of the future, if it means that we find ourselves also restrained in a world in which we do not have complete confidence?' Wright, on the other hand, argued that caution and compromise would be necessary and important, and raised the fundamental question of whether international law should aim to establish 'a world society with certain common standards' or should aim 'to promote the co-existence of territorial units that have different standards in respect to culture and truth'. Fenwick responded, saying what troubled the West was 'the policy of intimidation and terrorism' across boundaries, and he asked Wright if he had ever heard what was going on in Czechoslovakia. Wright responded back: 'we should distinguish propaganda from aggression.'[23]

On the topic of UN involvement in the Korean War, Wright pointed out the gravity of the cost, the duration of fighting, the loss of life, and the destruction visited upon Korea, concluding that it was difficult to denominate it 'an equivocal success'. Nevertheless, in the long run it might strengthen 'collective security and the capacity of the United Nations'. However, the UN's control was questionable, because General Douglas MacArthur was not a suitable leader under the UN supervision of military actions, he argued. Thus, he pointed out the danger of great powers' discretionary policy to treat the UN 'as an instrument of national policy'. This kind of policy would be 'tempting, especially to powerful states', and unless great powers restrain the temptation it would damage the United Nations and the system of collective security. Yet, at this point his concern lay more in American support for collective security rather than in its arbitrary use. He repeatedly pointed out that in a democracy the public's support for foreign policy would be indispensable, and the American people's misunderstanding and imperfect knowledge of collective security might lead to 'a general irresponsibility of the public'.[24] In addition, Wright thought that since an actual war was happening again, the public at large might easily think that it would be impossible to regulate war in general. Wright, however, stressing the historical development of legal regulation of war, argued that those who had been involved in the outlawry movement had not anticipated the Kellogg-Briand Pact would have an immediate effect, but 'they were thinking in terms of generations, not of decades'.[25] Around this time of growing tension

---

[23] 'Discussion' (1950) Proceedings, ASIL 117, 127–29, 132.
[24] Quincy Wright, 'Collective Security in the Light of the Korean Experience' (1951) Proceedings, ASIL 165.
[25] Quincy Wright, 'The Outlawry of War and the Law of War' (1953) 47 American Journal of International Law 365.

over ideological differences, Wright was not unmindful of the relationship between ideology and international law. He advocated tolerance for diversity, writing that international law should be based on the supposition that 'diverse religious, political and economic ideologies will co-exist in the world'.[26]

In the meantime, Fenwick assumed the presidency of the ASIL and his 1954 presidential address praised regional collective security, because it was 'simpler and more flexible than that of the United Nations'. Above all, his idea was based upon the supposition that the United States would be a benign hegemon. He believed that 'American States trust the United States to keep its word', and the latter would not act without 'prior consultation with the other members of the community' as well as 'in accordance with inter-American treaties and conversations'. In order to explain the superiority of regional collective security to a universal one, he summarized what had happened since the establishment of the UN. According to him, the basic foundation of collective security was that 'combined forces of the great majority of the nations' should not only be stronger than 'the forces of the law-breaker, but so much stronger that the law-breaker'. However, that was challenged by the new instrument of warfare—atomic weapons. Regarding the Soviet Union, he reiterated his position that the maintenance of the iron curtain constituted 'a major crime against the international community'. From the Korean War he drew positive implications for US leadership in a collective action, saying that even if 'the United States bore the heavier part of the resistance' it would not alter its collective character. Thus, he asked, 'May one, two or three countries be authorized to act in the name of community?' His answer was affirmative, because collective security necessarily resolved itself into 'collective confidence in those of the leading Powers' that could mobilize the forces to resist aggression.[27] Here, more definitely than ever, Fenwick supported the position that leading powers should bear the responsibility of collective action, and the most important power was the United States.

Under the circumstances, Wright for his part expressed his concerns about the future of the UN. He recalled his Swiss friend's remark after the San Francisco conference in 1945, conveying a sceptical view on the UN widely held in Switzerland. Wright explained that Swiss people had shared the sense of fear and danger that the UN would prove to be 'an empire which would be destructive of the liberties of small states'. If the five great powers achieved unity, they have capacity and authority to 'make decisions on the most important political matters affecting the very existence of the lesser states'.[28]

However, Wright could not develop any tangible and convincing legal discourse to combat the growing scepticism towards the UN. Under the conditions of the Cold War at the time, it would have been difficult to secure a unity of great powers,

---

[26] Quincy Wright, 'International Law and Ideologies' (1954) 48 American Journal of International Law 616.

[27] Charles G Fenwick, 'The Development of Collective Security, 1914–1954' (1954) Proceedings, ASIL 2.

[28] 'Addresses on Problems Involved in Review of the United Nations Charter: Remarks' (1954) Proceedings, ASIL 206, 207.

because collective security in actuality depended on 'voluntary action of Members in response to recommendations by the General Assembly under the Uniting for Peace Resolution'. Some sceptics argued that collective security was impractical and that states should instead arm themselves and rely on collective self-defence commitments in regional and traditional alliances. To this, he resolutely answered that 'this writer does not share this opinion'. Then he lamented that the prevention of war could not be 'effective unless the atmosphere of world opinion and international politics becomes more favorable to peace'.[29]

In the historic year of 1956, the fiftieth anniversary of the founding of the ASIL, it was Wright who assumed the office of its presidency. He highly praised the new development of international law, while noting 'but in practice the exigencies of international politics have obstructed the application of that law'. In keeping with his remark that 'to re-establish the authority of international law, creative effort is necessary', his fundamental faith in international law as well as lawyers' commitment was not shaken. Yet, he did not discuss much about the development of collective security, nor concrete problems. Rather he proclaimed the necessity of maintaining faith in international law as a fundamental organ that 'can ameliorate the conditions of the world'.[30]

At this memorable 1956 meeting, Secretary of State John Foster Dulles was again an honoured guest speaker. He remarked that he was very pleased to be there, following 'the tradition of close association of the Society with the Department of State'. Tracing the historical development of international law, he referred to the Hague Conferences, the League of Nations, the Kellogg-Briand Pact, and the UN. Toward the end of his speech, he described the present condition, under which only two countries, the United States and the Soviet Union, possessed atomic and thermonuclear weapons. He in particular noted that 'the relationship between the powerful weapons and the establishment of an effective international force' would be indispensable to 'punish violations of international law'. Therefore, building a community power would be important. He went on to say that because the world could not trust the Soviet Union, the United States should make it clear 'by word and deed through the United Nations and through collective defense associations' that the United States would use its power, even if it was only for the purpose of defending the community.[31]

In a remarkable contrast to Henry L Stimson and Cordell Hull, Secretaries of State in pre-war years, the speeches delivered by Dulles and Acheson before the Society did not stress the importance of international law for US foreign policy. Rather, concepts such as 'defence', 'forces', and 'collective actions' more frequently appeared and were the subjects of their appeals.

While Wright did not abandon his hope for the UN to prevent 'military reprisals, military interventions, and "preventive war," as well as imperial wars',[32] Fenwick

---

[29] Quincy Wright, 'The Prevention of Aggression' (1956) 50 American Journal of International Law 514.

[30] Quincy Wright, 'The Prospects of International Law' (1956) Proceedings, ASIL 2.

[31] John Foster Dulles, 'The Institution of Peace' (1956) Proceedings, ASIL 11.

[32] Quincy Wright, 'Intervention, 1956' (1957) 51 American Journal of International Law 257, 269.

was becoming more supportive of the hegemonic US position in Latin America. His commitment to United States-Latin American relations might have nourished his positive sentiment towards the regional system. After retiring from Bryn Mawr College in 1945, he served as director for the Pan-American Union (Organization of American States) Department of International Law and Organization from 1948 to 1962, and as a consultant from 1962 to 1973.[33] Fenwick contended that the United States had abandoned its unilateral interpretation of the Monroe Doctrine, and 'successfully' set up an inter-American collective security system. He was well aware of the fact that the asymmetric nature of the inter-American system in which 'one country has almost all the power and the rest have very little'. To him the key to overcoming this systemic paradox lay in enlightened US leadership, not in the system itself: 'The United States has pledged its word to use its power in strict conformity with the decisions of the Council of the Organization of the American States,' he argued.[34]

Toward the end of the 1950s, Wright seemed to become more sensible about the relationship between law and politics. It can be seen, for instance, in a series of lectures he gave at the Hague Academy of International Law. He observed that when the UN made a recommendation to respond to aggression, each member state would consider its political as well as its legal implications. Legal considerations were concerned with maintaining law 'which prohibits aggression as a continuing deterrent against potential aggressors' while the 'political point of view' would count upon 'immediate risks and costs to itself of military action to stop the aggressor'.[35]

In the stormy decade of the 1950s the old guard lawyers who had devoted their efforts to solidifying the framework of collective security in the interwar years and had high hopes for the UN were getting confused and increasingly divided. The events of the 1960s further accelerated the trend. Here, the Cuban Missile Crisis triggered confusion and differences among lawyers.[36]

Debates over the Cuban Quarantine of 1962

In October 1962 when the Kennedy Administration discovered that the Soviet Union was going to deliver to Cuba missiles with the estimated capability to reach American territory, it implemented a policy of 'quarantine' for ships heading to Cuba. President Kennedy proclaimed the reason for this policy was to act as a countermeasure to 'an explicit threat to peace and security of all the Americans'.

---

[33] *New York Times* (New York, 26 April 1973).

[34] 'Discussion' (1956) Proceedings, ASIL 72, 75–76.

[35] Quincy Wright, 'The Strengthening of International Law' (1959) Recueil des cours de l'Académie de Droit International 1, 81.

[36] For the changing trend of legal discourse in the 1960s, see Koskenniemi, *The Gentle Civilizer* (n 13) 510–17; Richard A Falk, 'The Adequacy of Contemporary Theories of International Law-Gaps in Legal Thinking' (1964) 50 Virginia Law Review 231, 232–38.

The Swedish government presented a contrary view, asserting that the act would be against the 'generally recognized principle of the freedom of the seas', and it refused to curtail its trade relations with Cuba.[37]

Abram Chayes, then a Legal Advisor at the Department of State, noted in the journal *Foreign Affairs* that neither the administration nor the OAS (Organization of American States) invoked Article 51 of the UN Charter, which authorized the right of individual or collective self-defence. Rather he argued that the act fell in the category of the action by regional organizations to preserve peace.[38] However, at the 1963 annual meeting of the ASIL, he shifted his position saying that 'the first and perhaps the hardest question to be asked about the Cuban quarantine' was whether law 'had anything to do with it at all'.[39] At the same meeting, former Secretary of State Dean Acheson remarked that the Cuban quarantine was 'not a legal issue'. Rather, 'the power, position and prestige of the United States had been challenged by another state' and 'law simply does not deal with such questions of ultimate power'.[40] Thus, when it became clear that US security was directly challenged by the Soviet action in Cuba, policy makers presented the issue as non-legal but, rather, political in nature.

At this 1963 ASIL meeting, it was Wright who presented a critical viewpoint regarding the US actions towards Cuba. 'The United States, by the quarantine of October 22, 1962', he claimed, clearly: 'resorted to a unilateral, forcible action, which cannot be reconciled with its objections under the United Nations Charter to settle its international disputes by peaceful means and to refrain from use or threat of force in international relations.' On the other hand, he was somewhat ambivalent and stated that while the United States lost 'its reputation for law observation', it gained 'some reputation for skillful diplomacy'. At the same time he speculated that the final agreement could have been resolved 'through diplomacy or the United Nations without illegal and dangerous unilateral action'.[41]

Fenwick again vocally expressed his differing position with Wright. To Fenwick's regret, despite his long years of cooperation with Wright in upholding international law, Wright often differed with him 'as to ways and means, and never more so than in this case'. He explicitly proclaimed that he agreed with McDougal this time, saying that the Cuban crisis was 'a clear case of self-defence, since the missile bases with atomic warheads were a "constructive armed attack" under Article 51 of the Charter of the United Nations'. 'The sheriff in our Western television shows', he continued, 'does not have to wait until a shot is fired when he sees the bad man reach for his gun.' Amusingly and visibly the United States was presented as a sheriff in Fenwick's remark.[42]

[37] Larman C Wilson, 'International Law and the United States Cuban Quarantine of 1962' (1965) 7 Journal of Inter-American Studies 485, 486.

[38] Abram Chayes, 'Law and the Quarantine of Cuba' (1962) 41 Foreign Affairs 552, 553–54.

[39] 'Remarks by Honorable Abram Chayes' (1963) Proceedings, ASIL 10.

[40] 'Remarks by the Honorable Dean Acheson' (1963) Proceedings, ASIL 14.

[41] Quincy Wright, 'The Cuban Quarantine' (1963) Proceedings, ASIL 9.

[42] 'Discussion' (1963) Proceedings, ASIL 17.

McDougal in turn stated that he found 'nothing in the history of Article 51 of the Charter to indicate that self-defense is limited to response to an armed attack'. He refuted Wright's interpretation, saying 'Professor Wright's interpretation of Article would require writing into the phrase "self-defense if an armed attack occurs" the words "actual" or "if, and only if".' Thus, he concluded 'the test of proportionality was clearly satisfied' in the Cuban case. On the other hand, Louis Henkin contended that Cuba might have 'shaken Mr. McDougal and others', but that 'the rule is at least as desirable and as important today as in 1945'. Louis B Sohn also pointed out that the issue was over how the Charter should be interpreted: 'One way is to interpret for survival; the other is to interpret in the best way in the long run for the world.'[43]

What made Wright and Fenwick take such different paths?[44] By this time Wright sensed that the attitude of the great powers towards international law was problematic. He wrote that the Cuban Quarantine, and the Suez and Hungarian episodes of 1956, showed 'the reluctance of a Great Power to observe its legal obligations' when dealing with 'unpalatable action or attitudes of small states', particularly when they were 'located in a position of strategic importance to the Great Power'.[45] To illustrate this case, Wright brought up the historical experience of the Manchurian Incident, and argued that international checks on unilateral declarations of self-defence were necessary: 'If this were not so, any war could be justified by calling it defensive.'[46] Quite ironically, this is exactly what his opponents in the interwar years—Thomas Baty and Edwin Borchard—had questioned and anticipated.[47] It sounded as if Wright implied what the United States was doing in the 1960s was not so different from Japan's action in Manchuria in the 1930s.

Relative Decline of Teaching of International Law?

While the events of the Cold War triggered debates over the state of international law, a significant reorganization process in the disciplines concerning international affairs was taking place in post-war American academia. Wright stressed the unchanging importance of the teaching of international law; however, some advocated the need to establish International Relations (IR) as an independent subject that stressed 'scientific' political science over international law.

In the immediate post-war period, the Council of Foreign Relations, a distinguished and influential think tank in the United States, was organizing a series of

---

[43] 'Panel' (1963) Proceedings, ASIL 147.

[44] For the issue of lawyers' different discourse, see Martti Koskenniemi, *From Apology to Utopia: The Structure of International Legal Argument* (Reissue with a new epilogue, Cambridge University Press 2005) 220–21, 590–96; Kennedy, 'When Renewal Repeats' (n 12) 402–03.

[45] Quincy Wright, 'The Cuban Quarantine' (1963) 58 American Journal of International Law 546–65.

[46] 'Discussion' (n 42).

[47] See Hatsue Shinohara, *US International Lawyers in the Interwar Years: A Forgotten Crusade* (Cambridge University Press 2014) 92–122.

meetings on the study of IR: in February 1946, they met in New York, Boston, and Philadelphia, and in May, they met in Chicago, Denver, Boston, and Berkeley. In total 126 participants from 76 institutions attended the meetings. The organizer of the meetings was Grayson Kirk of Columbia University. Hans J Morgenthau and Wright also attended the meeting held in Chicago.[48]

In 1948, the Social Science Research Council (SSRC), another influential academic institution in the United States, established a committee on IR, whose members included Wright, Kirk, Leo Pasvolsky (the Brookings Institute), Malcolm Davis (the Carnegie Endowment for International Peace), William Fox (Columbia University), and Rupert Emerson (Harvard University). As was seen by the fact that Wright, Pasvolsky, and a scholar from the Carnegie Endowment were involved in this project, its overall direction did not seem to completely exclude the study of international law and international organization.[49] Although this SSRC group had several meetings, its initiative discontinued in July 1950, partly because there were two different views on the orientation of IR: comprehensive and eclectic IR versus a claim for a more scientific approach.[50]

The fact that Wright himself became the president of the American Political Science Association from 1948 to 1949, even before assuming the ASIL presidency, might perhaps indicate the confusing condition over the state of the disciplines. His presidential address delivered in December 1949 was entitled 'Political Science and the Stability of the World'.[51] Wright also published a book, *The Study of International Relations*, in 1955. In its preface he recalled his long years of commitment to the field and stressed that the pre-war years had rich experiences in the series of Conference of the Teachers of International Law and Related Subjects under the auspices of the Carnegie Endowment. He frankly stated that his usage of the term—international politics—had been criticized but he reiterated that IR should not be confined to the newly ascending discipline of political science, arguing that IR should develop as a comprehensive and interdisciplinary field.[52]

In the meantime the Rockefeller Foundation sponsored a conference on the Theory of IR in 1954. Kenneth Thompson, a student of Morgenthau, was a major organizer. As he later recalled, two major factors resulted in the meeting: one was an increasing interest in a theoretical approach to political, economic, legal, and human relations in post-war years, and the other was the growing demand for theory readily applicable to policy.[53] Under his leadership and with the help of

---

[48] Grayson Kirk, *The Study of International Relations: In American Colleges and Universities* (Council on Foreign Relations 1946) 107–11.

[49] Nicolas Guilhot, 'Introduction: One Discipline, Many Histories' in Nicolas Guilhot (ed), *The Invention of International Relations: Realism, the Rockefeller Foundation and the 1954 Conference on Theory* (Columbia University Press 2011) 16–18.

[50] Guilhot, 'Introduction: One Discipline, Many Historians' (n 49) 16–19.

[51] Quincy Wright, 'Political Science and World Stabilization' in Quincy Wright (ed), *Problems of Stability and Progress in International Relations in International Relations* (University of California Press 1954) 115–20, 121–27.

[52] Quincy Wright, *The Study of International Relations* (Appleton-Century-Crofts 1955) vii–ix.

[53] Kenneth W Thompson, 'Toward a Theory of International Relations' (1955) 49 American Political Science Review 733.

Reinhold Niebur and Fox, the list of participants was finalized. Morgenthau, Fox, Arnold Wolfers, Niebur, Walter Lippmann, James Reston (the *New York Times*), and Don Price (the Ford Foundation) participated, while from the policy field Dean Acheson (then the president of the Rockefeller Foundation) and Paul Nitze were invited. The meeting proceeded under the chairmanship of Acheson. Both Acheson and Nitze wanted to have a concrete theory easily applicable to policy, citing the experiences of the Korean War.[54] Generally speaking, this conference was supported by those who were opposed to both legalistic and behaviourist approaches.

In the 1960s, as if synchronizing with the growing trend of supporting the policy oriented and 'scientific' approach in IR, the relative decline of international law in teaching was being recognized by some scholars of international law. One can find such concerns at the 1963 ASIL annual meeting. A panel 'Conference on Research and Teaching: The Application of Social Science Methods to the Study of International Law' took place. In this session Wesley L Gould of Purdue University pointed out the general decline of teaching of international law at political science departments in the United States. The ASIL had nominated a committee to investigate the condition of teaching and had distributed questionnaires to various academic institutions nationwide. Summing up the result of survey, Gould elucidated several viewpoints. Some mentioned the need of 'the use of the political scientist's tool as well as lawyer's' and others supported works of McDougal and Laswell and 'systems analysis and of national interest theory'. In addition he touched upon some concerns expressed by one respondent who had written that to encourage 'a major interest in international law might "limit the students' placement potential" '.[55]

Stanley Hoffman of Harvard University also pointed out at this session that 'the study of international law by social scientists concerned with international relations is in decline'. He mentioned four factors: 1) a sense of irrelevance of international law as a factor in world politics; 2) a sense of futility of traditional methods for teaching international law; 3) some lawyers tended to agree 'with the previous criticism that they themselves throw out the legal baby with the stale bath'; and 4) 'the trend among social scientists toward a kind of scientism'. Hoffman deplored the condition, stating that '[i]n my own department I am in a sad situation, I have a monopoly on teaching international law'. When he had a PhD student, he sometimes had to 'find somebody else to give the examination'. Despite his pessimistic observation, he concluded that it would be 'a mistake' if scholars of IR neglected international law.[56]

At another session of this 1963 meeting, though not directly addressed as a panel for education, Kenneth E Boulding of the University of Michigan's Department of

[54] Guilhot, *The Invention of International Relations* (n 49) 248–51.

[55] Wesley L Gould, 'International Law in Political Science Departments: A Brief Report and Commentary' (1963) Proceedings, ASIL 18.

[56] Stanley Hoffmann, 'The Study of International Law and the Theory of International Relations' (1963) Proceedings, ASIL 26, 47.

Economics (italics added), read a paper entitled 'The Role of Law in the Learning of Peace'. Stressing the concept of 'pay off', he argued that international law can function as a teaching process: 'If the law is to be successful, then it must itself be a teaching process, developing images of the integrative system.'[57] Following Boulding, Thomas C Schelling, a father of game theory, introduced the idea and logic of the 'game of chicken'. Schelling essentially argued that 'we would be better off with a good "chicken" player than a bad one'.[58] While the relative decline of teaching of international law was reported on, completely different discourse was being introduced at this ASIL annual meeting.

To these totally new and different approaches one commentator posed the question of whether world politics had changed so drastically as to reorient the way of thinking towards international relations completely. Wright, in turn, said in summary that Boulding characterized the control of force as a human problem while Schelling treated it as 'a mechanical problem'. In addition, after he repeated the need of education, he stressed the importance and relevance of the philosophy of John Locke, not Thomas Hobbes. He remarked that Schelling's view was based upon fear similar to Hobbes' view, and that he hoped that Locke's view should prevail instead.[59]

As was demonstrated by Boulding and Schelling's appearance at the Society's meeting, a new generation of IR scholars began to rear their heads, soon to be followed by Kenneth Waltz, who would present iconic structural realism, which highlighted the concept of anarchy. However, some later scholars critically argued that 'American' IR Theory was inclined to perpetuate a view in which war and conflict in international relations were natural and ubiquitous. Unfortunately it seemed that Wright was losing his battle against this current in the 1960s. The growing popularity and recognition of the 'scientific approach' led to the establishment of IR as an independent subject, and made legal and normative approaches less relevant and unpopular in the American IR community. Hegemonic discourse in IR was going to be increasingly set by US political scientists who claimed that 'scientific' IR should be offered at the department of political science.

It is beyond the scope of this chapter to examine comprehensively how the new trend in IR impacted the international law community.[60] However, to a degree the effect of new thinking was discernible in Fenwick's 1968 book, *Foreign Policy and International Law*. Although the work did not fully reflect upon scientific approach, it definitely indicated his inclination towards and respect for such notions as national interest and security. As the title clearly demonstrated, the term 'foreign policy' was an important concept for the book. While back in the late 1930s Fenwick argued

---

[57] Kenneth E Boulding, 'The Role of Law in the Learning of Peace' (1963) Proceedings, ASIL 92.
[58] Thomas C Schelling, 'The Threat of Violence in International Affairs' (1963) Proceedings, ASIL 103.
[59] Ibid, 111, 113.
[60] See Kennedy, 'The Discipline of International Law and Policy' (n 12), in particular a chart on 'International Legal Studies in the United States' at 30; Kirgis, *American Society* (n 20) 307; Wesley L Gould and Michael Barkun, *International Law and the Social Sciences* (Princeton University Press 1970).

that international law should defend the community's interest, in this book his balance shifted towards the direction that weighed more emphasis on US interests than those of the broader community. He defined the aim of foreign policy as being to secure interests, among which national security was more important than economic and social interests. He did not go as far as to contend that international law could solely be used for defending the national interest, but he wrote that international obligations should be observed in pursuing one's foreign policy. Nonetheless, he abandoned his hope for the UN, writing: 'We could no longer trust to the security of the Charter for our own immediate security'. Interestingly enough, no work by Wright was cited in the reference section of the book, even though he included those by Hudson, Hersch Lauterpacht, and James Brown Scott, as well as Hans Morgenthau's *In Defense of the National Interest*.[61]

Epilogue

Despite Wright's lonesome stand in the debate over the Cuban quarantine, his critical argument over the legality of quarantine of 1962 was soon recognized by fellow jurists, as if they were canonizing him as a heroic and iconic defender of international law. Richard Falk wrote that 'except for Quincy Wright' most of the authors appeared to 'mobilize legal arguments in support of a national position in a period of crisis'.[62] Larman C Wilson of Naval Academy also wrote that there was surprisingly '*almost* complete acceptance among the members of the American Society of International Law, especially the jurists and professors of international law' (italics original). However, he wrote that 'Professor Wright was the foremost, if not the sole, dissenter, arguing eloquently if not convincingly that the United States "quarantine" was in violation of international law'.[63] Even Fenwick acknowledged in his 1968 book that Wright was critical of quarantine while the majority of scholars supported it.[64]

Wright continued to fight and present a more outright critical view on US policy. Regarding the Vietnam War, he wrote that whatever they might call the US action in the country—intervention, reprisals, or collective defence—'the United States response by bombings in North Viet-Nam, which began in February, 1965, violated international law, the United Nations Charter, and the Geneva Agreement, if the latter were in effect'.[65]

---

[61] Charles G Fenwick, *Foreign Policy and International Law* (Oceana 1968) 50, 133–35.

[62] Falk, 'The Adequacy of Contemporary Theories of International Law-Gaps in Legal Thinking' (n 36) 234, fn 6.

[63] Larman C Wilson, 'International Law and the United States Cuban Quarantine of 1962' (n 37) 487, 490–91.

[64] Fenwick, *Foreign Policy and International Law* (n 61) 59, fn 14.

[65] Quincy Wright, 'Legal Aspects of the Viet-Nam Situation' in Richard A Falk (ed), *The Vietnam War and International Law* (Princeton University Press 1968) 288.

As was discussed in this chapter, Wright found great powers' attitudes towards and their use of international law controversial while Fenwick justified US official policy in the name of law. Fenwick took it for granted that law itself could comprise the elements of power. International law can be 'imperial' if necessary, but this empire would and should be trusted upon as an honest and benevolent one by its subordinates. Thus, he believed that under this American hegemonic order people would be better off than under a Soviet one. Wright in turn believed that international law can and should boldly walk into the realm of power and serve as a tool to regulate imperial actions, in particular its use of force. While he did not alter his fundamental position on international law since the interwar years, it is possible to argue that his legal discourse appeared as more 'utopian' under the changing political and academic context.

In the post-war years Wright's view was not as widely accepted as it had been during the interwar years. Rather, as Fenwick came to support McDougal, the latter and New Heaven School were gaining more currency. Furthermore, the rise of 'scientific' IR Theory helped to undermine the interdisciplinary approach that Wright advocated, in which law and politics could be inseparably addressed and explored. If there was an increase among lawyers lending intellectual support for American imperial policy, the condition cannot be explained solely by the internal disciplinary development of the field. There was a changing historical context with the growing tension in the Cold War, with policy makers presenting some issues as non-legal, as if they were telling 'law' to quietly step down from the stage. In addition, if an American empire needed legitimacy for the use of force, it was to be easily found in another developing academic discourse, namely 'scientific' IR. Concepts such as game theory, deterrence, security, and anarchy helped to nourish the rise of a different *Weltanschauung*,[66] which filtered into the post-war US international legal community, however intangible its effect may have been.

Bibliography

'Addresses on Problems Involved in Review of the United Nations Charter: Remarks' (1954) Proceedings of the American Society of International Law 206
'Discussion' (1950) Proceedings of the American Society of International Law 117
'Discussion' (1956) Proceedings of the American Society of International Law 72
'Discussion' (1963) Proceedings of the American Society of International Law 17
'Panel' (1963) Proceedings of the American Society of International Law 147
'Remarks by Honorable Abram Chayes' (1963) Proceedings of the American Society of International Law 10

[66] For the incompatible nature between the study of international law and IR, see Martti Koskenniemi, 'Law, Teleology and International Relations: An essay in Counterdisciplinarity' (2012) 26 International Relations 3, 26.

'Remarks by the Honorable Dean Acheson' (1963) Proceedings of the American Society of International Law 13

Acheson, Dean, 'The Development of International Community' (1952) Proceedings of the American Society of International Law 18

Boulding, Kenneth E, 'The Role of Law in the Learning of Peace' (1963) Proceedings of the American Society of International Law 92

Bradford, Anu and Posner, Eric A, 'Universal Exceptionalism in International Law' (2011) 52 Harvard International Law Journal 3

Bull, Hedley, *The Anarchical Society: A Study of Order in World Politics* (Columbia University 1977)

Byers, Michael and Nolte, George, *United States Hegemony and the Foundation of International Law* (Cambridge University Press 2003)

Carty, Anthony, 'Doctrine versus State Practice' in Bardo Fassbender and Anne Peters (eds), *The Oxford Handbook of the History of International Law* (Oxford University Press 2012)

Chayes, Abram, 'Law and the Quarantine of Cuba' (1962) 41 Foreign Affairs 550

Cohen, Warren, *Empire without Tears: American Foreign Relations, 1921–1933* (Alfred Knopf 1987)

Dulles, John Foster, 'New Aspects of American Foreign Policy' (1950) Proceedings of the American Society of International Law 48

Dulles, John Foster, 'The Institution of Peace' (1956) Proceedings of the American Society of International Law 11

Falk, Richard A, 'The Adequacy of Contemporary Theories of International Law—Gaps in Legal Thinking' (1964) 50 Virginia Law Review 231

Fenwick, Charles G, 'Freedom of Communication across National Boundaries' (1950) Proceedings of the American Society of International Law 107

Fenwick, Charles G, 'The Development of Collective Security, 1914–1954' (1954) Proceedings of the American Society of International Law 2

Fenwick, Charles G, *Foreign Policy and International Law* (Oceana 1968)

Ferguson, Niall, *Colossus: The Rise and Fall of the American Empire* (Penguin Books 2004)

Gould, Wesley L, 'International Law in Political Science Departments: A Brief Report and Commentary' (1963) Proceedings of the American Society of International Law 18

Gould, Wesley L and Barkun, Michael, *International Law and the Social Sciences* (Princeton University Press 1970)

Grewe, Wilhelm G, *The Epochs of International Law* (Michael Byers tr, De Gruyter 2000)

Guilhot, Nicolas, 'Introduction: One Discipline, Many Histories' in Nicolas Guilhot (ed), *The Invention of International Relations: Realism, the Rockefeller Foundation and the 1954 Conference on Theory* (Columbia University Press 2011)

Hoffmann, Stanley, 'The Study of International Law and the Theory of International Relations' (1963) Proceedings of the American Society of International Law 26

Hudson, Manley O, 'International Law at Mid-Century' (1950) Proceedings of the American Society of International Law 38

Johnson, Chalmers, *The Sorrows of Empire* (Metropolitan 2004)

Kennan, George F, *American Diplomacy 1900–1950* (University of Chicago Press 1951)

Kennedy, David, 'Thesis about International Law Discourse' (1980) German Yearbook of International Law 353

Kennedy, David, 'The Discipline of International Law and Policy' (1999) 12 Leiden Journal of International Law 9

Kennedy, David, 'When Renewal Repeats: Thinking against the Box' (2000) 32 Journal of International Law and Politics 335

Keohane, Robert, *After Hegemony* (Princeton University Press 2005)

Kirgis, Frederic, *The American Society of International Law's First Century 1906–2006* (Martinus Nijhoff 2006)

Kirk, Grayson, *The Study of International Relations: In American Colleges and Universities* (Council on Foreign Relations 1946)

Koskenniemi, Martti, *The Gentle Civilizer of Nations: The Rise and Fall of International Law 1870–1960* (Cambridge University Press 2001)

Koskenniemi, Martti, *From Apology to Utopia: The Structure of International Legal Argument* (Reissue with a new epilogue, Cambridge University Press 2005)

Koskenniemi, Martti, 'A History of International Law Histories' in Bardo Fassbender and Anne Peters (eds), *The Oxford Handbook of the History of International Law* (Oxford University Press 2012)

Koskenniemi, Martti, 'Law, Teleology and International Relations: An Essay in Counterdisciplinarity' (2012) 26 International Relations 3

Laswell, Harold D, 'Conditions of Security in a Bi-Polarizing World' (1950) Proceedings of the American Society of International Law 3

Negri, Antonio and Hardt, Michael, *Multitude: War and Democracy in the Age of an Empire* (The Penguin Press 2004)

New York Times (New York, 26 April 1973)

Schelling, Thomas C, 'The Threat of Violence in International Affairs' (1963) Proceedings of the American Society of International Law 103

Scott, Shirley V, *International Law, US Power: The United Sates' Quest for Legal Security* (Cambridge University Press 2012)

Shinohara, Hatsue, *US International Lawyers in the Interwar Years: A Forgotten Crusade* (Cambridge University Press 2014)

Thompson, Kenneth W, 'Toward a Theory of International Relations' (1955) 49 American Political Science Review 733

Wilson, Larman C, 'International Law and the United States Cuban Quarantine of 1962' (1965) 7 Journal of Inter-American Studies 485

Wright, Quincy to Manley O Hudson, 13 November 1942, Box 98, Folder 1, Papers of Manley O Hudson, Harvard Law Library, Cambridge, Massachusetts, US

Wright, Quincy, 'Freedom and Responsibility in respect to Trans-National Communication' (1950) Proceedings of the American Society of International Law 95

Wright, Quincy, 'Collective Security in the Light of the Korean Experience' (1951) Proceedings of the American Society of International Law 165

Wright, Quincy, 'The Outlawry of War and the Law of War' (1953) 47 American Journal of International Law 365

Wright, Quincy, 'International Law and Ideologies' (1954) 48 American Journal of International Law 616

Wright, Quincy, 'Political Science and World Stabilization' in Quincy Wright (ed), *Problems of Stability and Progress in International Relations in International Relations* (University of California Press 1954)

Wright, Quincy, *The Study of International Relations* (Appleton-Century-Crofts 1955)

Wright, Quincy, 'The Prevention of Aggression' (1956) 50 American Journal of International Law 514

Wright, Quincy, 'The Prospects of International Law' (1956) Proceedings of the American Society of International Law 2

Wright, Quincy, 'Intervention, 1956' (1957) 51 American Journal of International Law 257

Wright, Quincy, 'The Strengthening of International Law' (1959) Recueil des cours de l'Académie de Droit International 1

Wright, Quincy, 'The Cuban Quarantine' (1963) Proceedings of the American Society of International Law 9

Wright, Quincy, 'The Cuban Quarantine,' (1963) 58 American Journal of International Law 546

Wright, Quincy, 'Legal Aspects of the Viet-Nam Situation' in Richard A Falk (ed), *The Vietnam War and International Law* (Princeton University Press 1968)

14

Imperium sine fine: Carneades, the Splendid Vice of Glory, and the Justice of Empire

Benjamin Straumann*

International lawyers have gotten used to the idea that the historical origins of their discipline are implicated with imperialism and indebted to attempts to justify the exercise of unconstrained *raison d'état*. In my contribution I seek to show that debates about the justice of imperialism were indeed of foundational importance for the development of proto-international legal ideas, and that these debates were often conducted along the lines prefigured by the Roman thinker and statesman Cicero. Moral and legal argument concerning the justice of the Roman Empire was the fertile ground from which sprang early claims about binding rules in the international realm. As will become clear, from Augustine's *City of God* to Machiavelli there has always been a strand of political thought that sought to attribute Roman imperialism to the 'pagan' virtue of glory-seeking; for Machiavelli, glory-seeking provided a normative justification for Roman imperialism as well. However, most of the early modern European thinkers developed their ideas concerning international law in self-conscious opposition to that *raison d'état* strand of political thought, thinking instead in terms of the enforcement of peace and the imposition of legal order. These ideas owed more to Cicero and other Roman sources than to Machiavelli's celebration of the imperial expansion of the Roman republic.

The debate on the justice of Rome's empire and the arguments deployed in it do still have relevance for present-day debates concerning the legality or morality of modern imperialism, and deserve to be analysed by international lawyers curious about the normative and historical foundations of their discipline. As we shall see, the sceptical claim, already put forward in Cicero's *Republic*, that we do not really have reason to follow moral or legal precepts in the international realm—that really it would be irrational to do so—is of resounding topicality; usually it is presented as

* Many thanks to Peter Garnsey, David Lupher, Eric Nelson, and Chris Warren for their help. Classical authors and works are cited according to standard editions (*Oxford Classical Texts* and, where not available, Teubner). Abbreviations of classical sources follow Simon Hornblower and Antony Spawforth (eds), *Oxford Classical Dictionary* (revised 3rd edn, Oxford University Press 2003). Translations are referenced; if no reference is given, translations are my own. Some of this material has previously been published in chapter 7 of my *Crisis and Constitutionalism: Roman Political Thought from the Fall of the Republic to the Age of Revolution* (Oxford University Press 2016).

the view that given imperialism and other injustices, there is simply no justice to be had in the relations between states. The motivation behind this kind of scepticism is usually to unmask international interventions as cynical, imperialist power grabs that may be prudent and achieve the state's self-interest, but cannot claim to be just. The typical answer usually also follows the pattern we find in Cicero: some kinds of imperialism can indeed claim to be just, even by the sceptic's own lights. The sceptic seeks to force his opponent to acknowledge that his course of action, while clever, is unjust, and the imperialist aspiring to justice seeks to counter the sceptic by claiming that justice, not self-interest, is in fact both the motivation behind as well as the achievement of his or her actions. What is interesting about Cicero's way of dealing with these arguments is that he himself is clearly convinced that at least some kinds of imperialism are just but, at the same time and measured by the same criteria, he acknowledges that Roman imperialism exhibits deeply unjust features. By not accepting the sceptic's claims, Cicero opens himself, and Roman imperialism in general, up to moral criticism.

Greek political thought knows a prime example of perfectly unabashed cynical imperialism: the Athenians as presented by Thucydides in his history of the Peloponnesian War. In Thucydides' famous Melian dialogue the imperialist Athenians tell the inhabitants of the small neutral island of Melos that considerations of justice cannot be applied to international relations, at least not in cases where there are differences in power.[1] They resemble the sceptical claim rendered above, but this time in the service of imperialism: the Athenians tell the Melians that they are simply stronger and that considerations of justice do therefore not apply. Imperial powers rule by nature over their weaker competitors, and legal or moral norms are simply irrelevant in such a context. In what must be described as the first extant example of a philosophical treatment of the moral problem of imperialism, Cicero's dialogue *Republic*, Cicero made two participants in the dialogue argue in turn first for the necessity of *injustice* for states, both internally and externally, and then for the importance and applicability of *justice*. As far as we can tell from the fragmentary condition of the dialogue, Cicero's sceptic is mostly interested in attacking moral, or legal, universalism by claiming that any moral or legal norms that have any kind of normative pull on us are simply the norms of a given state and do not instantiate universal norms of justice, they simply establish what is convenient for a given community. The sceptic's opponent seeks to show that states cannot claim to be states without establishing just norms (as opposed to merely prudential ones); that at least some of these norms are of a universal nature; and that therefore imperialism can be normatively judged by these norms.

Cicero's dialogue was of course indebted to Plato's *Politeia*, where there could also be found a debate, between the sophist Thrasymachus and Plato's brother

---

[1] Thuc. 5.84–116. At 5.105 the Athenians are saying that by necessity of nature men who have power will always rule; and this principle they call a law (*nomos*) that they found already in existence and that will always be there. This is a version of what the sophist Callicles in Pl. *Grg.* 483e6 will call a 'law of nature' (*nomos tês phuseôs*) that is in favor of the strong against the weak—the first instance of the phrase 'law of nature', but the Athenians in the Melian dialogue come close.

Glaucon (who is channeling some of Thrasymachus' points) on the one hand and Socrates on the other, on whether injustice was more successful than justice, and on the standards of success. In Plato's dialogue as in Cicero's the attacks against justice come first and are followed by vindications of justice. Plato was not Cicero's direct model though, at least not nominally—the Academic sceptic Carneades was, who was active in the mid-second century BC. In the year 155 BC, Carneades had apparently been to Rome as a member of a Greek embassy and, feeling he owed the barbarous Romans a taste of Greek rhetoric and philosophy, had delivered two speeches before a Roman audience. The first speech must have praised justice, the second must have attacked it. In his *Republic*, Cicero refers to Carneades' speeches and has two of his protagonists represent the two Carneadean positions. However, as in Plato's work, the sequence in Cicero's dialogue reverses the Carneadean one; first the attack on justice, then the defence.

Cicero's is the first extant text to introduce the element of *imperialism* into the discussion; we have no reason to think that Carneades dealt with the question of the justice of empire in his own pair of speeches. Cicero, however, makes this the crucial feature of the debate on justice that takes place in the third book of the *Republic*: a participant in the dialogue by the name of Lucius Furius Philus represents Carneades and argues that justice does not exist, or if it did would equal stupidity; as an example he says that if Rome wanted to be just, she would have to give up her empire, which had been unjustly gained. In reply his opponent Gaius Laelius claims that Rome had gained the empire justly, by defending her allies in just wars,[2] and in accordance with natural law.[3] He also claims, in Augustine's highly influential rendering, that 'empire is just because servitude/subjection (*servitus*) is useful for such men and that when it is rightly done, it is done on their behalf, that is, when the right to do injury is taken away from wicked people: the conquered will be better off, because they would be worse off if they had not been conquered'.[4]

The debate, concerning itself with the justice of imperialism, has had considerable influence in the history of political thought. Reverberations of it reappear in Virgil, and very prominently in the Christian writers Lactantius (*c.*240–*c.*320) and Augustine (354–430). The way these last two framed the debate proved particularly influential, for the simple reason that it was primarily in their texts that fragments of book three of Cicero's dialogue have been preserved. The shape the debate assumed in Lactantius and Augustine was the shape the early modern writers on the law of nature and the law of nations came to be acquainted with. It was through Lactantius and Augustine that Gentili (1552–1608) came to know the debate, which in turn served as his model in his work *The Wars of the Romans* (1599). And it was on the

---

[2] Cic. *Rep.* 3.34f.   [3] Cic. *Rep.* 3.33=Lact. *Inst.* 6.8.6.

[4] Cic. *Rep.* 3.36=August. *De civ. D.* 19.21: *responsum est a parte iustitiae ideo iustum esse, quod talibus hominibus sit utilis seruitus, et pro utilitate eorum fieri, cum recte fit, id est cum improbis aufertur iniuri-arum licentia, et domiti melius se habebunt, quia indomiti deterius se habuerunt.* (James EG Zetzel tr, Cambridge University Press 1999), except for 'servitude/subjection' instead of Zetzel's 'slavery'. These are of course echoes of Aristotle's argument for natural slavery (*Pol.* 1.5–6, 1254a17–1255b15), but as for Aristotle, what is meant is not the actual, existing institution of slavery, but a normative 'ideal'; cf *Rep.* 1.37b.

basis of the normative framework Lactantius and especially Augustine had established for thinking about Roman imperialism and Roman virtue that Machiavelli (1469–1527) developed his views on republican expansionism, glory, and the preservation of the state. I shall present first some thoughts on the interpretation of the Carneadean debate as it appears in Cicero in order to then discuss its transmission by the Christian writers and finally the way it influences Machiavelli and Gentili.

In his influential interpretation of the Carneadean debate and its impact on later international thought, Richard Tuck has put forward the view that Cicero's 'final message', his defence of the justice of Roman imperialism, was 'likely to have been … that the apparent injustice of an imperial hegemony could be defended as being in the necessary interests of Rome'. This leads Tuck to claim that 'the Romans were the most powerful voices in antiquity in defence of what we may reasonably term this *raison d'état* view', a view he sums up as the 'idea that war could legitimately be made for imperial power and glory'.[5] In my chapter I will suggest that this is almost certainly wrong as an interpretation of Cicero and thus of the Carneadean debate, although it is an influential view that has been held, as we shall see, in various versions by Lactantius, Augustine, and Machiavelli. The idea that the Romans considered glory-seeking, *cupiditas gloriae*, as the driving force behind Rome's expansion can of course be found in Roman writers, especially in Roman historians. It might have been expressed most succinctly by Sallust, who wrote that once Rome lived under republican government, as opposed to kingly rule, 'it is hard to believe how quickly the city grew once liberty had been gained: so much had the desire for glory triumphed (*tanta cupido gloriae incesserat*)'.[6] But while Sallust famously explained the downfall of the Republic by reference to a moralizing account of the corrupting effect of imperial rule and the attending luxury,[7] the Carneadean debate offered a very different way of accounting for the demise of the Republic, with justice (or lack thereof), not glory, being the chief ingredient.

Tuck's view has been contested before. Taking a closer look at the Carneadean debate, however, is amply justified given its prominence in the early history of the law of nations. In an excellent article the classicist James Zetzel has argued that Cicero's rendering of the debate profoundly influenced Virgil's vision of Roman imperialism as it appears in the *Aeneid*. In particular Zetzel draws attention to the fact that in Virgil as well as in Cicero the 'Roman order may have triumphed, but not all the ways in which that triumph was achieved were admirable'.[8] This has consequences for the imperial power, Rome, herself—far from advocating the seeking of *gloria* and *raison d'état* (which should in any case not be equated, but this is too large a topic to address in this chapter), Cicero in his answer to Carneades offers a rather different vision.

---

[5] Richard Tuck, *The Rights of War and Peace: Political Thought and the International Order from Grotius to Kant* (Oxford University Press 1999), 22ff.

[6] Sall. *Cat.* 7.3: *Sed civitas incredibile memoratu est, adepta libertate, quantum brevi creverit: tanta cupido gloriae incesserat.*

[7] Sall. *Cat.* 52.19–23 (Cato's speech).

[8] JEG Zetzel, 'Natural Law and Poetic Justice: A Carneadean Debate in Cicero and Virgil' (1996) 91 Classical Philology 297, 312.

One of the key exhibits of Tuck's interpretation is a passage from Cicero's answer to Carneades in the *Republic* where the effect of death for states is contrasted with its effect on individuals:

For the state (*civitas*) ought to be established as to be eternal, and therefore there is no natural death of a state (*res publica*) as there is for a man, for whom death is not only necessary, but at times desirable. When a state (*civitas*) is removed, destroyed, extinguished, it is somehow similar (comparing small to great) to the death and collapse of the entire cosmos.[9]

Tuck thinks that this merely illustrates that 'sacrifice of the citizen' was considered a 'particularly glorious thing by all Roman writers'.[10] However, as Zetzel shows, the passage is set in the context of an argument about justice and its being in harmony with natural law and its being eternal, which is all in a very Stoic vein. This on the one hand serves to justify the integration of formerly independent cities and states into the Roman Empire.[11] On the other hand, however—and this is crucial for my argument—Cicero seems to be implying that Rome herself, when failing to live up to the standards of natural law sketched in the Carneadean debate, when failing to wage *just* wars in defence of her allies, that then Rome herself will have to fear for her survival.

At this point it bears mentioning that Cicero's dialogue, albeit written in the late 50s BC in a context of looming civil war and highly dysfunctional constitutional institutions, is actually set in the year 129 BC—also in the context of constitutional conflict, this time over Tiberius Gracchus' redistributive land reforms, when one of the protagonists of the dialogue, Scipio, must have been floated as a potential dictator to put everything back in place. However, this came to naught as the real Scipio died only a few days after the dramatic date of Cicero's dialogue (a historical fact actually alluded to by Cicero). His death destroyed hopes of a return to the old constitutional ways, and seems to serve as a watershed for Cicero; looking back to 129 BC from the late 50s, he seems to suggest that roughly 70 years earlier, everything could still have been saved. How? Interestingly, this is where he brings in international justice:

*Tiberius Gracchus, who paid attention to citizens, but neglected the rights and treaties of the allies and the Latins. If that license should become customary and spread more widely, and should transform our power from justice to violence (*imperiumque nostrum ad vim a iure traduxerit*), so that those who are now our willing subjects be held by terror (*ut qui adhuc voluntate nobis oboediunt, terrore teneantur*), even if those of us who are getting on in years are finishing our watch, I am still concerned about our descendants and about the immortality of the republic, which could be eternal, if our life remained in accordance with ancestral institutions and customs.[12]

---

[9] Cic. *Rep.* 3.34=August. *De civ. D.* 22.6. Trans. Zetzel.
[10] Tuck, *Rights of War and Peace* (n 5) 22.
[11] Zetzel, 'Natural Law and Poetic Justice' (n 8) 316.
[12] Cic. *Rep.* 3.41 (Zetzel tr, except he has 'laws' instead of 'institutions'). This is of course a part of the dialogue which has not been transmitted other than in the palimpsest found in 1819 by Angelo Mai (first ed, Rome/Stuttgart 1822), and the asterisk signifies the point at which the palimpsest passage starts abruptly.

Of course, given the dramatic date of the dialogue and the time of its writing, this implies that, in Cicero's view, by the late 50s, the *imperium* of the Romans had been transformed from *ius* (constitutional justice) to *vis* (violence) and that the once will-ing subjects are now simply held by terror. This contention needs to be seen in the historical context of two developments, both of which Cicero deplores. One was of a domestic nature and concerned the emergence, roughly from the time of the dra-matic date of the dialogue and the reforms of the Gracchi onward, of rival interpreta-tions of the basic constitutional norms of the Roman Republic. This constitutional crisis intensified from an initial violation of an important constitutional norm by Tiberius Gracchus until it culminated in a series of emergency measures, extraordi-nary military commands, and civil wars, starting with Sulla's march on Rome in 88 BC. By the late 50s, this had resulted in the breakdown or near-breakdown of many of the central institutions of the Republic. The other development concerned the relationship of the Roman Republic with its allies and provincial subjects. In the Social War (91–88 BC), Italian cities formerly allied with Rome fought against Rome in order to achieve Roman citizenship, which they had been denied. Gracchus' treat-ment of allies alluded to in the passage above should be situated in this explosive context; Cicero effectively reproaches Gracchus here with the kind of attitude vis-à-vis Rome's allies that had led to the bloody Social War. Gracchus here is portrayed as someone who, in the interest of demagoguery, seeks to satisfy the desires of the citi-zen masses by exploiting the allies and mistreating them. In the person of Gracchus, Cicero suggests, the violation of domestic constitutional norms and a violation of the rights of the allies and subjects of Roman Empire come together, with conse-quences that can be seen all too clearly in the dysfunctional world of the late 50s.

Cicero here certainly does not deploy the language of someone devoted simply to *gloria*, necessity, or *raison d'état*; quite to the contrary. Almost 10 years later, Cicero makes this clear in his highly influential philosophical work on practical ethics, the *De officiis*; here he unmistakably points out the tension between glory-seeking and justice, between especially military glory (*bellica gloria*) and the morally right (*honestum*), dissolving it in favour of the morally right.[13] Also, Cicero says, glory-seeking leads to injustice,[14] since 'no one who has gained glory through bravery by treachery and cunning' can be lauded, for 'nothing can be morally right that lacks justice'.[15] But Cicero's criticism of imperialist practices he deems unjust can be tracked throughout his work and political career. In a speech held before the (Roman) people in 66 BC, Cicero says:

It is impossible to exaggerate, citizens, the degree to which we are detested by foreign peo-ples, because of the greed and corruption of the men we have sent out to govern them in

---

[13] Cic. *Off.* 1.68: 'we must beware of ambition for glory; for it robs us of liberty.' Cf generally 1.62–69.

[14] Ibid, 1.64.

[15] Ibid, 1.62: *Quocirca nemo, qui fortitudinis gloriam consecutus est insidiis et malitia, laudem est adeptus; nihil enim honestum esse potest, quod iustitia vacat.* For a real-world example of the problems of conscience involved with unjust empire, see *Tusc.* 5.102 (statues illicitly gained in the provinces; cf also *Verr.* 4).

recent years. In all those lands, do you think there is any shrine that our magistrates have treated as sacred, any state they have treated as inviolable, or any private house they have treated as closed and barred to them? On the contrary, they actually go searching for rich and flourishing cities that they can find an excuse for declaring war on: that gives them their opportunity of plundering them.[16]

Four years earlier, Cicero had in fact prosecuted Gaius Verres, the corrupt Roman governor of the province of Sicily. Verres had to stand trial in 70 BC for misconduct, namely extortion, while holding office from 73 to 71 BC, and in order to put Cicero and his ideas on imperialism and justice in historical context, the nature of Verres' trial is highly significant and deserves brief discussion. Probably already from the year 149 onward and certainly by 122 BC, there was a legal mechanism in place by which provincials, that is, non-citizens, could bring Roman magistrates who had abused their office to trial before a special kind of court, the *quaestio de rebus repetundis*, which was governed by statute.[17]

Both the fact that provincials themselves had standing in these special permanent extortion courts and the fact that such courts should exist in the first place is certainly 'remarkable', and shows, according to the ancient historian John Richardson, that 'already under the Republic, the well-being of those *sub imperio*, under the control of the Roman people and its *imperium*-holders, was of concern to the senate and people'.[18] From 122 BC onward these jury courts had no longer simply civil but criminal procedures in place and became the model for later standing criminal courts in the late Roman Republic. They were the first permanent courts that were set up in the Republic as well as the first criminal courts. The concern with the 'well-being of those *sub imperio*', although certainly at least partly motivated by self-interested concerns about corruption and good governance, found thus expression in a pioneering legal procedure, which gives us an idea of what Cicero was aiming at when judging Roman imperialism. His own normative views and those expressed in the Carneadean debate were thus not merely confined to the realm of moral philosophy, but could also reasonably be interpreted to have a legal dimension. In one of his forensic speeches against Verres, held before the extortion court, Cicero in fact delivers some of his most damning depictions of the injustice of Roman imperialism, when he addresses the jurors and says:

In this beautiful city of ours, so well stocked with works of art, do you think there is a single statue, a single painting that was not taken from defeated enemies and brought here? On the other hand, the country houses of those men I am referring to are decorated and indeed stuffed with large quantities of beautiful treasures which have been looted from our most steadfast allies.[19]

---

[16] Cic. *Leg. Man.* 65 (DH Berry tr).

[17] For the text of the 123/122 BC law, see MH Crawford (ed), *Roman Statutes* (Institute of Classical Studies 1996) no 1.

[18] John Richardson, 'The Meaning of *imperium* in the Last Century BC and the First AD' in Benedict Kingsbury and Benjamin Straumann (eds), *The Roman Foundations of the Law of Nations* (Oxford University Press 2010) 27ff.

[19] Cic. *2Verr.* 5.127 (DH Berry tr).

It is obvious, from these and similar passages, that Cicero was indeed aware of the oftentimes criminal nature of Roman imperialism. It is equally obvious that his view that imperialism could be judged both morally and legally had not merely philosophical but also an institutional model to base itself on, such as the extortion courts. The model of these courts, it seems, underwrites for Cicero a normative view that allows both the justification as well as criticism of imperialism on legal grounds. The kind of imperialism that would seem to be justified, on this view, is one that is constrained, internally, by constitutional mechanisms of good governance that provide the foundations for imperial pacification. Glory-seeking and other martial virtues, by contrast, do not enter into the picture.

Virgil, whose *Aeneid* contains Jupiter's announcement that he had given the Romans *imperium sine fine*, 'empire without limit or end',[20] was heavily influenced by Cicero's stance. In the description of the shield of Aeneas at the end of book eight, Rome becomes the cosmos; in Zetzel's words, the victory of Augustus and the empire he pacified become 'the goal of world history and the center of the universe', portraying 'the end of history in both senses of the word "end" '.[21] Zetzel shows, however, that Virgil's vision is ultimately not all that Hegelian, but contains rather strong ambiguities proving any 'end of history' to be a false, naive hope. A further important strand of Virgil's propagandistic poem is the importance it attaches to the pacification of subjects, and to the imposition of *mos*, customary law; in one of the most famous passages[22] Anchises reminds Aeneas of the mission of the Romans:

> You, Roman, be sure to rule the world
> (be these your arts)
> to impose order on the foundation of peace
> to spare the vanquished and to crush the proud[23]

This is not about glory, but about the pacifying imposition of morality and, above all, constitutional order. Similarly, a few lines earlier Virgil has Anchises express strong misgivings about glory-seeking,[24] and in book 7, when Aeneas'

[20] Verg. *Aen.* 1.239. Cf Gentili, *WR* 2.2, 140/141, at n. 51, where, astonishingly, the lines of Virgil are not being quoted. There is an echo of these lines at *WR* 2.13, 350/351, however, where the imposition of peace and laws are said to have been the arts by which Rome grew: *Illis artibus Roma crevit: istis artibus Roma stetit.*

[21] Zetzel, 'Natural Law and Poetic Justice' (n 8) 310. On the shield, see also DA West, '*Cernere erat*: The Shield of Aeneas' (1975–6) 15 Proceedings of the Virgil Society 1.

[22] Which Augustine does not fail to quote either, but without stressing the aspects of peace, order, and the imposition of *mos*: August. *De civ. D.* 5.12. But cf *De civ. D.* 5.17, where the imposition of Roman laws and the security the Roman Empire provided are being lauded.

[23] Verg. *Aen.* 6.851–53: *tu regere imperio populos, Romane, memento/(hae tibi erunt artes), pacique imponere morem,/parcere subiectis et debellare superbos* (HR Fairclough tr, adapted).

[24] Verg. *Aen.* 6.817–23, where Lucius Iunius Brutus' killing of his own sons in the name of republican liberty is touched upon. Virgil's discomfort shows in his calling Brutus' spirit 'proud' (*animam superbam*), aligning him with kingly rule and Tarquinius Superbus. Augustine (*De civ. D.* 5.18) was to seize upon the passage in the *Aeneid*; so did, predictably, Machiavelli, without naming any source, in *Discourses* 1.16.4; 3.1.5, and especially 3.3.1. Machiavelli of course approved of Brutus' actions. Gentili also adduced the passage; Picenus (*WR* 1.4, p. 38) cites Anchises' claim that Brutus' glory-seeking had made him unhappy (*infelix*). In book 2 (2.4, 178ff.) Brutus is defended, and the authority of Augustine

son Ascanius is said to be 'inflamed with love of extraordinary praise', this makes him pursue Silvia's stag, which in turn triggers the war that lasts for the rest of the *Aeneid*, a catastrophic war very much modelled on the Roman civil wars of Virgil's youth.[25]

Once we get to the Carneadean debate as it appears in the Christian writers, in Lactantius and Augustine, we encounter additional layers added to it. The Christian apologist L Caecilius Firmianus Lactantius (*c.*250–*c.*325) in his *Divine Institutes*,[26] a work he was provoked into writing by emperor Diocletian's Great Persecution (which began in 303), quotes the central argument that is being put forward in the *Republic* against Carneades' sceptical, anti-imperialist stance verbatim—Cicero's Stoic[27] description of the natural law that serves as an objective yardstick for justice and according to which the empire has been gained justly.

> True law is right reason, consonant with nature, spread through all people. It is constant and eternal.... We cannot be released from this law by senate or people ... There will not be one law at Rome and another in Athens, one now and another later; but all nations at all times will be bound by this one eternal and unchangeable law.[28]

But Lactantius is not sympathetic to Cicero's theory of natural law. He only cites the passage from the third book of the *Republic* in order to then show that justice, properly understood, had in fact been absent from Rome. This was necessarily so, as pagans could not hope to achieve justice, which presupposed, for Lactantius, Christian piety and worship of the true god. For Roman pagans, in the absence of the Christian god, there could indeed be no reason to be just, Lactantius claims, conceding effectively Carneades' point. This is so because in the absence of heavenly rewards, which only await pious Christians, adhering to other-regarding norms of just behaviour is indeed, as Carneades had said, simply stupid and irrational. Lactantius is thus inclined to present Carneades' sceptical stance and his anti-Ciceronian arguments as effective as far as they go, both because he thinks that Cicero as a pagan could not possibly have refuted Carneades' scepticism, and because Lactantius, at the time of his writing the *Divine Institutes*, was of course highly hostile to the Roman empire of his own day, which was persecuting him and his fellow Christians. Lactantius goes on to say that 'if Cicero had also known or explained what instructions the holy law itself consists in as clearly as he saw its force and reason, he would have fulfilled the role not of a philosopher but of a prophet. That, however, he could not do, and so

---

doubted; the law of God has no claim to authority either (178: *neque nobis defendendi Romani sunt ad Dei legem*). There is no explicit reference to Virgil in book 2.

[25] Verg. *Aen.* 7.496: Ascanius is *eximiae laudis succensus amore*. Many thanks to David Lupher for this hint.

[26] On Lactantius and his work, see the excellent Introduction in Anthony Bowen and Peter Garnsey, *Lactantius: Divine Institutes* (Liverpool University Press 2003).

[27] Although Carneades is portrayed by Lactantius as mainly an enemy of Plato and Aristotle's ethical doctrines, Cicero claims that his main target were the Stoics: *Tusc.* 5.83.

[28] Cic. *Rep.* 3.33=Lact. *Inst.* 6.8.7–9: *Est quidem vera lex recta ratio, naturae congruens, diffusa in omnis, constans, sempiterna ... nec vero aut per senatum aut per populum solui hac lege possumus ... nec erit alia lex Romae, alia Athenis, alia nunc, alia posthac, sed et omnes gentes et omni tempore una lex et sempiterna et immutabilis continebit* (Zetzel tr).

we must.'[29] Of Carneades' sceptical anti-imperialist argument Lactantius wrote that Carneades did actually 'overthrow' 'all that was being said in its [justice's] favour'.[30] This was easily possible according to Lactantius because pagan justice 'had no roots; at the time there was no justice on earth, so that its nature and quality could not be identified by philosophers',[31] something that for Lactantius had of course changed with the arrival of Christianity. Lactantius' own argument against Carneades relied on the idea of a divine reward for virtue, which implied an anti-Stoic view of virtue as not being an end in itself.[32]

With Lactantius tilting the Carneadean debate dangerously in favour of Carneades' sceptical, Epicurean stance (at least in the absence of Christianity), it remained for Augustine to explain how the Romans could have been given their empire by God in the first place.[33] This was a major problem for the church father, not because he sought to justify imperialism, but because he had to explain how a pagan empire had been able to rule for an extended period of time the known world, notwithstanding the fact that they did not have the Christian god on their side. This was a problem for Augustine precisely because he was well aware of the ugly aspects of Roman imperialism—how was it possible that God had allowed Roman rule to persist, how could this be fitted into Augustine's eschatology? On the one hand, his theology of history sought to distance itself from the earthly, secular city, which was particularly important after the sack and near-collapse of Rome in AD 410: by 'uncoupling' the heavenly from the earthly city, Augustine tried to avoid Christianity being blamed for the calamity. On the other hand, there still remained a need to explain Roman success in the framework of this philosophy of history. Augustine, slightly more sympathetic to Cicero's defence against Carneades' sceptical argument than Lactantius had been, does not himself really try to refute Carneades' case against justice.[34] Rather, he integrates the debate into a historical view that accords the Romans some virtues due to which they have gained their empire—adherence to law is mentioned, but above all what Augustine thinks of as the pagan virtue par excellence, glory (*gloria* or *amor laudis*).

Augustine's account, given the above-described 'uncoupling' of Christianity from the earthly city, is of course ultimately very critical of the Roman Empire. Given the pagan nature of the Roman Empire the Romans could never achieve true justice.[35] But when he discusses '[b]y what virtues the ancient Romans gained the favour

---

[29] Lact. *Inst.* 6.8.11ff (Bowen and Garnsey tr).   [30] Ibid, 5.14.5f.

[31] Ibid, 5.14.5f.   [32] Ibid, 5.17–18.

[33] On Augustine's *City of God*, see Gerard O'Daly, *Augustine's* City of God: *A Reader's Guide* (Oxford University Press 2004); on his political thought, see Norman Hepburn Baynes, *The Political Ideas of St. Augustine's De Civitate Dei* (Historical Association 1968); Herbert A Deane, *The Political and Social Ideas of St. Augustine* (Columbia University Press 1963); RA Markus, *Saeculum: History and Society in the Theology of St Augustine* (Cambridge University Press 1989); Paul Weithman, 'Augustine's Political Philosophy' in Eleonore Stump and Norman Kretzmann (eds), *The Cambridge Companion to Augustine* (Cambridge University Press 2001).

[34] On Augustine's knowledge and use of Cicero, see Maurice Testard, *Saint Augustin et Cicéron*, 2 vols. (Études augustiniennes 1958). See also Brian Stock, *Augustine the Reader* (Harvard University Press 1996).

[35] August. *De civ. D.* 19.21.

of the true God, so that he increased their empire although they did not worship him',[36] Augustine quotes Sallust and answers that the Romans had been 'eager for praise' and 'sought unbounded glory'.[37] Augustine goes on to say, thereby creating a highly influential legacy whose impact can be felt, as we shall see, in Machiavelli,[38] that 'this glory they [the Romans] most ardently loved. For its sake they chose to live and for its sake they did not hesitate to die. They suppressed all other desires in their boundless desire for this one thing.'[39] A thirst for glory had first resulted in the Romans shaking off kingly rule and seeking liberty. 'But once they had freedom, so great was the passion for glory which arose that liberty seemed too little by itself unless they were also seeking dominion over others.'[40] It was for this reason, Augustine maintains in an utterly Sallustian vein, that the Romans gained first their liberty, and then their empire. While the Romans were virtuous in this sense and not corrupted by wealth, while their treasury (*aerarium*) was filled and their private wealth small (*tenues res privatae*), the empire grew.[41] But glory and the love of praise are virtues only in a very tenuous sense: Augustine does call glory-seeking a virtue of sorts,[42] but then almost immediately hedges his bets, quoting Sallust to the effect that ambition and glory-seeking, as opposed to avarice, was in fact 'a vice', albeit one 'that comes close to being a virtue'.[43] At times Augustine makes it clear, unambiguously, that glory is but a name the Romans used to hide crimes motivated by their lust for domination (*libido dominandi*).[44] As soon as pagan virtue no longer drove the Romans and was replaced by greed and luxury, the state grew poor and the private citizens rich, leading to the downfall Cato outlines in Sallust, a description Augustine quotes in the *City of God*.

By comparison, Augustine writes, developing an interesting and extremely influential idea,[45] glory-seeking and the love of praise can be 'regarded as virtues' in

---

[36] Ibid, 5.12: *Quibus moribus antiqui Romani meruerint ut Deus verus, quamvis non eum colerent, eorum augeret imperium* (WM Green tr).

[37] Ibid, quoting Sall. *Cat.* 7.6: *laudis avidi ... gloriam ingentem ... volebant*.

[38] For a good summary of the scholarly discussion of Augustine's influence on Machiavelli, with further literature, see John M Warner and John T Scott, 'Sin City: Augustine and Machiavelli's Reordering of Rome' (2011) 73 The Journal of Politics 857.

[39] August. *De civ. D.* 5.12: *hanc [gloriam sc.] ardentissime dilexerunt, propter hanc vivere voluerunt, pro hac emori non dubitaverunt; ceteras cupiditates huius unius ingenti cupiditate presserunt.*

[40] Ibid, 5.12: *Sed cum esset adepta libertas, tanta cupido gloriae incesserat ut parum esset sola libertas nisi et dominatio quaereretur.*

[41] Ibid, cf 5.15.

[42] eg at ibid, 5.12, when rendering discussing Sallust's view of Caesar: *In laudibus autem Caesaris posuit quod sibi magnum imperium, exercitum, bellum novum exoptabat, ubi virtus enitescere posset.* This is of course meant to give us Sallust's view, but Augustine here seems to acquiesce in the possibility of Caesar exhibiting virtue, although he does point out in the same chapter that Cato had been 'much closer' to real virtue than Caesar: *longe virtus Catonis veritati videtur propinquior fuisse quam Caesaris.*

[43] Ibid, quoting Sall. *Cat.* 11.1–2: *Sed primo magis ambitio quam avaritia animos hominum exercebat, quod tamen vitium propius virtutem erat.* For an intellectual history of ambition, see William C King, *Ambition, A History: From Vice to Virtue* (Yale University Press 2013).

[44] Ibid, 3.14: *Libido ista dominandi magnis malis agitat et conterit humanum genus. Hac libidine Roma tunc victa Albam se vicisse triumphabat et sui sceleris laudem gloriam nominabat ...*

[45] The idea of 'countervailing passions', where one vice or passion weakens or tames the others; the classic work on this is Albert O Hirschman, *The Passions and the Interests: Political Arguments for*

the sense that they limit or restrain (*cohibentur*) the greater vices.[46] The Romans, Augustine states, 'for one vice, that is, love of praise ... overcame the love of money and many other vices'.[47] Importantly, Augustine imputes to Cicero this exact notion of glory as the chief pagan virtue. He argues that 'men who do not obtain the gift of the Holy Spirit and bridle their baser passions by pious faith and by love of intelligible beauty, at any rate live better because of their desire for human praise and glory', and goes on to claim that Cicero also could not disguise this fact. '[N]ot even in his philosophical works', Augustine writes, 'did Cicero shrink from this pestilential notion, for he declares allegiance to it in them as plain as day.' By 'philosophical works' the church father here means Cicero's *Tusculan Disputations*, a highly rhetorical work, where Cicero makes a throwaway remark on the motivational power of glory which Augustine fastens upon.[48] Ultimately, glory-seeking remains a vice, or a pagan virtue at best; men 'like Scaevola, Curtius and the Decii' were merely 'citizens of the earthly city', who, in the absence of eternal life, could not be motivated but by glory.[49] As Pierre Bayle was to put it in his *Dictionary*, solidifying this strand of interpretation of Augustine, 'the good morals of some atheists' do not constitute 'any real virtues'—rather, these 'were only glittering sins, *splendida peccata*, as St Augustine has said of all the fine actions of the pagans'.[50]

We are now in a position to see clearly a tradition of thought, inspired by Sallust and given expression most prominently by Augustine, according to which glory-seeking was the true Roman virtue.[51] Augustine was helped in giving prominence to this idea by the contrast he could draw between it and his own Christian world-view. It is true that Augustine did mention the other, Ciceronian or Virgilian elements such as the 'imposition of laws on many nations', and the fact that 'the Romans too were not exempt from living under their own laws, the same laws that

---

Capitalism before Its Triumph (Princeton University Press 1977), especially 20–31, where Augustine's 'passing hint' at the idea is acknowledged (20).

[46] August. *De civ. D.* 5.13: *De amore laudis, qui, cum sit vitium, ob hoc virtus putatur quia per ipsum vitia maiora cohibentur.*

[47] Ibid, 5.13: *pro isto uno vitio, id est amore laudis, pecuniae cupiditatem et multa alia vitia conprimentes.*

[48] Ibid, citing Cic. *Tusc.* 1.4 (for a more representative take on Cicero's view of glory in that work, however, cf *Tusc.* 5.102).

[49] Ibid, 5.14: 'Since there was no eternal life for them, but merely the passing away of the dying, who were succeeded by others soon to die, what else were they to love apart from glory (*quid aliud amarent quam gloriam*), whereby they chose to find even after death a sort of life on the lips of those who sang their praises?'

[50] Pierre Bayle, *Historical and Critical Dictionary: Selections* (Richard H Popkin tr, Bobbs-Merrill 1965) 401. See also Pierre Bayle, *Dictionnaire historique et critique*, vol 4 (Amsterdam 1740) 627: 'Remarquez bien, s'il vous plaît, qu'en parlant des bonnes mœurs de quelques Athées, je ne leur ai point attribué de véritables vertus. Leur sobriété, leur chasteté, leur probité, leur mépris pour les richesses, leur zèle du bien public, leur inclination à rendre de bons offices à leur prochain, ne procédoient pas de l'amour de Dieu, & ne tendoient pas à l'honorer & à le glorifier. Ils en étoient eux-mêmes la source, & le but; l'amour-propre en étoit la base, le terme, toute l'analyse. Ce n'étoient que des péchez éclatans, *splendida peccata*, comme saint Augustin l'a dit de toutes les belles actions des Païens.' See Terence Irwin, *The Development of Ethics*, vol 1 (Oxford University Press 2007) 418–20, for an excellent discussion, arguing that Bayle did not interpret Augustine correctly.

[51] For guidance to Augustine's extraordinary and far-reaching influence on later Western thought, with literature, see now Karla Pollmann et al (eds), *The Oxford Guide to the Historical Reception of Augustine* (Oxford University Press 2013).

they imposed on others'.[52] But his emphasis, as well as his overall legacy, remained the focus on glory.

The idea of a dichotomy between this pagan virtue and Christian virtue was then taken up again and rendered very influentially by Machiavelli.[53] While for Augustine *gloria* remained highly ambivalent at best, Machiavelli gave it a straightforwardly sympathetic rendering.[54] Adopting Augustine's dichotomy between pagan and Christian virtue, but appraising pagan virtue in a way diametrically opposed to the church father, Machiavelli broaches the topic in a chapter designed to show how the Romans' virtue (as opposed to fortune) was instrumental in expanding their empire:

If one asks oneself how it comes about that peoples of old were more fond of liberty than they are today, I think the answer is that it is due to the same cause that makes men today less bold than they used to be; and this is due, I think, to the difference between our education and that of bygone times, which is based on the difference between our religion and the religion of those days. For our religion, having taught us the truth and the true way of life, leads us to ascribe less esteem to worldly honour. Hence the gentiles, who held it in high esteem and looked upon it as their highest good (*il sommo bene*), displayed in their actions more ferocity than we do ... [T]he old religion did not beatify men unless they were replete with worldly glory: army commanders, for instance, and rulers of republics.[55]

Worldly honour or glory, Machiavelli holds, constituted the highest end, or greatest good for 'the gentiles'. This is in line with Augustine, but it is of course rather polemical to impute this view to Cicero, who introduced the notion of the greatest good into Latin to render the Greek *telos*: an end in itself, that for the sake of which everything else is ultimately done. The fact that Machiavelli chooses the term *il sommo bene* is significant and betrays the polemical thrust. The *summum bonum* in ancient ethics is usually held to be the individual's well-being or happiness, his or her *eudaimonia*. The final good identified with virtue by various schools of ancient ethics, the aim being to dissolve any conflict between individual well-being and virtue, where virtue is understood as other-regarding morality. In line with this Cicero points out that 'when the Stoics say that the greatest good (*summum bonum*) is to live agreeably with nature, this means, in my view, the following: always to concur with virtue; and as for other things that are in accordance

---

[52] August. *De civ. D.* 5.17: *Neque enim et Romani non vivebant sub legibus suis, quas ceteris imponebant.* Augustine also quotes Virgil's verses on the mission of the Romans (*Aen.* 6.851ff), but does not dwell on the crucial aspect of the imposition of peace and constitutional order. On Augustine's use of Virgil, see Sabine MacCormack, *The Shadows of Poetry: Vergil in the Mind of Augustine* (University of California Press 1998), especially ch 5; see also Brian Stock, *Augustine the Reader* (n 34).

[53] For interpretations of Machiavelli's thought that differ in crucial ways from each other and from the line pursued here, see Paul Rahe, *Against Throne and Altar: Machiavelli and Political Theory in the English Republic* (Cambridge University Press 2008); and JGA Pocock's classic study *The Machiavellian Moment: Political Thought and the Atlantic Republican Tradition* (Princeton University Press 1975).

[54] My discussion is much indebted to Irwin, *Development* (n 50) 725–43, especially 729–31. See also Emile Perreau-Saussine, 'Quentin Skinner in Context' (2007) 69 The Review of Politics 106, especially 117ff.

[55] *Discourses* 2.2.6. I have used the following translation: *The Discourses of Niccolò Machiavelli*, 2 vols (Leslie J Walker tr, Routledge & Kegan Paul 1975).

with nature, to choose them if they do not conflict with virtue'.[56] The point is that when writing on virtue, Cicero has in mind, not Augustine and Machiavelli's pagan virtue with its concern for glory, but rather other-regarding virtue, what he calls the *honestum*.[57]

Machiavelli extols glory-seeking as a virtue that is apt to motivate citizens to preserve and expand their state.[58] For Machiavelli, therefore, this virtue is not an end in itself, but is instrumental to what he perceives as the ultimate, highest end: the preservation and expansion of the state. Glory can and should be sacrificed to the safety and preservation of the state.[59] Machiavelli defends exceptional means to save the state and adduces as an illustration Romulus' murder of Remus. Any 'action, however extraordinary, which may be of service in the organizing of a kingdom or the constituting of a republic' is justified in Machiavelli's view, and Romulus in killing Remus exhibited pagan virtue.[60] Augustine had also discussed Romulus' example, and agreed with Machiavelli that Romulus had been motivated by the desire to rule by himself and to acquire glory.[61] Augustine, of course, did not think the deed justified, least of all on the grounds of glory. Notwithstanding Augustine's talk of pagan virtue, Cicero's take on Romulus also resulted in a condemnation, on grounds of Stoic moral philosophy. In Cicero's view, Romulus' killing illustrates a case of conflict between expediency and what is right, where what seemed expedient won out:

[T]he appearance of benefit (*utilitas*) drove his [Romulus'] spirit; and when it seemed more beneficial (*utilius*) to him to rule alone than with someone else, he killed his brother. He abandoned both family obligation and humanity in order to secure something that seemed beneficial, but was not … He did wrong, then.[62]

Machiavelli's defence of such extraordinary measures oscillates between the position that considerations of justice either do not apply to the kinds of emergency situations he discusses (because the preservation and expansion of the state overrides justice as an end) and the position that the preservation and expansion of the

---

[56] Cic. *Off.* 3.13 (M Atkins tr).

[57] On Machiavelli's relationship to Cicero, see Quentin Skinner, *Machiavelli* (Oxford University Press 1981), 36–47; see also Marcia L Colish, 'Cicero's *De officiis* and Machiavelli's *Prince*' (1978) 9 Sixteenth Century Journal 81, who does not however emphasize the conflict between the two viewpoints sufficiently. Cf also Isaiah Berlin, 'The Originality of Machiavelli' in Henry Hardy (ed), *Against the Current* (Princeton University Press 2013) 33–100, who takes Machiavelli's pagan-Christian dichotomy at face value.

[58] *Discourses* 1.43. Cf 2.2.9. For an interesting comparison between Machiavelli and Francis Bacon's views on imperial expansion, showing Bacon's distrust of martial glory, see Michelle Tolman Clarke, 'Uprooting Nebuchadnezzar's Tree: Francis Bacon's Criticism of Machiavellian Imperialism' (2008) 61(3) Political Research Quarterly 367. Bacon thought that glory-seeking of this kind amounted to a 'satanical illusion and apparition' and was 'no better than a sorcery': ibid, 370.

[59] *Discourses* 3.41.

[60] *Discourses* 1.9.2. Cf 1.18.5–7 on extraordinary means. See Warner and Scott, 'Sin City' (n 38) 863–66 on Machiavelli's use of the Romulus example.

[61] August. *De civ. D.* 15.5. Cf *Discourses* 1.10.6.

[62] Cic. *Off.* 3.41. Romulus' course of action is only *seemingly* beneficial or expedient as there cannot be, on Cicero's assumptions, a real conflict between morality (*honestum*) and expediency; the *honestum* is necessarily beneficial (while the reverse does not hold).

state is itself something that is required by justice. The two positions are obviously inconsistent. As Terence Irwin has pointed out:

Machiavelli seems to argue that since extraordinary means are morally acceptable in emergencies, we ought to disregard morality altogether in all circumstances. The argument is not only unconvincing but also inconsistent; for if we think it matters to find moral grounds or permission for extraordinary means in emergencies, we cannot consistently suppose that moral considerations never matter.[63]

For all its ambiguity, it is reasonably clear that, overall, Machiavelli ultimately does come down in favour of the first position—that the preservation and expansion of the state is the ultimate goal and must therefore override considerations of justice. The second position merely amounts to a rhetorical ruse to make the first one more palatable to those incapable of noticing the inconsistency.

If his defence of 'pagan virtue', glory, and the preservation of the state is not, however, built on grounds of justice, then how does Machiavelli justify the idea that the safety of the state and imperialism constitute the *summum bonum*? One way of interpreting Machiavelli is to claim that he in effect makes a Hobbesian argument here for the importance of the state as a necessary condition for human self-preservation.[64] His views on glory and pagan virtue, however, are obviously in deep tension with Hobbes' proto-liberal views on individual prudence and practical rationality.[65] Machiavelli's position is shaped by Augustine's description of pagan virtue, with which Machiavelli entirely agrees, while of course diverging from Augustine's bleak normative assessment: as Warner and Scott write in an illuminating essay, Machiavelli 'celebrates Rome as unreservedly as Sallust while seeing it as clearly as Augustine'.[66]

A further important observation, which can be substantiated by reference to Machiavelli's discussion of Romulus' glory, is that Machiavelli's brand of republicanism is not at all committed to any pre-political norms; rather, the order of the state is itself permanently up for grabs, in the sense that most times seem extraordinary, the republic is permanently on the brink of corruption, and a (re)ordering of the 'constitutional' order is often warranted. Such a reordering is not itself bound by any higher-order constitutional norms, except for the preservation of the state. In stark contrast to Cicero's thought, Machiavelli's position points to a much more malleable view of the 'constitutional' order:

[S]hould a prince seek worldly glory (*la gloria del mondo*), he should most certainly covet possession of a city that has become corrupt, not, with Caesar, to complete its spoliation,

---

[63] Irwin, *Development* (n 50) 739.   [64] Irwin, *Development* (n 50) 734 suggests this.

[65] Resulting in rather different approaches to imperialism. Cf for a different interpretation of the relationship between Machiavelli and Hobbes, see Rahe, *Against Throne and Altar* (n 53). On Machiavelli and imperialism see Mikael Hörnqvist, *Machiavelli and Empire* (Cambridge University Press 2004), with further literature; see also David Armitage, *The Ideological Origins of the British Empire* (Cambridge University Press 2000) 125ff.

[66] Warner and Scott, 'Sin City' (n 38) 862. Machiavelli does not believe Sallust's picture of early, harmonious Rome, nor does he think that such a condition would have been desirable. In a Polybian way, he emphasizes the importance of conflict for stability.

but, with Romulus, to reform it (*riordinarla*). Nor in very truth can the heavens afford men a better opportunity of acquiring glory (*gloria*); nor can men desire anything better than this.[67]

Reordering the corrupt city with sole authority, regardless of higher-order constraints, is justified as long as the state is thus preserved. This stands in stark tension with the views, discussed above, held by Cicero and Virgil.

The same Augustinian framework on glory that can be shown at work in Machiavelli can also be found in the Spanish writers of the sixteenth century. Indeed, the debate at Valladolid in 1550–51 concerning the justice of the Spanish empire reflected in many important ways the key features of Augustine's view of the Roman Empire and of the Carneadean debate. Augustine's ambiguous account of the justice of the Roman Empire served as the main battleground, with both parties of the controversy trying to enlist him on their side. Augustine's 'unimpeachable'[68] authority made it difficult for anti-imperialist writers such as Domingo de Soto and Bartolomé de Las Casas to eschew his views as to why 'the ancient Romans gained the favour of the true god, so that he increased their empire'. One among many interesting adaptations of Augustine's view came from the jurist Vázquez de Menchaca. In his *Controversiae illustres* (1564) he explained Augustine's account by saying that the Romans were granted their empire by God not on the grounds of their 'vainglory' (*gloriae cupiditas*) in conquering it, but rather because, quite apart from their warfare, they were excelling other peoples in terms of other, moral virtues.[69]

The proponents of Spanish imperialism were conscious of Augustine's value, too. Sepúlveda, in his controversial dialogue *Democrates secundus sive de causis iustis belli apud Indos* (which nominally gave rise to the debate in Valladolid), combined Aristotle's theory of the natural slave[70] with Augustine's exemplary

[67] *Discourses* 1.10.9.

[68] The term is David Lupher's; see on the Roman empire as a model for the Valladolid debate his *Romans in a New World* (University of Michigan Press 2003), especially 103–49; the quote is from 65.

[69] See *Controversiae illustres*, vol 2, c 20, 31: *Neque ad rem quoque pertinet quod divus Augustinus de civitate Dei lib. v. c.xii. & c.xv. ait imperium Romanis ob morales virtutes suas datum fuisse ... Rursus non in praemium virtutum moralium, nam ipsi [Romani] pugnabant non tam virtutis quam inanis gloriae cupiditate, sicque illae actiones tam longe aberant a praemii remuneratione ut poena potius digniores forent, sed tamen interea Deus optimus maximus id permisit quod adhuc virtutibus aliis moralibus caeteras gentes excellebant, & tyrannidem Assyriorum aut Medorum aut Medes, Graecorum ad Romanos transferri permisit.* ('Nor is it relevant to this issue what the divine Augustine in *City of God*, book 5, chapters 12 and 15 claims, that the empire had been granted to the Romans by reason of their moral excellence ... On the contrary, not for the reward of moral excellence—for the Romans were fighting not so much out of a desire for virtue but for vainglory, so that their actions were so far away from the remuneration of a reward that they were rather more deserving of punishment—but still, God in the meanwhile permitted it because hitherto the Romans were excelling the remainder of peoples with regard to other moral virtues, and allowed the despotic rule of the Assyrians, Medes, and Greeks to be transferred to the Romans.'): Fernando Vázquez de Menchaca, *Controversiarum illustrium aliarumque usu frequentium libri tres*, vol 2 (F Rodriguez Alcalde ed, Talleres tipográficos 'Cuesta' 1931) (a transcription from the 1564 ed).

[70] See Lewis Hanke, *Aristotle and the American Indians* (Indiana University Press 1959); Brian Tierney, 'Aristotle and the American Indians—again' (1991) 12 Cristianesimo nella storia 295.

account of Roman imperialism to assert a civilizing mission as a just cause of war. After quoting from the *City of God* 13.5 Sepúlveda interpreted Augustine as saying that the Romans had gained their empire 'in order that by means of the excellent laws they observed and the virtue in which they excelled they might abolish and correct the barbaric customs and vices of many peoples'.[71] One hears the words of Cicero's Laelius filtered through Augustine.

When we now turn to Gentili and his highly polemical work on *The Wars of the Romans*, we encounter a treatise very much in the mould of the Carneadean dialogue in Cicero's *Republic*.[72] The Augustinian emphasis on glory as the chief Roman virtue is reflected in it, but—as opposed to Machiavelli's vision, and in line with Cicero's—ultimately clearly rejected.[73] In the first book, which constitutes an attack on Roman imperialism from the viewpoint of justice very much in the vein of Carneades, glory-seeking is identified as the chief trait of the Romans in the very first sentence:

There is a famous utterance of Cicero in a dispute about military affairs and political wisdom: 'Military excellence has engendered fame for the Roman people and eternal glory (*aeternam gloriam*) for the city; it has forced the whole world to obey this rule.'[74]

Similarly, referring explicitly to Cicero's *Republic* and to the distinction drawn in the Carneadean debate between civil justice, which is born of mere necessity and reflects simply a contractarian bargain, and natural justice, which if it even exists is identified by Carneades with foolishness, Gentili or rather the Carneadean accuser of book one addresses Cicero directly, in an accusatory tone:

Cicero, you will say and contend that civil—that is, cunning—justice existed in your state, but you will not persuade us that it was true, genuine justice, as Lactantius learnedly argues against you and as Augustine points out. 'A state cannot be enlarged without injustice'— among you Romans and for your benefit was that saying born.[75]

The quotation comes of course straight—or rather, by way of Augustine—from Carneades' sceptical attack as portrayed in Cicero's *Republic*. In book one Gentili

---

[71] Cited in Lupher, *Romans* (n 68) 114ff.

[72] See on this Benedict Kingsbury and Benjamin Straumann, 'Introduction' in Alberico Gentili, *The Wars of the Romans: A Critical Edition and Translation of* De armis Romanis (Benedict Kingsbury and Benjamin Straumann eds and David Lupher tr, Oxford University Press 2011); and David Lupher, 'The De armis Romanis and the Exemplum of Roman Imperialism' in Benedict Kingsbury and Benjamin Straumann (eds), *The Roman Foundations of the Law of Nations: Alberico Gentili and the Justice of Empire* (Oxford University Press 2010).

[73] Ptolemy of Lucca in his portion of *De regimine principum* also uses Augustine's framework and should be seen as a forerunner of the view propounded by Gentili. For Ptolemy, the constitutional rule spread by Roman republican imperialism simply *is vera iustitia* (*pace* Augustine), and serves as the chief justification of their empire. The whole world should, by natural right, be governed by the Republic and pacified by being brought under the 'single society of the Republic and its laws'. Glory is not an important end for Ptolemy.

[74] Gentili, *WR* 1.1, 8/9, citing Cic. *Mur.* 22.

[75] Gentili, *WR* 1.13, 118/119, alluding to August. *De civ. D.* 2.21. Interestingly, Augustine has *rem publicam regi sine iniuria non posse*, while Gentili writes *Augeri rempublicam sine iniustitia non posse*; Gentili's is the better report of what the debate in book three of the *Republic* is about.

also gives an account of the essence of Carneades' point, which he knew through Lactantius:

And thus Carneades quite properly told you, Romans, that if you wished to be just, you ought to return to those huts from which you first set forth, and you ought to surrender this empire of the world.[76]

Here, in book one, Lactantius' sympathetic report of the Carneadean attack clearly serves as the model and sets the tone. Gentili, too, discusses the example set by Romulus and does not fail to point out that Cicero had condemned Romulus' deeds in *De officiis*. He adds a further reference to this treatise, as support for the thoroughly anti-Machiavellian point that '[r]epulsive and criminal acts ought not to be done even for the sake of saving one's country'.[77]

Gentili's response in book two also follows the general path sketched by Cicero, namely a defence of Roman imperialism in terms of a universal natural law, which in Gentili's hands now is being identified with the Roman law of the *Corpus iuris*. There was of course no *Corpus iuris* in Cicero's day, but Cicero too thought that the law in force at Rome during the heyday of the Roman Republic was more or less identical with natural law.

Hence, the defence of the justice of Roman imperialism in the second book of *The Wars of the Romans* bases the justice of the Roman Empire on precisely the defence put forward in Cicero's *Republic* by Laelius, a defence known to Gentili through Augustine. The empire was 'seized by force of arms, but without wrongdoing', Gentili writes, and, helped by Augustine's ambivalence, he goes on to enlist the Bishop of Hippo and other 'theologians' for his cause:

Thus the interpreters of the law call the Roman Empire just, for it was obtained partly by agreement, partly by the sword. And the theologians and Augustine agree: 'It constitutes a just defense of the Romans for so many wars undertaken and waged that it was the necessity of protecting their safety and liberty, not greed for acquiring human glory, that forced them to resist enemies who attacked them violently.'[78]

Defending Romulus, Gentili in book two first makes room for doubt that Remus had been killed at all.[79] He then goes on to assume for argument's sake that Remus had indeed been killed by Romulus, but defends this action—against Cicero—as a lawful deed, where violence had been countered with violence (*per quam vim propulsata vis*) and Remus' killing was thus 'justifiable as an act of punishment'.[80] Note that unlike Machiavelli, Gentili does not justify Romulus' act on the Machiavellian grounds of 'reordering' the state in order to acquire glory; rather, he justifies the act on legal grounds. Self-defence can legitimately turn into punishment for the

---

[76] Gentili, *WR* 1.8, 68/69, citing Lact. *Inst.* 5.16.2–5.
[77] Gentili, *WR* 1.2, 24/25. Gentili must have had Cic. *Off.* 1.159 in mind, where moral concerns override even the protection of one's own country.
[78] Gentili, *WR* 2.2 , 162/163, citing August. *De civ. D.* 3.10.
[79] Ibid, 140/141, referencing the late antique pastiche *De origine gentis Romanae* 23.6.
[80] Ibid, 142/143.

aggression, Gentili believes, and this in turn provides the argumentative spring-board, as it were, for expansion and pacification.

In the last chapter of the second book, in the culmination of the defence of Roman imperialism, the attack that the Romans had not had a temple dedicated to Peace is rejected.[81] Gentili could not have known Emperor Augustus' altar to Peace, the *Ara Pacis*, which since the Fascist era has been so prominently on display in Rome. Augustus' propaganda would have vigorously enforced the point Gentili's defender of the justice of empire is trying to make, the point already made in Virgil's *Aeneid*: namely that pacification and the imposition of law carry the main normative weight, not glory.[82] Given how well Gentili knew Virgil, it is somewhat astonishing that he nowhere in *The Wars of the Romans* quotes the famous lines from the sixth book of the *Aeneid* quoted above (6.851–53); there are, however, prominent allusions to and echoes of the *Aeneid* in that work, especially in the thirteenth chapter of the second book,[83] where the imposition of peace and laws are said to have been the arts by which Rome grew: *Illis artibus Roma crevit: istis artibus Roma stetit.*

Gentili in the second book of *The Wars of the Romans* is also aligned with the almost Hegelian, teleological aspects of Virgil's view—the Roman Empire (or at least the spread of its rules) is the goal of history, while any other outcome is tantamount to slipping back into a state of nature. The imposition of law and peaceful order as a defence of Roman imperialism is supported by a speech taken from Tacitus where it is claimed that 'it is impossible to have peace among peoples without arms'. The only alternative to such a Virgilian, forceful, and imperial imposition of peace, Gentili thinks, is a state of nature, a state of nature he conceives in a proto-Hobbesian way as a war of all against all. The anthropological foundations for this view are taken from Tacitus as well: 'There will be vices as long as there are men', hence, 'should the Romans be driven out ... what can result but wars between all these nations?'[84] The resulting state of nature and war of all against all is then described by quoting Virgil:

But at last the empire was overthrown, and along with all other mortal affairs it had its end. But what had been predicted so long before by wise men, behold, when the Romans had been driven away ... But behold ... behold now the wars of all, of all peoples among themselves. 'Neighboring cities, the laws among them burst asunder, take arms; impious Mars

---

[81] Gentili, *WR* 2.13, 334/335.

[82] Augustus and his propaganda were much more influenced by considerations of *pax* than of *gloria* (Augustus' *Res Gestae* makes not a single mention of *gloria*, all the while dwelling on the importance of *Pax*, cf. *RG* 12, 13)—a precursor of Gentili and Hobbes, as it were. As Michael Peachin reminds me, in his *RG*, a document inscribed in bronze (like statutes), Augustus had arguably tried to establish a binding constitutional order for the empire. cf. also Augustus' edict in Suet. *Aug.* 28.2, where he aspires to be called *optimi status auctor* for having laid durable *fundamenta rei publicae*.

[83] *WR* 2.13, 350/351; cf *Aen.* 6.852: *hae tibi erunt artes.*

[84] Tac. *Hist.* 4.74 (from the same speech by Cerialis quoted by Gentili, *WR* 2.13, 346/347). On Gentili's use of Tacitus, Tacitean anthropology and his conception of the state of nature, see Kingsbury and Straumann, 'Introduction' (n 72), especially xvi–xviii; see also Karlo Tuori, 'Alberico Gentili and the Criticism of Expansion in the Roman Empire: The Invader's Remorse' (2009) 2 Journal of the History of International Law 205.

rages throughout the globe; as when chariots pour out from the starting pens, they go faster each lap; nor does anyone hold the halter; the chariot is carried along by the horses, and no one guides the reins.'[85]

Glimpses of this Virgilian theme can, I believe, also be detected in Thomas Hobbes' interest in the imposition of order and his accompanying intense distrust of glory (or pride, as he often calls it). As we know from John Aubrey, although Hobbes in later life had few books, he could always be expected to have copies of Virgil on his table.[86] Christopher Brooke has made it very clear that there is an 'Augustinian Hobbes',[87] for whom glory was a central concern. In fact, as Brooke points out, this is why Hobbes called his book *Leviathan* in the first place; Leviathan is 'King of all the children of Pride',[88] and while it 'might be God who humbles the proud, according to the text of the *Magnificat* … Hobbes assigns this task to the secular sovereign'.[89]

In Hobbes' famous suspicion that 'there was never any thing so deerly bought' as the 'learning of the Greek and Latine tongues'[90] there lies his rejection of Augustine's pagan virtues, and Hobbes is of course very much opposed to Machiavelli's embrace of glory and the pagan virtues. But Hobbes depends to a large extent on the Tacitean and Virgilian sentiments reported above.[91] With slight exaggeration it could be said that Hobbes' state of nature—as well as Gentili's dire world without Roman imperialism—strikingly resemble Machiavelli's ideal of the conflicted, glory-seeking Roman Republic.[92] By contrast, Hobbes' state is really a mechanism to crush the proud and impose peace. This is probably the most crucial characteristic of his thought that sets him apart from Machiavelli and the entire reason of state tradition.[93] For Hobbes, reason of state is part and parcel of his science of prudence where self-interest can act as much as a restraint as an authorization. In

---

[85] *WR* 2.13, 355. The quote is from Verg. *G.* 1.510–14 (Virgil's pessimistic rendering of the civil wars between the assassination of Caesar and Actium). Gentili's rendering of the last line is sloppy; he must have quoted from memory.

[86] Quentin Skinner, *Visions of Politics*, vol 3 (Cambridge University Press 2002) 42.

[87] Christopher Brooke, *Philosophic Pride: Stoicism and Political Thought from Lipsius to Rousseau* (Princeton University Press 2012) 69–75.

[88] Thomas Hobbes, *Leviathan*, vol 2 (Noel Malcolm ed, Clarendon Press 2012) ch 28, 496.

[89] Brooke, *Philosophic Pride* (n 87) 74.

[90] Hobbes, *Leviathan* vol 2 (n 88) ch 21, 334. Cf ibid, vol 3, ch 46, 1097, where Hobbes cites from Virgil's fourth *Eclogue* (4.36) to warn of the future (civil) wars if the teaching of 'Greek and Latin eloquence and philosophy' in universities is not going to be constrained.

[91] Which, as Hobbes realized, were connected with Emperor Augustus' programme. Hobbes writes that he 'observed in *Virgil*, that the Honor done to *Aeneas* and his companions has so bright a reflection upon *Augustus Caesar* and other great *Romans* of that time': Thomas Hobbes, 'Answer to Davenant's Preface to *Gondibert*' in Joel Elias Spingarn (ed), *Critical Essays of the Seventeenth Century*, vol 2 (Clarendon Press 1908) 58. I owe the hint to this passage to Chris Warren.

[92] Put the other way around one might say that for Machiavelli, there is no stark separation between a state of nature and a political state, which is precisely why extraordinary means are always in order and justified by a pervasive lack of trust.

[93] Justus Lipsius, as Brooke has suggested (*Philosophic Pride* (n 87) 36), is 'poised theoretically as well as chronologically between Machiavelli and Hobbes', as his Machiavellian outlook is tempered by considerations of security and the common good.

some limited sense Hobbes' willingness to breach conventional moral norms may itself be sanctioned by higher-level moral norms.[94]

To sum up, it seems to me that there are two important strands of thought emanating from the Carneadean debate, strands that had both their origins in the opposing views sketched in the original debate. One represents a Machiavellian concern with republican expansion and glory, which is ultimately deeply sceptical of normative arguments aiming at justice, the other a concern with the expansion of law and justice, one might say with the expansion of 'natural constitutional law',[95] and the imposition of peace. Richard Tuck's vaguely Straussian, or rather Augustinian, genealogy of international thought fails to keep those two apart; early modern republicans such as James Harrington, Walter Moyle, Algernon Sidney, other 'neo-Romans' and reason of state theorists such as Gabriel Naudé who were marching in Machiavelli's footsteps were also tracking the Roman historians, especially Sallust, Augustine's claims about glory as the chief Roman virtue, and Carneades' sceptical arguments. Natural lawyers such as Gentili on the other hand were much more interested in and convinced by the *refutation* of Carneades, a refutation Cicero had already sketched. This was a refutation based on a rebuttal of glory as an independent value and that insists on the value of pacification and the imposition of just legal norms. Hobbes, who for Tuck belongs to a tradition stretching from Machiavelli through Grotius, is a good example of this: his main interest is in peace, and his outlook, an almost Virgilian 'sparing of the vanquished and crushing of the proud' in order to escape the state of nature, is as far from elevating glory as is conceivable.[96]

These strands can be tracked into present international moral and legal argument. Self-declared so-called 'realists' harbour sceptical feelings about the existence of moral or legal norms that govern international politics; often they fail to make clear whether their scepticism is itself motivated by higher-order moral concerns, or whether it is owed to a thorough relativism à la Carneades. Thinkers and writers of a more moralistic bent, on the other hand, rarely fail to acknowledge the existence and normative pull of universal moral and legal norms. It is important to note, however, that there is no obvious upshot when it comes to the evaluation of imperialism; while criticizing imperialism presupposes universal norms, a 'realist' can coherently argue, in a Carneadean vein, that it would be irrational not to pursue imperialism if it leads to gain, or to pursue it if it is imprudent. By the same

---

[94] On Hobbes' relationship with the reason of state tradition, see Noel Malcolm, ' "Reason of State" and Hobbes' in *Reason of State, Propaganda, and the Thirty Years War: An Unknown Translation by Thomas Hobbes* (Oxford University Press 2007) 92. Malcolm makes the excellent point that unlike 'the "ragion di stato" theorists, Hobbes did not have to juggle with two opposing value-scales that proceeded on fundamentally different bases; rather, he showed how they were necessarily related within a single overall system': ibid, 120.

[95] This is the kind of law (*ius*) I take Cicero to be referring to in Scipio's famous definition (*iuris consensus*) at *Rep.* 1.39: '*Est igitur' inquit Africanus 'res publica res populi, populus autem non omnis hominum coetus quoquo modo congregatus, sed coetus multitudinis iuris consensu et utilitatis communione sociatus.*

[96] See on this Brooke, *Philosophic Pride* (n 87) ch 3.

token, moral or legal criticism of imperialism may, as in Cicero, harbour the seeds of a theory of a just imperialism: the very moral criteria that condemn certain kinds of imperial expansion may at times entail demands for a 'responsibility to protect' or similar interventionist aims.

Bibliography

Armitage, David, *The Ideological Origins of the British Empire* (Cambridge University Press 2000)

Bayle, Pierre, *Dictionnaire historique et critique*, vol 4 (Amsterdam 1740)

Bayle, Pierre, *Historical and Critical Dictionary: Selections* (Richard H Popkin tr, Bobbs-Merrill 1965)

Baynes, Norman Hepburn, *The Political Ideas of St. Augustine's De Civitate Dei* (Historical Association 1968)

Berlin, Isaiah, 'The Originality of Machiavelli' in Henry Hardy (ed), *Against the Current* (Princeton University Press 2013)

Bowen, Anthony and Garnsey, Peter, *Lactantius: Divine Institutes* (Liverpool University Press 2003)

Brooke, Christopher, *Philosophic Pride: Stoicism and Political Thought from Lipsius to Rousseau* (Princeton University Press 2012)

Cicero, Marcus Tullius, *On Duties* (M Atkins tr, Cambridge University Press 1991)

Cicero, Marcus Tullius, *On the Commonwealth and On the Laws* (JEG Zetzel tr, Cambridge University Press 1999)

Cicero, Marcus Tullius, *Political Speeches* (DH Berry tr, Oxford University Press 2009)

Clarke, Michelle Tolman, 'Uprooting Nebuchadnezzar's Tree: Francis Bacon's Criticism of Machiavellian Imperialism' (2008) 61 Political Research Quarterly 367

Colish, Marcia L, 'Cicero's *De officiis* and Machiavelli's *Prince*' (1978) 9 Sixteenth Century Journal 81

Crawford, MH (ed), *Roman Statutes* (Institute of Classical Studies 1996) no 1

Deane, Herbert A, *The Political and Social Ideas of St. Augustine* (Columbia University Press 1963)

Gentili, Alberico, *The Wars of the Romans: A Critical Edition and Translation of* De armis Romanis (Benedict Kingsbury and Benjamin Straumann eds and David Lupher tr, Oxford University Press 2011)

Hanke, Lewis, *Aristotle and the American Indians* (Indiana University Press 1959)

Hirschman, Albert O, *The Passions and the Interests: Political Arguments for Capitalism before Its Triumph* (Princeton University Press 1977)

Hobbes, Thomas, 'Answer to Davenant's Preface to *Gondibert*' in Joel Elias Spingarn (ed), *Critical Essays of the Seventeenth Century*, vol 2 (Clarendon Press 1908)

Hobbes, Thomas, *Leviathan*, vol 2 (Noel Malcolm ed, Clarendon Press 2012)

Hornblower, Simon and Spawforth, Antony (eds), *Oxford Classical Dictionary* (revised 3rd edn, Oxford University Press 2003)

Hörnqvist, Mikael, *Machiavelli and Empire* (Cambridge University Press 2004)

Irwin, Terence, *The Development of Ethics*, vol 1 (Oxford University Press 2007)

King, William C, *Ambition, A History: From Vice to Virtue* (Yale University Press 2013)

Kingsbury, Benedict and Straumann, Benjamin, 'Introduction' in Alberico Gentili, *The Wars of the Romans. A Critical Edition and Translation of* De armis Romanis (Benedict Kingsbury and Benjamin Straumann eds and David Lupher tr, Oxford University Press 2011)

Lactantius, *Lactantius: Divine Institutes* (Bowen and Garnsey tr, Liverpool University Press 2003)

Lupher, David, *Romans in a New World* (University of Michigan Press 2003)

Lupher, David, 'The *De armis Romanis* and the Exemplum of Roman Imperialism' in Benedict Kingsbury and Benjamin Straumann (eds), *The Roman Foundations of the Law of Nations: Alberico Gentili and the Justice of Empire* (Oxford University Press 2010)

MacCormack, Sabine, *The Shadows of Poetry: Vergil in the Mind of Augustine* (University of California Press 1998)

Machiavelli, Niccolò, *The Discourses of Niccolò Machiavelli*, 2 vols (Leslie J Walker tr, Routledge & Kegan Paul 1975)

Malcolm, Noel, ' "Reason of State" and Hobbes' in *Reason of State, Propaganda, and the Thirty Years War: An Unknown Translation by Thomas Hobbes* (Oxford University Press 2007)

Markus, RA, *Saeculum: History and Society in the Theology of St Augustine* (Cambridge University Press 1989)

Menchaca, Fernando Vázquez de, *Controversiarum illustrium aliarumque usu frequentium libri tres*, vol 2 (F Rodriguez Alcalde ed, Talleres tipográficos 'Cuesta' 1931)

O'Daly, Gerard, *Augustine's City of God: A Reader's Guide* (Oxford University Press 2004)

Perreau-Saussine, Emile, 'Quentin Skinner in Context' (2007) 69 The Review of Politics 106

Pocock, JGA, *The Machiavellian Moment: Political Thought and the Atlantic Republican Tradition* (Princeton University Press 1975)

Pollmann, Karla et al (eds), *The Oxford Guide to the Historical Reception of Augustine* (Oxford University Press 2013)

Rahe, Paul, *Against Throne and Altar: Machiavelli and Political Theory in the English Republic* (Cambridge University Press 2008)

Richardson, John, 'The Meaning of *imperium* in the Last Century BC and the First AD' in Benedict Kingsbury and Benjamin Straumann (eds), *The Roman Foundations of the Law of Nations* (Oxford University Press 2010)

Skinner, Quentin, *Machiavelli* (Oxford University Press 1981)

Skinner, Quentin, *Visions of Politics*, vol 3 (Cambridge University Press 2002)

Stock, Brian, *Augustine the Reader* (Harvard University Press 1996)

Straumann, Benjamin, *Crisis and Constitutionalism: Roman Political Thought from the Fall of the Republic to the Age of Revolution* (Oxford University Press 2016)

Testard, Maurice, *Saint Augustin et Cicéron*, 2 vols. (Études augustiniennes 1958)

Tierney, Brian, 'Aristotle and the American Indians—again' (1991) 12 Cristianesimo nella storia 295

Tuck, Richard, *The Rights of War and Peace: Political Thought and the International Order from Grotius to Kant* (Oxford University Press 1999)

Tuori, Karlo, 'Alberico Gentili and the Criticism of Expansion in the Roman Empire: The Invader's Remorse' (2009) 2 Journal of the History of International Law 205

Virgil, *Eclogues. Georgics. Aeneid: Books 1–6* (HR Fairclough tr, Harvard University Press 1999)

Warner, John M and Scott, John T, 'Sin City: Augustine and Machiavelli's Reordering of Rome' (2011) 73 The Journal of Politics 857

Weithman, Paul, 'Augustine's Political Philosophy' in Eleonore Stump and Norman Kretzmann (eds), *The Cambridge Companion to Augustine* (Cambridge University Press 2001)

West, DA, '*Cernere erat*: The Shield of Aeneas' (1975–76) 15 Proceedings of the Virgil Society 1

Zetzel, JEG, 'Natural Law and Poetic Justice: A Carneadean Debate in Cicero and Virgil' (1996) 91 Classical Philology 297

15

Scepticism of the Civilizing Mission in International Law

Andrew Fitzmaurice

It has been well documented that from at least the nineteenth century European nations adhered to a standard of civilization in their conduct of international relations or, rather, as Martti Koskenniemi argues, they used a *rhetoric* of civilization to justify their conduct of international relations and, in particular, to justify massive extensions of their empires.[1] That rhetoric was employed by numerous jurists to argue that the principles of international law were consistent with the civilizing mission. As Carl Schmitt observed, '*Civilization* was synonymous with *European* civilization'.[2] This sense that the superiority of European society justified its expansion had its origins, as many scholars have again shown, from at least the sixteenth century. The so-called standard of civilization continues to animate discussions of international conduct today and the rise of ISIS, or the 'Islamic State', in Syria and Iraq has led to an extraordinary surge in the language of civilization and barbarity as measures of political legitimacy. The association of the idea of civilization with progress and development has broad appeal.[3] Human rights discourse has provided a new standard of civilization in international relations just as development remains central to economic thought. However, as a number of critics have again observed, the dichotomy between civilized and uncivilized creates an inherent contradiction in the aspirations of international law to equality between nations and universality.[4]

[1] Martti Koskenniemi, 'Histories of International Law: Dealing with Eurocentrism' (2011) 19 Rechtsgeschichte 152, 156. See also eg: Carl Schmitt, *The Nomos of the Earth* (GL Ulmen tr, Telos 2003); Jörg Fisch, *Die europäische Expansion und das Völkerrecht* (Steiner 1984); Wilhelm G Grewe, *The Epochs of International Law* (Michael Byers tr, De Gruyter 2000) 445–82. More recently: Paul Keal, *European Conquest and the Rights of Indigenous Peoples: The Moral Backwardness of International Society* (Cambridge University Press 2003) 29; Antony Anghie, *Imperialism, Sovereignty and the Making of International Law* (Cambridge University Press 2005); Brett Bowden, *The Empire of Civilization: the Evolution of an Imperial Idea* (University of Chicago Press 2009).

[2] Schmitt, *The Nomos of the Earth* (n 1) 86.

[3] See Gerrit Gong, *The Standard of 'Civilization' in International Society* (Oxford University Press 1984) for a contemporary appeal to the need for a standard of civilization in international law.

[4] See eg: Reinhardt Koselleck, *Futures Past: On the Semantics of Historical Time* (Columbia University Press 2004) 160; Liliana Obregón, 'The Civilized and the Uncivilized' in Bardo Fassbender and Anne Peters (eds), *The Oxford Handbook of the History of International Law* (Oxford University Press 2012) 918; Koskenniemi, 'Histories of International Law: Dealing with Eurocentrism' (n 1);
International Law and Empire: Historical Explorations. First Edition. Martti Koskenniemi, Walter Rech, and Manuel Jiménez Fonseca. © Martti Koskenniemi, Walter Rech, and Manuel Jiménez Fonseca 2016. Published 2016 by Oxford University Press.

The rhetoric of the civilizing mission was central to the hegemony of European norms in the history of the law of nations.

My concern, however, is not with the many and well-documented examples whereby civilization was employed as a standard, or rhetoric, of international conduct. On the contrary, I am interested in the history of opposition to this idea and with scepticism and ambivalence concerning a standard of civilization as the basis for a law of nations and international conduct. Georg Cavallar has been prominent amongst the few historians to have examined opposition to the civilizing mission, pointing to what he describes as a 'strong cosmopolitan tradition' in the law of nations.[5] If by cosmopolitan we mean concern for others motivated by an understanding of citizenship or rights that originate from a universal human community—that is, rights that originate from beyond our own immediate political society—then it is important to point out that such sentiments have been historically closely associated with humanitarianism, which all too frequently collapsed into an effort to find a morally acceptable form in which sovereignty could be imposed upon peoples outside European political communities. In an earlier epoch, it is perhaps no surprise that Stoic cosmopolitanism flourished at the height of the Roman Empire. It is, however, questionable whether the term 'cosmopolitan' would be an accurate description of most of the critics of the civilizing mission. Insofar as those critics included early modern writers on natural law, some of whom are cited in Cavallar's 'cosmopolitan tradition', their concerns were more closely tied to a minimalist conception of universal rights of self-preservation than membership of and service to a universal human community. I will argue that many critics of the civilizing mission, from the sixteenth century to the nineteenth, were motivated not by concern for others as much as by self-interest: that is, by an immediate concern for their own political societies and only a secondary concern for others, if at all.

The civilizing mission was undoubtedly a product of Eurocentric understandings of culture and law, and to understand it one must consider the history of Eurocentrism, although they should not be conflated. It was possible, as we shall see, to be both Eurocentric and sceptical of the standard of civilization. At the

---

Emmanuelle Jouannet, *The Liberal Welfarist Law of Nations* (Cambridge University Press 2012); and Emmanuelle Jouannet, 'Universalism of International Law and Imperialism: The True-False Paradox of International Law?' in Petter Korkman and Virpi Mäkinen (eds), *Universalism in International Law and Political Philosophy* (Helsinki Collegium for Advanced Studies 2008).

[5] Georg Cavallar, 'Vitoria, Grotius, Pufendorf, Wolff and Vattel: Accomplices of European Colonialism and Exploitation or True Cosmopolitans' (2008) 10 Journal of the History of International Law 181, 209. From another perspective, Ian Hunter has criticized the level of philosophical coherence posited by postcolonial accounts of the civilizing mission conducted by European writers on the law of nations whom he portrays as concerned almost entirely with intra-European problems and the formation of territorial states rather than colonies and empires. See Ian Hunter, 'The Figure of Man and the Territorialisation of Justice in "Enlightenment" Natural Law: Pufendorf and Vattel' (2013) 23 Intellectual History Review 289; Ian Hunter, 'Law, War, and Casuistry in Vattel's *Jus Gentium*' (2011) 28(2) Parergon 87. While Hunter's critique is an important corrective, it should at the same time be said that Vattel's *Droit des gens* was written in the context of the tensions leading into the Seven Years' War, a conflict conducted between rival European imperial powers on a global scale, and the book was published in the early years of that conflict.

same time, some critics of the civilizing mission were inspired by a sceptical view of Eurocentrism. The Eurocentrism of international law poses almost insurmountable problems for the universality of international law. One response to those problems is to examine law and international society from a non-European perspective or, as Sanjay Subramanyam has argued, to reject the notion of the incommensurability of cultures and to explore the entangled histories of Europeans and non-Europeans.[6] This is what CH Alexandrowicz attempted at the level of international law.[7] I will argue that another important resource for critiquing Eurocentrism came from within writings upon the law of nations. There is a long history of European scepticism of Eurocentrism. There is also a long and related history of European scepticism of the idea of civilization as a measure of rights. Scepticism of Eurocentrism and scepticism of the civilizing mission were often closely aligned, but they were not the same thing. One did not always lead to the other. I will examine some of the early contributions to that history but I will focus on nineteenth-century writing on the law of nations which was ambivalent or sceptical about the civilizing mission. These authors questioned civility as a quality necessary to membership in the society of nations while others questioned the European monopoly upon the idea of civilization. Many of these authors cast doubt upon the standard and the rhetoric of civilization, and recognized it as rhetoric, or 'propaganda' to use their term. One cause for this scepticism was that some jurists and philosophers recognized the contradiction inherent in basing a system of law with universal aspirations upon the norms of European society. In other words, some jurists rejected the idea of civilization as a normative concept in the law of nations because they were concerned with the universality of the law of nations. They were not cultural relativists but they understood that international law must recognize a diversity of cultural practices in order for it to have universal claims. Other critics of the civilizing mission, such as Immanuel Kant, who were anti-imperialists were nevertheless Eurocentric. At the same time, some critics who promoted empire, such as JR Seeley, also rejected the civilizing mission because its aims were too broadly European rather than tailored to the interests of the nation state. The main conclusion to be drawn from this complexity is that discourses surrounding the civilizing mission were far more fragmented than recent accounts have credited.[8] Incoherence and the fragmentation of perspectives dominate European cultural and legal understandings of the

---

[6] Sanjay Subramanyam, *Courtly Encounters: Translating Courtliness and Violence in Early Modern Eurasia* (Harvard University Press 2012).

[7] 'Attempted' because he could be criticized for merely having trawled the practice of non-European states, and exchanges between European and non-European states, for principles which conform to European standards of the law of nations. For Alexandrowicz, see: CH Alexandrowicz, *The Law of Nations in Global History* (David Armitage and Jennifer Pitts eds, Oxford University Press 2017). For a more recent effort from this perspective, see: Arnulf Becker Lorca, *Mestizo International Law: A Global Intellectual History 1850–1950* (Cambridge University Press 2012); Arnulf Becker Lorca, 'Eurocentrism in the History of International Law' in Bardo Fassbender and Anne Peters (eds), *The Oxford Handbook of the History of International Law* (Oxford University Press 2012); Saliha Belmessous (ed), *Empire by treaty: Negotiating European expansion, 1600–1900* (Oxford University Press 2014).

[8] According to Paul Keal, MF Lindley attempted to account for this complexity by distinguishing between three periods of European legal arguments concerning empire: the first in which, Lindley argued, jurists from Vitoria to Grotius conceded that non-European peoples held sovereignty; the

non-European world. We may be able to describe the civilizing mission as the prevailing discourse of empire, certainly of nineteenth-century empire, but it was far from hegemonic.

I focus upon nineteenth-century scepticism of the standard of civilization in the law of nations because it is in precisely this period that we are told that positivism in hand with nationalism brought the Eurocentrism in the law of nations and the civilizing mission to a peak in which they nourished a new wave of imperialism. CH Alexandrowicz influentially argued that early modern natural law perspectives upon the law of nations were more favourable to a genuine universalism than nineteenth-century positivism. While natural law theories recognized the operation of law outside the state, positivists understood law to be the creation of the state and thus confined within its boundaries. Alexandrowicz's claim has been widely critiqued. Jennifer Pitts points out that natural law was only half of the early modern law of nations, alongside positive accounts of the law.[9] Hedley Bull argued that there was nothing universal about early modern European natural law.[10] These critiques have focused on Alexandrowicz's claims regarding the nature of early modern natural law. Scholars have not questioned his characterization of the nineteenth-century law of nations as inspired by fervent nationalism and a positivism hostile to natural law. Many nineteenth-century positivist accounts of law presupposed that laws are the creation of sovereign powers, and of nations, and thus encouraged a perception of laws as national rather than international. In this account, only states could bring law to those parts of the globe that were legal vacuums, ruled not even by natural laws or by a natural *jus gentium*. Positive accounts of the law could therefore be disposed to the civilizing mission and have been closely associated with the new wave of nineteenth-century imperialism.[11] Despite this broadly shared characterization of nineteenth-century international law, many jurists expressed deep misgivings about the standard of civilization. This may have been due in part to the fact that they were less beholden to positivism than Alexandrowicz and subsequent historians have claimed, although ambivalence about the civilizing mission was

second, in which eighteenth-century philosophers and jurists conceded partial sovereignty; and the third, in the nineteenth century, in which jurists denied sovereignty. Paul Keal adopts his understanding of Lindley's categories while conceding that they are flawed. See Keal, *European Conquest and the Rights of Indigenous Peoples* (n 1) 86. Lindley, it should be said, includes in his 'Class I' group, who 'recognize sovereignty in backward peoples', writers from Vitoria and Groitus through to numerous nineteenth-century jurists including Auguste-Wilhelm Heffter, Charles Salomon, and Gaston Jèze discussed in this chapter. See: MF Lindley, *The Acquisition and Government of Backward Territory in International Law* (Longmans, Green and Co 1926) 11–17. Indeed, the complexity of European attitudes to property and sovereignty in the non-European world defeats any such neat categorizations: see Andrew Fitzmaurice, *Sovereignty, Property and Empire 1500–2000* (Cambridge University Press 2014).

[9] Jennifer Pitts, 'Empire and Legal Universalisms in the Eighteenth Century' (2012) 117 American Historical Review 92, 100.

[10] Hedley Bull, 'The Emergence of a Universal International Society' in Hedley Bull and Adam Watson (eds), *The Expansion of International Society* (Clarendon Press 1984). See also Edward Keene, *Beyond the Anarchical Society. Grotius, Colonialism and Order in World Politics* (Cambridge University Press 2002) 28.

[11] Jennifer Pitts, 'Boundaries of Victorian International Law' in Duncan Bell (ed), *Victorian Visions of Global Order* (Cambridge University Press 2007).

shared by jurists from a spectrum of philosophical backgrounds including positivists and those who worked within the natural rights tradition.[12] Moreover, as we shall see, nationalist accounts of law and history could also lead to hostility to the civilizing mission.

The Idea of Civilization prior to the Nineteenth Century

Sixteenth- and seventeenth-century critiques of Eurocentrism were as likely to have been articulated by humanists influenced by Academic scepticism as they were by natural law writers. Indeed, writing against the background of the Wars of Religion, Michel de Montaigne and Pierre Charron provided some of the most celebrated critiques of Eurocentrism through their scepticism of the natural law tradition. There are some laws, Montaigne observed, which are 'called natural' but they are by 'these Mountains bound' and 'a lie in the world beyond them', and he added: 'of so infinite a number of lawes, there is not so much as one to be found … to be universally received, and by the consent of unanimitie of all Nations to be admitted'.[13] Charron declared: 'there is no opinion held by all, or current in all places, none that is not debated and disputed, that hath not another held and maintained quite contrary unto it'.[14] In the absence of clear moral standards, Montaigne, along with many late humanists, was drawn as much to the notion of self-preservation as he was to virtue as a guide to conduct. Self-preservation subsequently became central to the natural law theories of the humanist-educated Hugo Grotius and Thomas Hobbes as it would later be for Samuel Pufendorf's accounts of natural law.

Montaigne's and Charron's moral scepticism was often cited by subsequent critics of Eurocentrism, including Samuel Pufendorf, but also by nineteenth-century jurists. Pufendorf wrote against the background of the Thirty Years War that had decimated his native country and directed his political philosophy towards the establishment of principles that would bring stability and order to political life and would be blind to the theological and cultural differences that had been the causes of conflict. He brought aspects of that outlook to his discussions of European empire, arguing that claims to a superior culture, or civilization, were not a basis upon which to justify rule over other peoples. At the same time, while Pufendorf can be included amongst sceptics of the civilizing mission, he did not entirely reject the idea that European powers could legally acquire possessions in other continents. He therefore belongs amongst those jurists and philosophers who were sceptical about the civilizing mission while accepting other justifications for colonization. It is perhaps due

[12] Andrew Fitzmaurice, 'The Resilience of Natural Law in the Writings of Sir Travers Twiss' in Ian Hall and Lisa Hill (eds), *British International Thinkers from Hobbes to Namier* (Palgrave Macmillan 2009).

[13] Michel Eyquem de Montaigne, *Essays*, 3 vols (John Florio tr, LC Harmer ed, Everyman edition 1965) vol II, 297.

[14] Pierre Charron, *Of Wisdom: Three Books Written in French* (Samson Lennard tr, London 1625) 237–38. For Charron's scepticism, see Richard Tuck, *Philosophy and Government 1572–1651* (Cambridge University Press 1993) 87.

to this tension that he has been portrayed diversely as an apologist for 'colonialism', a critic of the justifications of empire, and as completely unconcerned by the extra-European world.[15] One could say that all these positions are simultaneously correct. Pufendorf was certainly most concerned by Europe but he did have something to say about the contemporary justifications for empire. He criticized Vitoria's claims that Europeans have a right to communication and commerce across the globe.[16] At the same time, in *De jure naturae et gentium*, while endorsing freedom of the sea he argued that princes may enter into trade pacts or refuse trade, as they prefer, and he noted that these principles apply equally where 'a European nation should make some portion of Africa or India its own, after the fashion which the nations usually recognize as imparting dominion, it has the right, if it shall see fit, to exclude all others from any access to it for purposes of trade'.[17] This is a very offhanded manner in which to acknowledge the justifications of European empires and it seems to be addressing the reality of state practice more than natural law principles, but it is nevertheless a form of acknowledgement. The passage is an implicit critique of Grotius' argument that the Dutch could trade in the East Indies regardless of Portuguese claims to dominion.[18] Rather than freedom of commerce being grounded in natural law as Vitoria and Grotius had argued, Pufendorf argued that the right of a nation to allow access to trade or to exclude other nations from trade was 'what we see observed in everyday practice, and there is nothing in it [that is: in the right to determine the openness or otherwise of trade] contrary to natural reason'.[19]

Pufendorf argued that just as self-preservation was the cause for creating civil society it was also the basis of its legitimacy. He criticized Aristotle for arguing that the law of nature was based upon the 'general agreement of all men or nations … and of civilized mankind'.[20] 'What people', he asked, 'endowed with enough judgement to preserve its existence, will be willing to acknowledge that it is barbarous.'[21] To this end, he cited Pierre Charron and Michel de Montaigne on the great diversity between cultures and the 'foolish' habit 'of condemning customs as barbarous or base for the simple reason that it does not agree with our own general customs and ideas'.[22] He continued:

In former days the Greeks, in their pride, looked down upon all other peoples as barbarians, and the Romans succeeded to their arrogance; and to-day in Europe some of us claim for

---

[15] On Pufendorf as an apologist for 'colonialism', see Richard Waswo, 'The Formation of Natural Law to Justify Colonialism, 1539–1689' (1996) 27 New Literary History 742, 754. On Pufendorf criticizing European justifications of empire, see Cavallar, 'Vitoria, Grotius, Pufendorf, Wolff and Vattel' (n 5) 198–200. On Pufendorf focused upon European questions, see Hunter 'The Figure of Man and the Territorialisation of Justice in "Enlightenment" Natural Law: Pufendorf and Vattel' (n 5).

[16] See Fitzmaurice, *Sovereignty, Property and Empire, 1500–2000* (n 8) 112.

[17] Samuel Pufendorf, *De jure naturae et gentium libri octo*, vol II (James Brown Scott ed, CH Oldfather and WA Oldfather trs, Clarendon Press 1934) Book IV, ch V, 568.

[18] See Hugo Grotius, *The Free Sea* (Richard Hakluyt tr, David Armitage ed, Liberty Fund 2004) ch 8: 'That trading is free by the law of nations among all or between any'.

[19] Pufendorf, *De jure naturae et gentium* (n 17) Book IV, Ch V, 568.

[20] Ibid, Book II, Ch III, 188–89.   [21] Ibid, Book II, Ch III, 189.

[22] Ibid, Book II, Ch III, 189–93.

ourselves to be superior to others in the development of our culture, while, on the other hand, there are peoples who rank themselves far above us.

This is not to argue that Pufendorf was a sceptic or moral relativist.[23] On the contrary, he rejected custom as a basis for the law of nations because he believed its true basis to be reason, but his understanding of human action in terms of self-preservation embraced a great diversity of cultures, albeit a diversity that was framed by a progressive anthropology.[24] If a people demonstrated sufficient judgement to preserve its own existence it was legitimate.[25]

In the first half of the eighteenth century, Christian Wolff, the most eminent authority on the law of nations, articulated a widely shared sentiment when he argued that '[i]t is plain, because it has to be admitted, that what has been approved by the more civilized nations is the law of nations'.[26] Wolff did not restrict this observation to European societies. For Wolff, natural law commands all humans to use their natural abilities to achieve the highest state of happiness and harmony with others.[27] We are obliged, he argued, to make our own decisions about how to govern ourselves and restrain our passionate nature, and for this reason each society has to be left to itself to make decisions about how to achieve these goals. According to Wolff, therefore, there is an obligation not only to respect the choice each society makes about its own organization but also to respect its pursuit of the perfectibility of human nature. He was adamant, in this respect, that any society is capable of using human reason to achieve those ends. Indeed, it was in part as a consequence of Wolff making precisely this claim about Confucian societies that he found himself exiled by Frederick I.[28] While Wolff's standard of civilization was not confined to Europe, it nevertheless demanded normative judgements of what constituted civility. He made a clear distinction between civilized and barbarian nations and he excluded the latter from the society and law of nations. 'Nations', he argued, 'ought to be cultured and civilized, not barbarous.'[29] He also distinguished an intermediate category, 'separate families', between barbarous and civilized nations—a category also adopted by Vattel in which both included North American natives.

---

[23] Istvan Hont, *Jealousy of Trade: International Competition and the Nation-State in Historical Perspective* (Harvard University Press 2005) 167–68 on Pufendorf's rejection of scepticism through the opposition between cultural diversity, on the one hand, and non-civil society on the other.

[24] Pufendorf's progressive anthropology is evident in his observations on 'Those people who to this day are but little removed from primitive community' and 'are somewhat barbarous and simple': Pufendorf, *De jure naturae et gentium* (n 17) Book IV, Ch IV, 554.

[25] Upon such a test all societies in the world might be deemed to be legitimate although, tellingly, later generations of Europeans would argue that certain indigenous peoples, for example in Australia, were a 'dying race', unable to preserve their own existence.

[26] Christian Wolff, *Jus gentium methodo scientifica pertractatum*, vol 2 (Joseph H Drake tr, Oxford University Press 1934) §20, 17. See also Richard Tuck, *The Rights of War and Peace: Political Thought and the International Order from Grotius to Kant* (Oxford University Press 1999) 188; and Bowden, *The Empire of Civilization* (n 1) 118–19.

[27] Knud Haakonssen, 'German Natural Law' in Mark Goldie and Robert Wokler (eds), *Cambridge History of Eighteenth Century Political Thought* (Cambridge University Press 2006) 270.

[28] Tuck, *The Rights of War and Peace* (n 26) 191; Wolff, *Jus gentium* (n 26) §55, 36.

[29] Wolff, *Jus gentium* (n 26) §54, 35.

Importantly, however, and in contrast to Vattel, Wolff did not agree that these people could have sovereignty imposed upon them from outside. He agreed that if they did not possess sovereignty they could not deny outsiders the right to travel through their lands but they could not be 'subjected to civil sovereignty against their will'.[30] Perfection was something that had to be pursued by each society and could not be imposed from outside. Here again we see not only that Eurocentrism and the civilizing mission were not always aligned but also that the standard of civilization as a condition of membership of the society of nations did not necessarily entail a civilizing mission. Such concepts did not work in a coherent intellectual system. They were part of fragmented and often contradictory attempts to think about European nations' relations with other peoples.

According to Cavallar and Francis Cheneval, Wolff's account of 'European relations to non-Europeans' are a 'triumph of intellectual cosmopolitanism'.[31] It would seem, however, that Wolff's concept of a *civitas maxima*, a global society, was animated less by cosmopolitan concern for the fate of others and more by the necessity for a universal system of common values if the conditions for self-preservation and self-perfection were to be realized. When Wolff wrote that 'no nation ought to do to another what it does not wish to be done to itself', he appealed not to a sense of a common humanity but to self-interest.[32] He immediately observed that failure to observe this rule would lead to any abuses a nation visited upon others, such as the appropriation of territory on the grounds that it had merely been hitherto unknown, would rebound upon the abuser. Nineteenth-century discussions of the standard of civilization often contrasted with Wolff either because they restricted the notion of civility to Europe—in such cases, 'civilized' meant 'European', as Schmitt argued[33]—or, at the other extreme, they rejected the idea of civility as a measure of international conduct.

In his youth, Immanuel Kant had been a student of the dominant Wolffian philosophical school, but he would take Wolff's emphasis on human perfectibility further and his critique is important to an understanding of many nineteenth-century jurists' opposition to the civilizing mission. Kant did not agree that the basis of rights was self-preservation but rather reason and human dignity. He used the idea of perfectibility to critique the state. In particular, he developed an understanding of the relation between property, sovereignty, and human perfectibility to condemn the imperial ambitions of contemporary states. In his reflections on the original acquisition of property, Kant asked whether 'we should not be authorized to found colonies, by force if need be' in order to establish a 'civil union' with other peoples and to 'bring these human beings (savages) into a rightful condition (as with the American Indians, the Hottentots and the inhabitants of New Holland [Australia])'.[34] 'Or', he added, '(which is not much better), to found colonies by

---

[30] Ibid, §310–13, 157–60.

[31] Cavallar, 'Vitoria, Grotius, Pufendorf, Wolff and Vattel' (n 5) 204; Francis Cheneval, *Philosophie in weltbürgerlicher Bedeutung* (Schwabe Basel 2002) 270–86.

[32] Wolff, *Jus gentium* (n 26) §309, 157.   [33] Schmitt, *The Nomos of the Earth* (n 1) 86.

[34] Immanuel Kant, 'The Metaphysics of Morals' in Immanuel Kant, *Practical Philosophy* (Mary Gregor ed and tr, Cambridge University Press 1996) 417.

fraudulent purchase of their land, and so become owners of their land, making use of our superiority without regard to their first possession.'[35] He reprised the natural law justification for colonization: namely, that 'nature itself (which abhors a vacuum) seems to demand it'.[36] Such claims, he argued, had driven the process whereby 'great expanses of land in other parts of the world' had become 'splendidly populated' when they would otherwise have remained unknown to 'civilised people' and continued 'forever uninhabited'. He then responded to this justification of empire, declaring it to be a 'veil of injustice (Jesuitism)' which would employ any means to achieve 'good ends' and which must be 'repudiated'.[37]

Kant elaborated his anti-imperial thought throughout his various works on moral philosophy.[38] He began with a Hobbesian notion that each civil constitution created a sovereign person whose autonomy must be respected.[39] His second preliminary article of perpetual peace condemned the appropriation of one state by another:

For a state (like the land on which it resides) is not a belonging. It is a society of human beings that no one other than itself can command or dispose of. Like a trunk, it has its own roots; and to annex it to another state as a graft is to do away with its existence as a moral person and to make a moral person into a thing, and so to contradict the original compact, apart from which no right over a people can be thought.[40]

In the *Metaphysics of Morals* he demanded: 'can two neighbouring peoples (or families) resist each other in adopting a certain use of land, for example, can a hunting people resist a pasturing people or a farming people, or the latter resist a people that wants to plant orchards, and so forth'.[41] Wolff and Emer de Vattel had previously drawn opposite conclusions on this question. Kant's response took Wolff's position: 'Certainly, since as long as they keep within their boundaries the way they want to *live* on their land is up to their own discretion.'[42] Critics of Kant nevertheless point out that his anthropology was Eurocentric, which was another point he held in common with Wolff, even if along with Wolff he did not confine the idea of civilized society to Europe (just as Wolff included barbarity as a potentially European characteristic).[43] Kant's Eurocentrism yet again underlines the divide between attachment to European values and support for the civilizing mission: it was possible, that is, to remain Eurocentric while criticizing

---

[35] Ibid, 417.   [36] Ibid, 418.   [37] Ibid, 418.

[38] Sankar Muthu, *Enlightenment against Empire* (Princeton University Press 2003) 186–200.

[39] Tuck, *The Rights of War and Peace* (n 26) 207–14.

[40] Immanuel Kant, 'Toward Perpetual Peace' in Kant, *Practical Philosophy* (Mary Gregor ed and tr, Cambridge University Press 1996) 318.

[41] Kant, 'The Metaphysics of Morals' (n 34) 417.

[42] Ibid; Muthu, *Enlightenment against Empire* (n 38) 198–99.

[43] On Kant as Eurocentric, see Walter D Mignolo, 'The Many Faces of Cosmopolis: Border Thinking and Critical Cosmopolitanism' (2000) 12 Public Culture 721; Enrique Dussel, 'Eurocentrism and Modernity (Introduction to the Frankfurt Lectures)' in John Beverley, José Oviedo, and Michael Aronna (eds), *The Postmodernism Debate in Latin America* (Duke University Press 1995); Emmanuel Chukwudi Eze, 'The Color of Reason: The Idea of "Race" in Kant's Anthropology' in Emmanuel Chukwudi Eze (ed), *Postcolonial African Philosophy: A Critical Reader* (Wiley-Blackwell 1996).

the civilizing mission and to insist that each people, nation, or family should determine its own destiny.

Crucially, in a discussion that had a profound impact upon some nineteenth-century international lawyers, Kant linked the violation of the right of colonized peoples to the violation of all rights:

Since the (narrower or wider) community of the nations of the earth has now gone so far that violation of right on *one* place of the earth is felt in *all,* the idea of a cosmopolitan right is no fantastic and exaggerated way of representing right; it is, instead, a supplement to the unwritten code of the right of a state and the right of nations necessary for the sake of any public rights of human beings and so for perpetual peace.[44]

The violations of colonized peoples' rights transgressed all peoples' rights and were a threat to the peace of all. Here Kant underlined one of the strongest grounds for opposition to empire from Vitoria through to the twentieth century: namely, fear of the repatriation of colonial injustices. Sovereigns who violated rights in colonial contexts would in time visit their abuses upon their own people or, for Kant, would already be violating the rights of the cosmopolitan community.[45] These anxieties were greatest at precisely the time that Europeans were fighting for the rule of law in their own societies.

Nineteenth-Century Opponents of the Civilizing Mission who were Sceptics of Empire

Many nineteenth-century jurists, philosophers, essayists, and historians were enthusiasts for the idea of historical progress and they concluded that civilized societies held a duty to spread the benefits of civilization throughout the globe. Numerous examples of such sentiments can be cited. In a series of works, including the essay 'Civilization', John Stuart Mill equated 'civilization' with the norms of European nations.[46] He argued that the characteristics of a 'state of high civilization' were 'the diffusion of property and intelligence, and the power of co-operation'. Indeed, these qualities were to be found in the 'principal countries of Europe, but especially in this island'.[47] This apparent hardening of Eurocentrism in the nineteenth century, in hand with nationalism, was reflected in works of international law, notably in the writings of Johann Caspar Bluntschli. Amongst his many offices, Bluntschli was a professor of constitutional law at Heidelberg, Counsellor to the Grand Duke Frederick I of Baden, and a member of the Baden parliament. He

---

[44] Immanuel Kant, 'Toward Perpetual Peace' (n 40) 330.

[45] Muthu, *Enlightenment against Empire* (n 38) 186–92 on Kant's cosmopolitan right and anti-imperialism.

[46] On Mill and civilization, see Pitts, 'Boundaries of Victorian International Law' (n 11) 76–77; Georgios Varouxakis, 'Great versus Small Nations: Size and National Greatness in Victorian Political Thought' in Bell (ed), *Victorian Visions of Global Order* (n 11).

[47] John Stuart Mill, 'Civilization' in *Collected Works of John Stuart Mill: Volume 8, Essays on Politics and Society* (John M Robson ed, University of Toronto 1977) 124.

strongly supported Prussian hegemony and Bismarck's policy of unification and he devoted his life to theorizing and valorizing the state. He was typical of liberal apologists for empire and supported the developing interest, within Germany, in overseas expansion in the 1870s.[48] In his statement of the 'fundamental principles' of international law, Bluntschli argued that 'civilized nations' are particularly called upon to develop common laws for humanity. 'The essence of civilization', he observed, 'consists, as Dante said, in the harmonious development of humanity'. International law', he continued:

> is one of the most precious fruits of civilization, because it is in essence an organisation of humanity. The pretension of European and American states to be, more particularly than all the others, the representatives and the protectors of international law, would be absurd, if it was not founded upon the more highly advanced civilization of those states.[49]

Bluntschli captured the circular logic of nineteenth-century Eurocentrism. The definition of civilization was to create harmony within humanity. International law created harmony within humanity. The codes of international law were therefore proof of civilization. International law was the creation of European states. European states were therefore custodians of the highest form of civilization. International law would be the means whereby civilization reached the savage places of the earth: 'humanity is destined to spread civilization on the earth'.[50]

Despite the great proliferation of such sentiment supporting the civilizing mission, many nineteenth-century jurists, philosophers, and historians critiqued both the idea of civilization and its incumbent duties. Some jurists opposed civilization as a standard of the membership of the society of nations at the same time that they critiqued empire. Others, while supporting European expansionism, thought that the idea of the civilizing mission was not a sound basis upon which to justify empire, or thought it an encumbrance to the true aims of expansion. I will first discuss cases in which jurists rejected both the civilizing mission and critiqued empire. This combined rejection was evident in the work of Auguste-Wilhelm Heffter (1796–1880). Heffter was born in Saxe, and later became Professor of Law at Bonn, Halle, and Berlin.[51] He was influential within the German Vormärz School of public law spanning 1815–48 and he remained an important authority on international law throughout the nineteenth century. As late as 1873 he became a founding member of the *Institut de droit international*.[52] He published his textbook on international law in 1844 when imperial designs beyond Europe were remote from Prussian political life and this distance may have facilitated the imperial critique. His text

---

[48] On Bluntschli 'parmi les modérés ou *libéraux*', see Alphonse Rivier, 'Notice sur M. Bluntschli' in Johann Caspar Bluntschli, *Droit international codifié* (4th edn, Librairie Guillaumin 1886) viii; and Martti Koskenniemi, *The Gentle Civilizer of Nations: The Rise and Fall of International Law 1870–1960* (Cambridge University Press 2001) 42–47.

[49] Bluntschli, *Droit international codifié* (n 48) 57.   [50] Ibid, 177.

[51] Ernest Nys, *Droit international: Les principes, les theories, les faits* (2nd edn, A Castaigne 1904), vol 1, 289–90.

[52] See 'Liste des members effectifs de l'institut de droit international, Octobre 1873' (1873) 5 Revue de droit international et de législation comparée 711.

was republished in 1873, the year the *Institut* was founded and when European powers were turning their attention to a new wave of imperial expansion, although the newly established German Empire under Bismarck was yet to begin exporting its sovereignty.[53]

In a discussion of empire that was widely noted amongst the *Institut de droit international* generation of jurists later in the nineteenth century, Heffter agreed with the principle originally stated by Francisco de Vitoria that European subjects 'can try to establish commercial relations with' non-European subjects and can 'stay with them in case of necessity, ask them for necessary objects and food, and even negotiate with them the voluntary cession of a piece of land which would be colonized'.[54] But he declared:

occupation could only be applied to goods that, though susceptible to ownership, have no master. [Occupation] can't be extended to people who could only be subjected [in a way that is] ... either voluntary or forced. Occupation is notably applied to areas or islands that are not inhabited or not entirely occupied, but no power on earth has the right to impose its laws upon wandering or even savage peoples.[55]

And in an explicit rejection of the civilizing mission he added:

Nature, it is true, does not forbid nations to extend their empire on earth. But nature does not give the right to only one of them to establish its domination everywhere it suits that nation. Propaganda about civilization, the development of commercial and industrial interests ... do not justify it either.[56]

Similarly, Edward Creasy, who became Chief Justice of Ceylon in 1860 and subsequently held the Chair of History at University College London, expressed grave doubts about the legal arguments used to justify European empire, although in contrast to Heffter, Creasy worked in the heart of the largest of the European empires. He dedicated his 1876 treatise on international law to the Secretary of State for the Colonial Department, the Earl of Carnarvon, reflecting a perception that the fortunes of empire were closely tied to international law and possibly also a hope that Carnarvon might implement some of Creasy's reformist views. Creasy's role in the administration of colonial law and the dedication of his work indicate that there was no simple alignment between expansionist interests and the views of jurists. In passages that he had first published four years earlier in *Imperial and Colonial Constitutions of the Britannic Empire: Including Indian Institutions*, Creasy argued that European occupation of non-European lands was justified 'in strictness to the taking possession of uninhabited or desert places only'.[57] 'The cases', he caustically

---

[53] Auguste-Wilhelm Heffter, *Le droit international public de l'europe* (Paris 1873) 39.

[54] Ibid, 142: 'Ses sujets peuvent chercher à nouer des relations commerciales avec ces derniers, séjourner chez eux en cas de nécessité, leur demander les objets et vivres indispensables, et même négocier avec eux la cession volontaire d'une portion de territoire destinée à être colonise.'

[55] Ibid, 142.   [56] Ibid, 142.

[57] Edward Creasy, *First Platform of International Law* (J Van Voorst 1876) 207. The passage, and many of those cited here from Creasy, were first published in Edward Creasy, *Imperial and Colonial Constitutions of the Britannic Empire: Including Indian Institutions* (Longmans, Green, and Co 1872) 63–65.

observed, 'in which the territories beyond Europe, now held by Europeans, were quite "desert and uninhabited" when first visited by Europeans, are rare and exceptional.'[58] 'In the vast majority of instances' he continued, 'the European "occupants" found native tribes already existing in the countries which were new to Europeans, but not new to human beings.'[59] It might be thought, he added, that in many instances large territories were 'roved over by a few sparse savages' who could not be considered as having occupied those lands so that 'the European newcomers gained a new title by occupancy'.[60] He responded to this Vattel-like objection by arguing: 'But in many cases the natives were in considerable numbers: they were often more or less agricultural, in some cases they had attained a high degree of peculiar civilization.' It could be fairly pointed out that here Creasy maintained some semblance of a stadial idea of history and civilization. He then cast doubt, however, upon the notion that Europeans should be the custodians of such ideas. The problem, he declared, was that the 'interpretation of the Law of Nations, as between European new comers and old-natives, was always pronounced by the European— that is, by the stronger party'. In other words, while native peoples held just titles, Europeans supplanted them through force: that is, through conquest. Creasy cited Chief Justice Marshall at length to this effect and concluded that '[a]ltogether the processes by which civilized Christians have supplanted heathen savages ... reflect little credit on our creed or on our culture' such that the 'mode' whereby such 'territories were originally taken is generally indefensible'.[61] European powers, he added, had no moral authority for criticizing the United States when 'there is much in the history of our settlements at the Cape, in Australia, in New Zealand, and elsewhere, which it is impossible to read without disapproval and shame'.[62] Creasy was a strong critic of his own nation's empire, as well as others. Yet, like Marshall, while regretting the brutality and injustice of conquest, he resigned himself to what he saw as the reality of administering the 'law of the land' and the protection of the indigenous peoples of conquered territories because the 'property of the great mass of the community' originated in conquest and 'could not be questioned'.[63] Creasy thus belongs to a category of jurists who were neither enthusiasts for the civilizing mission nor outright opponents of empire; jurists who subscribed to a Eurocentric view of stadial history but who did not believe that understanding of history justified the majority of cases in which European empires were extended over the globe, nor the behaviour of imperial interests.

Writing after the Berlin Conference on the partition of Africa in 1885, the French jurist, Charles Salomon, made one of the most sustained critiques amongst the international lawyers of his generation of the use of civilization to justify expansion. We know little about Salomon, other than the fact that he was a Bordeaux lawyer who belonged to a generation of European jurists many of whom, while unremarkable in most respects and possessing middling positions in faculties of law, were more worried about the threats posed to hard-won liberties of the European

---

[58] Creasy, *First Platform of International Law* (n 57) 208.   [59] Ibid, 208.
[60] Ibid, 208.   [61] Ibid, 211.   [62] Ibid, 214.   [63] Ibid, 213.

middle classes than by the wave of empire in the second half of the nineteenth century. In the sixteenth and seventeenth centuries, according to Salomon, all territories not inhabited by Christians were taken to be *res nullius*. In his own day, he said, an even more odious doctrine prevailed: namely, that all territories that were not civilized were treated as *res nullius*:

... the argument used nowadays by civilized peoples to justify and disguise the spoliation of the weaker races, is no longer religious interest, it is the interest of civilization: modern peoples have a civilizing mission to fulfil from which they cannot escape. One can sustain without paradox that the point of view of the sixteenth-century popes and princes was, in short, more legitimate than the position of nineteenth-century governments, that there was more sincerity and less hypocrisy in the former when they spoke about the mission that falls to them.[64]

He continued by pointing out that, while the use of religion to justify conquest at least appealed to a form of moral absolute, 'the idea of civilization, on the contrary, is variable and relative: nobody seriously argues that there is a sole civilization and that it is necessary that all men participate in its benefits'. Even at the time of Montaigne, he argued, Europeans claimed 'rights of civilization', and yet Montaigne had 'ridiculed the pretentions of those who call indigenous peoples Barbarians'. 'No word', he declared, 'is more vague and has been used to commit greater iniquities than the word civilization.' For a state, as for an individual, a shortcoming in 'education or development' was not a cause for the forfeiture of rights: 'the right of property for an illiterate is as inviolable as for a wise man; the rights of sovereignty for a people or a state half-civilized are as sacred as those of a Christian civilized state'.[65] In rejecting civilization as a basis for rights, Salomon seemed here to be accepting the force of the idea but he quickly corrected that impression: 'We speak of civilization as if there was one civilization absolute: we could cite many who believe they sit at the top of the ladder.' On the contrary, he concluded: 'je connais des civilisations, je ne connais pas la civilisation.'

Revealing the motivation for his scepticism, Salomon warned: 'Take guard! The pretended right of civilization could serve to legitimize the most grave attacks, even in Europe ... Is there not a German civilization, a Slavic civilization, a Latin civilization? Have we not often supported the incontestable superiority of one over the other?'[66] 'How could we deny', he argued, 'a right of civilization in relations between European peoples if it is legitimate, outside of Europe, to use such an argument to despoil savage peoples.'[67] The rights of a state, he pointed out, do not increase with its level of civilization. States today, he argued, had less right to speak of civilizing, religious, or humanitarian missions than at any other time in history because it was clear that they pursued above all their material interests and their commerce. When we hear that a state has intervened in the affairs of another people in the 'interests of civilization, we must always hear that it is acting for its own civilization and it pursues above all the development of its commerce'.[68] This,

---

[64] Charles Salomon *L'occupation des territoires sans maître* (Paris 1887) 193–4.
[65] Ibid, 195.   [66] Ibid, 192–96.   [67] Ibid, 196.   [68] Ibid, 197.

he pointed out, was how the charters given to African companies should be understood. Their purpose was to enrich the colonizers at the expense of a weaker people. How can a state such as Germany, he asked, speak of its civilizing mission and then delegate the 'direct action' of colonization to a commercial enterprise which seeks only its own enrichment? We must not have 'grand illusions', he observed, about the treaties concluded in Africa. Treaties must be freely consented to, not only in the 'absence of material violence' but also the 'indigenous chief must be aware of exactly of what he is doing'. Such conditions we 'encounter only exceptionally'.[69] Given, Salomon argued, that colonizers used the idea of civilization as a veneer over what was ruthless self-interest and the doctrine of might as right, then it was necessary to limit radically the doctrine of occupation to cases in which non-European peoples actually freely sought treaties ceding their sovereignty. Such treaties could not be made with 'a miserable tyrant who sells his subjects like slaves'.[70] Moreover, they could not cede rights other than those that can be ceded. In this discussion that recalled Kant's strict conditions on treaties made between Europeans and non-Europeans, Salomon insisted that cession must be made through free consent, and justly. These conditions, he drily repeated, 'we encounter only rarely'.[71]

Writing shortly before Salomon, the Swiss jurist Joseph Hornung, a professor of the history of law at Lausanne, was also concerned that abuses of the law of nations would rebound upon Europeans, although he believed that the threats that arise from abusing the rule of law would be external to Europe rather than internal. The fact that Hornung was a citizen of a European power without imperial ambitions may have facilitated his criticisms, although such expansionist interests did not always determine the views of jurists, as we see in cases such as Creasy and Salomon. Rather, national interests could be seen as being opposed to empire rather than aligned with it. Hornung has been seen as a humanitarian apologist for empire.[72] While he was highly critical of European colonizers, his criticisms instructed civilized powers on their responsibilities to the uncivilized. He has therefore been portrayed as inhabiting the 'prison house of paternalism' and participating in a discourse of exclusion and inclusion, whereby non-Europeans' lacked rights but, due to their common humanity, qualified for inclusion in European extensions of sovereignty and thus rights.[73] These portrayals are partly justified although they do not capture the complexity of Hornung's work. In his several essays on 'Civilisés et Barbares', Hornung called into question the portrayal of Europeans as civilized and non-Europeans as barbarian. Amongst many examples, he contrasted the behaviour of the Russians with the Ottomans. The Ottomans, he conceded, taxed subject peoples heavily and did nothing for them. Nevertheless, they 'at least' left them in possession of 'their languages, their religion, their schools, their customary laws, their local autonomy'. Russia, on the other hand, a member of the great powers of Europe, placed the law of nations 'at the service of its ambition, imposing on

---

[69] Ibid, 237.   [70] Ibid, 242.   [71] Ibid, 242.

[72] Koskenniemi, *The Gentle Civilizer* (n 48) 129–30; Pitts, 'Boundaries of Victorian international law' (n 11) 76.

[73] Koskenniemi, *The Gentle Civilizer* (n 48) 129–30.

all races that it governs (such as the Turkmen) its administrative system, its language and, when it can, its religion'.[74] They assumed that 'the barbarians have no rights' and on this basis they justified their 'exterminations' in the Caucasus and Turkestan, including the Yomud tribe in 1873.[75] Such behaviour, he observed, was not restricted to Russia, as other European colonizing powers conducted exterminations in Africa, Asia, America, and Tasmania.[76] It was the Europeans, in such cases, who behaved barbarously while non-Europeans, such as Turkey, proved to be relatively civilized. Part of Hornung's purpose, therefore, was to destabilize the very terms 'civilized' and 'barbarian' in the manner of Montaigne.

'International law', Hornung declared, 'is based upon the equality of sovereign states.'[77] Turkey, he pointed out, was a full member of international society, having been admitted, amongst other things, to the Concert of Europe in 1856 and having taken part in the Congress of Berlin in 1878 on 'the same standing as the other great powers'.[78] And yet, when the Ottomans' Balkan subjects complained, Europeans condemned Turkey 'as if it was an inferior and unequal state'. 'Writers hostile to Turkey', he continued, 'say that a Muslim state does not have the right to rest on Christian territory, and that Europe is right to take the part of its Christian subjects against the [Sublime] Porte ... Thus, it is because Turkey is a Muslim state that she cannot be equal to Christian powers, and those powers have a right to interpose themselves between Turkey and her subjects and to condemn her.'[79] 'Who cannot see', he exclaimed, 'how grave all this is!' The consequence of these claims would be to inaugurate a new principle that certain powers have the right to condemn a sovereign state 'in the case in which its subjects complain about it'.[80] Even, he lamented, the eminent founder of the *Institut de droit international*, Gustave Rolin-Jaquemyns, had condemned Turkey on this basis, 'leading us to wonder whether we live in the nineteenth century or the 13th'. Today, he pointed out, 'political and civil rights are everywhere rendered independent of religious belief' and yet here we find that international law has placed itself 'in a confessional perspective'.[81] Europe reproaches Turkey for making rights depend upon religion and then 'does exactly the same thing in the international order'.

At this point in his argument, Hornung turned away from the conflict between Europe and the Ottomans and asked what would be the consequences of applying these principles globally. His answer is surprising. What would we say, he asked, 'if Muslim states or the Buddhist states formed a coalition against Christians when they believed their coreligionists to be oppressed by Christians? We would return to the times of the Crusades and the wars of religion.'[82] There are two surprises here: first, that he believed that a significant number of 'civilized' states existed outside Europe and America and that they participated in international society; second, that he turned the question back onto Europeans. This was not, he argued, just a hypothesis. An Arab professor at Mecca had written a brochure calling on

---

[74] Joseph Hornung, 'Civilsés et barbares' (1885) 17 Revue de droit international et de législation comparée 1, 9.

[75] Ibid, 6.   [76] Ibid, 6–7.   [77] Ibid, 9–10.   [78] Ibid, 10–11.

[79] Ibid, 11.   [80] Ibid, 11.   [81] Ibid, 12.   [82] Ibid, 12.

Muslim powers to come together against the incursions of Christians. Raising the alarm further, he asked 'What if the Buddhists were to do the same':

A league between them, under the hegemony of China, is not impossible. China is becoming a military and maritime power equivalent to those of Europe. It possesses a racial unity and extreme cohesion and, with the states of Indochina, it forms a quarter of humanity. The principle that we propose can thus be turned against us, to the great peril of our civilisation.[83]

What we see here is not humanitarian sentiment expressed in a spirit of tutelage over non-European peoples (although Hornung at times made such appeals). Rather, we find the fear, also found in Salomon's writings, that abuses of the law of nations will rebound upon Europeans. For Salomon, the fear was that abuses would be repatriated to Europe. For Hornung, the dangers were larger. If Europeans did not support the formation of international law that respected the equality and inviolability of states, regardless of 'race and religion', then a day would come when they no longer dominated the international order and the same principles would be used against them.

It is true that Hornung envisaged a role for great powers to 'protect' weaker powers and he believed that this role would apply to Europe's relations, for example, to Africa. But, at the same time, this idea should not be abstracted in order to fit his work with a broader European civilizing mission. He argued that the 'glory of our times' was that 'tutelage of the weak' was a principle that was taken seriously in Europe and America, so that criminals and even animals were protected by states. Moreover, he argued, the formation of a 'juridical ensemble' by the powers of Europe allowed small Christian nations, such as his own Switzerland, to flourish under the 'protection' of the 'great powers', while outside that European law of nations only 'interest' ruled.[84] Hornung argued that 'human solidarity' dictated that these powers should have responsibilities on this global scale, particularly in the protection of 'degenerate' peoples, but rather than envisaging those responsibilities in terms of colonization he was concerned rather with the creation of a global 'state' or '*Societe des Nations, Volkerstaat, Volkergesellschaft*' of the kind described 'notably by Kant'.[85] This 'vast international organism' would include 'all the races' with the objective of securing 'common rights' and would be placed under 'the guarantee of civilised nations' which would presumably include Muslim and Buddhist 'states'. That world state 'with its law, its tribunal and sanctions, must extend to the limits of humanity'.[86]

The French jurist Gaston Jèze could not agree with Hornung. Writing in 1896, Jèze was at the time a relatively obscure figure, but he would later obtain prominence in French intellectual and political life and, as a Professor of Law at the Sorbonne, he pursued his criticism of Europeans' civilizing mission to the point whereby he represented Hailé Sélassié in the League of Nations in 1935 and 1936 in opposition to the invasion of Ethiopia by Italy.[87] Citing Hornung, Jèze conceded that 'Without doubt ... it is a handsome theory to declare that we must bring

---

[83] Ibid, 12.   [84] Ibid, 17.   [85] Ibid, 17.   [86] Ibid, 18.
[87] Marc Milet, *La Faculté de droit de Paris face à la vie politique, de l'Affaire Scelle à l'Affaire Jèze, 1925–1936* (LGDJ 1996); Pierre Péan, *Une jeunesse française. François Mitterrand, 1934–1947* (Fayard 1994) 45–61.

barbarians to civilisation' and 'Monsieur Hornung believes that civilized powers can intervene *collectively* in a 'disinterested intervention'.[88] In the eleven years, however, between when Hornung wrote at the time of the Berlin Conference on the partition of Africa in 1885 and the publication of Jèze's treatise on occupation in 1896, the exploitative nature of the race for Africa had become apparent, to Jèze at least. Do not the facts of everyday, asked Jèze, 'demonstrate the utopian character' of Hornung's proposal? 'We know', he added with heavy irony, 'the influence of commerce in Africa and the excellent results obtained by the great companies'.[89] Those companies, he argued, did not in the least recognize a civilizing mission and, on the contrary, declared their unique aim to deliver the highest possible dividends to their shareholders. 'We might hope', he added, that 'direct action by civilized states' might produce more satisfying results, but isn't it true 'that practice never corresponds to theory, no matter how generous it may be?'[90] Jèze observed that scepticism of the civilizing mission was long-standing:

As Vitoria already said in the sixteenth century, civilized powers have no more right to seize the territories of savages than savages have to occupy the European continent. The law of nations does not admit any distinction between the barbarians and the so-called civilized: men of all races, white or black, yellow or red, however unequal they are in fact have to be considered equal in the law.[91]

Citing Kant, he argued that 'we must not move from our only principle which is that all peoples, no matter who they are, have a right to respect for their territory and their sovereignty and that it is iniquitous to take that without their consent'.[92] Consent, he added, must fulfil the three conditions laid down by Kant for treaties: that is, '1. It must be free; 2. It must be knowing; 3. It must be conducted according to the customs of the country.'[93] He summarized: 'we decide in favor of the absolute right of the indigenous peoples. We believe the opposite theory does nothing but establish, on the pretext of civilization, the maxim "might is right" and violates, under the appearance of legality, the fundamental rule of racial equality'.[94] Dismissing the civilizing mission, Jèze concluded:

In the forward march of the civilized world, we must account for the inhabitants of the invaded countries. Barbarian peoples are not without rights. Under the pretext of civilization, we cannot deliver them to the calculations of an immeasurable ambition and to the most shameful speculative manoeuvres. Ideas of humanity and of social progress too often hide a spirit of scandalous plunder.[95]

Philanthropy was a veneer. Jèze, like Salomon, did not turn to humanitarian sentiment to motivate his opposition to colonial expropriation. He too was motivated by the danger that colonial abuses would be repatriated to the metropolis:

Otherwise, the argument turns against those who propose it. Isn't the right of civilization invoked even in Europe? Do we not hear certain chauvinistic spirits repeat that the

---

[88] Gaston Jèze, *Étude théorique et pratique sur l'occupation* (Paris 1896) 114.
[89] Ibid, 114.   [90] Ibid, 114–15.   [91] bid, 103.   [92] Ibid, *Étude*, 115.
[93] Ibid, *Étude*, 116.   [94] Ibid, *Étude*, 112.   [95] Ibid, *Étude*, 10.

civilization of this or that European country is superior to a neighbouring state? Must we not admit, under that pretext, that the strongest will crush the weakest?[96]

Nineteenth Century Sceptics of the Civilizing Mission who were Proponents of Expansionism

While many opponents of the civilizing mission were sceptics of empire, other critics did not oppose empire and colonization but nevertheless opposed civilization as a standard of the membership of the society of nations. Henry Bonfils (1835–97) strongly condemned the practices of European colonizers and rejected the civilizing mission but he sought a reformed kind of expansionism.[97] Bonfils was Professor of Law at Toulouse and wrote one of the most popular textbooks of international law in the late nineteenth century. He said that the 'so-called juridical subtleties' used in North America against the 'Red-Skins' and by 'a number of European powers against the habitants of Africa' were merely a veneer over the 'brutal use of force'.[98] At the same time, he rejected the civilizing mission, arguing that it was inadmissible to intervene on this basis in the affairs of another people, despite the support he noted that Bluntschli gave to that doctrine. 'This seductive thesis', he claimed, 'is too favourable to the violation of human freedom to be acceptable'.[99] Civilized people 'act without pity against races that are still barbarian'. While the 'pacific propaganda' is praiseworthy, Heffter, he said, had shown 'that no power on the planet has the right to impose its laws on even savage and wandering peoples'.[100] It is impossible, he continued, to accept that European powers have the right to impose their sovereignty in order to 'bring the benefits of civilization'.[101] While Bonfils rejected the civilizing mission in this way, he did not entirely reject European expansionism. 'It is through peaceful conventions', he concluded, that Europe must 'seek to penetrate in inhabited regions that are not yet under its influence'.[102] 'Protectorats' could be established through 'voluntary cessions' leaving the 'chiefs of the countries' in 'everyday control'.[103] Bonfils can be placed amongst those who rejected the civilizing mission and wave of empire that followed in its wake but at the same time admitted the possibility whereby European powers could expand through the cession of sovereignty. Like many liberals inspired by the notion of human perfectibility, Bonfils saw international law as the means to creating a vast association, an international community. But he rejected the Wolffian notion that that community could become a universal state.[104]

---

[96] Ibid, 115.

[97] Henry Bonfils, *Manuel de droit international public* (3rd edn, Rousseau 1901) 3. Note that this work was substantially revised by Paul Fauchille after Bonfils' death following the publication of the first edition.

[98] Ibid, 307.   [99] Ibid, 172.   [100] Ibid, 172.   [101] Ibid, 306.

[102] Ibid, 307.   [103] Ibid, 308.   [104] Ibid, 6.

Frantz Despagnet (1857–1906), Professor of Law at Bordeaux, played a role justifying the expanding French empire in Africa, although he can be placed amongst
those who critiqued empire at the same time that they excused it.[105] 'In our days',
declared Despagnet, 'many publicists and governments invoke a right of civilization against the resistance of barbarian peoples'.[106] 'But civilization', he continued,
'is a thing eminently relative that we cannot measure' as Montaigne, he added,
had beautifully shown. If we took this point of view of a right of civilization, he
reasoned, then 'each people would consider that they possessed the true civilization along with a right to impose it upon others'.[107] This would mean, in turn,
'if we accept that theory, that the German race would want to submit the Latin
races to German culture'.[108] Here we find echoes of Salomon's argument about the
potentially devastating long-term consequences of cultural chauvinism, which Jèze
would expand two years after the first edition of Despagnet's *Cours de droit international public* (1894).

Shortcomings of civilization, Despagnet reasoned, are an unhappiness for 'savage' peoples, 'not a reason for forfeiture of authority in robbing them of their
sovereign rights'.[109] He declared that nobody can occupy the territory of barbarian peoples and lamented that 'the true end of the occupation of territories is the
enrichment of the strong to the detriment of the weak'.[110] The 'pretended right to
spread civilization' had been used to 'despoil savage peoples of their sovereignty'.[111]
He concluded, therefore, that the 'propaganda of civilization' could only justify the
nourishment of pacific relations with barbarian countries, including the right of
communication and trade.[112] 'An absolute respect', he declared, 'was due to all sovereignty, even barbarian'.[113] While damning of the civilizing rhetoric of European
powers, Despagnet nevertheless took the claims of his own nation's imperial ambitions seriously and he sought a place for France in the international order whereby it
could recover its grandeur and yet pursue progress, justice, and peace.[114] The means
to reclaiming grandeur would be through protectorates.[115]

In the work of John Robert Seeley, Regius Professor of Modern History at
Cambridge, we find an explanation for why some imperial apologists opposed the
civilizing mission. In two lectures delivered in 1881 and 1882, at the height of
the new wave of imperialism, Seeley poured scorn on the idea of a civilizing mission. He published the lectures in his highly influential *The Expansion of England*
(1883) which became, as Duncan Bell puts it, 'the bible of Greater Britain' and a
'household book'.[116] While sceptical of the rhetoric of civilization, he was certainly

---

[105] On Despagnet, see Koskenniemi, *The Gentle Civilizer* (n 48) 272–73.
[106] Frantz Despagnet, *Cours de droit international public* (2nd edn, Larose 1899) 433.
[107] Ibid, 433.   [108] Ibid, 433.   [109] Ibid, 433.   [110] Ibid, 433.
[111] Ibid, 433.   [112] Ibid, 434.   [113] Ibid, 434.
[114] Frantz Despagnet, *La diplomatie de la troisième république* (Sirey 1904) viii; Koskenniemi, *The Gentle Civilizer* (n 48) 272–73.
[115] Frantz Despagnet, *Essai sur les protectorats* (Librairie de la Société du recueil général des lois et des arrêts 1896).
[116] Duncan Bell, *The Idea of Greater Britain: Empire and the Future of World Order, 1860–1900* (Princeton University Press 2007) 150.

an enthusiast for the progressive theory of history and he conceded that 'No one can long study history without being haunted by the idea of development, of progress'.[117] Any examination of the past centuries of English history, he argued, would do much to favour the view that 'the movement is progressive'.[118] On the other hand, he noted that it was difficult to define what that movement was and he found the 'old school of historians' unsatisfactory with their 'vague flourishes' to 'what was called the advance of civilisation'. These historians, he complained, gave no definition of civilization. They merely spoke in metaphors of light, thereby proposing a 'theory that was not serious, and which only existed for the purpose of rhetorical ornament'.[119] Even more strongly he declared:

It is a very fair sample of bad philosophising, this theory of civilization. You have to explain a large mass of phenomena, about which you do not even know they are of the same kind—but they happen to come into view at the same time;—what do you do but you fling over the whole mass a *word* which holds them together like a net?[120]

He explained that historians who use the word civilization carefully avoided defining it, preferring instead to use metaphors, so that they implied 'a living force of unknown, unlimited properties' which is 'enough to explain the most wonderful, the most dissimilar effects'.[121] Phenomenon such as the 'softening of manners', mechanical inventions, religious toleration, great literature and art, scientific discovery, and 'constitutional liberty' could all be explained with this one word: 'It was assumed, though it was never proved, that all these things belonged together and had a hidden cause, which was the working of the spirit of civilisation'. Seeley then pointed out that historians could have made a more convincing effort to demonstrate the connections between these phenomena. They might, for example, have shown that certain advancements in science and art flowed in the first place from the flourishing of political liberty. But this, he concluded, was not the problem with the idea of civilization. Rather, it was more simply that the proper subject of history is the state, not culture: 'I consider therefore that history has to do with the State, that it investigates the growth and changes of a certain corporate culture'.[122] Returning, then, to the question of the progress of history, Seeley asked whether the rise of liberty was the appropriate story for the 'progress of the English State'. The story of liberty, is certainly important, he argued, but it had distracted historians from the more important story of expansion, whereby a Greater Britain, 'a diffusion of our race and expansion of our state', had been established across the globe.[123] Here Seeley's hostility to the idea of civilization, and a civilizing mission for that matter, becomes apparent. Civilization, as he argued, was simply too diffuse a concept to capture the importance of English history. His aim was to encourage Britons to embrace their common racial and national origins and so create a greater British state. The idea of civilization would in fact weaken the features that 'Britons' across the globe shared by highlighting what they had in common with other exported

---

[117] JR Seeley, *The Expansion of England* (London 1883) 3.   [118] Ibid, 4.
[119] Ibid, 4.   [120] Ibid, 5.   [121] Ibid, 5.   [122] Ibid, 7.   [123] Ibid, 10.

European cultures and thereby diluting their commonality as Britons in a broader sea of civilization. For Seeley, the ends of nation and race were inconsistent with those of civilization.

The development of the progressive theory of history, which underpinned the civilizing mission, is undoubtedly one of the strongest currents in Western political thought over the past five hundred years. Many voices, however, including Pufendorf, warned of the dangers of a single understanding of progress, while others simply rejected the notion of civilization as a way in which we can think about relations between different societies. Yet others, such as Seeley, were reluctant to think about progress in terms of culture and were more concerned with national goals. I have contrasted, on the one hand, the critics of empire who were sceptical of the civilizing mission with, on the other hand, the apologists for expansionism who were also sceptical of the civilizing mission. One thing that these two perspectives shared, apart from their scepticism of the civilizing mission, was an understanding of empire in terms of interests. For Seeley, the civilizing mission was rhetorical nonsense that would distract from the proper pursuit of national interests which were the proper object of expansionism. Jurists such as Despagnet and Bonfils supported their own nation's interests in colonization while criticizing the civilizing mission of others. For Jèze and Salomon, and to some degree Hornung, the civilizing mission was insidious rhetorical nonsense that was designed to distract its audience from the interests that were the true object of expansionism. Interest has a history and its rise was closely tied to the rise of positivism.[124] Both interest and positivism were powerful motivations and justifications for empire.[125] But while interest was used to motivate expansion it was also used to oppose empire and some of the critics of the civilizing mission reveal that opposition. Given that interest was such a potent discourse of empire, it is all the more important to understand its power as an imperial critique.

Once the dichotomy between civilized and uncivilized is removed, as many critics wished—critics as diverse as Hornung, Jèze, and Salomon on one side, and Seeley on the other—the question remains whether international law would cease to be Eurocentric. The answer, clearly, is that it would not. It would continue to be a body of thought about relations between political entities that emerged from a largely European experience and from a European perspective upon empire and colonization. We have seen that it was possible to oppose the civilizing mission

---

[124] JGA Pocock, *Virtue, Commerce, and History* (Cambridge University Press 1985); Albert O Hirschman, *The Passions and the Interests: Political Arguments for Capitalism before its Triumph* (Princeton University Press 1997). Moreover, interest in the context of empire also has a history: see David Armitage, *The Ideological Origins of the British Empire* (Cambridge University Press 2000); Andrew Fitzmaurice, *Humanism and America: An Intellectual History of English Colonisation, 1500–1625* (Cambridge University Press 2003); Andrew Fitzmaurice, 'The Commercial Ideology of Colonisation in Jacobean England: Robert Johnson, Giovanni Botero and the Pursuit of Greatness' (2007) 64 William and Mary Quarterly 791; Andrew Fitzmaurice, 'Neither Neo-Roman nor Liberal Empire' (2012) 26 Renaissance Studies 479.

[125] Mónica Garcia-Salmones, *The Project of Positivism in International Law* (Oxford University Press 2013); Jennifer Pitts, *A Turn to Empire: The Rise of Imperial Liberalism in Britain and France* (Princeton University Press 2005).

while remaining Eurocentric. But the removal of the dichotomy would make that system significantly less Eurocentric, less focused upon European norms, and there is clearly a tradition of such thinking within the European history of international law available for this purpose. Importantly, these critiques were driven less by a cosmopolitan or humanitarian concern with the plight of non-European peoples and more by a sense either of the cost of Chauvinism to European interests or by a perception that the civilizing mission was inadequately adapted to the interests of the nation-state. In both cases, the critiques urge us to understand international law in terms that are sceptical of rhetoric and that are not driven by European norms. They urge states to act in accordance with their interests. The prospect of states only pursuing their own interests could be seen as antagonistic to a sense of an international community.[126] As some of these critics argued, however, the interests of a particular state are connected to the interests of peoples who live outside that state. For the state to act, therefore, in accordance with its own interests it must take the interests of those outside into account. One advantage of the rule of interest over that of civilization is that it is up to each state to define its own interests, to define its own idea of self-perfection, as Wolff put it, even as that idea implies living in a community with others.

Bibliography

'Liste des members effectifs de l'instiut de droit international, Octobre 1873' (1873) 5 Revue de droit international et de législation comparée 711

Alexandrowicz, CH, *The Law of Nations in Global History* (David Armitage and Jennifer Pitts eds, Oxford University Press 2017)

Anghie, Antony, *Imperialism, Sovereignty and the Making of International Law* (Cambridge University Press 2005)

Armitage, David, *The Ideological Origins of the British Empire* (Cambridge University Press 2000)

Bell, Duncan, *The Idea of Greater Britain: Empire and the Future of World Order, 1860–1900* (Princeton University Press 2007)

Belmessous, Saliha (ed), *Empire by treaty: Negotiating European expansion, 1600–1900* (Oxford University Press 2014)

Benvenisti, Eyal, 'Sovereigns as Trustees of Humanity: On the Accountability of States to Foreign Stakeholders' (2013) 107 American Journal of International Law 295

Bonfils, Henry, *Manuel de droit international public* (3rd edn, Rousseau 1901)

Bowden, Brett, *The Empire of Civilization: The Evolution of an Imperial Idea* (University of Chicago Press 2009)

Bull, Hedley, 'The Emergence of a Universal International Society' in Hedley Bull and Adam Watson (eds), *The Expansion of International Society* (Clarendon Press 1984)

---

[126] See eg: Anne Orford, *International Authority and the Responsibility to Protect* (Cambridge University Press 2011); Eyal Benvenisti, 'Sovereigns as Trustees of Humanity: On the Accountability of States to Foreign Stakeholders' (2013) 107 American Journal of International Law 295; Luke Glanville, *Sovereignty and the Responsibility to Protect* (University of Chicago Press 2014).

Cavallar, Georg, 'Vitoria, Grotius, Pufendorf, Wolff and Vattel: Accomplices of European Colonialism and Exploitation or True Cosmopolitans' (2008) 10 Journal of the History of International Law 181

Charron, Pierre, *Of Wisdom: Three Books Written in French* (Samson Lennard tr, London 1625)

Cheneval, Francis, *Philosophie in weltbürgerlicher Bedeutung* (Schwabe Basel 2002)

Creasy, Edward, *Imperial and Colonial Constitutions of the Britannic Empire: Including Indian Institutions* (Longmans, Green, and Co 1872)

Creasy, Edward, *First Platform of International Law* (J Van Voorst 1876)

Despagnet, Frantz, *Essai sur les protectorats* (Librairie de la Société du recueil général des lois et des arrêts 1896)

Despagnet, Frantz, *Cours de droit international public* (2nd edn, Larose 1899)

Despagnet, Frantz, *La diplomatie de la troisième république* (Sirey 1904)

Dussel, Enrique, 'Eurocentrism and Modernity (Introduction to the Frankfurt Lectures)' in John Beverley, José Oviedo, and Michael Aronna (eds), *The Postmodernism Debate in Latin America* (Duke University Press 1995)

Eze, Emmanuel Chukwudi, 'The Color of Reason: The Idea of "Race" in Kant's Anthropology' in Emmanuel Chukwudi Eze (ed), *Postcolonial African Philosophy: A Critical Reader* (Wiley-Blackwell 1996)

Fisch, Jörg, *Die europäische Expansion und das Völkerrecht* (Steiner 1984)

Fitzmaurice, Andrew, *Humanism and America: An Intellectual History of English Colonisation, 1500–1625* (Cambridge University Press 2003)

Fitzmaurice, Andrew, 'The Commercial Ideology of Colonisation in Jacobean England: Robert Johnson, Giovanni Botero and the Pursuit of Greatness' (2007) 64 William and Mary Quarterly 791

Fitzmaurice, Andrew, 'The Resilience of Natural Law in the Writings of Sir Travers Twiss' in Ian Hall and Lisa Hill (eds), *British International Thinkers from Hobbes to Namier* (Palgrave Macmillan 2009)

Fitzmaurice, Andrew, 'Neither Neo-Roman nor Liberal Empire' (2012) 26 Renaissance Studies 479

Fitzmaurice, Andrew, *Sovereignty, Property and Empire 1500–2000* (Cambridge University Press 2014)

Garcia-Salmones, Mónica, *The Project of Positivism in International Law* (Oxford University Press 2013)

Glanville, Luke, *Sovereignty and the Responsibility to Protect* (University of Chicago Press 2014)

Gong, Gerrit, *The Standard of 'Civilization' in International Society* (Oxford University Press 1984)

Grewe, Wilhelm G, *The Epochs of International Law* (Michael Byers tr, De Gruyter 2000)

Grotius, Hugo, *The Free Sea* (Richard Hakluyt tr, David Armitage ed, Liberty Fund 2004)

Haakonssen, Knud, 'German Natural Law' in Mark Goldie and Robert Wokler (eds), *Cambridge History of Eighteenth Century Political Thought* (Cambridge University Press 2006)

Heffter, Auguste-Wilhelm, *Le droit international public de l'europe* (Paris 1873)

Hirschman, Albert O, *The Passions and the Interests: Political Arguments for Capitalism before its Triumph* (Princeton University Press 1997)

Hont, Istvan, *Jealousy of Trade: International Competition and the Nation-State in Historical Perspective* (Harvard University Press 2005)

Hornung, Joseph, 'Civilsés et barbares' (1885) 17 Revue de droit international et de législation comparée 1

Hunter, Ian, 'Law, War, and Casuistry in Vattel's Jus Gentium' (2011) 28(2) Parergon 87

Hunter, Ian, 'The Figure of Man and the Territorialisation of Justice in 'Enlightenment' Natural Law: Pufendorf and Vattel' (2013) 23 Intellectual History Review 289

Jèze, Gaston, *Étude théorique et pratique sur l'occupation* (Paris 1896)

Jouannet, Emmanuelle, 'Universalism of International Law and Imperialism: The True-False Paradox of International Law?' in Petter Korkman and Virpi Mäkinen (eds), *Universalism in International Law and Political Philosophy* (Helsinki Collegium for Advanced Studies 2008)

Jouannet, Emmanuelle, *The Liberal Welfarist Law of Nations* (Cambridge University Press 2012)

Kant, Immanuel, 'The Metaphysics of Morals' in Immanuel Kant, *Practical philosophy* (Mary Gregor ed and tr, Cambridge University Press 1996)

Kant, Immanuel, 'Toward Perpetual Peace' in Immanuel Kant, *Practical Philosophy* (Mary Gregor ed and tr, Cambridge University Press 1996)

Keal, Paul, *European Conquest and the Rights of Indigenous Peoples: The Moral Backwardness of International Society* (Cambridge University Press 2003)

Keene, Edward, *Beyond the Anarchical Society: Grotius, Colonialism and Order in World Politics* (Cambridge University Press 2002)

Koselleck, Reinhardt, *Futures Past: On the Semantics of Historical Time* (Columbia University Press 2004)

Koskenniemi, Martti, *The Gentle Civilizer of Nations: The Rise and Fall of International Law 1870–1960* (Cambridge University Press 2001)

Koskenniemi, Martti, 'Histories of International Law: Dealing with Eurocentrism' (2011) 19 Rechtsgeschichte 152

Lindley, MF, *The Acquisition and Government of Backward Territory in International Law* (Longmans, Green and Co 1926)

Lorca, Arnulf Becker, 'Eurocentrism in the History of International Law' in Bardo Fassbender and Anne Peters (eds), *The Oxford Handbook of the History of International Law* (Oxford University Press 2012)

Lorca, Arnulf Becker, *Mestizo International Law: A Global Intellectual History 1850–1950* (Cambridge University Press 2012)

Mignolo, Walter D, 'The Many Faces of Cosmopolis: Border Thinking and Critical Cosmopolitanism' (2000) 12 Public Culture 721

Milet, Marc, *La Faculté de droit de Paris face à la vie politique, de l'Affaire Scelle à l'Affaire Jèze, 1925–1936* (LGDJ 1996)

Mill, John Stuart, 'Civilization' in *Collected Works of John Stuart Mill: Volume 8, Essays on Politics and Society* (John M Robson ed, University of Toronto 1977)

Montaigne, Michel Eyquem de, *Essays*, 3 vols (John Florio tr, LC Harmer ed, Everyman edition 1965)

Muthu, Sankar, *Enlightenment against Empire* (Princeton University Press 2003)

Nys, Ernest, *Droit international: Les principes, les theories, les faits* (2nd edn, A Castaigne 1904)

Obregón, Liliana, 'The Civilized and the Uncivilized' in Bardo Fassbender and Anne Peters (eds), *The Oxford Handbook of the History of International Law* (Oxford University Press 2012)

Orford, Anne, *International Authority and the Responsibility to Protect* (Cambridge University Press 2011)

Péan, Pierre, *Une jeunesse française: François Mitterrand, 1934–1947* (Fayard 1994)

Pitts, Jennifer, *A Turn to Empire: The Rise of Imperial Liberalism in Britain and France* (Princeton University Press 2005)

Pitts, Jennifer, 'Boundaries of Victorian International Law' in Duncan Bell (ed), *Victorian Visions of Global Order* (Cambridge University Press 2007)

Pitts, Jennifer, 'Empire and Legal Universalisms in the Eighteenth Century' (2012) 117 American Historical Review 92

Pocock, JGA, *Virtue, Commerce, and History* (Cambridge University Press 1985)

Pufendorf, Samuel, *De jure naturae et gentium libri octo*, vol II (James Brown Scott ed, CH Oldfather and WA Oldfather trs, Clarendon Press 1934)

Rivier, Alphonse, 'Notice sur M Bluntschli' in Johann Caspar Bluntschli, *Droit international codifié* (4th edn, Librairie Guillaumin 1886)

Salomon, Charles, *L'occupation des territoires sans maître* (Paris 1887)

Schmitt, Carl, *The Nomos of the Earth* (GL Ulmen tr, Telos 2003)

Seeley, JR, *The Expansion of England* (London 1883)

Subramanyam, Sanjay, *Courtly Encounters: Translating Courtliness and Violence in Early Modern Eurasia* (Harvard University Press 2012)

Tuck, Richard, *Philosophy and Government 1572–1651* (Cambridge University Press 1993)

Tuck, Richard, *The Rights of War and Peace: Political Thought and the International Order from Grotius to Kant* (Oxford University Press 1999)

Varouxakis, Georgios, 'Great versus Small Nations: Size and National Greatness in Victorian Political Thought' in Duncan Bell (ed), *Victorian Visions of Global Order* (Cambridge University Press 2007)

Waswo, Richard, 'The Formation of Natural Law to Justify Colonialism, 1539–1689' (1996) 27 New Literary History 742

Wolff, Christian, *Jus gentium methodo scientificia pertractatum*, vol 2 (Joseph H Drake tr, Oxford University Press 1934)

Index

Ingram Content Group UK Ltd.
Milton Keynes UK
UKHW020401210623
423792UK00005B/135